AN INTRODUCTION TO

AMERICA'S MUSIC

SECOND EDITION

AN INTRODUCTION TO

AMERICA'S MUSIC

SECOND EDITION

RICHARD CRAWFORD

UNIVERSITY OF MICHIGAN, ANN ARBOR

LARRY HAMBERLIN

MIDDLEBURY COLLEGE

W. W. NORTON AND COMPANY
NEW YORK · LONDON

W. W. NORTON & COMPANY has been independent since its founding in 1923, when William Warder Norton and Mary D. Herter Norton first published lectures delivered at the People's Institute, the adult education division of New York City's Cooper Union. The firm soon expanded its program beyond the Institute, publishing books by celebrated academics from America and abroad. By mid-century, the two major pillars of Norton's publishing program—trade books and college texts—were firmly established. In the 1950s, the Norton family transferred control of the company to its employees, and today—with a staff of four hundred and a comparable number of trade, college, and professional titles published each year—W. W. Norton & Company stands as the largest and oldest publishing house owned wholly by its employees.

Editor: Maribeth Payne
Associate editor: Justin Hoffman
Assistant editor: Ariella Foss
Editorial assistant: Michael Fauver
Manuscript editor: Jodi Beder
Project editor: Christine D'Antonio
Electronic media editor: Steve Hoge
Editorial assistant: Stefani Wallace
Marketing manager, Music: Amy Parkin
Production manager: Andrew Ensor
Photo editor: Nelson Colón
Photo researcher: Fay Torresyap
Permissions manager: Megan Jackson
Text design: Jillian Burr
Art director: Rubina Yeh

Composition: Jouve International, Brattleboro, VT
Manufacturing: Courier, Kendallville

Library of Congress Cataloging-in-Publication Data

Crawford, Richard.
  An introduction to America's music / Richard Crawford, Larry Hamberlin. — Second edition
      pages cm
  Includes bibliographical references and index.
  ISBN 978-0-393-93531-8 (pbk.)
  1. Music—United States—History and criticism.   I. Hamberlin, Larry.   II. Title.
III. Title: America's music.
  ML200.C72 2013
  780.973—dc23

                                        2012046036

W. W. Norton & Company, Inc., 500 Fifth Avenue, New York, NY 10110
www.wwnorton.com
W. W. Norton & Company, Ltd., Castle House, 75/76 Wells Street, London W1T3QT

1234567890

For Penelope B. Crawford, wife,
mother, musician—RC

And for my children,
David and Sarabeth—LH

ABOUT THE AUTHORS

Penelope Crawford

RICHARD CRAWFORD

Richard Crawford is a Distinguished University Professor of Musicology Emeritus at the University of Michigan. A past president of the American Musicological Society, he is also editor-in-chief of Music of the United States of America (MUSA), a series of critical editions. His books include *The American Musical Landscape* (1993) and *America's Musical Life: A History* (2001).

Vincent A. Jones IV

LARRY HAMBERLIN

Larry Hamberlin is Associate Professor of Music at Middlebury College, where he teaches courses in Western classical music, American music, jazz, and popular music. He is the author of *Tin Pan Opera: Operatic Novelties in the Ragtime Era*.

CONTENTS IN BRIEF

CONTENTS

COUNT BASIE AND HIS UNDISPUTED KINGS O

LISTENING GUIDES

PREFACE

In revising *An Introduction to America's Music* for this second edition, the authors have sought to strengthen the first edition's best features while adding new ones that expand the book's scope and its usefulness for both instructors and students.

A few core convictions have shaped our approach to the subject. First, we aim to tell a story that embraces many aspects of music making. It encompasses not only the creation of music but also performance, teaching, and an ever-changing music business—with a scope ranging from publishing and recording to instrument manufacturing and technological developments such as radio, television, and the Internet. Second, our story describes the musical activities of both musicians and their audiences. We are interested in how people *use* music socially and culturally to enhance a sense of individual and group identity. Third, we continually probe the boundaries drawn to separate different types of music and, by implication, different groups of listeners from each other.

The book's organization reflects the importance of this third point. While recognizing the neatness of splitting a narrative account of America's music into three stories—those of the classical, the popular, and the traditional or folk spheres—we hold that treating those spheres independently risks overemphasizing the boundaries between them. By maintaining a more-or-less chronological narrative, we show how the classical, the popular, and the traditional, even as they produce repertories that seem separate from each other, can also overlap and interact, resulting in music that blends traits from more than one sphere. Even as the approaches and values of each sphere evolve from one era to the next, their differences never vanish altogether but reappear within fresh, sometimes hybrid configurations of musical sound. By considering the range of musical approaches and styles in play during each time period, while tracing activity from earlier times to the present, we have done our best to write a nuanced account of America's music making as a vast playground of musical give and take.

The task of drawing an inclusive one-volume portrait of such a wide-ranging and diverse musical culture has not been a straightforward process. But, by taking that diversity seriously, we offer a certain kind of *first* word on the subject—which, after all, is the purpose of an introduction. Once the preliminaries are enacted, the acquainted parties may or may not choose to take their connections further. It is our hope that this book will serve as a framework that students—who likely already know a good deal about America's music—will find useful in deepening their connections with that music and the life that surrounds it.

USING THE BOOK

An Introduction to America's Music is designed to bring a rich understanding of American music to students of multiple musical backgrounds. To that end, several new features have been added for the second edition:

- The introduction includes a substantial **Talking about Music** section that explains fundamental concepts with an eye toward helping students build a vocabulary for describing what they hear. Musical terms introduced throughout the book appear first in **boldface** and are defined both in the text and in the **Glossary** located in the back of the book.
- There are four **Part Introductions**, which include concise overviews of artistic, political, and cultural developments within each time period, as well as **timelines** placing musical events in a chronological context.
- Each chapter ends with discussion questions and recommendations for further reading, listening, and viewing. A variety of **sidebars** offer different perspectives on the music and the people who make it:

- **A Closer Look** boxes center on instruments, technical features, and musical subgenres.

A CLOSER LOOK

The Banjo: African Origins of "America's Instrument"

As early as the 1650s European observers noted the presence among African slaves in the West Indies of instruments resembling both the present-day banjo and West African antecedents. North American accounts date back to the 1740s, and by 1810 written references to the banjo often lack descriptions, implying that the instrument was familiar to most readers. In its earlier forms, the banjo had a body made from a halved gourd, with an animal skin stretched over the opening and from one to six strings. Instruments of this description are identified by various names, some of which resemble its modern name: *bangil, bangar, banshaw, Creole-bania, banjar,* and *bonjaw.*

By the 1840s, the gourd sound chamber gave way to a wooden rim with a metal tension hoop and adjustable brackets much like a drum. Around the same time, whites also began to play the banjo. By the beginning of the twentieth century, a banjo manufacturer could proudly state that "what the mandolin is to Italy, and the guitar to Spain, the banjo is to America." That status inspired the title of a recent history of the banjo, *America's Instrument.* An irony of history is that today the instrument is associated almost exclusively with white performers.

✎ This "Creole-bania," made in Dutch Guyana before 1772, and now in the Rijksmuseum voor Volkenkunde, Leiden, Holland, is made from a gourd, a sheepskin, and gut strings.

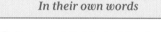

In their own words

John Coltrane on His Musical Goals

My music is the spiritual expression of what I am—my faith, my knowledge, my being.... When you begin to see the possibilities of music, you desire to do something really good for people, to help humanity free itself from its hangups.... I want to speak to their souls.

- **In their own words** boxes quote musicians and audience members speaking for themselves.

SPOTLIGHT ON HISTORY

- **Spotlight on History** boxes provide additional information on individuals, institutions, and musical trends.

Francis Hopkinson, Music Amateur

Perhaps the most devoted musical amateur in eighteenth-century America was Philadelphia native Francis Hopkinson, the University of Pennsylvania's first graduate, a lawyer and judge by trade, a patriot, and a signer of the Declaration of Independence. Hopkinson began playing the harpsichord at age seventeen, in 1754, hand-copying European songs and instrumental pieces, and by the early 1760s was good enough to join professional musicians in concerts. As an Anglican, Hopkinson served for a time as organist of Philadelphia's Christ Church, taught psalmody, and compiled sacred tunebooks for congregational singing. Music was Hopkinson's springboard for entry into Philadelphia's musical life, where, given the scarcity of professional performers, his ability and social position made him welcome.

In 1781, the last year of fighting in the American Revolution, Hopkinson produced a patriotic pastiche for solo singers, chorus, and orchestra called *America Independent, or The Temple of Minerva,* for which he fitted his own verses to music by others, including George Frideric Handel. But his musical ambitions also reached further, into the realm of original composition. As early as 1759 he was composing songs in two parts—with a keyboard accompaniment in which the right hand doubles the singer's melody and the left hand supplies a simple bass line—modeled on British songs he had copied out on his own.

For his *Seven Songs for the Harpsichord or Forte Piano* (Philadelphia, 1788), dedicated to George Washing-ton, Hopkinson wrote both words and music. A prefatory note declares: "I cannot, I believe, be refused the Credit of being the first Native of the United States who has produced a Musical Composition"—a claim referring to the nation born officially in June 1788 when the ninth state ratified the Constitution of the United States of America.

✎ Francis Hopkinson (1737–1791).

ABOUT THE LISTENING GUIDES

The book's eighty-eight **Listening Guides** highlight important features of the musical selections that accompany the text as CDs or streaming audio. Every selection has an easy-to-follow guide of events aimed at developing the critical skills that can deepen a listener's enjoyment of music.

Head includes CD and track numbers, Listening Guide number, Title, and Composer

Headnote calls out information on songwriters, performers, date of composition and/or recording.

"What to Listen For" boxes spotlight the big ideas.

Moment-by-moment descriptions, with cumulative timings and formal sections, guide student listening. Text and translations are included as appropriate.

| CD 2.3 | Listening Guide 10.2 | "Alexander's Ragtime Band" IRVING BERLIN |

DATE: 1911
PERFORMERS: Billy Murray, vocal, with studio orchestra
GENRE: ragtime song
METER: duple
FORM: verse and 32-bar *abac* chorus

WHAT TO LISTEN FOR
- instrumental accompaniment that resembles a military band
- key change at chorus, similar to that at the trio of a march or rag
- lyrics in stage Negro dialect

TIMING	SECTION	TEXT	COMMENTS
0:00	introduction		4-bar instrumental introduction based on the opening phrase of the verse.
0:10	vamp		A 2-bar phrase, played twice.
0:17	verse 1	Oh, ma honey…	Mild syncopation on "honey."
0:44	chorus a	Come on and hear…	Modulation to the subdominant resembles the similar modulation in a typical march.
0:58	b	They can play a bugle call…	Melody resembles a bugle call in bars 3–4.
1:11	a	Come on along…	Music is identical to the first *a*, with different lyrics.
1:25	c	And if you care to hear…	Quotation of "Old Folks at Home."
1:40	introduction and vamp		Return to beginning.
1:54	verse 2	Oh, ma honey…	The music of verse 1 repeats, with new lyrics.
2:21	chorus	Come on and hear…	As before.
3:16	chorus	They can play a bugle call…	Instrumental version of the chorus's *a* section, using Sousa-style countermelodies and woodwind trills. The vocalist sings only *b* and the second half of *c* (not indicated in the sheet music).

NOTE Edison cylinder, 1911.

"Listen & Reflect" questions stimulate thinking about musical styles and traditions.

Listen & Reflect

1. "Alexander's Ragtime Band" uses only the mildest syncopations—the same ones used, in fact, in Sousa's "Stars and Stripes Forever." As recorded here, the song gains even further ties to Sousa in its use of a military-style band. Yet the song was widely received by listeners at the time as a ragtime song. Why?
2. And what does that reception suggest about the attitudes of the musical public in 1911?

MEDIA RESOURCES

FOR STUDENTS

StudySpace is an easy-to-navigate website that gives students an organized study plan to master the material.

- **Chapter Outlines** help students keep track of their progress through the book
- **Review Materials** including flashcards and quizzes, help students test their own knowledge.
- **Streaming access** to all eighty-eight pieces in the core repertoire is included with every new book, and is organized on StudySpace in playlists by chapter.

A four CD set provides the complete recorded repertoire to students and instructors who want permanent, offline access to music.

FOR INSTRUCTORS

Instructor Site features all the art from the book in PowerPoint format and a Coursepack.

The Norton Coursepack provides multimedia content and assessment tools, including chapter outlines, flashcards, quizzes, and the playlist organizing streaming recordings for each chapter.

ACKNOWLEDGMENTS

Writing and revising this incarnation of the book has convinced the authors of the wisdom of the adage that two heads are better than one. Each of us has found in the other an ideal collaborator in the process of sifting, shifting, and repeatedly refining our material. But not even two heads can command all the knowledge, skills, and creative ideas that go into producing a textbook. We are grateful to all the scholars and teachers who read and commented on this material at various stages in its development, including Mark Katz, John Koegel, Charles Kronengold, Beth Levy, and Felicia Miyakawa. Students at Middlebury College provided valuable feedback on earlier versions of this book. Conversations with David Hamberlin and Casey Ryan led to new insights on recent musical trends. Sarabeth Hamberlin was an able translator and consultant on Hispanic music.

At W.W. Norton, Maribeth Payne proved once again why she is one of the most respected music editors in the business, keeping the project on track and the big picture in view at all times. Harry Haskell and Jodi Beder exercised a firm but gentle editorial hand on their authors' prose. Courtney Fitch, Ariella Foss, and Christine D'Antonio deftly moved the manuscript, in all its pieces, through editorial and production phases. The artwork has benefited from the creativity and expertise of Fay Torresyap and Nelson Colón. We offer our thanks as well to Ryan P. Jones of the University of Wisconsin, Eau Claire, for writing the online chapter outlines and quizzes.

For essential contributions to the project, some of them fundamental to its existence and others influential on its approach and content, Richard Crawford thanks Michael Ochs and Susan Gaustad of W.W. Norton, Dean Paul C. Boylan of the University of Michigan, the late Charles Hamm, the late H. Wiley Hitchcock, Samuel A. Floyd Jr., Jeffrey Magee, Tamar Barzel, Amy C. Beal, Mark Clague, William J. Crawford, Amy E. Crawford, Anne L. Crawford. Special gratitude goes to Penelope B. Crawford to whom the first edition of this book was dedicated. Professor Crawford also credits several generations of students at the University of Michigan, whose ideas about and responses to the American musical experience in academic dress have done much to shape the material in this book.

INTRODUCTION

ONE PEOPLE, ONE MUSIC?

On a cold January afternoon in 2009, more than 400,000 people gathered near the Lincoln Memorial in Washington, D.C., for a concert in celebration of the impending inauguration of president-elect Barack Obama. After an opening rendition of the national anthem by musicians of the armed forces, actor Denzel Washington greeted the huge crowd with these words, beginning with a paraphrase of Mr. Obama's first post-election speech from the previous November:

> We are not a collection of red states and blue states; we are the United States. We come here knowing that we are all in this together. So we named this ceremony that begins this inaugural week with three simple words that speak to who we are and to our future, and they are We Are One.

Yet the concert that followed seemed designed to demonstrate that, musically at least, the people of the United States are not one but many. The performers included rock stars, soul singers, rap artists, country crooners, gospel choirs, and a symphony orchestra.

The music they performed was equally diverse. Only a few songs were performed by the artists who had written them and made them famous: the Irish rock band U2 performed two of their own songs, and a blue-collar rocker from Indiana, John Mellencamp, sang his "Pink Houses," with its patriotism-tinged chorus beginning "Ain't that America." Most of the acts were duets and trios carefully chosen to combine musicians from different genres, often singing atypical material. Soul legend Stevie Wonder sang his own "Higher Ground," joined by Latina singer Shakira and southern R&B artist Usher. Country singer Garth Brooks took the stage with a mostly African American gospel choir to perform singer-songwriter Don McLean's "American Pie." After rapper and actress Queen Latifah spoke about another concert at the Lincoln Memorial seventy years earlier, by the great African American contralto Marian Anderson, the smooth balladeer Josh Groban, Trinidadian R&B singer Heather Headley, and the Gay Men's Chorus of Washington reprised Anderson's opening number at that concert, "America" ("My country, 'tis of thee"). Tom Hanks recited the words of Abraham Lincoln in a performance by the U.S. Armed Forces Symphony of Aaron Copland's *Lincoln Portrait*. Most bizarre, perhaps, was the vocal duet of country-pop singer Sheryl Crow and rapper will.i.am of the Black Eyed Peas, singing Bob Marley's reggae anthem "One Love" while pianist Herbie Hancock doodled dissonant avant-garde jazz in the background.

Pete Seeger, Bruce Springsteen, and a gospel choir sing Woody Guthrie's "This Land Is Your Land" in the *We Are One* concert at the Lincoln Memorial, January 18, 2009.

The concert's name, *We Are One,* evoked the motto on the Great Seal of the United States, *e pluribus unum* ("out of many, one"), to project a message of national unity. The musical content, however, stressed the *pluribus* more than the *unum.* If America is indeed a country where many peoples, from many lands, have united to form one whole, can the same be said for America's music? Does it even make sense to speak of "American music" as if that were a single, clearly defined category?

The tendency to think of music in terms of sharply separated styles or genres is perhaps stronger today than it has ever been. *Billboard,* a music-industry magazine, tabulates sales of recorded music in its influential weekly "charts" of hit singles and albums. Back in the 1950s, *Billboard* tracked record sales in three genres: pop, rhythm and blues, and country-western. Today, in contrast, each issue of *Billboard* includes sixty charts and distinguishes twenty-five distinct genres. For instance, "pop" is differentiated from "adult pop," which is not the same as "adult contemporary." Likewise, "rock," "hard rock," and "alternative" are separate categories, as are "Christian" and "gospel." (There are more charts than genres, in order to track different formats, identified as songs, radio songs, digital songs, albums, digital albums, and ringtones.)

A popular online music guide, AllMusic.com, makes even finer distinctions, dividing music into nine basic genres—pop/rock, jazz, R&B, classical, and so on—of which only one, "world," specifically designates music made outside the United States. The other eight genres are further divided into fifty-eight "styles," not counting non-U.S. categories. For example, pop/rock comes in thirteen styles—including alternative/indie-rock, folk/country rock, and psychedelic/garage—of which only two, Europop and British Invasion, exclude American music. The numbers really mushroom, however, when AllMusic divides the styles into subgenres. Alternative/indie rock, for instance, is broken down into fifty-four subgenres, of which only a few—such as New Zealand rock and Britpop—are out-

ALLMUSIC'S BLUES STYLES

Clicking on the word "blues" at AllMusic's home page leads the reader to the following list of eleven blues styles, subdivided into fifty-seven subgenres (not counting repetitions).*

BLUES STYLES	SUBGENRES
Chicago Blues	Acoustic Chicago Blues, Chicago Blues, Electric Chicago Blues Modern Electric Chicago Blues
Country Blues	Blues Gospel, Country Blues, Vaudeville Blues, Prewar Country Blues, Folk-Blues, Memphis Blues, Blues Revival, Work Songs, Prewar Gospel Blues, Songster
Delta Blues	Delta Blues, Electric Delta Blues, Finger-Picked Guitar, Modern Delta Blues
Early Acoustic Blues	Piedmont Blues, Acoustic Blues, Classic Female Blues, Acoustic Memphis Blues, Early American Blues, Dirty Blues, Prewar Blues
East Coast Blues	Jump Blues, Piedmont Blues, East Coast Blues, New York Blues,
Harmonica Blues	Electric Harmonica Blues, Harmonica Blues
Louisiana Blues	Louisiana Blues
Modern Electric Blues	Modern Electric Blues, Blues-Rock, Modern Electric Chicago Blues, Modern Delta Blues, Contemporary Blues, Modern Electric Texas Blues
Texas Blues	Electric Texas Blues, Texas Blues
Electric Blues	Early R&B, Soul-Blues, Electric Chicago Blues, Electric Blues, Electric Texas Blues, Electric Country Blues, Electric Delta Blues, Electric Memphis Blues, Electric Harmonica Blues, Urban Blues, New Orleans Blues, Swamp Blues, Juke Joint Blues, Detroit Blues, Slide Guitar Blues
Jump Blues/Piano Blues	Early R&B, Piano Blues, West Coast Blues, Jazz Blues, St. Louis Blues

*From www.allmusic.com/.

side the United States. The others include grunge, post-grunge, noise pop, math rock, and third wave ska revival. Under the major genre of blues may be found Chicago blues, electric blues, electric Chicago blues, modern electric blues, and modern electric Chicago blues. All in all, according to AllMusic, about 440 different types of music are made in the United States.

From this perspective, the "America's music" that this textbook purports to introduce is a chimera. Music journalism would lead us to believe that music is fragmented into myriad genres and subgenres. What's more, the audience for that music also appears to be splintered into tiny interest groups, each ready to defend its subgenre against others, whether arguing the relative merits of dark ambient and experimental dub or defending psychobilly from the proponents of cowpunk.

But such overenthusiastic categorizing distorts the picture of how most people in the United States actually experience music. In truth, hardly anyone is holed up in one tiny subgenre. In fact, the meaning of the term *genre* is itself difficult to pin down. Does it describe the sound of the music, or how it functions in society (church music, dance music, etc.)? Or does it have more to do with who is making and listening to it? By any of these measures, the boundaries of genres are permeable, to say the least.

Most of us encounter many different kinds of music in our daily lives. What's more, most of us enjoy more than one kind of music; if you don't believe that, check your friends' playlists—even the most diehard metalhead or techno lover will have a few surprising outliers. Moreover, as suggested by the prevalence of hyphens and slashes in the names of the AllMusic categories, music genres do not exist in a vacuum but are constantly interacting with one another. That's because musicians tend to enjoy the company of other musicians, both socially and professionally, and are inclined to listen to each other's work. It is these interconnections and interactions that we the authors find fascinating about America's music.

For that reason, this book approaches music making in the United States as one unified, albeit highly variegated, culture. The best way to understand our nation's music, we feel, is by studying its historical development across the centuries. It is true, of course, that certain divisions may be drawn within American music—if not 440 subgenres, then at least the three broad categories of classical, popular, and folk music that we have adopted as the underlying typology of this book. But even here, as we will explore in later chapters, those distinctions have more to do with the contrasting goals and ideals, both social and aesthetic, of the musicians creating the music and the audiences listening or dancing to it than with hard-and-fast stylistic boundaries. And sometimes the similarities between musical styles are more important than any surface differences.

The organization of this book, then, is roughly chronological, dealing first with the time from the arrival of Europeans through the Civil War, then the period between that war and the end of World War I, the decades between the two world wars, and finally the decades from the 1940s to the present. Although some individual chapters may focus on only one of the three broad categories of music, classical, popular, or folk, to the momentary exclusion of the other two, neighboring chapters guarantee that none of the categories stays out of the reader's attention for long. Treated in this way, American music can be seen to be characterized, throughout its history, by lively interactions between folk, popular, and classical spheres. American music, in fact, is much like the type of cooking preferred by the hero of Mark Twain's *Adventures of Huckleberry Finn*. Huck doesn't care for meals in which "everything was cooked by itself." Better, he says, to cook everything in one big pot: "In a barrel of odds and ends it is different; things get mixed up, and the juice kind of swaps around, and the things go better."

This book examines how musical juices kind of swap around. We're with Huck.

TALKING ABOUT MUSIC

The study of music, as the preceding section suggests, embraces the study of how people *use* music: how music functions socially to create a sense of individual and group identity, how it sets the tone of ritual events—not only inaugural concerts but also weddings, funerals, commencement ceremonies, and senior proms—as well as how it is passed on from generation to generation. But any worthwhile study of music must also delve into the actual sounds and the way they operate together to create musical meaning. To talk intelligibly about such matters, we need to develop at least a rudimentary technical vocabulary, a way of talking about specific musical features. The remainder of this introduction will help you lay the foundation for developing that vocabulary as you study the many types of music that have been made in the United States.

We may begin with the characteristics of a single musical sound—a **tone*** or, more casually, a **note**—and then proceed to talk about how musicians combine tones of varying characteristics to create more-complex musical structures.

Imagine a single note plucked on a guitar string. In your imagination, how long does that note continue to ring? Duration is an important characteristic of any tone, and this temporal aspect of music—how it unfolds in time—is called **rhythm**.

Is the note loud or soft? Volume, or **dynamics**, is another important characteristic of musical sound.

Is it a high note or a low note? **Pitch** is yet another characteristic of central importance in music, especially when tones of various pitches are combined to create *melody* and *harmony*.

Finally, imagine that guitar note once again, then imagine a note of identical duration, volume, and pitch, but played on a banjo. The difference between the two notes is one of **tone color**, or **timbre** (pronounced *tam'-ber*), another crucial element in how we experience music.

Now let's take a closer look at each of these characteristics, observing how musical patterns emerge by varying the characteristics of notes first in succession, then in simultaneous combinations. You can hear examples of these characteristics by listening to short segments of the recordings that accompany this textbook.

RHYTHM

Notes of varying duration can be combined to create different rhythmic patterns. Perhaps the simplest rhythmic pattern would be a steady succession of notes of equal duration, as at the beginning of "Twinkle, Twinkle, Little Star." Notice that after six notes of equal length, the seventh (on the word "star") is twice as long. That seven-note pattern—six shorts and a long—is then repeated, six times in all, to complete the song. This simple rhythm sounds child-like in "Twinkle, Twinkle," but in a psalm tune like Old Hundred (LG 1.2), a nearly identical pattern sounds sturdy and resolute, befitting the sacred text. (The names of hymn and psalm tunes are conventionally printed in small caps.) Conversely, the highly irregular rhythm of the piano part in Ruth Crawford

*Definitions of terms printed in **boldface** may be found in the Glossary on pp. A1–A13.

Seeger's "Chinaman, Laundryman" (LG 13.1), a song about racial and economic oppression, may strike you as anxious or jittery.

Most music presents these rhythmic patterns against the backdrop of a steady pulse, which divides musical time into equal units or **beats**. (The term *beat* can mean different things in different contexts, by the way, as can many of the terms discussed here.) Relatively long units are perceived as a slow **tempo**, or rate of speed, short units as a fast tempo. Music intended for dancing tends to express the beat emphatically, often with the use of drums or other percussion instruments. The zydeco band playing "Ful il sa" (LG 21.3) features a prominent drum set pounding out the fast, energetic beat. In Gil Evans's arrangement of *Summertime* (LG 16.3), the even notes of the string bass create a steady, relaxed underpinning for Miles Davis's expressive trumpet playing.

But not all music features a steady beat. Singers, especially when unaccompanied, may stretch out some notes for emphasis and hurry through others, constantly speeding up and slowing down, with the result that no clear sense of tempo emerges. Instead, the rhythm may more closely resemble the irregular patterns of speech. Such rhythmic elasticity, or **rubato,** can be heard to varying degrees in "The Liberty Song" (LG 2.1), "The Gypsy Laddie" (LG 9.2), and "Only a Pawn in Their Game" (LG 17.6).

An important feature of music with a steady pulse is its tendency to group beats into larger temporal units called **measures** or, more informally, **bars**. The first beat of each measure tends to carry the strongest **accent**, or emphasis; that initial beat is called the **downbeat**, by analogy with the downward motion an orchestra conductor makes with the baton to indicate it. The beat that precedes it (i.e., the last beat of the preceding measure), by a similar analogy, is called the **upbeat**.

Typically, all the measures in a piece of music have the same number of beats. The number of beats per bar determines the music's **meter**. Two beats per bar—the familiar "*one,* two, *one,* two" of a military march such as John Philip Sousa's *Stars and Stripes Forever* (LG 7.1)—signals a **duple meter**. Three beats per bar, or **triple meter**, lends a waltz-like feeling—"*one,* two, three, *one,* two, three"—to songs such as "After the Ball" (LG 7.3). Four beats per bar is the most common meter for all types of popular music of the past century; it can be heard in songs as different as Count Basie's fast-tempo *Lester Leaps In* (LG 15.4) and Curtis Mayfield's medium-tempo "Superfly" (LG 19.3). Some musicians prefer to use the term "quadruple meter" for music with four beats per bar, but we won't make such a fine distinction in these pages. The difference between two slow beats per bar and four fast beats can be hard to distinguish, so we'll use the term "duple meter" for both.

Just as beats are grouped together to form a larger unit (the bar), bars can be grouped to form an even larger unit, the **phrase**. And just as bars can consist of varying numbers of beats, phrases can encompass varying numbers of bars. That repeating seven-note rhythmic pattern in "Twinkle, Twinkle, Little Star" fills two bars of duple meter (four beats per bar) and can be thought of as a two-bar phrase. Notice that each musical phrase corresponds to a line of the lyrics. Here are the first two phrases:

measure:	**1**	**2**
first phrase:	Twin-kle, twin-kle,	lit-tle star
beats:	1 2 3 4	1 2 3 4

	3				**4**			
Second phrase:	How I		won-der		what you are			
	1	2	3	4	1	2	3	4

Most common, however, especially in music intended for dancing, is the four-bar phrase. In Leon Payne's "Lost Highway" (as sung by Hank Williams, LG 17.2), each poetic line in the lyrics corresponds to a four-bar phrase in the music. Here is the first stanza:

> I'm a rollin' <u>stone</u>, all alone and lost
> For a life of <u>sin</u> I have paid the cost
> When I walk <u>by</u> all the people say
> "Just another <u>guy</u> on the lost highway."

The first downbeat in each phrase corresponds, not to the first word of each line, but rather to the underlined syllable. When you listen to Hank Williams's performance, use the instrumental introduction to get a clear sense of where the beat is. When Williams sings the word "stone," start counting the beats as "*one,* two, three, four, *one,* two, three, four," and so on. After counting four groups of four (i.e., four bars of music—the first phrase), you should arrive at the point where Williams sings the word "sin."

Unlike the phrases of "Twinkle, Twinkle, Little Star," each of which begins directly on a downbeat, each phrase of "Lost Highway" begins with a few **pickup notes**, which precede and lead into the downbeat. A pickup note may coincide with the upbeat, or it may be on any unstressed part of the bar before a phrase's first downbeat. For example, the words "I'm a rollin'" are sung as pickup notes to the downbeat on "stone."

Equally important as a phrase's beginning is its ending, or **cadence**. A cadence may sound conclusive or inconclusive, depending on a variety of musical factors, including melody, rhythm, and especially harmony. A phrase ending that sounds final, whether or not it is actually the end of the piece, is called a **full cadence**; one that sounds inconclusive is a **half cadence**; and one that sounds as if it will be final but at the last moment substitutes a "wrong" chord for the expected one is a **deceptive cadence**.

Just as groups of beats form bars and groups of bars form phrases, groups of phrases can form larger structural units. In different kinds of music we may use different names to label those larger units. In "Lost Highway," for example, each group of four phrases constitutes a **stanza**: a section of music that can be repeated over and over, with new words each time around. (This is one of many terms music shares with poetry; we can also say that a stanza is a short section of poetry whose metrical and rhyme scheme is repeated; when the poem is set to music, the same music is used for each stanza.) Note the symmetry in "Lost Highway," which you may find in many other popular songs as well: four beats per bar, four bars per phrase, four phrases per stanza.

Now let's shift our focus in the opposite direction: to measurements smaller than the individual beat. In **simple meters** the beat is divided into two equal halves. Try counting "*one,* two, *one,* two," along with the simple duple meter of "Get Off the Track!" (LG 6.4). Now subdivide the beat by counting "*one*-and two-and, *one*-and two-and." Note that in the introduction, the lower part in the piano, played by the left hand, consists of two notes per beat, while the upper part, played by the right hand, subdivides the beat even further, into four notes per beat.

Contrastingly, **compound meters** divide the beat into three equal parts. Irish jigs display the "jiggety, jiggety" feeling of compound meter. The opening of Aaron Copland's "Morning on the Ranch" (LG 15.2) moves at a slower tempo than a typical jig, but you should still be able to count along with its compound duple meter: "*one*-and-a two-and-a, *one*-and-a two-and-a." Notice that most phrases begin with a pickup, and many beats are filled with two notes, one longer and one shorter; the longer note fills two-thirds of the beat, the shorter note the remaining third:

$$\text{a} \mid \textit{one}\text{-and- a } \textit{two}\text{-and- a} \mid \textit{one}\text{-and-a } \textit{two}\text{-and- a}$$

The difference between simple and compound meters is generally easy to hear, but an important exception may be found in the blues and in the many musical genres that draw on the blues, including jazz, gospel, and rock and roll. Characteristic of blues-related music is a shuffle rhythm, in which the meter is closer to compound than to simple: beats are often divided into three equal notes, or into two unequal notes that are not quite in the 2:1 ratio of "Morning on the Ranch." The subtle feel of that shuffle, or **swing**, enlivens the rhythms of "Walking Blues" (LG 14.1), *West End Blues* (LG 12.4), and "Talk about Jesus" (LG 14.2).

PITCH AND DYNAMICS

In scientific terms, a musical tone is created when a vibrating object (say, a guitar string) excites the surrounding air particles, creating a sound wave. The characteristics of that sound wave include its **frequency**, corresponding to how fast the object is vibrating, and its **amplitude**, corresponding to how energetically the object is vibrating—that is, how much distance it travels with each oscillation. Our ears perceive frequency as *pitch*: the faster the vibration, the higher the frequency and thus the higher the perceived pitch. A soprano's vocal cords vibrate faster than a bass's; a violin's strings vibrate faster than a cello's. The more energy that is expended in those vibrations, the greater the amplitude and thus the louder the volume or *dynamics*. An unplugged electric guitar can be played only at a low dynamic, but plug it into an electronic amplifier—thereby harnessing electricity to energize the vibrations—and it can be deafening.

Altering the dynamic level can transform music's effect. What would Sousa's *Stars and Stripes Forever* (LG 7.1) sound like if played at a whisper? Or what if that military band gave a thunderous rendition of "Jeanie with the Light Brown Hair" (LG 6.3)? Inappropriate dynamics can spoil the music.

Some music has an appropriate dynamic level that, once found, is sustained with little variation throughout the piece. Chuck Berry's 1957 song "School Day" (LG 17.4) has very little dynamic contrast; the entire song is most effective when played at a constant volume, preferably one that would annoy the parents of 1950s teenagers. Other music, though, exploits contrasting dynamic levels to convey a variety of musical ideas. Even the boisterous *Stars and Stripes Forever*

(LG 7.1) quiets down around the one-minute mark (1:00), then suddenly gets loud again at 1:29, the change in dynamic adding excitement to changes in other musical parameters as well. The second movement of Amy Beach's *Gaelic* Symphony (LG 8.1) begins very softly, but starting around 4:43 we hear a **crescendo**, a gradual increase in volume, which climaxes at 4:58 in a loud crash, followed by silence, then a return to the quiet dynamic of the opening. The closing moments (8:01 to the end) feature another crescendo, this one followed by a **decrescendo** or **diminuendo**, a gradual decrease in volume.

MELODY

If a sound wave's amplitude, or volume, has important musical applications, then its frequency, or pitch, is even more important. One of the defining features of any piece of music is its **melody**, or **tune**, which may be narrowly defined as a series of musical tones of varying pitch. But what makes a melody memorable is how it combines pitch and rhythm to create musical meaning.

This is evident even in "Twinkle, Twinkle, Little Star." The melody begins with two notes of the same pitch, then leaps up to a considerably higher pitch for the next two notes. The third pair of notes is slightly higher; then the melody drops back down to the pitch of the second pair for the long note on "star." (Even this simple song displays admirable artistry: the first break in the rhythmic pattern corresponds to the first return to a previously heard pitch.) The second phrase consists of pairs of notes dropping to successively lower pitches, until the next long note (on "are") brings us back to the opening pitch. The third and fourth phrases retrace the downward arc of the second phrase, and the fifth and sixth phrases are a literal repeat of the first two.

Another way to describe this melody would be to say that the first and fifth phrases have a rising **melodic contour**, the other phrases a falling contour. Each four-bar phrase in "Lost Highway" (LG 17.2) has a similar contour: a rise to a long note, then a fall to a second long note, lower in pitch than the first. The first long note in each of phrases 2 and 3 rises to a higher pitch than the corresponding note in the phrase before; phrase 4 returns to the pitch of the opening phrase. Just as we can describe the contour of each phrase, we can also describe the larger contour created by a series of phrases—in "Lost Highway," a three-step rise, then a fall.

A useful way to think about a melody is to observe the distances, or **intervals**, between adjacent notes. Small intervals, or **steps**, are easier to sing than wide intervals—**leaps** or **skips**. **Conjunct** melodies—consisting mostly of steps—tend to be easier to sing; an example is the song "America" ("My country, 'tis of thee"). **Disjunct** melodies—consisting mostly of leaps—are often harder to sing; "The Star-Spangled Banner," a notorious example, begins with six leaps in a row. All but one of those leaps are **thirds**, the interval formed by skipping over a pitch to the next available pitch; the name comes from counting three pitches: the one you start on, the one you skip, and the one you land on. The remaining leap is a **fourth**, formed by skipping over two pitches; the fourth lies between "you" and "see."

Another factor that makes the national anthem hard for many people to sing is its **compass** or **range**: the distance between a melody's highest and lowest pitches (its **apex** and **nadir**). The opening "O say" quickly leaps down to the nadir; even if you sing that opening as low in pitch as you comfortably can, you are likely to find yourself straining for the apex at "the rockets' <u>red</u> <u>glare</u>." That opening phrase moves in the melody's lower pitch area, or **register**; the rockets and bursting bombs occur in the melody's upper register. When the apex returns near the end, at "the land of the <u>free</u>," many ballpark soloists jump up to an even higher note, extending the tune's already wide compass, creating a new apex, and showing off their own vocal range. Is it an accident that they take such liberty on the word "free"?

Shifts in compass or range can also outline a melody's structure. The four phrases of "Happy Birthday" are nearly identical in rhythm, and the first three are also very similar in melodic contour. They differ, however, in their melodic compass: from the same starting pitch (in this case, the melody's nadir), each phrase uses progressively more disjunct motion to rise to successively higher pitches, with the third phrase climaxing on the melody's apex. The fourth phrase then relaxes with a falling contour and a narrower range. Likewise, although each phrase in "Lost Highway" (LG 17.2) has a similar contour, phrases 2 and 3 lie higher and higher in the tune's compass, reaching the apex about two-thirds of the way through, before phrase 4 returns to the low register of phrase 1.

TIMBRE

We may hear a melody played with perfect rhythm and pitch and at an appropriate dynamic level, yet find the performance unsatisfactory if the performer draws an unpleasant *timbre* from the instrument. Conversely, a particularly beautiful *tone color* can persuade us to forgive slight imperfections in pitch and rhythm.

ꙮ Cootie Williams, a longtime member of Duke Ellington's orchestra, using a plunger mute.

Timbre is a key element in how we perceive differences between musical instruments. Learning to identify the different instruments of the orchestra by ear can greatly increase your enjoyment of orchestral music. What at first can seem like an undifferentiated wash of sound takes on new meaning when you can follow the interlocking melodic lines of violins, clarinets, French horns, and so on. An awareness of timbre can also help distinguish different performance techniques on a single instrument, and even the signature style of specific performers. The trumpet, for instance, can be played either **open**, that is, in the usual fashion, or with a variety of **mutes**, objects placed in the bell of the instrument that have the effect of not only reducing the volume (hence the name) but also, and more importantly, altering the timbre in fascinating ways. Contrast the timbre of Louis Armstrong's open trumpet at the beginning of *West End Blues* (LG 12.4) with that of Miles Davis's muted trumpet on *Summertime* (LG 16.3). On *Black and Tan Fantasy* (LG 12.5), Bubber Miley extracts a phantasmagoric array of timbres from his trumpet using a "plunger-and-growl" technique, described in chapter 12 (his solo begins at 1:00 and gets particularly elaborate around 1:30).

To understand timbre, we need to take a close look at how musical instruments vibrate to produce musical tones. Visualize the strings of a violin when set into motion by a bow. If you could watch that string up close and in slow motion, you would see that it vibrates, not in a simple back-and-forth oscillation, but in a complex, sinuous motion. Acousticians analyze this motion as the sum of a series of simple oscillations, known as **partials**: the entire string length vibrating at one frequency, the two halves of the string each vibrating at double that frequency, the three thirds at triple that frequency, and so on. The slowest frequency, that of the entire string length, has the greatest amplitude and thus is by far the loudest, and it produces the pitch we perceive consciously: the **fundamental** pitch. But the higher frequencies, called **overtones**, though much softer, are present as well. The relative volumes of the partials—the fundamental and its overtones, which together make up the tone's **overtone series**—can vary considerably, and it is this phenomenon that we hear as timbre. The relative weakness of upper partials gives the flute its light timbre, for example, whereas prominent upper partials give the oboe its plangent nasality. Thus we can say that timbre is how we perceive the details of an individual tone's overtone series.

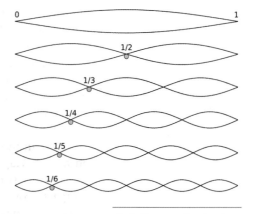

A diagram of a vibrating string, illustrating the first six partials.

With the voice, different vowel sounds correspond to different mixes of partials—that is, different timbres. Try singing long notes on a single pitch to the following vowels, with a breath after each: *oo, oh, ah, eh, ee*. With practice, you can hear the shifting of upper partials as you move from one vowel to the next. Now try singing *ah* first in the normal way, then "through your nose." That nasal quality is the result of giving extra emphasis to the higher partials of your voice. A slight nasality is a feature of much country singing, as can be heard in Dolly Parton's "Coat of Many Colors" (LG 19.2). If you compare her sound to Gladys Knight's in "I Heard It through the Grapevine" (LG 18.6), you can appreciate how vocal timbre can be a marker of different musical genres.

Timbre exists because all musical tones (with the exception of electronically generated sine waves) consist of multiple partials, related to one another by simple ratios: a fundamental frequency, a partial that vibrates twice as fast as the fundamental, another that is three times as fast, another four times as fast, and so on. Those simple numerical relationships not only govern the timbre of the single tone but also affect how different tones relate to one another. With this insight, we can take a closer look at the art of combining pitches.

PITCHES IN COMBINATION: SCALES, KEYS, HARMONY

Scales

If we take all the pitches in a melody and arrange them in sequence from the lowest to the highest (or vice versa), the resulting pitch collection is called a **scale**. The term comes from the Italian word *scala,* a ladder or staircase, and the analogy is apt: each pitch may be visualized as a rung in the ladder, and a melody's rising and falling contour as climbing up and down the ladder. Like actual ladders, musical scales can have varying numbers of rungs, or **scale degrees**; unlike the rungs of any good ladder, though, the degrees in most scales are not separated by equal distances. Counting the number of degrees in a scale and comparing the distances, or intervals, between them can tell us much about music that uses that scale.

Of all the possible intervals between two pitches, the **octave**—the distance between a pitch and another of exactly twice the frequency—has a unique feature. Our ears perceive notes an octave apart as being somehow "the same." For instance, when a group of men and women sing a melody together, the women usually sing pitches an octave higher than the men, yet we perceive their melody to be "the same." Consequently, if two notes in a scale are an octave apart, we can consider them to be "the same" note and count them as a single scale degree. By no coincidence, the octave is the interval between the first two partials in the overtone series.

Most music in the Western world draws on a system in which the octave is divided into twelve equal units, called **half steps** or **semitones**, the smallest interval in conventional music. (In chapter 19 we'll explore *microtonal* music, which uses even smaller divisions—but for now you can disregard **microtonality**.) The collection of all twelve pitches, equally spaced a semitone apart, is called the **chromatic scale**. Most melodies are based on a scale of fewer than twelve notes per octave, however. For example, the main tune of "Get Off the Track!" (LG 17.2, 0:07–0:15) uses only five pitches. That **pentatonic** scale is extremely common in folk songs and is not unusual in popular songs as well. The tune of "Lost Highway" (LG 6.4, 0:06–0:34) encompasses nine different pitches from its nadir (the very first note: "I'm a rollin' stone") to its apex ("When I walk by, all the people say"). Four of those pitches, however, are octave duplicates of other notes in the scale. If we discount those duplicate notes, there are only five discrete degrees in the scale: it's the same pentatonic scale heard in "Get Off the Track!" The black keys of the piano, incidentally, form a pentatonic scale.

Outside the realm of folk music, the most common scales are the two principal **diatonic** scales, **major** and **minor**. Both scales encompass seven scale degrees; the eighth note in the scale is the octave of the first note—that interval gets its name from the Latin word for "eight." Diatonic scales are a mix of whole steps and half steps (five of the former and two of the latter, to be precise); pentatonic tunes like "Lost Highway" have no half steps, only whole steps and thirds, the latter occurring where the scale skips over a note that would be present in a diatonic scale. Exactly where the half steps occur determines whether a diatonic scale is major or minor. The Christmas carol "Joy to the World" begins by working its way down a complete major scale; the interval from top to bottom is an octave. Melodies in the minor are somewhat less common; "When

👈 Pentatonic scales beginning on C and on F sharp. If you count the half steps between adjacent colored keys, you will notice that the interval pattern is the same in both scales.

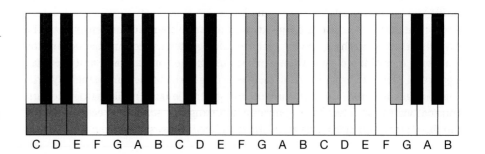

C D E F G A B C D E F G A B C D E F G A B

Johnny Comes Marching Home" is a widely known tune that uses the minor scale.

Most people perceive the minor scale as dark, tense, or sad in comparison to the brighter, more relaxed sound of major. After a short introduction in the major, the first section of James Reese Europe's *Castle House Rag* (LG 10.3, 0:04–0:19) begins in the minor but switches to major at 0:15. Can you hear that shift from dark to light near the end of the first section?

In the European classical tradition, the major and minor scales developed out of a medieval system in which major and minor (differently named) were only two of several possible diatonic scales, called **modes**. Some of those older modes resurface in folk music and especially in popular music from the rock era and later. For example, Santana's "Oye como va" (LG 19.1) uses a mode that resembles, but is not quite identical to, the minor scale. All the diatonic scales and modes, incidentally, can be played on the white keys of the piano.

Tonality and Key

A characteristic of melodies using any of the scales we've discussed is their tendency to come to rest on the first scale degree, called the **tonic**. Much as in the overtone series the fundamental is the pitch to which the higher partials are related, the tonic is the central note around which the other scale degrees are organized. We hear it as "home." A melody may or may not begin on the tonic, but it must end on the tonic to create a sense of resolution. Try singing "Happy Birthday" or any other familiar tune, stopping just before the last note. You can feel how the tune "wants" to resolve on the last note: that's the tonic.

You can think of the tonic as the center of a musical solar system—a sun around which the other scale degrees orbit like planets. The gravitational force that holds them together is called **tonality**, and it's a powerful organizer of much of the world's music.

Scales, as we have seen, can be thought of as patterns of intervals—whole steps and half steps, in the case of diatonic scales. All of these patterns can be built using as a starting point, or tonic, any one of the twelve semitones that divide the octave. Because of Historical Reasons Too Complicated to Explain, musicians label these twelve pitches using the first seven letters of the alphabet, adding "sharp" or "flat" to any of those letters to complete the set, for example, "C," "G," "B flat," "F sharp." Any piece of **tonal** music can thus be identified by naming which of the twelve possible notes it uses as its tonic; a piece based on the pitch D is said to be in the **key** of D. In classical music, the name of a piece often includes which diatonic scale it is based on; for example, a symphony may be in C minor, or a string quartet in E-flat major.

Just as the tonic functions as "home" for all the notes in a scale, a key may function as "home" in a piece of music that travels through several keys. The movement from one key to another—**modulation**—can create powerful musical effects. The moment in Sousa's *Stars and Stripes Forever* (LG 7.1) where the dynamic drops down to a soft level is also a moment where the music modulates from the "home" key to a lower key, increasing the sense of relaxation at this point in the march. Conversely, the New England contra dance musicians who play "Money Musk" (LG 2.2) raise the tune to a higher key after a few repetitions (at 1:37), injecting new energy into their performance.

Harmony

Very little of the music you have been listening to so far consists of melody and nothing else. Most music combines multiple voices or instruments, or uses instruments capable of sounding several pitches simultaneously, such as guitar or piano. The art of **harmony** involves combining pitches into simultaneities, or **chords**, and moving from one chord to the next to create **chord progressions**, or, in jazz lingo, **changes**.

An essential concept here is that of **consonance** and **dissonance**. A *consonant* chord is pleasing and harmonious to the ear, while a *dissonant* chord is harsh and unsettled. Most music mixes consonance and dissonance to create fluctuating levels of tension and relaxation. Dissonant combinations of pitches are legion; any toddler capable of reaching up to a piano keyboard will discover countless dissonances and play them with glee. Creating consonances, and mixing them with other consonances and just the right amount of dissonance to create pleasing chord progressions, requires considerably more craft.

The basic harmonic building block of tonal music is the three-note chord, or **triad**, consisting of a starting pitch or **root** and the pitches a third and a fifth higher. This combination occurs naturally in the overtone series, where the

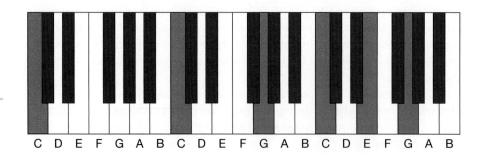

≫ The pitches of the first six partials as found on the piano's keyboard.

C D E F G A B C D E F G A B C D E F G A B

fourth, fifth, and sixth partials form a **major triad**. Lowering the middle pitch of a major triad by a half step results in a **minor triad**. Likewise, lowering the top pitch of a minor triad by a half step results in a **diminished triad**. Perhaps because all of its pitches resonate so well with the overtones of the root, the major triad sounds brighter or "happier" than the minor triad, whose third is not so resonant. The diminished triad, with both third and fifth out of kilter with the root's overtone series, sounds unstable and is treated as a dissonant chord.

Triads can be built on all seven scale degrees of a diatonic scale; some triads will be major, others minor, and one will be diminished. The all-important **tonic chord**, built on the tonic pitch, will be major in major keys, appropriately enough, and minor in minor keys. Two chords nearly as important as the tonic are those built on the fifth scale degree, or **dominant**, and the fourth scale degree, or **subdominant**. Although the remaining chords are useful, a huge number of folk and popular songs can be harmonized using only tonic, dominant, and subdominant chords, which are often labeled with roman numerals as I, V, and IV, respectively. In major keys, all three of these chords are major. In minor keys, all three are minor in theory, but in practice the dominant chord is usually changed to major.

Learning to identify chords by ear is an advanced skill that is not needed for this introductory study. But learning to hear the movement from one chord to another, even if you cannot name the specific chords being played, is useful and not hard to do. An excellent song for practice is one you have already come to know quite well, "Lost Highway" (LG 17.2). The following chart shows the sixteen bars of the first stanza with the lyrics and roman numerals to indicate where the song's three chords—I, IV, and V—occur:

(Four-bar instrumental introduction)			I'm a rollin'

1	2	3	4
stone	all a-lone and	lost	For a life of
I	I IV	I	I

5	6	7	8
sin	I have paid the	cost	When I walk
I	I	V	V

9	10	11	12
by	all the people	say	"Just another
IV	IV	I	I

13	14	15	16
guy	on the lost high-	way"	
I	I V	I	I

TEXTURE

Let's add just one last concept to our arsenal before we begin our discussion of America's music. That concept, **texture**, concerns the interactions between multiple melodic, harmonic, and rhythmic layers.

The simplest texture is **monophony**, meaning "one sound": a single melody, whether sung or played on an instrument. Jean Ritchie sings "The Gypsy Laddie" (LG 9.2) with no accompaniment of any kind; her rendition is *monophonic.* "The Liberty Song" (LG 2.1) also begins with a single voice; when other voices join in (0:13), they all sing the same melody, and for that reason the texture does not change but remains monophonic. The singer of "John Henry" (LG 14.4) accompanies himself by swinging an ax, but because the ax doesn't produce a specific pitch, we can still describe this as a monophonic texture.

When a prominent melody is heard over a discreet accompaniment, the resulting texture is called **homophony.** When Bob Dylan sings "Only a Pawn in Their Game" (LG 17.6) and accompanies himself on guitar, the texture is *homophonic*. The same is true when Sara Carter sings at the beginning of the Carter Family's "Can the Circle Be Unbroken" (LG 11.2). But when two other singers join in (0:24), they sing different pitches—they harmonize with the first singer. This texture, where multiple voices sing the same words in the same rhythm but with different pitches, is also called homophony. We can distinguish between these two kinds of homophonic textures by labeling the first **melody and accompaniment** and the second **hymn texture** or **block chords**. Hymn texture is also evident in OLIVET (LG 3.3)—fittingly, since that tune is a hymn.

Block chords can also be heard at the beginning of SHERBURNE (LG 3.1). But after only eight seconds, the voices seem to split apart: the basses sing alone for a moment (a brief bit of monophony), then the other voices join in one by one, each singing its own melodic line. All are singing the same words, but not at the same time. The effect is something like a round, such as "Row, Row, Row Your Boat" or "Frère Jacques." This *polyphonic* texture, consisting of multiple independent melodic lines, is considerably more complex than the block chords that came before. **Polyphony** is a feature of much classical music, but it can be heard as well in other types of music, such as early New Orleans jazz. The last section of King Oliver's *Dippermouth Blues* (LG 12.2) is a particularly adroit example of spontaneous-sounding polyphony.

USING THE LISTENING GUIDES

As you become acquainted with more of America's diverse musical traditions, you will have many opportunities to increase your technical vocabulary and refine your listening skills. A crucial means of doing so is through the use of the listening guides found in every chapter. There is a listening guide for every musical selection that accompanies this book. Each listening guide draws your attention to specific musical features, with timings to indicate formal divisions in the music and places where notable events occur. Thus it is important to listen to the selections with an audio player that indicates minutes and seconds. (Your player's readout may differ from the timings in the book by a second or two.)

This introduction covers a large number of concepts, but you shouldn't worry if your listening skills are not immediately up to the task of identifying them all by ear. At first, you might focus simply on perceiving the beat, hearing the meter, and feeling where phrases begin and end. With the listening guides to help you, the other skills will develop naturally out of your study. You may sometimes find it useful to pause the recording at the moments indicated in the listening guide, taking in the musical selection section by section. And you should count on listening to each selection multiple times, both with and without the listening guide in front of you.

With this goal of critical listening before us, we can now start our exploration of the history of music in the United States, beginning at a time when the nation did not yet exist.

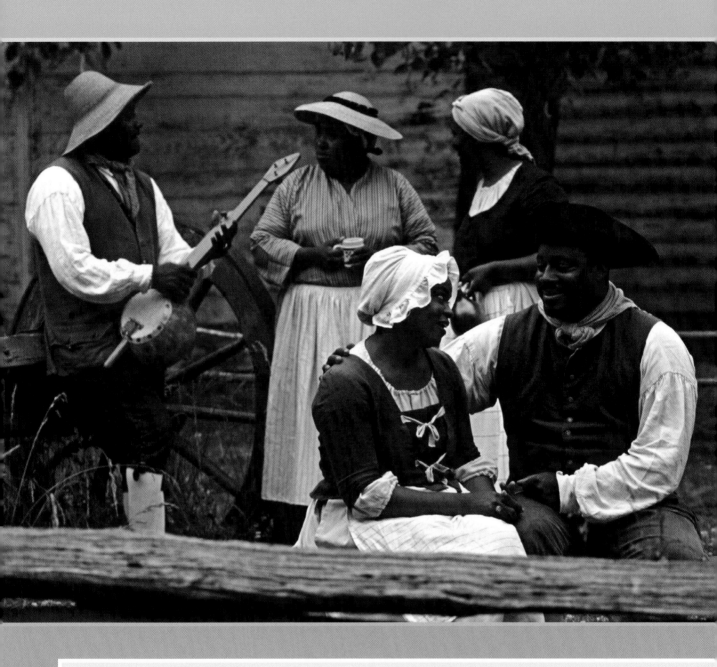

TIMELINE: 1540—1865

1540 Juan de Padilla teaches Indians in present-day New Mexico to sing plainsong

1698 *The Bay Psalm Book*, 9th ed., with printed music

1737–50 Charles Theodore Pachelbel active as organist in Charleston, South Carolina

1769 Junipero Serra begins the building of Franciscan missions in California

1770 Johann Friedrich Peter immigrates from Germany to Pennsylvania

1770 William Billings, *The New-England Psalm-Singer*

1787 First sheet music published in the United States

1801 Richard Allen, *A Collection of Spiritual Songs and Hymns*

1815 Founding of the Handel and Haydn Society of Boston

1820 Antony Philip Heinrich, *The Dawning of Music in Kentucky*

1822 [Lowell Mason], *The Boston Handel and Haydn Society Collection of Church Music*

1822 Founding of America's first resident opera company, in New Orleans

1825 First performance of opera in Italian in the United States

AMERICA'S MUSIC
FROM COLONIZATION THROUGH THE CIVIL WAR

Although native peoples had been making music in North America for centuries before the arrival of Europeans, the written history of music on the North American continent begins with documents by European explorers and settlers. The writings of Spanish and French missionaries describe not only the music of indigenous peoples but also the European-style music put to service in the efforts to convert them to Christianity. Music in the British colonies, meanwhile, arrived as a simple transplant from England, but began in the course of the first century of settlement to show traits that pointed to New World origins.

Developments in the colonies and the early republic tell the story of musicians searching for ways to be paid for their art without the established institutions that supported music in the Old World. A successful musical career such as that of Lowell Mason demanded not only musical ability but also an entrepreneurial spirit, business acumen, and a finger on the pulse of public taste. From early in the nation's history, a hallmark of music in the United States has been its active engagement with the marketplace.

In the decades before the Civil War, American music reflected the diversity of American society. Bands, orchestras, and choral societies presented music "of the highest class," as a Boston critic of the time called it, to urban audiences of growing sophistication. Southern slaves responded to hardship with music rooted in their African heritage. Working-class Northerners, many of Irish descent, adapted that slave music and dance to create a raucous stage entertainment, the minstrel show, that would resonate through American culture for many decades to come. Piano manufacturers and sheet music publishers catered to the tastes of a growing market for their merchandise, and their efforts would give rise to a popular music industry. By the end of the Civil War, the musical culture of the United States represented the rapidly industrializing, urbanized nation itself.

◀ African American music formed one part of the soundscape of colonial North America. Pictured here are present-day reenactors at Colonial Williamsburg with a reproduction of an early banjo.

---

ca. 1828 "Daddy" Rice creates the character Jim Crow

1831 Thomas Hastings and Lowell Mason, *Spiritual Songs for Social Worship*

1833 Founding of the Boston Academy of Music

1837 Lowell Mason begins teaching music in Boston public schools

1842 Founding of the New York Philharmonic Society

1842 The Hutchinson Family Singers begin touring

1843 The Virginia Minstrels perform the first full-length minstrel show

1844 B. F. White and E. J. King, *The Sacred Harp*

1846 End of musical activities in California missions

1850 Jenny Lind's U.S. tour, managed by P. T. Barnum

1851 Singing debut of Elizabeth Taylor Greenfield, "The Black Swan"

1854 Founding of Mason & Hamlin, manufacturer of reed organs and, later, pianos

1859 Dan Emmett introduces "Dixie" to the New York stage

1860 A resident opera company is established in San Francisco

1861–65 Civil War

"NATURE MUST INSPIRE THE THOUGHT"

Sacred Music in the European Colonies

Commercial and religious outreach spurred Europe's settlement of North America. The southern arm of the process was controlled by Spain, whose king and queen, hoping to extract riches from far-off lands, sponsored the voyage that sent Christopher Columbus to the Caribbean in 1492. The northern arm of settlement, beginning in the 1530s, took two different forms. Canada was colonized chiefly as a fur-trading venture under the direction of the French crown. Working with the Roman Catholic Church, which sent Jesuit priests to make Christians of American Indians and to minister to white settlers, the French turned the St. Lawrence River and its waterways into a delivery system for a business profitable in Old World markets. In the meantime, the English, who soon dominated the continent south of Canada, were far less systematic in their approach.

American history is not something that all happened west of the Atlantic Ocean; the territory that is now the United States was in reality an extension of European empires. Entrepreneurs in those nations, needing a labor force to extract the "new" continent's riches, encouraged their own people to settle there. They also brought slaves from Africa to enhance production and promote the increase in farming. Though geographically separated from Europe, America has for more than four centuries been tied economically, politically, and culturally to the Old World, forming a vast transatlantic arena in which the drama of western expansion has been played out. That fact looms large in the history of this country's musical life.

CATHOLIC MUSIC IN COLONIAL NORTH AMERICA

Two European nations were primarily responsible for the spread of Catholicism in North America: Spain in the South and Southwest, and France in the North and Midwest.

SPANISH COLONIZATION

For all the violence of the Spanish conquest in 1519 of the Aztecs in Mexico, the invaders did their work with the blessing of the Roman Catholic Church, which was vitally interested in converting the indigenous peoples to Christianity. Thus, the first Christian sacred music to take root in North America was that of the Roman Catholic liturgy, brought by priests attached to Spanish missions in the New World. Having established their capital in Mexico City, the Spanish created New Spain as a network of settlements ruled from the capital, with each town formed around a central plaza on which stood a church or cathedral. In these churches the people, who gradually came to include more and more *mestizos* (people of mixed blood) as well as Spanish and Indians, came to know the Roman rites of worship.

To make worship services as impressive as possible, the Roman Catholic Church encouraged public display. Monumental church buildings, bright images and flashing color, priestly garments, incense, large spaces within which speech and music could reverberate—all were welcomed into the Catholic tradition. As a part of that heritage, the church also favored musical elaboration, especially vocal **polyphony** (singing in two or more independent voice parts) and the use of an organ or other musical instruments. Moreover, until the Second Vatican Council of 1962–65, the Roman Catholic liturgy was celebrated throughout the world in Latin, helping to give it an aura of timeless formality, not to mention the practical advantages of having one liturgy and language for one international church.

By the early 1500s, the Spanish had installed the Roman rite in Mexico and were working to Christianize the native populations. As early as 1528, the Spanish-born Franciscan priest Juan de Padilla was teaching those near Mexico City to sing plainsong (Gregorian chant) and to participate in sacred choral partsinging. In 1540 Padilla crossed the Rio Grande into present-day New Mexico and began a similar project among the Moquir Pueblo and Zuni Indians. Nineteen years later, the Spanish launched a parallel effort in Florida, where the musician *Florida* and missionary Pedro Martín de Feria taught people near the present city of Pensacola how to sing parts of the liturgy in plainsong.

The Roman Catholic Church used sacred music not only to maintain and bolster the faith of the European settlers but also to familiarize indigenous peoples with white settlers' ways. In what is now Texas and New Mexico, Jesuit mis- *Texas, New Mexico* sions educated American Indians to participate in the missions' musical life. In 1630 Alonso de Benavides noted the presence of "schools for reading and writing, singing and playing all instruments," and by 1680 some twenty-five such missions existed across the Southwest.

In the latter 1700s the missionary effort spread farther west. In 1769 the Franciscan Junipero Serra, himself a trained musician, began the colonization of southern California as a part of New Spain. By the 1820s a network of twenty- *California* one Franciscan missions existed in California. The Roman Catholic liturgy, with appropriate music, was celebrated in the settlements until 1833, when the government in Mexico City secularized the missions, sold their lands, and sent the friars back to Spain. By 1846 musical activity in the settlements had ceased. While it lasted, however, music making in the California missions, rooted in plainsong

↬ Processions to mark the feast of Corpus Christi, such as this one in Guatemala in 2007, are still an important part of Roman Catholic practice throughout Latin America and elsewhere.

LG 1.1

but with plenty of polyphonic singing as well, displayed the variety of a flourishing colonial culture.

A good example of California mission music is "¡O qué suave!" (Oh, how gentle), which is preserved in several manuscript sources (LG 1.1). This anonymous **hymn**—a sacred song with a nonbiblical text—would have been sung during the elaborate outdoor processions that formed part of the celebration of Corpus Christi, a major Catholic holiday occurring in late May or early June. At each of four flower-strewn altars, a padre would raise up the communion bread and chalice, representing the body and blood of Christ, while poems were recited and music was played and sung. Unlike the liturgy performed inside the church, some of these hymns were not in Latin but in Catalan Spanish, the everyday language of the settlements. "¡O qué suave!" shows the influence of the *galant* style of mid-eighteenth-century European music: a graceful melody floats atop a simple homophonic texture, the harmonies move slowly and clearly, and the short phrases end gently. A stately triple meter suggests the sarabande, a formal European dance. This highly cultivated European-style music would probably have been performed by an ensemble of mostly American Indian singers and instrumentalists.

FRENCH COLONIZATION

In a parallel development to the Spanish missions, French Jesuit priests brought Roman Catholic worship to Canada. The long, harsh winters and rough terrain were not conducive to the kind of network of towns the Spanish had installed to the south; the French in Canada instead concentrated on setting up commercial outposts. In that arrangement, a trading center in Quebec City served as the chief link to the European market. Agents in France received fox, beaver, and mink furs as products of overseas investment, while in Quebec supervising agents monitored the white and American Indian trappers who fanned out through the Canadian wilderness to do their work. Jesuits followed the trappers'

| 🎧 | CD 1.1 | Listening Guide 1.1 | "¡O qué suave!" ANONYMOUS |

DATE: ca. 1800

PERFORMERS: Chanticleer (male voices, two violins, cello, organ, harp, guitar)

GENRE: Catholic hymn from California missions

METER: triple, then duple

FORM: **binary form** with varied repeats: AA'BB'

WHAT TO LISTEN FOR

- alternation of gentle and lively dance rhythms
- texture of paired melodic lines in thirds over a simple bass line
- light instrumental accompaniment

TIMING	SECTION	TEXT	TRANSLATION	COMMENTS
0:03	A	¡O qué suave y dulce estáis, altísimo Dios de amor!	Oh, how gentle and sweet you are, exalted Lord of love,	Homophonic texture: (1) a topmost melody with (2) a lower line moving mostly in parallel thirds (both lines sung and doubled by violins), over (3) a bass line (cello), with organ, harp, and guitar filling out the harmony. The two phrases are not quite symmetrical: 4 + 5 bars.
0:29	A'	Cuando muy fino ocultáis con la nube el resplandor.	when so delicately you hide with a cloud your brilliant splendor.	Varied repeat, with changes in rhythm. The phrases are extended to 6 bars each.
1:09	B			Change to a lively tempo and a dancelike duple meter. The performers here have opted to play this section through the first time with instruments only.
1:38	B'	Enciéndase y arda en mi corazón, mi amante Divino, mi rey, mi dueño y Señor, pues al incendio puro de tu dulce amor.	Let it ignite and burn in my heart, my divine love, my King, my Lord and Master, in the pure fire of your sweet love.	The B section repeats with the addition of voices.

NOTE Only the vocal parts are preserved in manuscript. For this performance, the music scholar Craig Russell (who is heard playing guitar) has added parts for instruments known to have been present in the missions.

Listen & Reflect

1. Does the music seem to reflect the mood or meaning of the text, and if so, how?
2. What features, if any, strike you as sounding particularly sacred or secular?

routes, helping to carry the flag of the French king into the heart of North America. And the sacred music they brought, by adding to the Roman Catholic Church's authority, proved useful in the settlement of New France.

EUROPEAN DESCRIPTIONS OF AMERICAN INDIAN MUSIC

European explorers, settlers, and missionaries in the New World left behind written descriptions that offer a glimpse of American Indian music making. Those descriptions can be understood only by keeping in mind the misconceptions that are likely to arise when members of separate cultures come into contact on a massive scale. Only with phonograph recordings and the first systematic attempts to notate their music (as described in chapter 9) did it become possible to begin to draw a more detailed picture of American Indian music history.

When Europeans encountered the people they hoped to displace, they were struck first by the differences between their own customs, dress, and behavior and those of American Indians. Measured against European values, the Indians were found wanting, an attitude that bred contempt and gave settlers an excuse to cheat, brutalize, and kill the peoples who were there before them. But the settlers also saw similarities, especially in the Indians' capacity for virtue (as the settlers defined it), a perception that led efforts to educate them in order to civilize them, and to convert them to Christianity in order to save their souls. It is in this context of "good Indians and bad Indians" (i.e., those similar to or different from their European observers) that historians have learned to read the first descriptions of Indian music making.

As early as the 1530s, a group of Spaniards traveling near what today is Big Spring, Texas, was greeted by "all the people . . . with such yells as were terrific, striking the palms of their hands violently against their thighs." They presented their visitors with "gourds bored with holes and having pebbles in them, an instrument for the most important occasions produced only at the dance or to effect cures, and which none dare touch but those who own them. They say there is virtue in them, and because they do not grow in that country, they come from heaven." Continuing west, the Spaniards met Indians in New Mexico who gave them a "jingle bell of copper" and two medicine rattles.

Another account from New Mexico in 1540 confirms the Indians' use of musical sound for specific functions, such as the ceremonial grinding of corn: "Three [Zuni] women come in, each going to her stone. One crushes the maize, the next grinds it, and the third grinds it finer. Before they come inside the door they remove their shoes, tie up their hair and cover it, and shake their clothes. While they are grinding, a man sits at the door playing a flageolet [an end-blown flute], and the women move their stones, keeping time with the music, and all three sing together."

These reports from the Southwest, written less than half a century after Columbus reached the Western Hemisphere, are some of the first evidence of American Indian instruments and uses of music. Although they say nothing about its sound, they give some idea of how music functioned in American Indian societies.

 This French engraving of American Indian farmers, appearing in Alain Manesson Mallet's *Description de l'Univers* (1683), reflects the "good Indian" image.

CALVINIST MUSIC IN COLONIAL NORTH AMERICA

If the American Southwest and California reflect the northern reach of New Spain, place names such as Detroit, St. Louis, and New Orleans serve as a reminder of New France's reach southward from Canada. But as important as both of these Roman Catholic realms were to the history of American development, the first Old World settlers to populate what is now the eastern United States were Protestants.

The Protestant Reformation of the early sixteenth century changed the religious, political, and economic face of Europe, leading to conflicts in which all sides remained convinced of their moral superiority. Sacred music seldom plays more than a small role in any such conflict, but as a part of public worship it does reflect fundamental ideas of the religious outlook it represents. In breaking with the Roman Catholic Church, Protestants took issue with some of the main premises of Roman worship.

Protestants challenged two key Catholic beliefs: (1) prescribed rituals foster true piety, and (2) God is best praised through sacred expression that pleases the senses. Reformers actually split on the role of ritual. German-speaking Protestants, under Martin Luther's leadership, and many in England who joined the Anglican Church (or Church of England) after King Henry VIII broke with Rome, maintained parts of the Catholic liturgy in translated form. Elsewhere in Europe, however, especially under the leadership of John Calvin, reform went further. Fired by the idea of "the priesthood of all believers," Calvinist groups in Switzerland, France, and the Netherlands wanted individuals and congregations to decide on liturgy for themselves. In the same spirit, they pledged their allegiance to the Holy Bible, not to church tradition. Protestants may have helped advance the cause of literacy by shifting the right to read and interpret the Scripture from the church to its members. According to the Calvinist vision, no human power should stand between God and the individual believer.

Calvinists scorned the notion that charming the senses in the name of religion could please God. Rejecting the idea that musical skill was worth cultivating in God's service, Calvin and his followers assigned music making to the congregation itself. And they found a style of singing suited to the abilities of most members. In comparison with the Catholic practice that it countered, Calvinist sacred music was simple and spare: no part singing, no instrumental accompaniment, and no singing of texts outside the **psalms**, a book of sacred songs in the Hebrew Scripture (Old Testament). Their practice of singing psalms in worship is called **psalmody**.

psalmody

The Calvinist ideal opposed musical professionalism—a stance that Catholics and "liturgical" Protestants, with their priests, choirs, organs, and fondness for elaboration, never took. In England, one Protestant group, the Puritans, hoped to reform the dominant Anglican Church by adopting a theology strongly influenced by Calvinist principles. Of the Puritans who settled in North America, one subgroup, the Pilgrims of Plymouth Colony, were driven to emigrate at least in part by a desire to worship in an environment where no state church existed. And that helps explain why the favored music of both Puritans and Pilgrims, in contrast to Anglican and Catholic music, was so plain.

PSALMBOOKS IN ENGLISH

Both Anglicans and Puritans were enthusiastic congregational singers. Their preferred **psalter** (book of metrical psalms) was *The Whole Booke of Psalmes, Collected into Englishe Meter* (London, 1562), versified by Thomas Sternhold and John Hopkins, until 1696, when Nicholas Brady and Nahum Tate produced their *New Version of the Psalms of David*. (The earlier work was then dubbed the "Old Version.") Both psalters turned the psalms into popular poetry, using rhyme and some of the same simple verse structures as the secular folk ballads that circulated in oral tradition (see chapter 2). These **metrical psalms**—the texts in the Old Testament Book of Psalms, versified in English and published in psalters—were to play a key role in American sacred music making through the seventeenth and eighteenth centuries.

The Pilgrims, who arrived in 1620 at Plymouth, Massachusetts, sang from a psalter translated by the Reverend Henry Ainsworth, a clergyman who had brought out *The Book of Psalms: Englished Both in Prose and Metre* in Amsterdam in 1612. Although its verses and tunes differed considerably from those of the "Old Version," the so-called *Ainsworth Psalter* shared several traits with the earlier book: its pocket size made it easily portable; it printed a tune with each psalm text so that those who read music could sing the tunes directly from the psalter; and it included far fewer tunes (39) than psalms (150). The first and last of these traits are true of all psalters that circulated in New England from then on. Ainsworth didn't need as many tunes as psalms because the psalms were cast in standard verse forms, or meters, so worshipers could sing many different texts to the same tune. As an art, then, music played only a secondary role in early New England psalm singing.

LG 1.2   The bone-simple OLD HUNDRED (LG 1.2) is one of the tunes in Ainsworth's psalter. Also found in the Church of England's "Old Version" and many English and American sacred tunebooks since, OLD HUNDRED traces its origin back to the 1550s and early French Calvinist psalm singing. It is commonly attributed to Louis Bourgeois, who compiled the music for a psalter Calvin himself published in Geneva in 1562. The tune is brief and straightforward enough to be perfect congregational fare, as proved by its continued use in Protestant worship today as the Doxology. No element is more basic to Western music than melody, and centuries of continuous use mark OLD HUNDRED as a good tune. The music consists of four phrases of equal length. The shapes of the phrases differ, but their rhythm is almost identical. Melodic movement is neatly balanced between conjunct (stepwise) motion and disjunct motion (skipping to a note other than an adjacent one), and between melodic rise and fall. Most of the motion is stepwise, but in each phrase, at least one skip occurs: a rising fourth in the first two phrases and a falling third in the next. In the last phrase, three skips of a third take place, two falling and one rising. That phrase, which also begins with an upward leap of a fifth to the melody's highest note, is by far the most active and serves as the melody's climax.

Calvinist doctrine dictated that psalm singing in church services should be in **unison**: a **monophonic** rendition of the plain melody only. The **homophonic** harmonized version heard here might have been sung by Puritan settlers in New England outside of church, as part of recreational music making.

🖎 The psalm tune OLD HUNDRED, first published in Geneva in 1561, supplied the music for Henry Ainsworth's version of Psalm 100 in 1612.

Pſalm. 100.

1. SHowt to Jehovah, al the earth. 2. Serv ye Jehovah with gladnes: before him come with ſing-ing-merth. 3. Know, that Jehovah he God is:

🎧 CD 1.2	Listening Guide 1.2	OLD HUNDRED ATTRIBUTED TO LOUIS BOURGEOIS

DATE: 1562

PERFORMERS: Gregg Smith Singers

GENRE: Protestant psalm tune

METER: duple

FORM: strophic

WHAT TO LISTEN FOR

- solid, straightforward rhythm
- simple but memorable melodic shape

TIMING	SECTION	TEXT	COMMENTS
0:00	phrase 1	Make ye a joyful sounding noise	Conjunct descent, then a leap up a fourth.
0:05	phrase 2	Unto Jehovah, all the earth;	Conjunct descent on a new starting pitch, then again a leap up a fourth.
0:11	phrase 3	Serve ye Jehovah with gladness:	Rising and falling conjunct motion, then a fall of a third.
0:16	phrase 4	Before his presence come with mirth.	Disjunct motion creates a climax, followed by a conjunct descent to the original starting pitch.

NOTE Only the first of Ainsworth's many stanzas is heard here; the same music would be repeated for all the others.

Listen & Reflect

1. Where do the lowest and highest pitches occur in OLD HUNDRED?
2. What interval do they form (that is, how far apart are they in terms of scale tones)?

The simplicity of OLD HUNDRED is not typical of the tunes in Ainsworth's psalter. Indeed, the difficulty of the book's melodies suggests that the original Pilgrims were accomplished singers. In fact, when the congregation in Salem, Massachusetts, voted in 1667 to give up *Ainsworth,* they cited the difficulty of the tunes. So did the Plymouth congregation itself in 1685, a consequence, according to claims by New England clergy of that day, of the settlers' isolation from their parent culture and the decline in singing ability that resulted.

Early New Englanders were even more troubled, however, by the psalters' nonliteral translations of the texts. Intent on following God's word faithfully, a group of clergymen from the Massachusetts Bay Colony collaborated on a new psalter that would more closely mirror the scriptural originals. The resulting collection, usually referred to as the *Bay Psalm Book,* was published in Cambridge, Massachusetts, in 1640. It was the first full-length book printed in the English-speaking colonies, and in its many revisions and reprints it supplied New England's congregations with texts for psalm singing well into the next century.

the Bay Psalm Book

A comparison of the prose beginning of Psalm 23 in the King James Bible with the versified form in the *Bay Psalm Book* illustrates how metrical psalmody works in practice:

KING JAMES VERSION	BAY PSALM BOOK (1651 EDITION)
The Lord is my shepherd;	The Lord to me a shepherd is
I shall not want.	Want therefore shall not I.
He maketh me to lie down in	He in the folds of tender grass
green pastures;	Doth make me down to lie.
He leadeth me beside the still waters;	He leads me to the waters still
He restoreth my soul.	restore my soul doth He;
He leadeth me in the paths of	In paths of righteousness, He will
righteousness for His name's sake.	For His name's sake lead me.

The *Bay Psalm Book*'s translators, following the example of Sternhold and Hopkins, Ainsworth, and others, set the psalm in four-line stanzas so that it could be sung **strophically**, that is, with all stanzas of text sung to the same music. (Psalm 23 fills five stanzas in the *Bay Psalm Book* version.)

The *Bay Psalm Book*'s translators did all they could to simplify psalmody for congregations. In that spirit, they set 125 of the 150 psalms in common meter, adding fourteen in long meter and another eight in short meter, leaving only three remaining psalms in unique meters. A congregation singing from the *Bay Psalm Book*, then, needed to know only a handful of tunes. These numbers indicate that tunes in seventeenth-century New England were chosen not to underline the meaning of the words but merely to provide a musical vehicle for their delivery.

THE OLD WAY VERSUS REGULAR SINGING

Metrical psalters were published to serve worshipers who could read. But by the 1640s, some New England congregations could get by with only one copy of a psalter. A single singer (sometimes called the **deacon** or **precentor**) would read

A CLOSER LOOK

Matching Tunes to the Text Meters of English Psalmody

Translators typically made each stanza four lines in length, with each line containing six or eight syllables, using the iambic (short-long) foot. The favorite meters were:

Common meter	8.6.8.6.
Long meter	8.8.8.8.
Short meter	6.6.8.6.

Psalm 23 in the *Bay Psalm Book* is a common-meter text; it could be sung to any tune in which the number of notes per phrase matches the syllabic pattern of the psalm text. OLD HUNDRED is a long-meter tune; it can be used for any metrical psalm versified in long meter—not just Psalm 100. This mix-and-match approach is fundamental to Protestant psalmody. For that reason, psalm tunes have names, conventionally printed in small caps, that rarely have anything to do with the texts to which they can be sung. In that respect, the name OLD HUNDRED is unusual.

or chant the psalm, a line at a time, to the congregation, who would sing each line back in response. Congregations may have begun **lining out**, as this practice came to be called, because too few worshipers could read the psalms, buy the books, or sing the tunes as they were written. Whatever the reason, the custom won acceptance as the clergy realized that without it there would be no congregational singing at all.

Lining out began, then, as a way of cueing congregation members on the texts they were to sing. Its impact on psalmody was enormous: first, it greatly slowed the pace of singing; second, it meant that the repertory was kept small because tunes had to be chosen from those that the worshipers already knew; finally, the music was entrusted to the leading singers, who did not necessarily read music themselves. As one observer of the time wrote, a tune might vary so much from one congregation to the next that "'tis hard to find Two that Sing [it] exactly alike." Lining out gave birth to a style in which the singers in a group freely elaborated a tune as they sang. This style, eventually labeled the **Old Way** of singing, won favor with many New England worshipers.

Although lining out eventually disappeared from New England churches, the practice has continued to the present day among a few extremely conservative religious groups. A recording from mid-twentieth-century rural Kentucky demonstrates a vocal practice that resembles the Old Way in some respects, though we should not assume that it matches exactly the singing of colonial New England congregations. The text of "Guide Me, O Thou Great Jehovah" (LG 1.3) is not a biblical psalm but a more recent poem written in the style of a metrical psalm: in other words, a **hymn**, in this case by the eighteenth-century Welsh Methodist evangelist William Walker. Written in 1745, it deviates from the pattern of older metrical psalms in two ways: each stanza has six lines instead of the customary four, and the meter is trochaic (long-short) instead of iambic (short-long).

LG 1.3

By 1720 some New Englanders were complaining that the Old Way had departed from the Puritan fathers' psalmody, which had been governed by the "rule" of musical notation. The Reverend Thomas Symmes recommended that **Regular Singing** (i.e., regulated singing—singing guided by rules), which carried the authority of notated music, replace the Old Way. Yet Symmes understood why people enjoyed singing as they did. In the Old Way, worshipers were able—within limits, of course—to decorate their praise of God as the spirit moved them.

The clergy's objection to the Old Way of singing inspired a burst of rhetoric on the subject: sermons, pamphlets, newspaper accounts, and Regular Singing meetings. But in this theological battle, unlike others of the time, the published words came from one side only: that of Regular Singing advocates, chiefly ministers

---

In their own words

Thomas Symmes on the Old Way of Singing, 1720

Singing-Books being laid aside, there was no Way to learn; but only by hearing of Tunes Sung, or by taking the Run of the Tune (as it is phrased). The Rules of Singing not being taught or learnt, every one sang as best pleased himself, and every Leading-Singer would take the Liberty of raising any Note of the Tune, or lowering of it, as best pleas'd his Ear, and add such Turns and Flourishes as were greatful to him; and this was done so gradually, as that but few if any took Notice of it. One Clerk or Chorister would alter the Tunes a little in his Day, the next, a little in his and so one after another, till in Fifty or Sixty Years it caus'd a Considerable Alteration.

CD 1.3	Listening Guide 1.3	"Guide Me, O Thou Great Jehovah" ANONYMOUS

DATE: unknown

PERFORMERS: George Spangler and the congregation of the Thornton Old Regular Baptist Church, Mayking, Kentucky

GENRE: Anglo-American lined hymn

METER: unmeasured

FORM: strophic

WHAT TO LISTEN FOR

- alternation of leader and congregation
- loose rhythmic coordination of voices

TIMING	TEXT	COMMENTS
0:00	Guide me, O Thou great Jehovah,	The leader slowly intones the first phrase of the tune, and members of the congregation gradually join in as they recognize the words and melody.
0:18	Pilgrim through this barren land.	The leader quickly calls out the second line of text, and the congregation responds by singing the words to the second phrase of the tune.
0:39	I am weak, but Thou art mighty; Hold me with Thy powerful hand. Bread of Heaven, Bread of Heaven, Feed me till I want no more.	The third line is similarly lined out, and the third phrase sung. The process continues with the fourth, fifth, and sixth lines.

NOTE Recorded in 1959. The recording fades out at the end of the first stanza.

Listen & Reflect

1. Many of the older metrical psalms fill six to eight stanzas. How long might it take to sing a complete psalm using the style of lining out heard here?

2. And how might we apply that insight to the clergy's objections to the Old Way of singing described in the text?

condemning a custom of worship that had slipped out of their control. Singers committed to the Old Way made no attempt to justify themselves in writing; they simply continued singing as they liked. In the meantime, the champions of Regular Singing argued that its order and solemnity would help to make public worship more pleasing in the sight of God. And they supported their opinions with references to the Bible.

When seen as a conflict pitting the clergy against the people, rules against customs, and control against freedom, the Regular Singing controversy stands as a colorful episode in New England's cultural history. But in the history of

American music, the outcome reached further, touching off a process of singing reform that reshaped New England psalmody.

THE SINGING-SCHOOL MOVEMENT

The Regular Singing controversy was one of many religious debates that marked early New England life. Cotton Mather, a leading American intellectual of the time, wrote in 1721 on the values of Puritan sacred music making. His endorsement of biblical texts stresses the importance of words over music. New sacred verses—hymns—should not replace divinely inspired ones, he believed, merely because they were more up to date. While he granted the possible merits of "devout hymns composed by the good men of our own time," they could not match the songs "prepared for us by the Holy Spirit of God."

For Mather and his allies, Regular Singing was a form of prayer. The orderly singing of a sacred text by a whole congregation, they believed, was pleasing in God's sight. But only a reform of congregational psalmody could lead to that result, because the Old Way lacked such discipline. And indeed, reform began in earnest around 1720, with two developments particularly helpful to the cause: psalm tunes were published in **tunebooks** to guard them from the whim of oral transmission, and singing instruction became available to congregation members.

In 1721 two books were published in Boston that emphasized sacred music over sacred verses. They included not only the tunes but also instructions in how to sing them. The titles reveal their purpose: John Tufts's *An Introduction to the Singing of Psalm Tunes* and Thomas Walter's *The Grounds and Rules of Musick, Explained.* Both volumes began with an introduction explaining the rudiments of singing: how to use one's voice as part of a congregation, including an explanation of the symbols in which the psalm tunes were written.

Tufts and Walter

The appearance of these two books began a new era in the history of Calvinist psalmody in the New World. Between them they bridged the gap between music as an art with a technical basis and a public ready to learn that technique. Those who wished to learn could now attend **singing schools**, which were aimed at beginners, were taught in the evenings in any available space, and typically lasted three months (a "quarter"). A singing master was not a clergyman but simply a musical individual (always male), perhaps recruited by aspiring singers or perhaps deciding on his own to organize a school and advertise for scholars, who paid a fee. Moreover, though it grew out of the church's needs, the singing school was from the start an institution distinct from the church.

By the early 1720s, then, the elements of a more disciplined psalmody had been introduced in and around Boston. In some congregations, reform went smoothly. Once a school was formed, the "scholars" persuaded other church members to follow their lead, and Regular Singing replaced the Old Way. But in others, the process could take years, even decades. With no popes or bishops to hand down decrees, questions about congregational singing and other matters of worship were put to a vote of church members, and the majority ruled. In Farmington, Connecticut, the congregation in 1727 upheld local independence by voting down Regular Singing as a practice "recommended by the Reverend Ministers of Boston"—by implication, big-city know-it-alls.

As it happened, singing schools proved more than instructional gatherings; they were also social occasions, providing a rare chance for young men and women to mingle. Supporters praised schools for offering "innocent and profitable recreation" that would help young people do something useful during the long winter evenings and wean them away from "idle, foolish, yea, pernicious songs and ballads." In the view of others, however, schools encouraged young people to be "too light, profane and airy," and to stay out late. Indeed, many who opposed Regular Singing saw it as a secular intrusion into a sacred realm.

choirs and congregations

Through the agency of singing schools, Regular Singing helped foster musical literacy and independent taste. By the 1760s these schools had spread widely in the colonies. By then, too, another organization was taking root: the meeting-house choir, formed not at the prompting of clergy or congregation but by the singers themselves. Choirs brought new energy and musical diversity to the meeting house, but almost from the moment of their appearance they also became targets of complaint: some parishioners found choir members' behavior secular and obnoxious. The youthfulness of choir members—many were in their teens and early twenties—may have had some influence on how older parishioners viewed their desire to sit, not with their families in the pews, but together as a group in the rear balcony, or gallery. Moreover, along with choirs came the gradual introduction of musical instruments into the meeting house—first the bass viol, or cello, to double the bass voices discreetly and help keep all the singers on pitch, and eventually fiddles, flutes, and other instruments, not playing independent instrumental parts but merely doubling the voices. Such a **gallery orchestra** compounded the growing distinction between choir and congregation.

As early as 1764 an observer described one Boston church choir as "a set of geniuses who stick themselves up in a gallery" and think that they have a right to do all the singing themselves, excluding the congregation. Eager to show off their skill as musicians, they considered the hymns sung by the congregation far too simple, favoring tunes that were more modern, elaborate, and worldly. They would, complained the writer, often perform "a light, airy, jiggish tune better adapted to a country dance" than to "chanting forth the praises of the King of Kings." Here, then, choir and congregation competed instead of complementing each other. The Boston choir confirmed the fear that once musical display won a toehold in the worship service, it would take its own course with little regard for the religious framework in which it had flowered in the first place.

A PHILADELPHIA TUNEBOOK

Given the long history of singing in New England meeting houses, it may seem strange that the first tunebook to address the needs of both congregation and choir was published in Philadelphia. That collection, titled *Urania, or A Choice Collection of Psalm-Tunes, Anthems, and Hymns,* was compiled in 1761 by James Lyon, a Presbyterian born in Newark, New Jersey, and a recent graduate of the College of New Jersey (later Princeton University). This sacred tunebook was far more ambitious than any that forty years of Regular Singing in Boston had inspired.

Philadelphia was the largest city in the English-speaking colonies, a dynamic settlement that grew steadily larger, unlike Boston, whose population remained

Henry Dawkins engraved this elaborate title page for James Lyon's *Urania* (Philadelphia, 1761).

stable from the 1740s to 1775. The religious culture of Philadelphia was also more tolerant and more diverse than Boston's, with substantial numbers of Anglicans, Lutherans, Methodists, Baptists, Roman Catholics, and Quakers, as well as Reformed "dissenters," including Lyon himself, whose Presbyterian faith marked him as a tolerant kind of Calvinist.

Urania was published by **subscription**, a commercial practice that allowed a work to be proposed for publication with a minimum of investment. To enroll subscribers, a publisher would offer copies of the book at a prepublication discount. Only if enough subscribers were found would the work then be printed, as was Lyon's 198-page volume in June 1761, with a list of subscribers in the front.

James Lyon's bold act of entrepreneurship lies behind this landmark of American music history. Not only did Lyon use commercial means to sell his book, but he also designed his collection for broad appeal. *Urania*'s musical contents offered something for every sacred singer: standard psalm tunes, left textless so that worshipers could sing them to their preferred psalter; plenty of choir music, including **anthems**—elaborate choral works by British composers, often with biblical texts; and hymn tunes apparently geared to home performance, as suggested on the title page: "adapted to the use of churches and private families." *Urania* was the first American tunebook to bring psalmody into the commercial arena, relying on subscription and advertising and tailoring its contents to attract customers. From a Puritan perspective, the process bears a distinctly secular flavor, but then, in 1760s Philadelphia the Puritan perspective carried little weight. *Urania* showed how psalmody, a mode of sacred expression, could find a niche in a public marketplace.

marketing psalmody

The absence in New England of any effort similar to Lyon's suggests how small a role musical learning had so far played in the tradition of psalmody. But that would soon change. By the 1760s singing schools and Regular Singing were spreading musical literacy and feeding interest in more-elaborate sacred music throughout the region, as suggested by the roster of church choirs formed in New England after midcentury, especially in Massachusetts. Boston's First Church had a choir by 1758, followed by many others through the next dozen years.

WILLIAM BILLINGS, AMERICAN COMPOSER

In 1770 a young Boston tanner and singing master produced a tunebook reflecting the vitality that had begun to flow into New England sacred music as Puritan restrictions fell away, music literacy spread, and secular attitudes grew more acceptable. *The New-England Psalm-Singer, or American Chorister*, by William Billings, is a true landmark. Though shorter than *Urania*, it came close to matching that book's variety, with everything from plain congregational tunes to long anthems that would tax the skill of any American choir. In musical content, however, the originality of Billings's book far outstripped Lyon's. Containing 127 compositions, all by Billings himself, *The New-England Psalm-Singer* was the first published collection of entirely American music and the first American tunebook devoted wholly to works by one composer. With its appearance, the number of American sacred compositions in print increased tenfold, and a region that had long fostered psalmody reclaimed leadership in sacred music.

Born in Boston in 1746, Billings attended school briefly, then learned the tanner's trade. As a musician he seems to have been self-taught. By age twenty-three he was teaching singing schools, an activity he pursued through much of his life. Billings's first tunebook, *The New-England Psalm-Singer*, reflects changes in New England culture that reached beyond music. By 1770, although some Puritan influence persisted, the region's moral purpose had found a new focus: resis-

resistance to Britain tance to Britain's rule of her American colonies.

The state of mind that led in 1775 to war with England could not have been predicted a dozen years earlier. In 1763, when the Treaty of Paris ended the French and Indian War, many colonists shared a feeling of pride in a hard-won Anglo-American victory. The British, too, looked for a new relationship with this fast-growing part of their empire. But while the Americans saw the departure of the French and Spanish as an opening of fresh opportunities, British officials believed that the time had come for England to receive a higher yield on overseas investments. The first of Parliament's money-raising measures—the Stamp Act of 1764, which increased taxes and duties on imports and exports—began a cycle of escalating grievances. Misunderstandings multiplied. What seemed to the British reasonable steps to govern their colonies were received by some Americans as unreasonable impositions of external authority. Such responses in turn brought stronger displays of power from the British. Positions gradually hardened, and extremists took over leadership on both sides.

Revolution Boston experienced new unrest in 1768, when customs commissioners asked for an armed guard to protect them as they performed their duties. British troops arrived in April. Although an uneasy peace was maintained, some Bostonians viewed the soldiers as an army of occupation. The Boston Massacre of 1770, where British soldiers fired into a crowd of protesters and killed five colonists, was one of several incidents that inflamed public opinion. During the next several years, conflict simmered as the British troops remained. The American public split into factions: "loyalists" who accepted England's right to rule her colonies as she chose, and "patriots" opposed to British rule. In April 1775 war broke out in Massachusetts between the British soldiers and local minutemen. When the smoke finally cleared in 1781, the colonies had won independence.

Striking an aggressively American note, *The New-England Psalm-Singer* bore the stamp of its time and place. The titles of many tunes refer to Boston and the surrounding area, including Massachusetts counties, cities, and towns, and Boston churches (NEW SOUTH, OLD BRICK). But even more unusual was the glimpse of himself that Billings offered his readers. In the book's introduction, he approached the public as a man of Boston and a musician of the New World. As Billings saw it, composers either were blessed with artistic inspiration or they were not. On "the rules of composition," he wrote: "*Nature is the best Dictator,* for all the hard dry studied Rules that ever was prescribed, will not enable any Person to form an Air [i.e., compose a melody] . . . without a Genius. . . . Nature must inspire the Thought." Confident of the "genius"—the intuitive inventiveness—that linked him with nature's inspiration, Billings then added: "For my own Part, I don't think myself confin'd to any Rules for Composition laid down by any that went before me."

Billings's "genius"

Billings also gained historical attention by launching his career on the eve of American independence in a city that played a key role in the conflict. Far from disguising his own sympathies, Billings celebrated them. The engraver of *The New-England Psalm-Singer*'s frontispiece, for example, was Paul Revere, strongly identified with Boston's patriot faction. Like James Lyon, Billings published his work by subscription, but he apologized in an advertisement for omitting the subscriber list from his book for want of space. Given Billings's links to Boston's patriots—he was also friendly with the arch-agitator Samuel Adams—it would be interesting to know whether subscribers ran chiefly to like-minded people or included a wider spectrum of Bostonians.

Billings as emblem

Patriot, composer, vivid personality, William Billings stands as an emblematic figure in American music history. When psalmodists and writers of his own time chose one man to exemplify their tradition, Billings was the natural choice. When later reformers wished to recall the supposedly crude beginnings of American music, Billings served their purposes too. More recently, when music historians have chronicled the origins of American composition, or when choirs have performed music of eighteenth-century Yankees, it is to Billings and his works that they have been most likely to turn. Billings stands foremost among our musical founding fathers, long on talent and historical charisma if short on polish and solemnity.

Billings struggled financially in his later years. Besides teaching singing schools and publishing tunebooks, during the 1780s he served the city of Boston as scavenger (street cleaner) and hog reeve (official in charge of controlling roving swine). The publication of his last tunebook in 1794 was sponsored by local singers as an act of charity toward him and his family. When Billings died in 1800, William Bentley, a Boston minister who had known him for thirty years, remembered the composer in his diary as "the father of our New England music." Bentley's obituary noted Billings's lack of "a proper education," his disturbing appearance ("a singular man, of moderate size, short of one leg, with one eye . . . & with an uncommon negligence of person"), and the air of defeat that marked his life's end ("He died poor & neglected & perhaps did too much neglect himself"). Yet Bentley could think of no rival who matched the impact of Billings, a man who "spake & sung & thought as a man above the common abilities."

LG 1.4

CHESTER (LG 1.4), from *The New-England Psalm-Singer,* shows Billings in action as both composer and poet. Written in long meter (8.8.8.8.), the hymn enlists God on New England's side in its quarrel with the mother country. The notion that in 1770 a sacred tunebook could include a piece with a text like CHESTER's shows how far the boundaries of psalmody had stretched since Cotton Mather's day, half a century earlier. Then, only divinely inspired texts had been allowed; now, a prophet of rebellion was opening up the tradition to new expressive territory.

Much of CHESTER's appeal lies in a melody (in the tenor part) whose profile is shaped by the dactylic rhythm (long-short-short) that begins all four of its phrases. Lying high in the voice, the melody reaches its apex (top note) in three phrases, encouraging full volume, just as the rhythm mandates a fairly brisk pace. Considering Billings's text, it is hard to imagine anyone singing this tune softly or slowly. And the tenor voice holds no monopoly on musical interest. The bass, for example, moves with sure melodic purpose in all four phrases, supporting the tenor tune. The treble (soprano), whose fourth phrase begins like the tenor's first, sings a melody almost as interesting as the main one. Only the counter voice (alto), whose role is to complete the harmony, lacks tunefulness.

CHESTER thus gave singers a confluence of independent, interlocking melodic lines, tailored to fit metrical verse, a fact important for worshipers and composers alike. But as a musical composition, it points up Billings's lack of artistic polish as well as his talent. For example, the most strongly stressed syllable in the

CD 1.4	Listening Guide 1.4	CHESTER WILLIAM BILLINGS

DATE: 1770

PERFORMERS: Gregg Smith Singers

GENRE: hymn from *The New-England Psalm-Singer*

METER: duple

FORM: strophic

WHAT TO LISTEN FOR

- marchlike rhythm
- block-chord texture
- melody in tenor

TIMING	SECTION	TEXT	COMMENTS
0:00	stanza 1 phrase 1	Let tyrants shake their iron rod,	The main tune (in the tenor) quickly rises to its highest note on the word "shake." On the word "iron," treble and tenor voices move in parallel fifths, forbidden in "correct" European styles.
0:07	phrase 2	And slav'ry clank her galling chains,	A four-note **melisma** (multiple notes sung on a single syllable) occurs on the harsh word "clank."
0:14	phrase 3	We fear them not; we trust in God,	The tenor's tune ends on its apex ("God").
0:20	phrase 4	New England's God forever reigns.	The tenor begins on the tune's apex and ends on its nadir (lowest note). Meanwhile, the treble echoes the tenor's melody from phrase 1.
0:27	stanza 4	The foe comes on with haughty stride Our troops advance with martial noise Their veterans flee before our youth And generals yield to beardless boys.	The music repeats, with new words.
0:54	stanza 5	What grateful off'ring shall we bring, What shall we render to the Lord? Loud hallelujahs let us sing, And praise his name on ev'ry chord!	A third time through the tune, with still new words.

NOTE Stanzas 2 and 3, omitted in this performance, are shown here.

Howe and Burgoyne and Clinton, too,
With Prescott and Cornwallis joined,
Together plot our overthrow,
In one infernal league combined.

When God inspired us for the fight
Their ranks were broke; their lines were forced.
Their ships were shattered in our sight
Or swiftly driven from our shore.

Listen & Reflect

1. Some of the five stanzas are political in content, some are religious, and some mix the two; is there a pattern, and if so, what is its effect?

2. Is this hymn well suited for liturgical use (i.e., for singing as part of a church service)? Why or why not?

second phrase is "clank," the stanza's least euphonious word. And then there are the parallel fifths between voices, forbidden by European "Rules of Composition" because they work against the lines' melodic independence. Billings, having sworn to follow "Nature" over "hard dry studied Rules," makes good on his pledge in the very first phrase, where treble and tenor move in a chain of four such intervals. We can imagine him weighing the alternatives—the sound of the whole versus the melodic integrity of individual voices—and choosing the first, perhaps because nothing better expressed the inflexibility of Britain's "iron rod" than the ring of those descending fifths.

composing in parts   CHESTER suggests how the method of composition Billings describes in one of his tunebooks worked in practice. He began by writing the tenor, or "first part," which he called "nothing more than a flight of fancy" to which other voices were "forced to comply and conform"—by forming harmonious consonances with the tenor rather than clashing dissonances. Billings then composed the rest of the voices so that they would partake "of the same air, or, at least, as much of it as they can get." In other words, Billings tried to infuse the other voices with melodic interest. But because they were composed *after* the tenor, "the last parts are seldom so good as the first; for the second part [the bass] is subservient to the first, the third part [the treble] must conform to the first and second, and the fourth part [the counter] must conform to the other three." By writing voice parts that kept singers musically engaged while still following accepted harmonic practice, Billings strove to reconcile the claims of nature and art—of inspiration and technique.

In his second tunebook, *The Singing Master's Assistant* (1778), Billings composed anthems paraphrasing Scripture to link the plight of present-day Bostonians with that of the ancient Israelites. The Old Testament Psalm 137 begins: "By the rivers of Babylon, there we sat down, yea, we wept, when we remembered Zion." In his *Lamentation over Boston*, Billings changed those words to "By the Rivers of Watertown we sat down & wept when we remember'd thee, O Boston." And later in the same piece, he took off from the Lamentations of Jeremiah:

> A voice was heard upon the high places, weeping and supplications of the children of Israel. (Jer. 3:21)
> A voice was heard in Roxbury which ecchoed thru the continent weeping for Boston because of their danger. (Billings)

Texts like these treated Scripture not only as God's word and a guide to spiritual inspiration but also as a historical epic that offered timeless parallels to current events.

PROTESTANT MUSIC OUTSIDE THE CALVINIST ORBIT

Although Calvinism dominated New England, the other former British colonies sustained a more diverse religious culture. Pennsylvania, founded by Quakers, cultivated a particularly high level of religious tolerance. Of the many groups practicing different faiths in the early republic, three developed especially distinctive musical traditions: the Anglicans, the Ephrata Cloister, and the Moravians.

THE ANGLICAN CHURCH

The Church of England supported a musical life on these shores very different from that of the Calvinists. Anglican worship followed a prescribed church calendar, and the content of many services was specified. The church was also hierarchical, with tiers of officials from the Archbishop of Canterbury on down. A church bureaucracy centered in London assigned clergymen to specific churches in the New World. (From 1786 on, American Anglicans called themselves Episcopalians.)

Anglicans in the New World, welcoming visual and musical display, recognized that organ music added impressiveness to their worship. As Francis Hopkinson, a prominent Philadelphia Anglican and himself an organist, put it: "I am one of those who take great delight in sacred music, and think, with royal David, that heart, voice, and instrument should unite in adoration of the great Supreme." Indeed, much of the history of early American church music centers on the organ: either the Calvinists' opposition to it or the financial investment needed to buy one. The high cost of importing an organ from overseas was only part of the expense, however, for churches with organs then had to find organists to play them. And that could mean hiring a professional musician with European training.

Hopkinson warned church organists to remember "that the congregation have not assembled to be entertained with [their] performance." But not all organists agreed, as shown by a 1781 description of an Anglican service in Philadelphia that reminded the disapproving observer of "a sort of opera, as well for the music as the decorations." Yet an organ could attract a skilled musician to a community, whose musical life might then be enriched by that presence. In 1737 St. Philip's Church in Charleston, South Carolina, hired as its organist Charles Theodore Pachelbel, a native of Germany and son of Johann, composer of the famous Canon in D. Pachelbel played at St. Philip's until his death in 1750. He also performed in public concerts, taught a singing school, and gave private lessons.

London organ builder John Snetzler completed this chamber organ in 1762. It is now found in the Congregational Church in South Dennis, Massachusetts.

THE EPHRATA CLOISTER

Other Protestant groups also led unusually active musical lives. Two such groups were Pennsylvania-based, German-speaking separatist societies that found havens in America, where they pursued their visions of Christian living. The first formed a cloister in Ephrata, Pennsylvania. Its founder, Conrad Beissel, was a prolific writer who used hymns to present his theological ideas. By the mid-1740s, Beissel, though untrained in music, had devised a system of composing sacred choral music with a soft, otherworldly sound. Conceived for his cloister

Conrad Beissel, founder and leader of the Ephrata Cloister in Pennsylvania, wrote both words and music for many hymns, which were elegantly copied in illuminated manuscripts such as this one.

members alone, Beissel's music was not published; rather, in a spirit of devotion, it was copied by hand, with elaborate decorations, in beautifully illuminated choral books that have been preserved.

THE MORAVIANS

Another group of musically inspired separatists were the Moravians, or Unitas Fratrum, who crossed the Atlantic in the 1740s and 1750s to create their own communities in Pennsylvania (Nazareth, Bethlehem) and North Carolina (Salem). Moravians encouraged the singing of elaborate anthems as well as congregational hymns. And as community life grew more settled, organs were introduced into the churches. David Tannenberg, a Moravian born in Saxony but a Pennsylvania resident from 1749, became one of the most important American organ builders, with at least forty-two instruments to his credit. Moreover, choral anthems were sometimes accompanied by orchestras formed by men of the congregation (musical instruments carried none of the secular taint here that disturbed the Calvinists). Such groups of instrumentalists also met outside worship services to play chamber and even orchestral music, most of it composed in Europe. By 1780 the Bethlehem **collegium musicum**—one such group, consisting of four violins, one viola, and pairs of violoncellos, flutes, oboes, French horns, and trumpets—was skilled enough to play symphonies by the day's leading composers: Haydn, Mozart, and the sons of J. S. Bach. Like the singers, collegium members were amateurs who performed to enrich a community life dedicated to God's glory.

Ich will dir ein Freudenopfer thun (I will freely sacrifice unto Thee; LG 1.5), by Johann Friedrich Peter, is a good example of a Moravian anthem. Peter, a native of Holland who was educated there and in Germany, was an exact contemporary of William Billings. He immigrated to America in 1770 at the age of twenty-four to serve Moravian communities in Pennsylvania. A schoolteacher who also filled several church positions, he directed music for the Salem, North Carolina, congregation between 1780 and 1790, and there he seems to have composed this work for four-voice choir (sopranos I and II, alto, and bass) and orchestra (strings with two French horns). Peter's anthem is **through-composed**: instead of literally repeating one or more sections of music, the composer continually spins out new music. Tying it all together, though, is one repeated musical figure: the rising melody to which the first words of the text are set. Played by the violins to start the anthem, this melody is also sung at the choir's first entrance. And from there, it returns often: in the instruments, in the voices, sometimes with the pitches changed but the rhythm intact, and sometimes in different keys. The natural interweaving of this figure throughout the piece points to the composing skill of Peter, whose six quintets for strings (1789) are the earliest known instrumental chamber music (one player per part) written in America.

Each of the traditions touched on in this chapter carried a different significance in its own day. The music of Spanish Catholic missionaries aimed to bring magnificent display that would impress American Indian converts and strengthen the faith of settlers in Europe's westernmost outposts. New England psalmody produced a homegrown tradition of singing and, eventually, of composing that served the needs of English-speaking Calvinists. Anglican church music created a niche for European-trained professionals. The Ephrata Cloister gave rise to a novel musical style. And the Moravians set up theocratic communities whose life owed much to cosmopolitan styles of music making. The variety of ways that colonists found to praise God through music reflected the diversity of American religious life itself.

This watercolor depicts Moravian bishop Jacob Van Vleck at the keyboard accompanying young singers who may be students at the school in Bethlehem, Pennsylvania, of which he was the principal.

🎧 **CD 1.5**	**Listening Guide 1.5**	*Ich will dir ein Freudenopfer thun* **JOHANN FRIEDRICH PETER**

DATE: ca. 1780s

PERFORMERS: Boston Baroque; Martin Pearlman, conductor

GENRE: Moravian anthem

METER: triple

FORM: through-composed

WHAT TO LISTEN FOR

- elaborate choral and orchestral texture
- absence of literal repetition
- modulating tonality

Ich will dir ein Freudenopfer thun,
und deinem Namen danken, Herr,
dass er so tröstlich ist.

I will freely sacrifice unto thee:
I will praise thy name, O Lord;
for it is good.

Psalm 54:6

TIMING	COMMENTS
0:00	Instrumental introduction anticipates the leading vocal melody, then turns to a more active instrumental idiom.
0:18	Sopranos enter with the leading melody; the lower voices enter a bar later in free imitation.
0:30	After a 2-bar instrumental interlude, the voices sing a varied repeat of their opening, then proceed to the second line of text.
0:43	Now the lower voices begin, and the sopranos enter a bar later.
0:49	On the word "Herr" (Lord), the music modulates to a higher key.
0:56	The opening instrumental introduction returns, now in the new key, then modulates to a darker, minor key.
1:05	Vocal phrase and answering instrumental phrase in the minor key.
1:16	The last, and longest, vocal section begins in the minor key and modulates back "home" to the tonic.
1:36	An instrumental **coda** (closing section) rounds out the anthem with a final statement of the leading melody.

Listen & Reflect

1. Compare this music with the other pieces discussed in this chapter. What can be inferred about the role of the congregation in the music of these different religious traditions?

QUESTIONS FOR DISCUSSION AND REVIEW

1. On the basis of what we hear in the actual music, what can we say about the different ways music functioned in the religious lives of Franciscan missionaries in California, Calvinist settlers in New England, and the Moravian communities in Pennsylvania and North Carolina?

2. An important aspect of the Old Way of singing is that it was fully participatory. There was no "audience" listening to the singing, unless that audience was the deity to whom the congregation directed their praise. What would be the difference between listening to the performance of "Guide Me, O Thou Great Jehovah" (LG 1.3), and participating in it? If there is an aspect of this musical practice that can be accessed only through participation, what might it be, and why would its adherents value it so highly?

3. OLD HUNDRED is a tune suitable for any text in long meter. Try singing the words of CHESTER to the tune of OLD HUNDRED. Now try singing the metrical translation of Psalm 100 (in LG 1.2) to the tune of CHESTER.

4. Three songs that have texts in common meter are "America the Beautiful," "Auld Lang Syne," often sung on New Year's Eve, and "Amazing Grace." Try singing the words of any of these songs to the tune of one of the others.

5. What does this experiment reveal about the New England psalmodists' mix-and-match attitude toward music and text?

FURTHER READING

Cooke, Nym. "Sacred Music to 1800." In *The Cambridge History of American Music*, edited by David Nicholls, 78–102. Cambridge: Cambridge University Press, 1998.

Crawford, Richard. "Introduction." In *American Sacred Music Imprints, 1698–1810: A Bibliography*, by Allen Perdue Britton and Irving Lowens and completed by Richard Crawford. Worcester, MA: American Antiquarian Society, 1990.

Knouse, Nola Reed, ed. *The Music of the Moravian Church in America*. Rochester, NY: University of Rochester Press, 2008.

Koegel, John. "Spanish and French Mission Music in Colonial North America." *Journal of the Royal Musical Association* 126, no. 1 (2001): 1–53.

Nabokov, Peter, ed. *Native American Testimony: A Chronicle of Indian-White Relations from Prophecy to the Present, 1492–1992*. New York: Viking, 1991.

Russell, Craig H. *From Serra to Sancho: Music and Pageantry in the California Missions*. New York: Oxford University Press, 2009.

Titon, Jeff Todd. "'Tuned Up with the Grace of God': Music and Experience among Old Regular Baptists." In *Music in American Religious Experience*. Edited by Philip V. Bohlman, Edith L. Blumhofer, and Maria M. Chow. 311–34. New York: Oxford University Press, 2006.

FURTHER LISTENING

Chanticleer. *Mission Road*. Warner Classics & Jazz, 2008. Californian mission music.

Songs of the Old Regular Baptists: Lined-Out Hymnody from Southern Kentucky. Smithsonian Folkways, 1997.

Wake Ev'ry Breath. New World Records, 1998. Choral music of William Billings.

CHAPTER 2

"OLD, SIMPLE DITTIES"
Secular Music in the Colonies and Early Republic

Americans make music in all sorts of settings, from concert halls to back porches. The kinds of music they make may vary according to place; a tavern song is out of place in church, like a string quartet at a football game. In some cases, however, music migrates easily from one social sphere to another, as when a song heard in the theater becomes a favorite to sing at home. This chapter examines various kinds of music Americans made in the decades before the American Revolution and during the early decades of the republic, looking at both private and public sites for music making. At this historical stage, the categories of public and private, professional and amateur, overlap in complex and revealing ways.

SONG, DANCE, AND HOME MUSIC MAKING

A key difference between music making in the Old and New Worlds lay in their systems of economic support. In Europe, society's ruling institutions—the church and the nobility—required music for their own purposes, and they paid musicians to supply it. In America, however, no national church existed, nor did any political structure with aristocratic continuity and clout. Lacking such sponsorship, musicians either made music their avocation or, if they aspired to be professionals, depended on their own entrepreneurial skills for the support and promotion of their art. The creation of a diverse musical life on these shores has largely been the work of musicians seeking to sell their services as performers, composers, teachers, instrument makers, or dealers of musical merchandise. In music, as in other walks of American life, the profit motive has been a vital source of creative energy, for better and for worse.

The number of customers for music grew during the 1700s as the population increased. But professional activity was concentrated in a few cities on the Eastern Seaboard—Boston, New York, Philadelphia, Baltimore, and Charleston—where immigrant musicians practiced what they had learned in Europe. And that fact points to something basic in America's musical life: from the start of European settlement, musicians here have been able to take for granted the ample supply of music from the British Isles and the European Continent, made available through oral tradition and written notation. Given a steady supply from Europe, there was little demand outside religious circles for music by American composers. Indeed, it apparently mattered little to singers and players that until long after American independence was won, very few of the songs, dances, or theatrical works they performed were composed here.

BROADSIDE BALLADS

An ocean separated early English-speaking settlers from the land of their origin, but not from its language or music. Songs from Great Britain were woven into Americans' lives, as a letter Benjamin Franklin wrote from London in 1765 to his brother Peter back home suggests. Peter had sent Benjamin some original verses, asking that an English composer be hired to set them to music. But in Benjamin's view, the verses called for a simpler tune than a London composer would write. If Peter had given his text "to some country girl in the heart of *Massachusetts,* who has never heard any other than psalm tunes or *'Chevy Chace,'* the *'Children in the Wood,'* the *'Spanish Lady,'* and such old, simple ditties, but has naturally a good ear, she might more probably have made a pleasing popular tune for you than any of our masters here." The songs Franklin names are all **ballads**: narrative songs in strophic form, with many stanzas of text sung to the same music. All three had originated in Great Britain in the early 1600s or before. That they were still circulating orally in North America in the 1760s testifies to their place in the hearts of the people. (Chapter 9 explores further the role of these traditional British ballads in America's musical culture.) *ballads*

Oral ballads existed outside any commercial network. But by the early 1700s a parallel tradition was thriving in America: that of songs sung to traditional ballad melodies but with new verses commenting on current events, printed on sheets called broadsides, and sold in the marketplace. These **broadside ballads** made popular songs widely accessible just as sheet music and phonograph records would in later times. Broadside ballads lacked the prestige that oral ballads came to enjoy. Their reputation was that of cheap commercial goods. The Reverend Cotton Mather complained in a diary entry in 1713: "I am informed, that the Minds and Manners of many People about the Countrey are much corrupted by foolish songs and Ballads, which the Hawkers and Pedlars carry into all parts of the Countrey." *broadside ballads*

Almost anything could inspire a broadside ballad. Colonial settlement, Indian wars, dissatisfaction with English rule, crime, love, and religion are some of the favorite subjects. In contrast to oral ballads, many broadside ballads show a cartoonlike quality of exaggeration, sometimes coupled with language or images that make later standards of public taste seem prudish. Such ballads were often used for political expression, circulating not only in broadsides but also in newspapers. For patriotism aroused passions well suited to the editorializing that broadside ballads invited. *subject matter*

In the years before and during the American Revolution, song after song, whether written from a patriot or a loyalist perspective, trumpeted the same claim: our side is virtuous and right, your side is corrupt and wrong; and if the difference can be settled only through combat, then let's fight. In the duel of words that accompanied rising political unrest, loyalists and patriots used the same stock of British song to argue for their cause. The songs that appeared on broadsides and in newspapers during these years provide a window on the founding of the American republic.

LG 2.1

Broadside ballads were based not only on traditional ballads but on any tune the public might know. John Dickinson's "Liberty Song" (LG 2.1), printed in the *Boston Gazette* in July 1768, was a takeoff on "Heart of Oak," a song written in 1759 to commemorate an English naval victory over France during the Seven Years' War. As the official march even today of both the British Royal Navy and the Canadian Navy, "Heart of Oak" bursts with patriotic pride, as the opening illustrates:

> Come, cheer up, my lads, 'tis to glory we steer,
> To add something more to this wonderful year;
> To honour we call you, as freemen not slaves,
> For who are so free as the sons of the waves?
>> Heart of oak are our ships, heart of oak are our men,
>> We always are ready;
>> Steady, boys, steady!
>> We'll fight and we'll conquer again and again.

Dickinson, a Pennsylvanian, struck a nerve when he fired a parody of "Heart of Oak" back at the British. Here is Dickinson's opening:

> Come, join Hand in Hand, brave AMERICANS all,
> And rouse your bold hearts to fair LIBERTY's Call;
> No *tyrannous Acts* shall suppress your *just Claim*,
> Or stain with *Dishonour* AMERICA's Name.
>> In FREEDOM we're BORN, and in FREEDOM we'll LIVE.
>> Our Purses are ready,
>> Steady, Friends, Steady,
>> Not as SLAVES but as FREEMEN our money we'll give.

Dickenson's thrust inspired a counterattack. In September 1768 the same Boston newspaper printed a loyalist version of "Heart of Oak" upholding the British cause and attacking the patriots:

> *Come shake your dull Noddles, ye Pumpkins and bawl,*
> *And own that you're mad at fair Liberty's Call,*
> *No scandalous Conduct can add to your Shame.*
> *Condemn'd to Dishonour. Inherit the same—*
>> In Folly you're born, and in Folly you'll live,
>> To Madness still ready,
>> And stupidly steady.
>> Not as Men, but as Monkies, the Tokens you give.

Today, the words and music cannot convey the emotional bite that these text-and-tune combinations must have carried in 1768. Dickinson's pro-American version takes a familiar, much-loved song and twists its meaning, while the loyalist version ridicules the new meaning with antipatriot venom. Bostonians would have been aware of how the patriot version turned an anthem of British self-congratulation into an indictment of Britain's policies, while the loyalist version implied that England, victor over a powerful European rival, could easily dismiss a minor family disturbance. In both cases, the melody and its associations gave an edge to political expression.

| CD 1.6 | Listening Guide 2.1 | "The Liberty Song" JOHN DICKINSON |

DATE: 1768

PERFORMERS: Arthur F. Shrader, with David Robertson, Edward Olsen, and Kenneth Lemly

GENRE: broadside ballad

METER: duple, but unmeasured in this performance

FORM: verse and chorus

WHAT TO LISTEN FOR

- alternation of solo verse and unison chorus
- rhythmic freedom of this performance

TIMING	SECTION	TEXT	COMMENTS
0:00	verse 1	Come join hand in hand ...	Solo singer.
0:13	chorus	In freedom we're born ...	The other voices join in on the unharmonized melody.
0:25	verse 2	Our worthy forefathers ...	Solo singer.
0:39	chorus	In freedom we're born ...	All voices.

NOTE The complete song has nine **verses** (musical sections that repeat with new words each time), each followed by an unchanging **chorus**. In this performance, only two verses are sung.

Listen & Reflect

1. Sing the quoted lyrics from "Heart of Oak" and the loyalist parody of "The Liberty Song" to the melody heard here. Does one set of lyrics seem to fit the melody better than the others? If so, how? And if not, what does that say about music-and-text relationships in these related songs?

Patriotic broadside ballads took their melodies not only from English songs but also from the vast body of dance music that circulated in Britain and its American colonies. For instance, "The Irishman's Epistle to the Officers and Troops at Boston," which appeared in the *Pennsylvania Magazine* of May 1775, only a month after war broke out, was sung to the tune of "Irish Washerwoman." In Philadelphia, far removed from the fighting, observers could look beyond the war's grim side and find humor in an event like the hasty British retreat from the colonials. In the second stanza, the song's Irish protagonist taunts the British Regulars, gleefully rubbing salt into their wounded pride:

How brave you went out with muskets all bright,
And thought to befrighten the folks with the sight;
But when you got there how they powder'd your pums,
And all the way home how they pepper'd your bums,
And is it not, honies, a comical farce,
To be proud in the face, and be shot in the arse?

DANCING AND DANCE MUSIC

For centuries, dance has been a lightning rod for American public opinion. Two controversial issues have repeatedly surfaced since the 1600s: dance's erotic dimension and efforts to keep it under control, and dance's connection with social class. Even though dance is being discussed here as a secular activity, it has long been a matter for debate in American religious life. Moreover, like clothing and manners, dancing has often served as a marker of social trends and fashion.

Before the Civil War, most American social dances came from Europe. More recently, they have originated chiefly on this side of the Atlantic, with new dances tending to be physically freer than the ones they replace (ragtime, discussed in chapter 10, is a prime example). In the story of popular dance's development in America, Puritanism has often been assigned a villain's role. Dances once denounced as instruments of the devil now appear quite proper, making objections raised against them seem quaint. Important issues were at stake, however, in the debates that dance has inspired.

Puritan attitudes toward dancing   The lack of common ground between social dance and the Puritan imagination may be traced to the belief that spirit and flesh are contrary forces locked in a perpetual struggle. Devout Puritans saw themselves as sinners dependent on the grace of God. Dance that celebrated the human body did so, they believed, at the soul's expense. Yet while mistrusting the spirit of dance, Puritans acknowledged that it could be effective as a way to discipline the young. In a tract with a title whose religious passion echoes through the ages—*An Arrow against Profane and Promiscuous Dancing; Drawn out of the Quiver of the Scriptures* (Boston, 1684)—the Reverend Increase Mather, father of Cotton, wrote that if "the Design of Dancing is only to teach children good Behaviour and a decent Carriage," then he could approve it. To keep "uncleanness" (i.e., sexuality) at bay, however, Mather recommends that girls and boys be taught separately, and by a pious teacher. The one adult Mather refers to in this passage is the dancing master. It was hard for Puritans to believe that grown men and women could dance together while still honoring and glorifying God.

For non-Puritans, however, dance has not always been considered a secular activity. African religions brought to North America by slaves gave dance a crucial role (see chapter 4). Many American Indian tribes have also relied on music and movement together to establish contact with the spiritual realm. Even within Anglo-American culture, the Shakers, a celibate sect founded in late eighteenth-century England that endured in this country into the early twenty-first century, were known for their sacred dancing.

Anglican attitudes toward dancing   Most Anglicans considered dancing to be a secular activity but did not share the Puritans' disapproval of it. In 1714 King's Chapel in Boston hired Edward Enstone from London as its organist, anticipating that his work would include dance instruction. There were also dancing masters in colonial Boston from the 1670s on, whatever the Puritans thought of them. At one end of the dance spectrum were skills taught formally by masters like Enstone that prepared people to attend social functions such as balls. At the other was a casual, informal pastime taking place at home and as part of festive occasions.

dance types   Dance manuals and musical sources reveal that Americans of the colonial era performed both **couple dances** and **country dances**. Couple dances, including the gavotte, the bourrée, and especially the minuet, were courtly affairs of French origin that called for precise, schooled movements. To perform such dances well was

British artist William Hogarth's painting *The Dance* (ca. 1745) depicts a "longways" country dance.

considered a social accomplishment that was possible only through instruction; those who did so thus had enough leisure time and money for lessons. By 1725, however, country dancing, a forerunner of square dancing and later New England contra dancing, had come into favor in England and the American colonies. Especially popular were "longways" dances, in which a line of men faced a line of women and patterns were traced collectively by the whole group.

As an extension of Britain's social structure, colonial society sought to follow Old World models in formal events like balls and banquets. The courtly French minuet, for example, might begin a ball, danced by the most important guests; other couple dances might follow. The rest of the evening was often given over to country dances, whose popularity increased on both sides of the Atlantic through the 1700s. But apparently these dances were not free from implications of class hierarchy either. In 1768 formal balls were discontinued for a time in New York "when consorts of General Gage and Governor Moore could not agree on who should stand first in a country dance."

Music for country dances, like the dances themselves, came from overseas, especially from the Anglo-Celtic traditions of England, Scotland, and Ireland. The music circulated both orally and in written form, including printed collections and manuscripts that musicians copied for their own use. The jig "Irish Washerwoman," for example, survives in many eighteenth-century copies, domestic and foreign, in print and in manuscript; several different longways country dances for the tune have turned up in American sources. Some of the tunes date back to the 1600s, and as already noted, broadside ballads sometimes borrowed their melodies from dance.

Another favorite country dance tune of the era was "College Hornpipe," which, like "Irish Washerwoman" and such ballads as "The Spanish Lady," survived changes of musical fashion.

Dance in a Country Tavern, by German-American painter John Lewis Krimmel (1786–1821).

A CLOSER LOOK

Characteristics of Country Dance Music

1. Steady, driving tempo.
2. Duple meter, either simple (2/4), as in the **reel** or **hornpipe**, or compound (6/8), as in the **jig**.
3. Regular phrases of predictable length, usually four or eight bars.
4. **Binary form:** two repeated sections, called **strains**, of eight bars each, *aabb*.

Also known as "Sailor's Hornpipe," "College Horn-pipe" was first published in London in 1766. At least six different American versions were printed in the years 1801–25, and in 1870 thirteen of the twenty American publishers in the Board of Music Trade listed editions for sale. Several decades later, composer Charles Ives (see chapter 8), remembering the fiddling at barn dances he had attended as a Connecticut boy in the 1880s, quoted "College Hornpipe" and other dance tunes in the "Washington's Birthday" movement of his *Holidays* Symphony. Today books of fiddle music still carry "College Hornpipe." And in cartoons, the appearance of a sailor on the screen is likely to call forth this tune.

"Irish Washerwoman," "College Hornpipe," and most other Anglo-Celtic fiddle tunes are in **binary form**; that is, they typically have two repeated strains of eight bars each (*aabb*). Owing to their identical length and form, many tunes used to accompany country dancing—or its later incarnation, contra dancing, still popular among folk enthusiasts throughout the United States and especially in New England—are more or less interchangeable, in the sense that a set of steps designed for one tune may be danced to many other tunes instead. A Scottish *LG 2.2* tune that doesn't fit that pattern is "Money Musk" (LG 2.2), whose odd structure—three strains of only four bars each—has kept it tied to the original country dance of the same name. The frequent appearance of "Money Musk" in American manuscript and printed tune collections suggests that both tune and dance were popular on this side of the Atlantic in the decades around 1800. Indeed, "Money Musk" still appears a favorite "chestnut" at contra dances. And in March 2009 contra dancers in the United States and several other countries created an "International Money Musk Moment," when groups were enjoying the old dance more or less simultaneously worldwide.

HOME AND AMATEUR MUSIC MAKING

Although documentation is sparse, there is evidence of music making in early American homes. Colonial Boston records indicate that many citizens owned musical instruments—keyboards (especially harpsichords), plucked and bowed strings, wind instruments, trumpets and drums—and the painting *A Musical Gathering*, most likely an eighteenth-century American work, depicts a home ensemble in action, with the punch bowl ready to be visited.

The scarcity of professional performers gave colonial Americans all the more reason to make music and hold dances in their homes. Like dancing masters, music masters, either itinerant or based in cities, supplied the necessary instruction, giving lessons in singing or on parlor instruments of the day: harpsichord, violin, flute, and guitar. In the years before the American Revolution, amateur music making seems to have increased, with dealers offering instruments, accessories, and printed music for sale and teachers advertising their services in the public press. A musically minded colonial who could pay for lessons had a decent chance to become a competent amateur performer.

🎧 CD 1.7	Listening Guide 2.2	"Money Musk" ANONYMOUS

DATE: 1700s

PERFORMERS: Rodney Miller, fiddle; Steve Woodruff, button accordion; Randy Miller, piano; Sandy Bradley, guitar; George Wilson, bass

GENRE: country dance tune

METER: duple

FORM: three repeated 4-bar strains: *aabbcc*

WHAT TO LISTEN FOR

- each statement of tune follows three-strain structure (with repeat of each strain)
- fiddler slightly varies each statement
- backup musicians provide harmony and rhythmic zest
- key change near halfway point injects new energy

TIMING	SECTION	COMMENTS
0:00	introduction	Two bars of music set the tempo and prepare the dancers.
0:02	first statement *aa*	
0:10	*bb*	
0:18	*cc*	
0:26	second statement	
0:49	third statement	
1:13	fourth statement	
1:37	statements 5–10	The fifth statement modulates to a new key, a fourth higher, raising the energy level; subsequent statements stay in the new key.

Listen & Reflect

1. The seasoned contra dance musicians heard here are accustomed to repeating a tune many times in the course of a dance. How do the players inject variety into the ten statements of the complete "Money Musk" tune?

2. What effect might their variations have on dancers, as opposed to listeners?

In early America, the word "amateur," rather than referring to someone less skilled than a professional, meant one who pursued music simply for love of it, as the Latin root *amare* (to love) suggests. The most illustrious member of that company was Thomas Jefferson, author of the Declaration of Independence and third U.S. president. Jefferson played the violin through much of his life, owned and maintained harpsichords, and collected a large library of music from which he and others performed. Among the music that Jefferson copied out in his own hand is the tune "Money Musk." In a 1778 letter to an acquaintance in Paris, he call : "the favorite passion of my soul" and told of his aspirations

🖎 Music was an important part of middle-class family life, as illustrated in this portrait of the Schuyler family, painted in New York by Ambrose Andrews in 1824.

for building musical performance more fully into the life of Monticello, his Virginia country estate. Jefferson saw music in America as standing "in a state of deplorable barbarism" compared with its place in Europe. He invited his correspondent to visit him or to send "a substitute . . . proficient in singing, & on the Harpsichord." To reconcile his "passion for music" with the constraints of his budget, he considered importing from Europe a domestic staff who could double as gardeners, weavers, stonecutters, and instrumental performers. Living in the country, Jefferson imagined a musical environment that would allow him to play and also to retain a "band of music" to gratify his appetite as a listener.

MILITARY, CONCERT, AND THEATER MUSIC

In the earliest years of the republic, much public music making took place in theaters, as part of dramatic performances. When music was performed for its own sake in a large meeting room, that room became, at least for the duration of the performance, a concert hall. Meanwhile, military music resounded outdoors.

MILITARY MUSIC

Musical instruments have long been used for outdoor communication. Drums, for example, played an important signaling role in early American life. In today's sonic world, where music's volume is often boosted by electronics, the sound of fifes and drums being played outside might not seem especially loud, but early accounts show that they were sometimes considered almost deafening. At a public ceremony to discipline a Continental soldier convicted of thievery in 1775, another soldier wrote that the drums "made such a report in my ears, when accompanied by such screaking of whifes [sic] that I could not hear the man next to me."

Francis Hopkinson, Music Amateur

Perhaps the most devoted musical amateur in eighteenth-century America was Philadelphia native Francis Hopkinson, the University of Pennsylvania's first graduate, a lawyer and judge by trade, a patriot, and a signer of the Declaration of Independence. Hopkinson began playing the harpsichord at age seventeen, in 1754, hand-copying European songs and instrumental pieces, and by the early 1760s was good enough to join professional musicians in concerts. As an Anglican, Hopkinson served for a time as organist of Philadelphia's Christ Church, taught psalmody, and compiled sacred tunebooks for congregational singing. Music was Hopkinson's springboard for entry into Philadelphia's musical life, where, given the scarcity of professional performers, his ability and social position made him welcome.

In 1781, the last year of fighting in the American Revolution, Hopkinson produced a patriotic pastiche for solo singers, chorus, and orchestra called *America Independent, or The Temple of Minerva*, for which he fitted his own verses to music by others, including George Frideric Handel. But his musical ambitions also reached further, into the realm of original composition. As early as 1759 he was composing songs in two parts—with a keyboard accompaniment in which the right hand doubles the singer's melody and the left hand supplies a simple bass line—modeled on British songs he had copied out on his own.

For his *Seven Songs for the Harpsichord or Forte Piano* (Philadelphia, 1788), dedicated to George Washington, Hopkinson wrote both words and music. A prefatory note declares: "I cannot, I believe, be refused the Credit of being the first Native of the United States who has produced a Musical Composition"—a claim referring to the nation born officially in June 1788 when the ninth state ratified the Constitution of the United States of America.

🎵 Francis Hopkinson (1737–1791).

Military uses for music may be divided into four categories: morale building (or *esprit de corps*), camp duties (which included signaling), public ceremonies, and recreation. On the first count, an eighteenth-century European general noted music's power to impart energy that lifts the spirit. Just as people could be inspired "to dance to music all night who cannot continue two hours without it," he wrote, musical sound could help troops "forget the hardship of long marches."

Music also proved a practical way to regulate camp duties. As armies increased in size, they became more cumbersome to control. Warfare required large groups of soldiers to be moved in an orderly way, and drum cadences worked better than oral commands. By the 1600s European armies had developed rhythmic and melodic signals such as reveille, retreat, and tattoo. The British military brought these signals to North America, where military leaders used them to communicate quickly with their men, both in and out of battle.

Military life relies a good deal on ceremonies. Parades that feature uniformed soldiers marching in time to music are a display of discipline and suggest invincibility. With no risk to life or limb, they contribute to an army's goal: to deter wars as well as to fight them.

Finally, a military unit is both a fighting force and a society, and its musicians have long performed at concerts, mealtime performances, evening entertainments, sports festivals, and riding exhibitions. In fact, the British and American military in the 1700s fostered two different kinds of ensembles, one functional and the other geared more toward aesthetic ends. **Field music**—which involved fifes and drums as in the 1775 ceremony described above—was played by musicians who belonged to the regiments and whose wages were paid out of army appropriations. *Harmoniemusik*—the German term is sometimes translated as "band of music"—was performed by an ensemble made up of pairs of wind instruments (oboes, horns, bassoons, occasionally flutes or clarinets) and required more polished players; they were hired by the officers, who paid for them out of their own pockets.

field music and **Harmoniemusik**

The field music, performed by marching musicians, was portable and loud—an ideal medium for building *esprit de corps,* controlling troop movement, and enhancing ceremonies. The band of music, less loud and portable but with a harmonized sound made by upper-, lower-, and middle-register instruments, offered wider possibilities; it was most useful for recreation, though it could also be an inspirational and ceremonial presence. When colonists formed militia units to fight in the American Revolution, they followed British custom, including the two-part division into field music and *Harmoniemusik.*

LG 2.3

On the accompanying recording for LG 2.3, a band of music plays the most enduring American instrumental composition of the 1700s, "The President's March," composed around 1793 by Philip Phile, an immigrant musician who worked in American theaters. In 1798 a Philadelphia judge, Joseph Hopkinson, set patriotic words to the march, beginning "Hail Columbia, happy land," and the combination of tune and text held a place as a favorite national song, "Hail Columbia," well into the twentieth century. The tuneful melody and sprightly march rhythm combine to create a piece of music suitable for both ceremony and entertainment. This performance uses instruments from the eighteenth century and modern reproductions: the flutes are wooden, not metal; all of the woodwinds have fewer keys than their modern equivalents; and the French horns have no valves. Keys, which open and close holes along the instrument's length, and valves, which add variable lengths of tubing, assist modern woodwind and brass players in producing a consistent tone and accurate **intonation**. Ezekiel Goodale, who published this arrangement in a method book for band instruments, noted that the "imperfect" wind instruments of his time required "the assistance of a good musical ear to blow . . . in tolerable tune."

Military music is a rare example of a secular institution's support of music making in eighteenth-century America. Some bands of music played in public concerts and at funerals; some even survived the war. When George Washington toured the United States in 1789, just before taking office as president, bands welcomed him almost everywhere. These ensembles played the full range of the day's music, from marches and patriotic songs to dance tunes. The band's ability

| CD 1.8 | Listening Guide 2.3 | "Hail Columbia" PHILIP PHILE |

DATE: ca. 1793

PERFORMERS: Members of the Federal Music Society, playing pairs of flutes, clarinets, French horns, and bassoons, with military side drum

GENRE: march

METER: duple

FORM: binary (AABB)

WHAT TO LISTEN FOR

- march rhythm
- varied timbres of mixed woodwinds and brass
- modulation away from and back to tonic

TIMING	SECTION	COMMENTS
0:00	A	Three phrases of four bars each: *abc*. The third phrase modulates up a fifth to the dominant key, where the A section ends.
0:22	A	Repeat.
0:45	B	Four phrases of four bars each, *dd'be*: *d* begins in a minor key; *d'* repeats *d* a whole step lower, bringing the music back to the tonic key, where it remains to the end; *b* repeats the middle phrase of the A section; *e* is a new idea that somewhat resembles the last phrase of the A section (*c*).
1:16	B	Repeat.

NOTE Arrangement for *Harmoniemusik* from Ezekiel Goodale, *The Instrumental Director*, 3d edition (Hallowell, Maine, 1820).

Listen & Reflect

1. How does this wind ensemble differ from present-day school or military bands?
2. What are the audible differences?
3. What impression would this ensemble make out of doors?

to travel and to exist in a variety of forms has made it a uniquely practical ensemble. In that spirit, band performances in early America were given in many different settings, both indoors and outdoors: coffeehouses, taverns, and theaters on the one hand, and parade grounds and pleasure gardens on the other. Taken together, field music and *Harmoniemusik* prefigure the later history of the wind band as it developed on American soil (see chapter 5).

CONCERT LIFE

Producing a public concert in eighteenth-century America, as today, required finding a venue, setting a date, securing performers, choosing music, and attracting customers. Concerts of the time were given chiefly by immigrants from Europe, who were familiar with such secular assemblies; they had only to transplant and adapt to the New World customs already familiar to them from the Old.

Concerts in the 1700s were not necessarily high-toned, formal events, and many were held in modest, often plain rooms with no stage and with temporary arrangements of chairs that might quickly be pushed aside for dancing when the concert was over. The first known public concert in the American colonies took place in Boston in 1729, in a room that a local dancing master used for assemblies. Not until 1754 did the city gain a real concert hall: a room in a building that was refurbished as "an elegant private concert-room." But even a room like this made Boston unusual. In most of eighteenth-century America, concert halls were concert halls only as long as the performance lasted.

benefit and subscription concerts

Benefit concerts, which could be organized quickly, were well suited to the conditions of musical life. Although the term today refers to a concert that raises funds for charity, in the eighteenth century it referred to concerts intended to turn a profit for the performers. The format allowed local organists, traveling professionals, or newly arrived singers in a theater troupe to star in nearly impromptu shows of their own making. The musician who arranged a benefit took the financial risk, paying the expenses and reaping the profits, if any. Benefit concerts were one-time happenings, which distinguished them from most **subscription concerts**, another eighteenth-century approach. The subscription format, like the subscription publications discussed in chapter 1, allowed organizers to hedge their bets: to issue a public proposal, often for a concert series, and then wait to see whether the response justified going ahead with the plan.

Other types of concerts included the charity benefit given to raise money for a worthy cause, such as aiding residents of the local poorhouse. Concerts were also given by musical societies: organizations formed to promote the art. The St. Cecilia Society of Charleston, South Carolina, for example, brought together amateur and professional musicians on a regular basis. Membership dues acted in effect as a subscription that supported musical performances, some of them open to the public.

The success of public concerts depended on whether their organizers could attract a sizable audience. From the very beginnings of American concert life, audience recruitment called for publicity, and one way to advertise was through handbills, which could be passed from person to person and posted as well. Unlike newspaper announcements, which survive in great numbers, however, few eighteenth-century handbills have been preserved.

newspaper ads

The earliest concert ads seldom go beyond the bare facts: Mr. X, for his own benefit, will present a concert at Y hall on date Z; tickets cost U shillings and may be purchased from Mr. V on W Street. After midcentury, however, promoters seem to have lost confidence that a straight factual report would attract an audience. A plea for customers might be framed as a personal invitation, as when a musician in Charleston announced in 1760 that he had "no Doubt, but that it will be in his Power to give the greatest Satisfaction to those Ladies and Gentlemen who shall honor him with their presence." Some announcements implied that public demand, not the organizer's pursuit of the Almighty Shilling, was the reason for a concert. A Philadelphia musician in 1757 headed his ad with the phrase "By particular desire"; and a concert there in 1770 was said to be given "at the request of several Gentlemen and Ladies." One ad cautioned: "This will positively be the only time of his performing, unless by the particular desire of a genteel company."

Public concerts of the eighteenth century emphasized variety, running more to short pieces than long ones. Most were two-part affairs, each part beginning and ending with as full an ensemble as possible, and mixing vocal and instrumental selections in between. Vocal numbers ranged from solo songs and opera arias to **glees** (unaccompanied songs for three or more solo singers). Instrumental numbers included solo keyboard pieces, chamber music, and pieces for orchestra, with "Concerto" or "Grand Symphony" meaning a one-movement excerpt, not an entire three- or four-movement work.

The program of a concert given on June 25, 1799, in Salem, Massachusetts, offers a glimpse of how a corps of seasoned troupers might plan a concert. This performance was a joint benefit for Catherine Graupner, a prominent theatrical singer, and Peter Albrecht von Hagen, instrumentalist and orchestra leader, both active in Boston.

The program follows the standard two-part format, with orchestral works beginning and ending each part. Soloists supplied variety, and five of the seven belonged to either the Graupner or the von Hagen family. The Graupner–von

---

In their own words

A Concert Program of 1799

PART 1ST

Overture, composed by . . . . *Pleyel*

Song by Mr. Munto . . . . *Dr. Arnold*

A Sonata on the Grand Forte Piano for 4 hands, by Mrs. von Hagen and Mr. von Hagen, jun.. . . . . *Kozeluch*

"By my tender passion," a favorite song in the Haunted Tower, by Mrs. Graupner . . . . *Storace*

Solo on the Clarinet, by Mr. Granger. . . . . *Vogel*

Lullaby, a favourite Glee for four voices, Mrs. Graupner, Mr. Granger, Mr. Mallet and Mr. Munto . . *Harrison*

Concerto on the Violin by Mr. Von Hagen . . . . *Jearnowick*

PART 2ND

Concerto on the Piano Forte, by Mrs. von Hagen . . . . *Haydn*

Columbia's Bold Eagle, a patriotic song, words by a gentleman of Salem.
    Music by Mr. Graupner and sung by Mrs. Graupner

Concerto on the Hautboy, by Mr. Graupner. . . . . *Le Brun*

The Play'd in Air, a much admired Glee in the Castle Spectre, by Mrs. Graupner,
    Mr. Granger, Mr. Mallet and Mr. Munto

Quartetto by Messrs. von Hagen, sen. and jun., Mr. Laumont, and Mrs. Graupner

"To Arms, to arms," a new patriotic song, written by Thomas Paine, A.M. sung by
    Mrs. Graupner and music by Mr. von Hagen, jun.

Finale . . . . *Haydn*

Hagen concert may be seen as an event in which Boston's two leading musical families took their act on the road to earn proceeds from an audience less familiar with their work than Bostonians were. Their program was designed to appeal to a broad range of audience tastes. Instrumental selections by leading European composers of the day testified to their artistic seriousness. Vocal selections, both solo and ensemble, expressed more-tender sentiments. And by placing new patriotic numbers on the concert's second half, the performers encouraged Salem's listeners to take pride in their American identity.

THEATER MUSIC

Theater companies enhanced the musical lives of their communities. When a company came to town, it arrived with singers and players who were also ready to perform in concerts (as the Salem program shows), participate in church music, and give music lessons. Some company musicians also became involved in publishing and the selling of musical instruments and sheet music.

The eighteenth-century American theater was an extension of the London stage. Some foreign performers toured the New World, then returned to the Old. Others settled here. Not until well into the 1800s did any appreciable number of American-born singers or players find a place on U.S. stages. And musical works by Americans had almost no place at all. New World residents whose musical works were produced onstage were all immigrants who had arrived in the country as experienced musicians.

Puritan attitudes toward the theater

Like dance, the theater provoked strong opposition. Puritan thought treated theater as a generally bad thing, symbolizing a preference for idleness and pleasure over hard work and thrift. For the Puritans, the theater was an institution that lured people away from worthier pursuits, such as churchgoing. Actors and actresses were considered vagabonds who threatened the stability of society. Faithful to illusion rather than truth, the theater posed social dangers that made it seem corrupt even to some who were devoted to other forms of art.

Nevertheless, the London-based English-language theater, especially Shakespeare, was the source of enduring theatrical activity in America. English traveling companies first appeared in the colonies in the mid-1700s, in Philadelphia, New York, Charleston, and Williamsburg, Virginia. New England resisted the effort for a time; between 1750 and 1793 a Boston law prohibited theater entertainments.

theatrical formats

By the 1760s theaters were being built to accommodate audiences in seats of varying location and price. A typical theatrical evening lasted four or five hours, starting with a long work (a tragedy, comedy, or drama with music) and ending with an afterpiece (a short work with music, such as a farce). Musical interludes were common; so were encores of favorite numbers. Straight plays often began with an overture, included music between the acts, and even featured songs. Eighteenth- and nineteenth-century Americans seldom formed the silent, respectful gathering of playgoers that we now expect to find in the theater. Early audiences freely shared their opinions with the actors and musicians. The work being performed seems to have been less important to them than the quality of their own experience. If they liked what they saw and heard, they clamored for more; if not, they demanded an end to it.

Favorite works of the British musical stage were also popular in America, including *The Beggar's Opera* (1728) by John Gay, which received its first American performance in New York in 1750. Gay's plot, characters, and lyrics challenged conventional notions of morality with comic precision. Like other **ballad operas**, its songs consist of new words set to familiar tunes, chosen not only for their melodies but also for their associations. For example, when Mrs. Peachum reviles her daughter Polly for marrying for love instead of wealth ("Our Polly Is a Sad Slut"), the tune Gay borrows is "Oh London Is a Fine Town," a satirical attack claiming that the city government's officials are totally corrupt. Knowing the tunes in their original version helped English audiences feel the sting of *The Beggar's Opera*'s social critique, and American audiences must have shared some of that experience (as they did again in the 1950s when Bertolt Brecht and Kurt Weill's 1928 updating of the play, *The Threepenny Opera*, was an off-Broadway smash).

Ballad operas concentrated on words and ideas, sometimes with society as a target. Another popular theatrical genre of the time, assembled from parts of other such compositions but placing a higher priority on music, was the **pasticcio**. A pasticcio that won great popularity on both sides of the Atlantic was *Love in a Village* (1762), a light romance with music supplied and arranged by the English musician Thomas Arne, first performed in Charleston and Philadelphia in 1766. Except for a handful of new pieces, Arne borrowed the music for *Love in a Village* from elsewhere. Most of all, he tapped a vein of lyrical song that flourished from the 1740s on in England's pleasure gardens (elegantly landscaped amusement parks).

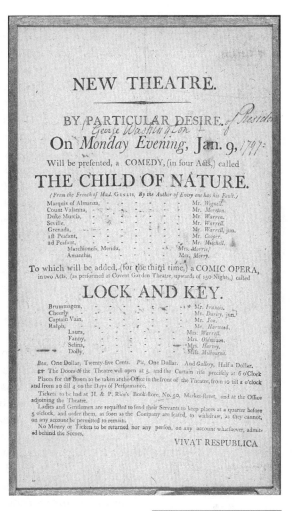

This program from Philadelphia's New Theater on January 9, 1797, shows what theatergoers of the time could expect from an evening's entertainment.

The third genre of musical theater work was the **comic opera**, or simply **opera**, which in the English-speaking world denoted a spoken play with a rather large amount of specially composed music. Despite the name, the plots are not so much humorous as melodramatic and sentimental, usually with a happy ending. A favorite comic opera was *The Children in the Wood*, with music by Samuel Arnold and a **libretto** (literally "little book," i.e., the words) by Thomas Morton. Premiered in London in 1793, it reached Philadelphia the following year. Taking its plot from one of the "old, simple ditties" Benjamin Franklin mentioned in his letter quoted earlier in this chapter, it replaces the original ballad's tragic ending with the villain's comeuppance and a tearful reunion for the title children, lost and refound, with their virtuous parents.

The early musical theater in America, like the spoken theater, was a branch of what is today called show business. While the names of the principal genres—ballad operas, pasticcios, and comic operas—may suggest distinct, self-contained art forms, all three types of musical stage work were aimed at audience accessibility. Performers, composers, and theater managers sought most of all to find and please audiences and to increase their size. Toward that end, musical stage productions featured plots with characters, good or evil, whom spectators could love or hate; players with a talent for comedy, singing, or dancing; a store of melody that was catchy if not already familiar; and a certain amount of spectacle.

By the 1790s, with companies established in Baltimore, Boston, Charleston, New York, and Philadelphia, the theatrical repertory was growing. New works were imported from overseas, while brand-new pieces were created by immigrant composers and playwrights on this side of the Atlantic. Established favorites were sometimes updated by replacing original numbers with newer ones or plugging in popular songs. Thus English works were routinely transformed in performance into Anglo-American ones.

professional actors

The glamour of the theater was an illusion created by players at work in a low-paying vocation. A typical stage performer made an annual salary of around $300, about the same as, or somewhat less than, that of an average American laborer in the 1790s. Unlike laborers, however, stage performers might be rewarded with benefits: performances whose beneficiary kept whatever proceeds topped expenses. A star's benefit might net as much as $500 or more; a decent yield for nonstarring players was $100.

Female actors were paid less than males. In an age when most theater works idealized the virtues of their heroines, an actress could not count on being treated with respect, onstage or off. No matter how important her role, her name always followed those of male actors on the bill. She was fair game for comments on her personal life and appearance and was expected to perform as long as possible during pregnancies.

theater managers

Company managers leased theaters from local proprietors, ran the company's day-to-day operations, took the financial risk, and reaped the profits if any. It was their job to decide the length of each evening's entertainment and the assignments of individual players, although they could be sure that their decisions would be debated and sometimes denounced by performers, critics, and audience members.

touring

The chief American companies spent the season in the major cities of the Eastern Seaboard and—after the Louisiana Purchase of 1803 made it part of the United States—New Orleans. Smaller companies were formed from their ranks for summer touring, which gave players year-round work. A memoir by actor-dancer John Durang describes what life was like in such an outfit. Between 1808 and 1816 Durang toured with a small company to towns in Pennsylvania and Maryland. Preparing seven or eight nights of entertainment, Durang's troupe ran through the repertory, then moved on to the next town, where they repeated it. They adapted "tragedys, comedys, farces, and operas" for smaller forces, offered their audiences dancing, pantomimes, and acrobatics, and even catered to some of their immigrant audiences with plays performed in German.

Into the 1820s, stock companies such as Durang's were still playing such venerable English works as *The Beggar's Opera* and *Love in a Village*. But newer works such as the British composer Henry Rowe Bishop's melodramatic opera *Clari, or The Maid of Milan*, with a libretto by the American actor and writer John Howard Payne, also entered the repertory. First performed in London in 1823, *Clari* opened six months later at New York's Park Theater and held a place on the American stage into the 1870s. One of its songs may explain the opera's success.

"Home, Sweet Home"

Bishop and Payne's "Home, Sweet Home," written to express the heroine's emotion as she returns home after being abducted, became one of the most popular songs of the nineteenth century.

Many Americans found "Home, Sweet Home" an apt reflection of their love of domesticity, which they claimed to value above exotic "pleasures and palaces."

And since the laws of the time held that the song could not be copyrighted in the United States because it originated in England, many American music publishers rushed their own editions into print. By 1870 American performers of virtually every stripe could buy a sheet music version tailored to their own needs. Singers interpolated the song into stage performances, seeking to touch the hearts of audience members for whom it was already a kind of anthem.

"Home, Sweet Home" was performed in most of the settings that made up America's musical landscape—the theatrical and concert stage, the parlor, the dance hall, the parade ground, the battlefield, the campfire—and was one of the best-loved melodies of the nineteenth century.

The history of secular music in the early republic traces a growing demand for professional standards of creation, performance, and presentation. The rising sophistication of musical tastes was by no means uniform among the varied populations of the young United States, however. The next chapter returns to the subject of sacred music to explore widening divisions in Americans' conceptions of the best qualities and purposes for devotional music.

QUESTIONS FOR DISCUSSION AND REVIEW

1. How did amateur and professional musical activities overlap in early America? Do amateur and professional musicians interact in any of the same ways today, and if so, how?

2. Contrast and compare social dancing in early and present-day America. Do different styles of dance mark different social groups, and if so, how?

3. Compare the presence of popular songs in early American theatrical genres with the use of contemporary popular songs in today's Broadway musicals, films, and television programs. Are there present-day equivalents of any of the three principal genres: ballad opera, pasticcio, and comic opera?

FURTHER READING

Camus, Raoul François. *Military Music of the American Revolution*. Chapel Hill: University of North Carolina Press, 1967.

Dizikes, John. *Opera in America: A Cultural History*. New Haven, CT: Yale University Press, 1993.

Keller, Kate van Winkle, with John Koegel. "Secular Music to 1800." In *The Cambridge History of American Music*, edited by David Nicholls, 49–77. Cambridge: Cambridge University Press, 1998.

McConachie, Bruce A. *Melodramatic Formations: American Theatre and Society, 1820–1870*. Iowa City: University of Iowa Press, 1992.

Porter, Susan L. *With an Air Debonair: Musical Theatre in America, 1785–1815*. Washington, DC: Smithsonian Institution Press, 1991.

Silverman, Kenneth. *A Cultural History of the American Revolution*. New York: Crowell, 1976.

Sonneck, Oscar G. *Early Concert-Life in America (1731–1800)*. 1907. Reprint. New York: Da Capo, 1978.

FURTHER LISTENING AND VIEWING

Music of the American Revolution: The Birth of Liberty. New World Records, 1976, 1996.

Music of the Federal Era. Members of the Federal Music Society; John Baldon, conductor. New World Records, 1978, 1994.

New England Chestnuts, vols. 1 & 2. Rodney Miller, fiddle, et al. Westmoreland, NH: Great Meadow Music, 2001. A reissue of two LPs from the early 1980s.

Searching "Money Musk" on YouTube (www.youtube.com) will turn up several videos from around the world of the "International Money Musk Moment" on March 14, 2009.

"HOW SWEET THE SOUND"

Sacred Music in the New Republic

A fter winning independence from England in 1783, Americans realized that the unique political circumstances of their lives offered fresh cultural possibilities, including musical ones. The idea of American musical distinctiveness was first embodied, as discussed in chapter 1, in the work of William Billings. This chapter explores how that idea, as it applies to the realm of Protestant sacred music, spread first among Billings's fellow psalmodists in New England and later throughout the territories of the new republic. As musical literacy grew, however, so did musical sophistication and a sense that the infant nation had far to go before it could match the mature musical culture of the Old World. In the same way that New England psalmody was the fruit of an earlier reform movement—the drive for singing schools to bring sacred singing under the control of musical notation—the spread of psalmody gave rise to new calls for reform. By the mid-1800s Protestant sacred music in America divided along lines reflecting not only sectarian differences but regional, class, and educational ones as well.

THE RISE AND FALL OF NEW ENGLAND PSALMODY

Though it began as early as 1720, the Regular Singing movement's call for musical literacy was slow to gain momentum. The printing of tunebooks grew gradually over the next decades. With peacetime came a new burst of energy from tunebook compilers, and the last two decades of the eighteenth century saw substantial growth, peaking in the first decade of the nineteenth century, when more tunebooks were printed than in the entire eighteenth century. A look at those tunebooks reveals that William Billings, for all his fame, was just one of many New Englanders who composed and published sacred music in the late 1700s.

YANKEE PSALMODISTS

Tunebooks, though overwhelmingly sacred in their texts, were intended to serve the needs of singing schools, which were not sacred institutions (and in fact they were too expensive for church use and their music too elaborate for any congregation). Many tunebooks begin with an explanation of the rudiments of music notation and then proceed from easy tunes to more and more difficult compositions. Tunebooks also served the needs of musical societies, groups of singers who banded together for the pleasure of exercising their skills. Rather than a branch of church music, then, psalmody shared certain traits with popular music.

From the mid-1780s into the early 1800s, tunebooks featured compositions by native-born Americans including Daniel Read, Lewis Edson, Justin Morgan, Timothy Swan, and others, who hailed from the towns and villages sprinkled across the Massachusetts and Connecticut countryside. In addition to their trades (Read was a comb maker and storekeeper; Edson a blacksmith; Morgan a farmer, schoolmaster, and horse breeder; Swan a hatter), they taught singing schools and wrote music, but without much exposure to the music making of the cities.

New England psalmody lacked the specialization found in later American music making. The composers, who had acquired their own musical learning in singing schools and through personal experience, were writing essentially for peers, friends, and neighbors. Thanks to subscription and informal interchange, even inexperienced composers could get their music into print. And though the singing was done for the greater glory of God, much of it took place outside public worship. The flexibility of boundaries that were later more sharply drawn—between sacred and secular, professional and amateur, composer and performer, creator and publisher—has led some to call the late eighteenth century a golden age of psalmody.

LG 3.1   Daniel Read's SHERBURNE (1785; LG 3.1) was a golden-age favorite. As it tells the story, a band of shepherds are working the night shift. It is a cold evening, the ground is hard, and they are bored. Suddenly they see a flash of light. And there hovers an angel, sent by God to report some startling news about His family. Read's setting, with its homegrown harmony and simple declamation, seems to encourage the performers to sing as people accustomed to sleeping on cold, hard ground themselves, as some of SHERBURNE's early performers doubtless were. In this composition, commonplace details and world-changing revelation blend into one experience.

SHERBURNE's musical idiom typifies a generation of Yankee composers. The opening shows two harmonic traits that are different from anything a European composer of the time would have written. One is a fondness for "open" sounds—harmonies that include only the root and fifth of a chord, omitting the third. That sound, the simplest of any consonance, resonates well and is easy to sing in tune. The second unusual trait is a freedom from certain orthodox harmonic conventions, as in the very first phrase, which ends with a chord built on the sixth note of the scale (on the word "night"), where a European-trained ear would have expected a triad on the fourth note.

fuging tunes   SHERBURNE is a **fuging tune**, an Anglo-American form beloved of psalmodists and singers of the period. Beginning with block chords, the texture explodes at its midpoint into a "fuge": a section where each voice part enters at

CD 1.9	Listening Guide 3.1		SHERBURNE DANIEL READ

DATE: 1785

PERFORMERS: Theatre of Voices; Paul Hillier, director

GENRE: fuging tune

METER: duple

FORM: strophic, each stanza divided into two sections

WHAT TO LISTEN FOR

- division of each stanza into a section in block chords and a polyphonic "fuge"
- melody in tenor

TIMING	SECTION	TEXT	COMMENTS
0:00	stanza 1	While shepherds watched their flocks by night, All seated on the ground,	Beginning with a stark "open" sonority, the four vocal lines move in nearly identical rhythm, creating a homophonic texture.
0:05		The angel of the Lord came down, And glory shone around.	Halfway through the text of stanza 1, the texture becomes polyphonic, with rhythmically independent vocal lines: the "fuge." The music is extended by repeating phrases of the text.
0:24		The angel of the Lord came down, And glory shone around.	The entire "fuge" repeats.
0:43	stanza 2	"Fear not!" said he, for mighty dread had seized their troubled mind . . .	The text of the "fuge" sections for stanzas 2–6 are not shown here. How easily can you make out the words by ear?
1:26	stanza 3	"To you, in David's town, this day is born of David's line . . .	
2:11	stanza 4	"The heavenly babe you there shall find to human view displayed . . .	The singers in this recording choose to sing this stanza at a softer volume.
2:55	stanza 5	Thus spake the seraph and forthwith appeared a shining throng . . .	A return to the full volume of the earlier stanzas.
3:39	stanza 6	"All glory be to god on high, and to the earth be peace . . .	
	NOTE Hymn text by Nahum Tate (1700).		

Listen & Reflect

1. As part of the shape-note tradition described later in this chapter, SHERBURNE has remained popular to the present day. View any of the amateur performances posted on YouTube and elsewhere. How do those performances differ from the sound of this professional choir? which do you prefer, and why?

2. SHERBURNE is sometimes sung with the counter (alto) voice omitted. Of the four vocal lines, why is the counter the one likeliest to be treated as optional? How does this reflect Billing's description of the psalmodists' compositional process, as related in chapter 1?

a different time, so that the text overlaps. (Because this is not quite the same as a proper European fugue, the Americans' idiosyncratic spelling is often used to make the distinction; the words are pronounced the same way.) The evenly accented notes of Read's "fuge" subject lend themselves to an energetic, even ecstatic vocal expression. Both the words and the act of singing joyfully praise God; it hardly seems to matter whether the singers are inside the meeting house or not. More a piece to be sung than listened to, SHERBURNE offers its singers more than a little sheer pleasure.

"ANCIENT MUSIC" AND REFORM

Nathaniel D. Gould

In a reaction against the lively singing of homegrown compositions like SHER-BURNE, a musical reform movement, based in New England, promoted a "correct" Europeanized taste. The clearest account of reform was written in the 1850s by Nathaniel D. Gould, a reformer and singing master. According to Gould, in the "dark age" ushered in around 1770 by Billings, people eager to hone musical skills for their own sake had wrested the control of singing from the clergy and the people. By 1800 public worship was plagued by nonsinging congregations, outspoken choir members, and a sprightliness in choral singing that encouraged competitiveness and pride. In that state of crisis, true Christians realized that the time had come to regulate and desecularize the singing in worship services. Beginning shortly after 1800 in Massachusetts, clergymen and other community leaders joined forces with "prominent singers" to advocate "ancient music," which they found ideal for kindling what they took to be a genuine religious spirit among congregation members.

"ancient music"

By **ancient music**, Gould meant European tunes composed decades, even centuries, earlier, and newer tunes whose simple style resembled that of the older favorites. Whereas American-composed psalmody was a recent creation, written by self-taught locals ignorant of proper harmony, ancient music was the work of Europeans and Old World training, embodying musical "science" that could withstand the test of time. And whereas some New England psalmody exhibited an infectious rhythmic snap, ancient music moved with a gravity better suited to the solemnity of public worship.

OLD HUNDRED (LG 1.2) was the quintessential piece of ancient music. "I have been informed," the reformer Andrew Law wrote in an essay, "that Handel said, he would give all his oratorios, if he might be the author of OLD HUNDRED." Although Handel is not known to have said any such thing, Law's statement carries a figurative truth. The pious sentiments of an oratorio like Handel's *Messiah* required many skilled musicians for their expression, but such sentiments, which Law valued above all else, lay open to anyone, trained or not, who sang OLD HUNDRED.

sacred music societies

New Englanders of the early 1800s often formed associations devoted to various causes. Debating societies, missionary societies, professional societies, and societies for moral improvement flourished throughout the region. So did sacred music societies—the Essex Musical Association in Salem and the Middlesex Musical Society in Boston, for example—and these groups helped reformers win more public attention and support than an individual like Andrew Law could ever hope to match. And ancient music, embodied in OLD HUNDRED and other tunes like it, gave reformers a rallying point.

Andrew Law and the Reform of Psalmody

A key figure in the transition from "golden age" psalmody to the reform movements of the nineteenth century was the Connecticut psalmodist Andrew Law (1749–1821). Though he graduated from Rhode Island College (now Brown University) in 1775 with a divinity degree, he took up the career of an itinerant singing master, leading singing schools along the Eastern Seaboard from Vermont to South Carolina. His letters reveal him to have been a zealous religious entrepreneur whose main disappointment was that he failed to profit financially from changes that he helped to introduce.

Law's career revolved around three innovations. First, when he began his work as a compiler, with the *Select Harmony* (1779), he placed American compositions side by side with British tunes, implying that the Americans and British were creative equals. Second, after experiencing a conversion in taste, he argued in *The Art of Singing* (1794) that "a considerable part of American composition is in reality faulty,"

largely owing to the New Englanders' fondness for "open" sonorities and their habit of placing the melody in the tenor part. Thereafter, Law systematically replaced American music in his tunebooks with British and moved the melody to the treble (soprano) part, where it could be more easily heard. Moreover, in *The Musical Primer* (1793) he called for a reform of American performance style: "The harshness of our singing must be corrected. Our voices must be filed."

Third, shortly after the turn of the century, Law made the most radical change of his career, abandoning standard musical notation and copyrighting his own system, in which the shapes of the notes, not their position on a staff, indicated the pitches to be sung. Unfortunately for Law, by the time he published his new system, a similar one was already on the market; William Little and William Smith's *Easy Instructor* (Philadelphia, 1801) would have a powerful impact on sacred music in the South. But that is a story for later in this chapter.

Gould names two tunebooks as spearheads of reform: *The Salem Collection of Classical Sacred Music* (Salem, 1805) and *The Middlesex Collection of Church Music, or Ancient Psalmody Revived* (Boston, 1807). Between them they contain a total of 185 compositions, and all but three are European in origin; in fact, almost the whole repertory is from the 1770s or earlier. And most of the music is harmonized in block chords, as are OLD HUNDRED and the "common tunes" of the early Protestant Reformation.

In contrast to most earlier American tunebooks, which were published under a compiler's name and whose introductions address readers on a more or less personal basis, *The Middlesex Collection* was compiled by the anonymous Middlesex Musical Society, and *The Salem Collection*'s contents chosen by a committee "whose names, were we at liberty to mention them, would add authority to the work." *The Salem Collection* apologizes for the current "general and most deplorable corruption of taste in our church musick"; and the preface to *The Middlesex Collection* intones, "The tunes here introduced are recommended by their antiquity, and more by their intrinsic excellence . . . for the spirit and flavor of old wine are always depressed by the commixture of new." Claiming to represent right-thinking Christians through the ages, the compilers imply that the best of all possible sacred repertories had already been in existence for generations.

reform tunebooks

The forces marshaled by reformers, including the clergy, influential laymen, and societies devoted to the cause, proved successful. Sacred tunebooks published in the Northeast after 1805 show a quick drop-off in American musical content and a corresponding rise in European. Addressing the public as an unnamed "we" and making pronouncements that brooked no argument, ancient music advocates won their purpose by launching a reform process in the name of religion.

EDIFICATION AND PRAISE

The reformers' approach raises a basic question: To what audience is sacred music addressed? Hitherto, the main goal of Christian sacred music was to praise God, and praise could be delivered in many forms. In a Handel oratorio, God is praised through the composer's artifice and the performers' skill. At the other end of the spectrum is the congregational hymn, which requires no great skill to perform but is deemed worthy because of the spirit in which it is sung. Such a spirit, whether confessing sin or making "a joyful noise unto the Lord," was certainly alive among New England choirs and singing schools, for all the criticisms that reformers leveled at their rowdy fuging tunes and anthems. Whether in oratorio, hymn, or anthem, the singing was directed toward the ear of the Almighty. But the reform of early nineteenth-century New England psalmody partakes of a different spirit—one centered not on praise but on edification. Rather than God, its main recipients were the worshipers themselves, and especially those seeking moral and social uplift.

Shortly after 1800, a split opened up in Protestant sacred music that was to have lasting reverberations in America. Those who made edification their ideal believed that worship was a solemn affair deserving its own kind of music, separate from secular music in sound, idiom, and style of performance. But Christians who held to praise as an ideal were inclined to understand sacred expressions, music included, as an extension of everyday life. The God they worshiped was more attuned to what was in the hearts of His worshipers than to the piety of their manner or the particular sounds with which they praised Him.

the Second Great Awakening

Nowhere was that attitude more evident than in the **camp meeting**. This new form of worship emerged from the Second Great Awakening, a surge of religious renewal between the 1780s and 1830 that brought a fervent Christianity to the northern, western, and southern fringes of the young republic. (An earlier series of religious revivals in the 1730s and 1740s is known as the Great Awakening.) Held in the countryside, camp meetings were gatherings at which frontier worshipers camped out for several days of prayer and singing in an atmosphere of spiritual renewal or revivalism. Crowds could be large, sometimes numbering in the thousands, and people might travel long distances to attend.

camp-meetings songs

Old-line Calvinism had held that only a certain number of Christians were predestined for salvation, while other souls burned in hell for their sins. The Second Awakening, in contrast, promoted the alternative of "free grace," opening the possibility of salvation to all sinners, dependent on an act of repentance and belief. Worshipers at camp meetings sang religious songs that expressed the emotion-filled moment of salvation, and they sang them without the benefit of any tunebook, by fitting simple sacred verses to familiar folk melodies. In time, the oral traditions of the camp-meeting praise song would leave their mark on the composition of notated sacred music.

On the one hand, the reform of sacred music in New England, as a move away from praise and toward edification, had shifted the focus toward human authorities and away from God. On the other hand, music centered on praise emphasized conviction and purity of heart over moral improvement. The pursuit of edification by musical means became a driving force in the churches and meeting houses of the urban Northeast, matched by the vigor with which evangelical revivalism's music of praise reached out to "plain folk" in the remote corners of the young republic.

SINGING PRAISES: SOUTHERN AND FRONTIER DEVOTIONAL MUSIC

In 1933 George Pullen Jackson, a New England–born professor of German at Vanderbilt University in Nashville, Tennessee, published a book—*White Spirituals in the Southern Uplands*—about a remarkable practice he had encountered among "plain folk" in the region. Gathering on weekends, groups of Southerners staged all-day "singings" of sacred music, and they brought their own books: oblong volumes of psalm and hymn tunes, fuging tunes, and anthems set mostly for four-part chorus with the melody in the tenor voice. They seated themselves according to voice part—treble (soprano), counter (alto), tenor, and bass—in a rectangle with open space in the middle. Into that space stepped a succession of singers from the ranks, each leading the group in two or three pieces. Typically, before adding the words to a piece, the group would sing the notes on four syllables: *fa, sol, la,* and *mi* (a form of solmization, as described in the box on page 72). Jackson, who found the singers' note-reading ability astounding, learned that most had attended singing schools. They tended to vocalize at full blast, paying little heed to voice quality and making no attempt to blend—but with no audience in sight, such things didn't seem to matter.

all-day singing

While the singing promoted by the New England reformers always included a human audience, which it tried to please and edify, singers in Jackson's Southern tradition made music to glorify God; theirs was an attitude of *praise*. According to their understanding, the power of the music and the absorbed concentration they brought to their singing made it worthy of the recipient, no matter how it sounded. Neither self-awareness nor an audience played any role, for when human judgments of musical quality began to be made, Jackson warned, "at that moment, this singing of, for, and by the people loses its chief characteristic."

music of praise

Conversations at the singings he attended helped Jackson understand what these gatherings meant to the singers. "Every time I go to one of these singings," one veteran confided, "I feel that I am attending a memorial to my mother"; when one of her favorite pieces was sung, it was "as if heaven itself hovers over the place." Pleasure in making music was also part of the attraction. But in the end, the spiritual environment seems to have left the deepest impression. Many of the people imagined heaven as "a place where they will meet again those beloved singers who have gone before, and sing again with them, endlessly."

SHAPE NOTES AND SOUTHERN HYMNODY

Jackson's research revealed these singings to be the tip of a historical iceberg. Rather than keeping pace with religious and musical change, people in the Upland South—which includes the Shenandoah Valley and parts of Maryland,

∾ The practice of shape-note singing remains strong today. Here, a participant leads singers arranged in the traditional square at a Sacred Harp convention in McMahan, Texas, in 1998.

Virginia, West Virginia, Kentucky, Tennessee, North and South Carolina, and Georgia, but not the coastal areas—had preserved a tradition dating back to New England in the 1700s.

With historical perspective, the Southern practice looks more like a transformation than a simple survival of the Northern practice. Psalmody had been sung in New England by rural people, city dwellers, college students, and Calvinist churchgoers of all ages, singing in the name of art as well as praise. In the Southern Uplands, however, **hymnody**—in effect, the psalmody of the nineteenth century, when hymn singing had eclipsed psalm singing—took root among rural plain folk with stern views of religion and generally old-fashioned ways. And perhaps nothing marks Southern hymnody as a countrified tradition more clearly than the musical notation in which it circulated.

shape notes

Many Southern tunebooks used the four-shape notation that Little and Smith's *Easy Instructor* had introduced in 1801. **Shape notes**, although they originated in the Northeast, were used there for only a short time, instead taking root in the Southern singing traditions, where for two centuries they have helped countless singers learn to sing accurately at sight from printed music books.

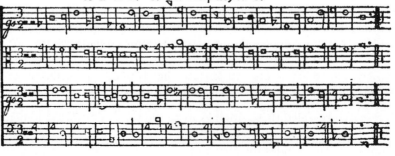

∾ The anonymous British psalm tune MEAR, as printed in shape notes in William Little and William Smith, *The Easy Instructor* (Philadelphia, [1801]).

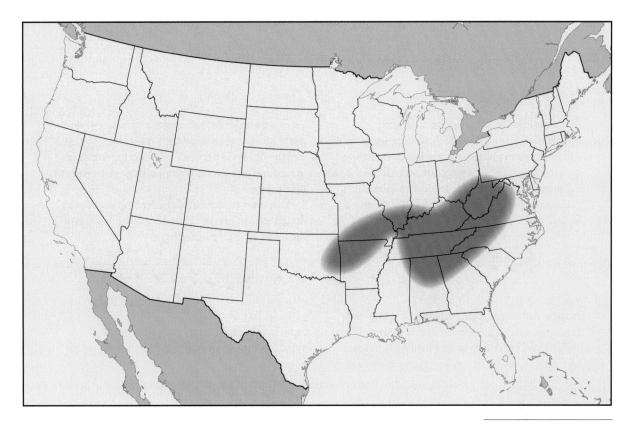

✎ The Upland South embraces the higher elevations of several states and is defined by culture and history as much as by geographical features.

Thanks to a mixture of regional, class, and religious prejudices, musical reformers soon branded shape notes a crutch needed only by ignorant rural singers. That attitude did not stop their spread, however, especially in regions where the reformers' message did not reach, such as New York State, New Jersey, Pennsylvania, and the Ohio River Valley. After 1810, as the frontier pushed westward, new shape-note collections began to appear in cities and towns farther and farther from Boston and Philadelphia. And while favorites from New England at first dominated the shape-note repertory, new tunes by local composers were also welcomed. The new pieces tended to emphasize the very features of New England psalmody that the reformers strove to eliminate: stark "open" sonorities, alternating with the harmonic collisions that could arise when each voice goes its own separate way. Ananias Davisson, the Virginia-born composer and compiler of *Kentucky Harmony* (Harrisonburg, Va., 1816), the first shape-note tunebook printed in the South, argued that such dissonances "answer a similar purpose to acid, which being tasted immediately before sweet [i.e., the open sonorities], give the latter a more pleasing relish."

Kentucky Harmony *(1816)*

Southern hymnodists were not the only composers to add to the sacred repertory. In 1805, Vermont composer and compiler Jeremiah Ingalls published *The Christian Harmony* (Exeter, N.H.). Inspired by the musical practices developed in the camp meetings of the Second Awakening, Ingalls filled his tunebook with **folk hymns**, in which religious words—many from the Baptist and Methodist preachers who led the wave of revivalism—were set to secular tunes. One such hymn combines a tune called INNOCENT SOUNDS with words by the English Methodist Charles Wesley, relating how timid worshipers have let the devil

Jeremiah Ingalls

A CLOSER LOOK

Fasola

Since the Middle Ages, the technique of **solmization**, or **solfège**, which assigns a particular syllable to each pitch in a scale, has been used to teach singers how to sing from notation. In the most common modern form of solmization, a major scale is sung on seven syllables: *do, re, mi, fa, sol, la,* and *ti* (repeating *do* at the octave):

do   re   mi   fa   sol   la   ti   do

In early America, singing masters taught note reading according to a four-syllable system of solmization called **fasola**, in which a major scale was sung *fa, sol, la, fa, sol, la, mi* (repeating *fa* at the octave):

fa   sol   la   fa   sol   la   mi   fa

Once singers knew their major and minor scales, could find the tonic *fa* and the *mi* just below it, and had the intervals between syllables ingrained in their vocal and aural memories, they were ready to read music.

Shape notes simplified the reading process by assigning a different-shaped notehead to each of the four singing syllables:

fa   sol   la   fa   sol   la   mi   fa

Singers who could coordinate shapes with syllables were spared having to figure out which note to sing.

take the best tunes and calling upon the religious faithful to reclaim them from Satan:

> Strip him of every moving strain,
> Of every melting measure;
> Music in virtue's cause retain,
> Risk the holy pleasure.

The music to which Ingalls set Wesley's stanzas is as sprightly as the title of the borrowed melody suggests: "Merrily Danc'd the Quaker."

Ingalls's book was not a success. Perhaps it failed in the marketplace because it appeared in New England at the very time the ancient music reform was taking hold, a movement whose spirit could hardly have differed more from the democratic energy of folk hymnody. Yet if folk hymns were out of step with the North's prevailing religious mood, they were welcomed in the hinterlands to the south and west. One of the most familiar and best loved today is NEW BRITAIN, known now by the opening words of the text it sets: John Newton's 1779 hymn "Amazing Grace." The **pentatonic** melody—using only five of the seven notes of the diatonic scale and thus avoiding the half steps—is characteristic of folk tunes from the British Isles, where it probably originated. As it first appears in the *Columbian Harmony* (Cincinnati, 1829), NEW BRITAIN is scored for three voices, omitting

"Amazing Grace"

the counter (alto). Each of its fourteen measures begins with a long note, often harmonized with an "open" sonority; many of the quicker notes that fill out each measure produce the fleeting dissonances that Ananias Davisson relished. The combination of the tune's simple beauty, the rugged harmonization, and a text that stresses divine grace—God's love embraced through contrition—makes "Amazing Grace" a quintessential expression of Southern praise singing.

PLAIN FOLK, PRAISE, AND *THE SACRED HARP*

The Southern shape-note tradition bore the stamp of revivalism as embodied in the Second Awakening. In fact, the shape-note tradition reveals the power of revivalism, not only because it encouraged the kind of worshipful singing that qualifies as praise but also because it indicates a leveling of class consciousness. Revivalism opened the medium of print to any American who had a message to deliver.

The idea of author and book buyer (i.e., singer) as social peers is reflected in the two tunebooks that brought shape-note hymnody to the Deep South: William Walker's *The Southern Harmony* (New Haven, Conn., 1835; compiled in South Carolina), and Benjamin Franklin White and Elisha J. King's *The Sacred Harp* (Philadelphia, 1844; compiled in Hamilton, Ga.). Both were printed in the North for lack of music-printing facilities in the regions where their authors lived. *The Southern Harmony* sold 600,000 copies by 1866. *The Sacred Harp* has been one of the great successes in American publishing history. King died before the book appeared in print; it went through three revisions and several editions under White's supervision, was revised further after his death, and is still in print today, used at singings around the country. The stories that circulated about the authors reveal *The Sacred Harp* as an icon of Upland Southern culture, a book "of, for, and by the people."

The Sacred Harp (1844)

Elisha J. King, a Georgia native and Baptist singing-school master, was a talented musician who has lived in memory through his association with the book. Benjamin Franklin White, the senior partner, was a native South Carolinian who moved to Harris Country, Georgia, around 1840. The youngest of fourteen children, White received only three months of formal schooling, yet managed to become editor of *The Organ,* the official newspaper of Harris County. Prominent as a singing master and editor, White also became a civic leader despite his lack of schooling. As he lay dying at seventy-nine, he was said to have "recounted all the mistakes as well as the good that had followed him throughout his life. He summed it all up in the words, 'The end has come and I am ready,'" departing

B. F. White

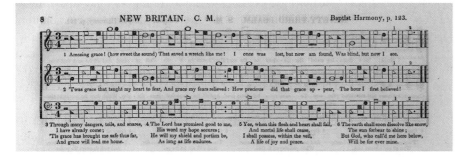

🎵 NEW BRITAIN, better known today as "Amazing Grace," as it was reprinted in William Walker, *The Southern Harmony* (1835); the melody is in the middle staff.

from this world only after singing the melody of SOUNDING JOY, which he had composed to words by Isaac Watts.

White seems to have achieved eminence in the Upland South as a typical figure, not an extraordinary one. A 1904 account of *The Sacred Harp*'s history indicates that he and King relied on their friends' and neighbors' taste in singing: the collection was shaped by gatherings in and around White's house, where people would "sing the songs long before they were published in book form."

The Sacred Harp emphasizes old favorites over new pieces. Familiar numbers in the third edition (1859) include OLD HUNDRED, Daniel Read's SHERBURNE, and folk hymns such as NEW BRITAIN and PLENARY, the latter a setting of Watts's funeral hymn "Hark! from the tombs a doleful sound" to the tune of "Auld Lang Syne." The third edition also contains WONDROUS LOVE (LG 3.2), a Southern folk hymn whose secular antecedent was a song about the pirate Captain Kidd.

LG 3.2

WONDROUS LOVE shows a kinship with camp-meeting songs in that it repeats short phrases of text. The poetic form is unusual, scanning as 12.9.6.6.12.9, corresponding to none of the typical meters of versified psalms or hymns. The first stanza's many incantations of "Oh! my soul!" and "for my soul" to the same short-short-long rhythm creates an exclamatory, awestruck mood. Just as important is the way the melody begins: with the first five words sung three times, each time at a higher pitch, and climaxing on the highest note of the piece precisely at the midpoint. The tenor melody's downward movement in the second half of the piece balances the first half's upward trajectory. That shape allows the text's main argument to unfold over a whole stanza, while hammering home, measure by measure, an emotional response to the miracle of Christ's sacrifice. By the stanza's end, only one phrase—"that caused the Lord of bliss"—has gone unrepeated.

text and melody

harmony

Also striking is the way the voices move, often locking together in parallel fifths and octaves, forfeiting the independence of line featured in earlier New England psalmody. But if the effect of intertwining voices is lost, a rugged power is gained, especially in the second phrase (repeated as the last phrase), where every interval between tenor and bass except the final one is a fifth.

vocal style

The impact is heightened by the full-throttle sound of the voices, as heard in folklorist Alan Lomax's 1959 field recording of an all-day singing in Fyffe, Alabama. The vocal production—at maximum volume, with no apparent attempt to blend the voices into a more conventional choral sound—is characteristic of the Southern *Sacred Harp* singing tradition. Also part of the tradition is the practice of male *and* female voices singing both the tenor melody and the treble (soprano) line, so that each part is doubled at the octave.

WONDROUS LOVE endures as a part of a singing tradition that distilled the attitude of religious praise into an untutored, heartfelt utterance.

Southern shape-note hymnody, or Sacred Harp singing, as it has also come to be known, has proved to be remarkably long-lived—displaced but never obliterated by later musical fashions. Even as George Pullen Jackson was "discovering" Sacred Harp singing in the 1930s, the composition of new tunes in this rugged folk style was very much alive. Indeed, one of the finest tunes in later editions of *The Sacred Harp* is SOAR AWAY, an inspired blend of folk hymn and fuging tune written in 1935 by A. Marcus Cagle of Villa Rica, Georgia.

The second half of the twentieth century saw a resurgence of interest in shape-note hymnody, with local and regional groups springing up throughout

| CD 1.10 | Listening Guide 3.2 | WONDROUS LOVE ANONYMOUS |

DATE: 1859

PERFORMERS: attendees at a singing convention in Fyffe, Alabama, in 1959.

GENRE: folk hymn from *The Sacred Harp*, 3d edition

METER: duple

FORM: strophic

WHAT TO LISTEN FOR

- block-chord texture
- rugged sound of parallel fifths
- use of **Dorian mode**
- doubling of tenor melody by women an octave higher

TIMING	SECTION	TEXT	COMMENTS
0:00	stanza 1	What wondrous love is this, oh! my soul! oh! my soul!	The singers establish their opening pitches, an open fifth, then begin the first stanza.
0:13		What wondrous love is this, oh! my soul!	The second phrase, corresponding to the second line of text, features pronounced parallel fifths between tenor and bass.
0:22		What wondrous love is this! That caused the Lord of bliss	The tenor melody reaches its highest pitch at the midpoint of the stanza, then begins its descent.
0:33		To bear the dreadful curse for my soul, for my soul, To bear the dreadful curse for my soul.	The tenor melody concludes by repeating the two opening phrases, with new words.
0:54	stanza 2	When I was sinking down, sinking down, sinking down, When I was sinking down, sinking down, When I was sinking down, Beneath God's awful frown, Christ laid aside his crown for my soul, for my soul. Christ laid aside his crown for my soul.	The music repeats with new words.

Listen & Reflect

1. Compare and contrast the vocal quality of these singers with the other examples of Protestant sacred music in this chapter and in chapter 1. How can you account for the differences, and what do they suggest about the singers' attitudes toward the performance of this music?

the United States and beyond to meet, often monthly, to sing from *The Sacred Harp.* Annual singing conventions today regularly draw hundreds of enthusiastic singers, not only in the South but even in New England, where many features of the music originated but long ago fell out of favor. The energy behind this new return to the past has more to do, generally speaking, with the discovery in recent decades of so-called "roots music" and its attendant cultural and social values—discussed in chapter 21—than with Christian religious expression.

nonliturgical setting   Yet while its subject matter is religious, the activity of Sacred Harp singing has always been nonliturgical. Even when singing meetings are held in a church, they are events distinct from worship services. Educationally speaking, Southern shape-note hymnody is a direct descendant of the Regular Singing movement that began in the 1720s with the aim of improving congregational singing, but liturgical use has never been its intent. It is quite different from the type of music sung by most American Protestant congregations today, which follows a different line of descent. That line may be traced from the reform movement of early nineteenth-century New England and the work of Lowell Mason. As the most important musical reformer in America's history, Mason stands as a key figure in music's development not only in American churches but also in American public schools.

EDIFICATION AND ECONOMICS: THE CAREER OF LOWELL MASON

Lowell Mason (1792–1872) is remembered not only as a significant reformer of sacred music but also as the "father" of public school music. His success in both areas was due to his grasp of the close ties between sacred and secular institutions in the United States. French writer Alexis de Tocqueville noted in his classic *Democracy in America* (1835) that whereas in France he had seen "the spirits of religion and democracy almost always marching in opposite directions," in America he found them "intimately linked together in joint reign over the same land." Nowhere was that more true than in the free institution of public schooling, which was steeped in the religious spirit. Mason's involvement in both church and school music thus seemed natural and complementary.

Moreover, when Mason enlarged his sphere of activity to include education, he vastly increased his range of potential customers. He also grew rich. Like the Yankee psalmodists before him, Mason approached sacred music with a commercial, entrepreneurial spirit. Unlike them, however, he recognized an opportunity to profit from the common ground between religion and free institutions, thereby discovering that edification could be big business.

MASON AS HYMNODIST

Born in Medfield, Massachusetts, Mason attended singing school as a youngster and also learned to play a variety of instruments, including the organ. In 1812, at age twenty, he left home and spent the next fifteen years in Savannah, Georgia, where he worked as a bank clerk, led church choirs, and studied harmony and composition with a German-born musician. There, while still in his late twenties, Mason compiled his first tunebook.

Mason found most of the music for his book in other publications, especially a London collection called *Sacred Melodies, from Haydn, Mozart, and Beethoven,* which adapted melodies by European masters to English hymn texts. Mason took pride in the musical know-how his collection displayed; in a letter to a friend, he boasted that he had harmonized the tunes correctly, "and I trust every false relation, and every forbidden progression will be avoided." Like Andrew Law, he saw harmonic correctness as a feature that separated the music of ignorant Yankee psalmodists from what the reformers considered **scientific music**—music based on theoretical knowledge rather than simply talent or practical experience.

"scientific music"

Because no Southern printer then owned a font of music type, Mason traveled north to Boston in 1821 in search of a publisher. The sponsor he found, Boston's Handel and Haydn Society, had been founded in 1815 to improve "the style of performing sacred music" and to promote American performances of music by Europe's "eminent composers" (see chapter 5). Appearing in 1822, *The Boston Handel and Haydn Society Collection of Church Music* won resounding success, and money from its sales helped support the society's activities for years to come. Although it was Mason's compilation, the tunebook appeared to be the work not of an individual but of a respected organization, thus giving it the same air of authority that marked earlier reform tunebooks such as *The Salem Collection.* As for Mason, the financial arrangement he worked out—profits were split equally between compiler and publisher—proved to be the cornerstone on which he built his career. By 1839, when the last edition was published (a new edition had appeared practically every year), Mason's share of the proceeds had reached approximately $12,000. And to that sacred collection Mason added others, each aimed at a different clientele.

the Handel and Haydn Society

In 1827 Mason left the banking trade and moved to Boston as leader of music in several churches and president of the Handel and Haydn Society. Not until the age of thirty-five, then, did Mason center his professional life on music. But through shrewd planning, talent, and energy, he entered his new calling at a level of income and prestige unprecedented for an American musician. Showing great talent as a hymn tune composer, he produced more than 1,100 tunes for congregations to sing, including BETHANY ("Nearer, My God, to Thee") and MISSIONARY HYMN ("From Greenland's Icy Mountains"). The line between works Mason composed and those he merely arranged is not always clear, however, as shown by ANTIOCH, the tune to which Isaac Watts's text "Joy to the World" is now sung as a Christmas carol.

Mason's hymns

When Mason first published ANTIOCH in 1836, he attributed the tune to Handel, although the melody has never been found in this form in Handel's compositions. Those who know Handel's *Messiah,* however, will hear echoes of it in the hymn tune. The opening four notes ("Joy to the world") resemble the opening of the *Messiah* chorus "Lift up your heads." And the melody sung later in the hymn to the words "And heav'n and nature sing" is close to the tune played by the violins at the start of *Messiah*'s opening tenor recitative, "Comfort ye, my people." From these fragments, Mason composed a new tune for Watts's text. Mason's tune starts high, with a burst of energy underlining the text's rapturous mood. His closing is also vivid. In fact, its word repetition, the dividing of text between upper and lower voices, and the energetic effect of the repeated notes all recall the fuging tune, a form by then long scorned by New England reformers. Yet its attribution to an "eminent composer" and "scientific" harmonization—avoiding open sonorities and parallel fifths—distinguish it from both older psalmody and Southern shape-note hymnody.

Other tunes of Mason's depart even further from the earlier style, a topic to be taken up later in this chapter, after exploring Mason's activities as a teacher and businessman.

MASON AS TEACHER OF CHILDREN

Like psalmodists and hymnodists before and after him, Mason taught singing schools in hopes of improving teenagers' and adults' musical taste through performance. Around the time that he moved to Boston, however, the newly instituted public schools there placed fresh attention on children, whose potential for making music had never received much notice. Mason grasped the advantages of teaching young children to sing before their taste was formed, so they could learn to appreciate "good music" as they developed their singing skills.

music in public schools

Around 1830 Mason formed the earliest known singing school for children, which he taught free of charge. The class grew quickly: from six or eight at the start to five or six hundred a few years later. And after a year of teaching gratis, he began to collect fees and to devote more of his energies to secular teaching, especially of children.

In 1833, in collaboration with George James Webb, an immigrant musician from England, Mason helped to found the Boston Academy of Music, which taught both sacred and secular singing. Soon he was offering teachers' classes through the academy and published his *Manual of the Boston Academy of Music* (Boston, 1834; eleven more editions by 1861) to serve them. The introduction of vocal music into public schools had been one of the academy's main objectives from the start, and in 1837, with three assistants, Mason approached the Boston school board and offered free singing classes in the city's public schools for the coming year. The success of that volunteer experiment led the board to declare vocal music a regular school subject in 1838 and to hire Mason and his associates as teachers. He taught music in the Boston schools until 1855.

🖎 Lowell Mason (1792–1872) not long after he moved from Savannah, Georgia, to Boston.

By all accounts, Mason was an outstanding teacher with a commanding personality. But what gave him authority as a teacher of other teachers was a systematic method of instruction. In honing his techniques, Mason learned much from William Woodbridge of Boston, who in the 1820s had studied the educational methods of the Swiss educator Johann Heinrich Pestalozzi, which were then being applied to music by German pedagogues. According to George F. Root, one of Mason's associates in the Boston public school venture, Woodbridge made Mason a promise: "If you will call together a class, I will translate and write out each lesson for you . . . and you can try the method; it will take about twenty-four evenings." Mason agreed, and the class was assembled. "Speaking to Dr. Mason once about this remarkable class," Root relates, "I asked him what those ladies and gentlemen paid for that course of twenty-four lessons. 'Oh, they arranged that among themselves,' he replied. 'They decided that five dollars apiece would be about right.' 'And how many were there in the class?' He smiled as he answered: 'About five hundred.'"

Mason was sometimes attacked for being mercenary, overpaid, or both. Root denied that he was either: "I do not believe he ever made a plan to make money, unless when investing his surplus funds. In his musical work it was . . . a clear case . . . of seeking first what was right."

MASON AS BUSINESSMAN

Lowell Mason seems to have been the first American musician who made a substantial profit from musical work. How he managed that remarkable feat is worth noting.

To earn a living in music, you have six basic choices: composing, performing, teaching, distributing (sales and publishing), writing about music, and manufacturing musical instruments or other goods. Mason's career was striking in that he took part in all of these occupations except the last. Yet while he was an active composer, performer (as church organist and choir leader), and writer on music, teaching and distributing music were the keys to his financial success and his widespread influence.

Long before Mason came on the scene, teaching was the foremost American musical profession. But the notion that it could also be profitable seems to have been Mason's invention, at least on this side of the Atlantic. The key lay in the large scope of the projects he tackled, which were often too big to handle alone. From the time he began children's classes, Mason used assistants, and by 1844–45 he was teaching singing in six Boston public schools while supervising ten assistants who taught in ten others. Mason's aides taught from his methods, used his books, and were paid by him from funds he collected from the school board. It seems likely that he took a cut of those funds for himself.

When Mason entered the book trade, profit was linked not to authorship but to financial risk. Hence, only publishers stood to reap substantial capital from successful books. Mason was never a publisher. Yet in view of the deal he worked out for *The Boston Handel and Haydn Society Collection*, he seems to have found ways to collect a larger share of the proceeds from his books than did other authors. Indications are that he earned substantial rewards as an author without taking a publisher's risk.

How wealthy did Mason become? In 1837 he was sufficiently well off to manage a European trip of several months that took him to England, Germany, Switzerland, and France. An 1848 list of Boston taxpayers valued his estate at $41,000, making him by far the richest musician in town. And *The Rich Men of Massachusetts*, a book published in 1852, set his worth at $100,000. Mason's tunebooks were regularly updated, and many of them continued to sell for years—especially *Carmina Sacra, or Boston Collection of Church Music* (1841), which logged sales of 500,000 by 1858. Mason traveled to Europe for a longer stay at the end of 1851, remaining there until the spring of 1853. When he returned to the United States, it was not to Boston but to New York, where he set up a new headquarters while he and his family settled in Orange, New Jersey. In 1869, three years before Mason's death, the plates of his copyrighted works alone were said to be worth over $100,000.

If Mason's publications produced a fountain of profit, he supplemented that income by taking part in conventions and so-called normal institutes for

A CLOSER LOOK

Pestalozzian Principles as Applied to Music

- Teach children to sing before they learn written notes.

- Make students active learners by having them imitate sounds.

- Teach one subject at a time, such as rhythm, melody, or expression, and practice each separately.

- Help students master each step through practice before moving to the next.

- Teach principles and theories *after* the practice.

Mason's wealth

the training of music teachers. Moreover, after midcentury the name Mason stood not only for Lowell but also for a substantial family enterprise. By the mid-1850s Mason Brothers publishing, set up by sons Daniel Gregory and Lowell Jr., was flourishing. And son Henry was a founding partner in Mason and Hamlin, a firm of reed organ makers established in 1854 that later, in 1883, entered the piano-making business. By looking forward to the musical needs of a wide range of Americans, Mason and his family prospered.

Lowell Mason's career traces a path from scarcity to abundance, achieved by targeting new customers while holding on to older ones; first singing schools and congregations, then children, adult secular singers, and finally teachers were courted as potential users of his books. In the 1830s he broadened the framework of hymnody to include secular edification, and by the 1850s Mason commanded a growing business network that he himself had partly invented. At the same time, as an acute businessman, he was able to modify his product to accommodate changing customer tastes. In the field of hymnody, that meant adapting to a new theological climate.

MASON AND THE HYMNODY OF NORTHERN REVIVALISM

With the rise of revivalism in the North came a sense that the standard hymns were no longer enough to speak for new religious sensibilities and their focus on free grace. As Protestants searched for new hymns, their first step was to shift the emphasis from an intimidating God to the joy of Christian salvation, substituting welcome for dread.

hymnals

Revivalism in the North left a mark on two tunebooks that appeared in 1831: *The Christian Lyre,* compiled by Joshua Leavitt, a Congregational minister in New York City, and *Spiritual Songs for Social Worship,* compiled by Thomas Hastings and Lowell Mason. Leavitt's collection was the first American tunebook to take the form of a modern **hymnal**, with music for every hymn and the multi-stanza texts printed in full with the music. Some of the music was original; the rest came from a variety of sources—New England psalm tunes, rural folk hymns, revival songs, and even popular songs such as "Home, Sweet Home" in sacred makeovers. Leavitt's book sold in the tens of thousands, and its format and contents were copied by other hymn collections for the next several decades.

In borrowing Leavitt's format, Hastings and Mason's *Spiritual Songs* managed also to compete with it successfully. The book contained four hundred hymns and tunes, many of them original, including a number by Hastings and by Mason. The texts, by Isaac Watts as well as later writers, summarized the main evangelical themes of the day more fully than any earlier revival hymnal.

Sacred tunebooks, from Lyon's *Urania* to *The Sacred Harp,* were published to serve singing schools, musical societies, singing conventions, and even meetinghouse choirs, but not worshiping congregations. The oblong shape, instructional introductions, and varied musical forms (fuging tunes, anthems) separate such books from hymnals used by congregations. Well into the 1800s, most congregational hymnals were wordbooks: metrical psalters or hymn collections printed without music. Some congregations still relied on a small stock of tunes learned by rote; some turned worship music over to a choir or organist. In either case, there was no need for tunes in hymnals. Leavitt's *Christian Lyre* and Hastings and

Mason's *Spiritual Songs,* however, were intended for congregations. Their success shows that revivalism brought fresh democratic energy into religious life.

Mason and his fellow reformer Hastings took the lead in creating a style of hymnody that preserved some traits of the preceding generation's ancient music while also appealing to the taste of worshipers in their own day. In a letter of 1837, Hastings wrote with satisfaction: "Europe has no style *strictly devotional* that compares at all with what we are cultivating in this country." Mason's OLIVET (LG 3.3), first appearing in *Spiritual Songs,* is a setting of Ray Palmer's text "My Faith Looks Up to Thee" that embodies that devotional style. Its three voices are not of equal melodic interest. Only the soprano melody has a clear profile; the alto mostly shadows that melody a third below, while the bass does little more than sing the root of each chord. The harmony follows European "scientific" principles at their simplest, emphasizing tonic and dominant chords. As with ancient music, Mason's setting poses no competition for the text and invites congregational singing.

LG 3.3

Yet the rhythm and structure of OLIVET are not those of ancient music. Instead of a bland succession of half or quarter notes, OLIVET features a dotted rhythmic motive in five of its seven poetic lines. And the rhythmic pattern and

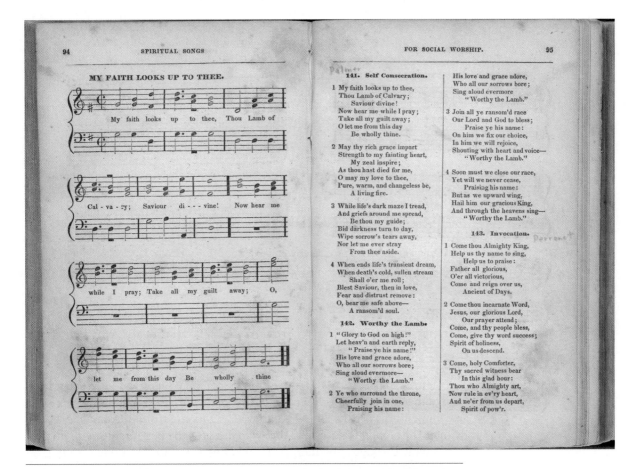

Lowell Mason's OLIVET, as it first appeared in *Spiritual Songs for Social Worship* (Utica, New York, 1831).

🎧 CD 1.11	**Listening Guide 3.3**		**OLIVET** LOWELL MASON

DATE: 1831

PERFORMERS: The Masonites; Larry Hamberlin, director

GENRE: congregational hymn

METER: duple

FORM: strophic

WHAT TO LISTEN FOR

- block chord texture
- melody in soprano

TIMING	SECTION	TEXT	COMMENTS
0:00	stanza 1	My faith looks up to three . . .	Mason's harmonization is in three parts (soprano, alto, bass), instead of the typical four-voice SATB texture of later hymnals. At mid-stanza, the men's voices drop out, leaving the women's voices harmonizing in thirds.
0:15		Now hear me while I pray . . .	
0:25		O let me from this day . . .	The men's voices return, to conclude the stanza in three-voice texture.
0:36	stanza 2	May thy rich grace impart . . .	In this performance, the tenors double the sopranos' melody an octave lower in stanza 2.
1:13	Amen	Amen.	A frequent addition to hymns that address God directly, i.e., prayers. The two syllables are sung to subdominant (IV) and tonic (I) chords, creating a plagal or "Amen" cadence.

Listen & Reflect

1. Does the melody of OLIVET fit any other psalm or hymn texts studied so far? Why or why not?

2. Apart from matching the right number of notes with the syllables, does the melody suit the hymn text in any other ways; that is, does the music convey the spirit of the words, and if so, how?

harmony are coordinated to serve a highly personal set of words. In the second half of the first verse of Palmer's text, the worshiper pleads with God: "Now hear me while I pray; / Take all my guilt away; / O let me from this day / Be wholly thine." The second line, sung to the same music as the first, seems more imploring, simply through repetition. The third line is even more urgent, calling on the highest note in the whole melody ("O let me from this day"). By the time a cadence relieves the tension, OLIVET has outlined a dramatic contour that supports the text's self-dramatizing demands.

MASON'S RIVALS, COLLABORATORS, AND LEGACY

Once Lowell Mason began exploring Americans' appetite for edification, other musicians recognized that a burgeoning market stood ready to be tapped. Thomas Hastings, Mason's sometime collaborator, shared similar goals, and his hymn tune TOPLADY (sung to the text "Rock of ages, cleft for me," by Augustus M. Toplady), which was also included in their *Spiritual Songs for Social Worship,* displays style features nearly identical to those of OLIVET. In his later years Hastings considered Mason a rival. A letter he wrote in 1848 sarcastically described Mason's idea of doing good as being in a position to "multiply and sell books."

Two younger men, both students of Mason's, built on his legacy of organized musical instruction. William B. Bradbury, a native of Maine, enrolled in the Boston Academy of Music and sang in one of Mason's church choirs in the early 1830s. After teaching music in Maine and New Brunswick (1836–40), Bradbury took a post as organist and choir leader in a New York Baptist church. There he established classes for children similar to Mason's in Boston. His first tunebook, *The Young Choir* (1841), continued that educational emphasis, and it was followed by others aimed at Sunday schools. The sales of Bradbury's tunebooks reached more than two million copies. Among the popular hymn tunes he composed are WOODWORTH ("Just as I am") and CHINA ("Jesus loves me! this I know"), the latter published in 1862. Bradbury also showed something of Mason's knack for business. In 1854 he helped to found a piano-making firm in New York, and in 1861 his publishing company opened in the same city.

William B. Bradbury

Another musician who carried Mason's message in new directions was George Frederick Root. Born in 1820 on a Massachusetts farm, Root grew up hoping to be a musician. Yet he never played organ or piano until, at age eighteen, he moved from his hometown of Sheffield to Boston, where his first teacher ordered him to begin teaching an even ranker beginner. After a brief struggle to make his "clumsy fingers" negotiate a keyboard, he began playing the last hymn in church services, apparently so the regular organist could leave to play another service. Root later explained his quick acceptance into the professional ranks as more a matter of opportunity than of talent. Lowell Mason had "just commenced what proved to be a revolution in the 'plain song' of the church and of the people," he recalled. And Mason's "methods of teaching the elementary principles of music were so much better . . . than anything . . . seen [before]" that those who were early in the field had very great advantage.

George F. Root

In Root's autobiography, Mason is his respected mentor, model, and eventually colleague. Root sang in the Boston Academy Chorus in 1838, and by 1840 he was teaching as one of Mason's assistants in the Boston public schools. The following year, Mason hired him as an instructor in one of his teacher-training conventions, and three years later Root moved from Boston to New York, where he led a church choir and taught from Mason's books in various schools, including "young ladies' academies" and the New York State Institution for the Blind. In 1853 Root enlisted Mason to be one of his collaborators at the first of several three-month normal institutes (courses for training teachers) in New York City.

Root granted that a hierarchy of musical genres existed, with European masterworks at the top. Indeed, he was a lover of the classics, especially Handel's *Messiah,* Mendelssohn's *Elijah,* and the works of Beethoven and Wagner. But he was also a practical man who had a clear sense of his own abilities, and early in the 1850s he realized that he had a choice to make. "A majority of the music-loving world," he knew, enjoyed only an "elementary" state of musical knowledge. Would he be selling out if he turned his efforts toward serving the majority, rather than the art of music?

Mason convinced Root that he would not. In the first place, a beginner's love of music was no less genuine than a connoisseur's, and in the second, a beginner's taste ought not to be despised. As Root came to understand, "all must pass" through the same hierarchy of musical genres, and very few reach the top. Moreover, the journey need not be one from bad music to good music but from simple music to more complex compositions. Root later wrote: "I am simply one, who, from such resources as he finds within himself, makes music for the people, having always a particular need in view." Root's idea of himself as a musician of the people eventually led him to compose popular songs, something that Mason never attempted.

edification and praise   Edification, in whose name Root toiled throughout his career, was a dynamic ideal in the first half of the nineteenth century. Yet its opposite number, praise, was equally, if not more, powerful in the realm of sacred music, as later developments will bear out. Already with Mason, Bradbury, and Root, the forces of edification were leading musicians out of the church and into schools and other sites of secular music making. Later chapters will explore those sites, both public and private. But first it is necessary to consider the musical achievements of Americans whose ancestors came not from Europe but from Africa.

QUESTIONS FOR DISCUSSION AND REVIEW

1. Boston's Handel and Haydn Society is still in existence today. After visiting the organization's website, describe how the society's original mission resembles its current activities and how it differs. How do the differences reflect changes in the United States in general and Boston in particular over the two intervening centuries?

2. Southern shape-note hymnody resembles the music of earlier New England psalmodists such as Billings and Read in some respects and differs in others. What are those similarities and differences?

3. Likewise, what are the similarities and differences between Southern shape-note hymnody and Northern reform hymnody?

FURTHER READING

Broyles, Michael. *"Music of the Highest Class": Elitism and Populism in Antebellum Boston.* New Haven, CT: Yale University Press, 1992.

Crawford, Richard. *The American Musical Landscape.* 2d edition. Berkeley and Los Angeles: University of California Press, 2000.

Gould, Nathaniel D. *Church Music in America.* 1853. Reprint. New York: AMS Press, 1972.

Jackson, George Pullen. *White Spirituals in the Southern Uplands: The Story of the Fasola Folk, Their Songs, Singings, and "Buckwheat Notes."* 1933. Reprint. New York: Dover, 1965.

Marini, Stephen A. "Hymnody and History: Early American Evangelical Hymns as Sacred Music." In *Music in American Religious Experience.* Edited by Philip V. Bohlman, Edith L. Blumhofer, and Maria M. Chow. 123–54. New York: Oxford University Press, 2006.

Miller, Kiri. *Traveling Home: Sacred Harp Singing and American Pluralism*. Urbana: University of Illinois Press, 2008.

Root, George Frederick. *The Story of a Musical Life: An Autobiography*. Cincinnati: John Church, 1891.

FURTHER LISTENING AND VIEWING

White Spirituals from the Sacred Harp: The Alabama Sacred Harp Convention. New World Records, 1977.

Word of Mouth Chorus. *Rivers of Delight: American Folk Hymns from the Sacred Harp Tradition*. Elektra/Nonesuch, 1979.

Hinton, Matt, and Erica Hinton. *Awake My Soul: The Story of the Sacred Harp*. DVD. Awake Productions, 2006.

CHAPTER 4

"MAKE A NOISE"

African American Music before the Civil War

As early as their first arrival in Virginia in 1619, Africans were imported to the New World with the idea of making agricultural opportunities such as tobacco growing more economically attractive. Though most Americans considered it morally wrong, slavery persisted as part of the economic engine that European settlement built on these shores. The Founding Fathers knew that slavery violated the republic's democratic principles, yet the constitutional debates of 1787–88 show that if it had been outlawed, some colonies would never have joined the union.

Slavery's evil touched everyone involved. In regions where blacks outnumbered them, the whites' sense of guilt mingled with fear. Slave rebellions in the Caribbean in the 1790s—especially the Haitian revolution, which began in 1791 and eventually ousted the French colonial government in 1803—sent shock waves through North American slaveholding society. Revolts were rare in the United States, but the threat of revolt was seldom absent. And when slaves did rebel, panic could lead to tighter repression.

American slaves came from a broad geographical area, stretching from the western Sudan (present-day Senegal) to Central and Southeast Africa as far as Mozambique and Madagascar. Most slaves came from West Africa—present-day Liberia, Côte d'Ivoire, Ghana, Togo, Benin, and Nigeria. The slave population thus included peoples with many different languages, religions, and traditions. For all their differences, however, these African peoples shared certain similarities in cultural expression. Their sense of community must also have been strengthened by the harshness of their lives in America. Custom and law here treated Africans' differences from each other as insignificant when compared with their differences from whites.

By 1850 almost one out of every six Americans was of African descent. The midcentury national census identified 3.6 million people—just over 15 percent of the population—as black, with 434,000 free and the rest slaves. Though concentrated in the South, most heavily on cotton and rice plantations, blacks were nevertheless present throughout the country. Yet white Americans everywhere generally agreed that blacks were inherently inferior. Even among slavery's opponents, few whites endorsed the notion of black-white equality. This attitude must be kept in mind in any discussion of black music making before the Civil

War. Black Americans preserved African cultural practices not only out of preference but also because whites discouraged their participation in Euro-American life. With chances for interaction limited, they relied on interactions with each other, and a strong African heritage was thus maintained.

There is scant documentation of the beginnings of African American culture, which, like American Indian culture, relied on oral transmission. Yet some observers left comments that allow historians to piece together an idea of black music making before the Civil War. Even before 1800, newspapers provide data on black musicians in the form of advertisements. Slaves, after all, were part of the American economy. And musical skills could increase a slave's market value, as the following ad from a Virginia newspaper in 1766 confirms: "TO BE SOLD. A young healthy Negro fellow who has been used to wait on a Gentleman and plays extremely well on the French horn." A Boston newspaper in 1745 carried a notice from an owner in Newbury offering a reward for the return of "Cato," who had disappeared a few days earlier: "about 22 Years of Age, short and small, SPEAKS GOOD ENGLISH AND CAN READ AND WRITE . . . has a smooth Face, a sly Look, TOOK WITH A VIOLIN, AND CAN PLAY WELL THEREON." This ad is a reminder that in colonial times slavery was practiced in the North as well as the South. But most of all, it was an attempt to keep Cato from gaining his freedom.

newspaper data

Cato's literacy may have made him exceptional, but his ability to play a European instrument was not entirely unusual. Advertisements in the *Virginia Gazette* between 1736 and 1780 carried more than sixty references to black musicians, of whom three-quarters were said to be violin players. The presence of African American fiddlers shows acculturation going on, with blacks mastering "white" instruments. It also points to a vocation taking shape: that of the black dance musician. In the North, music for formal dances and for dancing schools was routinely supplied by black musicians. In the South, meanwhile, blacks performed for dancing at their masters' balls, assemblies, and special "entertainments." Many of these players were slaves, which limited their ability to collect payment. But some were free and may be considered tradesmen of sorts. Already in the eighteenth century, then, black dance musicians were meeting a need in white society. And they must have been skilled, for only their success could explain why an institution as unbending as slavery would allow blacks the role of entertainer.

black musicians in the 1700s

THE AFRICAN ROOTS OF AMERICAN MUSIC

American slaves kept alive oral traditions rooted in Africa despite seemingly overwhelming obstacles. As early as the seventeenth century English slave traders developed the practice of transporting slaves to the West Indies for "seasoning," in which they were trained in Western modes of living. Most slaves in the United States, then, came here not directly from Africa but by way of the Caribbean; many, in fact, were second-generation slaves born in the West Indies. Once in this country, slaves were discouraged from communicating in their native languages. Likewise, slave owners generally suppressed the making of drums and other loud musical instruments for fear they would be used to signal uprisings. And even benevolent whites made efforts to supplant African cultural traditions with white practices in an effort to "improve" black Americans—often succeeding only in impressing on blacks a sense of their own cultural inferiority.

Yet the historical record shows that, these obstacles notwithstanding, African Americans preserved at least some aspects of African traditions.

It is a mistake, of course, to speak of "African traditions" as if they formed a monolithic whole—and the same is true of African American traditions. Africa at the time of the slave trade embraced a huge number of distinct peoples, speaking hundreds of languages, practicing myriad religions, and cultivating highly contrasting approaches to music making. Moreover, African music, like American music, is a dynamic, living cultural force that has changed over time. For these reasons, attempts to speculate on the sounds of slave music by drawing parallels between present-day African and African American musical practices pose insoluble problems for the music historian. Such efforts to fill gaps in the historical record must be taken with a grain of salt.

musical Africanisms   Nonetheless, it is possible to hear in the informal music making of rural African communities today certain commonalities with much African American music:

- *Music as a part of everyday life.* Music can accompany all sorts of activities: work, play, worship, and ritual.
- *Close interaction between performers and spectators.* Unlike a typical Western concert milieu, music making may uphold little distinction between those who are playing and singing and those who are dancing, shouting encouragement, and otherwise participating in the musical moment.
- *Call and response.* In a **responsorial** or **call-and-response** texture, a leader's musical phrase is answered (vocally or instrumentally) by the group. Although call and response is a musical pattern found throughout the world, it plays a particularly central role in much of both African and African American music.
- *Emphasis on voices and percussion.* Although a wide array of wind and string instruments are used, of greatest importance are voices and percussion instruments, including drums of all kinds, rattles, bells, and xylophones.
- *Polyrhythm.* In ensembles of drums and other percussion instruments, each instrument typically maintains a distinctive rhythmic pattern, which interlocks with the other instruments' rhythms to create a complex texture called **polyrhythm**.

Any of these musical tendencies, when found in music of the United States, may be considered an Africanism. The story of how Africanisms came to be part of the fabric of American music is necessarily speculative. But when historians carefully interpret what fragmentary historical record actually exists, that record reveals much about black music before the Civil War.

TRADITIONAL AFRICAN AMERICAN MUSIC MAKING

Present-day knowledge of the music of American slaves, as with earlier American Indian music, depends on accounts written by whites. One such account was that of New Englander Lewis Paine. During the summer of 1841 he visited a local plantation on a holiday and saw slaves dancing to a unique kind of accompaniment, called **patting juba**: placing one foot "a little in advance of the other, raising the ball of the foot from the ground, and striking it in regular time, while, in connection, the hands are struck slightly together, and then upon the thighs." Patting juba was a transformation of African drumming practice, using the human body as a substitute for the outlawed percussion instruments.

Travelers in the South were also struck by the way slaves sang while they worked. Frederick Law Olmsted in 1853 described a slave's **field holler** as "a long, loud, musical shout, rising and falling and breaking into falsetto." Communal **work songs** helped workers fulfill their tasks by pacing their activity, coordinating their movements, and rallying their spirits. Observers often described responsorial singing with strict rhythm and short phrases, the leader improvising calls and the group responding.

work songs

Slaves were "generally expected to sing as well as to work," recalled Frederick Douglass, born a slave in Maryland around 1818. "A silent slave is not liked by masters or overseers," he explained: "'*Make a noise*,' '*make a noise*,' and '*bear a hand*,' are the words usually addressed to the slaves when there is silence amongst them. This may account for the almost constant singing heard in the southern states." Douglass's statement points to the unique conditions in which blacks made music in antebellum America (that is, the United States in the decades before the Civil War). Aware that slaves' bodies were easier to control than their minds, masters could command singing to track their workers' whereabouts and monitor their mood. When slaves sang of brutality, injustice, or liberation within white hearing, they often disguised their meanings; it has long been understood that what slaves sang about was not always obvious from the words of their songs. To a slave, Douglass wrote, songs "represent the sorrows, rather than the joys of his heart; and he is relieved by them, only as an aching heart is relieved by its tears."

Work songs were sung by stevedores hauling cargo on or off ships, by field workers hoeing and weeding cotton, and by work crews clearing brush and timber with axes. After the Civil War, new work songs were created and old ones adapted by railroad crews driving spikes and by prison chain gangs repairing roads and performing other menial tasks. Though surely not identical to the songs of slavery, these later work songs offer the historian a glimpse of how those earlier songs might have sounded. Both before and after the Civil War, the job of the work song was to coordinate group efforts, such as the pull of the stevedores' ropes, and more generally to set a sustainable pace for repetitive actions such as swinging a hoe. A good leader needed a strong voice and an ability to remember or improvise long strings of calls. Most important, though, was an ability to combine a good sense of time with a knowledge of the work at hand in order to set and sustain the correct pace. A prisoner in the Mississippi State

---

In their own words 💬

Anonymous Portrayal of Stevedores in Mobile, Alabama, as They Unload a Steamboat, 1857

The men keep the most perfect time by means of their songs. These ditties, nearly meaningless, have much music in them, and as all join in the perpetually recurring chorus, a rough harmony is produced, by no means unpleasing. I think the leader improvises the words . . . he singing one line alone, and the whole then giving the chorus, which is repeated without change at every line, till the general chorus concludes the stanza.

Penitentiary at Parchman, interviewed in the 1940s by folklorist Alan Lomax, recalled of one leader: "He had a good voice, and he was an extra good worker. And the main thing about it, he would keep it, keep his song in time."

LG 4.1   In 1959 Lomax recorded a group of retired stevedores singing one of their work songs. "Carrie Belle" (LG 4.1) was also used in the field as a song for chopping or hoeing. The subject matter of the lyrics indicates that at least parts of the song postdate slavery, but the musical devices match earlier descriptions of African American work songs. The vocal parts display call and response, accompanied by a forceful exhalation (*"huh"*) on each pull of the rope. This simple texture is made more interesting by a rhythmic detail that suggests an African influence: the pulling of the rope is not on the downbeat but on the third beat of each four-beat bar, creating a kind of **syncopation**, the accenting of a beat or part of a beat that is usually unaccented. This feature, common in African American work songs, can also be interpreted as a kind of polyrhythm, in which the voice's downbeat ("Carrie Belle . . .") falls in one place, and the downbeat of the ropes falls in another.

The melody of "Carrie Belle" is pentatonic, and the group harmonizes their responses using notes of the pentatonic scale. But some of the pitches bend—especially the third degree of the scale—in a way that came later to be a trait of the blues.

REGIONAL DIFFERENCES IN ANTEBELLUM BLACK MUSIC MAKING

Black music making in North America before the Civil War varied with the conditions in which African Americans lived. The most dramatic difference existed between the North, where slavery was sparse, and the South, where it was entrenched.

THE NORTHERN UNITED STATES

By 1786 Pennsylvania and all states north except New Jersey had either abolished slavery or decided how they would do so. Blacks formed only a small minority of the population in the North. They worked alongside whites, though seldom accepted as social equals, and were able to enter some skilled trades.

Sacred Music in the North

In both North and South, religion loomed large in black-white relations. Whites disagreed about whether blacks should be Christianized, especially if they were slaves. Some believed that religious teaching would help reconcile slaves to their lot and make them more obedient, but others feared such instruction. Generally, however, Christian leaders favored the conversion of blacks. New York's Trinity (Anglican) Church was one place where evangelizing took hold early. In 1741 Trinity's organist, Johann Gottlob Klemm, instructed forty-three Negroes in psalmody. And two years later, the church's minister wrote that when the clerk rose to lead the congregation in psalm singing, "I can scarce express the satisfaction I have in seeing 200 Negroes and White Persons with heart and voice glorifying their Maker."

| CD 1.12 | Listening Guide 4.1 | "Carrie Belle" ANONYMOUS |

DATE: unknown

PERFORMERS: John Davis and seven other singers, St. Simon's Island, Georgia, recorded 1959

GENRE: traditional African American work song

METER: duple

FORM: verse and chorus

WHAT TO LISTEN FOR

- call and response
- rhythmic coordination of rope pulls

TIMING	SECTION	TEXT	COMMENTS
0:00	verse 1	Carrie Belle, don't weep Carrie Belle, don't mourn Don't you hang your head and cry.	The leader sings the first line, then the others join in on the second line. The sound of the rope pulls ("*huh*") marks the third beat of each bar.
0:23	chorus	Ain't gonna hurt nobody, oh no! Ain't gonna hurt nobody, oh no! I'm going to carry to the Alamo.	A very short signal from the leader cues in the other singers.
0:45	verse 2	Ever since I lay in the barroom door I said I'll never get drunk no more.	The music of verse 1 repeats, with new words.
1:07	chorus	Ain't gonna hurt nobody . . .	Both words and music are the same for each repetition of the chorus.
1:28	verse 3	Well, I pawn my watch and I pawn my chain then I pawn my diamond ring.	
1:50	chorus	Ain't gonna hurt nobody . . .	
2:11	verse 4	Carrie Belle, don't weep . . .	A repeat of verse 1.
2:32	chorus	Ain't gonna hurt nobody . . .	
2:53	verse 5	Ever since I lay . . .	A repeat of verse 2.
3:13	chorus	Ain't gonna hurt nobody . . .	

Listen & Reflect

1. What features of this music appear to be relatively fixed, and which seem to be more improvisatory? How can you tell?

2. Judging by what you hear, what can you say about the relationship between the leader and the rest of the group?

3. What does the tempo suggest about the nature of stevedores' work?

❧ Reverend Richard Allen (1760–1831), an ex-slave, compiled *A Collection of Spiritual Songs and Hymns,* the first such book prepared for a black congregation in America.

But the idea of blacks and whites worshiping together was opposed in many other places. Where more than a handful of blacks joined a white religious society, they were often assigned segregated seating. Black Christians in both North and South most typically worshiped in all-black congregations. The first of these were formed in the South in the 1770s and 1780s under Baptist preachers. In the North, blacks began in the 1790s and early 1800s to establish separate congregations, chiefly under Methodist sponsorship. The founding in 1816 of the African Methodist Episcopal (AME) Church in Philadelphia established a clear racial division in American Protestantism that persists today.

In 1801 the Reverend Richard Allen, one of the AME Church's founders, published a hymnal for Bethel Church in Philadelphia, the first such book assembled by a black author for a black congregation. It followed the format of metrical psalters such as the *Bay Psalm Book*: pocket-sized, devoted to multi-stanza poetry, and without music. Among the more than five dozen items Allen chose for his hymnal are familiar favorites by the British hymn writer Isaac Watts and others. But the hymnal also includes more than twenty texts that cannot be traced to any previous author, suggesting that Allen wrote some or all of them himself.

A few of these texts are printed with **refrains**: repeating lines at the end of each stanza or verse. Here, the refrains are two-line sections whose text may or may not relate to the subject of the hymn. Because a refrain is normally sung to the same words and music each time it appears, like a chorus but shorter and less independent, it can be learned quickly by ear; refrains are sometimes sung even by those who do not sing the verses. The alternating of a changing four-line verse with an unchanging two-line refrain suggests some kind of interaction. Perhaps a group might respond to a leader; or one group, bookless and singing refrains only, might respond to another group equipped with books and singing both verses and refrains. In any case, Allen's hymnal put into writing the oral practice of responsorial hymn singing.

Another practice cultivated by mixed groups of literate and nonliterate blacks was that of lining out. No doubt learned from the example of white congregations (see chapter 1), lining out was another type of responsorial hymn singing. The practice probably changed somewhat in its adoption by black churches. The Old Way of singing was marked by the loose coordination of voices singing more or less the same melody. In a present-day reconstruction of the Bethel Church's congregational singing as it might have sounded in Richard Allen's day, the texture of the Old Way of singing is conceived as **heterophony**, in which multiple voices simultaneously vary a melody, so much so that a vague harmony emerges. As sung by a choir of church elders and historians from the Smithsonian Institution, "Am I a Soldier of the Cross?" (LG 4.2), a hymn by Isaac Watts from Allen's hymnal, conveys a sense of communal religious fervor.

LG 4.2

Holiday Music in the North

Holiday celebrations gave African Americans another chance to make music of their own. In some colonies, blacks were given a break from their work schedules during local spring elections, and they staged secular festivals paralleling those of white society. A white observer in Newport, Rhode Island, caught the

🎧 CD 1.13	Listening Guide 4.2	"Am I a Soldier of the Cross?" ANONYMOUS

DATE: unknown

PERFORMERS: The Richard Allen Singers; Theodore King, precentor; recorded in 1992

GENRE: traditional African American lined hymn

METER: undefined

FORM: strophic

WHAT TO LISTEN FOR

- call and response between precentor and congregation
- free ornamentation of melody
- wordless interjections within and between lines of text

TIMING	TEXT	COMMENTS
0:00	Am I a soldier of the cross, A follower of the Lamb,	The precentor intones the first two lines of text. Nonverbal responses begin almost immediately.
0:10	Am I a soldier . . .	The congregation sings the first two phrases of the hymn tune.
0:58	And shall I fear to own His cause, Or blush to speak His Name?	Over the last notes of the congregational singing, the precentor speaks the third and fourth lines of text.
1:07	And shall I fear . . .	The congregation sings the third and fourth phrases of the tune.
1:53		Before the first stanza is ended, the precentor can be heard intoning the beginning of the second stanza as the recording fades.

NOTE: The recording fades out after the first stanza.

Listen & Reflect

1. Compare this performance with that of the Old Regular Baptists singing "Guide Me, O Thou Great Jehovah" (see LG 1.3). What are some similarities and differences?

spirit and sound of the music at an Election Day gathering there in 1756, noting its difference from white musical customs: "Every voice in its highest key, in all the various languages of Africa, mixed with the broken and ludicrous English, filled the air, accompanied with the music of the fiddle, tambourine, banjo and drum."

Another holiday for Northern blacks was known as the "Pinkster Celebration," held at Pentecost, seven Sundays after Easter. Pinkster festivities could fill several days. An account of one such celebration in Albany, New York, during the 1770s recalls a dance that lasted from noon until midnight or later. The dancers' movements gradually grew more "rapid and furious," fueled in part by their

Pinkster Celebrations

A CLOSER LOOK

The Banjo: African Origins of "America's Instrument"

As early as the 1650s European observers noted the presence among African slaves in the West Indies of instruments resembling both the present-day banjo and West African antecedents. North American accounts date back to the 1740s, and by 1810 written references to the banjo often lack descriptions, implying that the instrument was familiar to most readers. In its earlier forms, the banjo had a body made from a halved gourd, with an animal skin stretched over the opening and from one to six strings. Instruments of this description are identified by various names, some of which resemble its modern name: *bangil, bangar, banshaw, Creole-bania, banjar,* and *bonjaw.*

By the 1840s, the gourd sound chamber gave way to a wooden rim with a metal tension hoop and adjustable brackets much like a drum. Around the same time, whites also began to play the banjo. By the beginning of the twentieth century, a banjo manufacturer could proudly state that "what the mandolin is to Italy, and the guitar to Spain, the banjo is to America." That status inspired the title of a recent history of the banjo, *America's Instrument.* An irony of history is that today the instrument is associated almost exclusively with white performers.

🔊 This "Creole-bania," made in Dutch Guyana before 1772, and now in the Rijksmuseum voor Volkenkunde, Leiden, Holland, is made from a gourd, a sheepskin, and gut strings.

---

quaffing of "stimulating potions" that seemed to strengthen "all their nerves and muscular powers" and to make perspiration flow "in frequent streams, from brow to heel," before they dropped out when "extreme fatigue or weariness" set in. The music underlying this riot of physical stamina came from a drum and the drummer's "ever wild, though euphonic cry of *Hi-a-bomba, bomba, bomba,* in full harmony with the thumping sounds," which was "readily taken up and as oft repeated by the female portion of the spectators."

The description of a 1770s Pinkster celebration suggests a pattern of call and response between the drummer and the female spectators. The 1756 Election Day festival in Newport illustrates an additional Africanism: what has been called the "heterogeneous sound ideal," a preference for piling up different-sounding lines rather than blending them into one homogeneous sound. In this case the singing was accompanied by fiddle, tambourine, banjo, and drum, a combination poorly suited to blending. The Newport example, with its babel of African languages mixed with English and accompanied by instruments, also illustrates yet another African trait: the tendency to pack musical events as densely as possible into a relatively short time, thus filling all available musical space.

heterogeneous sound

The Albany Pinkster dance exhibits similar Africanisms. First, it makes bodily motion integral to musical performance: drumming and singing are tied so closely to the dancing they accompany that it is hard to say where music stops and physical motion begins. A second trait lies in the percussive use of the voice.

Black Professional Musicians before the Civil War

Even before the end of the Civil War brought freedom to Southern slaves, free blacks in the North had been finding niches in the American music business. One such musician, Francis "Frank" Johnson (1792–1844), a Philadelphia-born composer, bandleader, and performer on violin and keyed bugle, found such success as a self-taught leader of dance bands and concert ensembles that in 1837–38 he traveled to London, where he received from Queen Victoria a silver bugle in appreciation of his musical gifts. According to one Philadelphia observer, Johnson had "a remarkable taste in distorting a sentimental, simple, and beautiful song, into a reel, jig, or country-dance"; perhaps the "distortion" involved rhythmic complexities derived from the musicians' African heritage.

Another niche where a few black entertainers found work was the musical stage. William Henry "Juba" Lane became a full-fledged star as a dancer and tambourine player. Born around 1825, possibly in New York, Lane won fame as a teenager when English novelist Charles Dickens, then touring the United States, saw him perform in 1842 and called him "the greatest dancer known." Like Johnson before him, Lane toured England, where in 1849 his performances wowed critics, one of them wondering how Juba could "tie his legs into such knots, and fling them about so recklessly, or make his feet twinkle until you lose sight of them altogether in his energy."

A few African American musicians also began to appear on the concert stage, most notably Elizabeth Taylor Greenfield, also known as "The Black Swan." Born a slave in Natchez, Mississippi, around 1824, she was taken as a young child to Philadelphia, where she grew up free in a Quaker household. She received singing lessons as a girl and learned to play harp, piano, and guitar on her own. But it was her voice that caught listeners' attention: an instrument of wide range and unusual sound. In 1851 she settled in Buffalo, New York, where she made her concert debut. After touring in the northern United States and Canada, she traveled to England in the spring of 1853 for further study. Harriet Beecher Stowe, whose novel *Uncle Tom's Cabin* had been published the previous year and who was visiting England to promote the abolition of slavery, described a salon performance by "The Black Swan":

> Miss Greenfield's turn for singing now came, and there was profound attention. Her voice, with its keen, searching fire, its penetrating, vibrant quality, its timbre *as the French have it, cut its way like a Damascus blade to the heart. She sang the ballad "Old Folks at Home," giving one verse in the soprano, and another in the tenor voice. As she stood partially concealed by the piano, Chevalier Brunsen thought that the tenor part was performed by one of the gentlemen. He was perfectly astonished when he discovered that it was by her. This was rapturously encored.*

Stowe helped introduce Greenfield to socially prominent British patrons, and in 1854 Greenfield sang for Queen Victoria.

Returning to the United States, Greenfield continued a musical career that included concertizing, teaching in Philadelphia, and staging programs in the 1860s with an opera troupe. As the first black American concert singer to win acclaim on both sides of the Atlantic, Greenfield was able to parlay her English training and public experience into something of an American career as a vocal star.

✍ Elizabeth Taylor Greenfield (1824?–1876), ex-slave and concert singer, on the eve of her departure for Europe.

The drummer's repeated cry of *Hi-a-bomba, bomba, bomba*, creating a "full harmony" with the drum, suggests an approach to singing that is more rhythmic than melodic. Moreover, the women who are not dancing repeat this cry, feeding the rhythmic impulse further and illustrating the notion that African musicians tend to approach singing as well as instrumental playing in a percussive manner.

GREATER VIRGINIA

In the mid-1700s the region known as Greater Virginia, which included parts of today's Maryland and North Carolina, was home to some 400,000 people, of whom 35 to 40 percent were black. Except for the port of Baltimore, Greater Virginia lacked the cities that shaped the economy in the North; it was overwhelmingly rural, with most of the population gathered around the rivers that were used for shipping tobacco, the chief export crop. Though whites in the region imposed one social identity upon blacks, blacks' contact with each other was strong enough to sustain another.

conversion to Christianity

In the 1730s and 1740s a series of religious revivals known as the Great Awakening swept the colonies from Maine to Georgia, making both clergy and slave owners more inclined to consider slaves as potential Christians. By the 1750s the Reverend Samuel Davies, a Presbyterian minister in Hanover, Virginia, could point to success in his efforts to bring slaves into the Christian fold. "Ethiopia has also stretched forth her Hands unto God," Davies rejoiced in 1751. Congregational singing, he believed, helped attract slaves to his ministry. "The Negroes," he wrote, "above all the Human Species that I ever knew, have an Ear for Musick, and a kind of extatic Delight in Psalmody." A few years later, Davies again praised the singing of black members of his congregation, who, "breaking out in a torrent of sacred harmony," could provide a sound powerful enough "to bear away the whole congregation to heaven."

In 1853 Lewis Miller sketched this Negro dance in Virginia, picturing stately movements accompanied by fiddle, banjo, and bones.

The spread of the Christian faith seems to have done little, however, to restrain the black population's holiday celebrations. In 1774 a College of New Jersey graduate working as a tutor on a rural estate in northeastern Virginia contrasted the way Sundays were observed in New Jersey and Virginia. A Sabbath in Virginia did not seem to him to "wear the same Dress as our Sundays to the Northward," which were days of religious solemnity. "Generally here by five o-Clock on Saturday every Face (especially the Negroes) looks festive & cheerful—All the lower class of People, & the Servants, & the Slaves, consider it as a Day of Pleasure & amusement & spend it in such Diversions as they severally choose." The slaves might embrace those diversions wholeheartedly on any day of the week. A visitor to Virginia in 1784 expressed amazement that after a full day of work, a slave might walk several miles to take part in a dance where "he performs with astonishing ability, and the most vigorous exertions, keeping time and cadence, most exactly, with the music . . . until he exhausts himself, and scarcely has time, or strength, to return home before the hour he is called forth to toil the next morning." Perhaps slaves were willing to walk miles to attend dances because dancing for them was both recreational and spiritual—a chance to *perform* their sense of relatedness to community, gods, and ancestors.

SOUTH CAROLINA

Blacks heavily outnumbered whites in South Carolina, which more than any other colony resembled the plantation culture of the West Indies. Outside the capital, Charleston, blacks lived and worked in large, isolated groups, many of them on rice plantations. Black-white interaction in South Carolina was limited, but the lack of close oversight did not bring slaves any great amount of autonomy—especially after the Stono Rebellion of 1739, in which a black revolt left more than twenty whites and even more slaves dead. A report tells how the rebels emboldened themselves with music and dancing, using the drum to recruit other slaves to their cause. They came close to overthrowing their masters, who responded with greater repression. In earlier days, a few slaves had enjoyed the freedom to move from place to place, to earn money, raise food, and learn to read. But now controls were tightened. In hopes of reducing the disproportion of blacks over whites in South Carolina, the importing of new slaves was drastically cut.

Colonial efforts to Christianize South Carolina's slaves reached very few. In 1779 an observer called Negro slaves in South Carolina and Georgia "great strangers to Christianity, and as much under the influence of Pagan darkness, idolatry, and superstition, as they were at their first arrival from Africa." An account written in 1805 by John Pierpont, grandfather of the eminent New York banker J. P. Morgan, reports that on one local plantation different groups of slaves made different kinds of music, depending on the closeness of their ties to Africa.

LOUISIANA

Louisiana never belonged to the British Empire. Settled first by the French, the territory was controlled by Spain from 1762 to 1800, when it was returned to France, then sold to the United States in 1803 as part of the Louisiana Purchase. With its location and varied political history, Louisiana and its chief city, New

↳ This painting shows plantation slaves observing a holiday for dancing, accompanied by banjo and percussion. The painter and date of the picture, which was found in South Carolina, are unknown.

New Orleans

Orleans, acquired an ambiance unique in North America. Most of Louisiana's blacks were slaves, but some were not. And the presence of free blacks made legal and social distinctions less sharp and increased the possibilities for a merging of cultures. By 1800 New Orleans was a multiracial society with less rigid stratification than anywhere else on the continent; persons of mixed African and European ancestry could be found at most levels of society. During the nineteenth century, musicians were able to participate in white-organized musical activities, including balls and opera performances, regardless of their ancestry.

This openness also made it possible for blacks to gather for dancing and music making in public, in an expression of Africanness more open than elsewhere. As early as the 1750s such gatherings had become a Sunday custom. A witness to these Sabbath revels in 1799 noted the "vast numbers of negro slaves, men, women, and children, assembled together on the levee, drumming, fifing, and dancing, in large rings." And in 1804 another visitor wrote of the black population: "They assemble in great masses on the levee on Sundays, and make themselves glad with song, dance and merriment." But even in New Orleans there were restrictions on such public expressions. An 1817 statute limited black danc-

Congo Square

ing to Sundays before sundown, and only in Congo Square, a spacious common later renamed Beauregard Square and today a part of Louis Armstrong Park.

An account of a gathering in Congo Square comes down from Benjamin Latrobe, the architect who designed the U.S. Capitol building in Washington, D.C., and who spent many years developing a large-scale waterworks project in New Orleans. One Sunday afternoon in February 1819, he wrote, he heard "a most extraordinary noise," which sounded to him like "horses trampling on a wooden floor." When he investigated, it turned out to be an assembly of blacks, five or six hundred strong. They had formed themselves into rings, "the largest not 10 feet in diameter." In one ring, two women danced "a miserably dull & slow figure, hardly moving their feet or bodies." Two drums and a stringed instrument provided the music, and there was also singing: "The women squalled out a burthen [refrain] to the playing at intervals, consisting of two notes," in a call-and-response pattern resembling the way "the negroes, working in our cities, respond to the song of their leader."

Latrobe found nothing beautiful in the performance. "I have never seen anything more brutally savage," he wrote, nor "at the same time [more] dull &

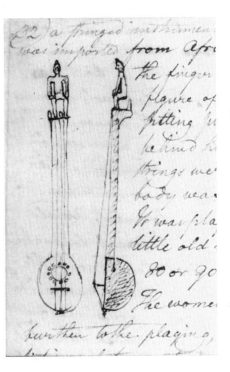

⤷ Benjamin Latrobe included sketches of the African instruments he saw played in New Orleans's Congo Square in his journal entry for February 21, 1819.

stupid." To his ear, the men's singing was "uncouth," the women's nothing more than a "detestable burthen . . . screamed . . . on one single note." Perhaps it was the strangeness of the whole affair that moved Latrobe to give so full an account, for he guessed that the singing "was in some African language," commenting that "such amusements of Sunday have, it seems, perpetuated here those of Africa among its inhabitants."

THE MUSIC OF BLACK WORSHIP

In addition to adapting the congregational singing practices of white churches, African American converts to Christianity created their own distinctive music for worship. Blending aspects of African and European music, just as they blended aspects of Christianity and African religions, black worshipers used these new sacred genres to express a uniquely African American religious experience. The music of black worship would have significant consequences as even more varieties of black music, and new audiences for that music, began to grow after the Civil War.

SPIRITUALS AND SHOUTS

the spiritual

Throughout the nineteenth century, white visitors to the South recorded their impressions of slave music in travel accounts. Here are found early descriptions of **spirituals**, African American sacred songs rooted in the experience of slavery. Peter Neilson, a Scottish trader who visited Charleston, South Carolina, in the 1820s, observed that "upon the evening of a Sunday, the song of praise may frequently be heard to issue from the hovel of the Negro, whilst all is quiet in the mansions of the wealthy." According to Neilson, the songs lacked the propriety of white hymn singing: "The religious fervor of the Negroes does not always break forth in strains the most reverential or refined."

But not all white descriptions of slave spirituals are disapproving. A native South Carolinian, Alexander D. Sims, delighted in hearing "the songs of Zion, at a distance, caroled in tones of sweetest melody by many co-mingled voices." At such times, "native harmony outvies instructed skill . . . such is the melody with which night after night the Negroes charm the ear." Ironically, his description comes from an 1834 pamphlet defending slavery as a moral institution. Compounding the irony is Sims's apparent unawareness that the words of many spirituals draw parallels between the Israelites' bondage and American slavery. Charlotte Brooks, a former slave, recalled in 1890 that as a child in Virginia she had heard a minister singing, "O where are the Hebrew children? Safe in the promised land"—words that make veiled reference to the free states in the North. Another spiritual she remembered also used images from the Bible that offered comfort to those longing for freedom:

> My God delivered Daniel, Daniel, Daniel
> My God delivered Daniel,
> And why not deliver me too?
> He delivered Daniel from the lion's den,
> Jonah from the belly of the whale,

> The three Hebrew children from the fiery furnace,
> And why not deliver me too?

Spirituals thus can be understood as both religious expressions and calls for action. In this way they anticipate the ties between black churches and the civil rights movement of the twentieth century. (See chapter 9 for the later history of the spiritual.)

A related feature of African American religious expression in the nineteenth century was sacred dancing. One early description comes from the 1849 travel account of James Dixon, a British missionary who visited a black church in Pittsburgh: "After the sermon the people sang some of their own peculiarly soft and melancholy airs. This excited them; and we had a remarkable scene. They leaped, I know not how high, and in a manner one would have thought impossible. But, more than this, they danced to their own melody, and in perfect time. . . . This looked strange to us sober people." Dixon appears to be describing the **shout**, or **ring shout**, a practice that continued among freed slaves after the Civil War. The term "shout" was applied primarily to the dance, and only secondarily to the music for the dance. Some scholars speculate that the name is derived from the Arabic word *saut* (pronounced "shout"), denoting the counterclockwise procession around the Ka'aba in Mecca, pointing to Islam's influence in West Africa and, by extension, on the American slaves who came from there. *the ring shout*

As preserved by groups in coastal Georgia to the present day, the shout consists of several elements. A leader, or **songster**, sets the tune, and the other singers, or **basers**, answer in call-and-response format and provide rhythmic hand clapping. Beside the songster sits a **sticker**, who beats a broom handle or other suitable stick on the wooden floor; the sticker's long-long-short (3 + 3 + 2) rhythmic pattern, heard in "Jubilee" (LG 4.3), is identical to the Cuban dance rhythm called the **habanera**, an indicator of Caribbean influence. (The habanera rhythm, also called *tresillo*, will play an important role in jazz, rock, and salsa.) The **shouters** shuffle slowly in a counterclockwise ring, using arm gestures to pantomime the words of the songster and basers. In "Jubilee," a shout song that apparently dates from around the time of emancipation in 1863, the songster sets a two-phrase call, in which the first phrase ends inconclusively and the second ends on the keynote or tonic. The basers answer with a two-phrase response, their second phrase also ending on the tonic. Hand claps and broomstick fill out a *LG 4.3*

In their own words

Shouting versus Secular Dancing

In a 1981 interview with folklorist Art Rosenbaum, James Cook, a 98-year-old deacon of a black congregation in McIntosh County, Georgia, explained the differences between the shouters' motions and secular dancing:

Back in the days of my comin' on in the shout, if you cross yo' feet you were dancin', but if you solid, move on the square, you were shoutin'. But if you cross yo' feet you were turned out of the church because you were doin' somethin' for the devil. . . . So you see those ladies didn't cross they feet, they shouted! And shouting is . . . praisin' God with an order of thanksgiving.

| CD 1.14 | Listening Guide 4.3 | "Jubilee" ANONYMOUS |

DATE: unknown

PERFORMERS: The McIntosh County Shouters; Lawrence McKiver, songster

GENRE: shout song

METER: duple

FORM: strophic

WHAT TO LISTEN FOR

- call and response
- habanera rhythm on broomstick
- polyrhythm of broomstick, hands, and feet

TIMING	SECTION	TEXT	COMMENTS
0:00		So I'm gon' sing one of the slave song' they like to sing, just after they come out of slave'—they sang this song, "Jubilee in the Mornin'."	Spoken introduction by the songster.
0:10	stanza 1	*Songster*: Jubilee, jubilee *Basers*: Oh, my Lord *Songster*: Jubilee in the mornin' *Basers*: My Lord, jubilee!	The songster sings the call, which changes in each stanza, and the basers respond with an unvarying refrain.
0:20	stanza 2	Jubilee in the evenin' (Oh, my Lord) Jubilee in the mornin' (My Lord, jubilee! *etc.*)	The baser's habanera rhythm, which began tentatively in stanza 1, grows forceful and steady. Hand claps and foot stomps become more audible.
0:29	stanza 3	Jubilee, jubilee Jubilee, jubilee	(From here to the end, the refrain is not shown in the text column.)
0:38	stanza 4	Walkin' members, walkin' Walkin' on your Jesus	
0:46	stanza 5	Shout, my children, 'cause yo' free My God brought you liberty	
0:55	stanza 6	Call me a Sunday Christian Call me a Monday devil	
1:03	stanza 7	Don' care what you call me So long Jesus love me	
1:12			The songster repeats the earlier stanzas in a new order: 3, 4, 5, 1, 2, 6, 7.

NOTE Recorded on St. Simons Island, Georgia, by Alan Lomax in 1983.

Listen & Reflect

1. Compare "Jubilee" with the other listening selections in this chapter. What do they have in common, and how do they differ?

polyrhythmic texture and suggest how American slaves, denied the percussion instruments that had played such a central role in their African musical heritage, found ways to transform and perpetuate that heritage despite the privations of bondage.

CAMP-MEETING HYMNS

The identity of black Americans as a group separate from white Americans was taken for granted until well into the twentieth century. Racial prejudice, fed by incomprehension, distrust, and fear, defined blacks, socially and legally, as a category of people with no chance of admission into white society. One result was that social activities in which whites and blacks engaged as partners were few and far between. As settlement pushed westward, however, a religious institution took shape that proved more hospitable than most white forums to blacks and their habits of expression: the camp meeting, described in chapter 3.

Although camp meetings were usually organized by Methodist and Baptist preachers who were ready to seek out "the plain folk" wherever they happened to live, the meetings were interdenominational and never part of any church's official program of worship. They caught on quickly: a leading Methodist of the day calculated that as many as four hundred camp meetings were held in 1811 alone.

The camp meeting set religion above race and welcomed black participants. Even in slave states, blacks took part, though generally on their own "shouting-ground," where religious meetings were held after the sermon. But while the camp meeting's egalitarianism is generally applauded today, it drew sharp criticism in its own time. In 1819 a tract appeared called *Methodist Error,* written by the "Wesleyan Methodist" John F. Watson, denouncing camp-meeting hymns. The music, he wrote, consisted of "merry airs, adapted from old songs, to hymns [i.e., hymn texts] of our composing." The religious enthusiasm these hymns kindled was no excuse for their shortcomings: "Often miserable as poetry," they were equally "senseless as matter." As for the merry airs, they were "most frequently composed and first sung by the illiterate blacks of the society," proof of their worthlessness.

The traits Watson singles out for attack are African: the reliance on oral transmission, the physical movement, and the responsorial repetitions, choruses, and "short scraps" of tunes. His critique indicates that the camp meeting, rather than establishing a particular kind of hymn singing and holding black worshipers to it, allowed them freedom to praise God as they saw fit—with spiritual and ring shout.

In their own words 💬

John F. Watson on Black Worship at Camp Meetings (1819)

In the *blacks'* quarter [of the camp meeting], the coloured people get together, and sing for hours together, short scraps of disjointed affirmation, pledges, or prayers, lengthened out with long repetitious *choruses*. These are all sung in the merry chorus-manner of the southern harvest field, or husking-frolic method, of the slave blacks; and also very like the Indian dances. With every word so sung, they have a sinking of one or [the] other leg of the body alternately, producing an audible sound of the feet at every step, and as manifest as the steps of actual negro dancing in Virginia, &c. . . . What in the name of religion can countenance or tolerate such gross perversions of true religion!

What galled Watson most was not the behavior of blacks at camp meetings but their influence. "The example has already visibly affected the religious manners of some whites. . . . I have known in some camp meetings, from 50 to 60 people crowd into one tent, after the public devotions had closed, and there continue the whole night, singing tune after tune, (though with occasional episodes of prayer) scarce one of which were in our hymn books." How could so many white worshipers sing hymns all night without hymnbooks? Apparently, by following the example of blacks, who did not depend on books in the first place. The hymns they sang relied on short, simple statements of music and text, with plenty of repetition, including call and response. The "endless" stream of sacred music sung by these transported souls seems to have come not from memorizing but from a kind of oral composition they had learned from blacks, using familiar formulas of tune and word. Watson's criticisms indicate that the camp meeting helped white Protestants learn something that black Protestants' African heritage was always asserting: that the key to sacred expression lay in awakening the proper spirit.

The story of the camp-meeting hymn reflects two complementary processes from which much of the distinctive quality of American music has flowed: blacks infusing Euro-American practices with African influence, and whites drawing on black adaptations to vitalize their own music making. The first of these two processes has been evident in this chapter. The second will become more and more evident in the following chapters, which take up white instrumental and vocal music in the antebellum years.

QUESTIONS FOR DISCUSSION AND REVIEW

1. What aspects of the music of American slaves show traces of African heritage? How did their musical practices change in the New World, and why?

2. What aspects of Euro-American music making were borrowed by slave musicians? How do their adaptations show signs of African influence?

3. Compare the social function of work songs with that of military music, as described in chapter 2.

FURTHER READING

Dargan, William T. *Lining Out the Word: Dr. Watts Hymn Singing in the Music of Black Americans.* Berkeley and Los Angeles: University of California Press; Chicago: Center for Black Music Research, 2006.

Djedje, Jacqueline Cogdell. "African American Music to 1900." In *The Cambridge History of American Music,* edited by David Nicholls, 103–134. Cambridge: Cambridge University Press, 1998.

Gura, Philip F., and James F. Bollman. *America's Instrument: The Banjo in the Nineteenth Century.* Chapel Hill: University of North Carolina Press, 1999.

Kmen, Henry A. *Music in New Orleans: The Formative Years, 1791–1841.* Baton Rouge: Louisiana State University Press, 1966.

Roberts, John Storm. *Black Music of Two Worlds: African, Caribbean, Latin, and African-American Traditions.* 2d ed. New York: Schirmer Books, 1998.

Rosenbaum, Art, and Johann S. Buis. *Shout Because You're Free: The African American Ring Shout Tradition in Coastal Georgia.* Athens: University of Georgia Press, 1998.

Southern, Eileen, ed. *Readings in Black American Music.* 2d ed. New York: W. W. Norton, 1983.

FURTHER LISTENING

McIntosh County Shouters, The. *Slave Shout Songs from the Coast of Georgia.* Folkways, FE 4344, 1984.

Prison Songs: Historical Recordings from Parchman Farm, 1947–48. Vol. 2. *Don'tcha Hear Poor Mother Calling?* The Alan Lomax Collection. Rounder, CD 1715, 1997.

Wade in the Water. Vol. 2. *African American Congregational Singing: Nineteenth-Century Roots.* Smithsonian Folkways, SF 40076, 1994.

"A LANGUAGE OF FEELING"

Cultivating Musical Tastes in Antebellum America

Music making, whether private or public, sacred or secular, served multiple functions in antebellum America. Just as Lowell Mason built a successful musical career by cultivating worshipers' desires for edification as well as praise, so other musicians sought to satisfy the aspirations of audiences for a more refined musical experience than the young republic had previously known.

This chapter examines the beginnings of a social process of separating a certain kind of music making from the broader tastes of the general public. It is fair to say that the usual names for music that appeals to a more specialized audience are freighted with connotations of elitism: "classical music," "art music," "cultivated music." These terms imply that other types of music are inferior. That attitude reflects a bias that may have been widely accepted in the past but is no longer consistent with the way most people think about or listen to music in their everyday lives.

We will first approach this topic by looking at the rise of the music publishing industry, where such distinctions were a matter not so much of elitism as of recognizing that there were different markets for different kinds of music. The chapter will then explore the birth of professional and semiprofessional performing ensembles in the United States—opera companies, bands, oratorio societies, and orchestras—and conclude with the life of America's first significant "classical composer," to the extent that that term can be applied to the colorful figure of Louis Moreau Gottschalk.

HOME MUSIC MAKING AND THE PUBLISHING INDUSTRY

By the mid-1800s, a substantial music business had taken shape to meet the desires of women and men, playing and singing at home, for recreation and amusement as well as edification. The spread of home music making belonged to a larger trend in the early 1800s, the growth of a middle class seeking a social order in which refinement and gentility could have a place. But home music making had been a business from the start, built around sheet music: not costly to publish or purchase, tailored to the skills and tastes of buyers, and hence an ideal artifact for a democracy.

The sheet music trade required several agents: composers and arrangers to create the music; publishers to produce and circulate it; teachers to give lessons in performing it (and also to sell it to their students); and manufacturers of musical instruments to play it. Each filled a necessary role, but publishers were the trade's chief architects.

ALEXANDER REINAGLE AND THE MUSIC BUSINESS

The beginnings of the sheet music trade in the United States can be traced to the year 1787 in the life of one immigrant musician: the English-born composer and performer Alexander Reinagle. When the thirty-year-old Reinagle arrived in the New World in the spring of 1786, no such thing as an American *music* publisher existed. Virtually all the composers then working in America were psalmodists whose music reached the public in tunebooks brought out by book publishers. Until 1787 all secular sheet music was imported. In that year, however, the first American-published sheet music was issued from the Philadelphia shop of engraver and metalsmith John Aitken. During the next five years, Aitken published sixteen items and had no competitors. But in 1793 musical artisans in New York, Boston, and Baltimore began to publish sheet music, and the United States from then on had its own music publishing trade.

sheet music publishing

Signs point to Alexander Reinagle as the instigating partner in Aitkin's publishing venture. For one thing, twelve of Aitkin's sixteen publications were composed by, arranged by, or printed for Reinagle. For another, when Reinagle took the post of music director for the New Theater in Philadelphia's Chestnut Street in 1793, Aitken stopped publishing sheet music. Reinagle's interest in the music business had surfaced soon after he landed in the New World. A newspaper notice from mid-1786 advertised for pupils "in Singing, on the Harpsichord, Piano Forte, and Violin" and proclaimed Reinagle's readiness "to supply his Friends and Scholars with the best instruments and music printed in London." Within a year, Reinagle had begun to take part in four distinct but interrelated aspects of the music profession: he composed and arranged music for home use, gave lessons to singers and players, involved himself in the distribution of music, and plugged the work of London instrument builders. His activity indicates that the American music business in the mid-1780s was still so rudimentary that one musician could take on almost the whole enterprise himself.

Two of Reinagle's works show that by the early 1790s he was already distinguishing music that could be sold to home buyers from music that could not. The first is a piano sonata he composed in Philadelphia, probably between 1786 and 1794. This work, most likely written for Reinagle himself to play in public concerts, reveals a command of the keyboard idiom of eighteenth-century European masters such as C. P. E. Bach and Joseph Haydn. The second piece, a song called "America, Commerce, and Freedom," was sung in *The Sailor's Landlady,* a stage work of 1794.

songs and sonatas

Reinagle's song was published soon after it was composed, while nearly two centuries elapsed before the piano sonata saw publication. Why would a song

~ Page 1 of the manuscript score of Reinagle's Piano Sonata no. 1 (Philadelphia, 1786–1794?). This work was not published until 1978.

go straight into print and a piano sonata by the same composer stay in manuscript? Because when this music was written, there was a market in the United States for songs and almost none for piano sonatas. Songs—short, melodious, simple to perform, and carriers of verse—combined traits that appealed to amateur performers, especially when they heard the songs sung onstage. But mastering a sonata required a good deal more skill, practice, and most likely lessons. Besides, good players could buy imported music by Old World composers. Who needed a piano sonata by Alexander Reinagle? While it is not known how Reinagle would have answered this question, there is no sign that he tried to get his sonatas into print.

In Reinagle's two compositions can be seen the divided heritage of composing as an occupation in the United States. In writing the sonata, Reinagle was acting as a member of the composing *profession,* whose ideal is tied not to economic outcome but to intellectual authority, including a composer's right to control performances through prescriptive written scores. In contrast, Reinagle's role in "America, Commerce, and Freedom" was more like that of a tradesman working to please customers. Composed for the theater, the song was expected also to appeal to amateur performers at home.

NOTATION AND MUSICAL CATEGORIES

Before the advent of the phonograph, musical notation was the key to musical commerce. Not until a piece was written down and printed could it become a commodity to be bought and sold. But musical notation can also embody the authority of the composer. Performers who played pieces like Reinagle's sonata followed the composer's instructions closely. In contrast, the score for Reinagle's song is less prescriptive. From the song's beginning to the instrumental tag at the end, the top line of the keyboard part does nothing but double the voice, and the lower line is a stripped-down, elementary bass whose only flash of independence is the string of quick repeated notes near the end. Not a single chord appears until the last two beats of the piece, a curious way to write for an instrument with chord-playing ability.

It is hard to imagine many accomplished players being content to perform the keyboard part of "America, Commerce, and Freedom" exactly as written. Some would surely add chords, decorate the melody, or enrich the bass. Others might double the bass line with a cello, or substitute guitar for keyboard, or extend the instrumental tag. Still others might sing the song unaccompanied, or move it to a different key. Significant departures from the score would be unacceptable in the sonata but were expected in the song. The score of "America, Commerce, and Freedom" was published and sold as an outline to be filled in by performers according to their abilities, tastes, and moods.

composers' music, performers' music

Given where the authority lies, Reinagle's piano sonata may be called a piece of *composers' music* and his song a piece of *performers' music.* Performers' music, while offering composers little control over performances, gave them access to customers in the marketplace. Composers' music offered artistic control but few

Reinagle's "America, Commerce, and Freedom," from *The Sailor's Landlady* (Philadelphia, 1794?) in its original sheet music printing.

if any customers, at least in Reinagle's day. From an economic standpoint, early American writers of composers' music were strictly on their own, while writers of performers' music worked at the behest of theater managers and publishers. By writing both kinds of music, Alexander Reinagle exercised the full range of his artistic and economic opportunities.

The field of opera offers a clear delineation between musical categories. Although many Americans in the antebellum years took opera to their hearts, most of them encountered operas not as integral works of art, faithful to a composer's score, but in altered form: as arrangements, pastiches, excerpts, and single numbers. Adaptation—the tailoring of the music to suit particular audiences and circumstances—was the key to opera's popularity in America. Composers' authority counted for little in the musical theater, for there the key to success lay in capturing an audience's attention. Opera and theatrical music in the first half of the nineteenth century, therefore, must be considered performers' music.

opera

Until the Civil War (1861–65), the idea of accessibility dominated the public performance of almost all music in the United States. Indeed, perhaps no development in musical performance was more important than the appearance in the latter 1800s of a new attitude that valued composers above performers and placed ultimate authority in written scores. Performers who followed such an ideal took audience enjoyment as secondary and judged performances on their faithfulness to the work as the composer was thought to have conceived it.

accessibility and fidelity

For composers, then, the major decision was between writing composers' music, with authoritative scores, or performers' music, intended more as a springboard for the interpretations of singers and players. For performers, the decision was whether to be ruled by the composer's score or to deviate from it in ways their audiences might find appealing. For both composers and performers, the attitude toward a work's notation was all-important. To what extent did composers expect deference to what they wrote down? Were performers more determined to seek a work's essence in the composer's notation or in communicating it to listeners? The answers to these questions reflected the existence of different kinds of musical works, which came to be grouped under such labels as "classical" and "popular."

the three spheres   Composers' music constitutes the **classical sphere**, built around an ideal that may be called *transcendence:* the belief that musical works can achieve enduring artistic stature; that such works form the basis for a worthwhile musical life; and that performers have a duty to sing and play them by following the composer's notation closely. Performers' music, in contrast, constitutes the **popular sphere**, whose chief premise is *accessibility,* giving authority most of all to the audience.

While the classical and popular spheres both depend on notation, a great deal of music in U.S. history has relied on oral transmission. This unwritten music—so-called folk music—makes up a separate domain: the **traditional sphere**. Music making in the traditional sphere tends to be connected with particular customs and ways of life. In its drive to preserve linguistic, cultural, and musical practices, the traditional sphere is ruled by a commitment to *continuity.*

Many musicians have pursued transcendence, accessibility, or continuity separately and for their own sake. Yet it is striking how often these goals have collided, intersected, coexisted, or blended. What kind of cultural transaction is taking place when a composer in the classical sphere "borrows" from the popular or the traditional sphere? Or when a popular song sustains itself until it enters the realm of folk music? Or when a recording makes a performance a candidate for transcendence? Circumstances like these have been commonplace in American music history. In fact, much of the music thought to be most fully American plays on the boundaries of the spheres—evidence that for musicians who make the music, the boundaries have practical consequences and really do exist.

ITALIAN OPERA IN THE UNITED STATES

On the night of November 29, 1825, a performance of Rossini's *Barber of Seville* at New York's Park Theatre marked the debut of a newly arrived opera troupe headed by the tenor Manuel García. The audience that had gathered to hear Count Almaviva serenade his beloved—"In the smiling sky / The lovely dawn was breaking"—actually heard "Ecco ridente in cielo / Spunta la bell'aurora." Garcia's troupe was singing Rossini's opera in the original Italian instead of the expected English translation. The implications of this fact reverberate through the later history of music in the United States.

the García troupe   A consideration of the new things the García troupe brought to New York makes clear why their visit was a landmark event. The Park Theatre was the first in the United States to offer opera sung by European-trained singers in the original Italian. In mezzo-soprano Maria García, the troupe also introduced New York's first star female singer. Though only seventeen, "the Signorina," as she came to be called, was already a commanding performer; since that day, star performers have loomed large on the American scene. A lively discussion in the press followed the García troupe's arrival. More than a new musical form, foreign-language opera was received as a social phenomenon that raised questions about economics, manners, and social class.

García rented the theater for two nights a week, sharing the stage with an English stock company already in residence. An orchestra of twenty-six accompanied the performances. By all accounts, the Garcías' opera season was neither a smashing success nor a failure; rather, it marked the start of a long struggle, lasting almost three decades, to establish Italian opera in New York. And on the eve of the Civil War, New York, New Orleans, and San Francisco were still the only American cities with resident opera companies of their own. Nevertheless, it is no exaggeration to call opera the most potent force to hit the American musical world in the nineteenth century.

Opera relies on the drama inherent in the notion of larger-than-life characters, with strong, sometimes beautiful voices, pouring out their emotions—love, rage, grief, exultation—on a grand scale, to music suited for such displays. Singers like Maria García earned adulation and moved audiences by making public spectacles of themselves. Their skill at communicating the human passions with utter conviction surely helped opera cut across social and class lines, attracting a wide range of listeners.

 Maria García (1808–1836), Spanish mezzo-soprano, came to the United States with her father's troupe in 1825, married Eugène Malibran in 1826, and returned to Europe in 1827, having achieved stardom on these shores. Highly acclaimed in Europe, she died from injuries suffered during a riding accident.

Another factor in opera's popularity was the interactive environment in which performances took place. By most accounts, audiences of the period were anything but silent and passive. "We (the sovereigns) determine to have the worth of our money when we go to the theatre," a Boston correspondent wrote in 1846. "Perhaps we'll flatter Mr. Kean [tonight] by making him take poison twice." Rather than mere spectators, audience members were participating witnesses who cheered favorite performers on, abused others, and expected calls for encores to be obeyed.

Opera is a form uniting drama, spectacle, and music, but it also is a bundle of elements that can be pulled apart and changed. The programs given around 1840 at New York's Olympic Theater reflect opera's adaptability. *The Roof Scrambler*, a parody of Vincenzo Bellini's *La sonnambula* (The Sleepwalker), was a particular hit there, as was *Fried Shots*, a parody of Carl Maria von Weber's *Der Freischütz* (The Freeshooter). In works such as these, performers twisted operatic dramas for comic effect, adapting music freely from the original scores. Offstage, the melodies, titles, subjects, leading characters, and plot elements of famous operas supplied hit musical numbers for the sheet music trade, for home performers to sing and for pianists and wind bands to play. (Bishop's "Home, Sweet Home," discussed in chapter 2, is an example from the English tradition.) As a theatrical form, opera struggled for a toehold on these shores. But as a frame of reference and a cornucopia of song, it enriched the theater and the musical scene as a whole.

The poet Walt Whitman celebrated opera's adaptability in "Italian Music in Dakota," a poem picturing a regimental army band stationed at the edge of a vast Western wilderness, playing operatic songs. Whitman fancies nature listening "well pleas'd" to the band's twilight performance. His recognition of the power of melody provides another illustration of how Italian opera won a place in the lives of nineteenth-century Americans.

OPERA STARS AND COMPANIES

In March 1826, on the night before her eighteenth birthday, Maria García married a merchant in New York. Several months later, the rest of the company left for an engagement in Mexico, and she, as Madame Malibran, stayed behind. Her performances had already received high praise; but now the young mezzo-soprano made the leap from singer to full-fledged star and won New Yorkers' hearts. With her chance to sing Italian operas gone, she learned English ones, showing skill as both actress and singer whenever she stepped onstage. Early in 1827 a critic wrote: "She not only knew her own part perfectly, but prompted the others, and directed the whole stage arrangement." Malibran was lauded for good taste, dignity of deportment, lack of exaggeration, charm, simplicity, ease, and grace—the first woman of the stage whom the American public accepted as "respectable." By the time she left for Europe in 1827, she was earning $500 per night in New York while still turning a profit for theater owners and managers.

A charismatic star like Malibran could make audience members feel that she was playing directly to them. Stars overshadowed other players—a fact that stock companies tried to minimize by passing lead roles around. Before Malibran, singers of star quality on the American stage had remained within the company's hierarchy, receiving higher pay than lesser players but still under the manager's control. The audience appeal of Malibran, however, shifted public attention toward herself and away from the company. As a result of the rise of such stars, the power of managers declined, and that of public opinion grew.

From the 1820s on, theatrical performance revolved more and more around stars, which meant that finding and presenting them became a key part of a manager's business. One could write the history of musical performance in America by tracing variations on the category of star: a singing actress like Malibran; an operatic tenor like Enrico Caruso; a jazz musician like Louis Armstrong; a rock-and-roll singer like Elvis Presley; a music video phenomenon like Michael Jackson. All of these individuals managed in performance not only to connect with audiences but to fill them with wonder and hence to assume a public image that was larger than life. In the nineteenth and early twentieth centuries, no other star-producing forum equaled that of the operatic stage.

OPERA IN NEW ORLEANS AND SAN FRANCISCO

Between 1827 and 1833 almost the only non-English operas in New York, Philadelphia, Boston, and Baltimore were presented by the company of the Théâtre d'Orléans from New Orleans, under John Davis's management. The company's summer tours brought to Northern audiences operas by French composers and carried on a tradition dating back to 1796 in New Orleans, when French opera was first performed in a local theater. New Orleans was home to many French and Spanish citizens—often called Creoles in those years, whatever their race—whose cultural ties to the United States were tenuous and who desired to remain culturally distinct from the Americans they scorned. In New Orleans, presenting French operas was a way to assert French identity.

Davis's company set a standard of high quality and lavish expense. In 1822 Davis traveled to France and brought back actors, singers, instrumentalists, and dancers, the latter for the ballets that French opera required. Beginning with the

Promoting a Star: P. T. Barnum and Jenny Lind

Star making requires not only a charismatic performer but also imaginative promotion. One of the great selling jobs in history took place in 1850, when the **impresario** P. T. Barnum presented Swedish soprano Jenny Lind to the American public. Initially resisting Barnum's proposal for a U.S. tour, Lind set her figure at the then-astronomical sum of $187,000, paid in advance. Barnum managed to raise the money and then, having secured her services, set about creating a demand for them.

Well before Lind's arrival, Barnum launched a publicity campaign that stressed the singer's virtuous Christian character and the prestige of opera singing. When Lind arrived on September 1, 1850, a crowd of thirty thousand greeted her ship in New York Harbor—the first of a series of mob scenes orchestrated by Barnum and his agents. Barnum's report of huge, enthusiastic gatherings created the impression that Jenny Lind tickets were always at a premium. He auctioned off, with great public fanfare, the first pair of tickets to a Lind concert in each city where she appeared, inviting cities as well as individuals to vie with each other's display of the value they placed on the arrival of Lind and her art.

In another masterstroke, Barnum fed "Lindomania" by announcing that she would donate to charity her share of receipts from her first U.S. concert. Thus Lind's arrival, persona, travels, and deeds were received not simply as an artistic or commercial venture but as *news,* reported throughout the country. Avid expectation, curiosity, and competitiveness moved people to buy tickets and shaped their reactions to her performances.

By peddling recitals of a foreign opera singer, Barnum created a cultural sensation that was also a commercial bonanza, involving not only concert tickets, sheet music, and pianos but also such Lind-endorsed products as gloves and stoves. Having taken a major financial risk, Barnum turned a profit of more than $500,000 from his connection with Lind.

Jenny Lind, the "Swedish Nightingale," whose 1850–52 U.S. tour was an artistic and marketing triumph.

1822–23 season, opera in the Théâtre d'Orléans was played by a resident company whose personnel were imported. Davis also sought out fresh repertory, giving American premieres of many works, chiefly French. To meet expenses, the company took to touring: first to Havana, Cuba, in 1824 and later to the Northeast. When Davis retired in 1837, his son took over management, and the troupe flourished into the 1850s. The theater closed after the Civil War.

Davis's competitor, James Caldwell, an English immigrant and erstwhile actor, had arrived in New Orleans in 1820 as head of a touring company from Virginia. In 1824 Caldwell began to play English-language opera at the 1,100-seat Camp Street Theater, in the city's new American section. In 1835 Caldwell built the St. Charles Theater and began to present traveling troupes there.

Local opera, then, flourished in New Orleans in both foreign-language and English forms until after the Civil War. Managers used the population's love of social dancing to attract audiences. The Théâtre d'Orléans had its own ballroom, and a ticket to the opera might also entitle the holder to attend a ball after the performance. A newspaper notice in 1836 reported: "Spectacles and operas appear to amuse our citizens more than any other form of public amusement—except balls." As well as enticing customers into the theater, social dances gave members of the opera orchestra more professional work.

San Francisco

Meanwhile, opera also gained a foothold on the continent's western edge. Many hundreds of miles separated San Francisco from the cities of the Midwest. Until the mid-1860s, it could be reached most easily from the East by two seagoing routes, both long and expensive: across the isthmus of Panama (in the days before the canal) or around Cape Horn. Communication by railroad, telegraph, and overland mail was not even established until after 1859. Thus the region was still a maritime colony of the East as well as a western frontier settlement.

In San Francisco's early years, men greatly outnumbered women. In the 1850 census, only 8 percent of California's population was female, many of those said to be women of ill repute. This state of affairs is explained by the discovery of gold in northern California early in 1848, when San Francisco was a village of five hundred. By 1851 thirty thousand people lived there, most of them men drawn by the prospect of getting rich quick. Thus San Francisco changed overnight from backwater to boomtown, a place where an expensive cultural form like opera could flourish.

Thomas Maguire

The city's first theater opened in October 1850. By the beginning of 1853, though fires had already burned three theaters to the ground, four more were operating. The man most responsible for establishing opera as an enduring local presence was Thomas Maguire, a New York native who moved to San Francisco in the late 1840s. He made his fortune not by striking gold but by running a successful saloon and gambling parlor and by building and renting out theaters. In 1856 the elegant new Maguire's Opera House opened, and four years later an Italian troupe took up residence there. Interested more in the power of what could happen onstage than in the financial bottom line, Maguire set his prices low: fifty cents or one dollar, at a time when the going local price for opera tickets ranged from one to three dollars. He later calculated that during the 1860s he lost $120,000 on opera.

In 1860 Maguire replaced his resident troupe with a new organization: the Maguire-Lyster Company, fashioned out of the traveling Lyster English Opera Company, on the one hand, and a complement of Italian and English singers who performed Italian opera in its original tongue, on the other. An orchestra of twenty-five played for both the English and Italian "wings." Instead of alternating nights of opera with nights of other popular entertainments, as was the norm at most opera houses, the Maguire-Lyster Company played opera every night, and to substantial crowds.

That year in San Francisco has been termed a year of wonders in the annals of opera. Maguire's Opera House, which seated 1,700, gave 145 performances. Attendance averaged 1,500 per performance, making a total of 217,000 seats sold in a city of 60,000. By comparison, in New York City today (population 8 million), the Metropolitan Opera, whose house seats 3,800, would have to build an additional fifty-two opera houses to accommodate an equivalent audience over 145 evenings. No American city, at any time, has shown a passion for operatic performance equaling that of San Francisco in 1860.

BANDS IN ANTEBELLUM AMERICA

Like opera, the wind band's public appeal is fundamental to its history. Indeed, the idea of a band that only connoisseurs can appreciate seems a contradiction in terms. For two centuries and more, American bands have been stoking enthusiasm by playing tunes that listeners already know in ways they can readily appreciate.

As the 1800s dawned, the U.S. military was still using wind instruments according to customs borrowed from the British army, with fifes and drums performing field music and somewhat larger ensembles—"bands of music"—playing *Harmoniemusik* (see chapter 2). With the reduction in size of the army following the revolution, military bands were maintained by state militias, essentially civilian groups. Many members of recreational town bands served in militia bands to fulfill their military obligations.

new instruments

The addition of two new categories of instruments transformed the sound of these nineteenth-century bands. The first were percussion instruments, the so-called **Janissary instruments** adopted from Turkish military bands in Europe: triangle, cymbals, and bass drum, which by the 1830s were standard in American ensembles, supplementing the traditional side or snare drum. The second were brass. Until the 1820s, brass instruments other than the trombone could not produce more than a limited number of notes, unless in the hands of highly trained virtuosos. But the development of keyed brass like the keyed bugle and the **ophicleide**, and valves for trumpets, **cornets**, and French horns, made it possible to play melody with much less training. With this increased flexibility, by midcentury the **brass band** was the typical American wind ensemble.

Adolphe Sax's invention of the **saxhorn** in Paris in the early 1840s furthered the brass band's vogue. Modeled after the upright tuba, saxhorns came in a full range of sizes, from high treble to low bass. (Sax's other important invention, the saxophone, would not become a common feature of bands until later in the century.) A brass band with cornets and saxhorns ranging from alto down to bass could achieve a uniform blend; percussion, and occasionally a clarinet as the sole woodwind, rounded out the ensemble. By the time of the Civil War cornets and saxhorns formed the core of the typical band.

performance settings

By the middle 1800s bands in the United States were serving functions that had nothing to do with the military. Bands can easily travel and reconfigure themselves, adapting themselves to many different settings: in early America they performed in theaters, private halls, hotels, resorts, parks, hospitals, and churches, and at sporting events, fairs, store openings, dinner parties, club meetings, and even funerals.

concert formats

Bands also played concerts, and here they followed the long-standing custom of varying the sound from number to number. During the 1850–51 season, for example, the sixteen-member American Band of Providence, Rhode Island, presented a series of concerts in a local hall. On one surviving program, the band offered a concert in two parts with six numbers on each. The first half consisted of a march, a vocal song, a cornet solo, a dance piece, another song, and an overture, in that order. Nineteenth-century band concerts embraced virtually all the musical genres that audiences of the time were likely to hear: marches, patriotic and popular songs, descriptive pieces, solos, transcriptions of orchestral and operatic works, and dance music.

LG 5.1

An example of the last-named genre is *Helene* Schottische (LG 5.1), which survives in an arrangement for a twelve-piece brass band: two E-flat cornets, seven saxhorns (three E-flat altos, two B-flat tenors, and basses in B-flat and E-flat), and percussion (three players on side drum, bass drum, and cymbals). The arrangement was written out during the Civil War by Walter Dignam, born in England in 1827 but an American resident from 1844. Dignam led the Second and Fourth New Hampshire Regiment Band in Virginia during the conflict. A skilled player, he intended the demanding first E-flat cornet part for himself. Played on instruments from the 1800s, the accompanying recording shows the delicacy, restraint, and beauty of sound possible from this kind of ensemble.

Each strain of this dance tune is eight bars long. Since the basic sequence of steps in the schottische (a type of polka) fills four bars, dancers could complete two sequences in each strain. For most strains, the instruments that accompany the melody outline the dancers' rhythm:

<u>step</u>-<u>step</u>-<u>step</u>-hop | <u>step</u>-<u>step</u>-<u>step</u>-hop | <u>step</u>-hop-<u>step</u>-hop | <u>step</u>-hop-<u>step</u>-hop

In the first two bars, they play a chord on each step and are silent for each hop. In bar 3, the bass instruments play for each step and the midrange instruments for each hop: oom-pah, oom-pah. Bar 4 may have either pattern, assuring variety.

militia and town bands

Many of the military bands during the Civil War were state militia bands whose members enlisted as a group, participated in the war as a unit, then returned home and continued to play, either in a militia band or a town band. Small towns north and south took pride in their local bands and often provided some degree of financial support, sometimes buying a set of saxhorns that were then lent to band members but remained town property. With their participation in all sorts of public functions, from concerts and dances to parades and holiday celebrations, town bands provided small-town Americans with music ranging from dance tunes to patriotic songs and lighter pieces in classical genres. For at least some audience members, exposure to operatic and orchestral music in band transcriptions whetted an appetite to hear the real thing.

CD 1.15	**Listening Guide 5.1**		*Helene* Schottische **ARRANGED BY WALTER DIGNAM**

DATE: ca. 1863–64

PERFORMERS: The American Brass Quintet Brass Band

GENRE: dance music

METER: duple

FORM: three-part or **ternary** with varied repeat: ABA′

WHAT TO LISTEN FOR

- mellow sound of nineteenth-century brass instruments
- characteristic schottische rhythm
- clearly delineated sections with much repetition
- use of contrasting keys

TIMING	SECTION	STRAIN	COMMENTS
0:00	A	*a*	The *piano* (soft) dynamic displays the cornets' and saxhorns' sweetness of tone. The first 4-bar phrase ends with an inconclusive half cadence; the second phrase begins like the first but ends with a more conclusive full cadence.
0:13		*b*	The *forte* (loud) dynamic and minor key provide contrast and make even sweeter the return of the opening strain.
0:26		*a*	The *a* strain returns.
0:40	B	*c*	The B section, or **trio**, typically modulates to the **subdominant** key (a fifth lower than the tonic), for an effect of relaxation. The 4-bar alternations of the opening strains here become 2-bar alternations of *forte* and *piano*.
0:53		*c*	The *c* strain repeats.
1:06		*d*	A **break strain**, as it would come to be known in later band music: a shift to a minor key and alternation of lower and higher instruments, building tension.
1:20		*c*	The *c* strain returns.
1:33	A′	*a*	The **recapitulation** of the *a* strain creates a sense of return.
1:47		*e*	A new continuation of the melody marks a departure: this is not a literal repetition of the A section.
2:00	coda		A drum roll and grandiose chords bring the schottische to an impressive, operatic close.

Listen & Reflect

1. What features mark *Helene* Schottische as functional music, appropriate for accompanying dancers?
2. What features make it suitable for nonfunctional (i.e., concert) performance?

AMERICA'S FIRST ORATORIO SOCIETY

the Handel and Haydn Society

On Christmas night in 1815, a concert took place in Boston's Stone Chapel that marked a new stage in Americans' recognition of music as an art. Some months earlier, the Boston Handel and Haydn Society had been formed to improve sacred music performance and promote the sacred works of eminent European masters. The society's first public performance, attended by an estimated one thousand, included excerpts from Haydn's *Creation* and Handel's *Israel in Egypt,* as well as the Hallelujah Chorus from Handel's *Messiah.* According to a Boston newspaper report, "The excitements to loud applause were frequently irresistible."

oratorios

The concert was a landmark event in the role it gave to composers. Reformers of psalmody had long been praising European musical science, but their interest lay in congregational singing, not in the complexities of **oratorios**: large-scale religious works for chorus, solo singers, and orchestra. The Boston Handel and Haydn Society set out to establish a place for Handel and Haydn as composers of oratorios, placing fresh emphasis on the music itself. Boston audiences could now experience musical sound that was both artistic and sacred in its evocative power.

The society's first concert was also unusual in bringing sacred music to an audience that entered the church as paying listeners and responded by clapping rather than praying. Thus began a tradition of oratorio performances that laid the groundwork for a concert life new to the United States.

As noted in chapter 3, Lowell Mason's offer to split the proceeds of his tunebook with the Handel and Haydn Society, which acted as publisher, proved a financial windfall for the partners. *The Boston Handel and Haydn Society Collection of Church Music*, which appeared in seventeen editions in as many years, beginning in 1822, enriched each by about $12,000 and helped underwrite the society's concert expenses. By 1827, when Mason moved to Boston as the society's president, the Handel and Haydn Society was Boston's foremost musical organization. It is still in existence today.

By publishing Mason's tunebook, the society was helping to raise the standard of singing in public worship, the era's main form of democratic music making. But in its concerts, the Handel and Haydn Society also showed Bostonians the quality and impact sacred choral singing could achieve. Except for a few soloists, the singers performing Handel's and Haydn's "scientific" music were amateurs, most likely drawn to oratorio by the sacred subject matter. Once enlisted, however, choristers were asked to sing demanding voice parts artistically and on pitch, with decent vocal sound and clear pronunciation.

democratic values

Just as reformers of psalmody took up the cause of European standards and "correct taste," some linked a European musical standard to refinement and gentility. But in the Handel and Haydn Society, composers were more than symbols of refinement; they were the authors of works that singers and listeners were coming to know through experience. Members of the chorus could seek religious exaltation while trying to improve their singing and learning great music. Thus the society promoted artistic skills in the name of religion, not refinement. Sacred subject matter, citizen involvement, and self-financing grounded the musical work of the Handel and Haydn Society in democratic values.

Congregations and Organists

Like oratorio societies, church choirs brought aesthetic pleasure to singers and listeners alike. But psalmodists remained wary of sacred choral singing's aesthetic side. If choirs strove only for a pleasant sound, Thomas Hastings wrote, "why, then, let us have at once the *prima-donnas* of the drama for our leading singers." Though Hastings was being ironic, by the time of the Civil War many urban churches boasted **quartet choirs**, in which professional soloists—a soprano, alto, tenor, and bass—replaced volunteer choirs. Professional singers brought into churches a mastery that amateurs could not match. But, evangelical leaders warned, some also displayed an insincerity that could blunt the religious impact of performances during worship service.

Another aesthetic force in nineteenth-century churches came from the organ loft, as more and more congregations made the largest financial investment in music that Americans of that era were ready to make. "Perhaps no work of man's," an enthusiast wrote of the organ in the mid-1830s, "can claim equal power of exciting and arresting the feelings." But that power also drew criticism. Hastings thought organists often became "dictators" over public worship and complained about the way some organists buried hymns in "massive peals of legato harmony."

As affluence grew in the United States, so did the grandeur of organs. In 1846 a Brooklyn builder completed a large instrument for New York City's Trinity (Episcopal) Church at a cost of $10,500. The Trinity organ, then the largest in the country, impressed both eye and ear. An observer who found the lowest pipes "big enough for a small family and room for boarders" wondered whether the organist intended "to save house rent" by living in one of them.

The opening of Trinity Church's giant instrument brought the organ's dual function of worship and artistry into conflict. Two days were set aside for a public display in which local organists were invited to play anything they chose. The result, one newspaper reported, included opera arias, "marches from military bands, and waltzes from the ballroom." Dismissing the display as "a farce," the report charged that the house of God had been turned into "an exhibition room." Like choral singing, organ playing was more than a means of sacred expression; it fostered both performing skill and an aesthetic sense. By the 1840s, thanks partly to opera and partly to the church, the idea of music as an art was beginning to take hold in concert life.

CLASSICAL INSTRUMENTAL MUSIC COMES TO BOSTON AND NEW YORK

Just as sacred music flourished in churches, other kinds of music were linked to the theater, the military, the school, and the parlor. But one kind of Old World music had no tie to entertainment, religion, education, or the home: instrumental music in what today is called the classical style. Originating in the latter 1700s, this music followed the design of a **sonata**: in three or four movements, and typically with no descriptive program. In Europe, Haydn, Mozart, and Beethoven raised the symphony, a sonata for orchestra, to prominence in the concert hall. For more intimate settings, they wrote string quartets (sonatas for two violins, viola, and cello), duo sonatas for violin and piano, and solo sonatas for piano alone.

In the hands of these masters, the sonata exemplified composers' music: a serious, discursive form, whose themes were presented, repeated, and developed to create a large musical structure. A growing appreciation of its artistic substance in Europe after 1800 eventually carried over to the United States. In the early 1800s, however, classical instrumental music was still new to America, and it posed difficulties for performers and listeners alike.

performances of Beethoven

By the 1830s a few American musicians and writers were starting to recognize Beethoven (who died in 1827) as a master. But before Americans could embrace Beethoven's works, there needed to be audience interest as well as a framework to support their performance. The way Bostonians overcame these obstacles may be shown by tracing the path that led to the first performance of Beethoven's First Symphony there in 1841.

One leader in the effort was John Sullivan Dwight (later the city's foremost music critic), an ardent music lover whose interest in philosophy combined with a passion for German poetry. In 1838 he published an English translation of poems by Goethe and Schiller, finding in their work a spiritual quality that convinced him "how life, and thought, and poetry, and beauty, are the inheritance of [humankind], and not of any class, or age, or nation." Dwight also saw certain musical works as universal. By 1837 he was convinced that Beethoven was a thinker on a par with Socrates, Shakespeare, and Newton. And he found in instrumental music "a language of feeling" that had reached its peak in works for orchestra. In 1841 Dwight described Beethoven's slow movements as uniquely eloquent music that was able "to hallow pleasure, and to naturalize religion." With such pronouncements, Dwight helped pave the way for regular performances of classical instrumental music.

✥ John Sullivan Dwight (1813–1893), a member of Harvard College's class of 1832 and an 1836 graduate of Harvard's Divinity School, became Boston's leading writer on music with the founding of *Dwight's Journal of Music,* which he edited from 1852 until 1881.

Institutional support came first from the Boston Academy of Music. Founded in 1833 to teach singing, the academy boasted Lowell Mason as its first professor. Its activities soon caught on with the public, and revenues from membership dues, classes for children and adults, and contributions were enough by 1835 to refurbish a local theater, supply it with a new organ, and set up the academy's headquarters there. An instrumentalist was hired to teach instrumental music, and singing instruction then became merely one stage in a farther-reaching project to enrich and diversify Boston's musical life. At the end of the decade an orchestra was assembled, and it was this orchestra of the Boston Academy of Music that gave the local premiere on February 13, 1841, of Beethoven's First Symphony.

The concert seems to have created no particular stir, but other orchestra performances followed. In 1842 a local newspaper reported that only a few years earlier the music of Haydn, Mozart, and Beethoven "would hardly have drawn an audience of fifty persons. Now, we see the hall filled an hour before the commencement of the performances . . . which speaks well for the increase of correct musical taste in our good city." The same article praised the Academy of Music's role in bringing about "this great revolution in musical taste." The academy's annual report for 1843 even suggested a link with personal virtue. Calling classical orchestral music "an intellectual and social enjoyment" of a high order, the report warned that rejecting such a worthy cultural force would be a "discouraging and painful symptom of the character of our population."

This last comment and others like it have led some scholars in recent years to conclude that, even more than a love of art, what stood behind the establishment of classical music institutions after the Civil War was the wish of some wealthy patrons to exercise social control by excluding people because of their class or ethnic background. That charge, however, seems not to apply to the Academy of Music. The academy was financed by its hundreds of members and devoted chiefly to activities in which those members participated: sacred singing, choir music, and elementary musical training. Its involvement in the whole range of music making, from simple to complex, reflected a political outlook that has been described as republicanism in Thomas Jefferson's mold. That view saw society as both hierarchical, in that the best-qualified citizens held authority, and egalitarian, in that all members of society were free to earn the position they deserved. Though the cultivation of classical instrumental music may have stood at the top of that hierarchy, any attempt to exclude people from the enjoyment of that music on the basis of class or ethnicity would have contradicted the principle of wholeness the Boston Academy of Music had embraced.

music and republicanism

Meanwhile, in 1842 a number of New York's leading musicians gathered to discuss the founding of an orchestra whose members would be permanent, unlike the ad hoc orchestras of the Boston Academy of Music. The constitution that resulted called for a structure of "actual" and "professional" members, who performed, and associate members, who attended rehearsals and concerts. The new ensemble, named the New York Philharmonic Society, was thus founded as a cooperative venture embracing both music-loving listeners (the name *philharmonic* means "loving harmony") and performers who welcomed the chance to play the best symphonic music. The United States' oldest professional orchestra, the New York Philharmonic gave its first concert in December 1842, opening with Beethoven's Fifth Symphony.

the New York Philharmonic

The new orchestra sought to edify players and audiences alike. With only four programs per season, the Philharmonic could be no more than a complement to any musician's livelihood. Yet its survival shows that it filled a need on the local scene. Moreover, the Philharmonic's early history is intertwined with the careers of many influential musicians, including Theodore Thomas, who will appear in chapter 8 as the premier conductor of his generation.

The activities of the Boston Academy of Music and the New York Philharmonic Society complemented the ideas of John Sullivan Dwight, who believed "in the capacity of all mankind for music," because music satisfied "a genuine want of the soul." Just as the Handel and Haydn Society had given Bostonians a chance to hear oratorios, the Boston Academy and the New York Philharmonic were now introducing the symphonies of Mozart and Beethoven to the public. In the early 1840s, with Dwight's idealistic notions in the air and an appetite for instrumental music apparently growing, there seemed reason to hope that American listeners of all stripes would come to embrace "music of the highest class." And already the United States was producing its first significant composers of instrumental music in the classical tradition: Anthony Philip Heinrich, William Henry Fry, George Frederick Bristow, and most famous of all, Louis Moreau Gottschalk.

Orchestras on Tour

Among the first European orchestras to tour the United States was the Austrian Steyermark ensemble, which arrived in Boston in 1846, twenty men strong (women orchestra players were rare throughout the nineteenth century). A Boston musician later recalled that they played "mostly light dance music, overtures, potpourris, and solos"—a program not much different from a typical band concert. When the Germania Musical Society, a polished twenty-five-man ensemble from Berlin, arrived in New York in October 1848, audiences heard somewhat more substantial programs. Playing more than nine hundred concerts in North America, for audiences of up to three thousand, the Germanians mixed dance music by Johann Strauss and others with overtures by Mozart and Rossini and more demanding works such as Beethoven symphonies. Even after the orchestra disbanded in 1854, its influence continued, for many of the members settled in American cities. One ex-Germanian led the New York Philharmonic for two decades, and another conducted the Boston Handel and Haydn Society from the 1850s through the 1890s. In this and in other ways, German immigrant musicians significantly improved the quality of classical performance and programming in nineteenth-century America.

Another landmark orchestral tour begin in the summer of 1853, when French-born conductor Louis Jullien arrived from England with twenty-six instrumentalists, to whom he soon added sixty American players. This huge orchestra and Jullien's flamboyant charisma made a vivid impression at the more than two hundred concerts they presented in ten months. Jullien's programming was not much different from that of other bands and orchestras of the time, but the size and quality of his orchestra made a profound impression on the critic John Sullivan Dwight, who warmly praised a New York concert he heard in October 1853: "To hear the great works of the masters brought out in the full proportions of so large an orchestra, where all the parts are played by perfect masters of their instruments, is a great privilege and great lesson." Less discerning listeners could enjoy lighter pieces such as Jullien's own composition "American Quadrille," a dance medley based on "Yankee Doodle," "Hail Columbia," "Hail to the Chief," and "Old Folks at Home." They also thrilled to Jullien's showmanship: at a "monster concert" given just before his return to Europe, the New York audience heard his "Firemen's Quadrille," whose final section featured a real blaze, complete with clanging bell and a battalion of firefighters rushing in to quench the flames.

Jullien's Concerts.

FIRST NIGHT OF THE GRAND ILLUSTRATED PROGRAMME.

QUADRILLE NAPOLITAIN.
Pianissimo!—JULLIEN

SOLO, CORNET-A-PISTON.
L'Adieu Maritime.—HERR KONIG

GALOPPE, AMAZON AND TIGER.
Descriptive of Hunting in South Africa.

THE GREAT EXHIBITION.
God Save the Queen!!

SOLO, CONTRA-BASSO.
On Themes from La Sonnambula—SIGNOR BOTTESINI.

SOLO, CONTRA-BASSO *(Encore).*
Carnival de Venise.—SIGNOR BOTTESINI.

FINALE

New-York Historical Society

Conductor Louis Jullien's New York concerts created an enthusiasm that, as these fanciful cartoons show, stopped short of artistic reverence.

LOUIS MOREAU GOTTSCHALK: A NEW ORLEANS ORIGINAL

In June 1857 New Orleans–born composer and pianist Louis Moreau Gottschalk was bound by ship from Cuba to St. Thomas when his vessel passed within sight of the island of Hispaniola. Gottschalk's first-ever glimpse of the Haitian coast brought to mind stories he had heard as a child. His mother was descended from an official of the French colonial regime that ruled the island until the slave rebellion of the 1790s overthrew it. "When very young," Gottschalk recalled in his journal, "I never tired of hearing my grandmother relate the terrible strife that our family, like all the rest of the colonists, had to sustain" when the slaves overwhelmed them. That memory led to another from Gottschalk's boyhood. "In the evening, the Negroes, myself, and the children of the house formed a circle around my grandmother. We would listen, by the trembling fire on the hearth, under the coals of which Sally, the old Negress [the Gottschalks' long-time slave], baked her sweet potatoes. . . . We listened to Sally so well that we knew all of her stories by heart, with an interest that has lasted till today." For Gottschalk, the "picturesque language," "exquisite originality," and "simple and touching melody" of Creole ballads he had learned in his youth went "right to the heart" and conjured up a "dream of unknown worlds."

Not only did Gottschalk remember his past; he also relied on it as an artistic source. The son of an English-Jewish father and a mother who was culturally French by way of Haiti, raised Roman Catholic in a household where blacks and whites mingled freely, Gottschalk recognized the artistic possibilities in his cultural background. In the annals of American composition, he is known for bringing indigenous themes and rhythms into music written for the concert hall. His shipboard reflections show that this practice was rooted in respect for the unique appeal of these supposedly primitive sounds.

GOTTSCHALK AND HIS MUSIC

Born in 1829 into a family that valued his musical talent, Gottschalk also had the good fortune to grow up in a lively musical environment. The population of New Orleans stood at 46,000 in 1830, supporting several full-time theaters and half a dozen dance halls—a mecca for musicians seeking employment. Local music stores sold instruments and sheet music, and they published the work of local composers. A touring circuit that connected New Orleans with New York and Havana brought many performing musicians to town. The city's streets and saloons were home to such informal music makers as fiddlers and banjo pickers. Organists played and choirs sang in Roman Catholic churches. Army bands offered a range of music from military to recreational. And African Americans congregated in Congo Square to keep alive their traditions of music and dancing. Thus New Orleans, with its mingling of Spanish, French, and free and enslaved black residents, enjoyed a highly diverse musical life, from artistically elegant to functional and homespun—a diversity that in the early twentieth century would give rise to jazz (see chapter 12).

New Orleans

Gottschalk's career was rooted in this musical richness. His mother took him to the opera, and he also picked up his musical language in front of the hearth

Anthony Philip Heinrich: America's Log House Composer

Among the musicians who played in the New York Philharmonic Society's first concert in 1842, one member of the viola section could lay claim to being the nation's chief composer of orchestral music. Anthony Philip Heinrich had by that year written at least a dozen such works, most of them still unperformed.

Born in Bohemia (today the Czech Republic) in 1781, Heinrich visited the United States in 1805 as a merchant and part-time musician and returned in 1810. After the Napoleonic Wars wiped out his family's fortune, Heinrich, at the age of thirty-six, decided to embark on a musical career—on the western frontier, rather than in the cities of the East. From Philadelphia he traveled in 1817 to Kentucky, where he lived alone in a log cabin near Bardstown and, inspired by his encounter with the wilderness, began to compose: at first songs and violin pieces, then piano pieces, and from the 1830s on, pieces for orchestra. In 1820 he published *The Dawning of Music in Kentucky,* a collection of vocal and instrumental pieces.

In 1823 Heinrich left Kentucky for Boston, where he served as a church organist, probably played in theater orchestras, taught, and published a new collection: *The Sylviad, or Minstrelsy of Nature in the Wilds of N. America.* A Boston reviewer, John Rowe Parker, praised the music's "boldness, originality, science, and even sublimity," arguing that Heinrich "may be justly styled the *Beethoven of America.*" To Parker, Heinrich "seems at once to have possessed himself of the key which unlocks to him the temple of science and enables him to explore with fearless security the mysterious labyrinth of harmony."

Heinrich's orchestral works draw Romantic inspiration from nature; some attempt to depict American Indian life, such as *Pushmataha, a Venerable Chief of a Western Tribe of Indians* (1831), *The Wild Wood Spirit's Chant* (1842), and *Manitou Mysteries* (1845).

Little performed in the composer's day or since, these works evince Heinrich's conception of himself as an artist striving not to please audiences but to serve the art of music. "Possibly the public may acknowledge this, when I am dead and gone. I must keep at the work with my best powers, under all discouraging, nay suffering circumstances."

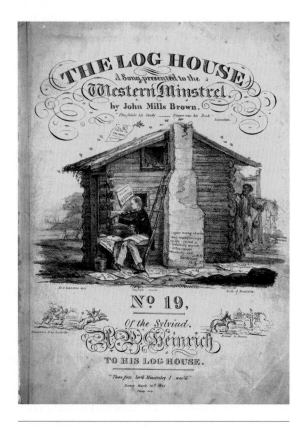

This image of Anthony Philip Heinrich (1781–1861) as the Log House Composer of Kentucky is found in his *The Sylviad,* a collection of pieces for keyboard, voice, and other instruments.

and around the city. He began playing piano at three and was soon taking lessons from a member of a local opera company. He also learned to play violin. Gottschalk sailed for France just after turning thirteen, ready for further musical education in Europe. His father had hoped that he would study at the Paris Conservatory, but the director rejected Gottschalk without an audition on the grounds that "America is only a land of steam engines." Soon, however, the boy was accepted as a piano pupil by a respected teacher. As the center where the world's leading pianists displayed their art, Paris proved the ideal place for Gottschalk to prepare for a virtuoso's career. When he made his own debut as a pianist in Paris shortly before his sixteenth birthday, the great composer and pianist Frédéric Chopin was in the audience.

Gottschalk's playing won approval, and he had also begun to compose. Starting with dance-based pieces, he paid homage to Chopin in a series of mazurkas and waltzes. Then in 1849 he based four new compositions on melodies he had learned in America: *Bamboula*, a description of the music and dancing in Congo Square; *La savane* (the Tropical Palm); *Le bananier* (The Banana Tree); and *Le marcenillier* (The Manchineel Tree)—all published in Paris under the name "Gottschalk of Louisiana." These pieces, which anticipate the efforts of later generations of composers to forge a distinctively American style of classical music, established Gottschalk as a musical representative of the New World in the Old. And they provide a glimpse of a young American artist discovering an approach suited to his talents as a composer who played his own works in public. Throughout his career, Gottschalk wrote music that was difficult for the player but easy on the listener.

By the end of 1852 Gottschalk was ready to return to the United States. The first concert he played after landing in New York took place in February 1853. Together with works by Liszt, Verdi, and others, plenty of Gottschalk's own music appeared on this program, including *Le bananier* and a "Grand Caprice and Variations" for two pianos on a popular tune of the day, *The Carnival of Venice*. As with other pianists of the time, Gottschalk's concerts seldom took the form of solo piano recitals, except where other skilled musicians were unavailable. He was joined in his American debut by a flute soloist, several singers, a pianist, and an orchestra.

One of Gottschalk's most appealing compositions is *The Banjo: An American Sketch* (LG 5.2), published in New York City in 1855. Seeking material with immediate impact, he chose two attention-grabbing elements: the sound of the banjo and a folklike pentatonic melody that strongly resembles Stephen Foster's well-known song "De Camptown Races," published five years earlier. (Either Gottschalk is borrowing Foster's tune or both composers are borrowing from a common folk source; see chapter 6.)

Formally speaking, *The Banjo* is an unbalanced piece. Its brief introduction, a fragment of the pentatonic tune (8 bars), is followed by a long section that imitates the banjo's sound (162 bars), then a shorter section presenting the complete melody and ending in a noisy burst of pianistic bravura (54 bars). If Gottschalk had wanted balance, he could have brought back the banjo imitation in a ternary form (ABA) or expanded the second section of his lopsided binary form. But neither would have churned up so much sheer excitement.

☙ Seven banjos, a tambourine, several pairs of bones, and a free-flowing pennant spell out the title of Gottschalk's "grotesque fantasie" *The Banjo: An American Sketch* in its first edition (New York, 1855).

LG 5.2

Fry and Bristow Defend American Music

When Gottschalk arrived in New York in 1853, that city was about to be caught up in a heated debate over the merits of American-made music. A principal voice in the debate would be William Henry Fry (1831–64), whose *Leonora*, an Italian-style grand opera in English, had premiered in Philadelphia in 1845. After eight years in Paris (roughly the same years that Gottschalk was there), Fry had settled in New York, writing music criticism for the *Tribune* and presenting a series of popular lectures on music with illustrations by an orchestra, chorus, band, and vocal soloists.

Fry's last lecture, in early 1853, closed with a tirade on American musical life, which Fry saw as hampered by, on the one hand, ignorant audiences raised on inferior music and, on the other hand, a dearth of native-born composers, owing to a lack of financial support and their own artistic timidity. Having long ago won political freedom, Fry argued, the United States now needed "a Declaration of Independence in Art." "Until American composers shall discard their foreign liveries and found an American school" of classical composition, he warned, "art will not become indigenous to this country, but will only exist as a feeble exotic."

On Christmas Eve 1853 Louis Jullien conducted the premiere of Fry's new *Santa Claus* Symphony, and when a critic dismissed it as undeserving of serious attention, the composer fired off a long, heated reply, sparking a controversy that continued for months in local newspapers and music journals. The debate invited Americans to think of concert life as a form of national expression. Was it enough simply to hear the music of European masters, or should a place also be reserved for homegrown talent? Fry denounced the Philharmonic Society for never having "asked for or performed a single American instrumental composition during the eleven years of its existence."

Fry's attack drew a quick rebuttal from a Philharmonic member, which was then answered sarcastically by George Frederick Bristow (1825–98), himself an American composer, an officer of the orchestra, and one of its violinists: "As it is possible to miss a needle in a haystack, I am not surprised that Mr. Fry has missed the fact, that during the eleven years the Philharmonic Society has been in operation in this city, it played once, either by mistake or accident, one single American composition, an overture of mine." Bristow wrote symphonies inspired by Mendelssohn, but with Mendelssohn's own symphonies available and still unfamiliar, the Philharmonic found no reason to perform Bristow's.

Fry and Bristow's advocacy of American orchestral music had a firm ideological basis but made little headway against the Philharmonic's cycle of supply and demand. Rooted in an ample supply of European masterworks, the orchestra created a demand for performances of more of the same. In the mid-nineteenth century, to perform untested music was risky, and the fragile economic status of orchestras argued against such risks. Not until later in the century would American composers begin to find a place in the concert hall.

The beginning of the piece's longest section is also unconventional. As a plucked instrument with gut strings, capable of rhythmic energy but not much volume, the banjo of Gottschalk's day called for close listening (see "A Closer Look: The Banjo," p. 94). Here it is as if the audience is invited to lean toward the music, concentrating on the details of Gottschalk's hushed imitation. Instead of a melody, he offers a rhythmically energized but harmonically static texture that evokes the timbre of plucked banjo strings. Though *The Banjo* was separated by distance, time, and a host of artistic conventions from direct African influence,

CD 1.16	Listening Guide 5.2	*The Banjo: An American Sketch* LOUIS MOREAU GOTTSCHALK

DATE: 1855

PERFORMER: Neely Bruce, piano

GENRE: character piece

METER: duple

FORM: binary

WHAT TO LISTEN FOR

- emphasis on pentatonic scale
- imitation of banjo picking
- long, nonmelodic A section and short, tuneful B section

TIMING	SECTION		COMMENTS
0:00	introduction		Loud octaves state shortened version of the pentatonic melody that will be heard again in the B section.
0:13	A	*a*	A dramatic drop in dynamic to *piano* marks the beginning of a long "picking" section in the lower register imitating the characteristic "bum-ditty" rhythm of traditional styles of banjo playing.
1:04		*b*	A burst of *forte* melody in the upper register features rapid repeated notes—difficult on the banjo and even harder on the piano.
1:33		*a*	The quiet "picking" suddenly resumes.
2:16		*b*	An exact repeat of the upper-register melody.
2:45		*a*	A shortened return of the "picking."
3:06	B	*c*	The complete 16-bar pentatonic tune hinted at in the introduction, closely resembling Foster's "De Camptown Races" (see LG 6.2).
3:22		*c*	The tune repeats, now in the upper register, and speeds up toward the end.
3:37		*c*	Once again in the upper register, now loud and fast.
3:50	coda		A burst of loud and fast hammering on the tonic chord brings the piece to a brilliant close.

Listen & Reflect

1. What aspects of this piece show African American influences?
2. What aspects place it firmly in the Euro-American tradition?

the piece's African American lineage, with its emphasis on rhythm and timbre over melody and harmony, is unmistakable.

The piece's overall form may be unusual, but its phrase-by-phrase unfolding is straightforward. Indeed, on that level, *The Banjo* is rooted in the conventions of dance music: a strict tempo, regular phrase structure, and lots of repetition. The steady beat and the four-bar phrases carry listeners comfortably ahead. And the music is at once familiar-sounding (the pentatonic tune), novel (the banjo imitation), and ingenious enough (the variety of banjo sounds) to hold their attention. Finally, the contrast between the piece's last roar and the delicacy of its "picking" sections dramatizes the vastly different capabilities of the grand piano—a technological marvel of the age—and the banjo itself, still in some quarters a homemade instrument in 1855.

GOTTSCHALK AND THE CLASSICS

Gottschalk's artistry was rooted in the sound of the piano. Explaining why he favored instruments made at the Boston factory of Jonas Chickering, he wrote: "I like their tone, fine and delicate, tender and poetic," adding that Chickering pianos allowed him to achieve "tints more varied than those of other instruments." These words point to the heart of Gottschalk's musical philosophy, which held timbre to be as important to a piece of music as were colors to a painting. Technique, though essential, was never enough. "Many pianists whose thundering execution astonishes us still do not move us," he wrote, because "they are ignorant of sound"—the surest means of touching listeners' hearts. With hard work, painters could learn to draw and musicians to play the right notes, but a command of timbre, which carried music's spiritual side, depended on intuition. "Color and sound are born in us," Gottschalk believed; they were "the outward expression of our sensibility and of our souls."

primacy of timbre   Gottschalk's belief in the primacy of timbre distanced him from the more Germanic outlook of John Sullivan Dwight, who once advised performers to play with "no show or effect" so that "the composition is before you, pure and clear . . . as a musician hears it in his mind in reading it from the notes." In other words, music is a composer's art; it should be judged by the way the composer has conceived it on paper. Though performance always involves interpretation, Dwight's outlook directed performers to look to the score, not their personal whims or the mood of the audience, for interpretive guidelines.

primacy of performance   In this clash of priorities, Gottschalk knew exactly where he stood. In 1862 he wrote, "Music is a thing eminently sensuous. Certain combinations move us, not because they are ingenious, but because they move our nervous systems in a certain way." In other words, for all the ingenuity preserved in composers' scores, music does its work in performance, occasion by occasion. Performers and composers can have no worthier goal than to form emotional links with their listeners.

touring   From his New York debut in 1853 until early 1857, Gottschalk traveled the United States, establishing himself as a charismatic presence in concert life and a prominent American composer. Complaints in his journal, however, suggest the price he and other stars paid for the rewards that came their way, including schedules crammed too full of concerts and train rides; hotels that roused guests with alarm bells and served indigestible food; bizarre audience behavior; and demands that popular numbers be endlessly repeated. But these were hazards of the profession. More frustrating to Gottschalk was the disparagement he received for performing his own compositions. Whatever his detractors might say, however, composing was fundamental to Gottschalk's musical nature. Being "cast in an original mold," he argued, he could hardly "abdicate his individuality," even if he tried.

As Gottschalk saw it, critics who championed the classics placed living composers, especially Americans, at a disadvantage. He knew, for example, that the very idea of classic works depended on who was defining them and how. In any discussion of the subject, Gottschalk wrote, he would insist on "reserving the right to ask you what you understand by the classics," for the label could be used as a "convenient club with which you knock on the head all those who annoy you." Aware also that a preoccupation with the classics threatened musical diversity, he asked, "Because the apple is a fruit less delicate than the pineapple, [would you] wish that there should be no apples?"

GOTTSCHALK'S LATER CAREER

During the sixteen years between his return from Europe and his death in 1869, Gottschalk never left the Western Hemisphere again, although he spent less than half of that time in North America. After touring the United States and Canada until 1857, he passed the next several years in the Caribbean, with long stays in Puerto Rico, Martinique, Guadeloupe, and especially Cuba, where he played many concerts, staged festivals, and even for a time managed the opera in Havana. Early in 1862 he returned to the United States and began a strenuous tour. At one point Gottschalk calculated that he had given eighty-five concerts in four and a half months and traveled fifteen thousand miles by train in a country where long-simmering sectional conflict had erupted into civil war. (An ardent foe of slavery, he supported the Northern cause.) Among at least a dozen new compositions he introduced in 1862 was "The Union," a war-inspired fantasy on national songs, featuring "The Star-Spangled Banner," "Hail Columbia," and "Yankee Doodle."

Gottschalk toured eastern North America until early 1865, then sailed for California by way of Panama, arriving in San Francisco in April. After performances in several California towns, June found him in Virginia City, Nevada, which he declared "the saddest, most wearisome, the most inhospitable place on the globe." Not long after his return to the coast, however, he was involved in an incident whose outcome made San Francisco seem even less hospitable than Nevada. That it involved a young woman will surprise no reader of his journal, which confesses that, from time to time during performances, his eyes might sweep the audience in search of feminine beauty. In September 1865 the pianist failed to return a local schoolgirl to her residence on time after an outing with another couple, offending local propriety to the point that vigilante justice was threatened. Though Gottschalk stoutly denied any wrongdoing, he took the precaution of fleeing by sea to South America, and there he spent the rest of his life, performing in Peru, Chile, Uruguay, Argentina, and Brazil. He died in Rio de Janeiro of pneumonia, aggravated by extreme exhaustion, after organizing and performing in a monster concert involving some 650 musicians. His death was marked by a hero's funeral.

No other American-born musician of the 1800s matched Gottschalk's impact, which continued after he died at the age of forty. Biographies were written, and his journal was edited and

Louis Moreau Gottschalk (1829–1869).

published. With the composer no longer alive to perform it, his music sustained a life of its own. Editions of his works were published in North and South America, Europe, and Cuba. But in the twentieth century his music dropped out of the concert repertory, and Gottschalk was gradually forgotten. In the 1970s, when dance impresario Lincoln Kirstein suggested that the New York City Ballet stage a work called *Cakewalk* using Gottschalk's music, the only one in the company who had even heard of the composer was George Balanchine, the great choreographer, who recalled hearing Gottschalk's music in his native Russia.

Gottschalk poses a challenge for historians and students of American music. On the one hand, there is no denying the wide swath that he cut in the international musical life of the 1850s and 1860s and later. Acknowledged as a superior pianist, he also won praise as a composer from both critics and listeners in Europe, South America, the Caribbean, and North America. His music delighted and moved audiences then, and it still sounds original today. On the other hand, Gottschalk is not widely performed nowadays, when the repertory of the concert hall and the teaching studio is often assumed to render the true verdict on musical quality. According to this line of thinking, whatever may be admired in Gottschalk's personality or approach to composition, the music has simply not been good enough to survive.

A case could also be made, however, that Gottschalk's eclipse has had more to do with historical fashion than with the worth of his music. His artistic pedigree is unique, blending the grassroots flavor of New World rhythms and melodies with the elegant sounds and textures of French pianism. That blend, however, went unappreciated by those who shared the Germanic outlook that gained strength after the Civil War. Once Gottschalk was no longer around to play it, his staunchly non-Germanic music lost its place in an American concert hall wary of music that, in the composer's own words, was "not yet consecrated." The product of a nation just beginning to develop cultivated musical tastes, Gottschalk's music would not survive subsequent changes in those tastes.

QUESTIONS FOR DISCUSSION AND REVIEW

1. What are the differences between "composers' music" and "performers' music"? How do different types of music embody the contrasting ideals of transcendence, accessibility, and continuity?

2. Italian opera introduced Americans to the phenomenon of the star performer. How did stardom in the nineteenth century resemble or differ from the present-day cult of celebrity?

3. What social forces may have contributed to the fashion for opera in antebellum San Francisco, at that time a comparatively small and remote city?

4. How did nineteenth-century bands differ from present-day high school, university, and military bands? What social functions do bands serve today, and how are those functions related to the role of bands in nineteenth-century life?

5. Contrast the origins, structure, and function of the Handel and Haydn Society, the Boston Academy of Music, and the New York Philharmonic Society. What goals did they have in common, and how did they go about achieving those goals in different ways?

6. What features of *The Banjo* are typical of classical music, and which are atypical? Generalizing from there, how were Gottschalk's attitudes typical of a classical musician's, and how were they atypical?

7. Discuss the merits and weaknesses of Fry's and Bristow's arguments in favor of American-made music. Do such arguments still need to be made today, and why or why not?

FURTHER READING

Ahlquist, Karen. *Democracy at the Opera: Music, Theater and Culture in New York City, 1815–60.* Urbana: University of Illinois Press, 1997.

Broyles, Michael. *"Music of the Highest Class": Elitism and Populism in Antebellum Boston.* New Haven, CT: Yale University Press, 1992.

Crawford, Richard. *The American Musical Landscape.* Berkeley and Los Angeles: University of California Press, 1993.

Martin, George Whitney. *Verdi at the Golden Gate: Opera and San Francisco in the Gold Rush Years.* Berkeley and Los Angeles: University of California Press, 1993.

Newman, Nancy. *Good Music for a Free People: The Germania Musical Society in Nineteenth-Century America.* Rochester, NY: University of Rochester Press, 2010.

Preston, Katherine K. *Opera on the Road: Traveling Opera Troupes in the United States, 1825–60.* Urbana: University of Illinois Press, 2001.

Starr, S. Frederick. *Bamboula! The Life and Times of Louis Moreau Gottschalk.* New York: Oxford University Press, 1995.

FURTHER LISTENING

Gottschalk, Louis Moreau. *Symphonies Nos. 1 and 2; Escenas Campestres Cubanas; Célèbre Tarantelle.* Hot Springs Festival Symphony Orchestra; Richard Rosenberg, conductor. Naxos American Classics, 2007.

The Yankee Brass Band: Music from Mid-Nineteenth-Century America. The American Brass Quintet Brass Band. New World Records, 1981.

CHAPTER 6

"THE ETHIOPIAN BUSINESS"

Minstrelsy and Popular Song through the Civil War

In the early 1850s Samuel Cartwright, a Louisiana physician, wrote an essay on diseases that were said to afflict black slaves, including "drapetomia" (running away) and "dysaesthesia aethiopica," which caused sufferers to "break, waste, and destroy everything they handle." These words could suggest that the writer was describing clever slaves who avoided work by convincing the master they were too stupid or clumsy for the job. But Cartwright intended no such irony. Proclaiming the theory of "polygenesis," he argued that each race was separate and distinct, rather than a variety of one species. In the southern United States, some accepted that theory as a proof that Africans were biologically inferior to Caucasians, and that being slaves was their natural destiny.

It is obvious today that polygenesis was simply a bit of fake science concocted to support racial prejudice. But the existence of this pseudo theory also points to deep conflicts in the feelings Americans had about race. In the early and middle 1800s, many white Americans were fascinated by the image of the African American slave. And that fascination—a mixture of curiosity, fear, love, and loathing—formed a key ingredient of blackface **minstrelsy**, the era's most popular form of entertainment. After a discussion of the minstrel show and its music, this chapter goes on to examine one facet of American music in which minstrelsy's influence was felt: the mid-nineteenth-century explosion of **parlor songs** intended for home music making.

BLACK, WHITES, AND THE MINSTREL STAGE

Minstrelsy, which originated with white performers pretending onstage to be black, has been called racist and exploitative entertainment. There is no question that race was fundamental to the minstrel show. Taking for granted the superiority of Euro-American culture, white minstrels relied on black-influenced song, dance, and humor to give their performances vitality. And there is no evidence that white minstrels shared profits with the black Americans whom they imitated. Yet neither racism—the belief that one's own ethnic stock is superior—nor economic exploitation fully explains minstrelsy's impact. For while entertaining audiences with jokes, skits, and music, minstrels also played on social issues. A black stage character could appear stupid one moment and cunning the next. On one level, the black face paint enabled white stage minstrels to amuse audiences by imitating black ways of talking, moving, dancing, laughing, singing, and playing musical instruments. On another, white minstrels learned that "blacking up" freed them to behave onstage in ways that polite society found uncivilized. They could also comment critically not just on black-white relations but on society in general: on politics, culture, and social class.

The spectacle of performers freed from social restraint could bring an unparalleled delight to audience members. In 1843 H. P. Grattan, an English actor, visited Buffalo, New York, and there, as part of an audience filled with boatmen, he watched a minstrel troupe perform. "So droll was the action, so admirable the singing, so clever the instrumentation, and so genuine was the fun," Grattan later wrote, "that I not only laughed till my sides fairly ached, but . . . I never left an entertainment with a more keen desire to witness it again."

The freedom enjoyed by performers included behavior not to be found in other kinds of theater. An English observer in 1846 described minstrels as "animated by a savage energy," their "white eyes roll[ing] in a curious frenzy." The frenzy was widely believed to have been inspired by black slaves themselves, who, as another observer wrote in 1857, were apt to "let themselves go" in "dervish-like fury . . . all night long, in ceaseless, violent exertions of frenetic dancing." In their unbuttoned manner, blackface minstrels of the 1840s and early 1850s had much in common with rock musicians from the 1950s on.

Three elements, then—the black mask, the chance for social commentary, and the creation of a zone of unbridled pleasure—combined to give blackface minstrelsy its appeal. Minstrelsy's subject matter was not so much whites' views of African Americans as whites' responses to the conditions of their own lives, delivered from behind a mask fashioned out of their notions about African American culture.

The late 1820s and early 1830s saw the creation of two stage characters who enjoyed a long life: Jim Crow and Zip Coon. Around 1828 an actor named Thomas D. "Daddy" Rice made theatrical history when, after noticing a crippled black stable groom's singing and weird dancing in Cincinnati, he memorized the first and tried to copy the second. He then bought clothes like those the stable hand wore, and finally, blacked up as "Jim Crow," he began doing an impersonation between acts of the play in which he was appearing. Audiences loved it, and Rice soon won fame as an "Ethiopian delineator" (the term reflects the eighteenth-century designation of sub-Saharan Africans as "Ethiopians"). The Jim Crow character became a self-satisfied Southern plantation hand who strutted the stage, unaware that his raggedy naïveté made him a buffoon in others' eyes.

The character Zip Coon was as urban and stylish as Jim Crow was rural and rough. Like Jim Crow, Zip Coon was boastful, and he appeared in garishly fancy clothes, including his "long tail blue" jacket, as one song has it. The adventures outlined in the song "Zip Coon"—sung by singing actor George Washington Dixon—include romance:

Among the blackface characters found onstage before the 1840s, when the minstrel show became a full evening's entertainment, one of the most prominent was the stylish, would-be sophisticate Zip Coon.

O its old Suky blue skin, she is in lub wid me
I went the udder arter noon to take a dish ob tea;
What do you tink now, Suky hab for supper,
Why chicken foot an posum heel, widout any butter.

O ole Zip Coon he is a larned skolar,
O ole Zip Coon he is a larned skolar,
O ole Zip Coon he is a larned skolar,
Sings posum up a gum tree an coony in a holler.

But this romance has more obstacles to overcome than the unsavory supper Suky puts on the table. One is that Zip seems too wrapped up in himself to be a serious lover. Another is that the music of "Zip Coon," the fiddle tune known as "Turkey in the Straw," fails to evoke even a hint that love can be tender.

The happy-go-lucky Jim Crow and the boastful, self-important Zip Coon were stereotypes on which whites could project racist fantasies about contented slaves in the South and "uppity" free blacks in the North. At the same time, however, Zip Coon could burlesque upper-class whites, and Jim Crow's dance could simply occasion an outburst of high spirits that lifted performers and audience above commonplace, everyday existence.

THE FIRST MINSTREL SHOWS

the Virginia Minstrels

The first full-length minstrel show was given in Boston in 1843 by Dan Emmet (fiddle), Billy Whitlock (banjo), Dick Pelham (tambourine), and Frank Brower (bones), billing themselves as the Virginia Minstrels. Despite the group's name, all four members had joined forces not in Virginia but in New York City's Bowery, whose entertainment district had already begun a long descent from respectability to disrepute with the infiltration of tough street gangs from the neighboring Five Points slum, the scene of intense rivalry between Irish immigrants and nativist gangs. In the pseudoscientific racist thinking of the time, the Irish were members of the Celtic race, distinct from and inferior to the Anglo-Saxon race and thus fit only for menial jobs scarcely different from the work assigned to slaves. It can hardly be coincidence that many of the early blackface minstrels were of Irish descent.

Honing their act in Bowery theaters and saloons, the Virginia Minstrels developed performing customs that were followed by many of the minstrel companies that sprang up in the wake of their success. The performers arranged four chairs on stage in a semicircle, with tambourine and bones at either end and fiddle and banjo in between, and filled their programs with short musical numbers. They divided an evening's entertainment into two parts, the first including a would-be topical speech, delivered in a stage Negro dialect. It was soon customary for a minstrel show's first part to concentrate on the Northern urban scene, with the second shifting to the South and closing with a lively plantation number. But however standardized the overall form, the flow of events in any given minstrel show lay with the performers. Each skit, song, and dance was a self-contained act. Ad-libbing and topical comments were part of the format, giving customers and players a sense of collaboration.

Within a few months of their debut, the Virginia Minstrels toured the British Isles, where audiences also welcomed blackface shows. And by the mid-1840s minstrelsy was sweeping the United States. In 1844 a troupe called the Ethiopian

Ground Rules of Blackface Minstrelsy

The writing of history encourages a mode of objectivity that exempts scholars from the burden of judging the actions of their historical subjects. But that pose can be hard to maintain where the commercial success of blackface minstrelsy is concerned. Scholarly protocols weigh against classifying even obvious oppression as evil. In this case, however, not only was a legally oppressed people denied personhood in a land constitutionally committed to democracy, but many of the distinctive ways these individuals found to cope with life under such a regime were, in effect, stolen from them by commercial entertainers as well. What the entertainers "borrowed" was an African-tinged persona—skin color, physical mannerisms, ways of moving and speaking and of making music—that, through the skills of artists like themselves, proved to be imitable and profitable too, because audiences throughout the English-speaking world found blackface minstrelsy delightful to watch and fun to imitate. It goes almost without saying that permission to borrow was not requested, nor did the lenders share in the profits. Moreover, the stage persona was grounded in the assumption of inferiority that racism carries with it. The sense of entitlement behind this transaction—in effect a large-scale pattern of humiliation and robbery—needs to be kept in mind as the story of "the Ethiopian business" unfolds.

Serenaders was invited to play at the White House. Spurred by popular demand, countless minstrel troupes were formed: the African Melodists, the Congo Minstrels, the Gumbo Family, the New Orleans Serenaders. Companies flourished along the Mississippi and in the cities of the Northeast, and the growing railroad system made touring easier. But the center of blackface entertainment was New York City; by the 1850s at least ten minstrel houses were open there, and a few companies enjoyed consecutive runs of several years or more.

Minstrelsy was the first musical genre to reverse the east-to-west transatlantic flow of performers. Until Americans began to perform on stages in styles invented here, a vast majority of stage performers were immigrants, chiefly from the British Isles. Minstrelsy, however, had no need for performers trained in the Old World. What it required were those who, like the four Virginia Minstrels, could step into the voice and the character of a stage "Ethiopian" and entertain an audience with comic turns, dancing, and the singing and playing of popular music.

That minstrel skills could not be gained through formal study is confirmed by the makeup of the original minstrel band: violin, banjo, tambourine, and bones. Only the violin was an instrument with established methods of instruction and a repertory of composed music. Yet the violin led a double life. As the fiddle, this bowed string instrument stood at the heart of Celtic American dance music, with its jigs, reels, and hornpipes. Like their country counterparts, minstrel fiddlers like Dan Emmett held their instrument loosely and more or less in front of themselves, rather than clamping it between chin and shoulder. As a minstrel-band fiddle, the violin was less a singing, lyric voice than a wiry, rhythmic one, played with little or no **vibrato**, the minute, rapid variation of pitch that lends expressivity to much singing and playing.

The banjo, as noted in chapter 4, migrated from Africa to the New World before 1700. No record of white banjo playing exists, however, before Joel

the minstrel band

the fiddle

the banjo

Sweeney began learning from slaves in Virginia, probably in the late 1820s; by the 1830s Sweeney was passing on their playing techniques to white performers like Billy Whitlock. The early minstrel banjo, which gave the ensemble its distinctive character, did not sound like a modern banjo. Its body was larger, the fingerboard had no frets, and its five gut strings were tuned well below the modern pitch. The sound was therefore fuller and suited to its role as a melody instrument.

bones and tambourine

That two of the early minstrel band's four members played small, portable percussion instruments testifies to the group's emphasis on rhythm, timbre, and body movement over melody and harmony. One member played **bones**: usually the rib or leg bones of a cow or pig, sawed into segments about six inches long. The sound, resembling that of castanets, is made by holding a pair of bones in either hand and clicking them together, enabling a skilled player to produce complex rhythmic patterns. It has long been a feature of Irish music, where modern players often use hardwood replicas or even metal spoons instead of actual bones, and the practice probably came to the United States from there. The tambourine, an ancient percussion instrument of Near Eastern origin, is a hand drum with metal jingles attached to the frame. It can be struck with the fingers for accents and also shaken to provide a layer of shimmering sound. Compared to a modern tambourine, the minstrel instrument was larger and had fewer jingles.

Judging by the instruments most often mentioned in ex-slave narratives, the four core instruments of the minstrel band were indeed those most commonly played by American slaves. That only one of the four was clearly of African origin serves as a reminder of the adaptability of African American culture in the early United States. The heterogeneous sound of the minstrel band resembles the similar ensembles described in early accounts of slave music making such as the 1756 Election Day celebration described in chapter 4.

SONGS OF THE EARLY MINSTREL SHOWS

The advent of the minstrel show brought a need for a new kind of stage song. The most popular new songs of the 1840s added to the cast of stereotyped black characters begun by Jim Crow and Zip Coon. "Miss Lucy Long" (1842) is a comic love song attributed to Billy Whitlock, the Virginia Minstrels' banjo player, who probably took the song in whole or in part from a folk source. The song's **persona**—the character who seems to be singing or narrating to the audience—praises the title character in ludicrous terms, offering to marry her but suggesting the limits of his love:

> Oh Miss Lucy's teeth is grinning
> Just like an ear ob corn,
> And her eyes dey look so winning!
> Oh would I'd ne'er been born. . . .
>
> If she makes a scolding wife
> As sure as she was born,
> I'll tote her down to Georgia
> And trade her off for Corn.

Miss Lucy would have been impersonated on the minstrel stage by a man, adding cross-dressing to racial masquerade.

Dan Emmett, the Virginia Minstrels' fiddler, took songwriter credit for "Old Dan Tucker" (1843), but like "Miss Lucy Long" it is probably of folk origin. The song introduces a boastful character who seems like a blackface version of the pioneer frontiersman, along the lines of the legendary, if not the factual, Davy Crockett:

> Down de road foremost de stump,
> Massa make me work de pump;
> I pump so hard I broke de sucker,
> Dar was work for Old Dan Tucker.
>
> So get out de way! get out de way!
> Get out de way, Old Dan Tucker!
> You're too late to come to supper.

The song's disjointed sequence of verses, which seemingly could be sung in any order with no effect on meaning, is characteristic of African American song and will be encountered again later in the blues (see chapters 11 and 14). Because the verses alternate between the first person and the third person, it is unclear whether the song's persona is Dan Tucker himself or an observer telling stories about him—not an unusual state of affairs in minstrel songs, which tend to embody the exhilaration of performance at the expense of narrative logic. The shifting point of view also suggests how solo songs may have turned into ensemble numbers in performance, with different members of the troupe singing different verses while others might add dance, pantomime, or even an interruption for a joke or riddle.

The line "Massa make me work de pump" evokes the reality of hard work in the lives of American slaves. "De Boatmen's Dance" (LG 6.1) is another minstrel song that draws on the working lives of African Americans, here the free men who labored on boats that carried cargo and passengers on the Ohio River and other waterways. Though greatly outnumbered by enslaved blacks—nearly 2.5 million by 1840—nearly 400,000 free blacks lived in the United States in 1840, divided about equally between the North and the South, most of them working the least desirable menial jobs. "De Boatmen's Dance" describes a life not only of labor but also of camaraderie and emotional release, even if the latter comes at risk of being thrown into the "calaboose," or jail. The lyrics show traces of black vernacular English and point to the song's likely folk origins, despite the sheet music's attribution to Dan Emmett.

LG 6.1

STEPHEN FOSTER AND THE "ETHIOPIAN BUSINESS"

At about the time Dan Emmett and the Virginia Minstrels were starting out on the East Coast, a teenage youth in Allegheny, Pennsylvania, was getting together with friends to stage amateur minstrel shows for fun. By the time he turned twenty-four, with several hits already to his credit, Stephen C. Foster had embarked on a songwriter's career, one of the most significant in this country's history.

"Gwine to Run All Night, or De Camptown Races" (1850; LG 6.2) was one of Foster's early minstrel show hits. Its verse-and-chorus form resembles "Old Dan Tucker" and "De Boatmen's Dance," but whereas Emmett's tunes are driven and aggressive, Foster's is jaunty and tuneful, with a memorable five-note

LG 6.2

| CD 1.17 | Listening Guide 6.1 | "De Boatmen's Dance" DAN EMMETT |

DATE: 1843

PERFORMERS: Vincent Tufo, fiddle; Percy Danforth, bones; Matthew Heumann, tambourine; Robert Winans, banjo; David Van Veersbilck, Peter DiSante, Brian Mark, Roger Smith, singers

GENRE: minstrel song

METER: duple

FORM: verse and chorus

WHAT TO LISTEN FOR

- driving rhythm
- heterogeneous sound of minstrel band
- alternation of solo and unison voices on verse and harmonizing voices on chorus
- lyrics in imitation of Negro dialect

TIMING	SECTION	TEXT	COMMENTS
0:00	instrumental introduction		After the fiddle plays a conventional 2-bar introduction, called "potatoes," the banjo and fiddle play a complete chorus and verse, with rhythmic accompaniment from tambourine and bones.
0:25	chorus	High row, de boatmen row, Floatin' down de ribber, de Ohio! High row, de boatmen row, Floatin' down de ribber, de Ohio!	The ensemble sings in informal harmony.
0:32	verse 1	De boatmen dance, de boatmen sing, De boatmen up to eb'rything. And when de boatmen gets on shore, He spends his cash and he work for more. Den dance, de boatmen dance! O dance, de boatmen dance. Dance all night till broad daylight An go home wid de gals in de morning.	A soloist sings the first quatrain of the verse alone, then the other voices join in unison for the second quatrain.
0:48	chorus	High row, de boatmen row . . .	The chorus returns in vocal harmony.
0:55	verse 2	I went on board de odder day To see what de boatmen had to say; An dar I let my passion loose An' dey cram me in de calaboose. Den dance, de boatmen dance! . . .	
1:10	instrumental interlude		An instrumental rendition of the chorus and verse, as in the introduction.

| | CD 1.17 | Listening Guide 6.1 | | "De Boatmen's Dance" DAN EMMETT |

TIMING	SECTION	TEXT	COMMENTS
1:33	chorus	High row, de boatmen row …	Harmonized.
1:40	verse 3	When de boatman blows his horn, Look out, man, your hog is gone; He cotch my sheep, he cotch my shoat, Den put 'em in bag and tote 'em to boat. Den dance, de boatmen dance! …	Like verse 1.
1:56	chorus	High row, de boatmen row …	Harmonized.
2:03	verse 4	De boatman is a thrifty man Dars none can do as de boatman can; I neber see a pretty girl in my life But dat she was a boatman's wife. Den dance, de boatmen dance! …	Like verse 2.
2:19	instrumental interlude		An instrumental rendition of the chorus and verse, as in the introduction, now with prominent bones.
2:41	chorus	High row, de boatmen row …	Harmonized.
2:48	verse 5	When you go to de boatmen's ball, Dance wid my wife or don't dance at all; Sky-blue jacket an' tarpaulin hat, Look out, boys, for de nine tail cat. Den dance, de boatmen dance! …	Like verse 1.
3:04	chorus	High row, de boatmen row …	Harmonized.
3:11	instrumental coda		The performance concludes with one last repeat of the verse melody, played instrumentally.

Listen & Reflect

1. Recall the English visitor's description (earlier in this chapter) of a minstrel performance for an audience of white boatmen in Buffalo. How might that audience have received this song?

2. What does the song tell us about a boatman's lifestyle?

3. How does race figure into the picture?

| CD 1.18 | Listening Guide 6.2 | "De Camptown Races" STEPHEN C. FOSTER |

DATE: 1850

PERFORMERS: Frederick Urrey, tenor, and John Van Buskirk, piano

GENRE: minstrel song

METER: duple

FORM: verse and chorus

WHAT TO LISTEN FOR

- jaunty, memorable melody
- piano accompaniment in imitation of minstrel band
- lyrics in imitation of Negro dialect

TIMING	SECTION	TEXT	COMMENTS
0:00	introduction		Piano's upper register imitates a fiddle, with the left hand providing the rhythmic accompaniment of the rest of a minstrel band.
0:06	verse 1	De Camptown ladies sing dis song, Doo-dah! doo-dah! De Camptown race-track five miles long, Oh, doo-dah day! I come down dah wid my hat caved in, Doo-dah! doo-dah! I go back home wid a pocket full of tin, Oh, doo-dah day!	All four lines of text are sung to the same pentatonic melody, while the punctuating **vocables** ("doodah," etc.) alternate half (unfinished) cadences and full (finished) cadences.
0:21	chorus	Gwine to run all night! Gwine to run all day! I'll bet my money on de bob-tail nag, Somebody bet on de bay.	Begins with a strikingly different, rising melodic line, then concludes with the same bit of melody used in the verse.
0:30	verse 2 and chorus	De long tail filly and de big black hoss, Doo-dah! doo-dah! Dey fly de track and dey both cut across, Oh, doo-dah-day! De blind hoss sticken in a big mud hole, Doo-dah! doo-dah! Can't touch bottom wid a ten foot pole, Oh, doo-dah-day! Gwine to run all night! . . .	Performers opt to slow the tempo for serio-comic "dramatic" effect in the second half of the verse.
0:57	verse 3 and chorus	Old muley cow come on to de track, Doo-dah! doo-dah! De bob-tail fling her ober his back, Oh, doo-dah-day! Den fly along like a rail-road car, Doo-dah! doo-dah! Runnin' a race wid a shootin' star, Oh, doo-dah-day! Gwine to run all night! . . .	As in all the verses, the piano accompanies the melody's solo phrases in the lower register, switching to the upper register for what would be the responses in a group performance.

| CD 1.18 | Listening Guide 6.2 | | "De Camptown Races" STEPHEN C. FOSTER |

TIMING	SECTION	TEXT	COMMENTS
1:19	interlude		Shortened return of introduction.
1:22	verse 4 and chorus	See dem flyin' on a ten mile heat, Doo-dah doo-dah! Round de race track, den repeat, Oh, doo-dah-day! I win my money on de bob-tail nag, Doo-dah! doo-dah! I keep my money in an old tow-bag, Oh, doo-dah-day! Gwine to run all night! . . .	

Listen & Reflect

1. What can you infer from the lyrics about the song's persona? Do you get any sense of the persona's race, gender, age, economic status, educational background, lifestyle, or outlook on life? What specifics about the song create those impressions?

2. How does this performance differ from that of "De Boatmen's Dance" (see LG 6.1)? What are the musical effects of those differences?

ascending figure that starts the chorus ("Gwine to run all night"). The sheet music presents the song with an accompaniment for piano, making it suitable for home performance, but the written vocal part reflects minstrel stage practice: the "doo-dah!" interjections in the verses are indicated to be sung by the group, creating a call-and-response texture characteristic of African American music, while the chorus is written in four-part vocal harmony, reflecting the informal vocal harmonizing of groups like the Virginia Minstrels. Even with these features, the song also works well as a vocal solo, exhibiting the flexibility that helped a song attain widespread popularity in antebellum America.

Though the differences between "De Boatmen's Dance" and "De Camptown Races" might be understood as a matter of different composing styles, they also reflect changes in minstrelsy between 1843 and 1850. "De Boatmen's Dance" represented the dominant voice of early minstrelsy: the black mask, linked with tough, unlyrical, folklike music, that invited white listeners to mock genteel social customs with fierce intensity. In the next few years, however, blackface minstrels vastly increased their audience, in part by broadening their musical repertory. Rip-roaring comic songs like "Miss Lucy Long" and "Old Dan Tucker" were still sung, but so were sad songs, love songs, sentimental songs, and even opera parodies. (The opera parodies mentioned in chapter 5, *The Roof Scrambler* and *Fried Shots,* were both blackface burlesques.) By midcentury the noisy, impromptu entertainments cooked up by Dan Emmett and the Virginia Minstrels were becoming a thing of the past. Moving into the center of American show business, minstrelsy evolved toward a more restrained kind of spectacle.

Stephen C. Foster (1826–1864), born near Pittsburgh on July 4, the nation's fiftieth anniversary, wrote more songs that won enduring popularity than any other American songwriter of the nineteenth century.

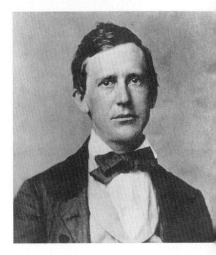

A song like "De Camptown Races," with a melody strong enough to hold performers closer to the prescribed notes, helped to channel unruliness into a more controlled mode of expression.

One who worked to widen minstrelsy's audience appeal was the impresario and performer Edwin P. Christy. Born in 1815 in Philadelphia, he perfected his blackface imitation as a comic singer in the 1830s, then founded his own troupe in the early 1840s. Acting as the group's manager, he also performed as **interlocutor** (master of ceremonies), played banjo, and sang. Christy's Minstrels toured for several years before opening in April 1846 in New York City, where a critic complimented them for "chaste, refined, and harmonious" singing. Offering family entertainment at cheap prices, Christy's Minstrels took up residence at New York's Mechanic's Hall for a seven-year run (1847–54).

Christy's Minstrels came to be the most successful minstrel band in America. The company embraced a wide variety of solo and choral music, including sentimental songs, glees, and arrangements of opera numbers. They came on the scene at about the same time Stephen Foster was publishing his first songs. Christy must have recognized that Foster's songs would appeal to the audiences his company was trying to attract, and Foster knew there was no better way to promote sales of his songs than to have them sung onstage by a famous company

The minstrel troupe led by Edwin P. Christy (1815–1862) introduced many of Stephen Foster's songs not only in the United States but also in England, as this British lithograph suggests.

SKEDADDLE.

THE CELEBRATED WALK ROUND.
SUNG & DANCED BY
THE CHRISTY'S MINSTRELS.
G.W. MOORE, J. CROCKER, J. RITTER & H. HAMILTON.
(PROPRIETORS.)

like Christy's. Thus, though they seem not to have met in these years, Christy and Foster became collaborators of a sort.

In 1850, when Foster became a full-time songwriter, he entered into an agreement that gave Christy's Minstrels exclusive first-performance rights to his new songs. In 1851 Foster allowed Christy to claim authorship of "Old Folks at Home," a song of huge popularity. The following year, though, he wrote Christy asking permission to restore his own name to its rightful place on the song's cover. "I find that by my efforts I have done a great deal to build up a taste for the Ethiopian songs among refined people," Foster told Christy. "I have concluded to reinstate my name on my songs and to pursue the Ethiopian business without fear or shame and lend all my energies to making the business live." Yet Christy refused Foster's request, going so far as to scrawl "vacillating skunk" on the back of Foster's letter. Indeed, until the copyright expired in 1879, sheet music printings of "Old Folks at Home" continued to name Christy as author and composer.

Foster has often been portrayed as the injured party in this matter: a young composer seeking only to be recognized for his achievements. But

Foster's "Old Folks at Home" (1851) shows his reliance on a single four-bar melody and the simplicity of the piano accompaniment, accessible to inexpert players.

Blackface Minstrelsy and *Uncle Tom's Cabin*

Through the minstrel show's early years, as anti-slavery sentiment grew in the North, Southerners hardened their allegiance to the institution of slavery. As the frontier moved west, bitter fights took place over whether slavery would be allowed in newly settled territories, which might then become states of the Union. Against this background, minstrelsy retreated from controversy that might have reduced its audience. Black characters were portrayed sentimentally, with contented Negroes fondly recalling the good old days on the plantation. Restless or unhappy blacks gradually disappeared from minstrel stages. By the mid-1850s the minstrel show was built around the notion that the plantation was blacks' rightful home, the only place where they could be truly happy and well cared for.

Politics, the economy, regional pride, and religion were all involved in the rising tension between North and South—as was literature, beginning with the publication in 1852 of Harriet Beecher Stowe's novel *Uncle Tom's Cabin, or Life among the Lowly*. Stowe tried in her work "to awaken sympathy and feeling for the African race, as they exist among us; to show their wrongs and sorrows, under a system so necessarily cruel and unjust as to defeat and do away the good efforts of all that can be attempted for them." A huge literary success in the North, *Uncle Tom's Cabin* was banned as subversive literature in some parts of the South.

Within weeks of its publication, plays based on Stowe's book began to appear on American stages, bringing to theatrical life characters like Uncle Tom, the saintly, trustworthy slave, and Simon Legree, the hard-fisted, hard-hearted slave driver. In 1854 Christy and Wood's Minstrels used Stowe's characters in a plantation sketch they called "Life among the Happy," which featured plenty of dancing, singing, and high spirits but made little use of Stowe's plot, omitting any reference to the cruelty and suffering of slavery, which had moved Stowe to write her novel in the first place.

To Stowe's readers, Uncle Tom was a powerful symbol of humanity. In the novel, Tom's master introduces him as "a good, steady, sensible, pious fellow. He got religion at a camp-meeting, four years ago, and I believe he really *did* get it. I've trusted him, since then, with everything I have." In contrast, by the time Emancipation was declared (1863), the character as portrayed on stage was aging, hard of hearing, and stupid—a feeble old man who came to dancing life at the sound of banjo music. A more striking symbol of the theatrical landscape in which black characters found themselves would be hard to find.

∾ "Tom shows"—minstrel-style stagings of *Uncle Tom's Cabin*—lasted into the twentieth century, as evidenced by this photo of a 1901 production with white actors portraying Simon Legree, Tom, and Emmeline, the latter two in blackface.

Christy's response is understandable. After benefiting for more than a year from Christy's fame and his plugging of the song (whose royalties Foster was receiving), here was Foster, who in an earlier letter had called himself "a gentleman of the old school," proposing to renege on a done deal.

The song that prompted this exchange reaches into new expressive territory. The persona, a displaced slave, sings of loneliness and longing, having no apparent plan to return to the home for which he yearns. Together the words and tune convey the emotional weariness that isolation can bring.

Foster's songs signaled the direction in which minstrelsy was headed by midcentury. Unlike Emmett, Foster played piano and conceived his songs at the keyboard. And in songs like "De Camptown Races" and "Old Folks at Home" he showed a knack for writing minstrel music suited to the talents and tastes of parlor performers. In the early 1840s Dan Emmett brought songs drawn from the countryside and circus into urban theaters. Now, around 1850, Foster had found an idiom that seemed equally at home on the stage and in the parlor. Foster's songs may have earned their initial success on the minstrel stage, but their continuing popularity was intimately bound to domestic music making.

THE SHEET MUSIC INDUSTRY AND PARLOR SONGS

In chapter 5 sheet music was described as inexpensive and thus a product ideal for a democracy. That statement holds true for the years after 1845, even though earlier in the century sheet music had been a luxury. Perhaps it would be better to say that having started out as a costly enterprise, by the mid-1800s home music making involving sheet music and pianos was a pastime accessible to many middle-class Americans. In the late 1820s the trade was turning out 600 titles per year, but the number grew to 1,600 annually in the early 1840s and 5,000 in the early 1850s. The threefold leap between 1840 and 1850 reflects a burgeoning demand.

The economics of sheet music publishing depended on a variety of factors, including copyright law. As first written, the law protected only authors who were American citizens or residents. A foreign hit like "Home, Sweet Home" was issued by many different publishers because no American edition of the song could be copyrighted. Therefore, it was cheaper for publishers to print foreign music than American music, which required them either to purchase rights from the composer or to pay a royalty on copies sold. The American appetite for European music owed much to the notion that Old World culture was superior, but the dollars-and-cents advantage to publishers was also a factor that cannot be ignored.

publishers and copyright

While money could be made in the sheet music trade, publishers complained that the business was risky. Indeed, all but a few of its products lost money. A notice of 1859 from Oliver Ditson & Co., a highly successful firm, emphasized risk: "Not one piece in ten pays the cost of getting up; only one in fifty proves a success." Success in the trade depended on these exceptions: the composer whose name helped to sell copies; the stage hit that transferred well to the parlor; the vocal or instrumental number that the public took to its heart. When one of their pieces struck pay dirt, publishers did all they could to exploit it, packaging the title and melody in as many different arrangements as possible. The enormous outpouring of sheet music during the century's second half testifies that, whatever the risks, publishing it could be lucrative.

MEN, WOMEN, AND PIANOS

By the 1820s the piano was on its way to becoming the quintessential parlor instrument of the nineteenth and twentieth centuries, in varied shapes and sizes: square pianos, uprights, spinets, consoles, and grands.

Chickering pianos

The pattern of growth in keyboard manufacturing paralleled that of the sheet music trade. At first an import and a luxury reserved for the few, keyboard instruments over the years became accessible to more and more people. Jonas Chickering of Boston began in the 1830s to mass-produce metal-framed instruments. By 1851 some 9,000 pianos per year were being made in the United States, with Chickering, the leading firm, producing 10 percent of that total. It has been estimated that one out of 4,800 Americans bought a new piano in 1829; in 1910, a year in which 350,000 pianos were produced, one out of 252 bought one.

Pianos were solo as well as accompaniment instruments, and a great deal of sheet music was published for piano alone. Between 1820 and the Civil War, three kinds of piano pieces dominated the repertory: **variation** sets, based on the melodies of popular songs, hymn tunes, or opera arias; dances, including waltzes, polkas, galops, cotillions, marches, and quicksteps; and a small amount of "abstract" music, especially rondos.

music in the middle-class home

In the late 1700s, the activity of a prosperous household involved a mixture of business and pleasure, including music. As business moved out of the house and into office buildings early in the nineteenth century, however, the bourgeois home became more a center for family and cultural activity. It came to be more common for husbands to leave home in the morning, spend their days in the competitive marketplace, and then return in the evening to domestic sanctuaries prepared by their wives. In removing their own work from the home, men gave up their involvement in much that happened there, while domestic affairs came to be considered women's work. Music making in the middle-class home was deeply influenced by the change.

women and domestic music making

Women in this social setting were responsible for raising children, managing household affairs, and beautifying their surroundings. The sheet music and piano trades thus came to assume that parlor piano was a female activity, and piano music published from the 1840s on was shaped by the trade's view of women's musical tastes and capacities. Was this an accurate view? It is impossible to tell; the publishers and composers who dominated the sheet music business were all male. But the music gives a good idea of the female sensibility that it was tailored to please.

One book from the 1700s distinguished women from men "by that *Delicacy*, express'd by *Nature* in their *Form*." Another claimed that "natural softness and sensibility" made women generally agreeable and disposed them toward a taste for beauty. That theme was repeated in countless nineteenth-century writings. An attraction to certain objects of beauty, such as flowers, was widely held (and not only by men) to be part of women's nature.

In the nineteenth-century parlor, music's purpose was more social than artistic, and touching the heart was among the highest social purposes of all. Composers and arrangers, fully allied with the popular sphere's credo of accessibility, were far more concerned with the feelings of players and listeners than with any concept of artistic originality or integrity. With the help of the piano industry, they tailored a growing repertory of sheet music for what they took to be the taste of female amateur pianists.

Yet for all the piano's prominence, the singing voice was the favorite home instrument of all, and the heart of the sheet music trade lay in the solo song with keyboard accompaniment. From early in the century through the Civil War, songs written for domestic performance—parlor songs—provide insight into the way Americans viewed themselves.

SONGS OF COURTSHIP AND SEPARATION IN ANTEBELLUM AMERICA

Then as now, a central topic of popular song lyrics was love and courtship. Representations of love relationships, however, have changed dramatically over the generations, as later chapters will bear out. In the nineteenth century, one favorite song genre in the home circle was centered on a mythic view of love harking back to the Middle Ages, when love between knights and ladies was ruled by a courtly code. Songs inspired by the lore of medieval chivalry began to appear early in the 1800s. John Hill Hewitt, born in New York in 1801 to a family of immigrant musicians, took this approach in "The Minstrel Return'd from the War," composed in 1825 in Greenville, South Carolina, and published around 1833 in New York. Choosing as his main character a minstrel-knight of yore (a minstrel was a medieval entertainer; blackface performers appropriated the name), Hewitt wrote a text that seems to have been inspired by the Christian crusades. His music begins like a march, then becomes more serenade-like as the knight woos his fair lady. In the fourth stanza, the hero lies mortally wounded on the battlefield.

chivalric love

By the mid-1830s songwriters were matching another kind of music to the imagery of archaic romance: an Anglo-Italian style similar to Henry R. Bishop's in "Home, Sweet Home." The influence of Italian opera brought to Anglo-American song a new source of grace and intensity, as well as a higher (but still accessible) tone. The gently arched shape of its melodies, as well as turns, trills, and other kinds of ornamentation, lent themselves well to cultivated vocal production.

influence of opera

Why would songs portraying brave knights and protected damsels have such appeal for Americans? Part of the answer is that both medieval courtly love and nineteenth-century courtship were based on separation of the sexes. Within courtly love's idealized realm, men and women acted as virtually different species, each governed by its own rules. In fact, chivalric courtship songs grew popular in America at a time when business was separating itself from home life. The distancing of men from women and the redefining of their roles made an impact on the language and decorum of romance. It now became possible to imagine men as gladiators who jousted in the public arena by day, then returned to domestic "bowers," where they sang and were sung to.

changing gender roles

As early as the 1820s, songwriters had begun adapting the courtship song for an American setting, taking separation, not medieval romance, as their main subject. Male lovers and their ladies might be separated by shyness (the love might be secret), the social code, physical distance (journeys often sparked love songs), or death, the ultimate separation. Almost all of these songs have a male persona and dwell on the pain of separation. Elevated speech, Italianate melody, and an image of pure, nonphysical love became standard ways to express a yearning for the beloved. The songs do not show lovers coming together, touching, freely conversing, or developing an erotic attachment.

Stephen Foster was a leading master of the courtly love song. His first published composition, "Open Thy Lattice, Love" (1844), for example, is a serenade, a song type originating in the Middle Ages. The melody traces a graceful curve in compound meter, and the rhythm, as in some Italian arias, invites the singer to take a flexible tempo. The accompaniment suggests the strumming of a guitar. In the text, the man camps at the woman's window while she stays protected inside. And that tension feeds the singer's romantic fantasy. He pictures a nighttime seaside scene with the two lovers sailing off into the sunrise, the stars keeping vigil just for her.

LG 6.3

One of Foster's classic songs of courtship, "Jeanie with the Light Brown Hair" (LG 6.3), deals with permanent separation. In the text, which Foster himself wrote, Jeanie has either gone away for good or died; her admirer is left with only memories of the look, the grace, and the sound of Jeanie to sustain him. The lover goes on to recall Jeanie's smile, but he reports nothing that she ever said or thought. Jeanie trips through meadows singing, dancing, and plaiting flowers, apparently all but oblivious to her suitor's presence.

But Foster's music makes this flimsy scenario work. The first section (lines 1 and 2 of the text) is strong enough to bear plenty of repetition. And Foster takes advantage of it, using a well-worn principle of musical form: statement, restatement, contrast, and return, or **aaba form**. The tune begins high in the singer's range, with "I dream" capturing in one stroke the sense of fantasy that the song portrays. The accompaniment's repeated chords act as a rhythmic foil for the vocal line, which, after emphasizing "dream," pushes ahead in quicker notes, then falls into phase with the accompaniment on "light brown hair." Foster's next gesture neatly matches music and words: the upward leap on "vapor" encourages the singer to try for a lighter-than-air sound while reinforcing the dreaming mode of the first line.

The song's first four bars show a grace that Foster at his best could command. By starting measure 3 on the downbeat, Foster gives "borne" the emphasis due the song's first active verb—an emphasis he supports with the first chord change since the voice entered. That chord begins a harmonic progression that moves away from the tonic, just as the summer air carries the dream of Jeanie. And the phrase-ending melodic cadence ("on the summer air") is sung to harmonies that change on every beat. Thus, in just four bars of singing, Foster has taken a familiar premise—a suitor dreaming of his absent lover—and set it to music so memorable that listeners are eager to learn what will happen next.

Cover art such as the winsome portrait on Stephen Foster's "Jeanie with the Light Brown Hair" (1851) was rare before the 1830s, but by midcentury it was a regular feature of sheet music.

CD 1.19	**Listening Guide 6.3**		**"Jeanie with the Light Brown Hair"** STEPHEN C. FOSTER	

DATE: 1851

PERFORMERS: Douglas Perry, tenor, and David Starobin, guitar

GENRE: parlor song

METER: duple

FORM: strophic; each stanza in *aaba* form

WHAT TO LISTEN FOR

- supple, expressive melody
- use of *aaba* form in each stanza
- each stanza closes with quasi-operatic rhythmic freedom and a cadenza

TIMING	SECTION		TEXT	COMMENTS
0:00	introduction			The guitar establishes the pensive mood with two bars of single notes and strummed chords.
0:08	stanza 1	*a*	I dream of Jeanie with the light brown hair, Borne like a vapor on the summer air;	The singer's first phrase is accompanied by simple chords, one on each beat. The phrase ends inconclusively on a half cadence.
0:24		*a*	I see her tripping where the bright streams play, Happy as the daisies that dance on her way.	The melody repeats with new words, as the accompaniment changes to broken chords, or **arpeggios**, in which the notes of the chord are played one after another. The end of the phrase modulates to the dominant key.
0:41		*b*	Many were the wild notes her merry voice would pour, Many were the blithe birds that warbled them o'er:	A new melodic idea occurs, while the guitar reverts to simple chords and the harmony returns to the tonic key. On the last word of the phrase the steady beat momentarily ceases, with a **fermata** in the notation indicating a held chord for the guitar.
0:59			Oh!	The singer climbs up the scale in free rhythm, much like an opera singer's **cadenza**.
1:04		*a*	I dream of Jeanie with the light brown hair, Floating, like a vapor, on the soft summer air.	The opening melody returns, with arpeggiated accompaniment. In the last line the tempo slows, and another fermata on "vapor" again suggests the rhythmic flexibility of operatic singing.
1:29	interlude			The guitar repeats the introduction between stanzas.
1:36	stanza 2		I long for Jeanie with the daydawn smile, Radiant in gladness, warm with winning guile;	A literal repeat of the music.

(continued)

| | CD 1.19 | Listening Guide 6.3 | "Jeanie with the Light Brown Hair" STEPHEN C. FOSTER |

TIMING	SECTION	TEXT	COMMENTS
		I hear her melodies like joys gone by, Sighing round my heart o'er the fond hopes that die: Sighing like the night wind and sobbing like the rain, Waiting for the lost one that comes not again: Oh! I long for Jeanie, and my heart bows low, Never more to find her where the bright waters flow.	
3:05	coda		Another statement of the introduction serves as a **coda**, or tag.

NOTE This performance follows one of the many versions of the song found in sheet music publications, this one for voice and fully notated guitar accompaniment (New York: Firth, Pond & Co., 1854). Only the first two of Foster's three stanzas are sung.

Listen & Reflect

1. How does Foster's song reflect the social values evinced by parlor songs in antebellum America?

2. In what ways does the performance support those ideals?

OTHER SONGS OF SEPARATION AND YEARNING

While songs of the later nineteenth century praise the triumphs of technology—steam engines, bicycles, balloons, and automobiles—many pre–Civil War songs tend to prefer the past. Stephen Foster's "The Voice of By Gone Days" (1850), for example, announces that then was better than now and claims the sound of that older voice as a tonic for the "weary hearted." The reason is that the singer's beloved, like Foster's Jeanie, has died—or, as these lyrics would have it, she has gone to join the angels' "bless'd and happy train."

"Woodman, Spare That Tree"

Poets and songwriters searched for subjects that would trigger nostalgic yearning, and one device was to focus on inanimate objects rather than people. Henry Russell's "Woodman, Spare That Tree" (1837), which sets a text by George Pope Morris, is an example. The English-born Russell both wrote and performed his own songs, perfecting his art in the United States during the 1830s. An accomplished keyboard performer, Russell accompanied his singing on a low-backed upright piano, which allowed him to face the audience. In his autobiography he named the statesman Henry Clay, known for his power to hold an audience spellbound, as his main inspiration.

Morris's poem for "Woodman, Spare That Tree" is written in the voice of a man hailing a woodcutter who is ready to swing into action:

Woodman spare that tree!
　　Touch not a single bough;
In youth it shelter'd me,
　　And I'll protect it now;
'Twas my forefather's hand
　　That placed it near his cot[tage],
There, woodman, let it stand,
　　Thy axe shall harm it not!

Russell directs that the song be sung "with much feeling and expression." After a long piano introduction, much in the *bel canto* style of the Italian opera composers Bellini and Donizetti, the melody is cast in four sections, *aabc*.

The threat of loss hangs over "Woodman, Spare That Tree": the prospect that an ancient, majestic thing, the site of family memories, will be destroyed. Russell apparently milked the song for all it was worth, sometimes offering a spoken prologue tying it to a real-life incident. The text leaves the tree's fate unresolved, and Russell used that uncertainty to create suspense in concerts. After one performance, he wrote, an audience member, "in a very excited voice, called [out], 'Was the tree spared, sir?' 'It was,' I said. 'Thank God for that,' he answered, with a sigh of relief."

The theme of yearning and loss also pervades some blackface minstrel songs, including "Carry Me Back to Old Virginny" and "Old Folks at Home." Favorite parlor songs on the same subject include "I'll Take You Home Again, Kathleen," "Silver Threads among the Gold," and "When You and I Were Young."

SONGS OF SOCIAL REFORM AND WAR

Equipped with a piano and supplied by a flourishing, resourceful sheet music trade, the American parlor also became an arena for the singing of operatic numbers, as well as religious, comic, and topical songs. Moreover, during the early and middle 1800s, movements took shape to abolish slavery and to reform the way Americans worshiped, their drinking habits, and the treatment of women in society. Popular song was enlisted in support of these movements. Indeed, the leading singers of activist songs in the pre–Civil War years were the Hutchinsons of Milford, New Hampshire, who began singing together for pleasure and then found that they could make a career out of it. Their reform music has caught recent historians' attention, partly because it anticipates the work of later protest singers such as Pete Seeger and the young Bob Dylan (see chapter 17). But the Hutchinsons were primarily entertainers who made their mark singing music of the day for paying audiences.

THE HUTCHINSON FAMILY AND SONGS OF SOCIAL REFORM

The Hutchinsons were inspired to enter the public arena in 1840 after attending a concert of the Rainer family, a traveling troupe from Switzerland who performed traditional songs in native costume. In 1842 the Hutchinson Family

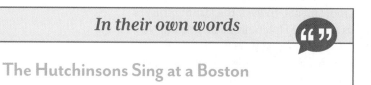

✎ From 1842 until sister Abby married in 1849, the Hutchinson Family Singers toured the United States and Great Britain, entertaining and edifying audiences with their songs.

Singers, a quartet made up of brothers Judson, John, and Asa and their young sister Abby, launched a career as a touring ensemble. Their travels, beginning in New England, took them down the Eastern Seaboard to New York, Philadelphia, and Washington, where in 1844 they sang at the White House for President John Tyler. In 1845–46 they performed in the British Isles, then returned and continued to tour the United States. Their heyday came to an end in 1849 when Abby married and left the troupe.

Entering a field dominated by foreign musicians, the Hutchinsons stressed their American origins. They seemed to play themselves onstage: members of a small-town New England family. A New York critic in 1843 praised their singing as "simple, sweet, and full of mountain melody."

The Hutchinsons' first reform-minded goal was to help reduce American consumption of alcohol, which in 1830 stood at nearly three times the per capita rate measured in 1975. During the 1830s reformers mounted an anti-drinking campaign, connecting drink to poverty, immorality, lack of family responsibility, and neglect of women and children. Their campaign succeeded: by 1845 consumption had dropped to one-fourth of what it had been in 1830. John Hutchinson took a nondrinking pledge in 1841, and from that time forward the family made a point of staying in temperance hotels when they toured. They also began early in their career to include anti-drinking songs in their concerts, and a few were published in sheet music form, helping to bring the message of sobriety into American homes.

The Hutchinsons also plunged into the fight against slavery. In 1843 they appeared at an antislavery rally in Boston's Faneuil Hall, joining with leading abolitionists, including ex-slave Frederick Douglass, who became a close friend. According to one eyewitness, slavery that day found no more forceful foe than the Hutchinson Family Singers. "Speechifying, even of the better sort," he wrote, "did less to interest, purify and subdue minds, than this irresistible Anti-Slavery music."

LG 6.4   One of the group's most effective rallying cries was "Get Off the Track!" (LG 6.4), sung to the tune of "Old Dan Tucker" and trading on that minstrel song's rough appeal. The sheet music, published in 1844, billed the piece as "a song for emancipation." When sung by the Hutchinsons, the song's impact could be overwhelming. An account written after the New England Anti-Slavery Convention in May 1844 leaves the impression that their performance was the emotional climax of the entire event.

At the same time that "Get Off the Track!" promoted antislavery fervor in general, it also acted more specifically as a campaign

In their own words   66 99

The Hutchinsons Sing at a Boston Antislavery Rally, 1844

And when they came to that chorus-cry, that gives name to the song, when they cried to the heedless pro-slavery multitude that were stupidly lingering on the track, and the engine "Liberator" coming down hard upon them, under full steam and all speed, the Liberty Bell loud ringing, and they standing like deaf men right in its whirlwind path, the way they cried "Get off the track," in defiance of all time and rule, was magnificent and sublime. . . . It was the cry of the people.

song in support of the radical abolitionist Liberty Party, whose candidate James Birney would win less than 3 percent of the popular vote in the 1844 presidential election. Along with multiple references to "liberty," evoking the party as well as the concept, Jesse Hutchinson Jr.'s lyrics warn that "Rail Roads to Emancipation / Cannot rest on *Clay* foundation," a swipe at Whig candidate Henry Clay, whose soft position on slavery alienated many abolitionist voters. The sheet music cover illustration shows a train whose engine, labeled LIBERATOR (a reference to William Lloyd Garrison's abolitionist newspaper of the same name), pulls a car labeled LIBERTY VOTES AND BALLOT BOXES, while in the distance a smaller train, its engine labeled CLAY, heads into a ditch. On top of that, Clay's Whig party had already produced its own campaign song that year, titled "Get Out of the Way!" and also sung to the tune of "Old Dan Tucker."

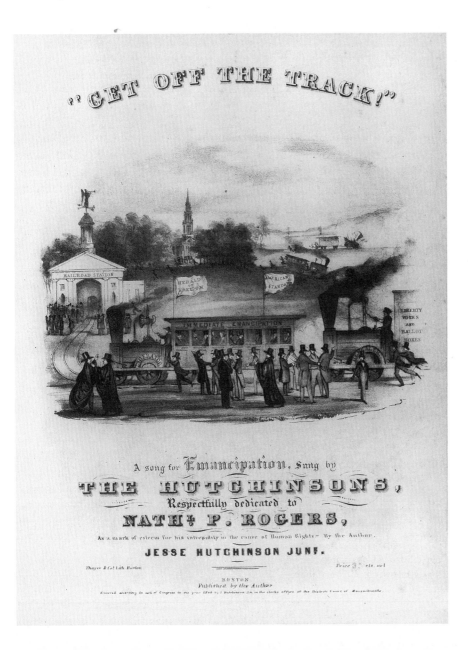

The Hutchinsons' emancipation song "Get Off the Track!," sung to the tune of the minstrel hit "Old Dan Tucker," made an especially strong impression at abolitionist meetings and rallies in the North.

| CD 1.20 | Listening Guide 6.4 | "Get Off the Track!" JESSE HUTCHINSON JR. |

DATE: 1844

PERFORMERS: The New Hutchinson Family Singers (George Berglund, Wayne Dalton, Bill Rollie, Judy Sjerven, voices; Linda Steen, piano; Robert de Cormier, director)

GENRE: song of social reform

METER: duple

FORM: strophic

WHAT TO LISTEN FOR

- alternation of solo voice and unison voices
- piano accompaniment in imitation of minstrel band
- political content of lyrics

TIMING	SECTION	TEXT	COMMENTS
0:00	introduction		The piano's introduction evokes the shrill fiddle and rhythmic accompaniment of the minstrel band.
0:07	stanza 1	Ho! The Car Emancipation Rides majestic thro' our nation Bearing on its train, the story, LIBERTY! A Nation's Glory Roll it along, Roll it along, Roll it along, thro' the Nation Freedom's Car, Emancipation.	
0:32	stanza 2	First of all the train, and greater, Speeds the dauntless *Liberator* Onward cheered amid hosannas, And the waving of Free Banners. Roll it along! Roll it along! Roll it along! spread your banners While the people shout hosannas.	Stanzas 2–5 begin each with a different solo voice, the other voices joining in for the second half of the stanza—the music that marks the chorus in "Old Dan Tucker."
0:57	stanza 3	Let the Ministers and Churches Leave behind sectarian lurches; Jump on board the Car of Freedom Ere it be too late to need them. Sound the alarm! Sound the alarm! Sound the alarm! Pulpit's thunder! Ere too late, you see your blunder.	
1:22	stanza 4	Rail Roads to emancipation Cannot rest on *Clay* foundation	

CD 1.20	**Listening Guide 6.4**		**"Get Off the Track!"** JESSE HUTCHINSON JR.

TIMING	SECTION	TEXT	COMMENTS
		And the *tracks* of *"The Magician"* Are but *Rail Roads* to perdition. Pull up the Rails! Pull up the Rails! Pull up the Rails! Emancipation Cannot rest on such foundation.	
1:47	stanza 5	All true friends of Emancipation, Haste to Freedom's Rail Road Station; Quick into the Cars get seated, All is ready, and completed. Put on the Steam! Put on the Steam! Put on the Steam! all are crying, And the Liberty Flags are flying.	
2:14	stanza 6	Hear the mighty car wheels humming! Now look out! *The Engine's coming!* Church and Statesmen! Hear the thunder! Clear the track! or you'll fall under. Get off the track! Get off the track! Get off the track! all are singing, While the *Liberty Bell* is ringing.	An *accelerando* adds excitement as the song nears its end.

Listen & Reflect

1. Steam-powered locomotives became common in the United States only gradually during the 1830s and thus were still somewhat novel in 1844. They were by far the largest, fastest, and most powerful machines in the experience of most Americans. How, then, might the train imagery have affected the impression the song made on the Hutchinsons' audiences? What sorts of images might a present-day song use to make a similar impression on today's audiences?

2. Given the obvious racism that pervades minstrelsy, what are the implications of Jesse Hutchinson's use of a minstrel tune for a song promoting the abolition of slavery?

3. In what ways does this song from 1844 resemble the 1768 broadside ballad known as "The Liberty Song" (see LG 2.1)?

Although "Old Dan Tucker" is in verse-and-chorus form, "Get Off the Track!" adds new lyrics every time the chorus rolls around; the resulting form is thus best described as strophic. The performers heard on the accompanying recording sing six of the song's eleven stanzas or **strophes**. Their performance holds closely to the sheet music, with only two significant changes: occasional harmonizing where the sheet music simply shows one vocal melody line, and an **accelerando**, a gradual increase in tempo, for the last stanza, vividly evoking the train's snowballing momentum.

As songwriters the Hutchinsons circulated their work in sheet music form, but their talent lay especially in public performing. When singing for an audience, they convinced spectators of the emotional truth of what they were hearing. Yet none of the compositions bearing their name gained lasting popularity.

SONGS OF THE CIVIL WAR

When war erupted in April 1861 between the Northern and Southern states, the sheet music industry responded with vigor. The songs of the Civil War, fueled by patriotic feelings and commerce, brought together in a new cause many of the themes associated with parlor songs: myth making, sentimentality, yearning, reform, and loss.

Song provided a way for the Union and the Confederacy to define their ideals. Just two days after Virginia left the Union on April 17, a pro-secessionist mob in Baltimore attacked a regiment of Union troops from Massachusetts, and in the fighting that followed, lives were lost on both sides. The incident inspired one of the first enduring songs of the war. James Ryder Randall, native Baltimorean, wrote the words just after the attack:

"Maryland, My Maryland"

> The despot's heel is on thy shore,
>   Maryland!
> His torch is at thy temple door,
>   Maryland!
> Avenge the patriotic gore
> That flecked the streets of Baltimore,
> And be the battle-queen of yore,
>   Maryland! My Maryland!

Randall's poem, immediately published in newspapers, urges fellow Marylanders to resist federal tyranny. His appeal is cast in elevated language familiar from the earlier courtship song, with some biblical diction mixed in:

> For life and death, for woe and weal,
> Thy peerless chivalry reveal,
> And gird thy beauteous limbs with steel,
>   Maryland! My Maryland!

In October 1861 Randall's words appeared in a sheet music version, set to the German Christmas song "O Tannenbaum" (O Christmas Tree).

"Maryland, My Maryland" is less patriotic than chauvinistic. Patriotic expressions reflect a love of country and concern for its well-being, but Randall's song is short on love and long on vengeance. Expressing total allegiance to one side and implacable hatred of the other, it calls fellow countrymen names—"tyrants," "vandals," "Northern scum"—that undercut the two sides' common ground. Its tone, found in both Northern and Southern songs, surely helped to create an emotional climate in which all-out war could be waged.

In a parallel vein, the pro-Union "Battle-Hymn of the Republic," with words by Julia Ward Howe, preaches how glorious it is to fall in step beside an omnipotent God marching into battle at the head of a virtuous (Northern) army. Howe's poem, which celebrates the birth and sacrifice of Jesus while also conveying the unforgiving tone of Old Testament prophecy, was published in January 1862. A few months later, these words, with the "Glory, Hallelujah" refrain added, were published in sheet music form, sung to a Methodist hymn tune of the 1850s. The music's character and the added refrain take the edge off the harsh message of Howe's words, and the cry of joy at the end of each stanza emphasizes camaraderie and high spirits over revenge. Like many enduring American songs, this one was made by several hands—poet, composer, arranger—some of them unknown.

"Battle-Hymn of the Republic"

"The Battle Cry of Freedom" (1862; LG 6.5) was written by George F. Root as a recruiting song for the Union army. Root's song offers a mix of soul-stirring ingredients: the flag, a collective cheer, the notion of fighting for a high ideal, a blunt statement of the Union's goal ("Down with the traitor, / Up with the Star"), and a refrain that, like "Glory, Hallelujah," could easily be learned on the spot. Written in march time, "The Battle Cry of Freedom" presents three memorable melodic ideas, associated with the words "Yes, we'll rally round the flag," "Shouting the battle cry of Freedom," and "The Union forever, / Hurrah boys, hurrah!" Every musical phrase is a statement or variant of one of these three, keeping the melodic energy at a high level. **Dotted rhythms**—the regular alternation of long and short notes, here subdividing the beat—tie the melodic phrases together, and the syncopation in the chorus on the song's highest pitch casts the word "forever" into relief with a climactic jolt. When these musical details, supported by purposeful harmony, are linked to the resonant phrases in the text, there is little mystery why "The Battle Cry of Freedom" became popular.

LG 6.5

The signature song of the Confederacy also originated in the North. "Dixie," attributed to Ohio-born minstrel Dan Emmett and introduced on a New York stage in 1859, found its way the following year to New Orleans, where it caused a sensation. Thus, even before the Civil War broke out, "Dixie" was a favorite Southern song. Here are the first verse and chorus as they appeared in the original sheet music:

"Dixie"

> I wish I was in de land ob cotton,
> Old times dar am not forgotten,
>> Look away! Look away! Look away! Dixie Land.
> In Dixie Land whar I was born in,
> Early on one frosty mornin,
>> Look away! Look away! Look away! Dixie Land.
>
> Dan I wish I was in Dixie,
>> Hooray! Hooray!
> In Dixie Land, I'll take my stand,
>> To lib and die in Dixie.
> Away, Away, Away down south in Dixie.
> Away, Away, Away down south in Dixie.

	CD 1.21	Listening Guide 6.5	"The Battle Cry of Freedom" GEORGE F. ROOT

DATE: 1862
PERFORMERS: The Gregg Smith Singers
GENRE: Civil War song
METER: duple
FORM: verse and chorus

WHAT TO LISTEN FOR

- stirring march rhythm with dotted notes
- alternation of unison singing in verses and block chord harmonies in chorus

TIMING	SECTION	TEXT	COMMENTS
0:00	introduction		The piano introduction is drawn from the last four bars of the chorus.
0:07	verse 1	Yes we'll rally round the flag, boys, we'll rally once again, Shouting the battle cry of freedom, We will rally from the hillside, we'll gather from the plain, Shouting the battle cry of freedom!	The voices sing the melody in unison, as it is presented in the sheet music.
0:24	chorus	The Union forever! Hurrah, boys, hurrah! Down with the traitor, up with the star; While we rally round the flag, boys, rally once again, Shouting the battle cry of freedom!	The chorus is sung in four-part block chords (homophonic texture), as notated in the sheet music.
0:40	interlude		The piano introduction is repeated between verses as an interlude.
0:47	verse 2	We will welcome to our numbers the loyal, true and brave, Shouting the battle cry of freedom! And although he may be poor, he shall never be a slave, Shouting the battle cry of freedom!	Unison.
1:04	chorus	The Union forever! . . .	Block chords.

NOTE This performance, by a male chorus with piano accompaniment, includes two of the song's four verses.

Listen & Reflect

1. Root's sheet music does not specify whether the verses should be sung by a solo voice or multiple voices in unison, and his four-voice arrangement at the chorus implies a mixed chorus of men and women. How might a performance by a soloist or mixed voices differ from this one?

2. Compare "The Battle Cry of Freedom" with "The Liberty Song" (see LG 2.1). How are these two wartime political songs similar, and how are they different? Along the same lines, how does this song compare with "Get Off the Track!" (see LG 6.4), which predates the war?

What made "Dixie" a Southern favorite? Why would white people fighting to preserve slavery express their solidarity in the comic dialect of a minstrel show slave? And why would a song without standard patriotic trappings command such allegiance? While there are no clear answers to these questions, it does seem that Emmett's song offered a myth of the South so inviting that Southerners wholeheartedly embraced it.

The words and images of "Dixie" picture the South as a place to love, supporting that view with homey details. The tune, however, is probably most responsible for the song's electric appeal. Neither a march nor a hymn, "Dixie" is a dance written to accompany the jaunty strut of a minstrel show **walkaround**, where performers cavorted in what was taken to be the manner of Southern plantation hands. When combined with its words, the tune kindles the kind of enthusiasm that has long made Southerners want to hoot and holler, wave banners, and throw hats in the air. The day after the South's military surrender in April 1865, President Abraham Lincoln was serenaded at the White House by jubilant citizens and several bands. After bantering with the crowd, Lincoln asked the bands to play "Dixie" because the North had recaptured it, and besides, he said, it was "one of the best tunes I have ever heard." But "Dixie" was never included in the North's spoils of war. By 1865 it was so firmly linked to the South and the mood of defiance that lingered long after the Confederate army surrendered that it could not be reclaimed by the nation as a whole.

Rather than centering on inspiration, patriotism, and revenge, many songs took the human tragedy of the Civil War as their theme. Some were set on the battlefield. Others dwelled on the feelings of those who remained at home. One of the most popular, Henry Tucker and Charles C. Sawyer's "Weeping, Sad and Lonely" (1862), is sung by the beloved of a Northern soldier who is away at the front. She addresses him as if in a letter:

"Weeping, Sad and Lonely"

> Dearest love, do you remember
> When we last did meet,
> How you told me that you loved me,
> Kneeling at my feet?
> Oh! how proud you stood before me,
> In your suit of blue,
> When you vow'd to me and country,
> Ever to be true.
>
> > Weeping, sad and lonely
> > Hopes and fears, how vain (yet praying)
> > When this cruel war is over,
> > Praying! that we meet again.

The singer goes on to confess that "many cruel fancies" haunt her. She imagines her soldier wounded, fearing that no one will comfort him. In the last verse, however, she decides that, fighting in a noble cause, he will receive the protection of angels. The perennial themes of romantic separation and patriotism are here brought together in a single parlor song.

Few songs of the Civil War try to deal with the connection between patriotic glory and the price that soldiers pursuing it are asked to pay. But one exception, "Tenting on the Old Camp Ground" by Walter Kittredge, looks beyond the standard language of heroism. The center of gravity is the refrain, where, rather than

"Tenting on the Old Camp Ground"

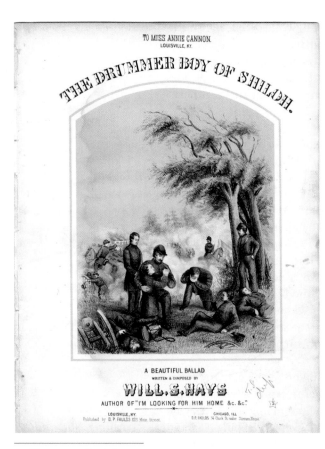

A BEAUTIFUL BALLAD

WRITTEN & COMPOSED BY

WILL.S.HAYS

AUTHOR OF "I'M LOOKING FOR HIM HOME &c. &c."

LOUISVILLE, KY.

Published by D. P. FAULDS 221 Main Street.

CHICAGO, ILL.

D. P. FAULDS 14 Clark St. under Sherman House.

〰 The cover of Will S. Hays's "The Drummer Boy of Shiloh" (1863) pictures the final prayer of a wounded noncombatant on the brink of death.

raising their voices in ecstatic, comradely shouts, soldiers sing in four-part harmony about war weariness. Although the song begins in a jaunty march tempo, that mood gradually loses steam, and the final lines are sung to rolled, sustained piano chords. Imagination combines with the idiom of the sentimental song to create a mood of numb resignation: an authentic response to the Civil War.

Testifying to the war's mindless brutality, a Rhode Island volunteer recalled what happened when several Union soldiers entered the house of a Confederate family in Fredericksburg, Virginia, and listened as a private played "really fine music" on the piano. "As he ceases playing, another says, 'Did you ever see me play?' and, seizing his rifle, he brings it down full force upon the keyboard, smashing it to splinters." That action signaled the soldiers to go on a rampage, destroying the remaining furniture in the house. It was in response to incidents like this one, as well as to battles in the field, that a song like "Tenting on the Old Camp Ground" explored the gap between the heroic and the sentimental, pondered what war could lead decent men to do, and thus reached a level of understanding that neither standard approach could manage.

QUESTIONS FOR DISCUSSION AND REVIEW

1. What problems may arise when we use minstrelsy to study nineteenth-century African American culture?

2. How did changing gender roles affect the nineteenth-century music industry?

3. What are some present-day examples of the use of music to effect social change? How are these examples similar to or different from the songs of the Hutchinson family or Civil War songs?

4. Looking back to the time line at the beginning of Part 1, which of these events had you heard of before reading the ensuing chapters? What can you connect in some way to your own musical life?

FURTHER READING

Cockrell, Dale. *Demons of Disorder: Early Blackface Minstrels and Their World.* Cambridge: Cambridge University Press, 1995.

Finson, Jon W. *The Voices That Are Gone: Themes in Nineteenth-Century American Popular Song.* New York: Oxford University Press, 1994.

Gac, Scott. *Singing for Freedom: The Hutchinson Family Singers and the Nineteenth-Century Culture of Antebellum Reform.* New Haven, CT: Yale University Press, 2007.

Kasson, John F. *Rudeness and Civility: Manners in Nineteenth-Century Urban America.* New York: Hill and Wang, 1990.

Lott, Eric. *Love and Theft: Blackface Minstrelsy and the American Working Class.* New York: Oxford University Press, 1995.

Mahar, William J. *Behind the Burnt Cork Mask: Early Blackface Minstrelsy and Antebellum American Popular Culture.* Urbana: University of Illinois Press, 1999.

Nathan, Hans. *Dan Emmett and the Rise of Early Negro Minstrelsy.* Norman: University of Oklahoma Press, 1962.

Watkins, Mel. *On the Real Side, Laughing, Lying, and Signifying: The Underground Tradition of African-American Humor That Transformed American Culture, from Slavery to Richard Pryor.* New York: Simon and Schuster, 1994.

FURTHER LISTENING

The Early Minstrel Show. New World Records 80338-2, 1985; CD reissue 1998.

TIMELINE: 1861–1918

1861 Reverend Lewis C. Lockwood publishes "Go Down Moses" in an abolitionist newspaper

1865 Founding of the Theodore Thomas Orchestra

1867 Publication of *Slave Songs of the United States*

1868, 1870 Fourteenth and Fifteenth Amendments extend citizenship and voting rights to African American men

1871 Founding of the Fisk Jubilee Singers

1876 Ira Sankey, *Gospel Hymns*

1877 Thomas A. Edison invents the phonograph

1879 Bureau of Indian Ethnology created at the Smithsonian Institution

1881 Founding of the Boston Symphony Orchestra

1882 First performances of "Buffalo Bill Cody's Wild West"

1882 Theodore Baker, *Über die Musik der nordamerikanischen Wilden* (On the Music of the North American Indians)

1883–98 Francis James Child, *The English and Scottish Popular Ballads*

1884 M. Witmark & Sons, Tin Pan Alley publisher, founded in New York City

1890 Massacre at Wounded Knee, South Dakota

AMERICA'S MUSIC
FROM THE CIVIL WAR THROUGH WORLD WAR I

fter the Civil War, the United States entered a phase of geographic expansion, as western territories became states; population growth, with an attendant increase in the size and number of major cities; and economic development, as new technologies spurred the nation's industrialization. Connected to these changes, and in contrast to the antebellum years, America's musical culture in the period from the Civil War to World War I witnessed a more pronounced separation between the three spheres of music making. In the classical sphere, the establishment of permanent orchestras, opera companies, and music conservatories provided the institutional support for new generations of skilled composers and performers. In the popular sphere, publishers of parlor songs laid the groundwork for a popular music industry in which sheet music, the standard stock in trade, was eventually joined by new products that resulted from emergent technologies: piano rolls and phonograph records. In the traditional sphere, pioneering ethnologists created the first archives of folk music, revealing the abundance of music making outside the classical and popular marketplaces. From the music of American Indians to the British ballads of Appalachia, and from the Spanish songs of the Southwest to the spirituals of former slaves, American folk music began to be written down, recorded, and studied as part of the nation's cultural heritage. Despite this heightened differentiation, however, the three spheres of classical, popular, and traditional music continued to interact in complex and mutually enriching ways.

◄ By 1900, innovations in printing made colorful sheet music covers the norm for popular song publishers.

1891 Leopold Vincent, *Alliance and Labor Songster*

1892 John Philip Sousa forms the Sousa Band

1893 Alice C. Fletcher, *Study of Omaha Indian Music*

1896 Edward MacDowell becomes the first professor of music at Columbia University, composes *Woodland Sketches*

1896 Ernest Hogan, "All Coons Look Alike to Me"

1896 *Plessy v. Ferguson* legalizes segregation

1896 Boston Symphony Orchestra premieres Amy Beach's *Gaelic* Symphony

1903 Will Marion Cook's *In Dahomey* opens on Broadway

1909 Revision of copyright law grants composers rights to mechanical royalties

1911 Alice C. Fletcher and Francis La Flesche, *The Omaha Tribe*, a pioneering work of ethnomusicology

1914 Irene and Vernon Castle, *Modern Dancing*

1916 Harry T. Burleigh, *Jubilee Songs of the United States of America*

1917 Cecil Sharp and Olive Dame Campbell, *Folk Songs of the Southern Appalachians*

1918 Frances Densmore, *Teton Sioux Music*

1918 *Sinbad*, starring Al Jolson, opens on Broadway

CHAPTER 7

"AFTER THE BALL"

Band Music, Gospel Hymns, and Popular Songs after the Civil War

Following the Civil War, the United States underwent a transformation from a primarily agricultural to a primarily industrial economy. Cities grew, while the proportion of people living in rural areas shrank. The public sphere became more commercialized, with greater emphasis on nationally distributed consumer goods. In the face of these changes, music continued to assert traditional small-town values and the tenets of old-time religion, even as the means for producing and disseminating that music were changing. This chapter describes some key features of that transformation: the professionalization of the wind band, the origins of gospel hymns patterned on popular song, the rise of the phonograph and vaudeville as new ways to popularize music, and the consolidation of the popular music industry in New York City.

BAND MUSIC AFTER THE CIVIL WAR

In August 1898 a newspaper in Wayne County, Pennsylvania, carried a poem that declared the Keystone Band of Lake Como, in the state's northeast corner, one of the town's chief assets.

> The grand old town of Como lies resting 'neath the hills,
> While its waters run on daily, in quiet rippling rills;
> And its sights and scenes are glorious—in fact, are simply grand,
> But there's one thing does excel all else—it's the music of its band.

Local pride stands behind this glimpse of an amateur group that played for summer picnics, winter entertainments, and civic occasions as they arose. People outside Lake Como may not have thought much of the Keystone Band, but the group was valued at home because the isolation of rural towns encouraged self-sufficiency. Local bands affirmed local self-respect. In newspapers of the time, there are almost no critical reviews of any band performance.

The Keystone Band stands in a line that began in the 1700s with local militia bands, blossomed during the Civil War into a national patriotic movement, and continued as an amateur pastime even after elite professional wind bands came into prominence (see chapters 2 and 5). The professional band, directed in the postwar years by such bandleaders as Patrick S. Gilmore and John Philip Sousa, brought polished musical performances to the ears of more Americans than any other ensemble. But behind bands like Sousa's lay a vast network of amateur groups that, like church choirs, were part of many people's musical experience as performers and listeners.

Between the Civil War and World War I, the wind band flourished, for it was well matched to the character of town and city life. As technological progress gave people more leisure time, civic functions multiplied: parades, picnics, dedications, store openings, as well as concerts, dances, and other social functions. By playing music that the public enjoyed, at a volume that could be heard outdoors, a band enlivened these occasions. In cities, the performers might be professionals who played in theater orchestras during the winter season. In villages and towns, players of all ages were recruited to form amateur bands. Band instruments were relatively inexpensive, and the music required only modest technique. The playing of amateur bands reverberated across the land in these years, bearers of a tradition of democratic music making that has continued into the twenty-first century.

Lookout Mountain, Tennessee, is the site of this 1864 photograph of a Civil War brass band's performance.

PATRICK S. GILMORE

At the same time that amateur bands were on the ascendancy, other musicians were working toward raising the band's artistic and professional status. A key figure in steering the wind band's course after 1865 was Patrick S. Gilmore, a bandmaster who proved that the band could cut loose from military affiliation and succeed as an independent ensemble in the public arena.

Born in Ireland in 1829, Gilmore immigrated to the United States in 1849 as a cornetist. He settled in Boston and began in the early 1850s to lead bands, including the Salem Brass Band, which he took over in 1855. The next year, Gilmore engaged the keyed-bugle virtuoso Ned Kendall in a public competition. Neither was judged to have won the contest, but with a shrewd gift for promotion, Gilmore parlayed his challenge into public recognition for himself and the cornet.

In 1858 Gilmore resigned from the Salem Brass Band and founded Gilmore's Band, which made its debut at the Boston Music Hall in April 1859. The group was a professional ensemble, with the leader in charge of both its artistic and business sides. Gilmore conducted the band, supplied uniforms for his thirty-two players, chose the music, booked engagements, and handled all other details. He also collected the profits.

The outbreak of the Civil War in April 1861 interrupted the successful routine of Gilmore's band, which became part of a Massachusetts regiment. When all volunteer military bands were mustered out of the Union army in August 1862, Gilmore and his musicians returned to Boston, playing concerts to sustain public morale. In 1864 he accompanied a band to New Orleans, where he staged a giant musical event celebrating the inauguration of a new governor: a performance by a "Grand National Band" boasting some five hundred players and a chorus of five thousand schoolchildren.

Gilmore's grandiose streak was soon to find an even grander focus. In June 1869, mindful that the war's end had not soothed the bitterness between North and South, he organized a National Peace Jubilee in Boston, a musical event of unprecedented scope. Gilmore assembled vast forces: an orchestra of five

the National Peace Jubilee

hundred, a band of one thousand, a chorus of ten thousand, and many famous soloists. Over a five-day span, an ambitious program of concerts took place, including symphonic music, oratorio excerpts, band music, and the singing of schoolchildren. The program for one of the concerts reveals that, for all his emphasis on gargantuan effects, Gilmore took care to vary his selections. The concert began with a huge orchestra featuring some four dozen trumpeters on the solo part of a French operatic overture. A choral hymn followed, and then a newly composed march for band and orchestra combined. Next came a soprano aria, providing a contrast so that the following number—Verdi's "Anvil" Chorus, with a hundred Boston firefighters pounding real anvils—could roar forth in all its splendor. Gilmore then relied on the patriotic familiarity of "Hail Columbia" for a finale.

The National Peace Jubilee of 1869 testifies to the wind band's prominent place in American life. For it was a bandleader who conceived and organized this event, an artistic and financial success for which an entire region pooled its musical resources. While the sheer number of musicians involved was remarkable, so was the participation of all manner of music makers: European-born conductors, solo singers and players, church musicians, whole choirs, public school teachers, orchestra players, bandsmen, and children—not to mention the Boston Fire Department. Gilmore, the only musician in Boston with ties to such a wide community, was the catalyst that made the enterprise work.

JOHN PHILIP SOUSA

Until his death in 1892, Gilmore led one of the first professional wind bands in the United States. And in 1892 John Philip Sousa formed the band that set the professional standard from that time forward. Sousa is a key figure in American music history. As a prolific composer for the stage and concert hall, he put his stamp on a well-known popular form: the march. As a conductor, he thrilled audiences with a blend of showmanship and polished performance. When Sousa arrived on the scene, the wind band was already a leading provider of music to the public, but by the time his performing career ended in 1931, the professional band was a thing of the past, and an amateur reincarnation—the school band—had begun to flourish.

Born in 1854 in Washington, D.C., the son of a U.S. Marine Band member, Sousa began playing violin as a boy. He studied in a local conservatory of music and at age fourteen entered the Marine Band's apprenticeship program. Discharged from the Marine Corps in 1875, he settled in Philadelphia, played in theater orchestras, developed his conducting skills, and returned to Washington in 1880, at the age of twenty-five, as leader of the Marine Band. During his dozen years in that post, Sousa also composed prolifically, especially marches and operettas, the lighter cousins to grand opera. In 1892 he moved to New York and formed his own band, which at first contained forty-six members, including some who left Gilmore's band when the leader died. By the 1920s Sousa's band numbered about seventy.

Sousa and his men proved a popular draw at fairs and expositions, settling in for weeks at a time. The band also spent half the year or more touring North America by rail. European trips were organized in the early 1900s, and a world tour in 1910–11. With concerts seven days a week and usually twice a day, Sousa's tours were not for the faint of lip. During one week-long swing through southern Michigan in 1913, the band played fourteen concerts in twelve cities.

John Philip Sousa
(1854–1932)

Boasting shiny instruments and dressed in military-style uniforms, Sousa's men projected a spit-and-polish demeanor and played as if they were a single, well-tuned instrument. In concerts, Sousa liked to begin with a classical work such as an overture. When the number ended and applause began, rather than leaving the stage, he would turn back to the musicians, call out the name of the first encore—perhaps a popular song arrangement or a Sousa march—and give the downbeat before the applause had died away. That encore might be followed by another; or Sousa might move on to the next number printed in the program. Not knowing what music to expect, the audience was kept in a state of anticipation. And so were the players.

The second scheduled number typically featured an instrumental soloist. Next came another ensemble piece, such as a suite by Sousa—perhaps his 1910 work *Dwellers of the Western World,* whose three movements are titled "The Red Man," "The White Man," and "The Black Man." A vocal selection usually followed, sung by the band's soprano soloist, and a rousing instrumental number completed the first half. Except for the last, all these selections were encored. The second half continued in a similar vein. From a variety of music—classical and popular, vocal and instrumental, soft and loud, solo and ensemble—Sousa the conductor wove collages of sound on the spot, responding to the occasion and the atmosphere in the hall.

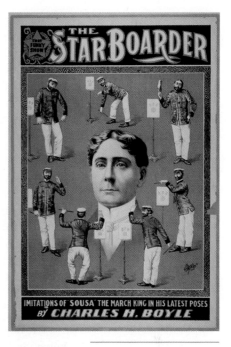

Sousa's flamboyant conducting made him a favorite of cartoonists and impressionists.

Spontaneity and showmanship aside, Sousa's band had the skill to play classical works originally written for orchestra. Sousa liked to say that as well as entertaining audiences, he hoped to educate them. Richard Wagner, whom Sousa once called "the Shakespeare of music," was a particular favorite; the band also played Sousa's arrangements of Edvard Grieg and Richard Strauss, not to mention older works like Bach's Toccata and Fugue in D Minor.

Although Sousa made no attempt to hide his distaste for ragtime dance (see chapter 10), he was willing to include ragtime music in his concerts. Audiences seemed to love ragtime, and Sousa believed that his band's performances raised the music above lower-class origins. The concept of "high" and "low" musical values was embraced by many musicians and critics of that day, including Sousa. In 1899 he likened a syncopated tune to a low-born woman made respectable by the band's attentions. "I have washed its face, put a clean dress on it, put a frill around its neck," Sousa wrote. "It is now an attractive thing, entirely different from the frowzly-headed thing of the gutter."

Sousa's marches

Sousa's best-known compositions are his marches. Like dance music, the **march** is music for the movement of human bodies, and like most popular dance music it features a steady beat, regular phrase structure, and repeated sections. For Sousa, however, the beat of his marches was not just steady; it was "military." Growing up in the nation's capital, Sousa was six years old when the Civil War began. He spent his youth and young manhood connected with the Marine Band, which his father served and he himself would conduct. His capturing of a martial tone in marches like "The Gladiator" and "The Gallant Seventh" summoned others to celebrate America's fighting spirit, through which, he believed, democracy had been won and would be preserved.

In all, Sousa composed 136 marches, three-quarters of which follow a standard musical form that he adopted around 1880, though he did not invent it.

march forms

A brief, four-bar introduction is followed by two repeated strains (AABB), often sixteen bars each. Next comes the trio, in a new key and sometimes ushered in by a short transition. The trio begins with a singing, **cantabile** melody for the third strain (C), which typically is played simply and softly. Sousa's marches then follow one of two options. The singing melody may simply be followed by a fourth strain (D), in the key of the trio but now blossoming into the sound of the full band. This "short" or "regimental" march form may be diagrammed as follows:

Introduction | AABB | (transition) CCDD

In a "long" or "military" march form, the singing trio melody leads into a contrasting break strain, sometimes called a "dogfight," in which high and low instruments exchange short, choppy phrases at a loud dynamic level and with agitated, unsettled harmony. The singing melody then returns in a triumphant blaze of glory. Another pass through the break strain and the triumphant melody brings the march to a close. The long form thus may be diagrammed as follows (with D indicating the break strain):

Introduction | AABB | CDCDC

The Sousa band consisted of three instrumental sections—trumpets, trombones and euphoniums, and clarinets—that might carry a melody, with the rest (flutes, saxophones, French horns, tuba, and percussion) filling in the texture. In peak moments of a Sousa march, the main tune is often doubled in two octaves or even three, while other voices present one or more countermelodies. The musical space, chopped into units of predictable length, brims with melody and **counterpoint**—a prime reason Sousa's marches are still relished today.

Catchy tunes are another key feature: most were written by Sousa himself, but more than a quarter of his marches quote melodies that were already well known or composed for another purpose. The *Revival March* of 1876, for example, is built around the gospel hymn "Sweet By and By," and *Ancient and Honorable Artillery Company* (1924) features "Auld Lang Syne." In several other marches, Sousa recycled melodies composed for his operettas—for example, the *El Capitan* march (1896) borrows melodies from his operetta *El Capitan*, written the previous year. By far Sousa's most successful stage work, *El Capitan* toured North America for four years and played another six months in England. As with other popular music of the day, Sousa and his publishers milked the marches for commercial gain by arranging them for an astonishing variety of combinations. Published in both band and orchestra arrangements, the *El Capitan* march was also available for piano (two, four, or six hands); banjo; guitar; guitar duet; mandolin; mandolin and piano; mandolin, piano, and guitar; mandolin and guitar; two mandolins and piano; two mandolins and guitar; zither; and two zithers. Sousa copyrighted each of these versions separately; most were aimed at the vast market of amateur performers.

march arrangements

LG 7.1

In *The Stars and Stripes Forever* (1897; LG 7.1) Sousa composed an American classic by inventing for the trio a memorable, songlike melody (the C strain) and then playing it off against a contrasting break strain (D). Cast in two halves, the trio's melody fills thirty-two bars of duple meter, comprising four phrases of eight bars each in the pattern *abac*. The melody traces a climactic curve through those four phrases. At first it moves entirely in **conjunct** motion—movement by

| CD 1.22 | Listening Guide 7.1 | *The Stars and Stripes Forever* JOHN PHILIP SOUSA |

DATE: 1897
PERFORMERS: The U.S. Marine Band
GENRE: march
METER: duple
FORM: long march

WHAT TO LISTEN FOR

- multiple strains, each melodically distinct and each repeated
- key change at trio
- contrasting texture at break strain
- addition of countermelodies (piccolo, then trombones) at repetitions of trio strain

TIMING	SECTION	COMMENTS
0:00	introduction	Four-bar introduction: full band playing a single melodic line in octaves, then dividing into harmony. Syncopation in bar 2 foreshadows later syncopation
0:03	A	Sprightly 16-bar melody in trumpets, doubled in high woodwinds; second half (bars 9–16) alternates soft and loud in 2-bar units.
0:17	A	Literal repeat of A.
0:31	B	New 16-bar melody stated by trumpets and trombones in octaves. Syncopation in bar 5.
0:46	B	Repeat of B adds contrasting soft and loud dynamics in 4-bar units.
1:00	trio C	Subdominant key. Lyrical 32-bar melody. Syncopation at bar 13.
1:29	D	Break strain (24 bars): New texture of alternating low- and high-register instruments, agitated harmony, active rhythms.
1:51	C	Lyrical melody combined with a new countermelody in piccolos suggesting Revolutionary-era fifes.
2:19	D	Repeat of break strain.
2:41	C	Lyrical melody combined with piccolo countermelody and new low-register countermelody in trombones.

Listen & Reflect

1. How does Sousa make use of the resources of the wind band; in other words, what makes this music particularly well suited to the wind band?

2. Conversely, what are some features of this music that might survive if it were played by any of the other instrumental combinations mentioned in the text in relation to Sousa's march *El Capitan*?

3. In other words, what features of this music are entirely independent of the sound of the wind band?

steps and thirds—in circular, undulating melodic shapes that avoid the tonic pitch, A flat. A touch of syncopation and the largest interval yet, a descending fifth, mark the halfway point (bars 14–16). The second half begins like the first, but the range continues to widen. The tonic A flat is heard for the first time at bar 24, and having avoided it for so long, Sousa now finds two ways to emphasize it. First, he sets it at the top of an octave leap (bars 26–27), the melody's largest interval. Second, after holding that high note for more than a bar, he invents a new, fast-moving motive centered on the tonic and moving in **disjunct** motion—with more leaps—to bring the tune to a resolute close in a rush of activity.

Sousa follows the trio with a break strain that is virtuosic for the lower brass, unusually active in rhythm and harmony, and without a hint of tunefulness—strongly contrasting with the trio's lyric mood. When the trio returns, it sounds all the more fresh with the addition of a new countermelody in the piccolo section. After the break strain is heard again, the trio tune returns once more, this time with percussion in full cry and a new low-register trombone countermelody to balance the piccolos on top. *The Stars and Stripes Forever* goes out with the band's full artillery blazing: a deft blend of lyric melody, historical reference (the piccolo sound recalls fifes), and military clamor.

amateur and professional bands

With Sousa's marches among the varied pieces in their repertories, both amateur and professional bands flourished at the turn of the century. Amateur bands included lodge bands, industrial bands, ethnic bands (German, Italian, African American, even American Indian bands), children's bands, and institutional bands, including prison groups. Around 1913 the young Louis Armstrong was playing cornet in a reform school band in New Orleans. Professional groups included not only military and concert bands like Sousa's but also circus bands and even family bands that toured on entertainment circuits. New Hampshire–born Helen May Butler, a violinist and cornetist, organized and led a professional Ladies Military Band during the century's early years. The band's concert performances between 1900 and 1913 include 203 appearances in Boston, 110 in Buffalo, 126 in St. Louis, and 130 in Charleston. Presenting "music for the American people, by American composers, played by American girls," Butler and her musicians bucked stereotypes of the time by showing that women could endure the hardships of touring life and please enough paying customers to survive in the music business.

SOUSA AND RECORDED MUSIC

Thomas A. Edison invented the phonograph in 1877. By 1890 bands were beginning to make recordings, and Sousa, as the leader of two famous bands, took part. By mid-1892 he had conducted the U.S. Marine Band in more than two hundred recordings, and the Sousa band made more than four times that many between 1897 and the early 1920s. Yet Sousa disliked the phonograph and conducted very few of his own band's recordings. As an artist-businessman, he faced a choice: should he block the band from recording altogether, or should he use the medium to keep the band's name before the public? In choosing the second course, Sousa recognized the power of recordings to attract audiences to his concerts. He quelled his own doubts by turning the band's recording sessions over to other conductors, chiefly band members.

What were Sousa's qualms about recordings? For one thing, recording technique around 1890, when Sousa was first involved, was so primitive that little thought could be given to artistry. With the invention of the electric microphone still more than three decades in the future, musicians had to crowd around a horn that directed sound to a needle that cut grooves in the recording disc or cylinder—a purely mechanical (nonelectric) process, more or less the reverse of the playback process. Recordings might do a fair job of capturing a solo singer or instrumentalist, but the sound of a full band was beyond the limits of the era's technology. Besides, the reproduction of multiple copies from one master recording was a process still under development. A photo of the Marine Band making cylinder recordings shows ten Graphophone machines arranged in front of the band. After an announcer shouted the title of the selection, the band would perform the work in an abridgement that lasted about two minutes. New wax cylinders were then placed on the machines, and the process was repeated. In this way, ten recordings of a march could be made every few minutes.

early recordings' limitations

Sousa mistrusted an enterprise that placed music in the service of technology. He also deplored the record companies' refusal in those early days to pay composers for the use of their works, and he lobbied hard for a change in copyright law that would be more favorable to composers. The 1909 copyright revision included new language granting composers rights to "mechanical" royalties for the reproduction of their music in player piano rolls and phonograph records—a term, still in use today, redolent of a time when people listened to music played on a wind-up contraption.

the 1909 Copyright Act

But more than that, Sousa considered recordings an assault on the ecology of musical life. He testified at a congressional hearing in 1906 that the phonograph was discouraging many Americans from doing their own singing and playing, a trend that could "ruin the artistic development of music in this country." Sousa remembered growing up in Washington at a time when "in front of every house in the summer evenings you would find young people together singing the songs of the day or the old songs." But now, he complained, "you hear these infernal machines

Published in 1891, this photograph shows the U.S. Marine Band recording in the Washington studio of the Columbia Phonograph Company. Note the multiple recording horns.

going night and day." In Sousa's view, the change was bad for the art of music, which ought to develop "from the people." "If you do not make the people executants," he told the congressmen, "you make them dependent on the machines."

Near the end of his life (he died at age seventy-seven in 1932), Sousa could look back on his active years as a time of robust growth for amateur performance in America. Music teaching was widespread, and a vast range of music and musical information was published. The instrument business, from pianos to winds and strings, was booming. Choral societies existed in virtually every sizable city. Glee clubs, choruses, and banjo and mandolin clubs flourished on college campuses. The piano was the parlor instrument par excellence, and many could play it. And amateur bands flourished. The growing appetite for music was being fed chiefly by amateur singers and players for their own delight and edification. But Sousa worried that the phonograph's encouragement of consumption without participation threatened the base of amateur performers whose love of music sustained the work of professionals.

participation versus consumption

By the time the United States entered World War I, tours by Sousa, other professional outfits, and circus bands, plus the growing circulation of phonograph records, had brought the sound of polished wind ensemble playing to more and more listeners. And bands were only part of the tide of professional music making that swept across the nation at the dawn of the twentieth century. Theaters were built where audiences could gather to watch and listen. Railroads now linked communities large and small, creating a national market for records and other consumer goods. Entrepreneurs, centered increasingly in New York City, used that transportation network to bring musical entertainment to more and more customers. By the early 1900s, popular entertainment was well on its way to becoming modern "show business." The workings of this new entertainment industry depended on a new approach to creating and marketing popular songs.

POPULAR SONGS AFTER THE CIVIL WAR

In the years following the Civil War, the sheet music trade seems to have lost interest in the central issues of the day. The hardships of war widows and ex-slaves, the bitterness of Southern whites, and the travails of American Indians may have been acute social realities, but they were not the stuff from which song hits were fashioned. Songwriters returned instead to subjects popular in the 1820s and 1830s: nostalgic or cautionary dramas or vignettes.

The verse-and-chorus form of Stephen Foster and his contemporaries remained as prominent after the war as it had been before. The key to popular song composition still lay in inventing a brief, catchy musical statement, usually four bars long, and then repeating it: the main statement was heard in the introduction, the verse (usually more than once), the chorus, and the piano tag, if there was one. Formal ingenuity thus counted for little; redundancy was welcomed and embraced.

"Silver Threads among the Gold" (1873), with words by Eben Rexford and music by Hart P. Danks, is a good example of the standard recipe. The graceful, **legato** (smooth) melody fits the sentimental subject—the ripeness of married love. The verse outlines an *aaba* structure, with each section four bars in length.

The chorus repeats the second half, *ba,* and the framing piano introduction and tag state the main idea as well, for an overall form of

intro	verse	chorus	tag
a	*aaba*	*ba*	*a*

The words of the chorus also repeat the lines that begin the first verse. All this repetition makes for a structure in which love is a force of stability: a haven shielding partners from the ravages of time.

INDUSTRIALIZATION AND THE RISE OF GOSPEL MUSIC

During the years between the Civil War and World War I, the United States became the world's foremost industrial nation. As industry advanced, agriculture declined. By 1910, when manufacturing jobs were on the rise, farm workers made up only 31 percent of the labor force, compared with 53 percent in 1870. Changes in the nation's economic and social structure touched all aspects of American life, music included. Industrialization brought more people into cities, where industries were concentrated. As that trend continued, the popular song trade came more and more to be ruled by the tastes of city dwellers.

Industrialization did more than shift workers from the countryside to the city; it changed the nature of work and, in the process, alienated many workers. A machinist testified in 1883: "The different branches of the trade are divided and subdivided so that one man may make just a particular part of a machine and may not know anything whatever about another part of the same machine." Wages for such workers were low and job security nonexistent, at the same time that industrialization brought great wealth to a few and raised the country's standard of living. Such working conditions form the background for a key religious development of the postwar years: the Protestant urban revival movement—sometimes called the Third Great Awakening—which also borrowed from the popular song and sheet music trade.

Revivals aimed at bringing the gospel—the glad tidings of Jesus and the kingdom of God—to unchurched Americans of all social and economic classes. One of the movement's leaders was Dwight L. Moody. Born in 1837 in Massachusetts, Moody moved to Chicago in the mid-1850s, where he prospered in the shoe business. He began Christian work with the YMCA (Young Men's Christian Association) and in 1864 founded a nondenominational church. Moody's preaching emphasized God's love, soft-pedaled his wrath, and cultivated sentiment over theology. He also favored simple, popular hymns like William Bradbury's "Jesus Loves Me."

In the early 1870s Moody held evangelical meetings in Great Britain, accompanied by his musical director, Ira Sankey, who led group singing and sang solos while playing the reed organ. The effect of these meetings was enormous. Kindling a national

Ira Sankey (1840–1908) leads the singing at an 1877 revival at the Boston Tabernacle presided over by evangelist Dwight L. Moody (1837–1899), visible to Sankey's right.

gospel hymns

revival in Scotland, they made Moody and Sankey famous, and soon they were making evangelical tours of the United States. Singing played a key role in the work of turning sinners into Christians. Moody and Sankey and other traveling evangelists found in **gospel hymns**—sacred songs in popular musical dress—a way to give their audiences easy access to Christianity's spiritual truths. Gospel hymns fed a desire to connect with God in an attitude of praise, with little concern for edification.

By 1875 evangelical revivalism was not only a religious force to be reckoned with but also a successful business in the United States. Huge crowds flocked to Moody's meetings, where they heard massed choirs trained by Sankey. In 1876 Sankey gathered the hymns he had used in Britain, added some by like-minded colleagues, and brought out *Gospel Hymns*, a collection that was to be a best-selling hymnal until well into the twentieth century. With copies being sold at Moody's meetings, royalties of some $360,000 were paid during the book's first ten years in print, proceeds that helped finance the duo's evangelical work.

LG 7.2

One of the book's selections, "Sweet By and By" (LG 7.2), is a daydream of heaven by a composer outside the revivalist circle. Joseph P. Webster composed "Sweet By and By" in 1867 to words by S. Fillmore Bennett. The music sustains the reverie of Bennett's text, avoiding complication: only three chords are used (tonic, dominant, and subdominant), and not a single added sharp or flat disturbs the diatonic melody and harmony. Equally important is the unbroken rhythmic flow. Webster instructs performers: "With much feeling and in perfect time." This is an unusual direction, for slowing the tempo is a standard way to emphasize feeling in a sung text.

"Sweet By and By" follows a familiar form: piano introduction, unison verse, and harmonized chorus. Its main interest lies in the chorus, which introduces the title phrase and main message, and whose length is doubled by a repeat—all features of post–Civil War popular songs, increasingly so as the century progressed. An echo effect between male and female voices invites singers and listeners to savor a rosy view of eternity: believers will meet on a "beautiful shore" when their days on earth are over. An air of serene confidence radiates from this hymn.

THE RISE OF TIN PAN ALLEY

Although several cities were the home of music publishers throughout the nineteenth century, by the late 1800s New York City had emerged as the capital of a new kind of publishing, one that focused exclusively on popular songs. **Tin Pan Alley**, the nickname given the publishing district that took shape in New York around 1890, is also an apt metaphor for an approach new to the trade: populist in tone, noisy with the sound of song pluggers, and shameless in the pursuit of commercial advantage. Tin Pan Alley's economics, like its atmosphere, differed from that of older publishing firms. The nineteenth century's flagship music publisher was Oliver Ditson & Co. of Boston. From its founding in the 1830s, Ditson's business grew spectacularly, and by 1890 the company had bought the catalogues of more than fifty other publishers and set up new firms in Philadelphia, New York, Chicago, and Cincinnati. Ditson published many popular songs, but they made up only a fraction of the firm's comprehensive catalogue.

| CD 1.23 | Listening Guide 7.2 | "Sweet By and By" JOHN P. WEBSTER |

DATE: 1867

PERFORMERS: Harmoneion Singers; Neely Bruce, director

GENRE: gospel hymn

METER: duple

FORM: verse and chorus

WHAT TO LISTEN FOR

- verse-and-chorus format of popular song
- devotional lyrics
- placement of title phrase for easy memorability
- vocal harmonies as chorus

TIMING	SECTION	TEXT	COMMENTS
0:00	introduction		4 bars; piano anticipates the main idea of the verse.
0:12	verse 1	There's a land that is fairer than day, / And by faith we can see it afar; / For the Father waits over the way / To prepare us a dwelling place there.	8 bars; men's voices in unison.
0:40	chorus	In the sweet by and by, / We shall meet on that beautiful shore; / In the sweet by and by, / We shall meet on that beautiful shore.	8 bars; four-part mixed chorus. Printed repeat is not observed in this performance.
1:07	verse 2	We shall sing on that beautiful shore / The melodious songs of the blessed; / And our spirits shall sorrow no more, / Not a sigh for the blessing of rest.	8 bars; women's voices in unison.
1:35	chorus	In the sweet by and by . . .	8 bars; four-part mixed chorus. Again, no repeat.
2:04	verse 3	To our bountiful Father above, / We will offer the tribute of praise / For the glorious gift of His love / And the blessings that hallow our days.	8 bars; men's voices in unison.
2:31	chorus	In the sweet by and by . . .	8 bars; four-part mixed chorus. Sung twice. Webster's score gives the following direction: "In the repeat, diminuendo gradually to the end."

Listen & Reflect

1. What features, if any, does this gospel hymn share with the music of earlier hymnody, such as SHERBURNE, WONDROUS LOVE, or OLIVET (see LGs 3.1–3)?

2. Are there any features shared with antebellum minstrel and parlor songs, such as those of Stephen Foster (see LGs 6.2–3), and if so, what are they?

New York's West 28th Street, nicknamed "Tin Pan Alley," was the home of many music publishers, including the Remick and Whitney Warner companies, seen in this photo from around 1915. Also visible are the offices of the *New York Clipper*, the first American newspaper devoted to the entertainment industry, and the William Morris Agency, a "talent agency" representing performers that is still active today.

As the century's end approached, the company had grown into a colossus that took pride not only in its financial strength but also in its service to the edifying art of music. Ditson would eventually collapse under the weight of its lofty goals and huge inventory.

In contrast, M. Witmark & Sons of New York City, founded in 1884, traveled light. Undistracted by thoughts of duty, the Witmark firm originated in a hunger for profit and a personal snub. In the mid-1800s a traveling minstrel troupe hired a fifteen-year-old boy soprano named Julius Witmark. The youth struck a deal with New York publisher Willis Woodward that, for a share of the proceeds, he would sing a particular song in Woodward's catalogue as often as possible during the troupe's upcoming national tour. Witmark made good on his part of the bargain, and the song enjoyed strong sheet music sales. But all he got from Woodward in return was twenty dollars and a dismissive pat on the shoulder. Julius and his brothers retaliated by opening M. Witmark & Sons, using their father's name because they were all under legal age.

Catching the flavor of Tin Pan Alley's commercial origins, this story also illustrates how its location in New York City allowed songs to be promoted. When a theatrical troupe was in New York recruiting personnel, looking for new material, and planning its next tour, a music publisher would enlist a troupe member to plug one of his songs. As the troupe toured, the publisher made sure copies of the song were on hand at each location. Then when that song later became a hit, thanks in part to the singer's efforts, the publisher reaped the rewards from sales of the sheet music. In contrast to Ditson, Tin Pan Alley firms published only popular songs, pouring much of their energy and money into promotion.

Music publisher Edward B. Marks, drawing on forty years' experience, published in 1934 a memoir that describes these fundamental changes in the popular song trade in the 1890s. Marks saw the songwriters of early Tin Pan Alley as careless businessmen who, instead of retaining rights to their songs and collecting royalties, often sold them outright to a publisher for ready cash, which they then squandered. Songwriters wrote "according to the market," Marks charged, and yet at the same time believed themselves superior to the public "to whom they pander." Publishers were also a mixed lot. In pre–Tin Pan Alley years, Marks recalled, the leading figures had been old-school gentlemen. But to survive in the "particularly insane business" of the 1890s and later, it helped to be "more of a Bohemian." A salesman at heart, Marks himself relished life in the trade: the personal associations, rivalries, adventures, and risks that fueled a high-energy enterprise, where the possibilities of financial bonanza or ruin were always present. To get performers to keep plugging the songs in his catalogue, Marks visited an average of "sixty joints a week," while Joe Stern, his partner in the firm of Joseph W. Stern & Co., dropped in at some forty more.

As Marks and his competitors scrambled to sell their songs in Tin Pan Alley's marketplace, the amusement world was changing in ways that deeply affected the popular song trade. Aware that sizable audiences could now be reached outside New York, theatrical producers began sending more of their shows on regional and national tours (see chapter 10's discussion of the early Broadway musical). In August of each year, theater owners from around the country went to New York and competed to lure "direct from Broadway" companies to their towns. As the number of shows on the road increased, booking agents emerged as middlemen to coordinate their touring. Six of these giants joined together in

1896 to form the Syndicate, a group that controlled most major theaters in New York and many outside. By 1906 the Syndicate boasted a network of some seven hundred theaters nationwide, and touring on its circuit was coming to be an orderly process, directed from New York. The Syndicate didn't just schedule the shows; it also controlled their content down to such details as the removal or addition of songs.

Consolidation also took place in variety entertainment, known by the turn of the century as **vaudeville**. Its roots lay in New York's music halls, concert saloons, beer gardens, and variety houses where Marks plugged his songs. Vaudeville also owed much to the large numbers of immigrants who had arrived by boat from Europe. In the form that crystallized around 1900, vaudeville combined a wide range of performers—comedians, jugglers, acrobats, actors, animal trainers, dancers, singers, and instrumentalists of every nationality—into an evening's entertainment at cheap prices. A standard vaudeville format called for nine acts, each running fifteen minutes or less. Shows often began with a "dumb act" (i.e., one with no spoken material—dancers, pantomimes, or acrobats) while late-comers straggled in; from there the show would build, with a climactic eighth act that featured the star. Following the headliner, an intentionally anticlimactic dumb act would act as the "chaser" to clear the hall so the entire show could be repeated for a new audience. A particular group of acts, or "bill," might play a given theater for one night or several weeks, depending on the community's size and the main star's drawing power.

As the Syndicate had done for musical theater, the Keith-Albee organization brought order to vaudeville when in 1906 it formed the United Booking Office of America, connecting thousands of performers and theater managers. In 1927 Keith-Albee combined with the Orpheum circuit, which played a similar role in the West. A smaller circuit in the South, the Theater Owners Booking Association (TOBA), brought black talent to black theaters and audiences, a market that Keith-Albee and Orpheum never tried to serve. Vaudeville czars held such power

vaudeville

☙ In the early 1900s venues across the country, such as the Grand Theater in Buffalo, New York, offered variety entertainment for low prices.

over performers who played their circuits that comedian Harpo Marx once said that to him the head of the Keith-Albee empire seemed "more powerful than the president of the United States."

In what was fast becoming national show business, stage performers were considered the most effective boosters of sheet music sales, and song publishers competed fiercely for their attention in New York City. For by 1900 Tin Pan Alley publishers knew well the riches that one best-selling song could bring.

THE ANATOMY OF A HIT: "AFTER THE BALL"

In 1892 banjo player and songwriter Charles K. Harris, living in Milwaukee, wrote a song that became the hit of the decade. Harris recalled later that the number took shape from an idea that had popped into his mind: "Many a heart is aching after the ball." With that line as a starting point, he fashioned a story in three long verses, each followed by a shorter chorus. Then, since his own grasp of musical notation was shaky, he solicited the help of a local arranger to provide a score and a piano accompaniment. Disenchanted by earlier experience with New York publishers, whose royalty payments he had found too small, Harris decided to publish the song himself. His strategy for plugging "After the Ball" (LG 7.3) proved excellent. A road company was playing a Broadway show in Milwaukee, and Harris arranged a meeting with the cast's leading baritone. The singer agreed to sing the new song in the show, and his first performance drew a five-minute standing ovation, with six encores of the chorus. With strong financial inducement from Harris—a promise of five hundred dollars and a share of the income from sales—the singer made "After the Ball" a part of every performance.

LG 7.3

More than any American popular song before it, "After the Ball" was an economic bonanza. Orders for the song poured in as the road company moved toward New York. Oliver Ditson ordered 75,000 copies, and John Philip Sousa programmed an arrangement of the song for his band at the 1893 World's Columbian Exposition in Chicago. Before long, Harris was earning $25,000 a month from sales, and on the strength of his success decided to open a popular song publishing business in New York, where he moved permanently in 1903.

The song's sheet music cover pictures a dance floor filled with men and women dressed in formal finery. Some couples whirl vigorously, others are locked in close embraces, and others seem occupied with gossip and flirtation. The picture suggests the display of personal charms in a competitive public arena, an image that separates "After the Ball" from earlier songs of courtship and love. Moreover, the song is a **waltz,** a dance in triple meter that called for partners to embrace and thus in 1892 carried erotic overtones. Harris's lyrics tell a story that dramatizes the misunderstandings that can occur in the sexualized atmosphere of the ballroom.

"After the Ball" struck a responsive chord in its time. Perhaps audience members and amateur performers found appeal in the story or the proverb-like moral delivered by the chorus. But it is the music that brings emotion to a tale that might otherwise be taken as a sermonette. While the lilting ball music maintains the illusion of calm control, the words portray feelings as fragile as the glass dropped by the song's disappointed lover. The long narrative verse floats on sustained tones

🎵 Once Charles K. Harris's "After the Ball" (1892) became a hit, Harris brought out an edition with an illustrated cover that hints at the erotic overtones of the waltz craze.

| 🎧 | CD 1.24 | Listening Guide 7.3 | "After the Ball" CHARLES K. HARRIS |

DATE: 1892

PERFORMER: George J. Gaskin

GENRE: popular song

METER: triple

FORM: verse and chorus

WHAT TO LISTEN FOR

- triple meter "waltz time"
- semi-operatic vocal technique
- limited audio fidelity of early recording
- truncation of song to fit on cylinder

TIMING	SECTION	TEXT	COMMENTS
0:00	announcement	"'After the Ball,' sung by Mr. George J. Gaskin."	Announcement was a common feature in early recordings.
0:04	introduction		8 bars; the piano anticipates the first 4 bars of the verse, before closing with a burst of quicker notes suggesting the ballroom's whirling energy.
0:10	verse 1	A little maiden climbed an old man's knee Begged for a story—"Do Uncle please. Why are you single; why live alone? Have you no babies; have you no home?" "I had a sweetheart, years, years ago; Where she is now, pet, you will soon know. List to the story, I'll tell it all, I believed her faithless after the ball."	64 bars, divided into four sections of 16 bars each: *aa' ba''*. The *b* section begins on a minor chord, adding a hint of pathos.
1:05	verse 2	Bright lights were flashing in the grand ballroom, Softly the music, playing sweet tunes. There came my sweetheart, my love, my own— "I wish some water; leave me alone." When I returned dear there stood a man, Kissing my sweetheart as lovers can. Down fell the glass pet, broken, that's all, Just as my heart was after the ball.	Although the sheet music indicates that the chorus should follow each verse, the pianist plays only a 4-bar interlude before verse 2.
1:56	chorus	After the ball is over, after the break of morn— After the dancers' leaving; after the stars are gone; Many a heart is aching, if you could read them all; Many the hopes that have vanished after the ball.	32 bars, *aa'a''b*. The performers modulate to a new key, not indicated in the sheet music, intensifying the contrast between verse and chorus.
	verse 3	Long years have passed child, I've never wed. True to my lost love though she is dead. She tried to tell me, tried to explain;	(not recorded)

(continued)

🎧 CD 1.24	Listening Guide 7.3		"After the Ball" CHARLES K. HARRIS

TIMING	SECTION	TEXT	COMMENTS
		I would not listen, pleadings were vain. One day a letter came from that man, He was her brother—the letter ran. That's why I'm lonely, no home at all; I broke her heart, pet, after the ball.	

Listen & Reflect

1. Does the character of the music suit the emotional content of the lyrics? Why or why not?
2. How does the story, as told here in a two-verse version, differ from the complete three-verse version?
3. Is the difference significant?

throughout its sixty-four-bar length, yielding to a catchier, faster-moving melody at the thirty-two-bar chorus. Evenly divided into four sections (aa'a''b), the chorus consists of three varied statements of that catchy tune, with the final section returning to the sustained notes of the verse to set the title line.

The Irish tenor George J. Gaskin, who had a successful career in the United States in the 1890s, was one of the first artists to record commercially produced cylinders for Thomas Edison. Among them is his 1893 rendition of "After the Ball." Gaskin's strong voice and clear diction, which may strike present-day listeners as overenunciated, enabled him to surmount the limitations of early recording technology.

Because the first music cylinders ran no longer than two and a half minutes, Gaskin and his unnamed accompanist perform a shortened version of the song: only two of the three verses and a single statement of the chorus at the end, all sung at a somewhat rushed tempo. As is evident from the full text—reproduced here with only a few corrections of the original sheet music's inconsistent punctuation—the story is not complete without the third verse. While there is time for a piano introduction, the sheet music's framing **coda**, or tag, at the end—an instrumental repeat of the last eight bars of the refrain—is absent.

POPULAR SONGS AT THE TURN OF THE CENTURY

As the opera and minstrel stage had done in an earlier day, musical comedy (see chapter 10) and vaudeville now provided the sheet music business's main marketing arm. But for all the changes in songwriting that took place—new subjects, fresh cover designs, more stars' endorsements, a growing emphasis on female glamour—Tin Pan Alley's ultimate goal remained the same as that of publishers and songwriters in the day of Stephen Foster and George F. Root: to sell sheet music to home performers in quantities as large as possible.

The variety of song types sung on American stages around the turn of the century was enormous: airs from opera and operetta, Victorian parlor songs, Tin Pan Alley numbers of every description, songs in foreign languages, songs from blackface entertainment, even religious songs. Each carried its own style of singing. Moreover, performers had their own techniques and mannerisms, and many stars owed their fame to a personal way of approaching songs. As in earlier days, popular songs were performers' music: outlines to be filled in according to each performer's personality and skill.

song types

For all their variety, however, the top-selling songs of the era have certain traits in common. Most are in major keys and share a familiar musical form: a brief piano introduction, followed by a verse (sometimes in the minor) and a chorus. Many are waltzes, most were published in New York, and with the occasional English exception, all are American in origin. They explore a wider range of moods than the era's popular nickname, the Gay Nineties, might imply. The cautionary theme of "After the Ball" is echoed more lightheartedly in "The Bowery" (1892), which warns of the dangers lurking in a notorious New York district where "they say such things, and they do strange things." Other songs reveal glimpses of life in Irish neighborhoods, as in "The Band Played On" (1895), "Sweet Rosie O'Grady" (1896), and "My Wild Irish Rose" (1899).

traits of hit songs

"After the Ball" is only one of many songs that deal with the separations of sweethearts, often by death. Perhaps the most unusual parted-lovers song is Paul Dresser's "My Gal Sal" (1905), in which death cuts short an unusual friendship. As described by the song's persona, "Jim," Sal was a person of mature years and plenty of experience:

> They called her frivolous Sal,
> A peculiar sort of a gal,
> With a heart that was mellow,
> An all 'round good fellow,
> Was my old pal;
> Your troubles, sorrows, and care,
> She was always willing to share,
> A wild sort of devil,
> But dead on the level,
> Was my gal Sal.

The kind of woman a man would describe in the language of male comradeship is rare in Tin Pan Alley song. But then, "My Gal Sal" rejects the romantic conventions that ruled the day's songs about women. We never learn why some called her frivolous, or why Jim hails her as wild, though excessive drinking and extramarital sex are implied. By Tin Pan Alley's code of conduct, these are signs of depraved character in a woman. But the song treats "old pal" Sal's behavior as if it were that of a man, who might not be condemned for such appetites.

The earthiness of "My Gal Sal" would have been rare in a Tin Pan Alley song a decade earlier. It was not that songs had previously ignored the possibility of sex outside marriage; rather, songs touching the subject treated their female characters as fatally stained. Between the Civil War and 1890, Edward Marks observed, "sniffly songs for the strayed sister, whom her virtuous co-females delighted to

✒ As the cost of photographic images declined, pictures of professional singers such as Rita Redmond were used more and more to plug sheet music editions of songs such as this well-known hit.

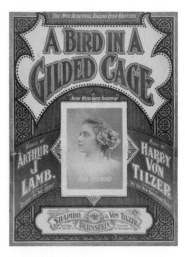

pity," were popular. In these numbers, "dishonor was always presented as the equivalent of death, which usually accompanied it in some form about the fifth verse." A song that comes close to Marks's description is "A Bird in a Gilded Cage" (1900). The female subject of this song dishonors the institution of matrimony by marrying "for wealth, not for love," and in the second of its two verses, she dies. The narrator pictures a cemetery, then muses on the "tall marble monument" marking the unfortunate woman's grave:

> And I thought she is happier here at rest,
> Than to have people say when seen:
> [*Chorus:*] She's only a bird in a gilded cage,
> A beautiful sight to see. . . .

Songs from a new group of songwriters and performers may have paved the way for "My Gal Sal." A generation of African Americans writing in the 1890s brought fresh energy to the music of Tin Pan Alley, helping to overturn some of the trade's inhibitions with unconventional subject matter and an intoxicating new musical style: ragtime, one of the subjects of chapter 10.

QUESTIONS FOR DISCUSSION AND REVIEW

1. In what ways do Sousa's marches belong to the popular music culture of their time, and in what ways do they affirm the values of classical music, as described in chapter 5?

2. How do gospel hymns reflect new developments in late nineteenth-century American society, and how do they affirm continuities from earlier eras?

3. What new elements altered the sheet music industry after 1890? How do changes in the entertainment industry reflect larger changes in turn-of-the-century U.S. society as a whole?

4. After 1890, a hit song could be hugely profitable for its publisher. Do turn-of-the-century popular songs reflect this newly commercialized environment, and if so, how?

FURTHER READING

Jasen, David. *Tin Pan Alley: The Composers, the Songs, the Performers, and Their Times: The Golden Age of Popular Music from 1886 to 1956*. New York: D. I. Fine, 1988.

Marks, Edward B. *They All Sang: From Tony Pastor to Rudy Vallee*. New York: Viking, 1934.

Marsden, George M. *Fundamentalism and American Culture: The Shaping of Twentieth-Century Evangelicalism, 1870–1925*. New York: Oxford University Press, 1980.

Schlereth, Thomas J. *Victorian America: Transformations in Everyday Life, 1876–1915*. New York: HarperCollins, 1991.

Sousa, John Philip. *Marching Along: Recollections of Men, Women, and Music*. 1928. Reprint. Westerville, Ohio: Integrity Press, 1994.

Warfield, Patrick. "John Philip Sousa and 'The Menace of Mechanical Music.'" *Journal of the Society for American Music* 3, no. 4 (November 2009): 431–64.

———. "The Sousa March: From Publication to Performance." In John Philip Sousa, *Six Marches*, edited by Patrick Warfield, xiii–xxxvii. Music of the United States of America 21. Middleton, WI: A-R Editions, 2010.

"TO STRETCH OUR EARS"
Classical Music Comes of Age

CHAPTER
8

By the late 1800s, musical institutions in the United States—professional orchestras, music conservatories, college music departments, and concert-promoting musical clubs—were providing the infrastructure for a new generation of composers and performers to develop their art in unprecedented ways. Beginning with the most influential American conductor of the nineteenth century, this chapter surveys the composers active in Boston and New York at the turn of the century and concludes with one of the most idiosyncratic of all American musicians: Charles Ives.

THEODORE THOMAS

The premier American conductor of the nineteenth century was Theodore Thomas, whose family immigrated from Germany in 1845. Thomas was recruited in 1853, at age thirteen, to play in Louis Jullien's orchestra, which was then taking New York by storm (see chapter 5). The following year he joined the first violin section of the New York Philharmonic Society. Within a few years he also was serving as concertmaster of the opera orchestra at New York's Academy of Music. Although Thomas played violin in public into his fourth decade, it was as a conductor that he made his mark. His musical outlook was also distinctive. Thomas took it as his mission to help raise musical standards so that the symphony orchestra's place in the United States would be secured. "Throughout my life," he wrote in 1874, "my aim has been to make good music popular."

Thomas mastered not only the artistic but also the business side of his trade. As conductor of the Theodore Thomas Orchestra (1865–90) he accomplished one of the more complex balancing acts in the history of American music, by controlling both its artistic and economic arms. In fact, Thomas's career challenges the notion that art and economics are separate things, for without a musical marketplace the Thomas Orchestra could never have survived. His great achievement was to discover within that marketplace an audience for the symphony orchestra.

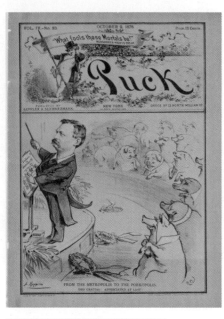

❧ When German-born conductor Theodore Thomas (1835–1905) left New York in 1891 to direct Chicago's new orchestra, one New York magazine called it a move "from the metropolis to the porkopolis."

Thomas found his audiences by blending idealism with pragmatism. Three related concerns dominated the Thomas Orchestra's early years: how the ensemble played, what it played, and where it played. Since much of the music he programmed was hard to play, the precise, polished performances he strove for relied on skilled players and time to rehearse them. To recruit the players most in demand, Thomas had to pay good wages, which hinged on the quantity of work he could provide them. Thus, as well as performing the classics in concert halls, from 1865 on the orchestra also made a specialty of outdoor concerts, mixing symphonic movements with overtures, dances, and lighter selections in settings where customers could smoke, drink, and socialize. Such concessions to public taste, Thomas believed, chipped away at barriers between audience and orchestra. At the same time, a full performance schedule enabled the Thomas Orchestra to improve until it outstripped all other American ensembles.

Yet Thomas was able to stay in business only by touring. In 1869 his orchestra made the first of many cross-country journeys, and through the 1870s the orchestra sometimes spent more than half the year on the road. While the touring life was difficult, the quality of the playing remained high. Russian pianist and composer Anton Rubinstein testified after an 1873 tour with Thomas that only the orchestra of the Paris Conservatory was the Thomas Orchestra's equal in personnel—"but alas, they have no Theodore Thomas to conduct them."

Thomas believed that listeners as well as performers benefited from the challenge of hearing symphonic music by Beethoven and other great composers: "faculties are called into action and appealed to other than those [the listener] ordinarily uses," absorbing attention and freeing listeners "from worldly cares." Recognizing that "the complexities of symphonic form are far beyond the grasp of beginners," Thomas planned his outdoor concerts with just such novices in mind: the concerts, featuring music with "very clearly defined melody and well-marked rhythms, such . . . as is played by the best bands," were meant to prepare inexperienced listeners "for a higher grade of musical performances." Charles Edward Russell, Thomas's biographer, remembered hearing an 1877 concert in the Mississippi town of his boyhood, including works of Mendelssohn, Berlioz, and Liszt: "Life was never the same afterward," for the audience had been shown that "there really existed as a fact, and not as something heard of as unattainable, this world of beauty, wholly apart from everyday experiences."

In Europe, most orchestras were local organizations financed by local resources and addressed to local audiences. But before a similar situation could arise in the United States, three elements had to come together: (1) a belief in the artistic importance of the symphony orchestra; (2) civic pride, centered in the feeling that an orchestra enriched community life; and (3) wealth, donated in recognition that the marketplace could not support an orchestra of the first rank. Thomas supported the first element by helping to establish the ritual elements in a symphony concert: an atmosphere of attentive restraint, a code of behavior and dress, and an understanding that performers aspire to honor the composer's artistic intentions. His search for the other two came to an end when Chicago businessman Charles Norman Fay asked if he would consider moving to Chicago to direct a full-time, permanent orchestra whose funding would not be supplied by Thomas himself. Thomas is said to have replied: "I would go to hell if they gave me a permanent orchestra." In response, Fay organized a group of financial backers, and in 1891 Thomas became the music director of the new Chicago Orchestra, later renamed the Chicago Symphony Orchestra, which he led until his death in 1905.

By that time, a classical sphere based on composers' music was established in America, and a number of cities boasted symphony orchestras. Musical life in centers like New York, Boston, Philadelphia, and Chicago seemed to be catching up with that of European cities, where broad public interest sustained a wide range of performing groups, concert halls, and conservatories. And succeeding such earlier musicians as Heinrich, Gottschalk, Fry, and Bristow was a new wave of American composers whose music could fully exploit these maturing musical resources. A center of activity for many of these younger composers was Boston.

THE SECOND NEW ENGLAND SCHOOL

Whereas earlier composers such as Gottschalk and Bristow had been isolated figures, in the late 1800s in and around Boston there arose the first real group of American composers since the Yankee psalmodists or the Moravians. Among those who deserve to be remembered are John Knowles Paine, George W. Chadwick, Arthur Foote, Horatio Parker, and Amy Cheney Beach, all native New Englanders. In a nod to their psalmodist forebears, these composers have come to be called the "Second New England School." To that group may be added New York–born Edward MacDowell, who lived and worked for a time in Boston.

CHADWICK AND "THE BOYS"

A 1907 article by George W. Chadwick, looking back to the 1890s, recalled how it felt to be part of this group. "Many a night after a Symphony concert," he recalled, they "gathered about the same table" in the Tavern Club, bantering in friendly exchange, "rejoicing in each other's successes, and working for them too." Chadwick portrays a community of equals who had fashioned a working environment of "mutual respect and honest criticism." The circle also included Theodore Thomas, who, traveling between Chicago and his summer home in New Hampshire, often stopped in Boston to enjoy the company of "the boys," as he called them. Although Amy Beach was excluded from this fraternal bonding, after a performance of her *Gaelic* Symphony in 1896 Chadwick pronounced the composition fine enough to make her "one of the boys" as well.

Several of the Boston composers were also skilled performers, chiefly pianists or organists, and their compositions were heard regularly in Boston on the programs of such local ensembles as the Boston Symphony Orchestra (founded in 1881), the Kneisel String Quartet, and the Handel and Haydn Society. Paine was a professor of music at Harvard, Chadwick the director of the New England Conservatory of Music, Foote organist at the First Unitarian Church and also a piano teacher, and Parker a professor of music at Yale and organist at Boston's Trinity Church—a dual career demanding much commuting by train.

Of that group gathered at the Tavern Club, Chadwick stands out today as the most notable figure, and in recent decades his music has enjoyed a modest revival. Born in 1854 in Lowell, Massachusetts, Chadwick grew up in circumstances that were far from prosperous. He left high school short of graduation to work for his father, a businessman who opposed his son's musical ambitions. While still working, Chadwick managed a part-time enrollment at the New England Conservatory, where he studied organ, piano, and harmony, and in 1872 he added an organist's job to the position in his father's company. In 1876–77 he taught at a college in Michigan. With the money he saved, he sailed to Germany, where he studied privately and at the Leipzig Conservatory in 1877–79, and in Munich with Josef Rheinberger in 1879–80. In 1880 he returned to Boston, took a job as a church organist, and then joined the faculty of the New England Conservatory, an association that lasted from 1882 until just before his death in 1931.

Chadwick's teachers at the Leipzig Conservatory had pegged him from the start as an extraordinary student. In June 1879 his *Rip Van Winkle* Overture for orchestra, performed on a graduation concert, was reviewed by a Leipzig critic as "uncontestably . . . the best of this year's compositions." His professors in Leipzig signed a report that reads in part: "Herr Chadwick possesses a completely exceptional talent for composition." Chadwick's talent for communicating in a concert hall would help make him a leader in Boston's musical life.

a "Yankee composer"

Chadwick was a "Yankee composer" in the sense that he was at home in European genres but approached them through an American sensibility. He developed virtuoso orchestration along European models, but many other traits of his style separated his music from German prototypes: a fondness for pentatonic and other gapped scales, African-Caribbean dance syncopations, and a musical sensitivity to the characteristic rhythms of English lyrics. From these, Chadwick evolved a personal approach that allowed him to write cosmopolitan music with an American flavor.

Recently Chadwick has been credited with creating an American symphonic style. Some evidence for that may be found in the first movement of his *Symphonic Sketches* (1904), to which Chadwick gave the title "Jubilee." Critic Henry Taylor Parker, who reviewed a performance in 1908, heard echoes of "Negro

The orchestra of the New England Conservatory in 1915, with an inset picturing its conductor, George W. Chadwick (1854–1931). The number of women in the orchestra testifies to the rising professionalism of female musicians early in the twentieth century.

tunes" and fancied that the work was set in an American farmhouse. A lively pentatonic melody resembles the refrain of Foster's "Camptown Races," and a slower section uses a Cuban habanera rhythm in the accompaniment.

But to say that Chadwick created an American symphonic style implies that other concert hall composers followed his lead, which none actually did. The faith in edification that ruled the concert hall, together with the notion that artistically serious music ought to be grave and dignified, were not, in the long run, in accord with Chadwick's personal approach. Could the standard Old World forms accommodate a more playful American mode of orchestral expression? Or did such music risk trivializing Americans' quest to find an honored place among the world's musical nations? In the thinking of most of Chadwick's contemporaries, the answers were no and yes, respectively.

Eventually, though, the American style Chadwick helped to invent found its niche. The leaders of the Hollywood film industry probably had little idea who George W. Chadwick was when films were outfitted with orchestral scores—first with live orchestras accompanying silent films, then, beginning in the late 1920s, with recorded soundtracks (see chapter 15). But they chose a musical style close to that of Chadwick's *Symphonic Sketches* and his Second Symphony: rooted in German Romanticism, tuneful in his Yankee manner, colorfully written for the instruments, and easily accessible to a general audience.

AMY BEACH AND AMERICAN MUSICAL DEMOCRACY

Amy Marcy Cheney was born in 1867 in West Henniker, New Hampshire. It did not take long for her mother, an accomplished pianist, to discover Amy's talent for music. Before she was two, the child was improvising harmony to Mrs. Cheney's lullaby. But she was determined not to push her daughter into music nor to exploit the child's talent in public. When she finally began giving Amy piano lessons at six, progress was swift, and before long the young girl was studying with a respected piano teacher in Boston. In 1883, at sixteen, she made her public debut, and two years later played a Chopin concerto with the Boston Symphony Orchestra. In the same year, 1885, she married Dr. Henry H. A. Beach, a forty-two-year-old widower, physician, and amateur musician. And for the next twenty-five years she lived an active, well-rounded musical life centered in Boston.

Beach had been writing music since she was four, and in her early teens she had taken a year's worth of lessons in harmony and counterpoint from a local teacher. As a woman in the nineteenth century, she found avenues for more formal study closed to her, so she acquired scores and books and taught herself to compose. After her marriage, she concentrated more on composition, though she still sometimes played in public. Beach composed well into her seventies, writing many songs and keyboard works, choral pieces, some chamber music, a piano concerto, a symphony, and even an opera. In 1895 her mother, always Beach's main musical adviser, moved in with the childless couple after Amy's father died, taking over household chores and leaving Beach free to compose.

Beach's settled life in Boston ended when her husband died in 1910, followed by her mother early the next year. In the fall of 1911, at age forty-four, she seized an independence she had never enjoyed before: she sailed for Europe, hired a manager, and began to play more often in public. After World War I forced her return to the

United States, she established a new home base in Hillsborough, New Hampshire. Beginning in 1930 she made New York City her winter home. When Beach died in New York in 1944, she left behind more than three hundred compositions and a record of pioneering achievements, as both a performer and a composer: she was the first American-trained concert pianist, part of the first generation of professional American female instrumentalists, and the first American woman to compose large-scale works for the concert hall. She was also one of the first composers, male or female, to use folk melodies to help create a distinctively American style.

music careers for women

Although women had taken an active part in America's music making during the eighteenth and early nineteenth centuries, most led their musical lives within severe limits. If Beach's generation was the first to produce professional women instrumentalists, that was because singers had previously been the only women encouraged to develop their skills to that level. If Beach was the first American-trained concert pianist, that was because the parents of talented males like Gottschalk sent their sons to Europe for their musical training. And if she was the first American woman to compose successfully in large-scale forms, that was because the men who controlled such opportunities had resisted the idea that a female composer could meet the demands of the symphony, concerto, oratorio, or opera—genres seldom approached by the few widely known female European composers, such as Clara Schumann.

"Can a woman become a great composer?" asked Louis Elson, Boston critic and member of the New England Conservatory's faculty, in his *History of American Music* (1904). "Will there ever be a female Beethoven or a Mozart?" In Europe, Elson reported, these questions had been answered "quickly and in the negative." Yet he doubted that men's capacities in music were superior to women's. "We venture to believe," he wrote, "that it has been insufficient musical education and male prejudice that have prevented female composers from competing with their male brethren in art." His evidence was the career of Amy Beach, which he had followed firsthand. As a child with extraordinary talent, she had shown the energy, confidence, and character to acquire professional skills that made her a peer of male colleagues. Thus Beach served in her own day as a symbol of what a woman musician could do if given the chance. Well known and tireless as both a composer and a performer, she set an example for other American women to take their talent seriously.

✎ This program of the Handel and Haydn Society of Boston places Amy Beach, composer of a new Mass in E-flat (1892), in the company of the European masters.

In later years Beach wrote music chiefly for the kinds of programs in which she herself performed. Yet large-scale works first distinguished her from her female predecessors, who by the 1890s had already composed many songs and piano pieces. Most of these works, including the Mass in E-flat (1892), the *Gaelic* Symphony (1896), and the Piano Concerto (1900), were written before Beach was thirty-five, a period coinciding with the Boston group's heyday. The Handel and Haydn Society premiered the mass, and the Boston Symphony Orchestra introduced the symphony and the concerto.

Looking back in 1917 on her *Gaelic* Symphony, Beach explained in a program note that the symphony's melodies "sprang from the common joys, sorrows, adventures and struggles of a primitive people. The simple, rugged and unpretentious beauty led me to 'take my pen in hand' and try to develop their ideas in symphonic form." These comments point to a fact unknown to the public when the symphony was premiered. Inspired by the Bohemian composer Antonín Dvořák, who during a three-year stay in the United States counseled American composers to tap the sources of folk music (see "Nationalism and the *Indian* Suite" later in this chapter), Beach borrowed most of the melodies in this work from elsewhere.

The symphony's second movement (LG 8.1) unfolds in three-part ABA form, slow-fast-slow, with a slow introduction and a brief coda. Easy to listen to the first time as well as the twenty-first, the movement boasts a unity of theme that compensates for the sharp change of mood and tempo that the middle section introduces. The melody of the A section, played by the oboe, is foursquare in phrase structure and predictable in form: statement, restatement, contrast, return (*aaba*), with the second half repeated. Beach based this tune on "Goirtin Ornadh" (The Little Field of Barley), a traditional Irish melody; with it she conveys the feeling of a lyric slow movement. But out of this reflective beginning grows a new, faster section in the character of a **scherzo** (a fast-tempo instrumental movement of light character, commonly an inner movement in a four-movement symphony, as it is here). The B section's melody, made up of rapid repeated notes, is heard immediately as a varied form of the A section's melody. Broken into fragments, reharmonized, and repeated in different instrumental colors, this melody moves through many keys in a whirl of musical development. Longer lines appear against it, but the rapid motion continues until interrupted by a silencing gesture. And now the lyric melody from the opening returns (A), with new harmonic shadings and fresh instrumental timbres. The coda, reintroducing the rapid repeated notes, brings the movement to a quick, whisper-like close.

Compared with most other American musicians, male or female, Beach lived a privileged life, despite the prejudice she faced as a woman. Her mother nurtured her talent from the start, and she was given the leisure and opportunity to develop her creative powers on her own. Once she married, a secure social position allowed her to play and to present her music in prestigious situations. Until 1911, when she made her first trip to Europe, Beach's musical career was that of an extraordinary amateur, performing for select audiences, including many friends and acquaintances. When she returned to the United States in 1914, however, the niche she had once filled in Boston no longer existed. She began to fashion a career that involved more public performances for the local musical organizations that grew up in the late 1800s and early 1900s.

From choral societies to teachers' associations and organists' guilds, musical organizations were a focal point for the energies and aspirations of both professional and amateur musicians and music lovers who sought to raise musical standards in the United States and spread the love of music throughout the general population. Beethoven clubs, MacDowell clubs, even Beach clubs sponsored meetings and concerts, published newsletters and magazines, and subsidized educational programs. Beach's first concert after returning from Europe took place at Boston's MacDowell Club, where she presented two groups of songs composed overseas. "An audience of 700 people rose *en masse* as she stepped upon the platform," a press account read, "and after an address, Mrs. Beach was showered with flowers." Free from the need to make a living or to run a household, Beach was one of few Americans able to devote herself to writing and performing music at a professional level without having to depend on the economic outcome. Her music found an audience too, as is shown by the substantial royalty checks she received in later years.

LG 8.1

Amy Beach (1867–1944).

| CD 1.25 | Listening Guide 8.1 | *Gaelic* Symphony, second movement
AMY BEACH |

DATE: 1896

PERFORMERS: Royal Philharmonic Orchestra; Karl Krueger, conductor

GENRE: orchestral music

METER: compound duple in the A sections, simple duple in the B section

FORM: ternary (ABA), with introduction and coda

WHAT TO LISTEN FOR

- lush timbres and wide dynamic range of romantic orchestra
- folklike quality of principal melody
- transformation of principal melody in contrasting B section

TIMING	SECTION	COMMENTS
0:00	introduction	Solo French horn, accompanied by strings, anticipates the A theme and sets a nostalgic mood.
0:24	A	Solo oboe, accompanied by clarinets and bassoons, states the A theme (*aaba* form).
1:13		Second half of the tune repeats (*ba*), with addition of flute and French horns, extended by a two-bar tag or codetta.
2:02	transition	Abrupt shift to faster tempo and new meter; a long trill in first violins, the other strings playing **pizzicato** (plucking the strings), then a rapidly rising, skittering figure in strings and winds.
2:18	B	Violins play the B theme, a variation of A, **arco** (with the bow), accompanied by pizzicato strings. Crescendo from *piano* to a loud passage for full orchestra, then diminuendo with orchestration returning to strings alone.
2:39		The B theme repeats.
3:00		Contrasting section begins with a fragment of A in the flute and a new continuation, answered by the violins; rapid modulations to distant keys add excitement.
3:18		Return of B, with new conclusion.
3:40		Developmental section begins with fragments of A in **augmentation** (with each note "stretched out" in slower rhythm), first in the French horn, then clarinet, then other solo instruments.
4:08		Passage for full orchestra slowly builds to a loud climax, then subsides.
4:34		B section closes with slow crescendo, arriving at a loud, accented chord on an unstable harmony, followed by silence.
5:02	transition	Return to the opening tempo and meter, again with solo horn and strings, plus clarinet.
5:26	A	The A theme returns in the English horn (a lower-pitched member of the oboe family), with low string pizzicato and high string **tremolo** (rapidly repeated notes). The three phrases describe an *abb* form.

	CD 1.25	Listening Guide 8.1	*Gaelic* Symphony, second movement AMY BEACH

TIMING	SECTION	COMMENTS
6:03		Theme in oboe, in the original key; three phrases, *abb*.
6:41		A new extension begins with the *a* phrase of the theme; crescendo to a loud chord. A descending line played by two clarinets leads to a duet for oboe and English horn that ends inconclusively.
8:01	coda	Return to the tempo of B.

Listen & Reflect

1. How does Beach use melody, harmony, rhythm, and orchestration to emphasize the Irish character of her borrowed theme?
2. How does she use those elements at other times to minimize the folk character?
3. Locate and listen to a recording of Dvořák's *New World* Symphony. Do any of its themes strike you as folklike?
4. How does Dvořák's treatment of those themes resemble Beach's symphony, and how does it differ?

EDWARD MACDOWELL

Although George Chadwick included Edward MacDowell in his list of "the boys," MacDowell's musical orientation ran against the classicist strain of German Romanticism—from Beethoven and Schubert through Mendelssohn, Schumann, and Brahms—that inspired the Bostonians. Instead, he identified with the "New German School" of Franz Liszt and Richard Wagner, which emphasized programmatic description and musical narrative over the classical sonata forms of symphony and string quartet.

years in Europe

In 1876 MacDowell's mother took her musically gifted sixteen-year-old son to Europe for more specialized training. He was accepted at the Paris Conservatory but disliked French instruction and moved to Germany two years later, studying piano in Wiesbaden and Frankfurt and taking composition lessons; from 1881 to 1882 he taught piano at the Darmstadt Conservatory. In July 1882, when he played his First Piano Concerto at a concert in Zurich attended by Liszt, the strong response surpassed anything MacDowell had imagined and changed the way he thought of himself as a musician.

Now MacDowell gave more and more attention to composing. By 1884 German publishers had issued some of his works, and other pianists had started playing them. In the same year, he married Marian Nevins, an American and a former piano student, and the couple settled in 1885 in Wiesbaden, where MacDowell taught piano and composed. Three years later, having lived nearly half his life in

Edward MacDowell (1860–1908) and his wife, the American pianist Marian Nevins MacDowell (1857–1956), who after his death established their summer home in Peterborough, New Hampshire, as the MacDowell Colony, a working retreat for composers, writers, and artists.

Europe, the twenty-seven-year-old MacDowell and his wife moved to Boston, where he launched an American career centered on composing but funded chiefly by piano teaching and performing.

In the spring of 1889 MacDowell premiered his Piano Concerto no. 2 in D Minor with the Theodore Thomas Orchestra in New York, followed a month later by a performance with the Boston Symphony. In July he presented the work again at the Paris Exposition Universelle in a concert of American music. When a respected New York critic wrote that the concerto deserved placement "at the head of all works of its kind produced either by a native or adopted citizen of America," some observers began to perceive the young composer as American music's Man of Destiny. In 1894, when he played his Second Piano Concerto with the New York Philharmonic, the conductor, Anton Seidl, a confirmed Wagnerite, declared MacDowell superior to Johannes Brahms as a composer. And two years later MacDowell played his First Piano Concerto in New York with the Boston Symphony, to great critical acclaim, on a program that also introduced his Second (*Indian*) Suite.

This concert proved a turning point in MacDowell's life. Now reckoned one of the country's leading musicians, he was offered the first professorship of music at Columbia University in New York City. In the fall of 1896 he plunged wholeheartedly into teaching but found that the job left him with little time for composing. Though he continued to write smaller pieces, no more orchestral works appeared. In conflict with Columbia's president over the music department's place in the university, MacDowell resigned in 1904 amid a commotion publicized in the New York press. Emotionally drained, and perhaps still feeling the effects of a traffic accident earlier in the year, he suffered a crisis in health. By December 1904 he was showing signs of serious mental illness, which gradually worsened. He died early in 1908 at the age of forty-seven and was buried near his summer home in Peterborough, New Hampshire, which, through Marian MacDowell's dedicated efforts, was made into an art colony in his memory.

While MacDowell's musical talents were uncommon, he also arrived on the scene at an opportune moment, as Americans were developing an appetite for classical music and building an infrastructure of ensembles, conservatories, concert halls, and opera companies to support it. The only missing element was a composer to signal the nation's musical maturity. Enter the young, handsome, charismatic—and modest—MacDowell, seemingly born to the role: impeccably schooled, with European training and reputation; an excellent performer of his own music; an artist of broad range who also wrote poetry and showed a knack for drawing. And his music had a sound of its own.

MacDowell obviously profited from the favored role that was thrust upon him, but eminence brought pressures, too, and they seemed to increase with the years. His Columbia post was a reward for creative artistry, but it imposed duties that swamped his creative vocation. After 1902 he began several new works but finished none of them. His illness was partly to blame, but MacDowell was also profoundly self-critical, with a mania for revising his compositions.

MACDOWELL AND MUSICAL NATIONALISM

Not long after his return from Germany, MacDowell found himself involved in a debate about the future direction of American music. When the debate began, suspicious of the idea of musical nationalism as an end in itself, he opposed "exclusively American" concerts, considering them more political events than artistic ones. In the long run, he believed, composers were better off having to *earn* performances purely on the basis of their work's quality.

Beyond musical politics, however, lay musical style. And here MacDowell aspired to the universality that European classics had achieved. In nineteenth-century Europe, nationalism and universality were closely connected. Music in the classical sphere was given a nationalist slant by borrowing material from local folk music, especially in newly emerging nations such as Poland, Russia, and Bohemia—in much the same way as each nation had its own language, folklore, music, flag, and institutions, while remaining part of cosmopolitan Europe. Indeed, it was their creation of a national flavor that brought composers like Frederic Chopin, Modest Musorgsky, and Antonin Dvořák international recognition. MacDowell aimed at a parallel kind of universality by "working toward a music which should be American," as he told the writer Hamlin Garland in 1896. "Our music thus far is mainly a scholarly restatement of Old-World themes; in other words it is derived from Germany—as all my earlier pieces were." MacDowell resolved to be an American composer in the way that Musorgsky was a Russian composer: by treating his own country as the equivalent of a peripheral European nation and bringing the landscape and indigenous American materials into his own European-based style. He perceived, in other words, that the road to universality led through nationalism.

European nationalism

MacDowell's *Woodland Sketches*, op. 51 (1896), reveal one way in which he claimed an American composer's identity. The work consists of ten short piano pieces whose titles refer to the American landscape and connect with the composer's personal experience. With such titles as "To a Wild Rose," "By a Meadow Brook," and "A Deserted Farm," the individual pieces register MacDowell's impressions of the New England countryside.

Woodland Sketches

In "To a Wild Rose" (LG 8.2), dissonances bring to MacDowell's sound image of a woodland flower just enough tonal ambiguity to cast an aura of mystery. Although MacDowell generally favored thick, complex chords, here the texture is transparent, with never more than five notes in a chord. MacDowell's music invites the listener to share his personal impression of a commonplace experience of coming upon a wild rose in its natural surroundings.

LG 8.2

The musical style of "To a Wild Rose" is rooted in European practice and no American melodies are quoted, yet the native lineage of this work is also clear. For all the years he spent in Europe, MacDowell was a born-and-bred American, and the New England countryside inspired the *Woodland Sketches* shortly after he told Garland that he was "working toward a music which should be American." What, then, constitutes American music? Is it a matter of style? nationality? subject? quotation of indigenous music? the composer's intent?

American nationalism

At least since the time of Gottschalk (see chapter 5), the question has sparked interest and controversy. So many different criteria have been used to measure musical Americanism that there seems little hope of finding a definition satisfactory to all. From one perspective, MacDowell's career and music show the composer's dependence on Europe; from another, the American identity of a

🎧 **CD 1.26**   **Listening Guide 8.2**   **"To a Wild Rose"** EDWARD MACDOWELL

DATE: 1896
PERFORMER: James Barbagallo, piano
GENRE: character piece for piano
METER: duple
FORM: ABAC

WHAT TO LISTEN FOR

- sustained mood with no sharp contrasts
- simple, delicate textures
- clear, songlike melody in foreground
- mildly dissonant harmony with touches of chromaticism

TIMING	SECTION	COMMENTS
0:00	A	An 8-bar melody, built on a short-short-long rhythm, avoids stepwise motion and the tonic pitch until its last note. Simple harmony with gentle dissonances, as in the second bar.
0:11		A variant of the 8-bar melody, with a somewhat higher contour. In bar 6, the left hand echoes the short-short-long rhythm.
0:23	B	12 bars, introducing more chromatic harmonies, climaxing in a 4-bar phrase that emphasizes the dominant chord, with a diminuendo on the piece's highest note.
0:44	A	Repeat of the opening 8-bar melody.
0:56	C	Chromatic melody related to B unfolds over a tonic **pedal point** (a long-held note with changing harmonies over it), then resolves in a quiet, gentle cadence.

NOTE From *Woodland Sketches*, op. 51.

Listen & Reflect

1. Is MacDowell's title an appropriate indicator of the music's character? Why or why not?
2. Aaron Copland's "Morning on the Ranch" (see LG 15.2) is a much later example of musical nature painting. Does it seem to share any aesthetic qualities with "To a Wild Rose"? Why or why not?

piece like "To a Wild Rose" seems indisputable; and from still another, both MacDowell and this piano piece reflect an interweaving of European and American traits on an equal footing.

NATIONALISM AND THE *INDIAN* SUITE

Several years before the *Woodland Sketches*, in an effort to compose music that did not sound German-inspired, MacDowell wrote an orchestral piece, the Second (*Indian*) Suite (1891), based on American Indian melodies. The melodies were drawn from transcriptions in Theodore Baker's 1882 dissertation on the music of North American Indians (see chapter 9).

MacDowell's suite contains five movements—"Legend," "Love Song," "In War-time," "Dirge," and "Village Festival"—each based on a theme he found in Baker. He once told an interviewer that of all his music, the "Dirge" pleased him most. MacDowell was not alone in judging this movement a success. His biographer called it "overwhelmingly poignant," and composer Arthur Farwell, who worked extensively with American Indian melodies himself, praised its "sheer imaginative beauty." The "Dirge" is for an absent son who has died. Since the preceding movement is about war, listeners are invited to think that he has been slain in battle. By extension, the "Dirge" can also be heard as a lament for the "vanishing Indian," written at a time when that population was at its smallest, in a state of complete subjugation to white conquerors.

MacDowell delayed the first performance for several years, for fear that "this rough, savage music" would not "appeal to our concert audiences." By the time the suite was premiered in 1896, the American visit of Bohemian composer Antonín Dvořák had brought the issue of musical nationalism into the public arena. Dvořák arrived in the United States in 1892 as director of the National Conservatory of Music in New York, and remained until 1895. He had been invited by Jeannette Thurber, a patron who, in setting up the National Conservatory, hoped to encourage the growth of national musical culture—if possible, with funding from the U.S. government.

Dvořák became a public advocate for musical nationalism in America. He showed particular interest in melodies native to the United States—especially African American plantation melodies and Indian tunes. In the spring of 1893 he told the *New York Herald* that, after eight months in America, he was "now satisfied . . . that the future music of this country must be founded upon what are called negro melodies. . . . There is nothing in the whole range of composition that cannot be supplied with themes from this source." Then, as if to show how composers on this side of the Atlantic might proceed, Dvořák wrote his Symphony no. 9, *From the New World*, inspired in part by African American and American Indian melodies and rhythms.

Dvořák and nationalism

MacDowell, who had finished his own *Indian* Suite two years before the well-publicized premiere of the *New World* Symphony in December 1893, took a dim view of the attention that Dvořák's ideas received. "Purely national music," he wrote, "has no place in art, for its characteristics may be duplicated by anyone who takes the fancy to do so. . . . We have here in America been offered a pattern for an 'American' national musical costume by the Bohemian Dvořák, though what the Negro melodies have to do with Americanism in art still remains a mystery." MacDowell objected to Dvořák's meddling and considered his prescription for national music shallow. "Music that can be made by 'recipe,'" he wrote, "is not music, but 'tailoring.'" Moreover, music based on tunes by slaves and former slaves might exude Americanism, but what would it say about the nation's character? On the other hand, he argued, the music of Indians pointed toward a heroic past, an unspoiled continental landscape, and an American people of independent spirit.

MacDowell and Dvořák

To MacDowell, the goal of musical nationalism should be elevating: to echo the "genius" of the nation. And that could be achieved only by composers "who, being part of the people, love the country for itself" and who "put into their music what the nation has put into its life." Furthermore, both composers and the public needed to seize "freedom from the restraint that an almost unlimited deference to European thought and prejudice has imposed upon us. Masquerading in the so-called nationalism of Negro clothes cut in Bohemia will not help us. What we must arrive at is the youthful optimistic vitality and the undaunted tenacity of spirit that characterizes the American man. This is what I hope to see echoed in American music."

Had he lived to see it, MacDowell might have been surprised to learn that the task of creating a national music from "negro melodies" would eventually fall to African American musicians—perhaps the central story of American music in the twentieth century. But it probably would have come as no surprise to Dvořák, who enjoyed a lively exchange of musical ideas with his African American students at the National Conservatory. In the meantime, a younger composer working in isolation was developing a much different approach to the challenge of writing American music.

CHARLES IVES

Charles Ives (1874–1954) attended the Hopkins Grammar School in New Haven, Connecticut, where he pitched for the school baseball team, a year before entering Yale. He is pictured here at left with Hopkins teammate Franklin Miles (1894).

Charles Edward Ives was born in 1874 in Danbury, Connecticut. George Ives, Charles's father, had studied music in New York City, led a military band from Danbury during the Civil War, then returned to his hometown to work as a bandmaster, performer, and teacher of music. Charlie, as family members knew him, showed uncommon talent on the keyboard, began composing at eleven, played snare drum in his father's band, and took his first post as a paid church organist at fourteen. In 1894, the year Charlie enrolled at Yale College, his father died, a loss he mourned for the rest of his life. After an academically undistinguished career at Yale, which included composition study with Horatio Parker, Ives graduated in 1898, moved to New York City, and began a career in business that led him into life insurance and estate planning.

Unconnected with New York's public musical life after 1902, when he gave up his last job as a church organist, Ives composed prolifically in private, at least until 1917, when an illness brought both his business and his composing to a temporary halt. Three years later, he printed, at his own expense, the large-scale Piano Sonata no. 2, *Concord, Mass., 1840–1860*, and a prose companion piece, *Essays before a Sonata*. In 1922 his self-published *114 Songs* appeared in print. Neither of these works drew much notice from critics, performers, or the public. Yet they were part of a large body of music unlike that of any other composer, living or dead, much of it radically forward-looking in style yet rooted in American musical traditions and history. In the 1930s younger American composers began to discover Ives, delighted to find an older figure whose music spoke with so distinctive a voice. As musicians gradually woke up to Ives's music—the *Concord* Sonata was not premiered until 1939, and in 1947 he won a Pulitzer Prize for his Symphony no. 3, composed some forty years earlier—they encountered a figure whose background was as unusual as his musical approach.

Ives credited his father with shaping his musical outlook. By Charles's testimony, George Ives had considered music a spiritually precious thing and conveyed his love for it to his son. And he was something of a visionary when it came to acoustics. Charles remembered an experiment of George's in which violin strings were "stretched over a clothes press and let down with weights," intended to produce quarter-tone subdivisions of the scale. George's teaching methods could also be unconventional. On the one hand, "Father knew (and filled me up with) Bach and the best of the classical music, and the study of harmony and counterpoint etc., and music history." On the other, "He would occasionally have us sing, for instance, a tune like *The Swanee River* [Foster's 'Old Folks at Home'] in the key of E♭, but play the accompaniment in the key of C. This was to stretch our ears and strengthen our musical minds, so that they could learn to use and translate things that might be used and translated (in the art of music) more than they had been." Such ear-stretching schemes taught Ives that euphony was not the only kind of harmony worth hearing; that two simultaneous streams of sound offered wide possibilities for focusing one's ear; and that even the most familiar Stephen Foster song could be defamiliarized.

IVES'S SONGS

The *114 Songs* is a collection of music written throughout Ives's life as a composer, presented in something close to reverse chronological order. As Ives declared in a "Postface" to the work, he had "merely cleaned house" to produce it. The variety of musical styles is enormous, from the simple consonances of the last song, "Slow March," the eleven-year-old composer's memorial for a deceased pet dog, to the massive, teeth-rattling dissonances of the opening song, "Majority," in Ives's most advanced (and for some listeners, off-putting) idiom. In between are sentimental songs, comic songs, hymns, songs in French and German, and many songs experimental in nature and unlike anything composed before, in the United States or anywhere else.

Although the contents of *114 Songs* exhibit great differences in style and substance, each song is unmistakably Ivesian. Indeed, according to Ives's musical philosophy, what a composition sounds like can never reflect more than part of the music's essence. "My God! What has sound got to do with music!" he bursts out in *Essays before a Sonata*. This paradoxical blast was Ives's response to the attitude that composers should tailor their music to performers. "It will fit the hand better this way—it will sound better," a violinist is supposed to have told Ives, provoking these often-quoted words. A bit later in the same paragraph he writes: "That music must be heard is not essential—what it *sounds* like may not be what it *is*." Clearly, any discussion of Ives's music must include aspects that reach beyond the realm of sound.

No single item from the *114 Songs* captures the tremendous scope of Ives's musical vision. In "The Circus Band," which recaptures boyhood impressions of a circus parade down Main Street, the singer represents the awestruck young bystander while the piano represents the band, playing a pair of Sousa-style marches, with an intervening drum roll-off (the signal for a parade band to begin the next march) imitated by the pianist thumping out thick handfuls of notes. The singer and the pianist provide two separate—and sometime not fully coordinated—musical layers, and the listener is encouraged to focus on one or the other, or on the seemingly chance convergences between the two. "Serenity," in contrast, sets a nineteenth-century hymn text by John Greenleaf Whittier to an incantatory melody accompanied by two dissonant chords that simply rock back and forth in hushed, fragile contemplation—another example of musical layering.

"The Housatonic at Stockbridge" was inspired by a walk Ives and his wife took along a riverbank in western Massachusetts shortly after their marriage. On that summer Sunday morning, he recalled, "we walked in the meadows along the

⤏ George E. Ives (1845–1894), father of Charles Ives, was a town musician and bandmaster in Danbury, Connecticut.

"The Circus Band"

"Serenity"

"The Housatonic at Stockbridge"

river, and heard the distant singing from the church across the river. The mist had not entirely left the river bed, and the colors, the running water, the banks and elm trees were something that one would always remember." The hymn tune being sung that morning, Ives recalled, was DORRNANCE, by Isaac Woodbury, a younger contemporary of Lowell Mason, and the singer's melody quotes that tune while the piano quietly flows along in an unrelated tonality—two tonalities, in fact, one in the lower register and a contrasting one in the upper. Here is yet another example of layering, to which is added a sense of multiple voices speaking through the music, the human voice of the singer and the voices of nature in the piano's complex texture.

Ives's quotations
        Because DORRNANCE was part of the experience that inspired "The Housatonic at Stockbridge," Ives's quotation of it is understandable. On one hand, his use of a hymn tune connects his music back through the ages to Bach and beyond, even to the origins of the European classical tradition in the late Middle Ages. But on the other hand, the example points to a larger question: Why did Ives, composing in the classical sphere, repeatedly quote melodies from the American popular and traditional spheres? Part of the answer lies in the spiritual power he felt came from the quotations. Believing that the purest-hearted performers were plain folks, singing and playing in the course of their everyday lives, Ives often quoted melodies that they loved and sang in their own way—including hymn tunes that most trained musicians scorned. His teacher at Yale, Horatio Parker, for example, said of "Sweet By and By" and similar gospel hymns: "I believe no lower level can be found than that of the . . . sickly sentimental hymn tune." Ives, in response, distinguished between such tunes as they existed on the page and as they were sung, writing of Parker (or someone like him) that "his opinion is based on something he'd probably never heard, seen or experienced. He knows little of how these things sounded. . . . It was the *way* this music was sung that made them big or little."

        As a boy, Ives had heard these melodies at outdoor camp meetings:

> The farmers, their families and field hands, for miles around, would come afoot or in their farm wagons. I remember how the great waves of sound used to come through the trees—when things like *Beulah Land . . . Nearer My God to Thee . . . In the Sweet Bye and Bye* [*sic*], and the like were sung by thousands of "let out" souls. . . . Father, who led the singing, sometimes with his cornet or his voice, sometimes with both voice and arms, and sometimes in the quieter hymns with a French horn or violin, would always encourage the people to sing their own way.

substance and manner
Ives's experience of communal singing, not written music, inspired these melodic quotations. He found in the spontaneity and freedom of such singing the spiritual power he came to call "substance." Ives explained:

> It wasn't the music that did it, and it wasn't the words that did it, and it wasn't the sounds (whatever they were—transcendent, peculiar, bad, some beautifully unmusical)—but they were sung "like the rocks were grown." The singers weren't all singers, but they knew what they were doing—it all came from something felt, way down and way up.

        While he never defined "substance" in so many words, Ives did offer many examples of "manner," the label under which he grouped technical skill, standard musical customs and forms, academic knowledge, and even sound itself. For Ives, the difference between music and sound, substance and manner, lay in attitude. Substance was a matter of putting your whole soul into the making of music, regardless of talent or skill. To say that hymns were sung "like the rocks were grown" was to suggest that the singers' feelings were so deeply grounded in belief and nature that they approached the geological. Hymns tapping such emotional depth could hardly be trivial, no matter what the professors said.

Ives quoted melodies to suggest the inner convictions that give perfor-   *LG 8.3*
mances substance in the first place. "The Things Our Fathers Loved" (LG 8.3), a song from 1917 to which Ives added the subtitle "and the greatest of these was Liberty," weaves together several quotations to conjure up a spiritual realm of music, "a place in the soul all made of tunes," as Ives's own lyrics have it. (Ives often set his own texts to music.) Those tunes range from Stephen Foster's "My Old Kentucky Home" and George F. Root's "Battle Cry of Freedom" to Paul Dresser's 1897 popular song "On the Banks of the Wabash," the hymn tune NETTLETON ("Come Thou Fount of Every Blessing"), and the gospel hymn "Sweet By and By." Ives combines these tunes in a through-composed form, in which the music constantly changes to suit the mood of the words, as opposed to strophic or verse-and-chorus forms based on repetition. He also alters the tunes in various ways. For example, the song opens with a quotation of "My Old Kentucky Home," but the first few melodic intervals are **inverted,** or sung "upside down," beginning with a descending line where Foster's song has a rising one. Ives also expands or contracts intervals, sometimes causing the melody to veer off key in surprising ways, as at the end of the same quotation, at the words "all made of tunes," where the last two notes are a half-step higher than they would be in a more literal quotation—perhaps an evocation of John Bell's impassioned voice.

The piano, during this opening quotation of "My Old Kentucky Home," supports the singer with simple, conventional chords in the left hand, while the right hand plays a variant of the singer's melody two beats behind the singer and in a different key, something like the way George Ives taught Charlie to "stretch his ears" with another Foster tune, "Old Folks at Home." And when the words allude to the "village cornet band," the piano comes in with "The Battle Cry of Freedom" one beat ahead of the proper place (according to the written music's bar lines), while the voice comes in one beat too late. The result evokes the off-kilter but spirited playing of an amateur town band.

Even more important than the tunes, Ives's words imply, are the values they reinforce. Ives chooses to quote a patriotic song ("The Battle Cry of Freedom"), two songs about specific places ("My Old Kentucky Home" and "On the Banks of the Wabash"), and two religious songs ("Come Thou Fount of Every

In their own words

Charles Ives on Music versus Sound

One of Ives's best-known stories reveals his distinction between substance and manner. A young man is questioning George Ives:

"How can you stand it to hear old John Bell (the best stonemason in town) sing?" Father said, "He is a supreme musician." The young man (nice and educated) was horrified—"Why he sings off the key, the wrong notes and everything—and that horrible, raucous voice—and he bellows out and hits notes no one else does—it's awful!" Father said, "Watch him closely and reverently, look into his face and hear the music of the ages. Don't pay too much attention to the sounds—for if you do, you may miss the music."

| CD 1.27 | Listening Guide 8.3 | "The Things Our Fathers Loved" CHARLES IVES |

DATE: 1917

PERFORMERS: Mary Ann Hart, mezzo-soprano; Dennis Helmrich, piano

GENRE: art song

METER: duple, often obscured by irregular rhythms

FORM: through-composed

WHAT TO LISTEN FOR

- shifting moods
- deliberate "disagreements" of key and rhythm between voice and piano
- use of quotations

TIMING	TEXT	COMMENTS
0:00	I think there must be a place in the soul all made of tunes of long ago;	"My Old Kentucky Home" in the voice, with the first few notes inverted. The piano echoes the melody in a different key.
0:19	I hear the organ on the Main Street corner,	Quotation of "On the Banks of the Wabash."
0:27	Aunt Sarah humming gospels;	Quotation of NETTLETON.
0:37	Summer evenings,	A suggestion of the richly chromatic style of Richard Wagner.
0:44	The village cornet band, playing in the square. The town's Red, White and Blue, all Red, White and Blue	"The Battle Cry of Freedom" (see LG 6.5), first in the piano and then in the voice as well. The piano is noticeably ahead of the voice. Gradually increasing speed and volume.
0:56	Now! Hear the songs! I know not what are the words But they sing in my soul . . .	The voice quotes "Sweet By and By" (see LG 7.2) while "The Battle Cry of Freedom" continues in the piano's upper register, over a thick, rolling, romantic keyboard texture. After the climax, a gradual slowing and softening.
1:14	. . . of the things our Fathers loved.	A return to the quiet mood of the opening. The final dissonance is very soft and gentle but lacks a conventional resolution.

Listen & Reflect

1. It is possible to read Ives's text as referring to three different times: a spiritual timelessness, the past, and the present. Where are these divisions in the song, and how does the composer use music to distinguish them?

2. Some commentators have interpreted the "now" of the song as 1917, the year Ives composed it. What current event in world history might have inspired this song, and how might that affect how the song is understood?

Blessing" and "Sweet By and By"). Love of country and home; devotion to family and to God—these are the communal values that music can express and sustain. But for Ives, these songs derive their moral force not so much from their lyrics as from their tunes. Even if their words are forgotten, Ives insists, the melodies still "sing in my soul of the things our Fathers loved."

IVES'S INSTRUMENTAL MUSIC

Ives's instrumental compositions reveal many of the same traits as his vocal works. Quotations, layering, and changes of voice abound, often leading to jarring contrasts—quotations from Beethoven symphonies, for example, next to fiddle tunes and gospel hymns—and dense overlappings. In *Putnam's Camp, Redding, Connecticut,* for orchestra, Ives creates the illusion of two bands, each playing a different piece, marching toward each other. In *The Unanswered Question* a single trumpet repeatedly intones the same angular figure over a string ensemble's consonant, organlike chords while four flutes respond with growing agitation to the trumpet's calls. Harmonic dissonance in *Putnam's Camp* comes to a head in a roar of cacophony, while in *The Unanswered Question* clashes between layers come and go, each time yielding to the serene euphony of the string background. In creating sounds that stretch the ears and minds of listeners, Ives was following the lead of his intellectual heroes, Ralph Waldo Emerson and Henry David Thoreau, who probed hidden unities and mysteries of human existence.

The Unanswered Question

The *Concord* Sonata, composed between 1904 and 1919 and printed in 1920 with the *Essays before a Sonata,* is the ultimate Ivesian synthesis. As Ives wrote, it "is an attempt to present (one person's) impression of the spirit of transcendentalism that is associated in the minds of many with Concord, Mass., of over a half century ago. This is undertaken in impressionistic pictures of Emerson and Thoreau, a sketch of the Alcotts, and a scherzo supposed to reflect a lighter quality which is often found in the fantastic side of Hawthorne." By honoring a group of New Englanders in an esteemed European form, Ives declared the universality of both. By commemorating literary Americans linked to transcendental philosophy, he suggested their influence on his own outlook. By combining sonata-style thematic development with quotation and layering, he proclaimed their compatibility and his own command of the composer's craft. By accompanying his sonata with a book-length introduction, he admitted that a composer of music like this had some explaining to do. And by having these items printed at his own expense rather than adding them to his stock of unpublished manuscripts, he made a bid for public recognition as a composer.

the Concord *Sonata*

For all its American subject matter, the *Concord* Sonata draws on the European musical past in its large outlines, which resemble such monumental nineteenth-century works as Beethoven's *Hammerklavier* Sonata. Only the last of its four movements, "Thoreau," breaks with the usual character of the European sonata. Instead of taking the decisive tone of a typical finale, the movement begins softly, mixes dreamy reflection with livelier moments, and fades away at the end, with the sound of Thoreau's flute echoing over Walden Pond.

The end of the *Concord* Sonata suggests a prophecy Ives made a few years later in the "Postface" to the *114 Songs.* The art of music, he wrote, was progressing, not

Charles Ives as photographed by W. Eugene Smith around 1947, when he was in his early seventies.

declining, and its progress would be understood best by people singing, playing, and composing in the course of their daily lives. Ives knew from experience the resistance his music would meet. But he could imagine a future in which his works could help people attune themselves to the spiritual dimension of human life in an interconnected universe.

Because Ives's music came to public knowledge long after it was written, the story of its discovery and performance belongs to a later time (see chapter 12). From the 1930s on, Ives's profile was recast more than once, as "new" works were discovered and views of them adjusted to fit the perspectives of composers, critics, and historians at that particular time. His contributions include a substantial body of music, some of it radically individual in style; an original aesthetic philosophy; and a symbolic presence that has served as a barometer of attitudes toward American composition for more than a half century since his death.

> ### In their own words
>
> ## Charles Ives on the Future of Music (1922)
>
> The instinctive and progressive interest of every man in art will go on and on, ever fulfilling hopes, ever building new ones, ever opening new horizons, until the day will come when every man while digging potatoes will breathe his own epics, his own symphonies (operas, if he likes it); and as he sits of an evening in his backyard and shirt sleeves smoking his pipe and watching his brave children in *their* fun of building *their* themes for *their* sonatas of their *life*, he will look up over the mountains and see his visions in their reality, will hear the transcendental strains of the day's symphony resounding in their many choirs, and in all their perfection, through the west wind and the tree tops!

QUESTIONS FOR DISCUSSION AND REVIEW

1. Compare and contrast the state of classical music in the United States in the periods before and after the Civil War.

2. What did the late nineteenth-century Boston composers have in common with each other? How was MacDowell like them in training, values, and output, and how was he different?

3. What circumstances in her life set Amy Beach apart from the other Boston composers and from MacDowell?

4. Listen to Dvořák's *New World* Symphony and MacDowell's *Indian* Suite. What are their similarities and differences?

5. What features mark Charles Ives's music as radically different from that of the other composers discussed in this chapter?

6. What musical traditions are connected with Ives's music? How are his attitudes toward these traditions expressed in his music and his writings about music?

FURTHER READING

Block, Adrienne Fried. *Amy Beach, Passionate Victorian: The Life and Work of an American Composer, 1867–1944.* New York: Oxford University Press, 1998.

Crawford, Richard. "Edward MacDowell: Musical Nationalism and an American Tone Poet." *Journal of the American Musicological Society* 49 (1996): 528–60.

Horowitz, Joseph. *Classical Music in America: A History of Its Rise and Fall.* New York: W.W. Norton, 2005.

Ives, Charles. *Essays before a Sonata, and Other Writings.* Edited by Howard Boatwright. New York: W.W. Norton, 1962.

MacDowell, Edward. *Critical and Historical Essays: Lectures Delivered at Columbia University.* 1912. Reprint. New York: Da Capo, 1969.

Magee, Gayle Sherwood. *Charles Ives Reconsidered.* Urbana: University of Illinois Press, 2008.

Yellin, Victor Fell. *Chadwick, Yankee Composer.* Washington, DC: Smithsonian Institution Press, 1990.

"ALL THAT IS NATIVE AND FINE"

American Indian Music, Folk Songs, Spirituals, and Their Collectors

The story of folk music in the United States, whether that of American Indians, African Americans, or European Americans, is inextricably bound up with the story of the people who collected, studied, classified, and defined that music. The concept of "the folk" as an object of study dates back to eighteenth-century Germany and especially to the writings of Johann Gottfried von Herder (1744–1803). Herder's notion of *das Volk* was closely tied to ideas of ethnic nationalism. For Herder, a nation consisted of a group of people united by a common language, geography, religion, and customs. In his view, the legitimacy of a political nation rested on the legitimacy of its ethnic nationhood, which in turn was rooted in the presumed antiquity of folk culture. Herder considered songs, tales, games, and other artifacts of folklore to be creations of the collective wisdom of the folk, dating back to a distant, nonhierarchical past.

Herder's Volk

As part of his interest in *das Volk,* Herder collected specimens of German folk culture, including folk songs. When he published a collection of folk song texts in the 1770s, he established a model for later students of folklore, who throughout the nineteenth century were more interested in the lyrics than in the music of folk songs. Also like Herder, those scholars understood folk songs to be composed not by one person but by a community, and to have been in existence for a long time; only in that way could they be valued as communal expressions of an entire people.

Herder's political philosophy pointed to the concept of popular sovereignty, a key component in the American Revolution. But his concept of ethnic nationality had little relevance for the United States as it loosened its ties to England and began to take on the features of a multiethnic nation. For folklorists in the nineteenth century, the United States was too young to have its own folk culture; it had merely transported Old World folk cultures to new shores, and the music of American Indians seemed too remote from European styles to be easily assimilated into a national music culture. Of course, from a present-day perspective it is easy to see that new and vital folk traditions were springing up in the New World. But for German-trained folklorists, "new folk traditions" was a contradiction in terms. Only with a change in the attitudes of collectors and students of folk songs could the discovery of American folk music take place.

AMERICAN INDIAN MUSIC AND ITS COLLECTORS

The decades after the Civil War saw the population of the continent's earliest residents, American Indians, swiftly decline in the face of war, disease, and poverty. But the same time period also saw the first systematic efforts of both Indians and non-Indians to preserve and understand their cultures, providing the first large body of detailed knowledge of traditional indigenous music.

AMERICAN INDIAN CULTURES SINCE 1830: CRISIS AND RENEWAL

American Indian societies suffered many hardships following the first contact with Europeans: the disruption of their culture, survival in an alien society, and struggles to adjust to minority status. So harsh was the Indians' lot that as the Civil War ended, many whites assumed that Indians were headed for extinction. Little more than 300,000 Indians were alive in 1865—a population merely one-tenth the size of the estimated 3 million residents of North America before European contact.

the Indian Removal Act

Much of that reduction was a direct result of U.S. policy. Beginning with the passage in 1830 of the Indian Removal Act, the government forcibly moved about 60,000 Indians from their homes in the southeastern United States to Indian Territory (present-day Oklahoma), an episode known as the Trail of Tears. But it soon became clear that movement westward would not be a permanent solution to the "Indian problem." During the 1840s whites moved west along the Oregon Trail, Mormons sought religious freedom in Utah, and prospectors flooded into California following the discovery there of gold. When Indian tribes resisted whites' westward expansion, the U.S. Army was deployed to move them onto reservations.

the General Allotment Act

In the decades after the Civil War, Congress abandoned the practice of making treaties with Indian nations, instead treating indigenous peoples as wards of the state and legislating on their behalf. (The Fourteenth Amendment, which in 1868 extended citizenship to former slaves, excluded most Indians.) New government policies were designed to deal with Indians on an individual or family basis rather than negotiating with autonomous tribes. In 1878 the General Allotment Act dissolved more than one hundred reservations by parceling out land that had been communally owned to individual heads of families. The results were disastrous for Indians, and by the 1890s they had lost 86 million acres of their former lands.

Indian boarding schools

Another part of the United States' policy was the creation of boarding schools for the education of American Indian children, beginning in 1878 with the Carlisle Indian School in Pennsylvania. The schools were approved by missionaries and social reformers who saw assimilation into the white mainstream as the best hope for the dwindling Indian population. But boarding school practices included transporting children far from their homes and families, forbidding them to speak in their native languages, and indoctrinating them in the attitude that their beliefs and traditions were inferior to Euro-American customs. Graduates, often meeting resistance from white society and encountering difficulties in rejoining their families, were caught between two worlds and at home in neither. Though well intentioned, the Indian boarding schools constituted an attack on indigenous culture.

And that was the peaceable aspect of the American Indians' saga. Even before and during the Civil War, the U.S. Army was engaged in the Plains Indian Wars, a series of hundreds of battles with western tribes. Beginning in the 1830s with the Comanche Wars, this episode in U.S. history includes the Dakota War of 1862–64, the Sand Creek Massacre of 1864, and the Battle of Little Big Horn ("Custer's Last Stand") in 1876. The Plains Indian Wars came to an ignominious end when the Seventh Cavalry massacred about 150 Lakota men, women, and children at Wounded Knee, South Dakota, in December 1890.

the Plains Indian Wars

In the same year, 1890, the U.S. Census Bureau announced that there was no longer an American frontier, no longer a line on the map separating white "civilization" from "untamed" Indian lands. The 1890s mark the low point in American Indian history, with the population decimated and cultural traditions in disarray. But the early years of the twentieth century saw indigenous peoples making advances, including the 1924 Indian Citizenship Act, which extended the rights of citizenship to nearly all Indians; the closing of the Indian boarding schools in the 1930s; the 1934 Indian Reorganization Act, which recognized the validity of tribal constitutions and bylaws; and the 1940 Nationality Act, which finally granted full citizenship to all American Indians. By 1940 the population figures were increasing, and today there are about 2 million Americans who self-identify as American Indian, Eskimo, or Aleut.

AMERICAN INDIAN MUSIC: THE CHALLENGES TO HISTORIANS

As noted in chapter 1, European descriptions of indigenous music making on the North American continent go back to the years of first contact in the early 1500s, and a sketchy history of American Indian music can be constructed from those accounts, flawed as they are by misconceptions and misunderstanding. But the story begins to change in the 1800s, when even as Indian life was being destroyed—or perhaps because of that destruction—Euro-Americans were discovering that the beliefs, tales, songs, dances, and material arts of these ancient civilizations had their own integrity and might well be worth preserving. The preservation effort, carried on chiefly by non-Indians, offers present-day observers their best window on earlier Indian music making, and it is with these nineteenth-century efforts that the history of American Indian music reaches relatively firm ground.

Three factors skew the historical record, however: the incompleteness of the surviving data, the difference between music in its natural habitat and outside it, and the contrast between native and non-native perceptions of Indian ways.

First, the record of American Indian music captures only a narrow slice of old and possibly highly varied traditions. When Europeans started settling in North America, aboriginal populations were both larger and more diverse than they were during the forced migrations and wars of the 1800s. At one time or another, North America has been home to as many as a thousand distinct tribal units, falling into roughly sixty different language families. Yet in only about 10 percent of those units is enough known about the culture to allow any reliable description of its music.

incomplete data

distortions in transcription

Second, an oral tradition of music is very different from music as it is preserved in **transcriptions** (performances "dictated" to a transcriber, who writes them down using music notation) and phonograph recordings. Writing and recording allow music that once existed only in live performance to be heard in other contexts, repeated as desired, and studied. But once a song is fixed in writing or on record, it takes on a permanent identity that it may never have enjoyed in performance. Emerging here is a phenomenon that will be a major theme of America's music in the twentieth and twenty-first centuries: the impact of recording technology on how listeners perceive music and, as a result, how musicians create it.

non-native perceptions

Third, until the late 1800s almost all of outsiders' knowledge about Indian music was filtered through the observations of people for whom it was a foreign mode of expression. When later scholars use those observations as the basis for secondary research, the possibility of introducing further distortions is all too real. With these caveats in mind, however, a great deal of valuable information can be gleaned from the work of the early preservationists.

EARLY WRITERS ON AMERICAN INDIAN MUSIC

The nineteenth century saw a significant increase in the quantity and quality of American Indian ethnography: writings about all aspects of Indian cultures. In the first half of the century the best writings are either by Indians themselves or by whites who enjoyed prolonged contact with them. The second half of the century witnessed two diverging treatments of Indian life: on the one hand, sensational and distorted portrayals presented in popular culture, and on the other hand, the more substantive work of scholars who brought anthropological methods to the study of music.

Lewis Cass

In 1822 Lewis Cass, governor of the Michigan Territory, quoted a Miami Indian song in an article on Native customs: "I will go and get my friends—I will go and get my friends—I am anxious to see my enemies. A clear sky is my friend, and it is him I am seeking." Aware that these words bore little resemblance to any song his readers would know, Cass explained how they were sung. His account squares with what we now know to be common Indian practices. The song has a specific purpose: to recruit volunteers for a mission of war. The text's brevity does not mean that the performance was short; Indians were known to repeat bits of text and music many times. **Vocables** (nonsemantic syllables) were also common, as was the song's use of a natural image—the sky, personified as a friend—rather than a narrative or literal description. Finally, Cass was struck by the unusual sound of the singing and attempted to describe it.

One observer who achieved close, sustained contact with Indian peoples was Henry Rowe Schoolcraft, who in 1823 married Jane Johnston, the mixed-blood granddaughter of

---

In their own words

Lewis Cass Describes a Miami Indian Song, 1822

There is a strong expiration of the breath at the commencement of each sentence, and a sudden elevation of the voice at the termination. The Chief, as he passes, looks every person sternly in the face. Those who are disposed to join the expedition exclaim *Yeh, Yeh, Yeh,* with a powerful tone of voice; and this exclamation is continually repeated during the whole ceremony. It is, if I may so speak, the evidence of their enlistment. Those who are silent decline the invitation.

an Ojibwa chief. By 1845 Schoolcraft's contact with Indians led to a combination memoir and ethnographic study, *Onéonta, or Characteristics of the Red Race of America,* which included an item called "Death Song," collected from Ojibwa sources. The song is a vivid statement in eighteen lines: the words of a warrior lying wounded after a battle, gazing at the sky, where he sees "warlike birds" who perhaps, Schoolcraft writes, represent his fellow warriors as they enter the territory of their foes, the Dacotahs or Sioux. The text concludes: "Full happy—I / To lie on the battlefield / Over the enemy's line." The neatly constructed poem, however, turns out to be a compilation. Knowing that readers found images of Indian stoicism poetic, Schoolcraft combined several sung moments into one song: evidence that his wish to document Ojibwa life vied with his urge to arrange it for public consumption.

Henry Rowe Schoolcraft

In 1847 George Copway, an Ojibwa born in Ontario whose parents were converted to Methodism by missionaries and who himself became a preacher in Illinois, published a memoir that included the five-line "George Copway's Dream Song":

George Copway

It is I who travel in the winds,
It is I who whisper in the breeze,
  I shake the trees,
  I shake the earth,
I trouble the waters on every land.

Copway said he received this song at age twelve from the god of the winds himself, who appeared in a dream and explained to him the song and its power. The notion of songs as personal possessions has not been rare among Indian peoples; nor is the belief that songs are carriers of prophecy.

Whites' views of Indians entered a new phase after 1855, which saw the publication of Henry Wadsworth Longfellow's *The Song of Hiawatha,* based on Henry Schoolcraft's researches. Selling thirty thousand copies during its first six months in print, *Hiawatha* became the most popular long poem ever written by an American. At a time when white settlement had largely wiped out traditional Indian ways of life east of the Mississippi, the poem introduced dramatic, elevated images of that life as it had existed earlier. Longfellow ascribed to Indians virtues admired by Victorian-era Americans, including manliness, courage, and integrity. Having prepared the way for white settlers, indigenous peoples had fulfilled their destiny and would now disappear, the poem implies, lingering only in memories built around myth.

The Song of Hiawatha

Recent opinion has judged Longfellow's images of Hiawatha and his people to be no truer than the older stereotype of Indians as savages. Nevertheless, the poem's popularity and staying power make it the central source for understanding how Americans in the eastern half of the continent viewed Indians from the mid-nineteenth century on.

⤳ George Copway (1818–1869), author of *The Life, History, and Travels of Kah-ge-ga-gah-bowh (George Copway): A Young Indian Chief of the Ojebwa Nation* (Albany, 1847).

AMERICAN INDIAN ETHNOGRAPHY AFTER 1865

The latter 1800s witnessed two new attitudes among white Americans. One, connected to show business and popular entertainment, trivialized indigenous cultures. The other was a scientific interest in American Indian life, rooted in idealistic curiosity and requiring trained workers and institutional funding.

✎ Alice Cunningham Fletcher (1838–1923), pioneer collector of music of Plains Indian nations, confers with Chief Joseph of the Nez Percé tribe.

Show business Indians, based on familiar images, grew more widespread as contact between Indians and white Americans decreased. Parodies of *Hiawatha* were standard fare, undermining the good intentions of Longfellow's flawed original, much as many stage versions of *Uncle Tom's Cabin* trivialized Harriet Beecher Stowe's sympathetic portrayal of the African American experience (see chapter 5). Another popular entertainment was "Buffalo Bill's Wild West," a traveling circuslike event staged by William "Buffalo Bill" Cody, a plains hunter turned showman. In Cody's shows, which began in 1882 and included real Indians, whites were the heroes and Indians the enemy in the grand finale, a reenactment of Custer's Last Stand. "Buffalo Bill's Wild West" set a pattern carried over into other popular forms, including dime novels, pulp magazines, and later, western movies. As in minstrel shows and other entertainments featuring "ethnic" (i.e., non-Anglo-American) characters, this strain of representation emphasized racial stereotypes.

The second response, which rejected stereotypes, took place chiefly at the U.S. government's initiative. Congress directed in 1879 that the Bureau of Indian Ethnology be created at the Smithsonian Institution in Washington, to find out more about the peoples with whom the army was still at war. During the 1880s and 1890s fieldworkers were dispatched from the nation's capital to document life in tribal settings. The drive to study Indians boosted the study of their music.

Theodore Baker

In 1882 Theodore Baker, an American music historian, published *Über die Musik der nordamerikanischen Wilden* (On the Music of the North American Indians), his doctoral dissertation at Leipzig University. Hailed as the first scholarly treatment of American Indian music, Baker's work contained transcriptions of songs he had heard on visits to a Seneca reservation in New York and the Carlisle Indian School in Pennsylvania. More than a decade passed, however, before a steady flow of similar studies began. A leader in that effort was Alice C. Fletcher, whose 1893 report on the music of the Omahas was the first of her many scholarly contributions. Emphasizing the subject's scientific interest, Fletcher and others gathered accurate data about the music. By the early twentieth century, reports and monographs on American tribal music were appearing regularly.

Alice C. Fletcher

Some idea of the process of collecting Indian music can be gained by looking at an Omaha song notated in 1884 by Fletcher. Born in 1838, Fletcher studied anthropology and was an assistant at the Peabody Museum in Cambridge, Massachusetts, when in 1881 she traveled to Nebraska for her first fieldwork with the Omaha people. The experience gave her a firsthand look at the sorry conditions in which many Indians lived, making her a strong advocate for reform and education. Fletcher's outlook was also influenced by her affiliation with the Bureau of American Ethnology, through which she administered grants of land to tribes in the western states. Fletcher did not at first think of her research as primarily musical. But she soon recognized the key role of music in Indian rituals and began transcribing melodies from the singers she met.

Fletcher's work owed much to her collaboration with Francis La Flesche, a man of mixed Omaha, Ponca, and French ancestry who grew up on an Omaha reservation. First meeting in 1881, the two combined forces to document Omaha traditions, culminating in their monograph *The Omaha Tribe* (1911). The transcription labeled "Ritual. Song of Approach" dates from an early stage of the collaboration. The musical source for this melody was La Flesche himself, who had learned the song in his youth. He sang it for Fletcher, who carefully notated not only pitches, rhythms, and syllables but also the singer's phrasing and accents.

Fletcher's interest in the melodies she collected grew over time, and she became intrigued by the question of where American Indian music belonged in the full range of human music making. In 1888 she wrote that "the Indian scale" could not be illustrated on the piano, and "there is no notation in common use that would make it feasible to describe it." Experience as a transcriber had taught her that rather than singing out of tune, Indians sang and heard music according to a logic that had so far eluded non-Indians. Because her Indian informants had a concept of **intonation**, or "in-tune-ness," different from that of Western music, Western notation could only approximate the pitch relationships she heard.

In the same year, Fletcher established contact with John Comfort Fillmore, a classical musician and teacher who believed that all music, Western and non-Western, written and nonwritten, shared a common harmonic basis. To Fillmore, Indians' departures from major and minor scales reflected "an underdeveloped sense of pitch discrimination" that was likely to mature in the future—an ethnocentric way of interpreting the differences in intonation that Fletcher had observed. Moreover, Fillmore heard harmonic implications in monophonic Indian melodies. When he first tried to harmonize Omaha melodies that Alice Fletcher had collected, he found that "no satisfactory scheme of chords could be made without implying the missing scale tones." The experiment convinced him that though Indian melodies seldom used all the notes in a standard major or minor scale—much like the pentatonic tunes found in both black and white American folk music—they were grounded in incomplete forms of those scales.

Alice Fletcher was persuaded by Fillmore's evolutionary hypothesis, at least at this point in her career. When her *Study of Omaha Indian Music* was published in 1893, only four of the collection's ninety-three melodies were left without accompaniment. The rest appeared with Fillmore's harmonizations, chiefly in the major mode.

The study of Indian music making was transformed after researchers started recording the music on Thomas A. Edison's cylinder phonographic machine. The recordings, begun around 1890 and continuing through the next century, are the basis of a major collection at the Smithsonian. The effort to preserve what remained of North America's oldest musical traditions seems all the more noteworthy when we consider the sheer foreignness of American Indian music to people outside their cultures and the delicate, highly demanding human endeavor musical fieldwork proved to be. In overcoming these two obstacles, scholars of American Indian music helped to establish fieldwork as the basis of a new discipline that emphasized ethnography, recording, transcription, and cultural and musical analysis. They stand among the key founding figures of **ethnomusicology**, a field that only in the 1950s would gain a foothold in academia.

Alice Fletcher's transcription of this traditional Omaha song was taken from a performance by her assistant, Francis La Flesche, in 1884.

the cylinder phonograph

〜 Frances Densmore, with an Edison cylinder machine, and Mountain Chief, leader of the Montana Blackfeet, in Washington, D.C., March 1916.

One pioneering ethnomusicologist was Frances Densmore, who began recording American Indian music in 1907 and by the time of her death at age ninety in 1957 had collected more than two thousand tribal songs. Her monograph *Teton Sioux Music* (1918) includes transcriptions and analyses of six hundred songs she collected at Standing Rock Reservation in South Dakota in 1911–14. One of those songs, "A Buffalo Said to Me," is also preserved on an Edison cylin-

LG 9.1   der (LG 9.1). The singer, Tatan ka-ohi tika (Brave Buffalo), was about seventy-three years old when he sang this song for Densmore's recording machine. His people, the Teton Sioux, also called the Lakota, are one of the seven distinct tribes that make up the Sioux nation, which in turn is part of the large Northern Plains Indian group. Since the eighteenth century the Lakota have lived in the area that is now North and South Dakota. Until the late nineteenth century they depended on the buffalo hunt for subsistence, supplemented with corn, which they received in trade with their eastern neighbors.

Densmore's cylinders are clearly a more accurate means of preserving American Indian music than transcription, which, as Alice Fletcher observed, falls short of capturing subtle nuances of performance, especially intonation. The recording of "A Buffalo Said to Me" reveals details about Teton vocal timbre, vibrato, and rhythmic nuance that are impossible to notate. Yet Densmore's primitive equipment was far from ideal. For instance, because the delicate recording machine was easily overwhelmed by sharp, percussive sounds, Densmore had to ask her informants to omit the drumming that was often an essential part of the musical texture. In her commentary for "A Buffalo Said to Me" she notes that Brave Buffalo also sang the song for her with a steady drumbeat that did not

In their own words

Frances Densmore Relates How Brave Buffalo Received Healing Power in a Dream

Brave Buffalo ... gave the following narrative concerning his first dream, from which he received his name:

> When I was 10 years old, I dreamed a dream, and in my dream a buffalo appeared to me. I dreamed that I was in the mountains and fell asleep in the shade of a tree. Something shook my blanket. It was a buffalo, who said, "Rise and follow me." I obeyed. He took a path, and I followed. The path was above the ground. We did not touch the earth. The path led upward and was smooth like smooth black rock. It was a narrow path, just wide enough for us to travel. We went upward a long distance and came to a tent made of buffalo hide, the door of which faced us. Two buffalo came out of the tent and escorted me in. I found the tent filled with buffalo and was placed in the midst of them.
>
> The chief buffalo told me that I had been selected to represent them in life. He said the buffalo play a larger part in life than men realize, and in order that I might understand the buffalo better day by day they gave me a plain stick (or cane) and told me that when I looked at it I should remember that I had been appointed to represent them. The cane was similar to the one which I now carry and have carried for many years. I would not part with this cane for a fortune....

Brave Buffalo said that the following song was given him in the lodge filled with buffalo, and that by it he received power to engage in the practice of medicine [Densmore's transcription and analysis follow].

Continuing his narrative, Brave Buffalo said:

> The buffalo in my dream told me that I would live to be 102 years old. Then they said: "If you are to show people the great value of the buffalo one proof which you must give them is a demonstration of your endurance. After properly qualifying yourself you will be able to show that weapons can not harm you, and you may challenge anyone to shoot you with arrows or with a gun."

Brave Buffalo said that on waking from his dream, he went home and thought the matter over seriously. After qualifying himself for the ordeal, he requested his relatives to erect a very large tent of buffalo hide in which he would give his demonstration and challenge anyone to shoot him with arrows. He clothed himself in an entire buffalo hide with the head and the horns. The whole tribe came to see whether anyone could wound him. Many tried with arrows, but could not do so. The arrows did not penetrate his skin. Several years later the test was repeated with guns, and Brave Buffalo stated that they were not able to injure him.

✎ At age 73, Brave Buffalo sang his dream song "A Buffalo Said to Me" for Frances Densmore at the Standing Rock Reservation, South Dakota, sometime between 1911 and 1914.

🎧 CD 1.28	Listening Guide 9.1	"A Buffalo Said to Me" TATAN KA-OHI TIKA (BRAVE BUFFALO)

DATE: ca. 1850

PERFORMER: Tatan ka-ohi tika (Brave Buffalo)

GENRE: Teton healing song

METER: irregular

FORM: iterative—music repeats with same words

WHAT TO LISTEN FOR

- descending melodic contour that begins near apex and ends near nadir
- use of gapped scale
- tense vocal quality

TIMING	SECTION	TEXT	TRANSLATION	COMMENTS
0:00	phrase 4 of partial statement	tatan ka wan hema kiya *he yo*	A buffalo said to me, *he yo*	Each song phrase has a descending contour with a held penultimate note. Phrase 4 begins near the apex and drops to midrange; the final note is the melody's nadir.
0:06	phrase 5	wahi nawa pin kte wanma yanka yo *he yo*	I will appear, behold me, *he yo*	Begins in midrange and ends on the nadir.
0:16	phrase 1 of full statement	wahi nawa pin kte wanma yanka yo *he yo*	I will appear, behold me, *he yo*	Begins on the apex and descends to midrange.
0:23	phrase 2	wahi nawa pin kte wanma yanka yo *he yo*	I will appear, behold me, *he yo*	Begins in midrange and ends like phrase 4.
0:30	phrase 3	wahi nawa pin kte wanma yanka yo *he yo*	I will appear, behold me, *he yo*	Identical to phrase 5.
0:38	phrase 4	tatan ka wan hema kiya *he yo*	a buffalo said to me, *he yo*	
0:44	phrase 5	wahi nawa pin kte wanma yanka yo *he yo*	I will appear, behold me, *he yo*	
0:51				Singer clears his throat.
0:55	second full statement			

NOTE Field recording by Frances Densmore, Standing Rock Reservation, South Dakota, 1911–14.

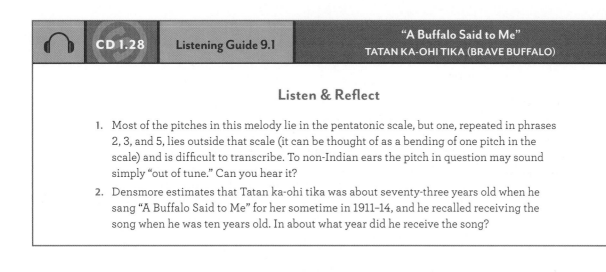

CD 1.28 **Listening Guide 9.1**

"A Buffalo Said to Me"
TATAN KA-OHI TIKA (BRAVE BUFFALO)

Listen & Reflect

1. Most of the pitches in this melody lie in the pentatonic scale, but one, repeated in phrases 2, 3, and 5, lies outside that scale (it can be thought of as a bending of one pitch in the scale) and is difficult to transcribe. To non-Indian ears the pitch in question may sound simply "out of tune." Can you hear it?

2. Densmore estimates that Tatan ka-ohi tika was about seventy-three years old when he sang "A Buffalo Said to Me" for her sometime in 1911–14, and he recalled receiving the song when he was ten years old. In about what year did he receive the song?

coincide with the pulse of the vocal part—not an unusual rhythmic complication in American Indian music.

Densmore apparently asked her informant to sing several repetitions of the song but did not attempt to synchronize the singer's beginning with the recording machine's. Her recording cylinder captured the end of one song statement and two complete statements, separated by the sound of the elderly Brave Buffalo clearing his throat. Thus the recording begins with the fourth of the song's five phrases.

Brave Buffalo's rather tense, nasal vocal timbre is characteristic of the Northern Plains, as is his practice of pitching the song high in his vocal range. The song's short, repetitive text, which mixes words with vocables, is also representative of Northern Plains music. The use of a **gapped scale**, in which some adjacent pitches are separated by a minor third, is common to nearly all Indian songs, not only those of the Plains Indians. A feature of Northern Plains songs particularly well represented here is what ethnomusicologists call the terraced descent: the tendency for each phrase to begin at or near the song's apex and descend stepwise, ending at or near the nadir. The place of the song in its culture—its healing function, the personal ownership of the song, and the understanding of its origin as supernatural—is also common to songs of the Northern Plains.

Northern Plains style traits

Fletcher, Densmore, and other pioneering ethnomusicologists developed bonds of trust and communication with hundreds of individuals, allowing them to collect thousands of examples of traditional music. By carefully analyzing each song, they built a body of knowledge that continues to be a resource for scholars today. Only after a huge amount of material had been amassed and classified did it become possible to speak with assurance about the general characteristics of that music.

ANGLO-CELTIC BALLADS AND THEIR COLLECTORS

The work of American folk song collectors began as the study of an Old World folk repertory: traditional ballads from the British Isles. Around the time of the American Revolution, as chapter 2 has already related, those "old, simple ditties" (in Benjamin Franklin's words) had furnished the tunes for new American lyrics, printed as broadside ballads. By the late 1800s, though, collectors were interested not so much in these reworkings as in their earliest British forms.

THE CHILD BALLADS

For Francis James Child, a ballad was a literary creation, and he did his collecting in libraries. Child was an 1846 Harvard graduate who pursued advanced studies in Germany and then returned to teach English at his alma mater. Searching through printed sources and manuscripts, he published the texts (not the tunes) of what he considered the oldest English-language ballads. Child's monumental work *The English and Scottish Popular Ballads* (five volumes, 1883–98) contains texts and commentary on 305 ballads and their variants. The repertory he collected is now known as the **Child ballads**.

"The Gypsie Laddie"   One Child ballad, "The Gypsie Laddie" (number 200 in Child's collection), tells of a band of gypsies stopping by the dwelling of an absent nobleman and singing so sweetly that his wife falls in love with one of them, runs off with him, and is then pursued by her husband. Child prints eleven versions and comments on their textual differences. The husband is called Lord Cassilis in three versions; Cassle, Castle, Corsefield, and Cashan in others; and in one collected in America, Garrick. The laddie is variously known as Johnie, Jocki, Faa (a last name), Gypsy Davy, and Gypsie Geordie. In some versions, the husband finds his lady, then hangs gypsies—fifteen of them, or sixteen, or seven. In some, the lady regrets her change in status. In another, the gypsy denies an interest in sex.

The dignified language of the ballads, together with their ancient lineage and the scholarship of Child and others, gave them academic prestige. And the disagreement over origins sparked intellectual debate. American versions of approximately one-third of Child's ballads were located, leading many to think of the ballad as the most important Anglo-American folk genre.

CECIL SHARP AND OLIVE DAME CAMPBELL

For Francis Child, ballads were a remnant of a lost past that now could be found only in libraries. But folk song study entered a new stage in the twentieth century, when scholars realized that the ballads belonged to a living tradition. The new collectors turned to the folk themselves for material, in an attitude of respect for oral tradition and the people who still carried it on.

A key figure among the new generation of collectors was the British scholar Cecil Sharp, whose career began in England under the aegis of the Folk-Song Society, formed in 1898 to collect and publish folk songs. Its founders were musicians determined, in the words of British composer Hubert Parry, to "save something primitive and genuine from extinction" and "put on record what loveable qualities there are in unsophisticated humanity." Parry called traditional folk music one of "the purest products of the human mind," though now in danger of being driven out by "the common popular songs of the day." Parry's themes—the age and authenticity of folk song, fear for its survival, the virtues of the folk, and nostalgia for a precommercial era—were sounded often by collectors in Britain and the United States. Indeed, these themes still echo in present-day notions, often unconscious, about authenticity and commercialism in music, as later chapters will explore.

In the early 1900s Sharp began to study the oral tradition that still existed in England and Scotland. His way of collecting a song was standard for his time: singers were asked to repeat what they had sung until Sharp had transcribed the melody accurately and written down a complete version of the text. Ballad scholars, with their background in literary criticism, were slow to adopt the Edison recording machines already in use by ethnomusicologists, and Sharp, although interested in ballad music as well as words, shared their bias against sound recording. In 1907 he published *English Folk-Song: Some Conclusions,* based on his own collection and analysis of some 1,500 examples. Sharp's study concludes that folk melody is based on the old medieval modes rather than major or minor scales and that folk songs were composed by individuals, then transmitted by a communal process.

Of the English and Scottish singers Sharp had encountered, only those over the age of seventy still remembered any of the old ballads, leading him to the conclusion that ballad singing would soon be a dead art form. That changed in 1915, though, when Sharp learned from Olive Dame Campbell, a Massachusetts native living in Appalachia, that a community maintaining an ancient folk song tradition existed in the mountains of North Carolina. Campbell, while studying the culture of the rural southern highlands with her husband, John C. Campbell, as part of a project to improve schools in the region, had noticed that some of the songs she heard there, sung by young and old alike, were versions of the Child ballads. The following year Sharp launched a collecting expedition in the western part of the state. The fruits of that trip appeared in *Folk Songs of the Southern Appalachians* (1917), a joint publication with Olive Campbell and the first major collection of the mountain people's music.

Counting both England and America, Sharp collected no fewer than twenty-eight versions of "The Gypsy Laddie." On September 1, 1916, in Flag Pond, Tennessee, he notated a version in seven stanzas with an added refrain. Here the emphasis is on the conversation between husband and wife when he catches up with her. No revenge is taken; no gypsies are hung. The wife refuses to return home and then, in the last two stanzas, regrets her decision. The next day, in Rock Fork, Tennessee, Sharp heard a five-stanza version whose melody is quite different, drawing out the first and third lines and repeating the fourth line of each stanza. The wife has left behind a child as well as home and husband. And the husband returns home alone, after repossessing her expensive shoes.

In no version of "The Gypsy Laddie" are listeners told why the lady might want to leave, nor does either of these examples describe her departure. Instead, husband and wife are plunged immediately into the consequences of her leaving. Characters speak in plain, formulaic language, with standard epithets, such as the "milk-white" horse the squire rides in both versions and the lady's "lily-white hand" in the second.

English folk song collector Cecil Sharp (1859–1924) paid several visits to America, transcribing songs from residents of Appalachia. Here, Sharp and his assistant Maud Karpeles (at right) collect from Mrs. Doc Pratt of Knott County, Kentucky, in 1917.

The various versions of "The Gypsie Laddie" point up a signal trait of balladry: the detachment with which many ballads relate their story. The strophic form itself is partly responsible, parceling out the tale in repeated patterns of verse. And rather than providing a commentary on the words, the tune serves as a neutral framework for their delivery, as in psalmody. All the ballad's action-filled events are announced to the same music; the repetitiousness keeps them all on the same emotional level. A sung ballad, then, is typically no exercise in animated storytelling but a sober, impersonal ritual.

LG 9.2   The version heard in the accompanying recording (LG 9.2) is sung by Jean Ritchie. The youngest of fourteen children in a musical family, Ritchie was born in 1922 in Viper, Kentucky, in the Cumberland Mountains. The family's singing was recorded in the 1930s by the folklorist Alan Lomax (see chapter 14), and in the 1940s Ritchie moved to New York, where she participated in the urban folk revival described in chapter 17. She became well known for her singing of traditional songs, sometimes unaccompanied, as here, and sometimes accompanying herself on guitar or Appalachian dulcimer (also called mountain dulcimer), a folk instrument with a diatonic fretboard, two drone strings, and a melody string, usually held in the player's lap.

Ritchie learned this version of Child 200 from a family member, Jason Ritchie. It does not correspond exactly with any of the versions preserved by either Child or Sharp, nor is its pentatonic melody one of the tunes written down by Sharp. Yet all of its events can be found in one or another of the many versions that have been collected. Its ten stanzas begin and end as narration, with the dialogue between husband and wife in the central stanzas. The closing stanza, in which the gypsy abandons his lover, is found in relatively few versions; the majority end with the lady staying with the gypsy.

Whereas in England Cecil Sharp had encountered only aging ballad singers, in the southern Appalachians he found the English ballad tradition still flourishing in the early twentieth century. Here the songs were "interwoven with the ordinary avocation of everyday life."

the value of folk music   Olive Campbell turned up some of the same ballads that interested Sharp, but she also collected other music she encountered in the mountains, including religious songs and hymns, popular music, and instrumental tunes. Campbell shared Sharp's belief that some of the songs in oral tradition were aesthetically better than others. She even imagined a social role that the better songs might play. In 1916 she wrote that the folk movement in the mountains "seeks the recognition and preservation of all that is native and fine. . . . We would like to have the people recognize the worth and beauty of their songs; we would like to have them displace the inferior music that is now being sung there." The "inferior" music of Tin Pan Alley and ragtime was part of a larger change that industrialization was bringing to Appalachia, as a way of life rooted in subsistence farming was being transformed into one dominated by coal mining.

Campbell was a key figure in the founding of Appalachian settlement schools, where rural children were taught to value their traditional crafts and folkways. A school Campbell founded in 1925 and named after her deceased husband, the John C. Campbell Folk School in Brasstown, North Carolina, continues today to teach folk crafts from basketry to blacksmithing, with a special emphasis on folk music.

🎧	CD 1.29	Listening Guide 9.2	"The Gypsy Laddie" ANONYMOUS

DATE: unknown

PERFORMER: Jean Ritchie, unaccompanied vocal

GENRE: Child ballad

METER: duple, treated flexibly

FORM: strophic

WHAT TO LISTEN FOR

- distinctive vocal timbre and technique
- strophic form: melody repeats for each stanza
- narrative lyrics

TIMING	SECTION	TEXT
0:00	stanza 1	An English lord came home one night Inquiring for his lady The servants said on every hand "She's gone with the gypsie laddie"
0:16	stanza 2	"Go saddle up my milk-white steed Go saddle me up my brownie And I will ride both night and day Till I overtake my bonnie"
0:33	stanza 3	Oh he rode east and he rode west And at last he found her She was lying on the green, green grass And the gypsy's arms all around her
0:50	stanza 4	"Oh how can you leave your house and land How can you leave your money How can you leave your rich young lord To be a gypsy's bonnie?
1:06	stanza 5	"How can you leave your house and land How can you leave your baby How can you leave your rich young lord To be a gypsy's lady?
1:22	stanza 6	"Oh come go home with me my dear Come home and be my lover I'll furnish you with a room so neat With a silken bed and cover"
1:39	stanza 7	"I won't go home with you, kind sir Nor will I be your lover I care not for your room so neat Or your silken bed or your cover
1:55	stanza 8	"It's I can leave my house and land And I can leave my baby I'm a-going to roam this world around And be a gypsy's lady"

(continued)

| | CD 1.29 | Listening Guide 9.2 | "The Gypsy Laddie" ANONYMOUS |

TIMING	SECTION	TEXT
2:12	stanza 9	Oh soon this lady changed her mind Her clothes grew old and faded Her hose and shoes come off her feet And left them bare and naked
2:29	stanza 10	Just what befell this lady now I think it worth relating Her gypsy found another lass And left her heart a-breaking

NOTE Recorded in 1961.

Listen & Reflect

1. Describe the qualities of Jean Ritchie's voice, which has been called a representative example of the "southern white mountain style" of singing. Does her vocal style suit the song she sings?

2. How does it support or detract from the story her song tells?

AMERICAN FOLK SONGS AND THEIR COLLECTORS

Even before Cecil Sharp ever set foot in America, Massachusetts-born scholar Phillips Barry had developed a more inclusive philosophy of ballad collecting. His work showed that whatever its origin, a song went through a process of communal re-creation when it entered oral tradition. In other words, even a relatively recent song by a known composer could be considered a folk song if it underwent changes as it passed from singer to singer. By working to document that process, Barry refocused the issue of repertory. He and other collectors—sometimes *song catchers* called **song catchers** by their informants—took the singers' own preferences as their starting place, thus recovering from oral tradition not only old ballads of English origin but also newer ballads composed in America. For song catchers like Barry, the folk process in America was alive and well and still creating songs.

FOLK SONGS OF THE AMERICAN WEST

The new songs of American origin often told stories that tied them to events in the nation's development. That was particularly true of songs that grew out of the westward expansion of the nineteenth century, when some 10 million Americans headed west.

"Sweet Betsey from Pike," one offbeat response to this epic migration, was first published by John A. Stone in 1858 in a San Francisco **songster** (a collection of song lyrics without music). The song relied from the start on oral tradition, for it was sung to the tune of "Villikins and His Dinah," an 1850 British music hall song in waltz time with a refrain made out of vocables. In setting new words to a preexisting tune of British origin, "Sweet Betsey from Pike" resembles "The Liberty Song" and other Revolutionary-era songs that had appeared in broadsides and newspapers. A key difference is the later song's lack of political agenda.

"Sweet Betsey from Pike"

In eleven stanzas, the song offers glimpses of a couple's trip across the continent, starting with their traveling party: "Two yoke of cattle, a large yeller dog, / A tall Shanghai rooster, and a one-spotted hog." Betsey's character locates her outside the world of the 1850s parlor song, where heroines tend to embody Victorian virtue. On the Overland Trail, only her determination, physical toughness, and self-reliant spirit let her survive. Sexual repression is absent from this song. As an unmarried couple traveling for months across the country, Betsey and Ike seem to face no barriers to lovemaking. Further, Betsey mocks Victorian norms by falling out of love with Ike, running away from Mormon leader Brigham Young (who wants to add her to his collection of wives), and responding with an earthy outburst to a California miner who invites her to dance. Betsey's confession that she's "chock-full of strong alkali"—a desert laxative—is not what one expects to hear from the belle of the ball.

To sing "Sweet Betsey" a person only needed to know the tune of "Villikins and His Dinah," whose many repeated notes fit the delivery of a comic text, and whose refrain placed nonsense syllables where a moral message might have been expected. Appearing in *Put's Golden Songster* along with other songs such as one about sailing to San Francisco to the tune of "Pop Goes the Weasel," "Sweet Betsey from Pike" flouted the very idea of elevation. Yet its emphasis on story recalls the traditional ballad, and like the much older Child ballads, "Sweet Betsey" entered the oral tradition, where old verses were dropped and new ones added.

Meanwhile, miners, loggers, homesteaders, Mormons, farmers, and soldiers all contributed to the large body of song that took shape in the American West. A particularly rich song repertory was that of cowboys. Some cowboy songs struck a realistic tone. For example, "The Captain of the Cowboys," written in 1873 to the well-known English tune "Captain Jinks," delivers a stern warning to inexperienced cowpokes:

cowboy songs

> If a visit to Blackjack Ranch you pay,
> By way of advice, just let me say,
> You'd better not come on branding day,
>   If beauty is your portion;
> For what with dust and what with blows
>   What with blows, what with blows,
> A dirty face and a broken nose
>   Will likely change your notion.

A cowboy song by Daniel E. Kelley, however, paints a picture far removed from dust and broken noses. Idealizing the out-of-doors, "Home on the Range"—the words and music were first published together in 1905—has come to be the best known of all western songs. "Home" reverberates through the song as it does through Bishop and Payne's "Home, Sweet Home," to which it surely owes a debt. The connection of life on the range to a vision of home elevates the

"Home on the Range"

🖙 Writer and folk song collector Charles F. Lummis (1859–1928), photographed in Los Angeles in 1903 with his daughter Turbesè and son Jordan.

cowboy into a mythic figure, and the song offers a peek into his dreams. To the superior men who live on the range, the song suggests, home is not just a domestic arrangement but a state of mind: a reward for mastering a perilous environment.

SPANISH SONGS OF THE SOUTHWEST

Long before westward expansion began, parts of the Southwest and southern California had been settled by people moving north from Mexico. And there, Spanish-language singing traditions flourished, separate from the English-language ones we have been discussing. Mexican American songs of the late 1800s can be glimpsed through the work of Charles F. Lummis, a Massachusetts native who crossed the country on foot in the 1880s and fell in love with the culture he found in the West. Lummis came to believe that life in California "before the gringo" arrived had been "the most beautiful life that Caucasians have ever lived anywhere under the sun." And he showed his love for the singing he heard there by collecting Hispanic folk songs.

A journalist by trade, Lummis started transcribing songs in Spanish soon after he arrived in Los Angeles in 1885. In the early 1900s he obtained a wax cylinder machine and hired trained musicians to notate the recordings he made. One who joined the project was American composer Arthur Farwell. Visiting Los Angeles on a 1904 lecture tour, Farwell was invited to Lummis's house, and there he encountered "a little world of Spanish-Californians and Indians." Farwell was enchanted by their songs. "I swam in the musical atmosphere of them—the suave or vivacious songs of the dwellers of the desert." Farwell spent the summers of 1904 and 1905 in Los Angeles transcribing hundreds of the melodies Lummis had recorded. Almost two decades passed before any were published, but *Spanish Songs of Old California* (1923), though containing only fourteen songs, was a noteworthy collection.

In the manner of folklorists, Lummis identified by name the singers he had recorded. At the same time, although recorded with guitar, the songs were published with piano accompaniments—an indication that Lummis and Farwell were more interested in having them sung than in preserving them for study. Indeed, by the early 1920s Farwell was involved in a movement to encourage community singing by amateurs. "In community song movements under my direction," he wrote, the Spanish California songs "have been sung, and are being sung, by large numbers of people year after year with increasing enthusiasm and delight." In Farwell's day, musical scholarship was still considered an accessory of performance. Preserving a song was first and foremost a step toward singing it.

Mexican American songs

The Mexican American songs collected by Lummis and arranged by Farwell offer glimpses of a sensibility different from anything found either in nineteenth-century American sheet music or in Anglo-Celtic ballads. In "La hámaca" (The Hammock) the singer lies in a hammock, musing about how sweet life can be when one is in love. And "El capotín" (The Rain Song) is as much about romantic disappointment as the weather. (Fearing that his passion is not returned, the singer pleads for an end to his misery while the music continues its sprightly raindrop imitation.) These songs were also musically distinctive, with flexible rhythm, melody, and form. Lummis and Farwell believed that the songs could enrich the experience of English-speaking Americans, for they conjured up "a world of romantic adventure" far removed from the Victorian values that dominated English-language songs of the post–Civil War years, treating love as one of life's great mysteries.

LABOR SONGS

During the late 1800s labor unions began to play a role in the struggle to control a changing workplace. Joining forces to seek better pay and working conditions, workers found that the threat of striking could be an effective bargaining tool. In the face of an unequal balance of power, they sang songs to boost morale and affirm solidarity. Labor songs, written for jobs ranging from mining to farming, are another source that fed into the stream of American folk music.

Leopold Vincent's *Alliance and Labor Songster* (1891) was compiled for use at meetings of the Farmers' Alliance, which by 1890 claimed more than three million members. One example from that collection, "The Right Will Prevail," sung to the tune of "Sweet By and By" (see LG 7.2), illustrates the uncompromising tone that labor songs usually took:

> When the Workingmen's cause shall prevail
> Then the class-rule of rich men shall cease,
> And the true friends of Labor will hail
> With a shout the glad era of peace.
> > Right will reign by-and-by,
> > When the Workingmen come into power;
> > Right will reign by-and-by,
> > Then the gold thieves shall rule men no more.

Readers will recognize an impulse for parody harking back to the broadside ballads of the 1700s. Here the author transformed a gentle affirmation of heavenly peace into an attack on capitalists. One can only speculate about the full range of meanings this song carried in 1891. For some, the use of "Sweet By and By" must have signified confidence: just as believers would go to heaven, workers would prevail over bosses. On the other hand, if triumph was to be postponed until some vague "by and by," perhaps others took this version more pessimistically, as in a later parody that promises: "There'll be pie in the sky when you die."

Since labor songs were militant, they were often sung to melodies whose original texts drew clear lines between right and wrong. Civil War songs were favorites. (Many labor songs were based on the "Battle-Hymn of the Republic" and on Root's "Battle Cry of Freedom" and "Tramp, Tramp, Tramp.") Other patriotic tunes were borrowed as well, including "America" ("My country, 'tis of thee," which in turn adopted its melody from "God Save the King"). As part of a

Songsters like this one, published in 1887, circulated pro-labor messages cheaply, relying on familiar music for much of their impact.

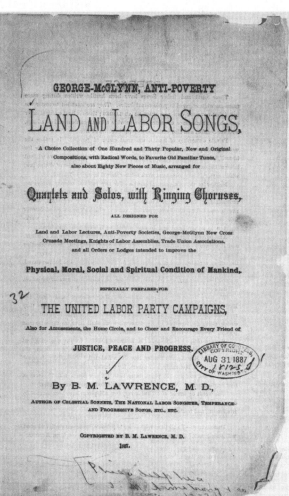

campaign to shorten working hours, the following lyrics were published for that melody in 1865:

> Ye noble sons of toil,
> Who ne'er from work recoil,
>   Take up the lay;
> Loud let the anthem's roar
> Resume from shore to shore,
> Till Time shall be no more,
>   Eight hours a day.

Management was not the only target of the nineteenth-century labor press. In 1893 a Philadelphia journal parodied a famous hymn, Arthur Sullivan's "Onward, Christian Soldiers," to attack Christian outreach. Here is the first stanza of "Modern Missionary Zeal," which reads like something out of the tumultuous 1960s:

> Onward! Christian soldiers;
>   On to heathen lands!
> Prayer book in your pockets,
>   Rifles in your hands.
> Take the happy tidings
>   Where trade can be done;
> Spread the peaceful gospel
>   With a Gatling gun.

songs of social critique

Thoughts like these proceeded from what amounted to an underground press, which attacked establishment beliefs. Labor songs thus reveal another face of American musical democracy: one that, rather than affirming the established social order, gives it a critical look and invites citizens to imagine that it could be otherwise. If European scholars had originated the idea that folk songs were the communal expression of a timeless society, then American folk music, as it developed in the nineteenth century, required extending that concept to include songs that critiqued society.

With their political agenda, labor songs share a bond with Revolutionary-era broadside ballads. But that bond is shared as well by a repertory that on its face appears to be more concerned with spiritual salvation than economic and political revolution. For the history of the African American spiritual is equally tied to the political struggles of a formerly enslaved people.

SPIRITUALS AND THEIR COLLECTORS: FROM CONTRABAND TO CONCERT HALL

Shortly after the Civil War began in April 1861, refugee slaves began seeking protection at Fortress Monroe, Virginia. Their masters demanded the slaves' return, but the fort's Union commander refused, calling them "contraband of war," or captured property. The now-freed blacks were put to work in the fort, but the military could not provide them enough shelter or clothing. So in August the American Missionary Association proposed a campaign of contraband relief, and soon the Reverend Lewis C. Lockwood arrived at Fortress Monroe as missionary to the ex-slaves. Lockwood's first encounter with Southern black singing

Lewis C. Lockwood

left a deep impression. "They have a prime deliverance melody, that runs in this style," he wrote in his first report: "'Go down to Egypt— / Tell Pharaoh / Thus saith my servant, Moses— / Let my people go.' Accent on the last syllable, with repetition of the chorus, that seems every hour to ring like a warning note in the ear of despotism."

Lockwood's report was published in October 1861 in a Northern abolition-ist newspaper. In December, the same paper printed a twenty-stanza transcrip-tion of "Let My People Go: A Song of the 'Contrabands'" in standardized English. "The following curious hymn," the notice reported, came from Lockwood, who had taken down the text "verbatim" from contraband dictation. Before the year was out, a sheet music version of "Go Down, Moses" was advertised for sale. The printed circulation of spirituals had begun.

"Let My People Go"

During the war and for some time after, the dissemination of these African American religious songs rooted in the experience of slavery depended on white advocates like Lockwood, who were eager to document the spirituality and creativity of African Americans. Therefore, the story of how spirituals moved beyond slave communities is revealed chiefly in the black singers' interaction with Northern white clergymen and teachers. White foes of slavery took the spirituals as evidence of the slaves' human capacity and their fitness to live as free Americans. In the struggle against slavery and its aftermath, "Go Down, Moses" and other spirituals signaled the involvement of Southern black people in what was to be a long campaign for equality.

Slave Songs of the United States (New York, 1867), collected and published by William Francis Allen, Charles Pickard Ware, and Lucy McKim Garrison, is the first of many anthologies in which black spirituals are preserved. It was the work of three Northern antislavery activists who worked during the Civil War to edu-cate freed slaves on the Sea Islands near Port Royal, South Carolina. Before arriv-ing at Port Royal, Massachusetts natives Allen and Ware had known little of black Americans or their music, but their duties gave them contact with both. Allen taught in a freedmen's school for more than eight months (1863–64), and Ware, his cousin, worked as a plantation superintendent on an island off the coast of South Carolina that had been liberated by the Union Army (1862–65). Garrison was the most accomplished musician of the three. Born in Philadelphia, she was a pianist and violinist who by age fifteen was giving piano lessons. The scholarly expertise behind *Slave Songs* was chiefly Allen's; Ware supplied the largest num-ber of transcriptions, while Garrison—with help from her husband, the literary editor of the staunchly abolitionist magazine *The Nation*—collected and edited transcriptions and saw the work through the press.

Slave Songs of the United States

Slave Songs contains 136 melodies with texts, arranged geographically. The introduction admits that the published melodies "convey but a faint shadow of the original," for the singers' inflections "cannot be reproduced on paper." Encountering a culture profoundly different from their own, the compilers still recognized it *as* a culture and worked to set down this repertory of "old songs . . . before it is too late," knowing that the songs' associations with slavery were making black people reluctant to sing them. The spirituals distinguished them-selves from white hymnody in the precedence given to rhythm. "The negroes keep exquisite time in singing," Allen wrote, "and do not suffer themselves to be daunted by any obstacle in the words." This comment is an early example of a principle later termed cultural relativism, which refuses to make cultural dif-ference a measure of quality in either direction.

Allen, Ware, and Garrison compiled *Slave Songs* to document a disappearing oral practice—much as Alice Fletcher, Frances Densmore, and other ethnographers would document American Indian music later in the nineteenth century. But *Slave Songs* was also the beginning of the process of turning black spirituals into a written repertory accessible to all. Soon that larger project of dissemination would be taken up by a new generation of educated African Americans.

THE SPIRITUAL TRANSFORMED

Fisk University in Nashville, Tennessee, founded in 1865 with a white faculty, was one of the schools organized by Northern missionary societies to educate the former slaves and their children. Dependent on donations from the North, the school struggled to find income in its early years. Then in 1870 the choir formed at Fisk under the direction of Northern-born faculty member George L. White performed at a national teachers' convention in Nashville to such enthusiasm that White began to imagine a fund-raising tour of the North by a select group of singers, emphasizing spirituals. In the fall of 1871 the Fisk Jubilee Singers set out on their bold venture. After performing in Oberlin, Ohio, for a convention of Congregational ministers, who were deeply touched by the singing, and receiving further endorsement from New York's leading clergymen, the Jubilee Singers became a sensation in the Northeast. Having far surpassed the college's financial expectations, they continued to tour for many years to come, including journeys to the British Isles and the European continent. Their performances during just their first seven years of touring enriched Fisk University by $150,000.

The professional demeanor of the Jubilee Singers helped them bring the past of Southern slaves to the notice of Northern Protestants, who responded to the spirituals' message of individual salvation. And Theodore F. Seward's arrangements, published in book form and sold at the concerts, could be sung by anyone. One chronicler writes: "Hills and valleys, parlors and halls, wherever they went, were vocal with jubilee melodies"—melodies tailored to suit audiences who might have found their original form less pleasing to cultivated sensibilities.

As pictured in the Fisk Jubilee Singers' repertory of spirituals, the slave's place in the world overlaps with that of the Christian sinner. Both view life as a hard journey, and both seek eternal peace when death brings release from this "vale of tears." A key difference is that while Christian sinners are weighed down by a sense of their own wrongdoing, slaves suffered more acutely from the wrongs of others. Nevertheless, white sinner and black slave held in common a sense of standing alone in a hostile world, and black spirituals appealed across cultural barriers by communicating how it felt to live in that state.

"Home" is a key notion in many spirituals. The slaves, though, sang not about the domestic institution that songs like "Home, Sweet Home" celebrate but rather about an *idea* of home.

Ⓢ The Jubilee Singers of Fisk University, Nashville, Tennessee, photographed around 1880.

Home might be eternal, as in "Deep River" and "Swing Low, Sweet Chariot"; or it might be in the world, as in "Got a Home in That Rock" or even "Steal Away," where it refers to freedom; or it might be either one, as in "Sometimes I Feel Like a Motherless Child."

A spiritual about the sufferings of Jesus invites listeners to imagine his torment. "He Never Said a Mumblin' Word" reviews the events of the Passion, including Christ's judgment before Pontius Pilate, the crown of thorns, the whipping, the nails, and two stanzas' worth of flowing blood. It is not hard to picture onlookers cringing at all this brutality while the victim silently accepts his fate:

> O they took my blessed Lawd,
> Blessed Lawd, blessed Lawd,
> O they took my blessed Lawd,
> An' he never said a mumblin' word,
> Not a word, not a word, not a word.

Spanning emotions from abject woe to joyful hope, the black spiritual stands as a remarkable legacy from one of American history's most degraded chapters. Writing on the spiritual in 1878, James Monroe Trotter, the first historian of black American music, reflected: "The history of the colored race in this country" proves that "no system of cruelty, however great or long inflicted, can destroy that sympathy with musical sounds that is born within the soul."

THE "NEW NEGRO," HARRY T. BURLEIGH, AND THE CONCERT SPIRITUAL

The founding of black colleges opened new educational opportunities for African Americans in the later nineteenth century. Higher education for blacks began before the Civil War, with the founding of Ashmun Institute (later Lincoln University) in 1854 and Wilberforce University in 1856. It flourished in the years immediately after the war with the creation of Fisk, Hampton, and Howard universities and Morehouse College, all founded before 1870, and by the end of the century included such notable institutions as Tuskegee Institute and Spelman College, both founded in 1881. To these must be added the small number of traditionally white institutions, such as Oberlin College, that admitted black students long before the civil rights movement of the mid-twentieth century brought an end to legal segregation in higher education.

black colleges

By the turn of the century, black and nonsegregated colleges had produced a generation of artists, writers, and intellectuals, born in the waning days of slavery or shortly after its abolition, whose achievements are remarkable by any standard of measurement. Writers and activists such as Booker T. Washington and W. E. B. DuBois spoke out eloquently on behalf of African Americans, and though they sometimes disagreed sharply about how to effect changes, they agreed that injustices against blacks demanded action. The new public image of the outspoken, educated, middle-class African American came to be called the "New Negro" and was a harbinger of the Harlem Renaissance of the 1920s and 1930s (see chapter 13). The ethic of working publicly to improve the conditions of African Americans pervaded all aspects of black culture around the turn of the century, music included.

black activism

An important handful of black musicians in the post-slavery period benefited from training at music conservatories like Oberlin, the New England Conservatory in Boston, and the short-lived National Conservatory in New York. Among their numbers were composers who wrote music in the classical European genres that was inspired by the African American experience. By imbuing their music with melodies and rhythms drawn from black folk music, these composers participated in the nationalistic movement advocated by Dvořák during his tenure at the National Conservatory in 1893–95. Among these black nationalistic composers were two students at the National Conservatory in those years: Will Marion Cook (see chapter 10) and Harry T. Burleigh.

Harry T. Burleigh

Born in Erie, Pennsylvania, in 1866, Burleigh developed musical tastes that were shaped in part by performances that took place in the wealthy home where his mother worked as a domestic servant, performances that at first he was able to hear only by standing outside the window. As a young man he sang professionally as a baritone soloist in churches and synagogues in Erie until, at the age of twenty-six, he became a scholarship student at the National Conservatory. In his second year there he worked as an assistant to Dvořák, who became acquainted with spirituals through Burleigh's singing; that acquaintance is evident in the *New World* Symphony, in which one theme reworks "Swing Low, Sweet Chariot." Burleigh sang at St. George's Episcopal Church from the 1890s until not long before his death in 1949, and also for many years at Temple Emanu-El, both in New York. He also worked as a vocal coach and as a music editor for the Italian-based publisher Ricordi. As a composer he produced songs and instrumental pieces and a significant body of spiritual arrangements, beginning with the 1916 collection *Jubilee Songs of the United States of America,* arranged for solo voice and piano.

Before Burleigh, published spirituals were presented either as unaccompanied melodies or in simple hymnlike harmonizations. In contrast, Burleigh's arrangements, whether for chorus or for voice and piano, use more sophisticated, varied textures and the rich, chromatic harmonies of late Romantic European music—the harmonic language of Dvořák. In the choral arrangements, voices are sometimes divided into more than the usual four parts, and the melody may be complemented by an upper countermelody, or **descant**, in the sopranos. In the solo arrangements, the piano accompaniments have the variety of texture and pattern found in the art songs of Schubert or Schumann. The finished product—the

the concert spiritual

concert spiritual—is an expression of African American experience that incorporates the manner of European classical music. Moreover, the performance of spirituals before Burleigh was the domain of groups devoted primarily or exclusively to that repertoire, such as the Fisk Jubilee Singers. By creating his arrangements on commission for various choral organizations and vocal soloists, Burleigh did much to add the concert spiritual to the repertory of classical vocal music.

Spirituals come in a variety of moods and styles, and so do Burleigh's arrangements. The rhythmic propulsion of "Go Tell It on the Mountain" and "Ride On, King Jesus!" breathes confidence that life's trouble can be surmounted and

LG 9.3

heaven lies within easy reach. "Deep River" (LG 9.3), in contrast, which begins with a drawn-out descent on the first syllable that can make the beat ambiguous, invites a performance that is freer in rhythm. The text views the Jordan River as a boundary between a life of toil and an afterlife of rest in heaven's "campground." The opening melisma and the energy required by the octave leap on "over" suggest a tough journey ahead, for the river is an abyss and the way home

| CD 2.1 | Listening Guide 9.3 | "Deep River" ARRANGED BY HARRY T. BURLEIGH |

DATE: 1913
PERFORMERS: The Howard University Chamber Choir
GENRE: concert spiritual
METER: duple
FORM: AABA'

WHAT TO LISTEN FOR

- pentatonic melody
- rich harmonies
- varied choral textures

TIMING	SECTION	TEXT	COMMENTS
0:00	A	Deep river, my home is over Jordan, Deep river, Lord, I want to cross over into campground.	Melody in the altos, over a lush homophonic texture in tenors and basses; the lower voices sing only a few of the words.
0:47	A	Deep river, my home is over Jordan, Deep river, Lord, I want to cross over into campground.	Solo alto sings the melody, sopranos sing wordless descant.
1:38	B	Don't you want to go to that gospel feast, That promis'd land where all is peace?	Louder, more rhythmically emphatic contrasting section in a minor key. For the first time, all voices declaim the words. The melodic apex, and the piece's climax, arrives on the phrase "that promis'd land"; the music then slows and subsides to a soft, inconclusive sonority on the word "peace."
2:16	A'	Deep river, Lord, I want to cross over into campground.	A return to the opening texture and mood, with the final phrase featuring the solo alto.

Listen & Reflect

1. What stylistic features does this arrangement of "Deep River" share with the antebellum black music studied in chapter 4?
2. What features are different?
3. How do the differences affect your response to the music?

strenuous. Burleigh's arrangement for mixed chorus (sopranos, altos, tenors, and basses), one of several he made of "Deep River," emphasizes blended choral timbre and rich harmony over rhythm. The pentatonic melody is sung over an accompaniment of lush chords, then repeated by a solo alto voice with the addition of a descant. A vigorous contrasting section follows—"Don't you want to go to that gospel feast?"—before the hushed, reverent-sounding opening mood returns to end the arrangement.

In the early years of the twentieth century, the concert spiritual represented the social progress made by African Americans in the decades following the abolition of slavery. Rooted in a past era of persecution, the words continued to have relevance for a people who in many ways were still treated as second-class citizens. The concert spiritual arrangements of Burleigh and others reinforced the image of the New Negro: cultivated, intelligent, articulate, and refined—the opposite of the minstrel-show stereotypes.

But another type of African American music was also entering the mainstream of popular culture at the turn of the century, one not so easily divorced from minstrelsy. That music, ragtime, is a central part of the story told in the next chapter.

QUESTIONS FOR DISCUSSION AND REVIEW

1. What specific features distinguish American Indian music from the types of music discussed in earlier chapters? Consider both the sound of the music and its uses. What are some similarities between American Indian and other kinds of music?

2. Explain why collectors using nineteenth-century European criteria for evaluating folk songs might either ignore American folk songs or consider them unworthy of study.

3. How were the efforts of the first collectors of black spirituals similar to those of the early collectors of American Indian music, and how were they different? How do these similarities and differences reflect the relative status in those years of the American Indian, African American, and Anglo-American populations?

FURTHER READING

Floyd, Samuel A. *The Power of Black Music: Interpreting Its History from Africa to the United States.* New York: Oxford University Press, 1995.

Foner, Philip S. *American Labor Songs of the Nineteenth Century.* Urbana: University of Illinois Press, 1975.

Kodish, Debora G. *Good Friends and Bad Enemies: Robert Winslow Gordon and the Study of American Folksong.* Urbana: University of Illinois Press, 1986.

Levine, Victoria Lindsay. "American Indian Musics, Past and Present." In *The Cambridge History of American Music,* edited by David Nicholls, 3–29. Cambridge: Cambridge University Press, 1998.

Logsdon, Guy, ed. *"The Whorehouse Bells Were Ringing" and Other Songs Cowboys Sing.* Urbana: University of Illinois Press, 1989.

Shirley, Wayne D. "The Coming of 'Deep River.'" *American Music* 15, no. 4 (winter 1997): 493–534.

Southern, Eileen. *The Music of Black Americans.* 3d ed. New York: W.W. Norton, 1997.

FURTHER LISTENING AND VIEWING

Healing Songs of the American Indians. Folkways FE 4251, 1965. Anthology of cylinder recordings by Frances Densmore.

Lost Sounds: Blacks and the Birth of the Recording Industry, 1891–1922. Archeophone, 2005.

Songcatcher. Directed by Maggie Greenwald. Trimark Pictures, 2000. A fictional story based on the work of Olive Dame Campbell and other early folk song collectors.

"COME ON AND HEAR"

Popular Music, Theater, and Dance at the Turn of the Century

In 1866 a French ballet company found itself stranded in New York City: the theater in which the dancers had been booked to perform had burned to the ground while the troupe was crossing the Atlantic. Meanwhile, a theater manager in the same city was discovering that the new play he had committed himself to—a pastiche of the Faust legend and Weber's opera *Der Freischütz*—was certain to be a failure without major surgery.

As luck would have it, each party came to the other's rescue, and when *The Black Crook* reached the public in September 1866 the supernatural scenes were greatly enlivened by female dancers in fairy costumes that, by the standards of the day, left little to the imagination. A motley mixture of **melodrama,** comedy, music, dance, and spectacle, *The Black Crook* became one of the nineteenth century's landmark stage successes, touring the United States through the end of the century and beyond. It also marked the beginning of a native tradition of musical theater that borrowed from European precedents without copying them slavishly.

Although it would be too much of a stretch to call *The Black Crook* "the first musical comedy," it did contain the building blocks of that yet-to-be-born genre. In the decades that followed, the American **musical comedy,** or simply the **musical,** would grow alongside an assortment of imported European stage entertainments, eventually finding a voice of its own, distinguishing itself from its British, French, and Austrian influences. By 1900, the key to that distinctive voice was the popular song, as codified by Tin Pan Alley songwriters. No musical show could succeed without appealing songs—songs that enjoyed an independent life outside the shows that introduced them. A history of musical comedy at the turn of the century is thus intertwined with the history of the popular song in the same years. Developments in the popular song, in turn, were closely tied to new styles of social dance. And pervading all three types of entertainment—theater, song, and dance—was an electrifying innovation in African American music: ragtime.

MUSICAL THEATER AT THE TURN OF THE CENTURY

It is possible to arrange the early twentieth century's various genres of musical stage entertainments into a hierarchy based on the cultural prestige claimed by their creators and performers. At the bottom was **burlesque,** in which the display of the feminine figure took precedence over other artistic considerations. Beginning as comic travesties of serious plays, burlesque shows would by the 1930s degenerate into striptease. A rung higher up the ladder was more family-friendly vaudeville, a variety style of entertainment presenting a succession of short acts, musical and nonmusical. Then came more elaborate and costly genres favored by the Broadway stage: **revue,** which presented variety, often with an overarching theme absent in vaudeville, and musical comedy, which involved characters and a story. At the top of the ladder were the genres linked most closely with the classical sphere and its emphasis on the role of the composer: **operetta** and, on the highest rung, opera.

OPERA AND OPERETTA

In 1903 Broadway song-and-dance man George M. Cohan wrote a patriotic number, "I Want to Hear a Yankee Doodle Tune," that included the following lines:

> Oh, Sousa, won't you write another march?
> Yours is just the melody divine.
> Now you can have your *William Tell,*
> Your *Faust* and *Lohengrin* as well,
> But I'll take a Yankee Doodle tune for mine.

Cohan could be sure that his audience would recognize *William Tell, Faust,* and *Lohengrin* as the names of famous operas. For while opera in the early 1900s was the most glamorous of musical genres, it was also part of the common culture. Tin Pan Alley produced many **novelty songs**—comic songs, often topical in subject matter—with operatic allusions, many of which made jokes that required at least a passing familiarity with opera. Like Cohan, the writers of those novelties could count on their audience's recognition of snippets of famous operatic tunes, allusions to operatic characters, and mention of operatic celebrities such as Enrico Caruso, from 1903 to 1920 the star tenor at New York City's Metropolitan Opera.

The Metropolitan Opera

The Metropolitan Opera had opened its doors in 1883. Backed by wealthy patrons, the new enterprise won a firm financial footing in the later 1880s by specializing in German opera, especially the music dramas of Richard Wagner. From the start, the opera company toured each year after concluding its New York season. In 1890, with a few Italian operas added to its repertory, the company traveled as far as San Francisco and Mexico. In a tour of twenty-three cities ten years later, the Metropolitan spent five months on the road. In 1906 the company was caught in the San Francisco earthquake, bringing an abrupt end to its April tour when sets, costumes, and most of the orchestra's instruments were lost.

Through much of the twentieth century, the opera repertory in the United States resembled the symphony orchestra's, emphasizing classic works rather than new ones. Yet during the 1910s especially, the Metropolitan encouraged

creative efforts of American composers. In 1911 the company presented Victor Herbert's *Natoma,* and also held a competition for an American opera, won by Horatio Parker's *Mona,* which was produced in 1912. In 1918 Charles W. Cadman's *Shanewis,* featuring American Indian melodies and based on a story involving cultural conflict, was successfully produced on the Met stage. None of these works, however, won an enduring place in the repertory.

As the Metropolitan was staging the classical sphere's most enduring musical dramas, a more accessible kind of show scored a major success on Broadway. *The Merry Widow,* a Viennese import by Franz Lehár, made its New York debut in 1907. And now **operetta**—also called **light opera** or **comic opera**—became a significant force on the popular musical stage. Featuring singers trained for opera, elaborate musical numbers, and plots carried by spoken dialogue, operetta was a European form that settled easily into formula. Rudolf Friml, another leading operetta composer, once said that the formula depended on "old things: a full-blooded libretto with luscious melody, rousing choruses, and romantic passions." *The Merry Widow* had these ingredients, and American audiences took it to their hearts. Within a few months of its New York opening, several road companies were playing Lehár's work on theatrical circuits, and its songs sold widely, both in recorded form—on cylinders, phonograph records, and piano rolls—and as sheet music.

Irish-born composer Victor Herbert was one of the Americans who competed successfully with the Hungarian-born, Vienna-based Lehár and the English team of W. S. Gilbert and Arthur Sullivan, whose operettas had long been favorites on the American stage. In his early years Herbert trained in Germany as an instrumentalist and composer, playing cello in European orchestras and composing classical works, earning the respect of his colleagues. He and his wife, an opera singer, emigrated in 1886 to the United States, where they performed with the Metropolitan Orchestra (she on stage and he in the pit), and Herbert later taught at the National Conservatory alongside Dvořák. He took over Patrick S. Gilmore's band when the leader died in 1892 (see chapter 7), and later conducted the Pittsburgh Symphony Orchestra. Herbert helped bring about changes in the music business by working, along with John Philip Sousa, for the passage of the 1909 copyright law that secured composers' royalties on the sale of recorded cylinders, discs, and piano rolls. In 1914 he helped to found the American Society of Composers, Authors, and Publishers (ASCAP), an organization that to this day ensures that composers are paid for performances of their music. And between 1894 and his death in 1924 he composed forty operettas.

Stranded in San Francisco by the 1906 earthquake, some members of New York's Metropolitan Opera Company try on California hats for size.

operetta

Victor Herbert

If opera belongs to the classical sphere and musical comedy and revue to the popular, operetta lands somewhere in between. Like musical comedies, operettas depend on speaking, not singing, to carry the plot—usually involving high-born characters who search for true love and find it. Yet operetta takes its emotional tone and vocalism from opera. The characters reveal that they are living in an exalted state by singing songs, duets, and choruses built around ringing high notes: proof of their ardent passion. Victor Herbert could write an operetta in 1910 (*Naughty Marietta*) and an opera in 1911 (*Natoma*) without making any radical change in his musical style.

Naughty Marietta fits Friml's list of ingredients perfectly: old things (it is set in 1780s New Orleans), a full-blooded libretto (Marietta, a disguised noblewoman, finds her lover through music), luscious melody ("I'm Falling in Love with Someone," "Ah! Sweet Mystery of Life"), rousing choruses ("Tramp, Tramp, Tramp," "The Italian Street Song"), and romantic passions (a jilted mixed-race beauty's plight exposes Louisiana's racial caste system).

Naughty Marietta opens at dawn on the central square of New Orleans. To hear the city wake up in Herbert's orchestration is to realize that he was a master of orchestral effect (his mastery is also apparent in his two cello concertos). Moreover, one vocal number in particular points up his ability to bring musical richness into comic opera without sacrificing immediate appeal. "I'm Falling in Love with Someone," a tenor song in waltz time, begins with a verse that could almost be that of a popular song, but the chorus moves quickly into deeper waters, including some bold melodic leaps, high tenor notes, and flexible tempo. The message of this theatrical love song may be intimate, but the chorus's journey from quiet midrange to ringing climax is a reminder that it was written to be felt in the farthest reaches of the hall.

Operetta remained popular on the Broadway stage through the 1920s, whether composed by Europeans like Lehár or Oscar Straus (*The Chocolate Soldier*, 1908), by the occasional native-born American like John Philip Sousa (*El Capitan*, 1896), or by European-born Americans like Herbert, Rudolf Friml (*The Firefly*, 1912; *Rose-Marie*, 1924; *The Vagabond King*, 1925), or Sigmund Romberg (*The Student Prince*, 1924; *The Desert Song*, 1925; *The New Moon*, 1928). After their initial runs on Broadway, several operettas were adapted as successful films in the 1930s and 1940s, some starring Nelson Eddy and Jeanette MacDonald. The best operettas also enjoyed long lives in both amateur and professional productions, tapering off in popularity only in recent decades. Even in its heyday, however, operetta shared the public's affection with its more informal cousins, musical comedy and revue.

Naughty Marietta

Sousa, Friml, Romberg

MUSICAL COMEDY

Just as they had in the eighteenth century, British imports dominated the American stage throughout the nineteenth century. And just as the old-fashioned ballad operas had given way to the newer operettas of Gilbert and Sullivan, those operettas by the 1890s were beginning to be eclipsed by a new style of direct-from-London entertainment: the musical comedy. Two things distinguished this new genre from the operetta. First, its settings and characters were contemporary. Instead of romantic nobility in faraway kingdoms, musical comedies featured well-to-do but not necessarily aristocratic young people whose romantic entanglements occurred in familiar settings, or at least what middle-class audiences would like to think of as familiar. Second, in place of the sweeping lyricism of operetta was a more conversational style of vocal writing, closer to the popular songs coming from Tin Pan Alley.

Although British musicals of the 1890s like *A Gaiety Girl* and *Florodora* are now long forgotten, their popularity and influence in the United States were significant. Their relaxed informality suited the American temperament, and the prominence they gave to the female chorus appealed to audiences brought up on *The Black Crook*, while maintaining a propriety that made them more suitable family entertainment. Most important, they provided a model for American composers interested in a theatrical genre that concerned itself with the here and now.

Most European imports, whether British musical comedies or Viennese operettas, arrived on Broadway with **interpolations**—added songs, generally not by the original show's principal composer and lyricist. Sometimes these interpolated songs replaced material that was judged unlikely to please American audiences, but that was not the only reason for adding them; indeed, even American-made shows in the early years of the twentieth century were frequently studded with interpolations. They sometimes appeared at the bidding of theater managers, anxious that a new show's score might lack potential hits. Other interpolations were added at the behest of star performers dissatisfied with what the show's authors had provided them. In this respect, all forms of musical theater—even opera, though the practice of interpolating arias was dying out—stood firmly in the realm of performers' music, not composers' music.

interpolations

A typical American musical comedy of this early period in the genre's development was *Sinbad,* which ran at Broadway's Winter Garden Theater for 404 performances in 1918–19. The music was by the Hungarian-born American Sigmund Romberg, who later would find his true métier in operetta after writing music for several musicals and revues. The lyrics were by the prolific but undistinguished Harold Atteridge, who also concocted the show's **book**, the musical comedy's plainly named equivalent of an opera's libretto. That is, he was responsible for what little book there was, *Sinbad* being notably short on plot or character development. Instead, the book functioned mainly to string together opportunities for elaborate staging—after starting at a Long Island dog show, the story moved on to the Grotto of the Valley of Diamonds and the Island of Eternal Youth, among others—featuring the chorus girls and the show's star attraction, Al Jolson.

⋹ Did the success of "Swanee" (1919) enhance Al Jolson's stardom, or vice versa? Likely, the answer is a bit of both.

Born Asa Yoelson in Lithuania in 1886, Al Jolson at age eight emigrated with his family to the United States, where his father had obtained a position as cantor at a Washington, D.C., synagogue. As a teenager he ran away to New York to enter show business, and in the early years of the century he worked his way up as a singer and comedian through burlesque and vaudeville to the legitimate stage. Jolson eventually became an immensely popular performer, not only in Broadway musicals but also in the new media of sound recordings, radio, and film. His portrayal of the title character in *The Jazz Singer* (1927), the first major sound film, marked the beginning of the end of the silent era in motion pictures (see chapter 15).

Sinbad introduced three big hit songs, all of them sung by Jolson. All three were interpolations by songwriters other than Romberg, brought into the show at the star's initiative. Jolson played an African American porter, a role he performed in blackface—a reminder of minstrelsy's long reach into later eras. By improbable plot devices, Jolson's black porter finds himself transported to Baghdad, where he meets Sinbad and other figures from the Arabian Nights. To establish the character's background, Romberg wrote "I Hail from Cairo," a comic song with a punch line about Cairo, Illinois. Early in the show's run, Jolson tired of this number and replaced it with a more emphatically Southern song, "Rock-a-Bye Your Baby with a Dixie Melody," with music by Jean Schwartz and lyrics by Joe Young and Sam M. Lewis, three Tin Pan Alley stalwarts. Still later in the run, that song was replaced with "My Mammy," by the same lyricists, with music by Walter Donaldson. Finally, after the show left Broadway and went on tour in 1920, the spot was filled with "Swanee," the first great hit for twenty-one-year-old George Gershwin, working with lyricist Irving Caesar. All three songs express a black persona's longing for a Southern home and family—the topic Stephen Foster had explored more than half a century earlier with "Old Folks at Home," a song directly quoted in "Swanee."

"Swanee"

All three songs also entered Jolson's permanent repertory, and he sang them for years on stage, screen, radio, and phonograph records. Although *Sinbad's* thirteen-month run made it a substantial hit show by the standards of the day, it then disappeared and has never been revived, whereas its interpolated songs, closely associated with Jolson but also sung and played by countless others, are still recognized by many music lovers today. Thus, like most early musical comedies, *Sinbad* was of lasting importance only as a delivery system for popular songs.

In the early years of the twentieth century, many of the best popular songs—whether introduced to the public in musical comedy, revue, or vaudeville—were imbued with the flavor of ragtime. The origins of ragtime lie in the activities of black musicians in the decades after the Civil War.

THE RISE OF RAGTIME

Before the Civil War, the popularity of the minstrel show (see chapter 6) had demonstrated a widespread fascination among white audiences with black music, even if that music was presented only through the distorted filter of white performers in blackface. Minstrelsy set the stage for the careers of professional African American entertainers after the war, both for better, in that minstrelsy had whetted audiences' appetites for real black entertainment, and for worse, in that African Americans had to accommodate their artistic expressions to minstrelsy's stereotypes of black culture. Either way, with the slowly rising fortunes of African Americans came new opportunities for black musicians.

BLACK MUSICAL ASPIRATIONS AFTER THE CIVIL WAR

Black musicians' difficult road to artistic recognition is inseparable from the struggles of the four million people who emerged from slavery at the end of the Civil War. Although new amendments to the Constitution guaranteed these new citizens full equal rights under the law, for decades to come those rights would exist more in theory than in practice. Sharecropping, in which tenant farmers worked land owned by absentee landlords, trapped many former slaves in a life of poverty scarcely better than their earlier condition. When Reconstruction ended in 1876, Federal troops were no longer present to ensure the voting rights of black men in the South. With the growth of white supremacist organizations such as the Ku Klux Klan came a corresponding increase in mob violence against blacks. Lynchings increased in number throughout Reconstruction and afterwards, reaching a peak in the 1890s, when each year more than eighty persons, mostly blacks accused but not convicted of serious crimes, were lynched. And the Supreme Court's decision in *Plessy v. Ferguson* in 1896 institutionalized the segregation of blacks and whites in public spaces—the "separate but equal" policy that soon came to be nicknamed Jim Crow, after the minstrel-show stereotype. As the black author and lyricist James Weldon Johnson saw it, "the status of the Negro as a citizen had been steadily declining for twenty-five years; and at the opening of the twentieth century his civil state was, in some respects, worse than at the close of the Civil War."

Jim Crow laws

Despite these obstacles, new professional opportunities for black musicians opened up in the late 1800s, providing the musicians were willing to withstand varying degrees of indignity. At one end of the spectrum was the musical savant and piano prodigy "Blind Tom" (Thomas Bethune, 1849–1908), who from childhood was exhibited as a curiosity by his owner-guardian: an uneducated slave, sightless from birth, with a large repertory of classical and popular pieces, all learned by ear, to which he added his own compositions and improvisations. As late as 1904 Blind Tom was still touring for the financial benefit of his former owners, who made a fortune exploiting his phenomenal musical abilities.

"Blind Tom" Bethune

At the other end of the spectrum was Matilda Sissieretta Jones (1868–1933), an operatic soprano, trained at the New England Conservatory, who performed at the White House for President Benjamin Harrison. She was nicknamed the "Black Patti," after the Italian diva Adelina Patti. Jones was barred from singing with any U.S. opera company because of the color of her skin; instead, she traveled extensively with her own troupe of African American performers, Black Patti's Troubadours, presenting a mixed program of operatic numbers and lighter fare.

Sissieretta Jones

Somewhere in the middle of the spectrum was the black minstrel show. Apart from a few isolated antebellum examples, only after the Civil War was minstrelsy opened to African American performers, who were expected to wear the customary blackface and conform to all the demeaning stereotypes of the minstrel stage. Minstrel troupes were almost always either all white or all black, and even the exceptional mixed-race troupes tended to segregate their shows, with white performers on the first half and black performers after intermission. By the turn of the century, a few black minstrel troupes had grown into large operations, performing mostly in the South. W. A. Mahara's Colored Minstrels announced their arrival at a town with a parade featuring a thirty-piece band led by bandmaster W. C. Handy, who would later become known as the "Father of the Blues" (see chapter 11). Minstrel bands, demanding high levels of musical skill and literacy, acted as proving grounds for black professional instrumentalists, composers, and arrangers. Moreover, the minstrel format encouraged musicians to find new ways to blend currently popular genres, such as the march, with music rooted in traditional African American idioms, which had been the basis of minstrelsy's appeal from the very beginning.

black minstrelsy

Once minstrelsy had opened the door for them, black performers gained admittance into other forms of stage entertainment, such as vaudeville and musical comedy. One composer of musical comedies who successfully drew on both

Will Marion Cook (1869–1944) brought the skills of a classically trained musician to an African American musical theater that boomed in New York from the mid-1890s until the early 1910s.

Euro-American and African American traditions was Will Marion Cook. Born in 1869 in Washington, D.C., Cook graduated from the Oberlin Conservatory in Ohio, studied violin in Berlin, and undertook advanced study at the National Conservatory during Dvořák's time there. At the World's Columbian Exposition in Chicago in 1893, he directed the performance of excerpts from his opera *Uncle Tom's Cabin*, now lost, with Harry T. Burleigh as one of the soloists. Despite these achievements, Cook found the classical sphere closed to him because of his race. Turning to show business, Cook lavished his skills on New York shows with black casts that, though now forgotten, contain music still worth hearing. *In Dahomey* (1903), the first black-produced show to run at a regular Broadway theater, made an international impact. After a warm reception in New York, it played for seven months in London, then toured England and Scotland before returning to the United States for more performances.

According to his contemporary James Weldon Johnson, Cook "believed that the Negro in music and on the stage ought to be a Negro, a genuine Negro," rather than a minstrel stereotype. And in that spirit, "Swing Along," a number from *In Dahomey* whose text Cook also wrote, uses syncopation and dialect to celebrate black folk culture:

Come along, Mandy, come along, Sue,
White folks watchin' an' seein' what you do,
White folks jealous when you'se walkin' two by two,
   So swing along, Chillun, swing along!

Well-a swing along, yes-a, swing along
   An'-a lif'-a yo' heads up high,
   Wif pride an' gladness beamin' from yo' eye!
Well-a, swing along, yes-a, swing along,
   From a early morn till night,
Lif' yo' head an' yo' heels mighty high,
   An'-a swing bof lef' an' right.

Though the stage Negro dialect may strike present-day ears as demeaning, "Swing Along" works within the conventions of its time to project an image of African Americans as justifiably proud, confident, and in possession of cultural achievements that could be the envy of white folks.

SCOTT JOPLIN

Of the remarkable generation of black musicians born shortly after emancipation, the one who most successfully brought music from the black folk tradition into the popular sphere was Scott Joplin. Born in 1867, Joplin would have heard traditional African American music as he grew up, the son of an ex-slave and his freeborn wife, near the Texas-Arkansas border, but he also took piano lessons from a local German-born music teacher. Joplin traveled in his early years as a minstrel troupe member, and in 1893 spent time in Chicago during the World's Columbian Exposition. Though evidence is sketchy, this gala celebration has often been cited as crucial in introducing the music soon to be called ragtime to a large audience. When the fair ended, Joplin traveled to St. Louis and from there to Sedalia, a central Missouri town where he lived from 1894 to 1901.

Sedalia was a railroad hub with a thriving community at the center of the region's commerce and transportation. Sedalia was also full of travelers in search of entertainment, and the city boasted two theaters as well as saloons and dance halls. During his late twenties and early thirties, Joplin enrolled in music courses at a local black college, played for dances, and worked for a time as a pianist in two of Sedalia's brothels. He also belonged to one of the city's two black social clubs, the Maple Leaf Club, to which he dedicated the *Maple Leaf Rag* (1899), his most famous composition.

When in 1896 the first syncopated songs were published under the "ragtime" label, the style was already familiar to those who knew black folk tradition; but for those who did not, ragtime brought the novelty of a fad. The next year, 1897, saw the first published instrumental rag, *Mississippi Rag*, by the white bandleader W. H. Krell, and shortly after, the first rag by an African American composer, Tom Turpin's *Harlem Rag*. Once ragtime numbers appeared in print, their impact was quickly felt. By the end of the decade ragtime songs and instrumentals were heard on the musical stage, in cylinder recordings and piano rolls, and in arrangements for ensembles like Sousa's band.

☙ Scott Joplin (1867–1917), the King of Ragtime.

Ragtime is thought to have been named for the "ragged rhythm" whose accents cut across the duple meter's alternating strong and weak beats. But a more recent theory holds that it was named, by its black practitioners, for the hoisting of handkerchiefs (rags) to signal a dance. The term seemed demeaning even to Scott Joplin, the declared "King of Ragtime." In 1908, for example, he wrote: "What is scurrilously called ragtime is an invention that is here to stay." Joplin made this comment in the *School of Ragtime: Six Exercises for Piano*, which gave to anyone who mastered its notation the key to the music's "weird and intoxicating effect." *School of Ragtime* explains syncopation as unusual groupings of rapid notes against a slower, steady beat, demanding that every note "be played as written." In publishing his piano rags, Joplin was pursuing three related goals: to give the music a salable form, to expand its range of customers, and to raise its status. For as long as ragtime stayed in the oral tradition, those who mastered it had only their skill as performers to sell.

School of Ragtime

Joplin's *Maple Leaf Rag* (LG 10.1), published in Sedalia in 1899, sold steadily through the remainder of the composer's lifetime and has afterward endured in the piano repertory. Like other instrumental rags, the piece evolved from the connection of syncopated rhythms to the form of the march. *Maple Leaf Rag* contains four strains, each sixteen bars long, each repeated at least once, and with the left hand providing a steady pulse for the right hand's rhythmic trickiness. The strict beat never flags, nor does the regular procession of square-cut phrases. But the melodies, harmonies, and textures offer variety and surprise. Rags, like marches, usually ease into the melody through an introduction, but the *Maple Leaf Rag* plunges right into the first strain. Likewise, piano ragtime is normally propelled by a left hand that alternates a low octave on the beat and a midrange chord after it, like the "oom-pah" of a military band's low brass. But here Joplin delays that pattern until the second strain. Also unusual in the first strain is the dynamic plan: a loud beginning, a drop of volume, and a crescendo back to the level of the start. The last six bars play on the lowered and raised third degree of the scale in a blues-like fashion, in an age before the blues took formal shape (see chapter 11).

LG 10.1

As in a march, the third strain of the *Maple Leaf Rag* is a trio that drops down into the subdominant key, a fifth lower than the tonic. Unlike marches and many rags, however, the new key does not usher in a singing, cantabile melody.

CD 2.2   Listening Guide 10.1   *Maple Leaf Rag* SCOTT JOPLIN

DATE: 1899
PERFORMER: Scott Joplin
GENRE: piano rag
METER: duple
FORM: AABBACCDD, 16-bar sections

WHAT TO LISTEN FOR

- syncopated rhythms over steady bass accompaniment
- multi-strain form similar to a march
- key change at trio, as in a march

TIMING	SECTION	COMMENTS
0:00	A	Steady two-note-per-beat rhythm in bass; faster, irregular, syncopated rhythms in treble. Just before the midpoint (0:08), a rising figure climbs from bass to treble. The second half consists of a 4-bar phrase played in the upper register, then repeated an octave lower, in the mid-register.
0:22	A	Repeat.
0:44	B	Falling melody in treble, standard "oom-pah" accompaniment in bass (alternating low octaves on the beats with midrange chords between the beats).
1:06	B	Repeat.
1:28	A	The A strain returns before the trio.
1:49	trio C	In the subdominant key. Treble alternates 2 bars of thick chords with 2 bars of a single-note melody, suggesting the kind of dynamic contrasts heard in a Sousa march.
2:11	C	Repeat.
2:34	D	Return to the tonic key, with more lyrical melody.
2:56	D	Repeat.

NOTE Piano roll by Scott Joplin, 1916.

Listen & Reflect

1. Like Sousa's marches, Joplin's rags were published in arrangements for a variety of instrumental combinations. Yet Joplin was a pianist and conceived his music for the piano. Dozens of performances of *Maple Leaf Rag* can be easily found on YouTube and elsewhere online, played by various wind and string instruments, as solos and in groups. Sample some of these, then consider what features of *Maple Leaf Rag*, if any, strike you as particularly idiomatic to the piano. Does the music seem better suited to some instruments or instrumental combinations than to others?

A CLOSER LOOK

Player Pianos and Piano Rolls

Piano manufacturing in the United States, already a healthy industry in the nineteenth century (see chapter 6), entered its boom years around 1900 with the popularity of the player piano: a mechanized "self-playing" instrument. The mass-produced player pianos of the early 1900s featured a pneumatic action, typically operated mechanically with pedals. Holes in a perforated paper roll acted as valves, allowing pressurized air to activate keys in the proper sequence. Of the 2.5 million player pianos sold in the United States between 1900 and 1930, most had a simple mechanism that produced an artificial-sounding music. More expensive and thus less common were "reproducing pianos," which could capture at least some of a pianist's expressive gestures; their variety of touch, dynamics, and pedaling could create lifelike performances. Yet even the simpler player pianos offered a home musical experience more vivid than that of the early phonograph, and player piano sales remained strong until the Great Depression of the 1930s.

Just as the phonograph created a market for records, the player piano created a demand for piano rolls. Master rolls could be created either from a pianist's live performance or by plotting the placement of holes visually and punching them manually. Often the two methods were combined: extra notes could be added to a pianist's performance after the fact, in a process analogous to the editing techniques of the later recording studio (see chapter 17).

Instead, the fourth strain comes as close to a songlike melody as any part of the rag. It also returns to the opening key, a common feature in a Joplin rag that never occurs in a Sousa march. Also standard in a rag but not in a march is a return of the first strain between the second and third strains. Compare the layout of a typical rag to the short (regimental) march form (see chapter 7):

Rag:	introduction | AA BB A | CC DD
Short march:	introduction | AA BB | (trans) CC DD

Accompanying Listening Guide 10.1 is a modern recording of a player piano "reading" a piano roll cut by Joplin himself in 1916. Although rolls made for high-end player pianos could reproduce a performer's nuances of dynamics, touch, and pedaling, the rolls made by Joplin lack those refinements. Moreover, Joplin made the rolls late in life, when his health was in decline, and they probably do not represent his playing at its best. Nevertheless, this piano roll gives the listener some idea of how Joplin wanted his music to be performed. It is worth noting, considering Joplin's written instructions to play his music exactly as notated, that his performance departs from the printed sheet music in many small particulars.

Joplin left Sedalia in 1901 and traveled through the Midwest for several years. In 1907 he settled in New York City, where he worked as a composer, arranger, and teacher until his death in 1917. *Treemonisha*, an opera for which Joplin wrote his own libretto, occupied much of his energy in those years. The opera is set in the Arkansas countryside near Texarkana—his childhood home. It centers on an embodiment of the New Negro named Treemonisha, a young woman who hopes to lead her community out of ignorance and superstition by teaching them the

Treemonisha

value of education, her emphasis on self-reliance fully in sympathy with the teachings of Booker T. Washington. Joplin called his work a grand opera. "I am a composer of ragtime music," he explained, "but I want it thoroughly understood that my opera 'Treemonisha' is not ragtime." Joplin announced plans for a 1913 performance by forty singers and an orchestra of twenty-five, but it never happened.

Joplin used to tell friends and rivals that he would be dead for twenty-five years before people appreciated his accomplishments. His prediction proved wrong by half, for more than fifty years passed before a ragtime revival took place in the 1970s with Joplin as its central figure. New recordings of his music were made; his rags were republished; *Treemonisha* was performed and recorded; ragtime orchestras were formed; and an Academy Award–winning film, *The Sting*, was released in 1973 with a score made up of Joplin's compositions. Although Joplin in his own lifetime never won the respect he sought for himself outside the popular sphere, his music has now earned its own kind of classic status.

POPULAR SONG AND DANCE IN THE RAGTIME ERA

Even before the first published instrumental rags, ragtime syncopations began to creep into the vocabulary of popular song. In part, this was the result of the opening up of minstrelsy and its descendants, vaudeville and musical comedy, to black entertainers. But the minstrel tradition put these young performers and songwriters in a bind. Its character types were too rigid to accommodate their talents, yet too widely accepted for black entertainers to ignore. Moreover, African Americans had to contend with a new kind of black character appearing in popular song during the 1880s: the "coon," a shiftless black male who could also be dangerous. The lyrics of so-called **coon songs**—to use the label then applied to songs with lyrics in stage Negro dialect—feature references to watermelon, chicken (usually stolen), alcohol, gambling, and other demeaning stereotypes of African American life. Having caught on with white audiences, coon songs were part of the legacy that younger black artists inherited when they entered show business.

"coon songs"

Any African American who worked in show business was faced with the conflict between needing to please an audience and knowing that many standard crowd-pleasing devices openly ridiculed black people's capacities and character. Entertainers dealt differently with the conflict. According to one Tin Pan Alley publisher, Edward Marks, leading figures like Bert Williams and George Walker were "outwardly resigned to all sorts of discrimination. They would sing 'coon,' they would joke about 'niggers,' they accepted their success with wide-mouthed grins as the gift of the gods." But the brothers James Weldon and J. Rosamond Johnson were different: "emphatically new Negro," as Marks saw it, and eager to change the caricature. "Their father was a minister—and they combined a clerical dignity, university culture, and an enormous amount of talent." The Johnson brothers "wrote songs sometimes romantic, sometimes whimsical, but they eschewed the squalor and the squabbles, the razors, wenches, and chickens. . . . The word 'coon' they banished from their rhyming dictionary, despite its tempting affinity with moon."

the cakewalk

The new generation of entertainers also inherited the **cakewalk**. Rooted in African tradition, this new way of moving onstage originated in a contest held during slavery times in which couples competed to show the fanciest strutting,

A couple in typical cakewalk pose graces the cover of Scott Joplin's *Ragtime Dance* (1902).

with the winners receiving a cake or some other prize. Long parodied in minstrel shows, the cakewalk was now being performed to ragtime. Just as the cakewalk is the high-spirited apotheosis of marching, ragtime infuses the rhythmic verve of march music with electrifying syncopation.

"May Irwin's Bully Song"

The characteristic cakewalk rhythm—a short-long-short pattern—enlivens "May Irwin's Bully Song," which the white performer May Irwin introduced in a Broadway comedy, *The Widow Jones*, in 1895. Two different sheet music cover images of Charles E. Trevathan's song depict the title bully as an overdressed dandy, a later incarnation of minstrelsy's Zip Coon, in his "long tail blue" coat, with one important distinction: where Zip Coon was portrayed holding a pair of pince-nez spectacles, the bully holds a straight razor, the stereotypical coon's street weapon of choice. This and other early Negro dialect songs consistently link cakewalk and other ragtime rhythms with demeaning portrayals of African Americans.

"All Coons Look Alike to Me"

As Marks noted, accommodation to the racist conventions of the coon song was for some black entertainers a necessary compromise for professional advancement. One of the leading black showmen of the time was Ernest Hogan, whose most famous song, "All Coons Look Alike to Me" (1896), is both demeaning to its black characters and unquenchable in musical liveliness. The subject is courtship. In the verse, the male persona tells ruefully how Lucy Janey Stubbles has dumped him for a "coon barber from Virginia." But her dismissal in the chorus mocks the very idea of love, except perhaps as a ploy to corral a partner for display in public and sex in private.

The song's cover shows a slim, pert Ms. Stubbles appraising several black men who, apart from their grotesquely distended lips, look entirely different from one another. The picture makes it clear that she is not really saying she can't tell her suitors apart. Rather, the difference that really matters—a willingness to spend money according to her wishes—cannot be seen by the naked eye. In an era when songs often idealized romance, an outlook like this, no matter how thickly layered with irony, took sheet music buyers into a realm of male-female relations beyond Tin Pan Alley limits.

The chorus made this song famous, for Hogan's title line, detached from the song, could be turned into a racial slur, dismissing a whole people in one jeering slogan. At the same time, the tune was strong and memorable enough for instrumental performance. In January 1900, New York's Tammany Hall played host to piano players from across the country, gathered for the Ragtime Championship of the World Competition. The three who reached the finals were required to demonstrate their skill by "ragging" "All Coons Look Alike to Me"—playing it with additional, possibly improvised, ragtime syncopations—for two minutes in front of the judges.

Hogan's music makes an especially strong impact in an alternative version of the chorus printed as a "choice chorus" in the sheet music. Here the accompaniment, full of rhythmic vitality, approaches the style that the following year would appear in the first published instrumental rags. With all the painful conflicts it represents, the song is an example of how, despite rampant racial prejudice and political oppression, African American culture continued to invent music that was not only complex but could even be joyful.

"Wait 'till the Sun Shines, Nellie"

In the following decade, ragtime syncopations began to infuse songs whose characters bear no ethnic markers and thus are conventionally construed as white. In "Wait 'till the Sun Shines, Nellie" (1905), Nellie, the girlfriend of Joe, is worried because she's bought a new gown to wear to a picnic, which is threatened by rain. Joe reassures her with the song's title line. Composer Harry Von

Tilzer uses a rag-derived syncopated motive to lend a slightly tentative quality to the verse, underscoring Nellie's fretfulness, which is shouldered aside by the chorus's confident arrival in striding, foursquare march time. Both the cover illustration and the lyrics, with their absence of stage Negro dialect, leave no doubt that Nellie and Joe are white. As the new century began, white Americans were finding themselves beholden to blacks for music that seemed, more than any other, to catch the modern spirit.

IRVING BERLIN

Despite its mild syncopations, "Wait 'till the Sun Shines, Nellie" was not perceived to be a ragtime song. In 1916 an observer wrote that in the early years of the twentieth century "only songs having to do with the negro" were considered to be ragtime. A series of hit songs with African American characters earned Irving Berlin a reputation during the 1910s as America's chief ragtime composer. After publishing several modestly successful ragtime songs, early in 1911 Berlin had his first smash hit with "Alexander's Ragtime Band," which has implied references to "the negro" (see below). But in his song "That Mysterious Rag," published that summer, no black persona is implied. Indeed, no black characters appear in any of Berlin's later ragtime songs. Moreover, from this time on, Berlin used the word "syncopated" instead of "ragtime" to describe his own songs in that vein. Syncopated songs soon came to symbolize the spirit of liberation that appeared in New York society, both black and white, and quickly spread elsewhere. And one mark of that new spirit was the craze for dancing.

In the second half of the nineteenth century most social dancing took place either at private functions or in dives that encouraged illicit behavior. But starting in the second decade of the 1900s, public dance halls opened in large numbers, and so did hotel ballrooms and dance floors in cafés, restaurants, and cabarets. A flood of new dances fueled the explosion. While dancing had formerly been an activity of learned steps, the new dances—many of them infused with syncopation and bearing such "animal" names as the foxtrot, turkey trot, bunny hug, and grizzly bear—encouraged more spontaneous movement. Women and men now began to move their whole bodies to the beat. And many new songs emphasized rhythm over melody. Popular music was now an extension of dancing as well as singing, playing, and listening.

Irving Berlin played a key role in this transformation. Having emigrated with his family from Russia to New York City at the age of five in 1893, he grew up in a Jewish neighborhood on the Lower East Side without much formal education. While still a teenager, Berlin published songs for which he wrote words, music, or both. Having a sharp business sense as well as talent and tenaciousness, he won such success that after a dozen years in the trade he established his own publishing firm, Irving Berlin Music, Inc. (1919). Describing his working method, Berlin once explained: "I get an idea, either a title or a phrase or

Irving Berlin (1888–1989), photographed between 1913 and 1919, when he and Ted Snyder were partners in the firm of Berlin and Snyder, music publishers on Tin Pan Alley.

melody, and hum it out to something definite." Unable to read or write music notation, he would then dictate the finished song to a musical secretary. But if "humming out" sounds like a casual process, Berlin's perfectionist streak made it anything but that. A friend recalls having more than once sat "beside Irving at his tiny piano" and listened while he composed. "He would go over and over a lyric until it sounded perfect to my ears. Then he'd scrap the whole thing and begin over again. When I asked Irving what was wrong, he invariably said, 'It isn't *simple* enough.'"

Berlin's song genres

To highlight the variety of Tin Pan Alley genres, an edition of the songs Berlin wrote between 1907 and 1914 divides them into groups: (1) ballads, (2) novelty songs, (3) ragtime and other dance songs, and (4) show songs. **Ballads** stood the closest in style and mood to the older Victorian songs; a **novelty song** sketched a brief, comic story, often pertaining to customs of the day; **ragtime songs** included all numbers with that word in their titles or that mention ragtime in their texts; and **show songs** were those performed in a stage production in Berlin's own day.

The years 1912–17 have been described as both the end of Victorian calm and the beginning of a cultural revolution. And Berlin's early work embodies both, mixing old-fashioned waltz songs and ballads with such novelties as "My Wife's Gone to the Country (Hurrah! Hurrah!)" and "If You Don't Want My Peaches (You'd Better Stop Shaking My Tree)." Ethnicity was a key subject in those years, for immigrants poured into New York's melting pot until 1914, when war broke out in Europe. The popular theater maintained black stereotypes from the minstrel show and added other groups, each with its own built-in story. Thus, in addition to Negro dialect songs with black characters, Berlin's early work includes songs with Italian, German, Irish, and Jewish personae, each singing in a stereotypical stage dialect, and even a few "rube" songs involving gullible country folk.

ethnic novelty songs

Three 1911 songs show Berlin celebrating the spirit of those eager to end American Victorianism once and for all. "Alexander's Ragtime Band" responds to the charisma of black musicians and the excitement of their playing. "That Mysterious Rag" recognizes the style's haunting traits and removes it from a racial setting. And in "Everybody's Doing It Now," ragtime is an infectious dance music—a fad uniting younger Americans in a spirit of uninhibited fun.

LG 10.2

To present-day audiences, "Alexander's Ragtime Band" (LG 10.2) may seem free of black references, but the name Alexander itself was associated with black minstrel-show characters, and the endearment "honey," in the very first line, was a common feature in Negro dialect songs but not in songs with white characters (the same was true of "baby"). Although the song lacks ragtime syncopations, it has a verse in one key and a chorus in the key pitched a fifth lower: the subdominant relationship found between the opening strains and the trio of a march, another reminder of how closely those two genres were connected. The urging of the text—"Come on and hear / Come on and hear / Alexander's Ragtime Band"—conveys the buzzing excitement that black influence brought to popular song. Most of all, Berlin's song registers the impact of black musical performance: Alexander's band can take a conventional bugle call, or the first phrase of Stephen Foster's "Old Folks at Home," and make it sound "like you've never heard before." Just thinking about Alexander and his bandsmen is enough to make the song's persona bubble with high spirits.

The recording of "Alexander's Ragtime Band" that accompanies Listening Guide 10.2 is typical of its era. The studio ensemble, which sounds like a small military band, backs up the singer with an arrangement that sticks close to the piano part in the published sheet music. The singer, Billy Murray, was a successful recording artist who seldom performed onstage. Rather, his appeal lay in his ability to enunciate words clearly and "hammer" his voice (as he put it) into the acoustic recording horn that was used in the years before the invention of the electric microphone in 1925. In short, his voice and technique were ideally suited to overcoming the limitations of early recording technology.

All the sections familiar from nineteenth-century popular songs—introduction, verse, and chorus—are present in "Alexander's Ragtime Band." The only new element is the **vamp**, a two-bar phrase that can be repeated an indefinite number of times until the singer begins the verse. The vamp comes from stage performance, where a singer might be telling a joke or finishing up some other stage business before launching into the song. For that reason, vamps in sheet music often carry the indication "till ready." Although not necessary in nonstage performances, the vamp became an expected part of popular song form and can be heard in this and countless other recordings of the era.

vamp

Another feature of "Alexander's Ragtime Band" was becoming a standard part of popular song structure in the second decade of the twentieth century: the thirty-two-bar chorus, divided into four equal sections of eight bars each. The *abac* pattern found here was becoming more common and would continue to be a standard pattern in later decades.

"That Mysterious Rag," written a few months after "Alexander," confirms the impact of ragtime but treats it as a kind of music that is more to be feared than relished. The text tells of a melody so disturbingly unforgettable that even sleepers are not immune: "If you ever wake up from your dreaming, / A-scheming, eyes gleaming, / Then if suddenly you take a screaming fit, / That's it!" Once planted in the brain, the music takes over, as if the victim were bewitched.

"That Mysterious Rag"

Although "Everybody's Doing It Now" contains relatively little syncopation, this song also emphasizes rhythm. The title, a daring *double entendre* for its day, refers to ragtime dancing. The verse notes the music's energizing effect: "Ain't the funny strain / Goin' to your brain? / Like a bottle of wine / Fine." And the chorus tells us that this electric new musical style—"Hear that trombone bustin' apart?"—was driving dancers to throw restraint to the winds:

"Everybody's Doing It Now"

See that ragtime couple over there,
Watch them throw their shoulders in the air,
Snap their fingers, honey, I declare,
It's a bear, it's a bear, it's a bear,
There!

While "Alexander's Ragtime Band" was the last of Berlin's ragtime songs to suggest that the new music was solely for African Americans, "That Mysterious Rag" and "Everybody's Doing It Now," by containing no evident ethnic markers of any kind, celebrate white America's infatuation with ragtime. But both songs also capture the *frisson* of danger: ragtime melodies are like drugs or diseases that can lead to mental derangement, and ragtime dances incite animalistic behavior that may stir illicit passions. Fears about the dangerous effects of ragtime music and dance often carried racist undertones, as in the assertion of Dr. Marion Palmer Hunt in 1897 that the best dancers were to be found among "untutored

| CD 2.3 | Listening Guide 10.2 | "Alexander's Ragtime Band" IRVING BERLIN |

DATE: 1911

PERFORMERS: Billy Murray, vocal, with studio orchestra

GENRE: ragtime song

METER: duple

FORM: verse and 32-bar *abac* chorus

WHAT TO LISTEN FOR

- instrumental accompaniment that resembles a military band
- key change at chorus, similar to that at the trio of a march or rag
- lyrics in stage Negro dialect

TIMING	SECTION		TEXT	COMMENTS
0:00	introduction			4-bar instrumental introduction based on the opening phrase of the verse.
0:07	vamp			A 2-bar phrase, played twice.
0:14	verse 1		Oh, ma honey...	Mild syncopation on "honey."
0:41	chorus a		Come on and hear...	Modulation to the subdominant resembles the similar modulation in a typical march.
0:55	b	*b*	They can play a bugle call...	Melody resembles a bugle call in bars 3–4.
1:08	a	*a*	Come on along...	Music is identical to the first *a*, with different lyrics.
1:22	c	*c*	And if you care to hear...	Quotation of "Old Folks at Home."
1:37	introduction and vamp			Return to beginning.
1:51	verse 2		Oh, ma honey...	The music of verse 1 repeats, with new lyrics.
2:18	chorus		Come on and hear...	As before.
3:13	chorus		They can play a bugle call...	Instrumental version of the chorus's *a* section, using Sousa-style countermelodies and woodwind trills. The vocalist sings only *b* and the second half of *c* (not indicated in the sheet music).

NOTE Edison cylinder, 1911.

Listen & Reflect

1. "Alexander's Ragtime Band" uses only the mildest syncopations—the same ones used, in fact, in Sousa's "Stars and Stripes Forever." As recorded here, the song gains even further ties to Sousa in its use of a military-style band. Yet the song was widely received by listeners at the time as a ragtime song. Why?

2. And what does that reception suggest about the attitudes of the musical public in 1911?

savages, the illiterate negroes and the patients in our lunatic asylums." From a black perspective, James Weldon Johnson wrote of his amusement in seeing white dancers trying to emulate what they saw as the "primitive" abandon of African Americans. Ragtime thus took its place as the first in a long line of popular music innovations in the United States that, in the eyes of their detractors, marked the end of civilization.

In their own words 💬

James Weldon Johnson on Ragtime Dancers

On occasions, I have been amazed and amused watching white people dancing to a Negro band in a Harlem cabaret; attempting to throw off the crusts and layers of inhibitions laid on by sophisticated civilization; striving to yield to the feel and experience of abandon; seeking to recapture a taste of the primitive joy in life and living; trying to work their way back into that jungle which was the original Garden of Eden; in a word, doing their best to pass for colored.

JAMES REESE EUROPE AND THE CASTLES

At the same time Irving Berlin was offering ragtime as an emblem of current fashion, a black musician working in New York was reminding the public of the music's African American roots. Born in 1881 in Mobile, Alabama, and raised in Washington, D.C., James Reese Europe played piano and violin but hoped most of all to be a conductor. Around 1903 he moved to New York and was soon conducting shows there. In 1910 Europe joined with others to create the Clef Club, a booking agency for African American musicians: the first real effort to harness the city's black musical talent. The club's roster of players in its peak years numbered more than two hundred, ready to form a dance orchestra at a moment's notice.

Europe's protégé, bandleader and singer Noble Sissle, remembered that before his mentor came into prominence, the New York social elite had favored Viennese waltzes, rendered by gypsy bands playing stringed instruments. But after members of white society heard Europe's syncopated music, they began hiring bands formed by members of the Clef Club. Europe and his men were hired because they were the best performers of the music their rich customers wanted to hear. "The wealthy people," Sissle explained, "would not take a substitute when they could buy the original."

While providing dance music for high-society entertainments, Europe became acquainted in 1913 with the white husband-and-wife professional dance team of Vernon and Irene Castle. Shortly after their marriage in 1911 the Castles had created a sensation in Paris by introducing the new ragtime dances. Two years later they were back in New York City, demonstrating a new style of dancing they had begun to develop by combining African American dance steps with European and Latin American dances such as the

James Reese Europe (1881–1919) poses as conductor with members of New York City's Clef Club (1914).

✒ Vernon and Irene Castle brought a new elegance to ragtime dance.

LG 10.3

tango. They popularized these dances first as exhibition dancers at society balls, then from 1914 at the Castle House, their exclusive Manhattan dance school, and in numerous magazine articles and photo spreads.

As codified in their 1914 book *Modern Dancing,* the Castles refined ragtime dance by replacing the vigorous movements of the "animal" dances with smoother, more graceful motions that were more palatable to cultivated tastes. Their debonair athleticism inspired a young generation to shake off the last vestiges of Victorianism and embrace a modernity in which both men and women could experiment with new gender roles: Vernon Castle combined grace and elegance with more-traditional concepts of manliness (which he later confirmed as a World War I flying ace), while Irene Castle embodied, not the frail domesticity of an earlier feminine ideal, but the freer, active, and youthful image of the new century's "New Woman." Together, they paved the way for such celebrated dance teams as Fred Astaire and Ginger Rogers (see chapter 15).

James Reese Europe's energetic yet polished orchestral ragtime was the perfect complement to the Castles' elegant dancing, and Europe's Society Orchestra was a fixture at the Castle House. When the Castles appeared in vaudeville, they insisted that Europe and his band accompany them, despite the objections of theater owners, who generally barred black performers from white theaters. Appearing onstage with the Castles at such first-rate theaters as the Palace and Hammerstein's Victoria, both on Broadway, Europe was in the vanguard of a long series of figures who would slowly erode the segregationist practices of the Jim Crow era.

Castle House Rag (LG 10.3) demonstrates the infectiousness of Europe's music for the Castles. As in the *Maple Leaf Rag,* constantly shifting syncopations enliven an unrelenting series of square-cut four-bar phrases. And like Joplin's rags, *Castle House Rag* draws on march form, with the same variant of repeating the A section before the trio. But Europe's rag also borrows two features of the march form rarely found in Joplin's rags: a transitional section leads into the trio, and a break strain heightens tension as in Sousa's *Stars and Stripes Forever.*

After a major-key introduction, the opening strain of *Castle House Rag* begins in a minor key before shifting back to the major. In other words, the third scale degree is alternately raised and lowered (the

---

In their own words

Suggestions for Correct Dancing from Irene & Vernon Castle's *Modern Dancing* (1914)

Do not *wriggle* the shoulders.
Do not *shake* the hips.
Do not *twist* the body.
Do not *flounce* the elbows.
Do not *pump* the arms.
Do not *hop*—glide instead.
Avoid *low, fantastic,* and acrobatic dips.
Stand far enough away from each other to allow free movement of the body in order to dance gracefully and comfortably.
The gentleman should rest his hand lightly against the lady's back, touching her with the finger-tips and wrist only. . . .
Remember you are at a social gathering, and not at a gymnasium.
Drop the *Turkey Trot,* the *Grizzly Bear,* the *Bunny Hug,* etc. These dances are ugly, ungraceful, and out of fashion.

CD 2.4   **Listening Guide 10.3**   *Castle House Rag* JAMES REESE EUROPE

DATE: 1914
PERFORMERS: The Paragon Ragtime Orchestra; Rick Benjamin, director
GENRE: orchestral rag
METER: duple
FORM: ABB'ACDC

WHAT TO LISTEN FOR

- energetic dance rhythm with ragtime syncopations
- structure similar to a long march, with break strain
- use of stop-time in trio

TIMING	SECTION	COMMENTS
0:00	introduction	4 bars. Cymbal crashes on the beat; winds and strings anticipate the A strain's melody.
0:03	A	16 bars. Begins *piano* in minor, then switches to *forte* in major for the last 5 bars. A woodblock reinforces the syncopations in the soft sections, followed by cymbals as in the introduction. No repeat of A in this performance.
0:18	B	16 bars. Sousa-like melody in trombone with an animated countermelody in flute, *piano* with crescendo to *forte*, ending inconclusively with a half cadence.
0:34	B'	As before, but ending with a full cadence. A single, short chord leads back to the A section.
0:50	A	
1:05	transition	4 bars. A syncopated figure taken from the end of the B section establishes the subdominant as the new key.
1:09	trio C	32 bars. Woodblock highlights the rhythmic gaps of stop-time.
1:40	D	8 bars. Dramatic break strain alternates high- and low-pitched instruments.
1:48	C	C returns at a louder dynamic level.

Listen & Reflect

1. What features of *Castle House Rag* make it particularly suitable for the dancing style of Irene and Vernon Castle?

most salient difference between major and minor) in a fashion that suggests the blues (see chapter 11). The subdued trio strain features **stop-time,** in which silences interrupt the steady marking of the beat in the bass and drums; the effect here is to enliven even the quietest part of the piece, keeping the dancers on their toes. Combining strings, winds, piano, and percussion, Europe's society orchestra created a timbral effect somewhere between Sousa's military band and the jazz-inflected dance bands yet to come in the 1920s.

When the United States entered World War I in 1917, Europe was asked to organize a band for the 15th New York Infantry Regiment (later reorganized as the 369th Infantry Regiment), an all-black military unit nicknamed the "Harlem Hellfighters." Sent to France to bring troops a taste of home, Europe's Hellfighters band was a huge success with the French people as well as the American soldiers. After the war, Europe and the Hellfighters band left the army and toured the United States, billed as "65 Musician Veterans of the Champagne and Argonne." In March and early May of 1919, part of the band recorded some two dozen selections, mostly popular songs, in New York under Europe's direction.

But the Hellfighters' saga ended abruptly in Boston on May 9, when a crazed band member stabbed Europe before a performance. He died later that day. The loss of this eminent musician was not taken lightly: Europe was the first African American to be honored by the city of New York with a public funeral. His funeral, like the short but brilliant career that preceded it, is emblematic of the rising status of black musicians at the beginning of the twentieth century. Despite many setbacks, those advances would continue as the new century progressed.

QUESTIONS FOR DISCUSSION AND REVIEW

1. Compare the relationship between music and dramatic situation in opera, operetta, and musical comedy.

2. Compare and contrast the careers of Harry T. Burleigh and Will Marion Cook.

3. What are the distinguishing features of instrumental ragtime? Of ragtime songs?

4. How did ragtime—the music, its social uses, and the imagery associated with it—change over the two decades from 1895 to 1915?

5. What are some more recent analogues to the public's discomfort with ragtime songs and dances? What are the shared features?

6. James Reese Europe's Society Orchestra recorded *Castle House Rag* in 1913, a recording available online and in some recent CD anthologies. It differs in many respects from the Paragon Orchestra's performance, which holds closer to the printed music. Locate the older recording and note the differences and their significance.

AMERICA'S MUSIC
FROM WORLD WAR I THROUGH WORLD WAR II

*I*n the years from World War I through World War II, expansions in communications technology—phonograph, radio, and motion pictures—transformed the musical culture of the United States. Phonograph records improved in quality as electrical recording developed through the 1920s, with important results. First, records gradually replaced sheet music as the popular music industry's chief commercial product, transferring to recording artists and record companies the central role that songwriters and publishers had held before. Second, burgeoning production of recorded music in all three spheres of musical activity—classical, popular, and traditional—created a rich legacy for present-day historians and music lovers. Recordings not only amplify the knowledge gained from musical scores and other written documents but also stand as artistic statements in themselves, worthy of appreciation, preservation, and study.

Equally transformative was the advent of radio and sound movies in the 1920s. Especially during the Great Depression of the 1930s, radio and movies offered relatively inexpensive entertainment to millions of Americans. Even more importantly, they constituted, after newspapers, the first new mass media: networks of communication that brought essentially the same content to all consumers regardless of regional, economic, or ethnic differences. The consequences were enormous for all three spheres of musical activity. Records, radio, and movies brought folk musicians before a much wider audience and led to a formerly unimaginable phenomenon: the professional folksinger. At the same time, classical musicians used the new media to democratize symphonic music. For a moment, at least, the boundaries between the classical and popular spheres became somewhat permeable, as composers like Aaron Copland wrote music for radio and movies, while George Gershwin showed that a Tin Pan Alley songwriter could reach the heights of symphonic music and opera.

◄ Along with radio and improved phonograph recordings, motion pictures became an important medium for music in the years between the world wars.

1931 William Grant Still, *Afro-American Symphony*

1933 John and Alan Lomax "discover" Leadbelly

1933–39 Fred Astaire and Ginger Rogers make nine films for RKO

1934 Virgil Thomson, *Four Saints in Three Acts*

1935 Gershwin, *Porgy and Bess*

1935 The U.S. government inaugurates the Federal Music Project

1936–40 Lester Young plays in Count Basie's orchestra

1938 Benny Goodman's orchestra performs at Carnegie Hall

1939 Marion Anderson's Easter Sunday concert at the Lincoln Memorial, Washington, D.C.

1941 Woody Guthrie, Pete Seeger, and others form the Almanac Singers

1942 First issue of *Cash Box*, a trade journal for the jukebox business

1943 Duke Ellington's *Black, Brown, and Beige* is performed at Carnegie Hall

1943 *Oklahoma!* opens on Broadway

1944 Copland, *Appalachian Spring*

1945 Mary Lou Williams records her *Zodiac Suite*

CHAPTER 11

BLUES, COUNTRY, AND POPULAR SONGS AFTER WORLD WAR I

Despite the economic and educational advances won by some African Americans by the turn of the twentieth century, many others continued to live in poverty and isolation. In one of the most remarkable developments in American music, blacks in the poorest region of the United States—the rural South—created the **blues**, a new kind of music that could express a wide range of powerful emotions. Blues music would influence nearly every style of music that developed in its wake.

Around the same time that blues artists were making their first records, rural white southerners began playing a new kind of music on radio and on records. At first called "hillbilly" and eventually relabeled **country music**, the new genre was eclectic from the start, borrowing freely not only from older Anglo-American folk styles but also from the blues.

The influence of the blues extended beyond the South to New York City's dual centers of the popular music industry, Tin Pan Alley and Broadway. There, a new type of song, introduced in musical comedy but transcending its theatrical origin, added the vocabulary of blues to earlier popular idioms, bringing a new expressiveness to popular music, in what has been called a golden era of popular song.

THE BLUES

The beginnings of the blues have been traced to the Deep South: to small towns and rural regions, Mississippi Delta plantations, and industries that demanded heavy manual labor. Lacking education, property, and political power in a segregated society, the creators of blues music led lives of hardship in rural isolation. Yet their songs take a resilient attitude toward separation and loss, with emotional responses that run the gamut from despair to laughter. The blues tradition is one of confrontation and improvisation.

Blues music took shape in oral tradition. The work song may be an ancestor; field hollers, sung by solitary workers, were also an influence. Apparently developed during the 1890s, early blues was accompanied by instruments, especially guitar, which provided a foundation of harmony and rhythm. Several performing techniques rooted in folk culture came to be earmarks of blues performance. First, blues involves a flexible approach to pitch, in which some notes of the melody are lowered, or "bent," for expression. Second, the blues included a variety of vocal timbres not found in other types of singing. Third, blues musicians developed a technique of call and response between voice and instrument. And finally, the rhythms are "swung": that is, each beat is divided, not into the even eighth notes of other styles, but into swung eighths, a relaxed long-short pattern sometimes called a shuffle.

To write down a blues song goes against the idea that the blues is a spontaneous kind of music. Yet current knowledge about the early history of the blues comes from printed sheet music, which predates the first blues recordings. Our survey of the blues thus begins with sheet music publications before 1920, then proceeds to the recording artists of the 1920s and, in chapter 14, of the 1930s.

EARLY BLUES PUBLICATIONS

A tale that demonstrates the folk origins of the blues was told by W. C. Handy, an Alabama-born musician who came to be called "the Father of the Blues." Not long after the turn of the century, he and his band were playing a dance in Cleveland, Mississippi, when "an odd request" reached the bandstand: "Would we object if a local colored band played a few dances?" Happy to be offered a paid break, Handy agreed, and three young instrumentalists, with "a battered guitar, a mandolin and a worn-out bass," took the stage. "They struck up one of those over-and-over strains that seem to have no very clear beginning and certainly no ending at all. The strumming attained a disturbing monotony, but on and on it went, a kind of stuff that has long been associated with cane rows and levee camps."

Handy could not imagine that anyone would find this music appealing, but he was wrong:

> A rain of silver dollars began to fall around the outlandish, stomping feet. The dancers went wild. . . . There before the boys lay more money than my nine musicians were being paid for the entire engagement. Then I saw the beauty of primitive music. They had the stuff the people wanted. It touched the spot. Their music wanted polishing, but it contained the essence. Folks would pay money for it. . . . That night a composer was born, an American composer.

After witnessing the effect of this humble music on a paying audience, Handy listened to the simple tunes more closely, wrote some down, and arranged them for his band. When he later published his own popular songs as sheet music, the blues began to be disseminated in printed form. Handy's story offers one version of how the marketplace discovered the blues.

The son of a Methodist minister in Florence, Alabama, Handy studied vocal music with a graduate of Fisk University, learned to play hymns on the organ, and received cornet lessons from a local bandleader. Once he left home, he directed the band for a black minstrel troupe (as described in chapter 10), taught music briefly at a black college in Huntsville, Alabama, and led dance orchestras in Mississippi and Tennessee. While in Memphis he adapted a folk song into a 1909 campaign song for a mayoral candidate, a song that in 1912 he published as "Memphis Blues," the first blues song in sheet music form. Two years later Handy followed that up with his greatest hit, "St. Louis Blues."

W. C. Handy

✎ W. C. Handy (1873–1958), as a youth of nineteen, when he played with a cornet band in Evansville, Indiana.

An enterprising businessman as well as a musician, Handy was his own publisher. He formed a sheet music company in Memphis with Harry Pace, and in 1918 Handy and Pace moved their company to New York, where their business became part of the thriving Tin Pan Alley scene. Rather than restricting his publications solely to popular songs in sheet music format, as most Tin Pan Alley publishers did, Handy pursued more prestigious projects as well. His collection *The Blues: An Anthology* appeared in 1926, and a book of spiritual arrangements came out in 1938. In the 1930s and 1940s he also wrote two books on African American music and an autobiography, *Father of the Blues* (1941). By the time of his death in 1958 W. C. Handy was one of the most respected black musicians in the United States.

At the same time, some critics have disparaged Handy because of his hyperbolic nickname, "Father of the Blues." To be sure, Handy never claimed to have created the blues. Instead, he played a crucial role in bringing an obscure folk music into the commercial mainstream, reaping considerable financial reward in the process. In doing so, he adapted the music he heard, dressing it up to meet the conventions of published sheet music—another practice that added to his controversial standing in American music. Compared to the blues recordings to come, Handy's notated blues songs have only a tenuous connection to their folk roots; by later standards, they seem to lack authenticity. But as later chapters will explore, the very concept of authenticity in folk and popular music is a highly contested topic in the twenty-first century. Still, Handy's songs can be heard on their own terms as songs that blend the qualities of the blues with the traits of other popular idioms.

In its sheet music form, "Memphis Blues" fits the standard verse-and-chorus format of the era's popular songs, complete with four-bar piano introduction and repeating vamp before the verse. Only in the chorus does "Memphis Blues" conform to conventions found in folk blues, such as the Delta blues of Robert Johnson (see chapter 14). Those conventions are more pervasive in "St. Louis Blues," where three of the song's four stanzas fit the pattern that came to be known as the "standard" blues: a twelve-bar chorus, comprising three four-bar phrases. Many blues songs follow longer or shorter patterns—eight-bar and sixteen-bar choruses are not unusual—but the twelve-bar pattern is by far the most common, hence the familiar term **twelve-bar blues**.

twelve-bar blues

A typical **blues chorus** can be identified by its phrase structure, textual form, and harmonic progression, all illustrated by "St. Louis Blues"; the style also includes certain melodic features.

MEASURE:	1	2	3	4
Harmony:	I	(IV)	I	I
Text:	I hate to see	de evenin' sun go	down.	

MEASURE:	5	6	7	8
Harmony:	IV	IV	I	I
Text:	Hate to see	de evenin' sun go	down.	

MEASURE:	9	10	11	12
Harmony:	V	V	I	I
Text:	Cause my baby	he done lef' dis	town.	

The three equal phrases of a twelve-bar blues chorus typically accommodate a three-line lyric, one line for each phrase (although other lyrical patterns are not unusual). In its archetypal form, a blues stanza repeats the opening line of text for the second phrase, then introduces a new, rhyming line in the third phrase that completes the idea. In other words, the stanza is a couplet with the first line repeated. Some writers describe this lyrical structure as AAB; care must be taken, however, not to confuse this description of lyrics with the similar use of letters to denote musical forms such as *aaba*.

Blues melodies generally deliver the words in the first half of each four-bar phrase, leaving the second half open for an instrumental response, sometimes called a **fill**. The result is the call-and-response dialogue found in many types of African American music.

Blues melodies also make prominent use of **blue notes**, lowered or "bent" versions of the third and seventh (and occasionally the fifth) scale degrees in the major scale. "St. Louis Blues" begins on the unaltered third degree of a major scale, but "sun" in bar 2 is sung to a blues third, a half step lower; the lowered pitch can signify both the setting sun and the persona's melancholy as the sun sinks from sight.

blue notes

Blues melodies tend to be sung to a standard series of chords, a **blues progression** built, in its simplest form, on three chords: tonic (I), subdominant (IV), and dominant (V), distributed across the three phrases as I——/ IV— I—/ V— I—. The placement of these chords at the beginning and middle of each phrase is crucial, but other chords are often inserted elsewhere to elaborate on the basic progression. One common variation is the addition of a subdominant chord in bar 2; sometimes that chord is added in bar 10 as well. Another common alteration is the addition of a dominant chord in the last bar, which has the effect of propelling the music into the next chorus; because it creates the sensation of demanding "one more time," the dominant chord in the last bar is sometimes called a **turnaround**.

blues progression

turnaround

The first and second stanzas of "St. Louis Blues" are set to identical music in Handy's sheet music. The fourth stanza uses the same blues progression and twelve-bar phrase structure, but with a new melody and a busier texture. Yet "St. Louis Blues," like "Memphis Blues," is more than just a succession of blues choruses. The third of the song's four strains is sixteen bars long and enlivened by a Latin rhythm associated with the tango. In 1914, the year Handy published "St. Louis Blues," the tango was enjoying popularity in the United States, thanks largely to its promotion by exhibition dancers like Irene and Vernon Castle. "St. Louis Blues" was a signature blues number, gaining worldwide popularity, and earning its composer royalties for the rest of his long life; it has been recorded countless times since its first recording in 1920.

RACE RECORDS AND CLASSIC BLUES

The early years of the century saw the fledgling phonograph industry undergoing its first "format war": the battle between cylinders and discs. By 1920 the latter had decisively edged out the former, though the Edison company continued

78-rpm single

to produce small numbers of cylinders through the next decade, alongside the more popular discs. The standard format for recorded music was now the 78-rpm single—a disc, usually ten inches in diameter, that spun at 78 revolutions per minute, yielding a playing time of about three minutes per side (twelve-inch discs, with a playing time of four and a half minutes, were in use for classical music but rarely for popular music). At first one-sided, 78s by 1920 were consistently manufactured with a second musical selection on the back or "flip" side, also called the **B side**. With the introduction of the electric microphone into the recording studio in 1925, the sound quality of recorded music advanced, and the market for records grew dramatically. By the mid-1920s the phonograph was a prized possession in many homes that otherwise might have few luxury items—much as pianos had been in earlier days.

Even before 1920 record companies had discovered that Americans would buy a wide variety of recorded music: everything from band music to opera, hymns, minstrel songs, and the music of immigrant groups. As the industry grew, it learned to market records by advertising to the audiences most likely to buy them. In 1920 the record industry discovered a new specialty group that grew rapidly into a shaping force in American music: the audience for records featuring African American performers singing and playing the blues.

A handful of black dance bands had made records before 1920, but those records had been marketed to the same general audience that also bought records by white dance bands. That changed after August 10, 1920, when Mamie Smith recorded "Crazy Blues" for the Okeh label. The record was advertised in black newspapers and at first was sold mainly by mail order. Although no attempt was made to reach the much larger white market, the record's sales reached a surprisingly high 70,000 copies in the first month. The appeal of black records for a black audience had been shown, and a new segment of the record industry

race records

was born: **race records**. If the term sounds derogatory to present-day ears, "race" in that day could signify pride in the era of the New Negro, when an advocate for African American advancement might be admiringly called a "race man" or "race woman."

The success of "Crazy Blues" created a demand for more race records, and soon Okeh was joined by other labels: Paramount and Brunswick/Vocalion, small independents like Okeh that focused primarily on black artists, and later Columbia, a major label that coined the term "race records" to distinguish that line from its other genres. The largest record company, Victor, was slow to enter the field, buying out Okeh in 1926 and starting its own race-record division, Bluebird, in 1932.

The audience was there: in the mid-1920s, by one estimate, African Americans were buying 10 million records per year. Though often lacking the economic resources of whites, black record buyers, according to one retailer in the South, "outbought whites in record consumption 50 to 1"—an exaggeration, no doubt, but proof of the high value those consumers placed on race records.

classic blues

The vast majority of race records were blues numbers. And at first, most of those blues records followed the pattern set by "Crazy Blues": a female vocalist with instrumental backing, ranging from one piano player to a "combo" of five or six "pieces" (instruments). The record companies found most of their blues artists working for the Theater Owners Booking Association (TOBA), which dominated the black vaudeville circuit, thus this style of blues performance is sometimes referred to as **vaudeville blues**. Alternatively, as the first flowering

of blues on records, it is often called **classic blues**. All the well-known classic blues singers were women: Mamie Smith, Gertrude "Ma" Rainey, Bessie Smith, Ethel Waters, Alberta Hunter, and many others. They recorded a variety of material, including Tin Pan Alley pop songs, but most of their songs are twelve-bar blues.

Perhaps the greatest of the classic blues singers was Bessie Smith, nicknamed "Empress of the Blues." Born in Tennessee in 1894, at age seventeen she became a dancer for a vaudeville troupe that featured Ma Rainey. By the early 1920s Smith had begun performing as a singer. In 1923 she made her first record for Columbia, "Downhearted Blues." Within six months it sold 780,000 copies. For the next decade she recorded prolifically and performed widely, although the popularity of classic blues singers declined after 1929.

Smith's 1925 recording of Handy's "St. Louis Blues" (LG 11.1) showcases her rough, expressive voice. She emphasizes key words with swooping glides, heavy vibrato, and subtle shadings of pitch, especially on the blue notes. Accompanying her are two instrumentalists: Fred Longshaw, not at his customary piano but at the harmonium, a reed organ that sounds out of place in a blues context, and Louis Armstrong, a New Orleans–born cornetist who was soon to have a major impact on his own. Smith and Armstrong interact in a call-and-response texture, with Smith singing in the first half of each four-bar phrase and Armstrong improvising fanciful "licks" (flourishes) in the second half. The wheezy harmonium robs the recording of some of the rhythmic verve characteristic of other classic blues records, but Smith's heartfelt vocal and Armstrong's imaginative fills more than compensate.

The relationship of this performance to Handy's composition reveals key aspects of the blues aesthetic. Smith alters Handy's lyrics and often flattens out

⤷ Gertrude "Ma" Rainey (1886–1939) was a Georgia native and one of the first classic blues singers. The Georgia Jazz Band, with which she is pictured here, includes pianist Thomas A. Dorsey, later a leader in the field of gospel music (see chapter 14).

LG 11.1

CD 2.5	Listening Guide 11.1	"St. Louis Blues" W. C. HANDY

DATE: 1914; recorded 1925

PERFORMERS: Bessie Smith, vocal; Louis Armstrong, cornet; Fred Longshaw, harmonium

GENRE: classic blues

METER: duple

FORM: AA'BA"

WHAT TO LISTEN FOR

- Smith's voice: rough timbre, bent notes, slides
- Armstrong's cornet: in call and response with Smith's vocals
- 12-bar blues choruses, with one 16-bar minor-key strain

TIMING	SECTION	TEXT	COMMENTS
0:00	strain 1 (A)	I hate to see the evening sun go down, I hate to see the evening sun go down, It makes me think I'm on my last go round.	Introduction is a single one-bar V chord. First strain uses a variant of Handy's melody emphasizing the blue third. Basic blues progression uses added chords in the second bar of each phrase; the last two bars feature descending chromatic chords ending on the dominant turnaround.
0:48	strain 2 (A')	Feeling tomorrow like I feel today, Feeling tomorrow like I feel today, I'll pack my grip and make my getaway.	Melodically and harmonically similar to strain 1.
1:32	strain 3 (B)	St. Louis woman wears a diamond ring, Pulls her man around by her apron string. Wasn't for powder and this store-bought hair, The man I love wouldn't go nowhere, nowhere.	Minor-key 16-bar strain contrasts with the surrounding blues choruses. Harmonium becomes more active but does not use Handy's tango rhythm.
2:26	strain 4 (A")	I got them St. Louis blues, just as blue as I can be. He's got a heart like a rock cast in the sea, Or else he would not go so far from me.	Increased raspiness in voice, rhapsodic cornet fills, and rhythmic energy in harmonium.

NOTE The lyrics are reproduced here as Smith sings them, with many small deviations from the sheet music version.

Listen & Reflect

1. Each of the three performers has a distinct function within the overall texture. Describe those functions and how they interact in performance.

his melodic line, as in the second phrase of the opening stanza, where Smith reduces Handy's melody to basically two notes—the tonic and the lowered third—but bends the blue note to powerful effect. Likewise, Longshaw does not restrict himself to Handy's basic blues progression, instead inserting additional chords in the second bar of each phrase and an elaborate turnaround at the end of the first two choruses. Freest of all is Armstrong's improvised commentary, which corresponds to nothing in Handy's sheet music. Father of the Blues though he may have been, Handy is merely an attendant to the Empress and her cohort in this supreme example of performers' music.

HILLBILLY: THE INVENTION OF COUNTRY MUSIC

After the unexpected success of Mamie Smith's "Crazy Blues" in 1920 proved the existence of a market for race records, the search was on to find more blues performers who could match her in sales. Smith's label, Okeh, hired Ralph Peer to comb the rural South as a talent scout—or, as industry lingo would later have it, as an **A&R** (artists and repertoire) man. With two engineers and a carload of portable recording equipment, Peer would arrive in a southern town, set up an improvised recording studio, and allow himself to be interviewed by the local newspaper, whose free publicity spared his company the expense of advertising his presence.

Ralph Peer

While auditioning blues musicians in Atlanta in the summer of 1923, Peer was persuaded to record an entirely different sort of performer: a fifty-five-year-old white entertainer called "Fiddlin' John" Carson. With no accompaniment other than his fiddle, Carson played and sang a traditional dance tune, "The Old Hen Cackled and the Rooster's Going to Crow," and an 1870s minstrel song, "The Little Old Log Cabin in the Lane." Carson's playing was marginally adequate, Peer thought, but his singing was "plu-perfect awful." Peer saw no commercial potential in the two sides Carson recorded, but an Atlanta record distributor persuaded him to press five hundred copies for local sale.

"Fiddlin' John" Carson

When the distributor ordered more copies a few days later, reporting that the first five hundred had all been sold, Peer belatedly assigned the record a serial number and placed it in the Okeh catalog for national distribution. Eventually, the record sold several thousand copies, and a new market had emerged in the record industry. Whereas race records were by, for, and about African Americans, this new music was created by and marketed to rural white southerners. Okeh and the other labels that soon competed in this market tried out various names for the music through the 1920s: "old-time tunes," "old southern melodies," "old familiar tunes," "mountain songs and jigs," "popular ballads and mountaineer tunes." But the label that stuck, at least through the 1920s and 1930s, was the one coined by Ralph Peer, drawing on a colloquialism with mocking overtones: **hillbilly records**.

hillbilly records

Just as race records would develop into a variety of African American popular styles after World War II, hillbilly records would later develop into the genre known today as country music. But in the years between the two world wars, the boundaries between country music and other genres were not clearly marked. On the contrary, hillbilly records embraced a wide diversity of styles and influences. Like many other types of American music, country music, from the beginning, found its strength in hybridity.

CREATING HILLBILLY MUSIC

old-time music

Although hillbilly records were a new phenomenon in the 1920s, the music on them was purported to be much older. Indeed, marketing terms such as "**old-time music**" indicate that the music's old-fashioned quality was a primary selling point. But just how old was it?

Addressing that question soon leads to two related ones: Is old-time music folk music, and are the performers on hillbilly records folk musicians? As chapter 9 has implied, what is or is not folk music depends on what the person who is doing the asking hopes to find. For some of the song catchers, a folk song had to be a British ballad of great antiquity; for others, a folk song could be of more recent origin. But even in the latter case, a folk song had to demonstrate its connection to traditional styles of singing, playing, and songwriting. Even a new song, in other words, had to sound old.

folk and country compared

The key difference between folk music and early country music lies perhaps not so much in the music itself, nor in the musicians who created it, but in the goals and attitudes of the outsiders who brought the music to a wider audience. Folk song collectors framed the music they loved in opposition to the mass-market popular music of Tin Pan Alley, which was then in its ascendance. Folk music, they argued, represented an older, purer culture untainted by the commercialism of the twentieth century. Their attitude could not be further from that of the record industry executives, such as Ralph Peer, who created hillbilly records. For Peer, who didn't care for hillbilly music—his disdain is evident in the term he used for it—the music of rural white southerners was valuable only as a commodity that could turn a profit. Any distinction, then, between the folk music of rural white southerners and country music, at the moment of its birth, has more to do with how the music was bought and sold than with its musical features. But a too-narrow focus on economics obscures what musical differences in fact existed. Because A&R men cared little about cultural purity, they were willing to sell to the hillbilly market anything its customers were willing to buy. For that reason, hillbilly records document the eclectic, wide-ranging tastes of their buyers. Some of the music fits neatly into the category of folk, but much of it does not. To understand the variety of music captured on hillbilly records, it is useful to consider first how music was disseminated in the rural South at the beginning of the twentieth century.

SPREADING MUSIC AROUND THE RURAL SOUTH

The most powerful force in creating a shared musical culture throughout the United States in the nineteenth century was the sheet music industry. But sheet music's reach depended on musical literacy, the music lessons that promoted literacy, and the ownership of musical instruments, especially the piano. Such advantages were beyond the reach of many Americans, especially in the least prosperous regions of the country. For a song originally published as sheet music to reach that population, it had first to enter the oral tradition; simply put, most poor people could learn a song only by hearing someone else sing it.

stage entertainment

Alongside the sheet music industry was a lively tradition of stage musical entertainment that afforded just such opportunities for disseminating new songs. Both the minstrel show and its offspring, vaudeville, were primarily urban phenomena, however; only in cities, large or small, could theaters and the populace to fill them be found. For country folk, infrequent visits to the city offered a rare chance to catch up on current musical trends.

By the latter part of the nineteenth century, however, enterprising entertainers had found means of bringing their acts directly to rural audiences. One means was the circus, with its brass band and other musical acts. Another was the **medicine show**, in which a traveling peddler of patent cure-alls would draw an audience for his sales pitch by offering free entertainment. A third was the **tent-repertory show**, or tent-rep, a collection of vaudeville acts that traveled circus-style by horse and wagon, and later by truck, pitching a tent near a small town and performing for a few days before moving on. Musical acts in tent-rep reflected the passing fads of vaudeville, everything from Alpine yodelers to Hawaiian guitarists. By all of these means, but especially the tent-rep show, rural southerners supplemented their traditional musical fare with newer popular selections: sentimental parlor songs and waltzes, raucous minstrel tunes, and by the turn of the century, the ragtime-influenced popular songs of Tin Pan Alley.

tent-repertory shows

Whereas these forms of entertainment brought new musical repertories from the urban North to the rural South, another musical institution, the fiddle contest, remained a regional southern event. Dating back to the 1730s and still attracting large audiences today, fiddle contests and their music became an emblem of southern regional identity.

fiddle contests

In addition to these rural entertainments, two technological innovations profoundly altered home music making for virtually all Americans: phonograph and radio. Although the phonograph was the earlier of the two inventions, for poor whites the more affordable radio exerted a stronger influence from the start. Throughout the United States, radio stations provided a way for local musicians to build their audiences, and radio listeners enjoyed hearing music performed by people like themselves. At the same time, some radio stations in those unregulated years before World War II broadcast immensely powerful signals that could be received hundreds or even thousands of miles away, and local musicians sometimes discovered that they had fans far from home.

In 1923 radio station WBAP in Fort Worth, Texas, created an influential new radio format when it broadcast an hour and a half of square dance music led by a former Confederate army officer and old-time fiddler, M. J. Bonner. An enthusiastic audience demanded more, and the **radio barn dance** was born. The following year saw the inauguration of the long-lived *National Barn Dance* on WLS in Chicago. In 1925 a station in Nashville began its own version, the *WSM Barn Dance,* which two years later would undergo a fateful name change. Following NBC's nationally syndicated *Musical Appreciation Hour,* WSM announcer George D. Hay made the following transition to the barn dance: "For the past hour we have been listening to music taken largely from grand opera, but from now on we will present 'The Grand Ole Opry.'" Rechristened *The Grand Ole Opry,* the program today is the longest-running radio show of all time.

radio barn dances

THE HILLBILLY REPERTORY

Hillbilly records featured the same types of songs and performers as heard on the radio barn dances. At first, most of the performers were amateurs who earned little or nothing from their music and made their living as farmers, laborers,

Radio: Music for the Millions

Guglielmo Marconi made the first successful radio transmissions in the 1890s, but not until after World War I did the commercial radio industry begin to take shape. When radio broadcasting began in 1920, only about 4 percent of American homes had radio receivers, but by 1934 about 60 percent of households owned radios. Meanwhile, the number of broadcasting stations grew from five in 1921 to 765 on the eve of World War II. Connecting them were networks such as the National Broadcasting Company (NBC) and the Columbia Broadcasting System (CBS), both of which would later expand into television.

Radio programming in the first two decades relied less on recorded music than on live entertainment: news, comedy, drama, and music of all kinds. In addition to the networks' nationally distributed offerings, stations also featured local entertainers, often in regularly scheduled programs lasting fifteen minutes or less. A favorite format was "song and patter," in which a group of musicians would alternate musical selections with jokes, plugs for the sponsor, and informal small talk. Radio stations thus promoted the spread of a more homogenized national mass culture while nurturing more specialized local music scenes.

and—a disproportionately large group—cotton mill workers. Only later did the professional country musician come on the scene.

string bands

Hillbilly records in the 1920s generally feature either a solo vocalist, self-accompanied or with one or two other musicians, or a **string band**, an ensemble of two or more instrumentalists who may or may not sing as well. Virtually all string bands gave pride of place to the fiddle, the quintessential country lead instrument. Duos of fiddle and banjo were common, harking back to the pair of melodic instruments found in the minstrel band. Nearly as common were fiddle-and-guitar duos. The guitar was something of a newcomer to the southern Appalachians: it was a rarity there until after World War I, when returning soldiers brought home instruments they had obtained in the wider world. Larger string bands might include a second fiddle or guitar; string bass and mandolin were still unusual additions, although later they would become standard in the bluegrass band, a descendant of the old-time string bands.

event songs

Both amateurs and professionals drew on a diverse repertory of song types. Alongside the old Anglo-Celtic ballads discussed in chapter 9 were newer narrative songs, so-called **event songs**, inspired by recent occurrences. As in the old ballads, murdered lovers figure prominently in event songs, as do robberies, kidnappings, family feuds, and even the assassinations of Presidents Garfield and McKinley.

A particularly rich topic for event songs was disaster: mine explosions, shipwrecks, and train derailments. Vernon Dalhart's 1924 Victor recording of "Wreck of the Old 97," about a 1903 railroad disaster in Virginia, inaugurated a long-running fashion for train songs in country music. The record's B side was another widely imitated number, "The Prisoner's Song" ("Oh, if I had the wings of an angel / Over these prison walls I would fly"). Prison songs, like train songs, would have a prominent place in the country repertory for decades to come; Johnny Cash's "Folsom Prison Blues" (1955) manages to combine the two genres.

Whereas ballads, old or new, were generally sung in the impassive, undramatic tone of traditional folk singers, a more emotive vocal style was sometimes applied to such sentimental numbers as "The Prisoner's Song." Sentimental songs complemented the previous century's parlor-song repertory with newer compositions in a similar vein. Nostalgia, family solidarity, tragic love, and religious affirmation are hallmarks of the sentimental country song.

In contrast to both ballads and sentimental songs were the lively instrumental dance tunes of the string bands. Old Anglo-Celtic fiddle tunes made their appearance, transformed by southern fiddling traditions, which emphasized a rhythmic "saw stroke" bowing technique and **double stops**, in which two strings are sounded simultaneously, so that the melody is heard against a droning background note. Newer fiddle tunes found their way onto hillbilly records as well, many of them drawn from minstrelsy, such as "Turkey in the Straw," an instrumental version of the minstrel song "Zip Coon." *fiddle tunes*

String bands often drew their vocal repertory from minstrelsy as well, or from its later Tin Pan Alley descendant, the Negro dialect song. Most of these are comic songs, often with bawdy lyrics celebrating a dissolute lifestyle, as also heard in many blues records. Like the performers of minstrelsy and turn-of-the-century Tin Pan Alley ethnic novelties, hillbilly musicians used racial masquerade to express the lure of sexual promiscuity, hard drinking, and even, occasionally, the use of drugs such as cocaine—proclivities hard to own up to in the intensely religious culture of the rural South. *minstrelsy and Tin Pan Alley*

The tone and subject matter of early country songs, then, cover a wide spectrum, from pious sentimentality to raucous immodesty. The breadth of subject matter is no better illustrated than in the work of the first two country acts to achieve stardom. By pure coincidence, both acts were discovered by Ralph Peer within days of each other.

THE BIG BANG IN BRISTOL

Ralph Peer spent the summer of 1927 touring Georgia and Tennessee in search of new talent for Victor's race and hillbilly catalogs. Arriving in Bristol, Tennessee, near the Virginia border, in late July, he was the subject of a front-page story in the *Bristol News Bulletin* that attracted musicians from as far away as Kentucky and North Carolina. Among them were two acts that, each unknown to the other and representing two distinct strands of early country music, recorded for Peer in the first few days of August: the Carter Family and Jimmie Rodgers. The popularity of their records transformed country music from a small specialty market into a major segment of the American music industry. The discovery of these two major forces in the same town in the same week has been called "the Big Bang of country music."

THE CARTER FAMILY

Traveling to Bristol from their home in Virginia less than thirty miles away were the three members of the Carter Family: A. P. Carter; his wife, Sara Dougherty Carter; and Sara's cousin Maybelle Addington Carter, who was also married

The Carter Family, including A. P. Carter, his sister-in-law Maybelle (left), and wife Sara (right, who also played autoharp). Residents of the Clinch Mountains of Virginia, the trio won fame in the South after they began to record in 1927.

to A. P.'s brother. As a singing trio, the Carters had been entertaining local audiences for some months before approaching Ralph Peer. What they had to offer Victor was unlike anything that had previously been heard on hillbilly records.

Sara Carter, with her strong, deep alto voice, generally took the vocal leads while providing a light background accompaniment on guitar or autoharp, a type of zither. Maybelle Carter sang backing vocal harmonies and stood out as the trio's most gifted instrumentalist. Her distinctive style of guitar playing came to be known as **Carter style** or "thumb-and-brush" picking: a melodic line plucked on the bass strings with the thumb, the melody notes alternating with chords strummed on the higher strings with one or two fingers. Sometimes Carter ornaments the melody with a **hammer-on**: she plucks a string just before placing her finger forcefully behind a fret, creating a characteristic "boing" sound.

The sound of the Carter Family's records gives the impression that A. P. was the least important member: he doesn't play an instrument, his bass voice is somewhat tremulous and always in the background, and his rhythm and pitch are uncertain. But in fact he was the driving force behind the success of the Carter Family. A farmer at the time the trio came to Bristol, A. P. had earlier traveled while working for a railroad and as a fruit tree salesman, collecting songs with the interest of an avid amateur singer and fiddler. So great was his interest that he even made expeditions solely to hunt for songs, which for several years he collected with the aid of African American blues guitarist Leslie Riddles.

As an amateur song catcher, A. P. Carter collected everything that caught his fancy: ballads, sentimental songs, minstrel songs, gospel hymns, and blues. All of these song types went into the Carter Family's repertory, usually after passing through A. P.'s reworking. Not content simply to preserve old songs, he used them as raw material to be reshaped into a new musical product. The advantages of his method were multiple: while creating distinctive material that audiences would link to the Carter Family, A. P. also copyrighted the songs, thus earning songwriter royalties on Carter Family records in addition to his cut of the performer royalties.

By present-day standards, this practice amounts to plagiarism, and that may in fact be a fair assessment. But any judgment of A. P. Carter's business practices must also consider his position at a historical moment when musical worlds collided: the traditional sphere, in which authorship is communal, informal, and not of primary importance, and the popular sphere, in which ownership is a controlling economic factor. Arising here are legal and ethical issues around musical ownership that are still with us.

Examining a typical Carter Family song shows how A. P. took older material as a starting place and arrived at something uniquely his own. "Can the Circle Be Unbroken" (LG 11.2) was one of the Carter Family's signature songs, a staple of the country repertory. Most performers after the Carters, however, change the chorus to begin "*Will* the circle be unbroken"—the title of a 1907 gospel hymn whose melody closely resembles A. P.'s. The folklike, gapped-scale melody is also found in an African American religious song, "Since I Laid My Burden Down," first recorded in 1928 and memorably performed by blues singers such as

LG 11.2

CD 2.6	Listening Guide 11.2	"Can the Circle Be Unbroken" THE CARTER FAMILY

SONGWRITER: A. P. Carter

DATE: recorded in New York, 1935

PERFORMERS: Sara Carter, vocal and guitar; Maybelle Carter, vocal and guitar; A. P. Carter, vocal

GENRE: country music

METER: duple

FORM: verse and chorus

WHAT TO LISTEN FOR

- same music for verse and chorus
- alternation of solo voice on verses and vocal harmony on choruses
- Carter-style guitar playing
- occasional triple-meter bars

TIMING	SECTION	TEXT	COMMENTS
0:00	introduction		A bar and a half of solo guitar establishes the key and tempo: alternating bass notes on the beat and strummed chords between the beats. Throughout, Sara's second guitar is almost inaudible.
0:04	verse 1	I was standing by the window...	Sara's low voice is somewhat emotionless, in contrast to the sentimentality of the lyrics, which set a scene of bereavement.
0:24	chorus	Can the circle be unbroken...	Three-part hymn-style, block-chord harmonization.
0:43	instrumental chorus		Maybelle plays the melody, ornamented with hammer-ons, on the bass strings, alternating with energetic strummed chords on the higher strings.
1:02	verse 2	Lord, I told the undertaker...	The return to Sara's solo voice signals a continuation of the story told in the verses.
1:22	chorus	Can the circle be unbroken...	The harmonized group singing gives the chorus the quality of commenting on the story.
1:40	verse 3	I followed close behind her...	The use of a solo voice suits the subjective, first-person narrative.
1:59	chorus	Can the circle be unbroken...	The group singing suits the more communal idea expressed by the lyrics.
2:17	instrumental half chorus		Only the second phrase (bars 5–8) of the chorus.
2:26	verse 4	Went back home, Lord...	The story ends with no resolution.
2:45	chorus	Can the circle be unbroken...	Slight *ritardando* signals the end.

Listen & Reflect

1. On their own, the four verses and four statements of the chorus sung here would fall about thirty seconds short of the typical three-minute running time of a 78-rpm single. The two guitar interludes form one solution to the problem of filling out the record. What would be some other possibilities, and what musical differences might result from them?

Mississippi John Hurt. Whether the composer of the gospel hymn, Charles Gabriel, took the melody from folk practice or vice versa is impossible to determine, but it surely did not originate with A. P. Carter.

The lyrics of Carter's chorus begin with a phrase almost identical to the hymn's title, but the resemblance ends there. Whereas the hymn focuses on the reunion of family members in the afterlife, A. P.'s song focuses on earthly bereavement: the death of the song persona's mother. Despite the chorus's assertion that "there's a better home awaiting in the sky," the song's emotional gravity is centered in the grief and loss expressed in the verses. Rather than simply reworking the hymn, Carter has taken the title as a point of entry for the creation of a different song.

the Carters' vocal style

The Carter Family's singing style and the song are perfectly suited to each other. Sara Carter's straightforward, unemotional alto evokes the deadpan performance tradition of Anglo-Celtic ballads. The chorus features all three singers harmonizing in the three-voice texture of old-fashioned southern shape-note hymnody: a central melodic line with a higher countermelody, over a structural bass line. (Compare the setting of NEW BRITAIN ["Amazing Grace"] illustrated in chapter 3.) A. P. had learned to read shape notes from his uncle, a singing-school master, and Sara and Maybelle had surely also grown up with the sound of shape-note hymnody, which in their day was merging with the later gospel hymn repertory. A Carter Family innovation was to apply this style of harmonizing to secular songs—often pious and moralistic, but definitely not hymns—and accompany it with Maybelle's driving guitar.

Each of the song's eight-bar verses comprises two musical phrases, *aa'*, corresponding to the two lines of a rhymed couplet. The chorus uses the same music as the verse. A rhythmic oddity recurs throughout: here and there, a bar consists of three beats instead of the usual four. Such irregularities are common in the singing of early blues and country musicians but usually are disregarded as momentary aberrations of solo performance. Here, though, all three performers drop a beat together, and the dropped beat is always in the same places: in the sixth bar of the verse, and in the second and sixth bars of the chorus. By dropping beats where they do, the singers press on to complete the phrases with added urgency.

"Can the Circle Be Unbroken" represented a departure for hillbilly records, which before 1927 had emphasized either vocal solos or, more commonly, string band instrumentals with only incidental singing. Hereafter, many country acts would imitate the Carters' harmonized singing, sentimental songs emphasizing family and traditional moral values, and energetic guitar picking.

JIMMIE RODGERS: AMERICA'S SINGING BRAKEMAN

Recording the Carter Family on August 1 and 2 would have been enough in itself to make Ralph Peer's 1927 field trip to Bristol a historic occasion. But to top it off, on August 4 another musician walked into the makeshift Victor studio in Bristol to make his first records. Those records would make Jimmie Rodgers the first undisputed solo star of country music.

Born near Meridian, Mississippi, in 1897, Jimmie Rodgers picked up music informally in poolrooms and barbershops as a child. After winning a talent contest at the age of twelve, he ran away from home to join a medicine show. Brought back home, he joined his father's railroad work crew, and over the next

Jimmie Rodgers (1897–1933), the first country singing star, capitalized on his early years as a brakeman by occasionally posing and performing in railroad garb.

decade he worked a variety of train jobs that carried him throughout the South and Southwest, as far as the Pacific Coast. When tuberculosis ended his railroad career, Rodgers devoted himself more fully to music, playing banjo and guitar in a variety of small ensembles and working his way to Asheville, North Carolina, where he had a radio show on WWNC.

As a member of a string band, Rodgers traveled to Bristol to play for Peer. When the band members argued over what name to use on their records, Rodgers parted company with the others and persuaded Peer to record him as a solo act. He sang two sentimental waltz songs to his own guitar accompaniment that day, "The Soldier's Sweetheart" and "Sleep, Baby, Sleep." The second song, of uncertain origin, combines a strophic lullaby with a yodeling refrain, reminiscent of J. K. Emmet's once-famous "Lullaby" from *Fritz, Our German Cousin*, a stage success of the 1870s. Emmet's song survived into the phonograph era and no doubt was familiar to Rodgers and other rural music lovers. Alpine yodeling had been a feature of touring singing acts such as the Tyrolese Minstrels as far back as the 1830s. That Rodgers chose to audition for Peer with such antiquated material speaks to the persistence of older forms of entertainment in the rural South of the 1920s.

auditioning for Peer

When Victor released Rodgers's two Bristol recordings in October, Rodgers traveled to New York City and contacted Peer, informing him that he was ready to record more sides. One of the four songs he recorded there eventually sold more than one million copies. Originally titled simply "Blue Yodel," it was later renamed "Blue Yodel no. 1 (T for Texas)" after its success inspired a series of related songs. By combining the blues with yodeling, Rodgers put a twist on the twelve-bar blues that was new to the record industry.

In his thirteen **blue yodel** records, Rodgers sometimes sings a standard blues chorus—a rhymed couplet, with the first line repeated—followed by a few bars of yodeling. In others, such as "Blue Yodel no. 8 (Muleskinner Blues)" (LG 11.3), he sings the couplet in the first two phrases of each chorus, yodeling for the third phrase. "Muleskinner Blues" begins as a dialogue between the foreman of a railroad construction crew and a job applicant looking for work as a mule driver or "skinner" (mule-powered wagons were then standard equipment in railroad construction). The applicant's ethnicity would have been apparent to any listener at that time: he addresses the foreman as "captain," a common black locution, and the foreman in turn calls him "Shine," a derogatory term referring to shoe shining, an activity in which whites and blacks frequently came into contact, always with the black person in a position subservient to the white customer.

blue yodels

LG 11.3

The subsequent verses are in the voice of the muleskinner, who brags about his prowess in driving mules, thus echoing the boasting theme found in many songs drawing on African American folk traditions. Mention of the "good gal" who awaits his paycheck leads to a verse of dialogue between the muleskinner and his gal, in which the line about turning down the damper (to reduce the heat in a wood stove) recalls the veiled sexual references of classic blues records. The reference to a Stetson hat, for present-day listeners, may evoke the image of a cowboy; in the early years of the twentieth century, however, hats manufactured by the Stetson Company were status symbols and appeared often in African American songs—most notably the traditional ballad "Stagger Lee," in which the title character kills another man over a Stetson hat. Similarly, Louis Armstrong recalled the status conferred by a Stetson hat among musicians in the early days of New Orleans jazz.

| CD 2.7 | Listening Guide 11.3 | "Blue Yodel no. 8 (Muleskinner Blues)" JIMMIE RODGERS |

SONGWRITER: Jimmie Rodgers
DATE: Recorded in Los Angeles, 1930
PERFORMER: Jimmie Rodgers, vocal and guitar
GENRE: country music
METER: duple
FORM: strophic blues

WHAT TO LISTEN FOR

- combination of blues choruses and yodeling
- simplified version of Carter-style guitar playing
- ragtime-influenced harmonies in instrumental introduction and interlude

TIMING	SECTION	TEXT	COMMENTS
0:00	introduction		8 bars (plus pickup notes), using a chord progression characteristic of ragtime.
0:11	chorus 1	"Good morning, Captain." "Good morning, Shine" "Do you need another muleskinner out on your new mud line?"	Opening melodic phrase includes a prominent blue note. The two lines of text fill two phrases of the blues chorus; the third phrase (0:26) is yodeling.
0:34	chorus 2	I like to work, I'm rolling all the time I can carve my initials on a mule's behind	Like chorus 1, but with more-elaborate yodeling in third phrase.
0:56	chorus 3	Hey little water boy, bring that water round If you don't like your job, set that water bucket down	3-phrase blues chorus extended to create 4 phrases: harmony of phrase 2 repeats with yodeling; final phrase continues yodeling.
1:25	chorus 4	Working on the good roads, a dollar and a half a day My good gal's waiting on a Saturday night, just to draw my pay	2-phrase blues chorus: instead of yodeling, proceeds directly into guitar interlude.
1:39	interlude		16-bar guitar solo begins with a single-line melody on the upper strings and ends in bass register, with the ragtime harmonies of the introduction.
2:01	chorus 5	"I'm going to town, Honey, what you want me to bring you back?" "Bring a pint of booze and a John B. Stetson hat."	5-phrase blues chorus: phrases 1–2 with lyrics; phrase 3 with spoken "Bring it to me, Honey"; phrases 4–5 like phrases 3–4 of chorus 3.

| | | CD 2.7 | Listening Guide 11.3 | "Blue Yodel no. 8 (Muleskinner Blues)" JIMMIE RODGERS |

TIMING	SECTION	TEXT	COMMENTS
2:33	chorus 6	I smell your bread a-burning, turn your damper down If you ain't got a damper, good gal, turn your bread around	Return to 3-phrase structure of choruses 1 and 2. Melody of phrase 2 varied by ascending to a new apex, the blue third.

Listen & Reflect

1. How does Rodgers build musical interest over the three minutes of this record?
2. What elements of Rodgers's performance resemble Bessie Smith's "St. Louis Blues" (see LG 11.1), and what elements differ?

Rodgers's "thumb-and-brush" guitar playing resembles the Carter style, though without Maybelle Carter's rhythmic security. Single notes on the bass strings mark the two beats in each bars, with chords on the higher strings falling between the beats—the accompaniment pattern of the left hand in ragtime piano, transferred to the guitar. Short bass runs enliven the texture, and Rodgers even attempts a guitar solo in the second half of the record.

Rodgers's phrasing

Characteristic of Rodgers and his many country imitators is a flexible approach to blues phrasing. Although the three phrases of the twelve-bar blues chorus are easy to distinguish, some phrases contain more than four bars. The first chorus, for example, consists of 5 + 6½ + 5 bars. While many black country blues singers similarly stretched or contracted phrases, their use of varied guitar textures smoothed over any sense of irregularity (see chapter 14 for a discussion of country blues). Rodgers's steady "boom-chang" texture, in contrast, draws attention to the sometimes lurching rhythm.

In short, both music and lyrics of "Muleskinner Blues" draw deeply from African American culture. In his railroad jobs Rodgers had worked in close contact with black laborers, and his absorption of black folkways is evident in many of his records. Rodgers's blue yodels demonstrate how country music, though considered then and now perhaps the "whitest" of popular music genres, from its inception was tied to black music.

Rodgers's song types

The music and subject matter of the blue yodels stand in contrast to the songs of the Carter Family. Rodgers did record nostalgic songs similar to favorite Carter Family themes, especially songs about family ties and chaste, often unrequited love. But many of his most successful songs celebrated the wandering life and the lure of drinking, gambling, and violence. Even more than the Carter Family, Jimmie Rodgers embraced country music's full spectrum of subject matter.

Rodgers's records also demonstrate the eclecticism of early country music. In addition to solo records, he often recorded with small ensembles, sometimes

steel guitar

a second guitar or a fiddle, resembling the string band sound. Sometimes he is accompanied by a **steel guitar**: a guitar modified so the strings are well above the fingerboard, held in the lap and played with a metal slide held in the left hand. This instrument, also called a **Hawaiian guitar**, was popularized on the mainland by Hawaiian musicians who toured in vaudeville and tent-rep shows, such as Joe Kaipo, who recorded several songs with Rodgers.

Other Rodgers records use jazz instrumentation; in "Blue Yodel no. 9 (Standing on the Corner)," his singing and yodeling are accompanied by Louis Armstrong on cornet. Collaborations between white and black musicians were rather unusual on records at that time and virtually never seen on stage. Putting Armstrong and Rodgers together was the brainstorm of Ralph Peer, who made his money in both hillbilly and race records.

Rodgers recorded for only six years before succumbing to tuberculosis. By the time he died in 1933, country music had established itself as a significant part of the record industry. Its second decade would build on the successes of Rodgers and the Carter Family, continuing the styles they pioneered and adding new ones.

THE CLASSIC AMERICAN POPULAR SONG

A key requirement for a hit show tune was its ability not only to function dramatically in its original stage setting but also to stand on its own. The first quality—dramatic suitability—links musical comedy to opera and operetta, though in fact the early musicals place only the lightest dramatic demands on their songs, as the case of *Sinbad* and its interpolations suggests (see chapter 10). As an independent song, a show tune might achieve hit status by exhibiting the best qualities of any other popular song of the time: simplicity, memorability, just enough distinctiveness, and a lyrical subject that audiences found interesting. Like Tin Pan Alley, Broadway embraced ragtime. And with the rise of the blues, popular song and the musical found a new means of expressivity. From the 1920s until well after World War II, many popular songs would display some degree of blues influence.

standards

The best show tunes of that period have escaped the usual fate of the popular song by surviving to the present day as so-called **standards** in the repertories of jazz and cabaret singers and instrumentalists. Because these songs have proven to have enduring value for so many people, the period from the 1920s through the early 1950s is sometimes called the golden era of the **classic American popular song**, a term practically synonymous with "standard." Not every standard began life as a show tune, but most of them did. Their longevity stands in stark contrast to the short lives of most of the shows that launched them. For that to change, a show's songs needed to be part of a larger artistic vision. A landmark musical, perhaps the first to generate multiple hits and sustain a long life on the stage, is *Show Boat* (1927).

MUSICAL COMEDY MEETS OPERETTA: *SHOW BOAT*

An example of the new up-to-date musical comedy of the 1920s was *Lady Be Good!* (1924), with songs by George and Ira Gershwin. The lighthearted tale about a stage brother and sister featured dancer and singer Fred Astaire and his real-life sister,

Adele. George Gershwin's concert piece *Rhapsody in Blue* had premiered earlier that year (see chapter 13 for a discussion of his life and career as a composer of concert pieces), and now he and his lyricist brother Ira were trying their hand at a Broadway show. The result was groundbreaking. George's mastery of an up-to-date song style touched with jazz and blues elements was matched by Ira's lyrics in a fresh vernacular idiom, carefully fitted to his brother's music. The American musical theater had found a fresh native idiom, and the show delivered two standards, both marked by bluesy melodies and harmonies: "Oh, Lady Be Good!" and "Fascinating Rhythm."

Lady Be Good! premiered on December 1, 1924, and the very next evening saw the premiere, a few blocks up Broadway, of *The Student Prince,* a Viennese-style operetta with music by Sigmund Romberg and lyrics by Dorothy Donnelly. *Lady Be Good!* ran for nine months (330 performances), *The Student Prince* for a year and a half (608). *The Student Prince* was revived on Broadway in the 1930s and again in the 1940s, and for decades was a staple of amateur theater groups; *Lady Be Good!* never returned to Broadway, and only in recent years have historically minded organizations mounted revivals. Yet the Gershwins' musical comedy produced two standards, whereas only diehard operetta fans can whistle a tune from Romberg's score.

Before the decade was out, the gulf between *Lady Be Good!* and *The Student Prince* was bridged by another composer-author team in a work that blended new elements effectively with old ones: *Show Boat,* which received its New York premiere in 1927. The author of *Show Boat's* book and lyrics, Oscar Hammerstein II, had already scored major operetta hits in collaborations with Rudolf Friml and Romberg. The composer, Jerome Kern, was an American who had gotten his start in London, supplying interpolations for British musical comedies. In the late 1910s Kern had written a series of musicals for Broadway's Princess Theatre that captured the contemporary tone of British shows with the added value of Kern's songs, which blended Viennese lyricism with the rhythmic vitality of the new Castle-style dance music.

Based on a novel by Edna Ferber, *Show Boat* is set in the Midwest, spans an era from around 1890 to the 1920s, and concerns a bittersweet romance between Gaylord Ravenal, a Mississippi River gambler, and Magnolia, whose father is the captain of a steamboat that travels the river presenting stage melodramas—a showboat. From the beginning of act 1, *Show Boat* uses the conventions of both operetta and musical comedy while reaching beyond both in subject matter. Audiences for musical comedy would expect a curtain-raising chorus sung by a bevy of beauties and their beaus, and *Show Boat* delivers that in crisp British style, but only after a strikingly different opening chorus, in which black stevedores sing about the backbreaking work of loading cotton. Ravenal then enters with a suave aria marking him as an operetta tenor; though he is no prince, his manner suggests the aristocracy of the Old South. His subsequent scene of flirtation with Magnolia leads to a soaring duet for soprano and tenor, "Make Believe," in the purest operetta style.

The gambler departs, and Magnolia, lovestruck, asks a stevedore named Joe (a baritone) what he thinks about Ravenal. Joe tells her to ask the river "what *he* thinks." And then Joe sings "Old Man River." As personified in this song, the river is a mighty force, indifferent to human struggles. The sober melody and the philosophical text, which work together in the style of a traditional Negro

From 1924, when they wrote *Lady Be Good!* until George's death in 1937, the Gershwin brothers, Ira (left) and George, collaborated on songs for musicals, movies, and the opera *Porgy and Bess.*

Jerome Kern

Show Boat's
blend of genres

FLORENZ ZIEGFELD
PRESENTS
SHOW BOAT
ADAPTED FROM EDNA FERBER'S NOVEL OF THE SAME NAME

BOOK & LYRICS BY
OSCAR HAMMERSTEIN 2nd
MUSIC BY
JEROME KERN

ENSEMBLES & DANCES BY
SAMMY LEE
SETTINGS BY
JOSEPH URBAN

T. B. HARMS
COMPANY
NEW YORK

🐚 As with earlier shows, songs from Kern and Hammerstein's *Show Boat* (1927) were sold individually as sheet music for amateur performers. This "composite cover" was made to be used for any one of five songs from *Show Boat* (listed on the cotton bale in the lower right).

LG 11.4

spiritual, lend authority to Joe and support his view of the characters' trials and tribulations.

The scene quickly changes to the kitchen of the showboat, where the next number, "Can't Help Lovin' Dat Man," is sung by Julie LaVerne, the showboat's sultry mezzo-soprano songstress. Spiced with blue notes, the song becomes a marker of racial identity. The black cook, Queenie, marvels that she has never heard "anybody but colored folks" sing that song. And soon, unmasked as a woman with African American parentage who has been passing for white, Julie is forced to leave the showboat.

"Make Believe," "Old Man River," and "Can't Help Lovin' Dat Man," presented in rapid succession, were conceived for particular characters and moments in *Show Boat*. The first song uses operetta style for white characters, the second alludes to the spiritual for a black character, and the third introduces blues elements for a mixed-race character. Yet for all their differences in style, all three are similar in form, a verse alternating with a thirty-two-bar chorus: the popular song format established by Tin Pan Alley. Each song serves a dramatic function in its theatrical context yet was also able to circulate independently, in both sheet music and recordings, as a stand-alone pop song.

In popular songs of the 1920s, the verse is less important than the chorus. Outside the theatrical setting, performers sometimes omitted the verse altogether and typically repeated the chorus once or more to fill out a performance. In many classic American popular songs, a verbal phrase recurs at the beginning or end of most of the four sections in the thirty-two-bar chorus. The repeated words are almost always the title of the song and thus help imprint the song on the listener's memory. In a single chorus of "Can't Help Lovin' Dat Man," the title phrase is sung three times, always to the same melody.

In *Show Boat*, the mulatto character Julie sings the first verse and chorus of "Can't Help Lovin' Dat Man," and Queenie answers with her own verse and chorus, which in turn lead into an extended dance and ensemble. Tess Gardella, the Italian American actress who played Queenie in the original production of *Show Boat* (the only performer to appear in blackface), recorded the song in 1928 under her stage name, Aunt Jemima. On that record (LG 11.4), she sings the two verses back to back, followed by two statements of the chorus. Instead of the stage version's full theater orchestra, the backing ensemble here is a small ensemble typical of 1920s jazz (see chapter 12).

ROMANTIC LOVE IN THE CLASSIC POPULAR SONG

Most show songs that won popularity in the years between the two world wars were songs about romantic love. Courtship, treated almost as a ritual in many earlier songs, now emerged as an absorbing, sometimes mysterious personal

CD 2.8	Listening Guide 11.4	"Can't Help Lovin' Dat Man" JEROME KERN AND OSCAR HAMMERSTEIN II

DATE: 1927
PERFORMERS: Tess Gardella, vocal; Hymie Farberman, trumpet; Jim Cassidy, trombone; Sam Feinsmith, alto saxophone; Rube Bloom, piano; Tony Colucci, banjo
GENRE: Broadway show tune
METER: duple
FORM: verse and chorus

WHAT TO LISTEN FOR

- 12-bar blues verse, 32-bar *aaba* chorus
- influence of blues singing on vocal style
- accompaniment by jazz ensemble

TIMING	SECTION	TEXT	COMMENTS
0:00	introduction		Solo trombone hints at the rhythm of the chorus.
0:05	verse 1	Oh listen sister . . .	12-bar blues, with call and response in phrases 2–3. Accompaniment stresses all four beats of the bar, a "quarter-note throb" that for Broadway composers signified the blues.
0:29	verse 2	The chimney's smokin' . . .	12-bar blues chorus.
0:53	chorus	Fish gotta swim . . .	32-bar *aaba*. Each *a* section ends with the title phrase, with blue note on "man." Gardella sings Kern's written melody with only a few alterations.
1:57	chorus		First **half chorus** (*aa*) played instrumentally. In second *a* section, accompaniment shifts into the Charleston dance rhythm.
2:29		When he goes away . . .	Gardella returns at the **bridge** (*b*) to sing a final half chorus (*ba*), departing more freely from Kern's melody.

Listen & Reflect

1. How does Gardella's vocal technique resemble that of blues singers like Bessie Smith (see LG 11.1)? How does it differ?

adventure. The demand for love songs on Broadway was great, both in revue and in musical comedy, since the plots of virtually all of the latter involved characters seeking someone to love. As one New York tunesmith put it, the songwriter's craft lay chiefly in saying "I love you" in thirty-two bars.

Songwriters approached love from a variety of angles. Richard Rodgers and Lorenz Hart's "My Heart Stood Still" (1927) dwells on the experience of love at first sight by suspending time—freezing the frame, in effect. Hart responds to the short phrases of Rodgers's melody, which hint at breathlessness, with lyrics consisting almost entirely of one-syllable words, each *a* section of the *aaba* chorus ending with the title words. George and Ira Gershwin's "The Man I Love" (1924), in contrast, is pure anticipation, as a woman reveals her romantic dream of a future love. Both songs depend on time-worn clichés, which are then transcended by the songs' graceful, self-aware expression.

romance and individualism

The new emphasis on this kind of romantic love accompanies the rise of individualism. Before around 1880, most Americans had little reason to doubt that the ties linking people to their family, community, church, and occupation formed the main social reality of their lives. Between 1880 and 1900, however, these connections began to loosen, and from the 1920s on, Americans were increasingly likely to downplay traditional social ties and define themselves in personal terms.

By the end of World War I, songwriters were absorbing this spirit of individualism. The portrait of love that came to dominate the Broadway stage and Tin Pan Alley concentrated on lovers who were infatuated and preoccupied with each other beyond anything else, who dwelled in a world of two—sometimes only one, if the love affair had ended, as in Cole Porter's "What Is This Thing Called Love?" or, as in the Gershwins' "The Man I Love," if it had yet to begin. Family, friends, society, and community barely existed in this world.

enriched harmony

The new subject matter called for new musical expression, especially in the realm of harmony, where an enriched musical vocabulary that Edward MacDowell had called a "shadow language" had appeared. Using chords with sevenths, ninths, and added or altered tones, songwriters tapped into harmony's power of suggestion in a way that intensified emotions, especially that of yearning.

European influences

The enriched harmony of the classic American popular song came primarily from the songwriters' contact with the European classical sphere. Kern, Gershwin, Rodgers, and Porter all received classical training, and German and Russian compositions of the later nineteenth century and early modern French works were part of their musical experience. Composers such as Liszt, Tchaikovsky, Puccini, and Ravel had enlarged the harmonic vocabulary of Western music in general, and popular songwriters borrowed from their palettes. The kinship between European romanticism and the idiom of the American popular song is reflected in the way songwriters use chromaticism to intensify progressions that lead the listener, in a regular pattern of tension and release, from one phrase to the next. Further enriching that European-style harmony, however,

blues influences

was a native element: the blues, evident not only in the blue notes of the melodies and harmonies but also in the new, more improvisational vocal styles embraced by popular singers.

Popular songs of the golden era celebrated individuals who loved with a passion strong enough to overshadow other social connections. And the music suggested that love with such high expectations had to be more dynamic than stable. Whatever the lyrics might say, the harmonic richness that bathed them reminded listeners that romance between "free" modern individuals could be perilous. Just as the simple diatonic idiom of an earlier age's parlor songs pointed outward to the network of home, family, and religious relations, the restless, bluesy harmonies of Broadway and Tin Pan Alley, joined to sophisticated lyrics, seem to point inward.

QUESTIONS FOR DISCUSSION AND REVIEW

1. What are the stylistic characteristics of the blues (melody, harmony, phrase structure, lyrics, performance techniques, etc.)? Which elements are shared by the recorded performances of "St. Louis Blues," "Muleskinner Blues," and "Can't Help Lovin' Dat Man," and which are not?

2. Compare the attitudes and practices of folk song collectors like Cecil Sharp and Olive Dame Campbell (see chapter 9) with those of A&R men like Ralph Peer.

3. Summarize the role of communications technology in the development of country music.

4. What are the distinguishing features of the classic American popular song? Consider melody, harmony, structure, lyrics, subject matter, and dramatic function.

FURTHER READING

Banfield, Stephen. "Popular Song and Popular Music on Stage and Film." In *The Cambridge History of American Music*, edited by David Nicholls, 309–44. Cambridge: Cambridge University Press, 1998.

Gioia, Ted. *Delta Blues: The Life and Times of the Mississippi Masters Who Revolutionized American Music*. New York: W.W. Norton, 2008.

Handy, W. C. *Father of the Blues: An Autobiography*. New York: Macmillan, 1941.

Havighurst, Craig. *Air Castle of the South: WSM and the Making of Music City*. Urbana: University of Illinois Press, 2007.

Huber, Patrick. *Linthead Stomp: The Creation of Country Music in the Piedmont South*. Chapel Hill: University of North Carolina Press, 2008.

Kenney, William Howland. *Recorded Music in American Life: The Phonograph and Popular Memory, 1890–1945*. New York: Oxford University Press, 1999.

Malone, Bill C. *Country Music, U.S.A.* 2d rev. [i.e., 3d] ed. Austin: University of Texas Press, 2002.

FURTHER LISTENING AND VIEWING

Lost Sounds: Blacks and the Birth of the Recording Industry, 1891–1922. 2 CDs. Archeophone ARCH 1005, 2005.

Times Ain't Like They Used to Be: Early Rural and Popular American Music, 1928–1935. Sherwin Dunner and Richard Nevins, producers. DVD. Yazoo, 1992. An anthology of short films featuring early country, blues, and old-time musicians.

MODERN MUSIC AND JAZZ IN THE 1920s

Between the debacles of World War I and the 1929 stock market crash, Americans enjoyed more than a decade of prosperity and technological innovation. The ethos of the 1920s embraced an optimistic thirst for novelty and a corresponding rejection of seemingly outmoded strictures of the past. Nowhere was the sense of new possibilities greater than in two otherwise dissimilar spheres of musical activity: classical music's venture into modernism, and the combining of blues and ragtime to create jazz.

MUSICAL MODERNISM

In the years before World War I several European composers—the Austrian Arnold Schoenberg, the Russian Igor Stravinsky, the Hungarian Béla Bartók, and the Frenchman Erik Satie, among others—had rejected key aspects of the romantic tradition, which had long dominated Western concert halls and opera houses, in favor of new aesthetic values that came to be called **modernism**. The works of these modernist composers tended to favor fragmented melodies, dissonant harmonies, and irregular rhythms. Across the Atlantic, a movement took shape to introduce into the concert hall music by the European modernists and their American counterparts.

Modernist music did not conform to romantic notions of aesthetic beauty, and most performers and audiences did not welcome it at first. Nonetheless, during the first half of the twentieth century, as some of these European works gained a foothold in American concert halls, a number of émigré and native-born composers in the United States were embracing modernism in a spirit of experimentation that links their work to the earlier music of Charles Ives (see chapter 8). Though much of it still sounds surprisingly unconventional, the best of this music has proven to have lasting value both on its own merits and through its influence on later classical, jazz, and popular music.

LEO ORNSTEIN

Although Ives had been experimenting with modernist devices even before 1900, he did his composing outside of a professional musical life, and his work was acknowledged only much later. Instead of Ives, a composer recognized more widely at the time as an American modernist was Leo Ornstein. Born in the Ukraine in 1893, Ornstein emigrated in 1907 to the United States, where he studied music at the Institute of Musical Art, the New York conservatory that later became known as the Juilliard School.

Beginning at age nineteen, Ornstein produced a series of radically modernist works, mostly solo piano pieces that he performed himself. Characteristic features of his music include **atonality**, or the avoidance of any clear key center; **tone clusters**, created by pressing adjacent piano keys, sometimes with all five fingers of the hand; highly dissonant harmonies; and, instead of traditional classical structures, forms that tended to meander. Like the earlier romantic and impressionist composers, however, Ornstein favored descriptive, poetic titles, which help shape the listener's response to what otherwise might be bewildering sonorities. In his *Three Moods* (1914), for example, the individual movement titles—"Anger," "Grief," and "Joy"—are an aid in interpreting the unconventional music.

atonality

tone clusters

Ornstein composed his most radically modernist pieces before 1920. Afterward, he retreated to a more conservative style and directed most of his energies to teaching at his Ornstein School of Music in Philadelphia (where one student in the 1940s was the visionary jazz saxophonist John Coltrane, discussed in chapter 18). Ornstein thus played only a small part in the organized modernist movement that emerged after 1920. His slow fade into obscurity was reversed in the 1970s when the music historian Vivian Perlis brought his music to the public's attention, and a spurt of creative energy led to several new compositions late in Ornstein's remarkably long life. He died in 2002 at the age of 108.

THE ULTRAMODERNISTS: VARÈSE, RUDHYAR, RUGGLES

Among the leaders in modern music in the 1920s were composers from Europe who moved to the United States—chiefly to New York City—and promoted the cause of new music on these shores. Aggressively nontraditionalist, they and like-minded native-born American musicians came to be known as the **ultramodernists**. The most prominent was Edgard Varèse, who arrived in New York from Paris in 1915. Varèse, fellow French émigré Carlos Salzedo, and some others with ultramodern leanings founded the International Composers' Guild in 1921 to serve "composers who represent the true spirit of our times," as Varèse announced in a manifesto. He criticized performers for often being more interested in judging new music than understanding it. "Not finding in it any trace of the conventions to which [they are] accustomed," he wrote, they denounce new music as "incoherent and unintelligible."

Edgard Varèse

If finding sympathetic performers was difficult, finding receptive listeners was even more so. The premiere in New York of *Hyperprism* in 1923 sparked an uproar in the audience, which heard nothing comprehensible in the onslaught

Hyperprism

Charles Tomlinson Griffes

One important composer of the World War I era had little connection to the modernist movement. When Charles Tomlinson Griffes, the thirty-five-year-old director of music at the Hackley School for Boys, north of New York City, died of an abscessed lung in 1920, he was only beginning to become widely known as a composer. Several of his compositions had been performed in New York: in 1917 *Sho-Jo* (a stage pantomime) and *Five Poems of Ancient China and Japan* for voice and piano, and the following year a new piano sonata. In 1919 *The Pleasure-Dome of Kubla Khan* was played by the Boston Symphony Orchestra, and the *Notturno für Orchester* by the Philadelphia Orchestra. If his older contemporary Charles Ives drew on the experience of a New England boyhood, Griffes's outlook was more cosmopolitan, as these titles suggest. Though his career was cut short by early death, his substantial body of work demonstrates that in his lifetime a place existed in America's musical culture for a composer in the classical sphere whose work, like Amy Beach's (see chapter 8), was neither tied to folk or popular music nor part of the modernist movement.

---

of dissonance and rhythmic complexity produced by Varèse's ensemble of nine wind players and seven percussionists. The title signaled the composer's fascination with science (subsequent titles would include *Octandre, Intégrales, Ionisation,* and *Density 21.5*), and Varèse saw himself—like Milton Babbitt and other composers to be considered in Part 4—as something of a musical scientist, conducting research into unexplored properties of music, or, as he preferred to call it, "organized sound."

In Varèse's compositions massive dissonant chords are used as blocks of sound that are juxtaposed with other sounds, forming patterns and relationships that have nothing to do with traditional notions of tonality, in which the tension of dissonance resolves into the relaxation of consonance. Instead, Varèse's atonal music offers a listening experience that, though jarring, is also invigorating. Unusual sonorities, punctuated by staccato blasts of unpitched percussion "noise" and the whine of sirens, evoke urban modernity and effect a radical break with the past. Thus Varèse aimed to "represent the true spirit of [his] times."

Dane Rudhyar

Another Franco-American member of the International Composers' Guild was Dane Rudhyar. Rudhyar emigrated from Paris in 1916, just one year after Varèse, and by 1920 had settled in California. He was a devotee of Theosophy, a mystical movement founded in New York in the 1870s by the Russian-American Helena Blavatsky that combined interest in Eastern religions with explorations into the psychic and occult. Where Varèse looked to science for inspiration, Rudhyar found in spiritualism a similar inspiration to create a highly dissonant, nontraditional-sounding music. His piano composition *Three Paeans* (1927) "deals with Energies," he argued, "not with so-called Form." In a series of articles, collected into the books *Dissonant Harmony* (1928) and *The New Sense of Sound* (1930), Rudhyar expressed his ideas about music's effect on the soul, ideas that influenced a generation of modernist American composers and that much later resurfaced in New Age music.

Carl Ruggles

Of the native-born American ultramodernists, one of the most original was Carl Ruggles. Ruggles was born in Massachusetts, conducted and taught briefly in

Minnesota and New York, but lived most of his adult life in semi-seclusion in Vermont. He was a friend of Varèse—until a falling-out with that irascible artist led to a closer alliance with Rudhyar—and of Charles Ives, who stopped composing in the 1920s just as the younger ultramodernists were beginning to discover his music. Like Ives, Ruggles had become aware of the new modernist movements in Europe only after having formulated his own highly dissonant, nontraditional style, which is well displayed in his best-known work, the orchestral *Sun-Treader* (1931).

HENRY COWELL

Although he reached his musical maturity outside the influence of Varèse, Henry Cowell shared with the older composer an enthusiasm for musical experimentation that was scientific in its rigor yet thoroughly romantic in its visionary idealism. Born in California in 1897 to bohemian parents, Cowell spent much of his early life in poverty and had little formal schooling. Nonetheless, his unusual talent and intellect came to the attention of a Stanford University psychologist when Cowell was in his early teens. Funds raised by Stanford faculty members and others allowed him to study music with Charles Seeger, a composer on the faculty at the University of California at Berkeley, who encouraged Cowell's fondness for experimenting. (Seeger acted as a coach for several ultramodernist composers, among them Carl Ruggles and Ruth Crawford; see chapter 13.) At an early age, Cowell later explained, he had decided to use "a different kind of musical material for each different idea that I have." The result was that "even from the very start, I was sometimes extremely modernistic and sometimes quite old-fashioned, and very often in-between."

Cowell won a reputation first as a composer-performer who treated the piano like no one before him, not even Ornstein. *The Tides of Manaunaun* (ca. 1917)

In this photo from the 1920s, composer Henry Cowell (1897–1965) demonstrates his technique of creating tone clusters with fist and forearm.

features tone clusters made by pressing down the forearm on the keyboard to produce blocks of sound spanning more than an octave. *Dynamic Motion* (ca. 1916), representing the New York subway, calls for the player to hammer out clusters with fists, forearms, and elbows in the manner of a virtuoso. *Aeolian Harp* (ca. 1932) and *The Banshee* (1925), on the other hand, use the piano more like a harp than a percussion instrument, calling for the performer to play directly on the strings as well as the keyboard. Between 1916 and 1919, Cowell also worked on a treatise exploring fresh acoustical possibilities in the overtone series, published in 1930 as *New Musical Resources.*

LG 12.1

The Banshee (LG 12.1) takes its inspiration from Irish legend, like many pieces by Cowell, the son of an Irish immigrant. A banshee is, in Cowell's words, "an Irish family ghost, a woman of the inner world" who arrives to claim the soul of someone who has just died. Cowell's score calls for the performer to stand in the crook of a grand piano and play directly on the strings, entirely in the lower half of the instrument's range. Meanwhile, an assistant sits at the keyboard and holds down the damper pedal, thus disengaging the dampers, which ordinarily stop a string from vibrating when a key on the keyboard is released. As a result, the strings, once set into vibration, continue to ring until they naturally die down, creating a resonant shimmer.

On first impression, *The Banshee* sounds like an improvisation. Only on repeated listenings does its traditional construction become apparent: it follows the centuries-old plan of a **theme and variations**. Three musical ideas or segments constitute the "theme" (to borrow a traditional term that seems somewhat out of place here). Then follow two "variations," or elaborated repetitions of the theme. The sonic climax occurs at the beginning of the second variation. Lasting less than three minutes, *The Banshee* begins softly, builds up to high intensity, then fades away.

Though the music sounds free and unstructured, Cowell specifies tempo, dynamics, pitch, and methods of tone production in precise detail. The designation *tempo rubato* at the beginning indicates that the player should treat the rhythm flexibly, with slight accelerations and decelerations rather than a steady pulse. Cowell's instructions call for sweeping the strings with the flesh of the finger or with the nail. Sometimes the hand sweeps across many strings, either in one direction or back and forth. Sometimes one string (or more) is stroked lengthwise or plucked like a harp. Melodic fragments and even chords float to the surface in this sonic exploration.

Cowell and world music

By the late 1920s Cowell was drawing on folk and non-Western music, including Chinese, Japanese, African, South Indian, and Javanese as well as Irish music. The *United Quartet* (1936) makes use of **ostinatos** (repeating melodic and rhythmic figures), drones, and stratified textures in ways that help to explain his claim, clothed in the ethnocentric language of the time, that the work "should be understood equally well by Americans, Europeans, Orientals, [and] higher primitives." Cowell spent the years 1936–40 in San Quentin State Prison after being convicted for having sex with a teenage boy, a charge for which he was later pardoned. He remained active there as a musician and composer. In 1939 he wrote several works for percussion ensemble at the request of composer John Cage, who was then musical director for a dance company in Seattle.

Once released from prison, Cowell married the ethnomusicologist Sidney Robertson, who introduced him to the music of William Walker's shape-note

CD 2.9 | Listening Guide 12.1 | *The Banshee* HENRY COWELL

DATE: 1925
GENRE: character piece for piano
PERFORMER: Anthony De Mare, piano
METER: notated in duple meter, but undefined aurally
FORM: theme and variations

WHAT TO LISTEN FOR

- emphasis on timbre and texture, more than pitch
- unusual performance techniques
- form determined by contrasts of texture and dynamics rather than melody or harmony

TIMING	SECTION	SUBSECTION	COMMENTS
0:00	theme	*a*	6 bars, each beginning with a very soft sweep from the lowest string to one in the midrange. The player then runs a finger along the length of that midrange string, producing a wailing pitch. A descending melody can be faintly discerned.
0:23		*b*	While the right hand sweeps back and forth across the strings, the left hand plucks out a forlorn three-note melody.
0:36		*c*	5 bars; as in *a*, each bar begins with an upward sweep, but now the player runs the fingers of first one hand and then the other along not one but three strings, forming ghostly chords. Crescendo to bar 5, in which the player uses the fingernail to produce an even eerier sound.
0:50	variation 1	*a'*	Louder than before, and with each note of the melody played first with the nail and then with the flesh of the finger.
1:10		*b'*	Both hands sweep up and down over the strings, followed by the forlorn plucked melody, to which a fourth note is added.
1:23		*c'*	The three-note chords are now five-note clusters. The last cluster is very loud, and the tempo increases.
1:38	variation 2	*a"*	Very loud and very fast, the descending melody returns as thick clusters.
1:55		*b'*	The forlorn plucked melody returns in its original form, but the sweeping accompaniment is now played with the flat of the hand instead of a single finger.
2:08		*c'*	The original three-note chords return, now outlining the descending melodic pattern of *a*. Diminuendo to silence.

Listen & Reflect

1. Cowell could have given this piece a generic title such as "Etude" or "Theme and Variations." Does the descriptive title affect how you listen to the piece? Does it help or hinder your appreciation of it, and why?

2. Although the theme-and-variations structure of *The Banshee* is thoroughly traditional, its sound world is strikingly nontraditional and can be disorienting even for listeners nearly a century after it was composed. Would the piece be as effective without that traditional structure?

tunebook *Southern Harmony* (1835). Between 1944 and 1964 Cowell wrote, for various instrumental combinations, eighteen *Hymns and Fuguing Tunes,* inspired by early American hymnody, as well as eighteen of his twenty symphonies. He and his wife traveled widely, in 1956 surveying the music of Ireland, Germany, Greece, Turkey, India, Pakistan, Iran, and Japan with the support of a foundation grant, and in 1961 representing the United States at international conferences on music in Tehran and Tokyo. These travels led to such late works as *Ongaku* (1957), in which Western instruments imitate Japanese ones, and *Persian Set* (1957), for a chamber orchestra that includes the *tar,* a Persian string instrument.

While seeking to live "in the whole world of music," as he once put it, Cowell was also a tireless advocate for his fellow American composers. As editor of the journal *New Music* from 1927 to 1936, he published the scores of many, including Ruth Crawford, Carl Ruggles, and Charles Ives, whose biography he and his wife brought out in 1955. Cowell also promoted new music concerts through composers' societies. He wrote hundreds of articles, gave countless interviews on behalf of new music, and served as an overseas ambassador for the work of his American colleagues. And he taught composition, both privately and through institutions, counting among his pupils Burt Bacharach, John Cage, George Gershwin, and Lou Harrison.

Henry Cowell's career demonstrated that neither European-based modernism nor American nationalism was broad enough to encompass the creative imagination of American composers between the two world wars. In fact, working outside the classical sphere, some of that era's most innovative musicians were developing a new kind of American music with a fresh, arresting sound and a name to go with it: jazz.

THE RISE OF JAZZ

The origins of the syncopated dance music called **jazz** remain a matter for speculation. But virtually all authorities agree that the city of New Orleans played a key role and that its African American citizens took the lead.

New Orleans   Among the traits that made New Orleans musically unique were its French and Spanish heritage, a long-standing devotion to opera, the presence of many free blacks in pre–Civil War years, and their freedom to assemble for various festivities (see chapter 4). Education and musical training were also available to some blacks. Yet it would be wrong to imagine that blacks and whites mingled freely in the post–Civil War years. A caste system based on color and language split New Orleans's black citizens into French-speaking, lighter-skinned Creoles who lived downtown and darker-skinned English speakers, many of them migrants who had moved from the country into uptown New Orleans neighborhoods.

In the early 1900s, then, three distinct groups of New Orleans musicians—white, black, and Creole—were playing the ensemble dance music from which jazz evolved. While they shared instrumentation, repertory, and some audience members, contact between these groups was limited.

It seems likely that jazz grew out of ragtime dance music as musicians in the city began playing it early in this century. Dances imported from Paris in the 1840s such as the polka, the schottische, and the quadrille had long dominated the New Orleans scene. In the 1890s, however, new dances began replacing them—especially the one-step, a simple walking and gliding movement well suited to ragtime. Later, the fad for "animal" dances such as the turkey trot called for a new, earthier accompaniment.

Another distinguishing trait of the New Orleans music scene lay in the expressive ways that black New Orleans musicians found to play dance music. Even before 1900 visitors to the city mentioned local musicians' aptitude for melodic playing. Perhaps some players' melodic inventions, together with new rhythmic emphasis, brought a different character to their performance of ragtime. Yet pinpointing when, where, and how jazz music first diverged from ragtime, and from blues music as well, is difficult if not impossible, for even in those early years "jazz" referred to a way of performing that was improvised, not written down. From the beginning, jazz was the quintessential performers' music.

💮 The Piron and Williams Orchestra of New Orleans, around 1915. Members include (standing) Jimmie Noone, clarinet; William Ridgley, trombone; Oscar Celestin, cornet; John Lindsay, bass; (seated) Ernest Trepagnier, drums; A. J. Piron, violin; Tom Benton, mandolin-banjo; John A. St. Cyr, banjo; and (in front) Clarence Williams, piano.

A typical turn-of-the-century New Orleans dance ensemble was led by a violinist, joined by several wind instruments, plus a **rhythm section** of drums, guitar or piano, and double bass (the last usually bowed rather than plucked) that provided the harmonic and rhythmic underpinning. Gradually, following a national trend of replacing guitar and double bass with the banjo and the tuba, New Orleans dance bands also dropped the violin and adopted the saxophone family. As the 1920s dawned, melody was generally assigned to the cornet player, who was often the band's leader.

By that time, the three melodic voices of the New Orleans jazz ensemble's **front line**—cornet, clarinet, and trombone—had assumed contrasting roles and performing styles. Joe "King" Oliver (1885–1938) and other cornetists of his generation born in the city played the lead melody without much variation. The clarinetist wove a countermelody, often in rapid, even notes over a wide range of the instrument but focusing on the upper register to stay clear of the cornet's lead. Clarinets were sometimes missing from pre-1920 New Orleans ensembles, but never trombones, which played in **tailgate** style, with frequent smears (glides through several adjacent pitches) and a mixture of countermelody in the tenor range and doubling of the bass line. The players' drive for expressivity may be heard in the earliest recordings made by Oliver, Sidney Bechet, and others, which incorporate blue notes and portamento (melodic slides) into a fluent, sometimes eloquent melodic style.

Dippermouth Blues (LG 12.2), recorded in 1923 by King Oliver's Creole Jazz Band, is an exemplary recording of this early New Orleans jazz idiom. The form is simple: a four-bar introduction, nine choruses of twelve-bar blues, and a two-bar tag at the end. The first two choruses, plus the fifth and ninth, are played by the full ensemble in the texture called **collective improvisation**, closely identified with New Orleans jazz. Honoré Dutrey's tailgate trombone leads into the first chorus with an upbeat smear, then fills in dead spots between the phrases of Oliver's cornet lead to keep the momentum going. Meanwhile, clarinetist

LG 12.2

collective improvisation

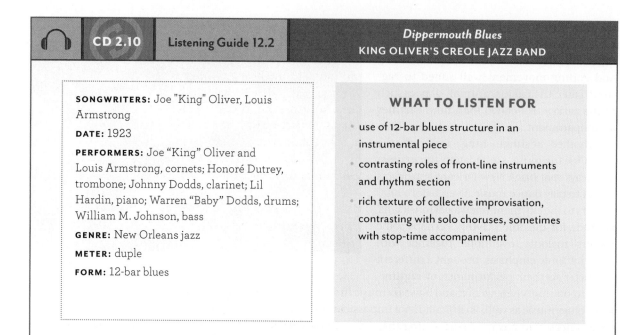

CD 2.10 | **Listening Guide 12.2**

Dippermouth Blues
KING OLIVER'S CREOLE JAZZ BAND

SONGWRITERS: Joe "King" Oliver, Louis Armstrong

DATE: 1923

PERFORMERS: Joe "King" Oliver and Louis Armstrong, cornets; Honoré Dutrey, trombone; Johnny Dodds, clarinet; Lil Hardin, piano; Warren "Baby" Dodds, drums; William M. Johnson, bass

GENRE: New Orleans jazz

METER: duple

FORM: 12-bar blues

WHAT TO LISTEN FOR

- use of 12-bar blues structure in an instrumental piece
- contrasting roles of front-line instruments and rhythm section
- rich texture of collective improvisation, contrasting with solo choruses, sometimes with stop-time accompaniment

TIMING	SECTION	COMMENTS
0:00	introduction	Four bars, divided into a two-bar falling pattern, then two bars of expectant chords. Trombone smear leads into first chorus.
0:04	choruses 1–2	The full ensemble in collective improvisation.
0:35	choruses 3–4	Clarinet solo over stop-time accompaniment.
1:06	chorus 5	Collective improvisation; Armstrong is playing lead while Oliver prepares for his solo.
1:21	choruses 6–8	Oliver's solo; each chorus expands the range upward, increasing the intensity. Chorus 8 ends with a spoken break.
2:07	chorus 9 and tag	Collective improvisation, extended by two-bar tag.

Listen & Reflect

1. In Bessie Smith's recording of "St. Louis Blues" (see LG 11.1), each of the three musicians has a distinct function within the ensemble. How are they analogous to the various functions performed here by the members of the Creole Jazz Band?

Johnny Dodds carries on another dialogue with Oliver, weaving an independent line, generally higher in range than the lead and with phrasing that dovetails with Oliver's in a manner of call and response.

The other five choruses are devoted to solos. Johnny Dodds takes the third and fourth choruses while the rest of the band accompanies him in stop-time (short punctuating chords separated by silences). After another chorus of collective improvisation comes the most celebrated part of *Dippermouth Blues*: Oliver's cornet solo in choruses 6–8. All of the Oliver trademarks are here. The solo is played with a variety of muted effects, placing the emphasis on timbre; prominent among those effects is the "wah-wah" sound of the **plunger mute**, the rubber end of a plumber's helper, which Oliver uses to partially open and close the bell of the trumpet, sounding eerily like a human voice. There is also a focus on the middle register, especially in his first solo chorus, which worries the blue third much as Bessie Smith does in "St. Louis Blues" (see LG 11.1). This was a "set" solo: a melody in the style of an improvisation that Oliver worked out and repeated when his group performed this piece—and that other musicians sometimes emulated when playing it.

plunger mute

Oliver's last chorus ends with a two-bar **break**: a brief span of time during which the accompaniment drops out, creating a gap in the otherwise continuous musical fabric. Breaks are typically filled with an instrumental solo, but here the bass player, Bill Johnson, shouts, "Oh, play that thing!"

break

The limitations of acoustic recording (in 1923 the electric microphone was still two years in the future) make the piano and bass all but inaudible and force drummer Warren "Baby" Dodds to restrict himself to woodblock—drums overpowered the delicate recording equipment. Digital restoration has done something to clarify the murky sound of the original. Still, only intermittently audible is the twenty-one-year-old musician playing second cornet to Oliver's lead: Louis Armstrong, who has already appeared in chapter 11 accompanying Bessie Smith and who was soon to leave Oliver's organization for a brilliant solo career. Oliver thought enough of his deferential sideman to name this tune after him: "Dippermouth" was one of several nicknames bestowed on Armstrong in reference to his large mouth, along with "Gatemouth" and "Satchel Mouth," the latter misheard by a British reporter when Armstrong was touring England and transformed into "Satchmo," the name long used by the jazz virtuoso's adoring fans.

Dippermouth Blues and the other sides recorded by Oliver's band at the Gennett Studio in Richmond, Indiana, in 1923 are a landmark in the history of jazz. Not only do they represent the first major set of recordings by black jazz musicians, but they also seem to have broken the color barrier. From 1923 on, the music of black jazz performers as well as white was preserved and circulated on record. The Oliver band's remarkable blend of freedom and discipline has been taken as another kind of landmark: an exemplar of classic New Orleans jazz.

JAZZ AND THE PUBLIC

Well before these black New Orleanians began recording, the American public had discovered jazz as a riotous new form of popular entertainment. In late 1916 the Original Dixieland Jazz Band was hired for an engagement in New York, and in 1917 they became the first jazz group to make recordings, for Victor. The ODJB, made up of five white New Orleans players (cornet, clarinet, trombone, drums, and piano), caused a great stir. *Livery Stable Blues* featured rooster sounds from the clarinet, cow moos from the trombone, and a horse neighing from the cornet. In the hands of the ODJB, jazz was thus introduced as a nose-thumbing parody of standard music making, and the public found the result hilarious.

denunciation of jazz

In the years after World War I, jazz was seen in some circles as a symptom of civilization's decline. Many community leaders, both white and black, had opposed ragtime, and now they made jazz a target. One complaint linked jazz with the illegal liquor trade that sprang up after Prohibition became law in 1920. With its eccentric sounds, earthy rhythms, and the encouragement of brazen dance styles, jazz came to be linked with the moral drift that educators and the clergy had been deploring since the war's end.

In wartime Americans had united against the common German foe. But peace brought new complexity and social unrest. As African Americans migrated in large numbers from the southern countryside into the cities of the North in search of better jobs, they changed the culture of the areas where they settled. And they met resistance from whites. The Ku Klux Klan—whose constitution pledged "to unite white male persons, native-born Gentile citizens of the United States of America"—was reorganized in 1915, and by 1924 its membership reached 4.5 million. It was hardly a coincidence that in 1924, the year of the Klan's greatest popularity, the denunciation of jazz was also at its peak.

Yet jazz, for some a symbol of moral decadence, shared with gospel music a grounding in the blues (see chapter 14). Blues musicians tapped a vein of human emotion deeper than the divisions between the sacred and the secular, the moral and the immoral. And that depth of expression could be found as well in jazz.

FOUR GIANTS OF EARLY JAZZ

Within the first decade of recorded jazz, the new music underwent a series of transformations. The story of that rapid maturation can be told by tracing the lives of a few of the key personalities in early jazz. In those years artists of the highest caliber molded the music to reflect their aesthetic goals, some emphasizing compositional intricacy, others improvisational freedom; some developing the sound of the ensemble, others perfecting the soloist's art.

JELLY ROLL MORTON: JAZZ COMPOSER

Storyville

Born in 1890 in New Orleans of Creole parents, Ferdinand Joseph Lamothe, better known as Jelly Roll Morton, received formal music lessons as a child and began playing piano at age ten. While still in his teens he continued his informal education in Storyville, where he also gained his first professional experience as a pianist. Called "the District" by locals, Storyville was a neighborhood where legalized prostitution formed the center of an array of rough entertainment, including saloons and gambling houses, that supported a lively demand for music. Although jazz did not originate in the District, it flourished there. After the federal government closed Storyville down in 1917, a decline in the number of venues spurred many talented musicians to leave New Orleans. Morton himself, in fact, had traveled in black vaudeville and cabaret entertainment as early as 1907, visiting many parts of the country, as far west as California.

Chicago

Morton was employed for a time in Chicago during World War I. He returned there in the spring of 1923, making his first recordings and publishing his compositions through a Chicago firm. In 1926 he organized the Red Hot Peppers for an epic set of Victor recordings. Record sessions could be haphazard affairs in those days, but not when Morton was the leader. Baby Dodds, the group's drummer, recalled that Morton worked "on each and every number" in rehearsal until he was satisfied. "You did what Jelly Roll wanted you to do, no more and no less."

Morton moved to New York in 1928. But in an environment dominated by large dance orchestras, his emphasis on the New Orleans style was considered old-fashioned. Work opportunities gradually dried up, and Morton fell into obscurity, convinced that he was the victim of a voodoo curse. He resurfaced in 1938, opening a small jazz club in Washington, D.C. Morton also presented himself at the Library of Congress, anxious that his role in the history of jazz—he claimed to have invented it—be documented. In a landmark encounter, he was interviewed at length by folklorist Alan Lomax, illustrating his recollections at the piano. During a trip to California in 1940 he became ill and never recovered. His death in Los Angeles in July 1941 was hardly noticed by the jazz community.

Jelly Roll Morton and His Red Hot Peppers, who recorded New Orleans–style jazz in Chicago in 1926–27.

At a time when solo improvisation based on a composition's harmonic structure was gaining importance in jazz, Jelly Roll Morton maintained composition as the music's vital force, with improvisation in a secondary role. "My theory," Morton announced, "is to never discard the melody." Thus spontaneity in his music stemmed not only from improvising on harmonic changes but also on embellishing the melody, and on the varied repetition of whole sections. Morton's preference for melodic variation and sectional construction reflected his attachment to ragtime, whose rhythm, melody, and multi-strain forms he absorbed growing up, and which he continued to draw upon throughout his career.

Morton's compositional prowess is on display in *Black Bottom Stomp* (LG 12.3), the first of his Red Hot Peppers recordings from 1926. The title refers to a then-popular dance of African American origin, the Black Bottom, whose music made use of what Morton called the "Spanish tinge": a hint of Latin American or Caribbean rhythm, which he considered an essential element of jazz. The Black Bottom rhythm resembles both the habanera, audible in the ring shout "Jubilee" (see LG 4.3), and the Charleston, another popular African American dance style of the 1920s. But the Spanish tinge is only one rhythmic feature of *Black Bottom Stomp*: Morton and his musicians vary the rhythmic sense by using stop-time; by having the bass line alternate between two strong beats to the bar (on beats 1 and 3) and four, the latter called a **walking bass**; and, in the last section, emphasizing beats 2 and 4 in the drums, the so-called **backbeat**.

The structure of *Black Bottom Stomp* resembles the multi-strain format of marches and ragtime, including a key change in the middle to suggest a trio. But where rags and marches typically have four strains, Morton's tune has only two, labeled A and B in the listening guide, providing material for multiple variations. The composed A section is followed by two variants showcasing solo cornet and clarinet respectively, and the B section is heard in no fewer than seven contrasting versions. Increasing and decreasing the number of instruments playing at a given time and spotlighting different soloists, Morton creates variety not only between sections but within them as well; a sixteen- or twenty-bar segment may encompass several shifts in texture, volume, and rhythm. The result, for a close listener, is akin to a constantly changing musical kaleidoscope.

LG 12.3

the "Spanish tinge"

walking bass

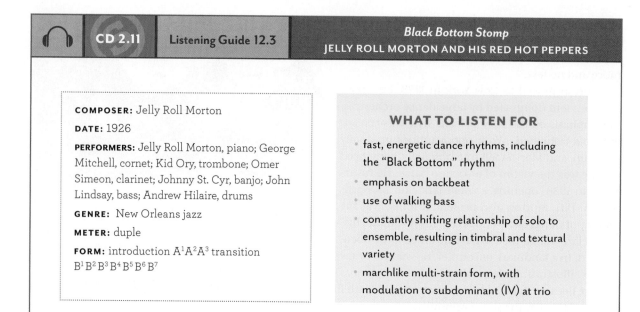

CD 2.11   **Listening Guide 12.3**   *Black Bottom Stomp*
JELLY ROLL MORTON AND HIS RED HOT PEPPERS

COMPOSER: Jelly Roll Morton

DATE: 1926

PERFORMERS: Jelly Roll Morton, piano; George Mitchell, cornet; Kid Ory, trombone; Omer Simeon, clarinet; Johnny St. Cyr, banjo; John Lindsay, bass; Andrew Hilaire, drums

GENRE: New Orleans jazz

METER: duple

FORM: introduction $A^1 A^2 A^3$ transition $B^1 B^2 B^3 B^4 B^5 B^6 B^7$

WHAT TO LISTEN FOR

- fast, energetic dance rhythms, including the "Black Bottom" rhythm
- emphasis on backbeat
- use of walking bass
- constantly shifting relationship of solo to ensemble, resulting in timbral and textural variety
- marchlike multi-strain form, with modulation to subdominant (IV) at trio

TIMING	SECTION	COMMENTS
0:00	introduction	Four bars, played twice, setting the fast tempo and raucous mood.
0:07	A^1	An 8-bar composed section, played twice, with the ensemble in block chords; four sustained chords precede a series of faster chords in cakewalk syncopation (short-long-short).
0:22	A^2	A variant of the A section, with cornet solo in place of the sustained chords of A^1; the first solo is accompanied by the rhythm section, the second solo by trombone and rhythm section in stop-time.
0:37	A^3	Another variant of A: clarinet solo, accompanied by rhythm section with prominent banjo; first appearance of the Black Bottom/Spanish tinge/Charleston rhythm. The accompaniment begins each 8-bar half in stop-time; the first half finishes with 2 bars of walking bass, the second with 2 bars of full ensemble.
0:51	transition	Modulation to the subdominant key (IV), as in a march; 4 bars.
0:54	B^1	New section, in collective improvisation style over a (mostly) walking bass; break for cornet and trombone in bars 7–8; 20 bars total. In the last 2 bars, the full ensemble plays a turnaround figure in the syncopated Black Bottom rhythm.
1:14	B^2	Clarinet solo, with rhythm section; clarinet break in bars 7–8, full ensemble in last 2 bars.
1:33	B^3	Solo piano, with full ensemble in last 2 bars; Morton's ragtime-style left hand is easy to hear.
1:50	B^4	Cornet solo, with full ensemble accompanying in stop-time; cornet break in bars 7–8; a few "extra" notes suggest that this section was under-rehearsed.
2:09	B^5	Banjo solo, with bass alternating 2-beat and 4-beat (walking bass) patterns; banjo break in bars 7–8; full ensemble in last 2 bars.

CD 2.11	**Listening Guide 12.3**		***Black Bottom Stomp*** **JELLY ROLL MORTON AND HIS RED HOT PEPPERS**

TIMING	SECTION	COMMENTS
2:28	B⁶	Full ensemble in collective improvisation style; cymbal break in bars 7–8.
2:47	B⁷	Tailgate trombone smears and tom-tom on the backbeat; the energetic trombone break in bars 7–8 inspires a hot response from the clarinet in the following bars.
3:05	coda	The out chorus expands the usual 2-bar closing figure into a 4-bar coda.

Listen & Reflect

1. Because the full ensemble is playing identical rhythms in A¹, it is apparent that that section was composed, not improvised. Simply by listening, how certain can one be whether musicians are improvising or playing precomposed material elsewhere in *Black Bottom Stomp?*

2. In terms of structure and arrangement, how does *Black Bottom Stomp* resemble *Castle House Rag* (LG 10.3) on the one hand and *Dippermouth Blues* (LG 12.2) on the other? Using your ear as a guide, compare the amount of composition and improvisation in each of these three records.

3. Compare the recorded sound of *Dippermouth Blues* with that of *Black Bottom Stomp*. Though separated by only three years, the first was recorded acoustically (with a horn instead of a microphone) and the latter electrically. What differences can you hear?

Moreover, Morton's Red Hot Peppers numbers display his awareness of the artistic possibilities of the phonograph record. The three-minute duration of *Black Bottom Stomp* is filled not only with musical variety but a sense of narrative rise and fall, leading to a climactic **out chorus,** a final statement of the B strain that brings the music to a fever pitch. Though Morton allowed his musicians plenty of improvisational freedom in their solos (as they attested later in interviews), he maintained a composer's firm grip on the large-scale structure of his records. Working at the dawn of electrical recording, Jelly Roll Morton anticipated the achievements of composer/record producers to be discussed in Part 4.

LOUIS ARMSTRONG: JAZZ SOLOIST

Except for their hometown, Jelly Roll Morton and Louis Armstrong held little in common. They were men of different generations and temperaments. They took different musical approaches, their career paths differed sharply, and there is no record of the two working together. Yet both of these New Orleans natives reached artistic fulfillment in Chicago, a northern city whose environment allowed jazz to flourish, both commercially and artistically.

Louis Armstrong was born in poverty in New Orleans in 1901, the son of a laborer who deserted the family and a mother who worked as a domestic and

New Orleans

perhaps as a prostitute. While Armstrong grabbed some schooling as a boy, he claimed as his real diploma the common sense and consideration he learned from his mother. Armstrong went to work at the age of seven. He also formed a vocal quartet with friends, who sang on street corners for tips. In 1913 he was declared delinquent and sent to the Colored Waifs' Home for Boys, a local reform school, where he received his first instruction in music. He left home two years later as a cornet player determined to make a career as a musician. When cornetist King Oliver left New Orleans for Chicago in 1918, Armstrong took Oliver's place in a band led by trombonist Edmund "Kid" Ory. In 1922 Oliver, who was leading his Creole Jazz Band in a Chicago cabaret, invited Armstrong to join his group as a second cornetist.

Chicago
Chicago's jazz scene was rooted in the African American population on the city's South Side. In 1910 approximately 44,000 black residents lived there. Between 1916 and 1919 the Great Migration from southern states added thousands more, so that by 1920 the count stood at almost 110,000. This demographic shift, besides strengthening local black political influence, also ushered in the city's jazz age. Cabarets, vaudeville and movie theaters, and dance halls were opened to serve the growing market for black musical entertainment. And by the later 1910s some of these establishments were featuring the energetic, syncopated, often raucous-sounding dance music that, under the name of jazz, was gaining national attention.

black-and-tans
The cabarets in which Chicago's jazz scene flourished were South Side "black-and-tans," where black and white customers mingled. Some clergymen condemned the cabarets as dens of iniquity, yet they brought jobs and paying customers to the South Side. And they supplied residents with professional entertainment, cast in familiar idioms of speech, humor, dancing, and music. The undisputed leaders of the Chicago jazz scene, however, were black musicians, and they deeply impressed young white jazz musicians, including banjoist and guitarist Eddie Condon. Condon's description of King Oliver's band playing at the Lincoln Gardens in 1922 has often been quoted: "It was hypnosis at first hearing. Everyone was playing what he wanted to play and it was all mixed together as if someone had planned it with a set of micrometer calipers."

Thanks to his association with Oliver, Armstrong's reputation began to grow, especially after the band began recording in 1923. The next year, Armstrong left the Creole Jazz Band for the Fletcher Henderson Orchestra in New York. But late in 1925 he returned to Chicago and for the next several years performed in clubs and theaters while also leading record dates with small groups, at the same time making the switch from the mellow-sounding cornet to the brighter, louder trumpet. The sixty-five recordings that Armstrong and his Hot Five and Hot Seven groups made in 1925–28 are now recognized as musical classics.

Armstrong moved to New York in 1929 and soon appeared in *Hot Chocolates*, a Broadway revue. Then he embarked on a career as a solo entertainer: a jazz trumpeter who also sang, led a big band, hosted his own radio show, and appeared in films, all with supreme musicianship and a personality that seemed to welcome and embrace the audience. He also toured the world for the U.S. State Department in the 1950s. A heart attack in 1959 slowed his pace somewhat, but he kept performing until a few weeks before his death. When Armstrong died in 1971, he could claim an audience as large and varied as that of any musician in the world.

The Hot Five and Hot Seven
Armstrong's Hot Five and Hot Seven groups, like Jelly Roll Morton's Red Hot Peppers, were studio ensembles put together for the express purpose of making

records; with a single exception, they never played live engagements. To listen to Armstrong as the leader of the Hot Five and the Hot Seven is to understand why he became one of the most influential of all American musicians. In 1927, for example, he recorded *Struttin' with Some Barbecue* with four other players. The piece begins and ends with ensemble choruses in the New Orleans mode, full of call-and-response interchange. In between, the trombonist and clarinetist each play a solo half a chorus long, and Armstrong plays a complete solo chorus. His role in *Struttin'* is far more prominent than was Oliver's in *Dippermouth Blues*; his lead cornet in the ensemble sections takes center stage by virtue of its powerful sound and rhythmic energy, and his solo's inventiveness outshines that of his fellow players.

Armstrong's impact could be dazzling. Trumpeter Max Kaminsky, after hearing him live for the first time in 1929, recalled having felt "as if I had stared into the sun's eye." Examples of Armstrong's solo artistry in these years are legion. Among them is *West End Blues* (LG 12.4), a tune by Oliver that Armstrong recorded in 1928 with pianist Earl "Fatha" Hines and three other musicians. With the addition of the Pittsburgh-born Hines to the Hot Five, Armstrong finally had a colleague who came close to matching his inventiveness and virtuosity. Hines transformed the ragtime-based style of most early jazz pianists, developing his own nervous, unpredictable manner based on cascading runs and what came to be known as his "trumpet style": melodic lines played in octaves, for greater volume, with octave tremolos (rapid alternation of the two notes an octave apart) that approximated a trumpet player's vibrato.

LG 12.4

West End Blues opens dramatically with an unaccompanied solo in free rhythm—a cadenza—that immediately sets Armstrong above other trumpeters of his time. This cadenza was so influential that learning to imitate it was for decades a standard part of any jazz player's training—and not just trumpeters, as evidenced by Charlie Barnet's 1944 version of *West End Blues*, in which the entire big band leads off by playing Armstrong's cadenza in unison. Armstrong's 1928 recording follows this spectacular opening with a sudden change of mood, as the band relaxes into a subdued blues. The first chorus begins with Armstrong delivering King Oliver's melody straight. He turns the second four-bar phrase into an unadorned call and a florid response. And in the third phrase, the serene melody is dissolved by Armstrong's decorations.

Later choruses include a trombone solo, a delicate call-and-response duet between the clarinet and Armstrong, who sings his responses in vocables—**scat singing**—and a rippling solo chorus by Hines on piano. The last chorus, played by everyone, starts with another surprise: Armstrong begins the melody an octave higher than before, sustaining a high B flat for almost four bars. Then the tension is released in an improvised burst, based on a repetitive figure that seems to break loose from rhythmic restriction, floating freely above the accompaniment. Armstrong's climactic conclusion manages to sound both spontaneous and inevitable.

The musical synthesis that Armstrong achieved in the latter 1920s drew on three sources that were already present in the music of Chicago's South Side. The first was the African American oral tradition, with its practice of signifying, which in musical terms means taking a preexisting melody, harmony, rhythm, or form and changing it in a way that amounts to a musical comment: a

꩜ Louis Armstrong and his Hot Five, including Lil Hardin, piano; Kid Ory, trombone; Johnny Dodds, alto sax and clarinet; and Johnny St. Cyr, banjo.

| CD 2.12 | Listening Guide 12.4 | *West End Blues* LOUIS ARMSTRONG AND HIS HOT FIVE |

SONGWRITER: Joe "King" Oliver

DATE: 1928

PERFORMERS: Louis Armstrong, trumpet, vocal; Earl Hines, piano; Fred Robinson, trombone; Jimmy Strong, clarinet; Mancy Carr, banjo; Zutty Singleton, drums

GENRE: New Orleans jazz

METER: duple

FORM: 12-bar blues

WHAT TO LISTEN FOR

- striking, attention-getting opening cadenza
- emphasis on solos over ensemble; no collective improvisation
- trumpet playing and singing keep Armstrong in the spotlight

TIMING	SECTION	COMMENTS
0:00	introduction	Dramatic cadenza for trumpet alone, then an anticipatory chord from the full group.
0:14	chorus 1	Trumpet plays Oliver's composed melody, with increasing departures.
0:49	chorus 2	Trombone solo, emphasizing smears.
1:23	chorus 3	Call-and-response duet between clarinet in low register and scat singing.
1:57	chorus 4	Piano solo. Phrase 1, fast, light runs; phrase 2, "trumpet-style" octaves, with tremolo at the end; phrase 3, return to lighter texture.
2:31	chorus 5	Phrase 1, trumpet holds high note; phrase 2, series of falling figures against the beat; phrase 3, piano solo.
3:03	coda	Full group in a closing gesture, ending with cymbal "clop."

Listen & Reflect

1. *Dippermouth Blues* (see LG 12.2) and *West End Blues* are similar in instrumentation and in form: a series of 12-bar blues choruses with short introduction and coda. What features make the two recordings sound so different?

gesture of affirmation, surprise, irony, or even mockery. The second influence came from the cabarets, where Armstrong learned how to be an effective entertainer. Those who worked in Chicago's competitive show business needed to be able to make artistic statements that would impress club managers, contractors, and bandleaders. Jazz musicians there learned to work out solo statements that would instantly grab the spotlight.

The third influence was the demand for instrumental virtuosity. According to songwriter Hoagy Carmichael, Armstrong owed much of his technical command to the prodding of Fisk University–educated Lil Hardin, the jazz pianist to whom he was married from 1924 until the 1930s. "Lil worked the fat off Louis," Carmichael wrote. "She got a book of the standard cornet solos and drilled him. He really worked, even taking lessons from a German down at [the American Conservatory of Music, at] Kimball Hall, who showed Louis all the European cornet clutches." Carmichael's comments reveal Armstrong as a performer who was eager to learn all the tools of the trade. Armstrong himself, in a 1961 interview, attributed his attitude to being "from New Orleans, where the musicians were very serious about their music. . . . All of my life in music, whatever happened to me that's right today come from observin' other musicians that was playing something."

It has sometimes been assumed that the black oral tradition, the demands of audience taste, and formal musical training are incompatible. Indeed, each influence has been described here as if it belongs to a separate musical domain: the traditional, popular, and classical spheres. Yet in Louis Armstrong's musical consciousness, these influences and their values of continuity, accessibility, and transcendence were uniquely blended, each playing a role in the work of one of the century's most remarkable artists.

BIX BEIDERBECKE: JAZZ LEGEND

The Chicago jazz scene also gave birth to the career of white cornetist Leon "Bix" Beiderbecke. Louis Armstrong once wrote, "The first time I heard Bix, I said these words to myself: There's a man as serious about his music as I am." Born in 1903 into a prosperous Iowa family, Beiderbecke began piano lessons at the age of five, but, finding his teachers' approaches to classical music unappealing, he lost interest and in fact never learned to read music fluently until late in life. In his teen years, recordings by Nick LaRocca and the Original Dixieland Jazz Band caught his ear, and he taught himself cornet by playing along with them. His parents, unhappy with their son's musical taste and academic performance, sent him to Lake Forest Academy, north of Chicago. Here he discovered the city's jazz scene; he also confirmed his resistance to school and fondness for alcohol. After being expelled from the academy in 1922, Beiderbecke stayed in the Midwest, living wherever he could find work playing jazz. Catching on with other young musicians who emulated black players, he began recording in 1924 with the Wolverines Orchestra. Over the next several years he won admiration from musicians and knowledgeable fans for his warm sound and melodic originality.

In 1927 a leading New York bandleader, Paul Whiteman (see chapter 13), hired Beiderbecke, along with a few other jazz improvisers, to enliven his dance orchestra's performances. Between 1927 and 1929 he made many influential recordings with Whiteman and with various groups in New York. By the time he left Whiteman in 1929, however, heavy drinking had taken its toll, and Beiderbecke was able to work only sporadically from then until he died in the summer of 1931.

Although Beiderbecke was little known by the public while he was alive, his memory took on a mythic aura. Starting among musicians, the legend spread to the general public after the appearance of Dorothy Baker's novel *Young Man with a Horn* (1939), based loosely on Beiderbecke's life and later made into a movie. His talent, alcohol consumption, short life, and almost mystical devotion to music helped to create the myth that would make Beiderbecke a symbol of the Roaring Twenties.

Leon "Bix" Beiderbecke (1903–1931), legendary jazz cornetist from Iowa.

It was no accident that the first legendary jazz musician was white. (The memory of an even earlier figure—Buddy Bolden, a turn-of-the-century black New Orleans musician—also became the object of a mythologizing cult, but that came later.) In the 1930s the general public would hardly have looked on a black figure as a symbol of the tortured, romantic genius. Armstrong and Oliver could claim by birthright the African American folk traditions whose reservoir of melody and rhythm nourished their performances; the same was true, though somewhat more complicated, for Morton, a Creole. But a white who became a jazz musician had to make a more self-conscious break with his social and musical background; he had to construct his own artistic base.

By the late 1930s, when the Swing Era had pulled big-band jazz into the forefront of popular music (see chapter 15), work for white jazz musicians was plentiful. But big-band work, based on written arrangements, lacked the spontaneity of the small New Orleans and Chicago jazz ensembles. Jazz musicians who improvised well and resisted popular formulas were now looked on not just as entertainers but as artists. As the audience for swing-band music grew, so—among some aficionados—did the belief that it was artistically inferior to earlier jazz. And Bix Beiderbecke became a symbol of one who had taken the artist's path, in spite of limited technique and a disorderly personal life.

the Beiderbecke legend

The Beiderbecke legend has continued to evolve. One view has the cornetist actually refusing a musical education and aspiring to a kind of downward mobility, while another finds him more a victim of isolation than one who chose it, unable to connect with any tradition that spoke to his own sensibilities. There is no denying the power of Beiderbecke as a symbol of bohemian artistry crushed by the music business's commercial demands, even though, on closer inspection, he looks more like a remarkable intuitive artist who lost faith in the instinct that first sustained him. Yet whatever the truth of the Bix legend, its existence suggests that by the latter 1930s some white jazz musicians were finding it useful in helping them shape their own artistic identities, and fans of jazz were taking the music seriously.

DUKE ELLINGTON: JAZZ BANDLEADER

Whereas jazz in New Orleans and Chicago focused on relatively small ensembles, the New York scene was dominated by larger dance orchestras, beginning before the jazz age with groups such as James Reese Europe's Society Orchestra (see chapter 10) and continuing into the 1920s with the Paul Whiteman Orchestra, which drew Bix Beiderbecke to New York, and the Fletcher Henderson Orchestra, which did the same for Louis Armstrong. Henderson's orchestra began a long-term engagement at the Roseland Ballroom in midtown Manhattan in 1924: a black band playing for white audiences. Thanks to arrangements by Don Redman and soloists like Armstrong and tenor saxophonist Coleman Hawkins, Henderson could include hot jazz numbers in a menu of waltzes, popular songs, and more conventional dance music. Henderson's is considered the first dance orchestra that, while playing written arrangements, achieved the rhythmic lilt, or swing, of the blues tradition. But by the end of the decade, another New York jazz orchestra had gained even more prominence. Led by Duke Ellington, this group was to be a presence on the music scene from the 1920s into the 1970s.

Washington, D.C.

Edward Kennedy Ellington, born in Washington, D.C., in 1899, once wrote: "When I was a child, my mother told me I was blessed, and I have always taken

The Fletcher Henderson Orchestra, New York, 1924–25. The trumpet player in the middle of the back row is Louis Armstrong.

her word for it." He started piano lessons at seven, studied commercial art in high school, and began playing piano professionally with Washington-area dance orchestras at seventeen. He seems always to have had a talent for leadership.

New York

In 1923 Ellington moved to New York. For the next several years he led groups in midtown clubs. He also began to record. Late in 1926 Ellington hired as his manager Irving Mills, who belonged to a white music-publishing family. Personal connections with bootleggers enabled Mills to book Ellington and his musicians into the Cotton Club in Harlem, where the band entertained white audiences, playing for dancing and floor shows over the next three years (1927–30). It was here that Ellington hit his stride as a composer. Working with such distinctive-sounding Ellington's sidemen musicians as saxophonists Harry Carney and Johnny Hodges, clarinetist Barney Bigard, trumpeters Bubber Miley and Cootie Williams, and trombonist Joe "Tricky Sam" Nanton, he fashioned an ensemble that, while playing a varied repertory, specialized in his own original music. Between 1932 and 1942 Ellington traveled the United States, made two successful European tours, and recorded extensively with a fourteen-piece orchestra: six brass (three trumpets, three trombones), four reeds (two alto saxophones plus a tenor and a baritone sax, all doubling on clarinet), and a rhythm section of four (his own piano, plus double bass, guitar, and drums). Through these years he produced larger works to complement his short instrumental pieces and popular songs such as "Mood Indigo," "Sophisticated Lady," and "Take the A Train" (the latter composed by Billy Strayhorn, who joined the band as a composer and arranger in 1939). In 1943 Ellington began a series of annual Carnegie Hall concerts with *Black, Brown, and Beige*, a fifty-minute suite in five large sections, commemorating the history of African people in the New World. (We'll have more to say about Ellington's concert music in chapter 13.)

Ellington's sidemen

After World War II, Ellington enlarged his band, even as economic conditions forced many big bands out of business. Touring both at home and abroad, playing dances, concerts, and festivals, the band maintained a core of older favorites in its repertory. Meanwhile, Ellington continued to write new compositions, including the score to Otto Preminger's film *Anatomy of a Murder* (1959). In the 1960s Ellington began to be noticed in the halls of official American culture. He was awarded the Presidential Medal of Freedom (1969), won honorary doctorates from universities, and was elected to the National Institute of Arts and Letters. In the years since his death in 1974 he has been more and more widely recognized not only as a leading figure in the jazz tradition but also as an important twentieth-century composer.

Ellington as colorist

Strayhorn, Ellington's close collaborator, observed that "Ellington plays the piano, but his real instrument is his band." Indeed, Ellington sought tonal "charisma" from his players, and he worked to discover timbres that would seize listeners' attention. Encouraging his band members to develop distinctive personal timbres, Ellington then combined those colors with a painterly touch. Experience taught him that some musicians revealed their inner selves most deeply in their sound, and that audiences knew it. Audience response to the first note of a solo by alto saxophonist Johnny Hodges, for example, "was as big and deep as most applause for musicians at the end of their complete performance."

Ellington appreciated the collaborative role of his audiences. "I travel from place to place by car, bus, train, plane," he wrote, "taking rhythm to the dancers, harmony to the romantic, melody to the nostalgic, gratitude to the listener." And he knew how rhythm can bring musicians and audience members into sync: "When your pulse and my pulse are together, we are swinging, with ears, eyes, and every member of the body tuned into driving a wave emotionally,

◈ Edward Kennedy "Duke" Ellington (1899–1974), composer and bandleader, in a publicity photo taken in 1934.

compellingly, to and from the subconscious." In Ellington's view, musicians performed their best for knowledgeable listeners—especially on those rare occasions when "audience and performers are determined not to be outdone by the other, and when both have appreciation and taste to match."

But again, distinctive timbre—sometimes called "the Ellington effect"—was Ellington's trump card, making his band instantly recognizable and emotionally potent. The chief architect of the Ellington effect as it emerged in "East St. Louis Toodle-Oo," a composition of the latter 1920s, was trumpeter Bubber Miley. Miley had discovered that by buzzing his lips, gargling, and humming at the same time, he could "growl" through his trumpet, a sound he shaped further with a plunger mute for "wah-wah" effects. By combining this with a "pixie" mute in the bell of the instrument, which added a pinched quality to the timbre, Miley achieved his distinctive **plunger-and-growl** technique, an extension of King Oliver's fascination with various muted timbres. "Tricky Sam" Nanton made the technique equally effective on the trombone. Ellington loved this sound and maintained it in his arsenal of effects after Miley left the band.

plunger-and-growl

The plunger-and-growl sound is prominent in *Black and Tan Fantasy* (LG 12.5), an Ellington composition from 1927. It begins with Miley's tightly muted trumpet playing a paraphrase of "The Holy City," an 1892 sacred song that was popular with vocal recitalists both black and white, here transformed into a doleful lament over a twelve-bar blues progression in the minor mode. In complete contrast is the slinky major-mode strain that follows on alto sax, the quintessence of urbane sophistication. Then comes a series of major-mode twelve-bar blues choruses for Miley, Ellington, and Nanton, finishing up with a quotation from Chopin's "Funeral March."

LG 12.5

The combination of such disparate elements suggests that Ellington may have had in mind a **program**: some extramusical content such as a story, picture, or person that the music describes. Ellington wrote many programmatic pieces throughout his career, sometimes describing the program explicitly, sometimes not. *Black and Tan Fantasy* combines a religious song with the blues, and in that sense crosses the boundary between sacred and secular. Because a "black and tan" was a nightclub that catered to both black and white patrons, the title might refer to crossing racial boundaries. Or, by combining colors and a classical genre designation in the title, Ellington may be signifying on Gershwin's *Rhapsody in Blue,* written three years earlier, a piece that crosses the boundary between jazz and classical music (see chapter 13). With nothing more to go on than a provocative title and evocative music, attentive listeners are free to discover their own meanings in Ellington's richly textured composition.

The sound of plunger-and-growl was an important part of the "jungle music" the band played to accompany the Cotton Club's exotic floor shows. In *Concerto for Cootie* (1940), written to show off the talents of Miley's replacement in the band, Cootie Williams, the growl is liberated from the jungle and used as one of many timbral qualities at Williams's command. *Ko-Ko*, a minor-mode blues number from the same year, opens with a menacing sound built on the foundation of Harry Carney's room-filling baritone sax. Another kind of Ellington sound is heard in a family of pieces

On the road with Ellington. Card players in this candid railroad-car shot include singer Ivie Anderson, drummer Sonny Greer, and Ellington himself.

	CD 2.13	Listening Guide 12.5	*Black and Tan Fantasy*
			DUKE ELLINGTON AND HIS ORCHESTRA

COMPOSER: Duke Ellington

DATE: 1927

PERFORMERS: Duke Ellington, piano; Bubber Miley, Louis Metcalf, trumpets; Joe "Tricky Sam" Nanton, trombone; Otto Hardwick, Rudy Jackson, and Harry Carney, saxophones; Fred Guy, banjo; Wellman Braud, bass; Sonny Greer, drums

GENRE: New York big-band jazz

METER: duple

FORM: 12-bar blues with a contrasting 16-bar strain

WHAT TO LISTEN FOR

- eerie, voice-like timbre of trumpet and trombone using plunger-and-growl technique
- alternation of minor and major modes
- contrasting 16-bar non-blues strain
- quotations of non-jazz tunes at beginning and end

TIMING	THEME	COMMENTS
0:00	chorus 1	Minor-mode paraphrase of "The Holy City"; melody in muted trumpet, harmony line in muted trombone, over chords on every beat of 4-beat bar.
0:25	B strain	16-bar major-mode melody featuring Hardwick's sweet alto sax, with thick vibrato and portamento, over banjo chords on every beat and bass notes on beats 1 and 3 of each bar. A break at bars 7–8 is filled with chromatic chords for the full band.
0:57	chorus 2	Choruses 2–6 are in major. Miley begins his solo with a long-held, tightly muted note for 4 bars, then uses plunger mute for wah-wah effects.
1:21	chorus 3	2-bar trumpet phrase is punctuated by cymbal (1:25); Miley continues to growl.
1:46	chorus 4	Ellington takes a piano solo in **stride** style (see chapter 14).
2:10	chorus 5	Nanton's trombone solo begins tightly muted, then opens; the third phrase contains an eerie whinny and speechlike closing gesture.
2:35	chorus 6	Miley returns for a solo filled with growling and stuttering repeated notes.
2:56	coda	4-bar return to the minor mode quoting Chopin's "Funeral March."

Listen & Reflect

1. What are some similarities and differences between *Black and Tan Fantasy* and the other early jazz pieces in this chapter, especially in terms of their structure and their musical effect?

slow in tempo, rich in harmony, delicately blended in timbre, and meditative in atmosphere, of which "Mood Indigo" (1930) is the most famous.

These are only a few of the more than 1,100 pieces that Ellington composed and copyrighted in the course of his long career. In about 20 percent of those works, he shared authorship with musicians who played with him, and he collaborated with others on the rest. Even when Ellington received the sole composer credit, collaboration lay at the heart of his music making. For as well as imagining fresh combinations of timbre and pitch, Ellington composed by working with his musicians so that their tonal personalities—their particular sound, way of playing, and inventiveness—actually helped to create the music. When trumpeter Fred Stone spent a few months with Ellington in 1970, he reflected that the band was the only outfit he knew "where you are not required to match the sound of the previous member. You must function as an individual."

The 1920s were a time of relative prosperity. One aspect of the decade's optimistic outlook was a thirst for novelty that encouraged musicians to experiment and innovate. That encouragement bore fruit in spheres of musical activity as different as ultramodernism and jazz. With the stock market crash of October 1929, however, musicians of all stripes faced new challenges: how to remain creative and productive while making a living under the straitened circumstances of the Great Depression.

QUESTIONS FOR DISCUSSION AND REVIEW

1. What are the characteristics of modernist music? Who were the leading ultramodernists, and what distinguishes their music from more traditional compositions?

2. Listen again to Sousa's *Stars and Stripes Forever* (LG 7.1). How does the final strain of that march resemble the collective improvisation heard in *Dippermouth Blues* (LG 12.2) and *Black Bottom Stomp* (LG 12.3)?

3. Compare Jelly Roll Morton, Louis Armstrong, and Duke Ellington in terms of two musical polarities: improvisation versus composition, and solo playing versus ensemble playing.

4. Several pieces discussed in this chapter rely on blues music, but the result is somewhat different in each case. How would you characterize these various treatments of the blues?

5. A musician active in a genre that many people associated with disreputable lifestyles and illegal activities, Bix Beiderbecke led a short life marked by substance abuse and early death. What later figures in popular culture does this profile bring to mind? What are some similarities and differences?

FURTHER READING

Broyles, Michael, and Denise Von Glahn. *Leo Ornstein: Modernist Dilemmas, Personal Choices.* Bloomington: Indiana University Press, 2007.

Crawford, Richard. *The American Musical Landscape.* Berkeley and Los Angeles: University of California Press, 1993. Chapter 6.

Floyd, Samuel A. *The Power of Black Music: Interpreting Its History from Africa to the United States.* New York: Oxford University Press, 1995.

Gushee, Lawrence. "The Nineteenth-Century Origins of Jazz." *Black Music Research Journal* 14 (1994): 1–24.

Kenney, William Howland. *Chicago Jazz: A Cultural History, 1904–1930.* New York: Oxford University Press, 1993.

Oja, Carol J. *Making Music Modern: New York in the 1920s.* New York: Oxford University Press, 2000.

Peretti, Burton William. *The Creation of Jazz: Music, Race, and Culture in Urban America.* Urbana: University of Illinois Press, 1992.

Teachout, Terry, *Pops: A Life of Louis Armstrong.* Boston: Houghton Mifflin Harcourt, 2009.

Tucker, Mark. *Ellington: The Early Years.* Urbana: University of Illinois Press, 1991.

FURTHER LISTENING

Morton, Jelly Roll. *The Complete Library of Congress Recordings by Alan Lomax.* 8 CDs. Rounder Records 11661-1888-2, 2005.

CONCERT MUSIC BETWEEN THE WORLD WARS

In the decades between the two world wars, classical music in the United States underwent profound transformations. Symphony orchestras saw the rise of the celebrity conductor, an elevation of the performer to a standing in the classical sphere once reserved for the composer. At the same time, some composers, both ultramodernists and conservatives, responded to the Great Depression with a new populist spirit that placed a higher value on connecting their music to the lives of ordinary Americans. And some Americans made music that confounds the familiar division into classical, popular, or folk categories.

This chapter begins with a consideration of how the Great Depression altered the relationships between composers, performers, and audiences in the classical sphere, with a focus on one ultramodernist, Ruth Crawford Seeger, as an exemplar of the classical musician's struggle to balance advanced musical techniques with political relevance. Next we take up George Gershwin, a composer whose music, perhaps more than that of any other American artist, resists the usual categories. To conclude, this chapter surveys concert works by African American composers with strong ties to jazz and folk traditions.

SYMPHONY ORCHESTRAS, CELEBRITY CONDUCTORS, AND THE NEW MEDIA

As described in chapter 8, in the latter 1800s Theodore Thomas and other conductors established the American symphony orchestra as an ensemble grounded in European classics. The years 1890 to 1930 saw the establishment of permanent orchestras in such cities as Dallas, Detroit, San Francisco, and Seattle. Symphony orchestras were supported by a combination of box-office receipts and private gifts. The role of wealthy citizens was crucial, yet orchestras survived because members of the general public also supported them. And as orchestras thrived, conductors emerged as star performers.

Like other performers, conductors were publicly defined as charismatic artists. Yet conductors also had to face tough intellectual and aesthetic issues. Were modernist composers the legitimate heirs of Beethoven and Wagner? Would programming their "revolutionary" new works be worth the risk of losing public support for symphony orchestras? Did American composers deserve a larger place on concert programs? Questions like these, debated by musicians and critics, were far from academic ones for conductors, who based their programming on the answers. The careers of three illustrious conductors who led major orchestras during the first half of the century—Arturo Toscanini, Serge Koussevitzky, and Leopold Stokowski—show that these questions could be answered in different ways.

Arturo Toscanini

The Italian-born Toscanini (1867–1957) first came to the United States in 1908 as principal conductor at the Metropolitan Opera, a post he held until 1915, when he returned to Italy. A worldwide traveler and performer, he directed both La Scala opera house in Milan and the New York Philharmonic until his disgust with the Fascist takeover of the Italian government caused him to leave Italy and make the United States his permanent home. In 1937 the National Broadcasting Company, which operated one of the country's largest radio networks, created an orchestra expressly for Toscanini, now seventy years old. And from then until he retired in 1954, he conducted the NBC Symphony in concerts, in radio and television broadcasts, and on recordings.

Toscanini's reputation outstripped that of any other classical musician of his day. He was sometimes proclaimed the "greatest conductor of all time," and the promotional forces behind the NBC Symphony helped spread that message. In performance, Toscanini was noted for his energy, the command he brought to the podium, his demands for perfection, and his musical memory. Adding to the legend were his abiding hatred for political fascism and his towering rages when rehearsals went badly. Toscanini conducted the music of virtually every major classical and romantic composer as well as a smattering of works by such modern masters as Richard Strauss, Claude Debussy, Maurice Ravel, and Serge Prokofiev.

Serge Koussevitzky (1874–1951) began conducting in his early thirties. He left his native Russia after World War I and settled in Paris, forming an orchestra that included in its programs new scores by French and Russian composers, including Prokofiev and Stravinsky. In 1924 he was named conductor of the Boston Symphony Orchestra, a post he held until 1949. Aaron Copland, whose music he championed, later wrote that Koussevitzky combined skill on the podium with "his passion for encouraging whatever he felt to be new and vital in contemporary music." That included works by living American composers such as Roy Harris, Walter Piston, Samuel Barber, and William Schuman, not to mention commissions of works by Stravinsky and other leading Europeans. In the summer of 1940 the Berkshire Music Center opened at Tanglewood, a Massachusetts estate, with Koussevitzky as director and Copland as assistant director. In later years, contemporary composers including Paul Hindemith and Olivier Messiaen taught there as guests. Koussevitzky has been praised for the emotional power he brought to performances, especially of Russian music and the music of French composers such as Debussy.

Serge Koussevitzky (1874–1951), conductor of the Boston Symphony Orchestra from 1924 to 1949, in action.

The London-born Leopold Stokowski (1882–1977) came to the United States in 1905 and in 1909 was named music director of the Cincinnati Symphony Orchestra. Three years later, Stokowski began a twenty-five-year stint as conductor of the Philadelphia Orchestra. If Toscanini was known as a servant of the composer's score, Stokowski was known for showmanship. Tall and striking, he made his Philadelphia string section famous for its singing sound. In 1940 he appeared on-screen in Walt Disney's *Fantasia* shaking hands with Mickey Mouse. A champion of twentieth-century music, Stokowski conducted over two thousand first performances—mostly of works by American composers. Among the premieres were works by Griffes, Ives, Varèse, Copland, and Cowell, as well as the American premieres of Stravinsky's *Rite of Spring*, Mahler's Eighth Symphony, Berg's *Wozzeck*, and Schoenberg's *Gurrelieder*. A musician of great vitality, he continued to conduct until shortly before his death at age ninety-five.

❦ Leopold Stokowski shakes hands with a deferential Mickey Mouse in Walt Disney's animated film *Fantasia* (1940).

These sketches portray three very different figures. Toscanini was a passionate champion of the classics. Koussevitzky was drawn to new musical experiences, and he cultivated friendships with composers. Stokowski came to hold an aggressively democratic philosophy, which he linked to technological progress. Believing that most adults had "difficulty absorbing ideas and impressions," Stokowski did much of his crusading for new music at concerts aimed at young listeners.

The contrasting careers of these three conductors show the symphony orchestra between the wars as an arena with established norms that was also open to fresh approaches. They also are a reminder that the most prominent names in the American classical sphere were performers, such as violinists Fritz Kreisler and Jascha Heifetz, pianists Arthur Rubinstein and Vladimir Horowitz, and singers Amelita Galli-Curci, Ezio Pinza, and Kirsten Flagstad. Most were foreign-born; all made their reputations presenting European masterworks to audiences in Europe and the United States. Live performance remained the public's chief point of contact with classical music, though after electrical recording replaced the acoustic process in 1925, listeners could experience something closer to concert-hall sound at home.

The new medium of radio broadcast a wide variety of music, most of it popular but certainly not all. In 1926 NBC presented Koussevitzky and the Boston Symphony in the first live network concert, attracting a million listeners. Five years later, NBC paid $100,000 for the right to broadcast grand opera live from the Metropolitan in New York; soon these were among the most popular broadcasts on daytime radio. In the 1800s

In their own words

Leopold Stokowski on Music's Universal Appeal (1943)

Music is a universal language—it speaks to everyone—is the birthright of all of us. Formerly music was chiefly confined to privileged classes in cultural centers, but today, through radio and records, music has come directly into our homes no matter how far we may live from cultural centers. This is as it should be, because music speaks to every man, woman, and child—high or low, rich or poor, happy or despairing—who is sensitive to its deep and powerful message.

arrangements, excerpts, and simplifications had made operas and symphonies into fare for the general public. By the 1930s, thanks to new kinds of musical transmission, such works were being widely listened to in their original versions—as composers' music.

COMPOSERS, THE GOVERNMENT, AND THE MARKETPLACE DURING THE GREAT DEPRESSION

In 1923, two years after the founding of the International Composers' Guild, a group of American composers, finding Varèse's idea of the time's "true spirit" too exclusive, left the guild and formed the League of Composers. Their stated goal, "to bring the entire range of modern tendencies before the public," indicated a broad platform that embraced more traditionalist styles as well as ultramodernism. Both groups shared an interest in internationalism with a third organization, the Pan American Association of Composers, founded in 1928, whose manifesto called for composers "to make still greater effort toward creating a distinctive music of the Western Hemisphere." The creation of these three organizations, all based in New York, signaled that composers in America were now banding together, regardless of nationality, in the name of modernism.

Also founded in 1928 was yet another organization devoted to modern music that cut across a broad stylistic spectrum: the Copland-Sessions Concerts, named after its two founding composers, Aaron Copland and Roger Sessions. The organization produced ten concerts between 1928 and 1932. Sessions, an American who was living in Europe during that period, wrote music that displayed his mastery of the new vocabulary of European modernism. His dissonant, chromatic idiom testified to his belief in continuous stylistic evolution as a "universal principle" that outweighed nationalism, which he considered a mere

🎵 Composer Aaron Copland (1900–1990) in the 1930s.

"accident of locality." Aaron Copland, on the other hand, became a leading proponent of a music that spoke to a wide audience in a musical language that sounded distinctly American. Copland's two-pronged search—for a musical style that had an American accent and that had broad communicative power—came to be a dominant theme of American composition in the 1930s.

The 1930s was also the era of the deepest economic depression in U.S. history. The country had emerged from World War I as a creditor nation—one that took in more money from overseas than it spent. And the economy boomed during the 1920s: the United States saw a 50 percent increase in manufacturing output, and by 1929 was producing major shares of the world's coal, petroleum, hydroelectric power, steel, and natural gas. In October 1929, however, the stock market collapsed. And when many banks failed during the next couple of years, production, consumption, and investment declined, unemployment rose sharply, and confidence in the economic future crumbled. Farming, heavy industry, and the blue-collar workforce in general bore the brunt of the hardship.

The Great Depression made a deep impact on musical life. Some larger institutions such as symphony orchestras and the Metropolitan Opera survived on patronage and a growing pool of listeners, reached through radio broadcasts and recordings. New-music activities, however, struggled to attract financial backing; of the four modernist organizations mentioned earlier, only the League of Composers lasted beyond the early 1930s. With less money in the hands of audience members (who could listen to radio broadcasts for free), work for performers evaporated. Meanwhile, the invention of sound film in 1927 removed the need for the players who had previously accompanied silent films in orchestra pits.

Between 1929 and 1934 about 70 percent of all musicians in the United States were unemployed, a trend the American Federation of Musicians, the national musicians' union, was powerless to buck. In 1935, as part of the massive relief effort of the Works Progress Administration (WPA), the national government took action, enacting Federal Project Number One as a way of supporting out-of-work writers, artists, musicians, and historians. Created with public money, Federal One exposed some parts of the country to original artworks, live theater, and symphony orchestras for the first time. One arm of the initiative was the Federal Music Project, which at its peak employed sixteen thousand musicians and funded twenty-eight symphony orchestras, as well as many dance bands and folk-music groups. More than a million music classes were given to 14 million students. As a silver lining to economic distress, the years of the Great Depression brought more abundant access to classical music than Americans had ever enjoyed before.

the Federal Music Project

Adversity also led composers to write in more conservative styles and focus on regional and national subjects. Virgil Thomson, a Kansas City native who studied at Harvard and then in Paris under the eminent pedagogue Nadia Boulanger (also the teacher of Copland), displayed his own brand of modernism in the *Sonata da chiesa,* a dissonant chamber work of 1926. But a decade later, scores for two government-sponsored films, *The Plow That Broke the Plains* (1936) and *The River* (1937), confirmed his credentials as a composer who could write American-sounding music.

Virgil Thomson

Thomson's most notorious work was the opera *Four Saints in Three Acts* (1934), to a libretto by American expatriate Gertrude Stein, whom he met in Paris. Set in sixteenth-century Spain, the opera celebrates the lives of St. Teresa and other religious figures while following no perceptible plot. Thomson declared his opera's style "simple, melodic, and harmonious . . . after twenty years of everybody's trying to make music just a little bit louder and more unmitigated and more complex than anybody else's." In one unforgettable moment, a soloist and male chorus alternate singing, to a gentle, folklike melody, the lyric "Pigeons on the grass, alas," words whose incongruity seems calculated to baffle and delight at the same time. Thomson's midwestern roots and Harvard education were mixed with strong Gallic sympathies; he particularly admired French composer Erik Satie, noted for satire and musical simplicity.

During the 1930s a sense of cultural unity grew among Americans. Economic hardship had something to do with this trend, and so did reduced immigration. President Franklin D. Roosevelt was elected in 1932 by a coalition that crossed ethnic and class lines, including blacks as well as whites and many blue-collar workers. Federal One programs found artistic worth where it had been overlooked in the past, in folk culture and local life. Murals in post offices featured American themes. Painters and photographers such as Thomas Hart Benton and Dorothea Lange took ordinary people in American settings as their subjects. While artistic works such as these portrayed the United States as an array of local settings, each with its own character, citizens were encouraged to think of such localities as examples of a larger American consciousness.

Roy Harris   Such was the background for the nationalism of Roy Harris—born in Oklahoma, raised in California, trained in Paris—who aspired to compose on behalf of all Americans. An essay he wrote in 1933 claims that "wonderful, young, sinewy, timorous, browbeaten, eager, gullible" American society was in the process of finding a common racial identity that would override local differences. In Harris's view, rhythm was the key that separated Americans from Europeans—especially the "asymmetrical balancing of rhythmic phrases." Moreover, he wrote, pointing to aspects of his own works, American music showed a fondness for modal harmony and a tendency to avoid definite cadences, features evident in his Third Symphony (1939), one of the most celebrated compositions of his generation.

Aaron Copland   Nowhere is the shift from the ultramodernism of the 1920s to the more accessible populism of the 1930s more apparent than in the music of Copland. After spending the early 1920s studying in France with Nadia Boulanger, Copland returned to the United States in 1924. In January 1925 he saw his first major premiere, the Symphony for Organ and Orchestra, by the New York Symphony Orchestra conducted by Walter Damrosch, with his teacher, Boulanger, at the organ. At the conclusion of the bristling, dissonant symphony, Damrosch turned to the audience and remarked, "If a young man in his twenties can compose a piece like that, by the time he is thirty he should be ready to commit murder." Throughout the 1920s Copland continued to write music that was uncompromisingly modernist, even when, in works like *Music for the Theatre* (1925) and the Piano Concerto (1926), he incorporated elements of jazz.

With the advent of the Great Depression Copland's socialist sympathies deepened, and his aesthetic goals shifted as well. At the invitation of the Mexican composer Carlos Chávez, Copland visited Mexico in 1932, and over the next five years he worked on an orchestral piece inspired by his visit to a Mexico City dance hall. Chávez conducted the premiere of *El salón Mexico* in 1937, and Koussevitzky and the Boston Symphony Orchestra played the U.S. premiere the following year. What happened next was a surprise, as Copland later recalled:

> One year after publication in 1938, Boosey [and Hawkes, Copland's British publisher] put together a list of orchestras that had played *El salón Mexico*: fourteen American orchestras ranging from the BSO to the Women's Symphony in Chicago; two radio orchestras; and five foreign ensembles. Never in my wildest dreams did I expect this kind of acceptance for the piece.

Yet Copland had tried from the start to make *El salón Mexico* audience-friendly. Using local melodies for themes, he kept them recognizable, and he stayed within the major-minor tonal system. Only the asymmetrical rhythms and occasional "wrong-note" harmonies sounded modern, and these gave the traditional elements new life and vigor.

In this and other compositions of the 1930s and later, Copland found a way to merge his modernist interests with music that appealed to conservative tastes. Four large-scale works of the period reveal a New World stamp by borrowing American folk and popular melodies. In two ballets about the West, *Billy the Kid* (1938) and *Rodeo* (1942), cowboy and western tunes appear. *A Lincoln Portrait* (1942) for orchestra, featuring a narrator who speaks words of Abraham Lincoln, quotes Stephen Foster's "Camptown Races" and a New England folk song, "Springfield Mountain." *Appalachian Spring* (1944), a ballet set in rural Pennsylvania during the nineteenth century, contains a set of variations on the Shaker tune "Simple Gifts."

Thomson, Harris, and Copland in these years all belonged in the camp of stylistic conservatism. Yet each had his own sound and approach, and each found ways to advance his musical language in the direction of modernism without alienating the general audience for music. The more conservative aspects of their music can be understood as a response to the political and cultural mood of Depression-era America. Similar political concerns, however, are also evident in one of the most important ultramodernist composers of the 1930s: Ruth Crawford Seeger.

> ## In their own words
>
> ### Aaron Copland on Composers and Audiences in the 1930s
>
> The old "special" public of the modern-music concerts [of the 1920s] had fallen away, and the conventional concert public continued apathetic or indifferent to anything but the established classics. It seemed to me that we composers were in danger of working in a vacuum. Moreover, an entirely new public for music had grown up around the radio and phonograph. It made no sense to ignore them and to continue writing as if they did not exist. I felt it was worth the effort to see if I couldn't say what I had to say in the simplest possible terms.

A MUSICAL REVOLUTIONARY: RUTH CRAWFORD SEEGER

In 1914 a thirteen-year-old girl in Jacksonville, Florida, wrote a poem in which she imagined her future as a novelist, a poet, and a musician not only performing on "a great opera stage" but also "singing to children my own." Though she would produce no novels or poems as an adult, young Ruth Crawford seemed somehow aware of her future as a composer, an author of books of musical arrangements, and a mother and stepmother to three important musicians. Her adolescent poem also anticipated the tug-of-war between professional and family demands that would shape her career.

While studying piano and composition at the American Conservatory of Music in Chicago during the 1920s, Crawford heard lectures and concerts by visiting musicians Henry Cowell and Dane Rudhyar (see chapter 12), and she began writing piano pieces inspired by Rudhyar's mystical liberation of dissonance. When some of her pieces were included on League of Composers and Copland-Sessions programs, Crawford was drawn into the circle of New York ultramodernists. In 1929 she moved to New York to study with Charles Seeger, and in 1930–31 she lived in Berlin and Paris, where she met such leading European modernists as Alban Berg and Béla Bartók. By the time she married

Seeger in 1932, shortly after her return from Europe, Ruth Crawford had already written some of the most remarkable music composed by any American.

CHARLES SEEGER'S "DISSONANT COUNTERPOINT"

Although Charles Seeger wrote no significant compositions, his ideas provided an intellectual framework that aided the artistic achievements of other musicians, especially Henry Cowell, Carl Ruggles, and Ruth Crawford Seeger. The core of his compositional theory he termed **dissonant counterpoint**. Whereas traditional counterpoint was concerned with combining multiple melodic lines in such a way as to achieve maximum euphony, Seeger inverted those rules to assure maximum dissonance—what Cowell called "shifting the center of gravity from consonance to dissonance." Moreover, Seeger extended the idea of dissonant counterpoint to other elements besides pitch. If pitches can be juxtaposed in dissonant relationships, he asked, is it possible to do the same with rhythms, dynamics, and timbres? The result would be music in which the various melodic lines would interact in complete independence from one another.

The danger, of course, is that such "dissonated" music (to use Seeger's term) would simply fall apart, with each instrument or voice going off in its own direction. But in Crawford's mature works, the highly dissonated musical lines paradoxically weave together to form a strong fabric with an intricate pattern. The analogy is Crawford's own: she compared one of her compositions to a Persian rug.

String Quartet 1931

That composition, *String Quartet 1931,* begun during her stay in Europe and completed shortly before her marriage to Seeger, is Crawford's masterpiece. In the third movement, the four instruments—two violins, viola, and cello—play sustained notes with unsynchronized rising and falling dynamics, drawing the listener's ear from one instrument to another, creating a melody whose successive notes are played by different instruments. The result is what Arnold Schoenberg called *Klangfarbenmelodie* (tone color melody): a melody that is a succession of not only pitches but also timbres. Moreover, the movement extends the traditional notion of a **canon**, in which a melody is stated in all the voices or instruments one after the other (as in a round such as "Frère Jacques"). Here, it is not the pitches of the melody that are stated in canon but the dynamics, the rising and falling swells of sound.

Because the technical aspects of her later music are so complex, verbal descriptions tend to make Crawford's mature compositions sound like purely intellectual exercises. Yet she never lost the spiritual intensity of her earlier, Rudhyar-inspired pieces. Writing to her student Vivian Fine in 1931, Crawford asserted, "Music must flow. It must be a thread unwinding, a thread from no one knows just where. It must not be a problem in mathematics, writing music."

A PEOPLE'S MUSICIAN

Like Copland and many other musicians in the 1930s, Charles and Ruth Crawford Seeger were drawn to leftist political causes, at least in part as a response to the economic depression. As the folk singer Pete Seeger, a son of Charles's from his first marriage, later recalled, "I came home from school and I found Father and Ruth up to their ears in radical politics." Active in the Workers Music League, which was affiliated with the American Communist Party, Charles described himself and Ruth as "very loyal fringe members of the Communist front."

The political climate of the Great Depression gave urgency to radical ideals of collective action and militancy. Now, in retrospect, the advocacy groups for modernist music in the 1920s seemed effete and self-regarding. What was the point of writing music simply for oneself and a tiny group of like-minded devotees? Instead the question became, how can modernism be put into the service of the revolutionary struggle?

For Ruth Crawford Seeger, one attempt to answer that question resulted in a pair of songs for voice and piano she called *Two Ricercari,* borrowing an antique term for music that relies on intricate counterpoint—dissonant counterpoint, in her case. Written in 1932, both songs are settings of poems by H. T. Tsiang, a Chinese dissident. The first, "Sacco, Vanzetti," refers to two Italian American anarchists who were executed for murder in 1927 after a notoriously politicized trial; Ben Shahn completed his famous painting *The Passion of Sacco and Vanzetti* in the same year that Crawford wrote her song. The second, "Chinaman, Laundryman" (LG 13.1), sets a poem that first appeared in the communist newspaper the *Daily Worker* in 1928 and was reprinted the next year in Tsiang's *Poems of the Chinese Revolution.*

Both poems are examples of a period genre called "worker's recitation," filled with exclamations and exhortations directed both to the listener and to characters within the poem's narrative. Tsiang's poems are somewhat heavy-handed, but Crawford's music transcends their limitations.

"Chinaman, Laundryman" is in the voice of an immigrant Chinese laundry worker who is exploited by his capitalist boss. Some of its themes—longing for a relative back home, recognition that working conditions may be equally exploitative here as in the home country—resonate with debates that recur through the long history of immigrant labor in the United States. While drawing on the reality that many Chinese Americans in those years worked in the laundry trade, the poem counters the period's stereotypic portrayal of Chinese men as feminized—suited only for "women's work"—and thus inferior to masculine white males. At the same time, a poem in which an oppressed worker raises not hammer and sickle but wash brush and iron could have had a special appeal for Crawford, one of the few women striving to create modernist music.

Crawford's setting of "Chinaman, Laundryman" explores a musical terrain opened up by the concept of dissonant counterpoint. It comprises two melodic lines, one sung by the voice and the other played in octaves by the piano. The vocal line is in duple meter, the piano in a faster triple meter; the two meters and

☙ Ben Shahn, *The Passion of Sacco and Vanzetti* (1932). Whitney Museum of American Art, New York.

| CD 2.14 | Listening Guide 13.1 | "Chinaman, Laundryman" RUTH CRAWFORD SEEGER |

DATE: 1932

PERFORMERS: Nan Hughes, mezzo-soprano; Joel Sachs, piano

GENRE: ultramodernist song

METER: changing

FORM: through-composed

WHAT TO LISTEN FOR

- antagonistic, nonsupportive role of piano
- use of *Sprechstimme*
- vocal contrast between worker's words and bosses' words
- overtly political text

TIMING	TEXT	COMMENTS
0:00	"Chinaman!" "Laundryman!"	Boss's voice signified by rising melodic contour and high vocal register, here sung unaccompanied.
0:07	Don't call me "man!" I am worse than a slave. Wash!— Wash!— Why can I wash away the dirt of others' clothes but not the hatred of my heart? My skin is yellow,— Does my yellow skin color the clothes? Why do you pay me less for the same work? Clever boss! You know how to scatter the seeds of hatred among your ignorant slaves. Iron!— Iron!— Why can I smooth away the wrinkle of others' dresses but not the miseries of my heart? Why should I come to America to wash clothes? Do you think Chinamen in China wear no dresses? I came to America three days after my marriage. When can I see her again? Only the almighty dollar knows! Dry!— Dry!— Why do clothes dry, but not my tears? I work twelve hours a day, he pays fifteen dollars a week.	Piano enters with the worker's words, sung to descending phrases in a lower register. Nine-pitch row is rotated at first within a narrow range, which gradually opens outward and downward. Brittle rhythms are mechanical yet unpredictable.

	CD 2.14	Listening Guide 13.1	"Chinaman, Laundryman" RUTH CRAWFORD SEEGER

TIMING	TEXT	COMMENTS
1:04	My boss says: "Chinaman, go back to China, if you don't feel satisfied! There, unlimited hours of toil: two silver dollars a week, if you can find a job."	Boss's voice: rising phrases in high register.
1:24	Thank you, boss,—for you remind me. I know bosses are robbers ev'rywhere!	Worker's voice, descending phrases in a lower register.
1:33	Chinese boss says: "You Chinaman, me Chinaman, come work for me,— work for your fellow countryman! By the way, you 'Wong,' me 'Wong,' do we not belong to same family? Ha! Ha! We are cousins! O yes! You 'Hai Shan,' me 'Hai Shan,' do we not come from same district? O come work for me;—I will treat you better!"	Chinese boss's music shares the features of American boss: high register and ascending melodic contours.
2:03	Get away from here! What difference when you come to exploit me?	Worker's voice.
2:08	Chinaman! Laundryman!	Dramatic pause, then a return to the opening music and the voice of the American boss.
2:18	Don't call me "Chinaman!" Yes, I am a "Laundryman!" The working man! Don't call me "Chinaman!" I am the worldman!	With the worker's reply, the piano resumes its machinelike relentlessness.
2:30	"Chinaman!" "Laundryman!"	The opening music again, at an even higher pitch.
2:40	All you working men! Here is the brush made of study. Here is the soap made of action. Let us all wash with the brush! Let us all press with the iron! Wash! Brush! Dry! Iron!	When the worker exhorts workingmen, he takes on a characteristic of the boss: the rising melodic contours.
3:02	Then we shall have a clean world!	Piano breaks off; the worker speaks the closing words unaccompanied, a privilege previously reserved for the boss.

NOTE Crawford's song alters several lines in Tsiang's poem. The text appears here as she set it.

(continued)

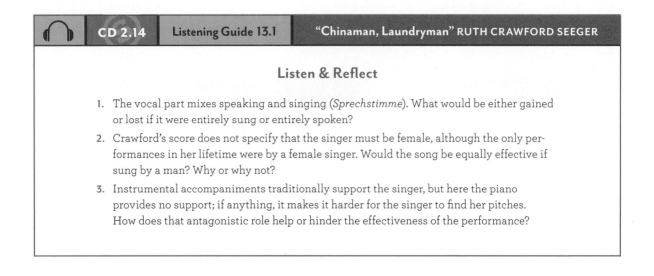

CD 2.14   **Listening Guide 13.1**   **"Chinaman, Laundryman"** RUTH CRAWFORD SEEGER

Listen & Reflect

1. The vocal part mixes speaking and singing (*Sprechstimme*). What would be either gained or lost if it were entirely sung or entirely spoken?

2. Crawford's score does not specify that the singer must be female, although the only performances in her lifetime were by a female singer. Would the song be equally effective if sung by a man? Why or why not?

3. Instrumental accompaniments traditionally support the singer, but here the piano provides no support; if anything, it makes it harder for the singer to find her pitches. How does that antagonistic role help or hinder the effectiveness of the performance?

tempos converge on the downbeat of each bar, then diverge. The vocal notation indicates some notes to be sung on precise pitches and other notes to be spoken following a less precise contour; the mixture of singing and speaking creates an expressionistic effect called **Sprechstimme**, which Arnold Schoenberg had used powerfully in his 1912 work *Pierrot lunaire,* a favorite of the American ultramodernists.

serialism

The piano part displays Crawford's original adaptation of Schoenberg's most famous innovation: **serialism**. The serialism of Schoenberg meant arranging all twelve notes available within the octave into a fixed pattern or row, which could then be manipulated by quasi-mathematical means to generate a stream of constantly changing pitches that, though thoroughly atonal, would be unified by their derivation from the original row. In "Chinaman, Laundryman," Crawford modifies Schoenberg's serialism by creating a nine-pitch row. Each bar of the piano part contains either nine notes or silence. The first bar (after three bars of silence) states the original row; the second bar states the row beginning with the second note and ending with the first; the third bar states the row beginning with the third note and ending with the first two; and so on. After working through all the rotations, the whole process repeats, with the original row now transposed down a half step. Moreover, the nine notes of each bar fall into one of three rhythmic patterns, which also are rotated according to a quasi-mathematical scheme.

While in traditional accompanied song, a high-register vocal melody is often supported by accompanying chords in the lower and middle registers, here the relationship is the opposite, with the piano's melody generally higher than the voice, dipping down into the vocal register only a few times in the song. The resulting "dissonated" texture suggests a programmatic intent: the singer's free-flowing declamation may represent the individual worker, who struggles against the implacable operation of the capitalist "machine," represented by the brittle, rigidly structured music of the piano. Put to a political purpose, this highly intellectual yet powerfully emotional song proves that for Crawford, writing music was no mere "problem in mathematics."

The composition in 1932 of "Chinaman, Laundryman" marked the end of Crawford's most productive period as a composer. She would compose only sporadically over the remaining two decades of her life. It is hard not to infer a connection between the redirection of her energies away from composing and her marriage to Seeger, followed by the births of their four children. Crawford later referred to the period of her life beginning in 1933 as her time of "composing babies."

Equally significant, perhaps, was the philosophical shift taking place among politically radical modernist musicians. Shortly after his marriage to Crawford, Charles Seeger began to express his disillusionment with the aims of modernism in his columns for the *Daily Worker*. "Dissonant writers" like his wife, he wrote in 1933, were a "defeated faction" in their battle with the traditionalists. At the same time, he and Henry Cowell helped form the Composers' Collective, a group that aimed to create a "proletarian music" whose centerpiece would be "mass songs," simple songs with propagandistic lyrics, traditional enough to be suitable for collective singing but lightly spiced with hints of modernism—an updating of the labor songs described in chapter 9. Although a number of composers tried their hands at mass songs—in 1934 Aaron Copland composed "Into the Streets May First"—proletarian music never caught on with a larger audience, leftist or otherwise.

the Composers' Collective

By the mid-1930s Seeger had decided that the music best able to serve the masses was not modernist, indeed was not classical music in any sense. He redirected his efforts toward the study of folk music, and Ruth Crawford Seeger joined him in that study. Although that change removed her from the historical narrative of classical music in the United States, at the same time she and her family became key figures in a different narrative: that of the transformation of folk music in the mid-twentieth century, a story taken up in the chapter 14.

GEORGE GERSHWIN

George Gershwin was born in Brooklyn in 1898 to Jewish parents who had emigrated from Russia. His boyhood was marked by an interest in athletics and an indifference to school. Music was seldom heard in the Gershwin household until around 1910, when the family bought its first piano so that older brother Ira could learn to play it. But George soon took over the instrument. He progressed quickly and about 1912 began lessons with a teacher who recognized his talent and introduced him to the world of classical music. In 1914, however, Gershwin left high school and went to work for a Tin Pan Alley publishing firm. Hired as a **song plugger**—a pianist who demonstrated new songs for potential performers in vaudeville and musical comedy—he spent endless hours at the keyboard, which improved his playing. Plugging songs also gave the young musician an excellent education in songwriting, and before long the teenager was trying his hand at songs of his own.

song plugger

GERSHWIN'S POPULAR SONGS

In 1917 Gershwin found work as a rehearsal pianist on Broadway, where his flair for songwriting was noticed. The following year, a prestigious publisher offered him a weekly salary for the right to publish songs he might compose in the future. When Al Jolson interpolated Gershwin's "Swanee" into the musical *Sinbad* (see chapter 10), the twenty-one-year-old Gershwin scored his first hit.

George Gershwin (1898–1937), pianist, songwriter, and composer; portrait by Arthur Kaufmann, 1936.

Gershwin's songwriting career followed a rising trajectory. At first he was able to place interpolated songs into musical comedies and revues. Their popularity led to opportunities to write complete scores for full-length musicals; a major success was 1924's *Lady Be Good!* (see chapter 11), and several others followed throughout the next decade. And as it did for other songwriters such as Irving Berlin and Jerome Kern, success on Broadway led eventually to offers from Hollywood, where Gershwin spent most of the last year of his life composing songs for films, most notably *Shall We Dance,* a 1937 dance musical starring Fred Astaire and Ginger Rogers.

Of the hundreds of songs Gershwin wrote throughout his career for Tin Pan Alley, Broadway, and Hollywood, several stand out as masterpieces of the classic American popular song. Graceful, sometimes blues-tinged melodies fill such romantic ballads as "The Man I Love," "Someone to Watch over Me," and "Embraceable You." Clever, energetic syncopations mark up-tempo numbers like "Fascinating Rhythm" and "I Got Rhythm." Between those two extremes lies a Gershwin specialty, the relaxed, jazz-tinged song in medium tempo, such as "Nice Work If You Can Get It" and "They Can't Take That Away from Me," songs perfectly suited to the understated singing of Fred Astaire, for whom they were written. The quantity and quality of these hits place Gershwin firmly in the pantheon of classic American songwriters, along with Berlin, Kern, Cole Porter, Richard Rodgers, Harold Arlen, and Hoagy Carmichael.

RHAPSODY IN BLUE

In November 1923 the Canadian mezzo-soprano Eva Gauthier presented in New York's Aeolian Hall a "Recital of Ancient and Modern Music for Voice" that mixed classical and popular music. Her modern selections included songs by Bartók and Schoenberg, plus a set of six songs billed as jazz, including Berlin's "Alexander's Ragtime Band" and two numbers by Gershwin, who accompanied her in that part of the program. The American songs delighted Gauthier's audience, and so did Gershwin's performance in his first concert-hall appearance. Playing from sheet music, the young pianist took off from what was written on the page in a way that sounded spontaneous. Gershwin's freewheeling approach to performance—he played in the style of an improvisation, though many details were most likely planned—owed much to jazz, and it brought to the recital a sense of fun not often heard in the concert hall.

LG 13.2

Three months later, on February 12, 1924, again in Aeolian Hall, Gershwin played the featured piano part in the premiere of his *Rhapsody in Blue* (LG 13.2), a "jazz concerto" commissioned for the occasion by Paul Whiteman, the leader of an immensely popular dance orchestra. Billing his concert "An Experiment in Modern Music," Whiteman courted and gained the attention of New York's music critics. With discussions of jazz music very much in the air, it is no surprise that the unveiling of a new jazz-flavored concert piece by an up-and-coming young songwriter attracted public notice. What is surprising, however, is that Gershwin's work lived up to the ballyhoo of preconcert publicity. Bringing together three separate strands of musical development—the rise of blues as a popular song form, the spread of jazz as an instrumental music, and the push

| CD 2.15 | Listening Guide 13.2 | *Rhapsody in Blue* GEORGE GERSHWIN |

DATE: composed and recorded in 1924

PERFORMERS: George Gershwin, piano; Paul Whiteman Orchestra; Paul Whiteman, conductor. Instrumentation: solo piano; three reeds (doubling saxophones and clarinets of all sizes, oboe, and heckelphone); two trumpets (doubling flugelhorn); two French horns; two trombones (one doubling euphonium); tuba; string bass; two pianos (one doubling celesta); banjo; drums (doubling timpani); eight violins (one doubling accordion)

GENRE: concert music

METER: changing

FORM: through-composed in four large, continuous sections

WHAT TO LISTEN FOR

- mixture of jazz, blues, popular song, and classical elements
- brilliant solo writing for piano
- colorful orchestration by Ferde Grofé
- use of short motives to unify the various themes

TIMING	SECTION	THEME	COMMENTS
0:00	introduction	Ritornello	Clarinet low trill, rising with a smear to the high note that begins an incomplete statement of Ritornello theme. (A **ritornello** is a recurring section in a classical composition.) The second bar of the theme (0:10) uses the ragtime-derived rhythmic motive.
0:31		Stride	French horns introduce Stride theme, whose repeated notes emphasize blue notes (lowered third and seventh scale degrees).
0:41		Ritornello	Fragment of Ritornello theme in muted trumpet, interrupted by solo piano.
0:48		Tag	Solo piano enters in a dreamy mood with the Tag motive, quickly interrupted by full band's loud statement of the Ritornello theme. Piano resumes, in a more playful mood, and is joined by solo violin and a few other instruments.
1:18			A cadenza builds anticipation for the first complete statement of the Ritornello theme.
1:40		Ritornello	Ritornello theme appears in complete *aaba* song form: two statements of the *a* theme by the solo piano (answered by bass clarinet playing the Tag), a bridge (2:01), and a return of the *a* theme that stops one chord short of complete closure.

(continued)

CD 2.15	Listening Guide 13.2			Rhapsody in Blue GEORGE GERSHWIN

TIMING	SECTION	THEME		COMMENTS
2:18				Another cadenza, then complete Ritornello theme by the full band (2:49).
3:15	scherzo	Train		A lighthearted theme in *aaba* form, played over a chugging banjo beat. The *a* sections feature muted trumpet with growls, accompanied by a syncopated three-note saxophone motive. The bridge (3:26) features slap-tongue tenor sax and clarinet.
3:35				Transition: rising piano runs alternate with the clarinet's anticipation of the Stride theme.
3:51		Stride		Full *aaba* form. At the end of the first two *a* sections, trombones hint at the Ritornello theme.
4:11				Transition: Three falling statements of bluesy melody in soprano sax, muted trumpet, and muted trombone with wah-wah effect.
4:25				Cymbal crash, marking the end of the record's first side, coincides with a cut of 32 bars, eliminating one of the *Rhapsody*'s themes.
4:26		Stride		Side 2 begins with piano cadenza, then dreamy solo statement of Stride theme (4:44) stops one bar short of completion.
5:17				Cut of 102 bars of the scherzo, skipping ahead to make a transition that slows down the syncopated rhythmic motive in preparation for the Love theme.
5:25	slow movement	Love	*a*	Large-scale *aaba* form. Each *a* section is a statement of the Love theme, which begins with the rhythmic motive in augmentation. The following long notes are accompanied by a three-note motive in the French horns resembling the one that accompanied the Train theme.
6:00				Ends inconclusively, with a violin solo over shifting harmonies.
6:10		Love	*a*	Like first *a*, but with fuller scoring.
6:43				Ends inconclusively, with pizzicato strings and celesta over throbbing, syncopated chords in the piano.
6:51			*b*	Piano solo: slowly rising scale over a development of the three-note accompaniment motive.
7:05		Love	*a*	Piano solo continues in a rhapsodic, romantic texture.

| CD 2.15 | Listening Guide 13.2 | | *Rhapsody in Blue* GEORGE GERSHWIN |

TIMING	SECTION	THEME	COMMENTS
7:28			Ends inconclusively, as piano states the rhythmic motive in a falling sequence over an agitated, syncopated accompaniment.
7:41			Transition: Piano cadenza (heavily cut for the recording) leads directly into the final section.
7:53	finale	Love	Trombones, then all the brass, play theme, transformed into an energetic call to action. The music builds in intensity, climaxing in a dissonant scream.
8:21		Tag	The piano's opening music (from 0:48) returns, now very agitated.
8:41		Stride	Piano's final solo moment, an emphatic return of the Stride theme.
8:48		Ritornello	A grandiose return of the very opening, played by the full band at top volume. As the final chord grows in volume, the piano concludes with the bluesy Tag.

NOTE This recording cuts the work in order to fit on two sides of a twelve-inch 78-rpm record. In this listening guide, the names of sections and themes do not come from the composer but are borrowed from the analysis in David Schiff, *Gershwin: Rhapsody in Blue* (1997).

Listen & Reflect

1. In what ways does this performance of *Rhapsody in Blue* resemble jazz records from the 1920s, such as Ellington's *Black and Tan Fantasy* (see LG 12.5)? In what ways does it resemble classical music?

2. Listen to any recording of the symphonic version of *Rhapsody in Blue* (i.e., with Grofé's later orchestration). How do changes in the orchestration affect the piece's overall impression? Compare the performance style of Gershwin and Whiteman's band to the performers on the more recent recording. What differences can you hear?

for modernism in the classical sphere—*Rhapsody in Blue* has come to be reckoned both an American classic and a piece emblematic of its time.

Working hurriedly—accounts vary, but at the most Gershwin had only a couple of months from commission to performance—the composer envisioned a single-movement piece that would feature his own piano playing. The title, suggested by his brother and songwriting partner, Ira, is a playful reference not only to the blues but also to the painter James Whistler, who gave his canvases musical titles like *Symphony in White*. Following standard practice on Broadway, but certainly not in the classical sphere, Gershwin wrote out the orchestra's music for two pianos, then passed it on to Whiteman's leading staff arranger, Ferde

title

Grofé, who orchestrated the piece for the idiosyncratic Whiteman ensemble, some of whose members played as many as four or five instruments.

structure   The name **rhapsody** is generally used by composers to indicate a one-movement piece with no set form, but expressive and spontaneous in effect. Some recent commentators have pointed out that *Rhapsody in Blue* contains four linked sections that resemble a symphony's fast opening movement, playful scherzo, melodious slow movement, and energetic finale; in this manner it is reminiscent of the First Piano Concerto and other pieces by Franz Liszt, whose music Gershwin had studied in his youth.

motives   Two thematic elements, or **motives**, recur in all of the *Rhapsody*'s themes, either singly or together. One motive is a seven-note syncopated rhythm (short-short-short-*long*-short-short-short) derived from ragtime. The other is a four-note melodic fragment that emphasizes a blue note, the lowered seventh degree of the major scale. In Gershwin's time this fragment was already familiar as a song tag akin to the response portion of a call-and-response interchange. In short, ragtime and blues—the African American building blocks of jazz—permeate *Rhapsody in Blue*.

style   Throughout Gershwin's *Rhapsody*, the musical material plays upon the widely accepted boundaries separating the classical, popular, and traditional spheres. From the opening clarinet smear through the blues-tinged themes to the syncopation that enlivens tunes and transitions, the work claims African American music as part of its pedigree. Gershwin's experience as a songwriter also leaves its mark on the work's harmony and melody, with phrases and periods cast in the four-, eight-, and sixteen-bar units of popular song. Finally, the work's title and length, as well as its sections of near-symphonic development and virtuoso piano writing in the vein of Chopin and Liszt, show the influence of the European piano concerto. They also reflect the concertgoing that began early in Gershwin's teenage years, his classical training on piano, and the private study of harmony and later classical composition through much of his working life. Gershwin's references are not borrowed tune quotations but evocations of different musical styles; this is the work of a composer who understood and believed in the artistic worth of all three spheres of American music.

a landmark premiere   Whiteman's "Experiment in Modern Music" was a concert with a purpose: to illustrate that the group's jazz stylings were not just good dance music but American music worth listening to sitting down, in a concert hall. That was what the brochures handed out at the concert asserted, and that was what New York's music critics were there to weigh in on. As the capstone of Whiteman's experiment, the premiere of *Rhapsody in Blue* was a landmark event in American music history. The music critics validated that impression, first by showing up at a concert they would probably have skipped had Whiteman not held public rehearsals to get them involved, and then by writing seriously about the work—some praising it warmly (the New York *Sun*'s W. J. Henderson called it America's answer to Stravinsky in the "modern music" vein), and others roundly criticizing it. Whiteman played the piece in public no fewer than eighty times in 1924 and frequently thereafter. A phonograph record, made in April 1924 with Whiteman's orchestra and Gershwin himself, saw a steady growth in sales until by 1928 or so it was realizing substantial "mechanical royalties." By the end of the 1920s there was no more famous piece of music in the United States than the *Rhapsody,* and it has never really gone out of fashion. Indeed, in its later reorchestration, again by Grofé, for a more-or-less standard symphonic ensemble, *Rhapsody in Blue* entered the orchestral repertory and became the twentieth century's most performed piece of American concert music. A hybrid of classical music, blues, and jazz, *Rhapsody in Blue* offers performers more than one way to emphasize its divergent elements.

PORGY AND BESS

Beginning with *Rhapsody in Blue* in 1924, Gershwin pursued a dual career as a popular songwriter and a composer of concert works. Entrusting the job of orchestration to an assistant was standard procedure in the hurried schedules of Broadway and Hollywood, and Gershwin continued to do so for his musical comedies and his movie music. But he did his own orchestration for all of his concert works after the *Rhapsody*: the Concerto in F for piano and orchestra (1925), the **tone poem** *An American in Paris* (1928, partly composed during Gershwin's visit to that city), and the *Cuban Overture* (1932), among others.

Orchestration by the composer is only one of the features that distinguishes *Porgy and Bess* (1935) from Gershwin's stage musicals. Gershwin called *Porgy and Bess* a "folk opera"; the work's precise nature was contested from the start. Gershwin's Broadway background led some to doubt whether he was up to a full-fledged operatic challenge. The score called for opera singers, but the show played nightly in a Broadway theater. Knowledge that massive cuts took place before the New York premiere has also fed the view that the work is more a succession of musical numbers than an operatic whole, as has the popularity of some individual numbers. Moreover, commercial success for *Porgy and Bess* first came after Gershwin's death—in 1937, at age thirty-eight—when, stripped of its recitative, it was played as a Broadway musical: a drama of separate musical numbers linked with spoken dialogue. Not until 1976 did the complete opera reach the stage, in a landmark production by the Houston Grand Opera, which the previous year had presented the first full production of Scott Joplin's *Treemonisha* (see chapter 10).

Based on a libretto by Dubose Heyward, from his novella *Porgy* (1925), *Porgy and Bess* features music of remarkable variety. The memorable melodies of the best-known numbers have made them enduringly popular. These songs include "Summertime," a lullaby that invokes the spirituals of slavery times; "My Man's Gone Now," sung by the widow of a man killed in an onstage brawl; Porgy's banjo song "I Got Plenty o' Nuttin'," in *aaba* form (as is "My Man's Gone Now"); and the love duet "Bess, You Is My Woman Now." The principals of the opera are also members of a larger community, virtually always onstage, whose character Gershwin portrays in communal songs. Instead of borrowing traditional spirituals, Gershwin wrote new ones, ranging from songful exaltation ("Leavin' for the Promise' Lan'") and consolation ("Clara, Clara") to stark desolation ("Gone, Gone, Gone") and even chanted prayer ("Oh, Doctor Jesus"), inspired by Gershwin's visits to black churches in South Carolina while he was composing the work. There is also a picnic episode where the amoral drug peddler Sportin' Life gets the community, softened up by a day of carousing, to join him in a mockery of biblical teaching, sung in call-and-response dialogue full of blue notes ("It Ain't Necessarily So").

Gershwin's use of African American folk songs as a model for the music of *Porgy and Bess* was widely acknowledged from the start. Not until more recently,

a "folk opera"

best-known numbers

influences

since the uncut opera's first performance in 1976, have opera lovers come to appreciate its reliance on other sources as well. Gershwin acknowledged the influence of Bizet's *Carmen* and Wagner's *Die Meistersinger,* to which recent scholarship has added *Wozzeck,* an expressionistic opera by the Viennese modernist composer Alban Berg. Gershwin met Berg during his 1928 European visit, studied his atonal music closely, and attended *Wozzeck*'s introduction to the United States in a 1931 concert performance conducted by Leopold Stokowski in Philadelphia. More than any other single work, perhaps, *Porgy and Bess* demonstrates Gershwin's ability to forge a distinctive personal style from a huge range of diverse influences.

Gershwin achieved celebrity in his lifetime as a songwriter, a dazzling pianist, and a composer of concert music and opera. His friend and fellow songwriter Kay Swift once said that "he heard his music simultaneously through his and yours and anyone else's ears." That empathy between composer and audience helps to explain not only the music's popularity but also its remarkable afterlife, judging by the number of recordings, arrangements, and concert performances of Gershwin's music from his lifetime to the present. Through the history of his music's performances and recordings, Gershwin emerges as one of the most significant composers of the twentieth century.

BLACK CONCERT MUSIC AND THE HARLEM RENAISSANCE

Our study of African American music so far has emphasized the folk and popular spheres. But in the years between World War I and World War II, black musicians also worked to establish a beachhead in the concert hall. The cultural movement known as the Harlem Renaissance—under way by around 1920 and led by black intellectuals including philosopher Alain Locke, social scientist W. E. B. DuBois, and poet and author James Weldon Johnson—focused primarily on the arts. Cultural achievement, the leaders hoped, would crack the seemingly impregnable wall of racism, for once black writers, painters, and composers showed their mastery of classical techniques, whites would be forced to give up their stereotype of black inferiority. The Harlem Renaissance's aesthetic ideal prescribed work that reflected the artists' black heritage but in culturally prestigious (i.e., European-derived) forms. That call to action resulted in the creation of an impressive body of music rooted in both European classical and African American folk traditions.

WILLIAM GRANT STILL

The generation's most versatile black composer was William Grant Still. Born in 1895 in Mississippi, Still grew up in Little Rock, Arkansas. He attended Wilberforce College and the Oberlin Conservatory in Ohio. Later formal study included lessons with George Chadwick and Edgard Varèse. Still earned his living in popular music, however, beginning in 1914 as a dance orchestra performer. In 1916 he worked as an arranger for W. C. Handy's music-publishing company in Memphis, producing the first band version of *St. Louis Blues.* In 1919 Still accompanied Handy to New York, where he continued in the publishing business and played in Handy's bands. He joined the Black Swan Phonograph Company in 1921 as manager and arranger, and from 1921 to 1923 he played oboe in the pit orchestra of Eubie Blake and Noble

Sissle's *Shuffle Along,* the decade's most successful black Broadway show. An accomplished professional arranger and composer, Still also continued to compose classical works, including ballets, operas, symphonies, chamber music, and vocal pieces. The premiere of his *Afro-American Symphony* in 1931 by the Rochester Philharmonic Orchestra with Howard Hanson conducting marked the first time in history that a major orchestra performed a symphonic work by an African American composer.

Afro-American Symphony

Somewhat like *Rhapsody in Blue,* the *Afro-American Symphony* uses materials derived from African American music to build a structure patterned after European models. Here the model is the traditional four-movement symphony, and each of Still's four movements corresponds to the classical norm. The first movement (LG 13.3) follows the time-honored sonata form established by Haydn and Mozart in the eighteenth century: an exposition in which two themes establish contrasting key areas, a development that takes the themes through sometimes agitated transformations, and a recapitulation in which the themes return in more recognizable form and in the home key. (Like some nineteenth-century composers, Still reverses the order of the themes in his recapitulation.)

LG 13.3

Unlike any European symphony, however—and unlike *Rhapsody in Blue,* for that matter—the *Afro-American Symphony* begins with a theme in the twelve-bar structure of a blues chorus. Still's second theme is an original melody in the style of a Negro spiritual—not the first time such a theme appears in a symphony, since Dvořák's *New World* Symphony does the same, most famously in the slow movement's English horn solo. The very opening of Still's symphony, for unaccompanied English horn, might be interpreted as an acknowledgment of his debt to Dvořák. Indeed, the *Afro-American Symphony* seems to fulfill Dvořák's prophecy of an American concert music rooted in African American folk idioms.

Still's use of those folk idioms extend to orchestration and timbre. He scored his work for a standard symphonic ensemble, but several details reveal his background in theater and dance orchestras. Trumpets and trombones use **Harmon mutes,** giving them a pinched, nasal timbre common to jazz bands but rarely heard in the concert hall. The percussion section includes a vibraphone, a metal instrument something like a xylophone that was just beginning to be taken up by jazz performers. In addition to the standard pair of hand-held cymbals, Still calls for a suspended cymbal struck with a stick, producing a sound more familiar from the dance band's drum kit. Also familiar from popular music is the sound of a snare drum played with wire brushes. By these means, the sound of the symphony orchestra is imbued with popular elements.

FLORENCE PRICE

Still's symphony was a landmark work of the Harlem Renaissance, setting a precedent for others to follow. One of the first to benefit from the attention beginning to be paid to black concert musicians was Still's somewhat older contemporary Florence Price. Born in 1887 in Little Rock, Arkansas, Price studied with Chadwick at the New England Conservatory and taught at various southern colleges before moving to Chicago in 1927. In 1932, the year after the premiere of Still's *Afro-American Symphony,* Price's Symphony no. 1 in E Minor took first prize in a composition contest, and it was premiered the following year by the Chicago Symphony Orchestra.

Symphony No. 1

A wife and a mother, Price supported her efforts as a composer of concert music by working where work was to be found, including teaching, writing

| CD 2.16 | Listening Guide 13.3 | *Afro-American Symphony*, first movement (Moderato assai) |
| | | WILLIAM GRANT STILL |

DATE: 1930

PERFORMERS: Fort Smith Symphony; John Jeter, conductor

GENRE: concert music

METER: duple

FORM: sonata form

WHAT TO LISTEN FOR

- use of sonata form
- 12-bar blues structure for the first theme of the movement
- reference to the spiritual in second theme of the movement
- colorful orchestration, including solo English horn and Harmon mutes for trumpets

TIMING	SECTION	SUBSECTION		COMMENTS
0:00	introduction			Solo English horn sets pensive mood.
0:27	exposition	first theme		12-bar blues theme in solo trumpet with Harmon mute; lightly syncopated blues harmonies in French horns.
1:04				Blues theme repeats in clarinet, with call-and-response answers in flute and piccolo.
1:47		transition		Blues theme motive in violins. Increasing agitation with movement to new tonality.
2:24		second theme	*a*	New theme, in *aba* form, in oboe, emphasizing the notes of the pentatonic scale and suggesting the style of a spiritual.
2:58			*b*	Slightly faster and in minor, as violins extend the spiritual melody, then relaxing with flute ensemble and return to major.
3:25			*a*	Melody in cellos, followed by a minor-key variation in the harp; exposition ends softly in G minor.
3:55	development			Suspended cymbal begins the development, with a short transition to the minor key.
4:08				Violins and French horns trade off new melody, related to opening blues theme.
4:39				Climax, with full orchestra at its highest dynamic. Tension subsides gradually: brass drop out, followed by solos for English horn, clarinet, then bass clarinet accompanied by celesta.
5:10	recapitulation	second theme		Spiritual theme, now in the violins and in tonic key but in minor.
5:46		transition		Bassoons begin transition; then strings take up a slow shuffle rhythm, reinforced by a snare drum played with wire brushes and a soft backbeat on the suspended cymbal.

CD 2.16	Listening Guide 13.3	*Afro-American Symphony*, first movement (Moderato assai) WILLIAM GRANT STILL

TIMING	SECTION	SUBSECTION	COMMENTS
6:03		**first theme**	Blues theme now with all three trumpets with Harmon mutes and a more swinging rhythm.
6:40	coda		Harp leads into a short closing section, with bass clarinet on blues theme underneath high strings, then clarinets. Woodwinds, then strings, create a final blues-tinged cadence. The last chord contains an added sixth, common in popular music but unusual in classical harmony.

NOTE Still originally titled this movement "Longings" and attached the following lines from a poem with the same title by the African American poet Paul Laurence Dunbar (1872–1906):

> All my life long twell de night has pas'
> Let de wo'k come ez it will,
> So dat I fin' you, my honey, at last,
> Somewhaih des ovah de hill.

Listen & Reflect

1. What do you think it might have meant to William Grant Still, an African American composer, arranger, and performer, to write a movement of a symphony built around a theme based on the twelve-bar blues structure? What do the resources of an orchestra bring to this traditional genre?

2. The epigraph by Dunbar uses black dialect, a literary device that presents an obstacle for many present-day readers, for whom such language suggests offensive stereotypes. Can any parallels be drawn between the language of Dunbar's poem and the musical language of Still's symphony?

popular songs, and a stint as a silent movie accompanist. During a long career that lasted until her death in 1953, she also continued to compose. Her list of compositions includes four symphonies and other orchestral works, chamber pieces, solo works for piano and organ, choral pieces, and art songs.

Along with her contemporaries William Dawson and Roland Hayes, Price also carried forward the development of the concert spiritual as begun by Harry T. Burleigh. Her arrangements were taken up by a new generation of performers, which included not only Hayes, a classically trained tenor, but also Paul Robeson and Marian Anderson. Robeson was a singer, actor, and political activist whose commanding, cultivated baritone voice conveyed the dignity and emotional force of a music that expressed long centuries of oppression. Anderson was one

concert spirituals

of the greatest African American singers of opera, art songs, and spirituals. Her recording and concert performances of the spiritual "My Soul's Been Anchored in the Lord" added considerably to Price's renown as an arranger.

CONCERT WORKS BY JAZZ MUSICIANS

William Grant Still and Florence Price were primarily classical musicians who also worked in the popular sphere, partly from inclination and partly because racial discrimination limited their concert-hall careers. In contrast are individuals remembered today as jazz musicians who also wrote concert works. While their compositions, like those of Still and Price, reflect the values of the Harlem Renaissance, they also reveal the influence of Gershwin, whose *Rhapsody in Blue* paved the way for other popular artists who aspired to cross the cultural boundaries that separated composers' music from performers' music. Like Gershwin, they produced concert works based on materials drawn from the popular sphere.

James P. Johnson   James P. Johnson (1894–1955) was one of the creators of **stride**, a virtuosic style of jazz piano that descended from ragtime. Along with Willie "The Lion" Smith, Luckey Roberts, and other pianists, Johnson developed stride in the adversarial **cutting contests** that attracted spectators to Harlem's rent parties, social events in which each guest contributed a small fee to help the hosts pay their rent. In addition to flashy piano pieces like "Carolina Shout" (1921), which quickly became a standard in the stride repertory (and whose title refers to the traditional ring shout; see chapter 4), Johnson also wrote successful popular songs, including the 1923 dance hit "The Charleston."

Just as Gershwin's visits to Harlem to hear Johnson and other stride pianists contributed to the musical language of *Rhapsody in Blue,* the success of that pathbreaking work inspired Johnson to try his hand at writing for the concert hall. *Yamekraw: A Negro Rhapsody,* composed by Johnson and orchestrated by William Grant Still, received its premiere at Carnegie Hall in 1927 with the solo piano part taken by Johnson's protégé Thomas "Fats" Waller, soon to become one of the most popular performers and songwriters of the Swing Era. Although *Yamekraw* was followed by two symphonies, a piano concerto, and a one-act opera (*De Organizer,* 1940, to a libretto by Langston Hughes), none of Johnson's concert music enjoyed critical or popular success during his lifetime, nor has it since. The loss of many of the unpublished scores makes a reassessment difficult today, but recent reconstructions of *Yamekraw* and *De Organizer* show Johnson to have been an inventive composer, if an unschooled one, capable of genuine power and depth of expression.

Duke Ellington   A musician who found greater success in merging jazz and concert music was Duke Ellington, whose 1943 concert suite (or "tone parallel," as he called it) *Black, Brown, and Beige* was mentioned in chapter 12. Long before that piece reached Carnegie Hall, however, Ellington had been experimenting with extended musical compositions on phonograph records. Until the long-playing 33⅓-rpm disc became common in the 1950s, classical works, much longer than popular songs, often required two or more record sides for a single movement. In that respect, if no other, Gershwin and the Whiteman band's recording of *Rhapsody in Blue* would have given a listener the feeling of classical music. Likewise, Ellington's *Creole Rhapsody* (1931), by filling both sides of a ten-inch 78-rpm disc, announced

Marian Anderson Gives a Lesson in Tolerance

Despite a distinguished early career in Europe and the United States, where she had sung with the New York Philharmonic in the 1920s, Marian Anderson continually confronted setbacks caused by racial discrimination. In 1939, after the Daughters of the American Revolution denied Anderson the use of Washington's Constitution Hall because of her race, First Lady Eleanor Roosevelt resigned from the organization and President Franklin Roosevelt approved plans for Anderson's recital to take place on the National Mall. There, on Easter Sunday, 1939, seventy thousand people gathered to hear Anderson's rich contralto voice. One newsreel reported the event with the headline "Nation's Capital Gets Lesson in Tolerance."

Contralto Marian Anderson (1897–1993) at the Lincoln Memorial, Easter 1939, with Secretary of the Interior Harold Ickes, who introduced her with the words "In this great auditorium under the sky, all of us are free."

---

that its composer had aspirations beyond the three-minute limit of most popular recordings.

Four years later, with *Reminiscing in Tempo,* Ellington reached even further, creating a composition nearly thirteen minutes long and spanning four sides. His *Diminuendo and Crescendo in Blue* (1937) again fills a single record, with "Diminuendo in Blue" on one side and "Crescendo in Blue" on the other. Like *Creole Rhapsody,* the title self-consciously invokes Gershwin's *Rhapsody in Blue,* but the music is grounded in the twelve-bar blues, the jazz tradition's most familiar form, with its three phrases of four bars each, its characteristic harmonic progression, and the implied call and response in each phrase. Ellington uses this form, on which many players in his band were capable of improvising at length, as the basis for an ingeniously shaped piece in which improvisation plays only a small role.

The opening of "Diminuendo in Blue" illustrates something that clarinetist Barney Bigard once said of Ellington: "At first, just after I joined Duke . . . I used to think everything was wrong, because he wrote so weird." By changing some element in each of the first four choruses —adding measures, delaying a harmonic arrival point, or switching the expected ordering of calls and responses— Ellington sows seeds of doubt in his listeners. Are we hearing blues choruses or not? We cannot be sure until chorus 5 arrives.

"Diminuendo in Blue" moves from dissonance to consonance, from loud to soft, from density to sparseness, from rhythmic disruption to smoothness, and from formal ambiguity to formal clarity. In contrast to traditional classical structures

Diminuendo and Crescendo in Blue

🎜 A gifted composer, Mary Lou Williams (1910–1981) demonstrates the powerful left hand that also made her a formidable boogie-woogie pianist.

such as sonata form, where the music begins with clear, stable harmony and rhythm only to be disrupted by later events, Ellington's piece begins on a note of manic disconnection, settles into a groove, hits a point of calm, and then (after the listener turns the record over) reverses the process in "Crescendo in Blue." And it is unified not only by the blues harmonic progression that underlies all twenty-two of its choruses but also by the melodic motive that begins the entire piece, returns briefly in chorus 7, then reappears at the beginning of the "Crescendo" and is heard in five of its twelve choruses.

Because Ellington wrote these extended compositions for his big band instead of a symphony orchestra and—until *Black, Brown, and Beige*—primarily for phonograph records instead of the concert hall, listeners were comfortable assigning his music to the popular sphere even while acknowledging its high artistic ambitions. And he expended similar artistic care on many of his shorter compositions, such as *Ko-Ko* (1940), a set of minor-key blues variations with virtually no improvisation that nonetheless is universally perceived to be jazz, not classical music. Even the grandly conceived projects of Ellington's later years—concert suites like the Shakespeare-inspired *Such Sweet Thunder* (1957) and the series of three Sacred Concerts composed between 1965 and 1973—did little to change Ellington's status as America's premier *jazz* composer.

Ellington's influence had an immediate impact on other jazz musicians. One was Mary Lou Williams (1910–1981), a brilliant pianist and arranger for leading big bands such as those of Benny Goodman and Ellington himself. After reading a book about astrology, she was inspired to compose her *Zodiac Suite*, in which each movement portrays musician friends who share a common sun sign. The first movement, "Aries," for example, is a portrait of both Ben Webster, then playing tenor sax in Ellington's band, and Billie Holiday. Williams premiered the *Zodiac Suite* in the early 1940s on her weekly radio show in New York City, one movement per week, and in 1945 recorded it as a set of six 78-rpm discs. The tiny label that released the album was run by Moe Asch, a political leftist with a taste for both jazz and folk music, a field in which he would play an important role in the postwar years. Though she recorded it with a standard trio (piano, bass, and drums),Williams clearly imagined a more expansive scoring, which she was able to indulge the following year, when the New York Philharmonic performed three movements of the suite at Carnegie Hall.

Ellington and Williams demonstrated that a jazz artist could win the kind of "highbrow" respect usually reserved for classical musicians without leaving the popular sphere. In that regard, their music marks a seismic shift in cultural values in the United States. Beginning with jazz criticism in the 1930s and increasingly in the postwar years, the cultural hierarchy would gradually be dismantled, as the best musicians came to be appreciated as artists regardless of their musical style.

QUESTIONS FOR DISCUSSION AND REVIEW

1. What are the significant differences between the accomplishments of Arturo Toscanini, Serge Koussevitzky, and Leopold Stokowski? What did their careers have in common that distinguishes them from Theodore Thomas (see chapter 8)?

2. Describe the impact of the Great Depression on classical music making in the United States. How did it affect both composers and performers?

3. What are your thoughts about political subject matter in musical compositions, or any type of art, for that matter? Does the artistic setting affect the political message? Conversely, does the political message strengthen or weaken the work's aesthetic value?

4. In recent years Marcus Roberts, Herbie Hancock, and other jazz pianists have repositioned *Rhapsody in Blue* as a jazz piece by interpolating long, freewheeling improvisations. View one of their performances on YouTube or elsewhere. How does such an interpretation alter the balance of jazz and classical elements in Gershwin's composition?

5. What are some characteristics that unite the African American creators of concert music described in this chapter? How do they differ from one another?

FURTHER READING

Hisama, Ellie. "The Politics of Contour in Crawford's 'Chinaman, Laundryman.'" In *Gendering Musical Modernism: The Music of Ruth Crawford, Marion Bauer, and Miriam Gideon*, 60–98. Cambridge: Cambridge University Press, 2001.

Horowitz, Joseph. *Classical Music in America: A History of Its Rise and Fall*. New York: W.W. Norton, 2005.

Keiler, Allan. *Marian Anderson: A Singer's Journey*. New York: Scribner, 2000.

Oja, Carol. J. *Making Music Modern: New York in the 1920s*. New York: Oxford University Press, 2000.

Pollack, Howard. *Aaron Copland: The Life and Work of an Uncommon Man*. New York: Holt, 1999.

Reynolds, Christopher. "*Porgy and Bess:* An American *Wozzeck*." *Journal of the Society for American Music* 1, no. 1 (February 2007): 1–28.

Schiff, David. *Gershwin: Rhapsody in Blue*. Cambridge: Cambridge University Press, 1997.

Smith, Catherine Parsons. *William Grant Still*. Urbana: University of Illinois Press, 2008.

Tick, Judith. *Ruth Crawford Seeger: A Composer's Search for American Music*. New York: Oxford University Press, 1997.

BLUES, GOSPEL, COUNTRY, AND FOLK MUSIC IN THE GREAT DEPRESSION AND WORLD WAR II

As we saw in the previous chapter, many musicians in the classical sphere responded to the populist climate of the Great Depression by embracing an aesthetic of outreach. Their music, whether ultramodernist or conservative in style, attempted to speak to a broad audience, and its subject matter often addressed the lives of plain folk. This chapter considers the music of those plain folk, beginning with the rural blues records of the 1930s and ending with the more politicized work of folk musicians before and during World War II. It also explores two genres closely tied to folk roots: gospel and country music.

COUNTRY BLUES

The classic blues recorded in the early 1920s represented the first wave of blues recordings. By the mid-1920s a different kind of blues performer began showing up on race records: typically a male singer accompanying himself on guitar, sometimes with a second performer on harmonica, mandolin, or guitar. **Country blues**, the style of blues associated with this type of performer, takes its name from the performers' rural origins, though in fact many had migrated to southern cities, and urban settings probably were important for the music's development. Whereas sales of classic blues records began to wane at the end of the 1920s, records of country blues—especially **Delta blues**, associated with the Mississippi River Delta region—remained strong sellers through the Great Depression.

Blind Lemon Jefferson

One of the first country-blues musicians to make records was Blind Lemon Jefferson, a Dallas-based street performer who traveled to Chicago to record for the Paramount label. When four blues songs that Jefferson recorded in March 1926 became hits, selling many thousands of copies, the search was on for similar artists. A record store owner had recommended Jefferson to Paramount;

now music retailers throughout the South began acting as paid talent scouts for record companies. The most successful of these men was Henry C. Speir of Jackson, Mississippi—the same dealer who boasted of selling fifty records to black customers for every one sold to a white customer (see chapter 11). The list of musicians "discovered" by Speir reads like a who's who of Delta blues: Charlie Patton, Son House, Tommy Johnson, Willie Brown, Skip James, and the most legendary of all Delta bluesmen, Robert Johnson.

Many tales have surrounded Robert Johnson's short life—he died in 1938 at the age of twenty-six. In the decades since his death, researchers have combed the South seeking out birth and death certificates, retracing Johnson's travels, and interviewing anyone who knew or claimed to have known the elusive bluesman. The contradictory stories they have unearthed only add to the mystery of Robert Johnson. For starters, it is not easy to collect accurate data for a poor, southern African American of the early twentieth century with such a common name. Adding to the difficulty is Johnson's penchant for using assumed names and never staying long in one place. As his fellow blues musician Johnny Shines attested, sheer wanderlust may have kept Johnson on the move.

Johnson himself may have originated or at least encouraged the most famous legend about his life. As the story goes, Johnson was an inept would-be guitarist until one fateful midnight when he met Satan at a crossroads and sold his soul in exchange for musical prowess. Those who had once derided him were now amazed by his abilities, and for a few years Johnson traveled widely, displaying phenomenal creative powers, until the moment in August 1938 when he suddenly and dramatically took ill, crawling on the floor and howling like a dog until the devil claimed his soul. By hinting that his music had otherworldly overtones, Johnson ascribed to himself the mystery and power of the supernatural. But a more mundane explanation of Johnson's early death is no less colorful: he was poisoned by the husband of a woman to whom Johnson was paying too much attention.

As for his attainment of musical abilities, the music offers proof of Johnson's self-teaching method: he developed his techniques by listening to race records and imitating them. His wide stylistic palette shows the influence of not only local Mississippi bluesmen but also other, more distant artists that Johnson was likely to have heard only through recordings. In other words, Robert Johnson was part of the audience for race records before he was a recording artist himself.

"Walking Blues" (LG 14.1) displays Johnson's dexterity as a singer and guitarist. His voice croons, growls, moans, and yodels, with the occasional spoken aside. The vocal line exercises great rhythmic freedom, now rushing ahead, now pulling back, always against the steady backdrop of the guitar's lower strings, which lay a rock-steady rhythmic foundation while the upper strings provide melodic fill, Johnson plays **slide** or **bottleneck guitar**, gliding a metal or glass object along the strings, thus allowing the guitar to imitate the swooping vocal

Robert Johnson

> ## In their own words   ❝ ❞
>
> ### Johnny Shines on Robert Johnson
>
> Robert was a guy, you could wake him up anytime and he was ready to go. . . . You say, "Robert, I hear a train, let's catch it." He wouldn't exchange no words with you; he's just ready to go. . . . It didn't make him no difference, just so he was going. He just wanted to go.

LG 14.1

| CD 2.17 | Listening Guide 14.1 | "Walking Blues" ROBERT JOHNSON |

DATE: 1937
PERFORMER: Robert Johnson, vocal and guitar
GENRE: country blues
METER: duple
FORM: strophic 12-bar blues

WHAT TO LISTEN FOR

- unusual distribution of lyrics over the three phrases of each chorus
- variety of vocal timbres and effects
- slide guitar

TIMING	SECTION	TEXT	COMMENTS
0:00	intro		A bar of high **triplets** (three notes per beat), a bar of chromatic descending notes, and a bar of dominant harmony, creating a sense of expectation.
0:06	stanza 1	I woke up this morning feeling round for my shoes Know by that I got these old walking blues, well	Opening couplet sung against even beats in the bass strings of the guitar.
0:17		Woke this morning feeling round for my shoes	Slide used to give the subdominant note vibrato in bars 1–2; bars 3–4 feature quiet yodeling fill on upper strings.
0:26		But you know by that I got these old walking blues	Subdominant and dominant notes in the bass with strong vibrato, and the yodeling fill reappears.
0:36	stanza 2	Lord I feel like blowing my old lonesome home Got up this morning, my little Bernice was gone Lord I feel like blowing my lonesome home Well I got up this morning whoa all I had was gone	Guitar accompaniment from stanza 1; in phrase 2, the vocal yodel on "blowing" makes the following fill sound like an echo of the voice.
1:05	stanza 3	Well leave this morning if I have to whoa ride the blind I feel mistreated and I don't mind dying Leave this morning I have to ride the blind Babe I been mistreated baby and I don't mind dying	Raspier vocal timbre; phrases 2 and 3 have a new melodic figure on the upper strings, emphasizing the blue third.
1:32	stanza 4	Well some people tell me that the worried blues ain't bad Worst old feeling I most ever had Some people tell me that these old worried old blues ain't bad It's the worst old feeling I most ever had	Accompaniment reverts to the pattern of the first two stanzas.

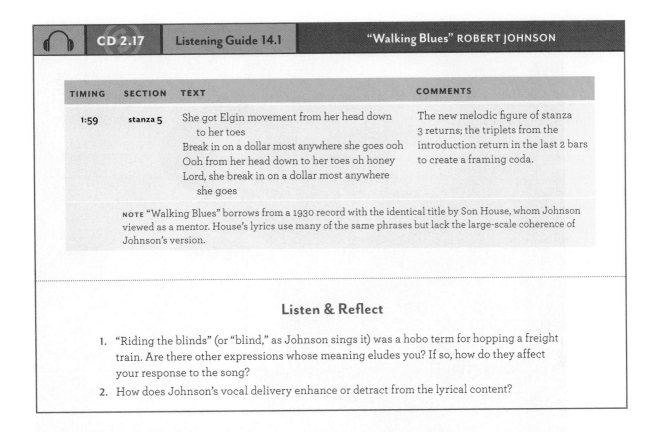

TIMING	SECTION	TEXT	COMMENTS
1:59	stanza 5	She got Elgin movement from her head down to her toes Break in on a dollar most anywhere she goes ooh Ooh from her head down to her toes oh honey Lord, she break in on a dollar most anywhere she goes	The new melodic figure of stanza 3 returns; the triplets from the introduction return in the last 2 bars to create a framing coda.

NOTE "Walking Blues" borrows from a 1930 record with the identical title by Son House, whom Johnson viewed as a mentor. House's lyrics use many of the same phrases but lack the large-scale coherence of Johnson's version.

Listen & Reflect

1. "Riding the blinds" (or "blind," as Johnson sings it) was a hobo term for hopping a freight train. Are there other expressions whose meaning eludes you? If so, how do they affect your response to the song?

2. How does Johnson's vocal delivery enhance or detract from the lyrical content?

lines. (Like most slide guitarists, he favors "open" tunings, with the strings retuned to produce a major chord.)

Each of the five stanzas in "Walking Blues" is set to a twelve-bar blues chorus; Johnson's single alteration of the basic blues progression is an arrival on the subdominant chord at the beginning of the third phrase, withholding the expected dominant chord until the second bar. Somewhat unusual is the distribution of the text across the three phrases: both lines of the couplet are sung in the first phrase, with the first line repeated in phrase 2 and the second in phrase 3. In other words, instead of playing an instrumental fill in bars 3–4, as he does in bars 7–8 and 11–12, Johnson anticipates the second line of the couplet. This places emphasis on the words, and those words reveal another aspect of Johnson's craft.

Like most country-blues songs, "Walking Blues" draws on a common fund of verbal formulas, beginning with a standard opening, "I woke up this morning." But where many blues performers recycle stock phrases in a seemingly arbitrary sequence, so that stanzas can be sung in almost any order with no loss of meaning, Johnson crafts a series of stanzas that develop the opening imagery, fleshing out an ever more detailed picture of the persona's mental distress: his urge to leave, then his reason for leaving—a woman who has left him and thus mistreated him—and finally a description of the woman's physical attributes, which he compares to the finely calibrated mechanism, or movement, of an Elgin watch. Only the fourth stanza feels out of place; it seems to belong to a different song, which could be titled "Worried Blues." "Walking Blues" demonstrates a key element of

Robert Johnson (1911–1938), left, with fellow blues musician Johnny Shines (1915–1992).

A CLOSER LOOK

Blues Piano and Jug Bands

If the iconic country-blues figure is the lone bluesman who creates music with only his voice and his guitar, at least two other important early blues styles deserve mention here. One is the piano style developed in the South and called **boogie woogie** or sometimes **barrelhouse**, after the rough taverns where it was developed. Charles Edward "Cow Cow" Davenport and Clarence "Pinetop" Smith, both born in Alabama in the 1890s, played instrumental numbers and accompanied their own singing and that of others with a propulsive bass line in the left hand and syncopated chords, melodic fills, and insistent repeated octaves in the right hand. Smith's tune *Pinetop's Boogie Woogie* was taken up by numerous pianists and jazz bands for decades after Smith first recorded it for Vocalion in 1928.

An important ensemble genre is the music of **jug bands**, groups of various sizes that typically mix string instruments such as guitar, banjo, fiddle, or mandolin with kazoo, washtub bass, spoons, washboard, or other homemade or toy instruments. The foundation of the ensemble is a ceramic jug, which a skilled player can blow into with buzzing lips to produce a sound similar to the tuba. Vaudeville blues singers like Ma Rainey sometimes worked with jug bands, and jug band instrumentalists such as Big Bill Broonzy and Tampa Red went on to have solo careers as singer-guitarists.

Johnson's success: his ability to shape the spontaneous flow of folk blues into a compact artistic utterance that fits neatly on one side of a 78-rpm record.

When the record producer and concert promoter John Hammond tried to book Johnson for a concert at New York's Carnegie Hall in 1938, he learned that the bluesman had died shortly before under mysterious circumstances. Nevertheless, the concert—a fund-raiser for the leftist journal *New Masses* that was called "From Spirituals to Swing" and purported to illustrate the development of African American music—featured Johnson as a ghostly presence. Two of his records, one of them "Walking Blues," were played for the respectful audience gathered in the nation's most prestigious concert hall. Only a few months after his death, the posthumous elevation of Johnson's recorded legacy had begun. As later chapters chronicle, postwar developments in folk and rock music would demonstrate that Robert Johnson was one of the most influential of all blues musicians.

THOMAS A. DORSEY AND GOSPEL MUSIC

Blues and black **gospel music** share a melodic and harmonic idiom, a rhythmic approach, and a rootedness in traditional African American culture, but their functions are entirely different. Blues is a secular music, tied to work and entertainment; gospel is a sacred music, performed in worship. Blues speaks for individuals, gospel for communities. Where blues states problems of human existence, gospel solves them through Christian doctrine. Blues fits in many settings; gospel belongs to the church.

Black gospel music exemplifies the attitude of praise rather than edification. The music seeks to glorify the Almighty by offering the best—the most heartfelt, ecstatic, artful, and therefore worthy—in human expression. The emotionally direct yet disciplined musical stylizations of black gospel performers have proved to be among the most powerful expressions of praise in the modern Christian church.

Racial prejudice in America has sharpened class consciousness within black communities, and religious life has mirrored the social divisions. In Chicago, for example, middle-class blacks gravitated toward African Methodist Episcopal (AME) and Baptist churches, while working-class blacks—including migrants from the South—were more likely to join Pentecostal, or "sanctified," congregations. Middle-class black denominations modeled their worship customs on white churches: in the latter 1920s the choirs at two of black Chicago's largest Baptist congregations were singing sacred music by the likes of Handel and Mendelssohn. The ministers of these "old-line" churches favored a restrained preaching style and avoided traditional black worship music, except for arranged, notated spirituals. A different spirit was found in Pentecostal denominations such as the Church of God in Christ: congregation hymns were "gospelized" and the mood was ecstatic, with jubilant singing to drums and tambourines (or even pots and pans), hand clapping, foot stomping, and shouting, as in the days before Emancipation (see chapter 4).

Modern black gospel music took shape before World War II as mainstream denominations brought Pentecostal musical styles into their worship. A key moment was the performance in August 1930 of Thomas A. Dorsey's "If You See My Savior" at a convention of black Baptists in Chicago. Dorsey (sometimes called "Georgia Tom") was a Chicago musician and songwriter whose performing credits included a stint as pianist for Ma Rainey and who, from the early 1930s on, devoted himself entirely to sacred music.

Thomas A. Dorsey

In 1931 Chicago's Ebenezer Baptist Church hired a new minister from Alabama who hoped to introduce songs like those he had heard in the South. So in early 1932 a new choir was formed, accompanied by Dorsey himself. But when another Chicago minister invited Dorsey to do the same at his church, the choir director there objected to the secular basis of Dorsey's gospel style: "I felt it was degrading. How can something that's jazzy give a religious feeling? If you're in a club downtown, a nightclub, that's all right. That's where it belongs. But how can you associate that with God's word? It's a desecration." The transformation of music in Chicago's old-line churches did not happen without internal strife and dissent.

Later that year Dorsey joined with like-minded musicians to form the National Convention of Gospel Choirs and Choruses, dedicated to teaching the gospel style. That year also saw the founding of the Dorsey House of Music, the first publishing company devoted to black gospel music. Dorsey's ability to compose, improvise, and notate music; his command of blues-based rhythmic drive; his commitment to the church; and his understanding of sacred and secular music as two sides of the same

In their own words

Thomas A. Dorsey on the Relation of Blues to Gospel

If a woman has lost a man, a man has lost a woman, his feeling reacts to the blues; he feels like expressing it. The same thing acts for a gospel song. Now you're not singing blues; you're singing gospel, good news song, singing about the Creator; but it's the same feeling, a grasping of the heart. If it's in your public, they holler out "Hallelujah" or "Amen" in church. In the theater they holler "sing it again" or "do it again" or something like that.

coin—all of these made him the very model of a black gospel musician. At a time of cultural tension in Chicago's churches, Dorsey came forward with music that was authentically southern yet urbanized enough to counter the northern culture's push for European anthems.

For several generations Dorsey's gospel songs have offered black gospel singers an attractive body of music: songs in standard forms, with straightforward melodies and harmonies. The richness and excitement are supplied neither by the written music nor by the words, which both tend to be simple, but by the performers. "Talk about Jesus" (LG 14.2) is a good example of this type of gospel song: a verse followed by a chorus, which is then repeated with altered words. The approach to the subject is more down-to-earth than elevated; as seen by Dorsey, Jesus is no distant icon but a "friend of mine," a comrade who is "mighty fine."

LG 14.2

In her recording of "Talk about Jesus," Marion Williams provides her own piano accompaniment. Williams was fifty-nine years old when she made this recording in 1986. In 1993 she became the first singer to receive a "genius" grant from the MacArthur Foundation; she died a few months later. In this performance Williams starts quietly but is soon caught up in the spirit of her praise. By the start of the chorus she has established a powerful rhythmic groove, using her large, supple voice and an arsenal of techniques—blue notes, bent notes, offbeat melodic phrasings, register shifts, and even a growl (when "the tears come rolling out")—to express religious devotion in an inventive, heartfelt way.

Marion Williams

Gospel music offered rich opportunities for women as well as men, including solo singers Sallie Martin, Clara Ward, and Mahalia Jackson. Jackson, born in New Orleans and raised chiefly in Chicago, won fame during the 1950s and 1960s through recordings, tours, and broadcasts. Her voice and artistry made her the world's leading gospel singer in her lifetime and long after.

Mahalia Jackson

Roberta Martin's career in gospel music proved that singing was not the only role open to women. Born in 1907 in Arkansas, Martin moved with her family at age ten to Chicago, where piano study gave her a solid musical background. At Ebenezer Baptist Church in the early 1930s, she worked with Dorsey and

Roberta Martin

꙳ Thomas A. Dorsey (1899–1993), the "Father of Gospel Music."

CD 2.18 | Listening Guide 14.2 | "Talk about Jesus" THOMAS A. DORSEY

DATE: recorded 1986

PERFORMER: Marion Williams, vocal and piano

GENRE: gospel song

METER: duple

FORM: verse, chorus, chorus (ABB')

WHAT TO LISTEN FOR

- simplicity of harmony and verse-and-chorus form
- expressive performance using blues vocal techniques
- shaping of performance to reach an emotional climax in the second chorus

TIMING	SECTION	TEXT	COMMENTS
0:00	verse	On the road there was a cry…	Vocal begins quietly, with simple chords in the piano; halfway through, vibrato increases and glides, blue notes, and other vocal ornaments are introduced.
0:41	chorus 1	Talking about Jesus…	Melody moves into a higher register; Williams adds growls and bent notes as she increases the volume and rhythmic drive. The last line (1:11) displays a particularly wide range of vocal timbres.
1:20	chorus 2	I'm talking about Jesus…	Williams repeats the chorus, adding extra words and notes to the melody. The piano, while remaining in the background, develops a rocking, bluesy groove.

Listen & Reflect

1. "Talk about Jesus" uses neither the twelve-bar blues chorus nor the standard blues chord progression. As performed by Marion Williams, however, its affinity with the blues is apparent. What are the similarities?

accompanied a choir of youngsters. She also began showing a knack for leadership. In 1933 Martin recruited several male singers to form the Martin-Frye Quartet; gospel groups then consisted either of male quartets in business suits or female choruses in choir robes. By 1936 she was adding her own alto voice to the group, now called the Roberta Martin Singers, which she accompanied on piano. In the mid-1940s she added two women singers, marking the first combination of male and female voices in one ensemble. By then, Martin and her singers were also making records. Based in the area around Chicago, the group sang in churches, meeting halls, and religious revivals. They also toured by car from January to June, starting in either California or Florida and working their way back to the Midwest as winter gave way to spring.

Martin sang, played, and traveled with her singers until the late 1940s. From then on, she concentrated more on writing and arranging for them and running her own publishing business. Gospel was not only a performing style but also a musical repertory, and new songs boosted the music's appeal for singers and congregations. Martin composed some fifty gospel songs and arranged many more, putting her stamp on gospel's entry into a written tradition. Between 1939 and her death in 1969, she published nearly three hundred pieces of gospel sheet music. Unlike Dorsey, who issued only his own compositions, Martin published the songs her group sang regardless of the composer. Alone among musicians of her era, she seems to have recognized gospel music as an endeavor that could link spirituality, music making, and commerce in a single enterprise. (The example of musician-businessman Lowell Mason in the 1830s and 1840s comes to mind; see chapter 3.)

Martin's funeral has been seen as a symbol of black gospel music's place in American life: a blend of acceptance and obscurity. When she died in January 1969 at the age of sixty-two, fifty thousand Chicagoans passed through Mount Pisgah Baptist Church, where she was music director, to view the body, although no national newspaper or journal covered the event. Across the United States, gospel fans heard the news through word of mouth and on the radio.

Gospel music's roots lie in spirituals, ring shouts, and the blues; in turn it became a wellspring from which other African American musical traditions have flowed. Many who have excelled in jazz, blues, rhythm and blues, and soul have served their apprenticeship in the black church. And partly because gospel music making has been widely accessible to black Americans, its influence has been broad as well as deep. Gospel music was responsible for much of what came to be considered emblematic in American culture of the 1960s: from rock and roll's beat, drama, and group vibrations to the hymn singing at sit-ins and freedom marches.

COUNTRY MUSIC DURING THE GREAT DEPRESSION AND WORLD WAR II

Country music in its second decade continued to grow and diversify, despite the inhibiting effects of the Great Depression. Country performers, like other musicians, struggled with the near-collapse of the record industry, as sales dropped from 104 million records in 1927 to only 6 million in 1932. Helping to offset those losses, however, were gains in publishing, radio, and movies.

Realizing that newly composed songs could be much more profitable than recordings of traditional material, many country musicians in the 1930s followed the example of the Carter Family and Jimmie Rodgers (see chapter 11) by writing and copyrighting songs that could then earn royalties when performed by other musicians or printed in songbooks. Ralph Peer again played a significant role in this development, now as a publisher. The company he founded in 1928, Southern Music, handled the copyrights for songs not only by the artists Peer recorded for race and hillbilly records but also by mainstream jazz and popular musicians. In the 1950s, Southern Music would sign deals with many of the first rock and roll artists.

Also benefiting country musicians in the Depression years was the rise of **border blasters**, radio stations owned by U.S. citizens but located just across the Rio Grande from Texas and thus exempt from U.S. broadcasting regulations. The most powerful of the border blasters had signals powered by up to half a million

border blasters

Barbershop Quartets and White Gospel Music before World War II

Like solo gospel singing and the blues, gospel quartet singing draws on a secular anteced-ent: the **barbershop quartet**. Probably origi-nating in informal African American group singing in the 1800s, by the early twentieth century the bar-bershop quartet had become popular among both blacks and whites. Barbershop is a style of four-part singing for men (and occasionally women) in which a lead voice carries the melody, higher and lower voices (tenor and baritone) add harmony lines, and a bass voice provides harmonic underpinning and occasional countermelodies. Though its popularity had waned somewhat even before World War II, in the 1940s a revival movement led to a resurgence of both amateur and professional interest, and today the Barbershop Harmony Society, the largest of sev-eral such organizations, has about 30,000 members in North America.

Barbershop harmonizing also influenced a new form of white gospel music that arose with the huge urban revivals of the early 1900s, led by charismatic preachers like Billy Sunday. Unlike the older gos-pel hymns described in chapter 7, the newer gospel songs from around 1910 featured jaunty, march-like rhythms with some ragtime-style syncopation; optimistic texts stressing salvation and the joys of heaven; and the four-part texture of the barbershop quartet. Charles Gabriel, whose "Will the Circle Be Unbroken" was one source for the Carter Family's similarly titled song, was one of many composers whose gospel songs of this type were published by Homer Rodeheaver, Billy Sunday's music director.

Urban gospel songs found a ready audience in the rural South. They found their way into southern hymnals, especially by means of the newer seven-shape notation that in the late 1800s came into use alongside the older four-shape notation of *The Sacred Harp* (see chapter 3). The most important publisher of seven-shape gospel music was the Stamps-Baxter Music Company of Dallas, Texas, which, beginning in 1924, supplied written music for southern singing schools and conventions. Stamps-Baxter promoted its publications by sponsoring gospel music radio programs and by sending professional male vocal quartets on tours throughout the South to familiar-ize audiences with the latest gospel songs in their catalogue. By the end of the 1930s, the sound of the white male gospel quartet, performing either a cap-pella or with a ragtime-influenced piano accompa-niment, was a common feature of southern radio.

watts, ten times the legal maximum in the United States—signals that could be heard all the way to Canada and even, when the weather was right, around the world. Before they were finally shut down by the Mexican government in the 1980s, border blasters, or "X stations" (their call letters began with the letter X), were notorious for their characteristic programming blend of quack medicine peddlers, crackpot preachers, and country music (and later, rock and roll). From 1938 until they disbanded in 1943, the Carter Family took up residence in Del Rio, Texas, crossing the border twice daily to perform on XERA, owned and operated by "Doctor" John Romulus Brinkley, who used the station to advertise his goat gland cure for impotence. Border radio extended the audience for the Carters and many other country musicians far beyond the rural South, bringing them increased profits, if not cultural prestige.

motion pictures   Motion pictures offered another way for country musicians to reach a wider audience. Movies were a primary medium for the spread of new types of country music originating in the Southwest. In both feature films and the "shorts" that accompanied them, string bands and other hillbilly acts made occasional appearances as well. So profitable were such acts that even non-hillbillies tried cashing in on the craze, a trend parodied in a film musical, *Gold Diggers of 1933*. In one of the movie's scenes, a group calling themselves Zipky's Kentucky Hillbillies enter a Broadway producer's office seeking an audition. When their Yiddish accents give them away, the producer tells them to scram back to their old Kentucky home. The implication is that country music, on screen and elsewhere, had the power to attract persons born well outside the rural South.

COUNTRY MUSIC IN THE SOUTHEAST AND MIDWEST

Throughout the 1930s and 1940s, radio barn dances and shorter "song and patter" shows, originating mostly in the Southeast and Midwest, broadcast performances that developed the styles heard on early hillbilly records. For example, the characteristic sound of the string band was combined with the vocal harmonies of the Carter Family in a new format: the "brother" duo. Brother acts that gained popularity during the Great Depression included the Delmore Brothers (from Alabama), the Monroe Brothers (from Kentucky), and the Callahan Brothers and the Blue Sky Boys (both from North Carolina).

brother duos

All of these duos featured a lead vocal with a higher harmonizing tenor voice, closely blended to produce what became known as "the high lonesome sound." Moreover, many of these duos featured one brother playing guitar and the other playing mandolin, an instrument rarely heard on 1920s hillbilly records. During the 1930s the mandolin eclipsed the banjo, which, except in the hands of a few musician-comedians such as Louis "Grandpa" Jones, temporarily went out of fashion until an exciting new style of playing emerged in postwar bluegrass (see chapter 17).

Not all country vocal duos were brother acts. Two popular sister acts were the Girls of the Golden West (from Illinois) and the Cackle Sisters (from Minnesota). The Cackle Sisters sang first on WLS's *National Barn Dance* in Chicago and later on the nationally syndicated *Purina Mills Checkerboard Time*, where their distinctive novelty yodeling won them their stage name (the show's sponsor manufactured chicken feed). WLS in Chicago was also the radio home of Lulu Belle and Scotty, a husband-and-wife team whose comic skits and sentimental love songs made them one of the most popular radio acts of the 1930s.

sister acts

Musically and lyrically, these acts generally stayed within the broad categories already established for hillbilly music: ballads, sentimental songs, **breakdowns** (fiddle tunes played as virtuoso showpieces), and rowdy songs about drinking, gambling, and living outside the law. Event songs kept up with changing times: the Dixon Brothers' "I Didn't Hear Nobody Pray" (1938, recorded by Roy Acuff as "Wreck on the Highway" in the 1940s) describes a drunk-driving accident in which "whiskey and blood mixed together." In 1939 the Rouse Brothers, a duo from Florida that included fiddle instead of mandolin, recorded "Orange Blossom Special," a train song that alternates twelve-bar blues vocal choruses with a lively instrumental breakdown, an effective marriage of Anglo-Celtic and African American musical idioms. That first recording featured Ervin's imitation of a train whistle, and ever since, contest fiddlers have used "Orange Blossom Special" as an occasion for virtuoso display and mimicry of all kinds.

country genres

SINGING COWBOYS

Because so much of the early recording took place in the southern Appalachians, the name "hillbilly" seemed fitting for prewar country music. But not all of the music came from the southern uplands, and by the end of World War II the term was on its way out. Changes in the perception of this musical category are evident in *Billboard* magazine's name for its chart of top-selling country records in the 1940s. In 1944 the category was called "Folk Records," an obvious misnomer. In 1947 the name changed to "Hillbilly Records," and in 1949 it became "Country and Western," a designation that would last into the 1960s. The new term reflected the appeal for country audiences of musical genres originating in the West and Southwest.

A few genuine cowboy singers appeared on records in the 1920s. One, Goeble Reeves, claimed to have taught Jimmie Rodgers how to yodel. Rodgers had lived near San Antonio, Texas, for the last few years of his short life and sometimes performed wearing western gear. In the wake of his success, some of his younger imitators also adopted cowboy stage personae regardless of their actual backgrounds. Ernest Tubb, who grew up on a cotton farm in east Texas, performed in boots and ten-gallon hat, as did Hank Snow, who was born in Nova Scotia.

Gene Autry   The most successful of the Jimmie Rodgers imitators was Gene Autry. Born in Texas and raised in Oklahoma, Autry grew up on farms and could ride a horse, and his early job as a telegraph operator left him with enough free time to work on his guitar playing and singing. Tulsa's KVOO billed him as "Oklahoma's Yodeling Cowboy," even though his repertoire included few western-themed songs, leaning instead toward hillbilly numbers and Rodgers's songs. Autry's big break came in 1931, when he was signed to the WLS *National Barn Dance* and had his first hit record, "That Silver-Haired Daddy of Mine," an original song in the mold of Rodgers's "Daddy and Home."

Beginning in 1934 he took his cowboy persona one step further by appearing in the first of nearly ninety western films, most of them low-budget B movies, thus becoming, if not the first, then certainly the most famous singing cowboy in Hollywood. By 1940 Autry was one of the top box office draws in the United States. His film acting did not bring an end to his singing career, which continued with live performances, radio shows, and several hit records, ranging from traditional cowboy songs like "Home on the Range" to newly minted seasonal songs like "Rudolph the Red-Nosed Reindeer." Autry's recording of Johnny Marks's "Rudolph" would sell 2.5 million copies in 1949 and eventually reach ten times that number, making it the second-best-selling single of all time, topped only by Bing Crosby's 1942 version of Irving Berlin's "White Christmas."

western escapism   Like Tex Ritter, Roy Rogers, and other 1930s movie cowboys, and like cowboy-themed singing groups such as the Sons of the Pioneers, Autry invited listeners to indulge in gentle nostalgia for a West that had largely disappeared, even though the legendary days of the Wild West remained in living memory—barely half a century separated the Great Depression from the gunfight at the OK Corral or the death of Billy the Kid. A number of western songs were about the longing to be out west, rather than the actual experience of being in the West. The persona in Stuart Hamblen's "Texas Plains" (1934), for instance, seeks relief from the pressures of modern urban life:

> These city lights and these city ways are driving me insane
> I want to be alone
> I want to be back home
> Back on the Texas plains.

This 1947 movie poster gives second billing not to Gene Autry's love interest, Lynne Roberts, but to his horse, Champion Jr.

Similarly, Patsy Montana (Ruby Blevins, from Arkansas) had the first significant hit record for a solo female country artist with "I Want to Be a Cowboy's Sweetheart" (1935), a lively polka modeled on "Texas Plains":

> I want to be a cowboy's sweetheart
> I want to learn to rope and to ride
> I want to ride o'er the plains and the desert
> Out west of the Great Divide.

Western music catered to a public dissatisfied with the harsh economic realities of life during the Great Depression. Cowboy songs promised escape into a past that seemed somehow more honest and authentic than modern urban existence.

WESTERN SWING

If movie cowboys purveyed an idealized West for an urban audience, other types of music emerging from the Southwest reflected their audiences' more here-and-now concerns. Much of this new music came from Texas, western Louisiana,

and Oklahoma, where the discovery of vast oil reserves created an economic boom that offset some of the effects of the Great Depression. Hard work in the oil fields called for hard play, and relatively plentiful money combined with the repeal of Prohibition in 1933 to make that possible in the form of the cheap nightclubs known as honky-tonks.

Revelry in the honky-tonks demanded suitable music: driving rhythms for dancing and enough volume to be heard over the din of the crowd. Such music was provided either by live musicians or, increasingly, by the **jukebox**, a coin-operated phonograph that permitted listeners to choose among several selections. In the middle of the twentieth century, the jukebox was such an important source of revenue that the music industry kept track of which records got the most play, in specialized charts in either *Billboard* magazine or *Cash Box*, which began in 1942 as a magazine devoted exclusively to the jukebox trade.

One kind of music that came out of the honky-tonks was **western swing**, a combination of traditional fiddle music, blues, jazz, Tin Pan Alley song styles, the polka rhythms of Czech and German immigrants in the Southwest, and Mexican genres such as mariachi and conjunto (see chapter 21). Bob Wills, the central figure in western swing, started out in 1931 with a traditional string-band instrumentation and eventually expanded his band, the Texas Playboys, into a larger and louder musical organization. Taking a cue from the jazz-oriented swing bands that toured the Southwest, Wills added horns—sax, trumpet, and trombone—and a rhythm section of piano, bass, and drums. Like the big bands of mainstream popular music, the Playboys featured a singer, Tommy Duncan, who could croon popular songs and shout the blues like Jimmy Rushing, Count Basie's singer.

Wills also modified the string-band core of the Texas Playboys in his quest for greater volume and a jazzier sound. In place of one fiddle, the Texas Playboys often had two or three, allowing the alternation of jazz-influenced solos with a smooth section sound analogous to the reed and brass sections of a big band. Also significant was the band's use of electrically amplified guitar and steel guitar. The electric steel guitar was pioneered by Bob Dunn, a member of another popular western swing band, Milton Brown's Musical Brownies. Inspired by jazz musicians like Louis Armstrong and trombonist Jack Teagarden, Dunn had electrified a Hawaiian-style lap guitar, on which he played horn-like single-line melodic solos. The Brownies' 1935 "Taking Off" is sometimes cited as the first record featuring an electrically amplified instrument. Following Dunn's lead, Leon McAuliffe brought to the Texas Playboys a virtuoso technique on both steel guitar and standard electric guitar; the nineteen-year-old McAuliffe's "Steel Guitar Rag" (1936) was a Texas Playboys staple and a defining example of western swing.

Many of the elements of western swing can be heard in the Texas Playboys' 1940 version of "Corrine, Corrina" (LG 14.3), a blues tune first recorded in 1928.

☞ Before Patsy Montana, shown here putting her guitar at risk, women in country music were generally part of family groups or husband-and-wife duos. The cowgirl image helped audiences accept her as a solo performer.

electric guitar

LG 14.3

⤳ Bob Wills (with fiddle) leads his Texas Playboys. Visible are alto and tenor saxes, clarinet, bass, and electric guitar (an amplified hollow-body instrument rather than the solid-body guitar popularized since the 1950s).

Although the Playboys' horn section was absent from this recording session, the jazz influences are evident in solos for steel guitar, fiddle, and piano. While certain features of instrumental and vocal style sound country, other features resemble the big-band swing of the 1930s and 1940s. The combination of influences results in music that participates in the mainstream of popular music without losing its regional character.

Like "Muleskinner Blues" (see LG 11.3), the Texas Playboys' "Corrine, Corrina" displays the metrical irregularities common in the black country blues tradition, from which the tune is derived. Wills frequently, but not consistently, adds an extra beat to the even-numbered bars of his vocal choruses. (He usually left the singing to Tommy Duncan, but here he takes the vocal spotlight in addition to urging on his players with spoken interjections.) In contrast, the instrumental soloists, accustomed to playing for dancers, iron out the rhythmic wrinkles: in each instrumental solo chorus, every bar has two beats except the last, where an extra beat or two allows Wills to enter at his leisure for the next vocal chorus. Nevertheless, the composed instrumental ensemble chorus that opens the record and recurs near the end has extra beats in two of the twelve bars.

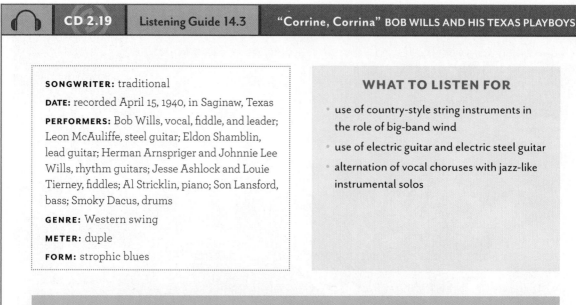

CD 2.19 | **Listening Guide 14.3** | **"Corrine, Corrina"** BOB WILLS AND HIS TEXAS PLAYBOYS

SONGWRITER: traditional

DATE: recorded April 15, 1940, in Saginaw, Texas

PERFORMERS: Bob Wills, vocal, fiddle, and leader; Leon McAuliffe, steel guitar; Eldon Shamblin, lead guitar; Herman Arnspriger and Johnnie Lee Wills, rhythm guitars; Jesse Ashlock and Louie Tierney, fiddles; Al Stricklin, piano; Son Lansford, bass; Smoky Dacus, drums

GENRE: Western swing

METER: duple

FORM: strophic blues

WHAT TO LISTEN FOR

- use of country-style string instruments in the role of big-band wind
- use of electric guitar and electric steel guitar
- alternation of vocal choruses with jazz-like instrumental solos

TIMING	SECTION	FEATURED VOICE OR INSTRUMENT(S)	COMMENTS
0:00	chorus 1	fiddle section	Three fiddles play the melody in close harmony, with short chords in the steel guitar, a texture analogous to the sax and brass sections, respectively, of a big band.
0:15	chorus 2	vocal	Wills sings the melody straightforwardly, then adds more blue notes as he goes. Steel guitar **comps** (plays accompanying chords) in the background.
0:33	chorus 3	steel guitar solo	Jazz influence: blue notes, bent pitches, syncopation, and fluid phrasing.
0:47	chorus 4	vocal	Fiddle fills behind the vocal.
1:05	chorus 5	fiddle solo	Solo in jazzy mood (although perhaps not improvised).
1:20	chorus 6	vocal	Piano comps behind the vocal.
1:39	chorus 7	piano solo	Stride style, with prominent, rhythmically driving left hand beneath right-hand melodies and chords.
1:54	chorus 8	vocal	Lead guitar and fiddle comp lightly behind the vocal.
2:13	chorus 9	fiddle section	Like opening chorus.
2:29	chorus 10	vocal	Light comping from both steel guitar and fiddle hint at the collective improvisation of New Orleans jazz.

Listen & Reflect

1. In choruses 1 and 9, which bars have an extra beat?
2. The record's format—opening and closing sections for the full ensemble, with a series of solos in the middle—resembles jazz records like *West End Blues* and *Lester Leaps In* (chapter 15). What similarities and differences do you hear between those recordings and "Corrine, Corrina"?

THE RISE OF URBAN FOLK MUSIC

During the interwar years, a new generation of folk song collectors extended their predecessors' efforts to include groups whose music had been overlooked. At the same time, radio and phonograph records altered the relationship between folk singers and their audiences. Finally, from those new audiences emerged an unprecedented kind of musician: the urban folk singer.

JOHN AND ALAN LOMAX AND THE ARCHIVE OF AMERICAN FOLK SONG

The late 1800s saw a rising interest in uniquely American traditions. In 1888 the American Folklore Society was founded, with the intent of gathering and publishing songs and stories from Anglo-American, African American, Indian, Mexican, and French Canadian cultures. After 1900 many state folklore societies were established, dedicated in large part to collecting and preserving folk songs from the Old World, especially Child ballads. In 1914 the U.S. Office of Education declared a "rescue mission" for folk songs and ballads, in the belief that they were an endangered species.

🎵 After accompanying his father, John Lomax, on a long folk-song-collecting trip in 1933, Alan Lomax (1915–2002) devoted himself to traditional music, including a 1948 radio program, *Your Ballad Man*.

By the latter 1920s it was clear to anyone paying heed that the United States was home to a rich, diverse assortment of music in the traditional sphere. One symbol of that recognition was the founding in 1928 of the Archive of American Folk Song at the Library of Congress in Washington, D.C. The idea seems to have come from Robert Winslow Gordon, a scholar and collector who was named the library's first sound archivist. Gordon, who had an academic background, had for years been collecting folk songs and writing about them in *Adventure,* a popular magazine focused on the out-of-doors.

After Gordon left his post at the archive in 1933, his replacement, John A. Lomax, turned the archive into a real force on the music scene. Born in 1867, Lomax grew up in Texas with a deep interest in black music. Graduating from the University of Texas in 1887, he worked in that school's administration and taught English at a Texas college, with time off for master's degree study at Harvard in 1906–7. Lomax's interest in cowboy songs led to a published collection in 1910. After his book appeared, he was elected president of the American Folklore Society and traveled and lectured widely. By the early 1920s Lomax had left the academic world for banking, though he continued to collect songs and ballads. In 1932, out of a job at age sixty-five, he convinced a New York publisher to support his plan for a comprehensive collection to be called *American Ballads and Folk Songs.* He then approached Carl Engel, chief of the Library of Congress music division, who agreed to furnish him with portable recording equipment if Lomax would deposit his recordings at the library. In July 1933 Lomax was named honorary consultant to the Archive of American Folk Songs for a stipend of one dollar per year.

Knowing that black folk songs were poorly represented in American collections, Lomax made them the focus of a four-month-long collecting trip that he and his son Alan, eighteen years old and a college student, began in the summer of 1933. In their search for African American musicians insulated from white traditions, they visited Southern penitentiaries and prison camps. In one Louisiana prison, the Lomaxes found the remarkable singer and guitarist Leadbelly. John Lomax arranged for his parole, and between 1935 and 1948 Leadbelly recorded many songs for the Library of Congress archive.

Leadbelly: Folk and Blues Troubadour

On a song-collecting trip to Angola State Prison in Louisiana in 1933, John and Alan Lomax became acquainted with Huddie Ledbetter (1888–1949), who went by the name Leadbelly (or Lead Belly). Impressed with his formidable musical skills and encyclopedic knowledge of blues and folk songs, the Lomaxes agreed to record his sung petition to Governor O. K. Allen, asking for an early release from his sentence for attempted homicide. In 1934 they conveyed the petition to Allen on a phonograph record, and Leadbelly was released (though state officials said the recording had nothing to do with their decision).

After a few months as John Lomax's driver on a recording expedition, Leadbelly began performing for the first time outside his native South. Beginning with a concert at Bryn Mawr College in Pennsylvania, he sang in New York and at other northeastern liberal arts colleges, with John Lomax acting as his manager. Leadbelly found his most enthusiastic audiences among leftist political organizations.

At Lomax's suggestion, Leadbelly developed the practice of introducing his songs with spoken introductions, often while he strummed his twelve-string guitar, with the intent of giving his listeners some necessary background for understanding the song's subject matter. This style of song presentation would become a standard feature of the urban folk revival that was yet to come. Leadbelly also introduced a number of songs that became favorites in the coming folk boom, including "Goodnight, Irene," "The Rock Island Line," and "The Midnight Special."

These performances made Leadbelly a significant folk musician who took his music outside its original cultural context and performed before an audience unfamiliar with his musical traditions. Leadbelly, Woody Guthrie, Cisco Houston, and the blues duo of Sonny Terry and Brownie McGee were among the key figures in American folk music in the mid-twentieth century.

꠱ Leadbelly (Huddie Ledbetter, 1889–1949) performs with his 12-string guitar for a private mixed-race audience in New York City in the 1940s.

In 1937 the Archive of American Folk Song, supported since 1928 by donations and outside monies, began receiving a stipend from Congress. Alan Lomax was hired as a staff member and remained there until 1942. During his long career Lomax worked indefatigably, making thousands of field recordings, compiling oral histories, writing books and articles, and producing radio programs and documentary films about folk music both in the United States and throughout the world.

Like his father before him, Alan Lomax continued to make field recordings of African American music in southern penitentiaries. On one visit to a work camp in Mississippi in 1959 he recorded a prisoner, Ed Lewis, singing the traditional work song "John Henry" (LG 14.4). Like much older ballads, "John Henry" exists in numerous versions that conflict in details but all tell the same basic story. John Henry is a powerful man who drives spikes with a hammer in the building of a railroad. Matching his strength with a steam-powered drill, he outperforms the machine but dies in the contest. In some versions the infant John Henry foretells his death, and in some versions his wife or girlfriend picks up his hammer and completes his job. In almost all versions, John Henry tells his boss, or captain, that he will accept the steam drill's challenge even though "a man ain't nothing but a man."

Lewis's version of "John Henry" situates the action on the Mobile and Ohio Railroad, but in most versions the action takes place on the Chesapeake and Ohio (C&O), built in Virginia and West Virginia in the 1870s, and specifically in the Big Bend tunnel, one of three long tunnels near the state line. Those tunnels were constructed with the labor of prisoners from the Virginia Penitentiary, and the historical John Henry, if such a person ever existed, would probably have been one of those prisoners. When the old penitentiary buildings were torn down in 1992, workers discovered the shallow graves of some three hundred prisoners, all buried in the 1870s, near a whitewashed building next to an old rail line, suggesting one verse found in some versions of the song:

> They took John Henry to the white house
> And buried him in the sand
> And every locomotive come roaring by
> Says there lies that steel-driving man.

Whether or not one of those graves held an actual John Henry, the legendary figure in the song became a powerful symbol of human strength and dignity in the face of the crushing forces of industrialization.

Lewis accompanies his singing of the pentatonic melody with the rhythmic swing of an ax. In stanzas 1–5, each ax stroke lands on the third beat of the bar. A six-beat pause before stanza 6 (while Lewis recalls the words?) shifts the meter of the sung melody so that the downbeat coincides with the ax strokes for a full stanza. At the beginning of stanza 7 Lewis delays an ax stroke for two beats so that it will once again fall on the third beat, which it does through the end of the song. The implication is that the third beat is the correct place for the emphatic stroke, not the downbeat, and that stanza 6 is a mistake in the performance.

In their own words

Alan Lomax on a Folklorist's Duty

He goes where book-learning is not. He lives with the underprivileged. He brings back the proof in their songs and stories and dances that these folks are expressive and concerned about the beautiful and the good. In doing so, he continually denies the validity of caste lines and caste barriers. . . . The folklorist has the duty to speak as the advocate of the common man.

LG 14.4

"John Henry"

CD 2.20	Listening Guide 14.4	"John Henry" ANONYMOUS

DATE: recorded at Mississippi State Penitentiary, 1959

GENRE: African American work song

PERFORMER: Ed Lewis, vocal and ax strokes

METER: duple

FORM: strophic

WHAT TO LISTEN FOR

- coordination of meter to ax strokes
- pentatonic melody
- strophic form

TIMING	SECTION	TEXT	COMMENTS
0:00	stanza 1	Whoa John Henry went up on the mountain You know that mountain it was so high Whoa John Henry he laid his hammer down he cried "Captain, a ten-pound maul is too small, O Lord, A ten-pound maul too small"	Recording begins with an ax stroke on beat 3, followed by three vocal pickup notes. The first syllable of "Henry" lands on the first downbeat, with a strong emphasis. Subsequent ax strokes are on beat 3 of each bar.
0:32	stanza 2	Whoa John Henry he says to the captain, "Captain, pay me my whole back day I will make more money on that IC Line I will on this M&O Whoa than I will on the M&O"	Vocal line becomes more ornate, apparent in the last two lines of stanza.
1:03	stanza 3	Well John Henry's captain told him, "I have a power steel driver down home Well John Henry now if you'll beat that power driver down Going to buy you a railroad of your own I'm going to buy you a railroad of your own"	Continues in the more ornate vocal style.
1:33	stanza 4	Well John Henry told his captain He says, "A man ain't nothing but a man 'Fore I would stand and see your power driver beat me down Would die with my hammer in my hand Whoa I would die with my hammer in my hand"	The return to simpler vocal style gives emphasis to text.
2:02	stanza 5	Oh well the people all hear my running Well now the train coming down the track Oh John Henry throwed his hammer on the ground and he lay Say, "Echo from my hammer coming back Oh that's the echo from my hammer coming back"	
2:35	stanza 6	Well John Henry had a buddy Said, "Buddy, why ain't you taking your time?" John Henry drilled down eighteen spikes While his buddy was only driving down nine Oh while his buddy was only driving down nine	Delay of stanza for a bar and a half (6 beats) shifts the meter so that the ax strokes now fall on the downbeat of each bar.

	CD 2.20	Listening Guide 14.4	"John Henry" ANONYMOUS

TIMING	SECTION	TEXT	COMMENTS
3:04	stanza 7	John Henry he told his shaker He said, "My shaker, you better pray If I misses this deal on a deal going down Tomorrow be your burying day, You'll know tomorrow be your burying day"	Delay of the first ax stroke by two beats puts it once again on beat 3 of each bar.
3:32	stanza 8	Well John Henry told his captain Said, "Just bring your steam driver down here And before I let your steam driver beat me down Going to die with my hammer in the wind I'm going to die with my hammer in the wind"	
4:00	stanza 9	John Henry he had a little woman And her name was Polly Ann John Henry taken sick and he had to go to bed Polly Ann drilled steel like a man Whoa Polly Anne drove steel like a man	
	NOTE Field recording by Alan Lomax.		

Listen & Reflect

1. In the same year he made this field recording, Alan Lomax also recorded a group singing "Carrie Belle" (see LG 4.1). What similarities and differences can you hear between these two work songs?

2. "John Henry" tells a story: it is both a work song and a ballad. What features does it share with "The Gypsy Laddie" (see LG 9.2) and how does it differ?

Alan Lomax reached maturity during the Great Depression and, just as the economy was recovering, saw war break out in Europe. He came to perceive folk music as the distilled political expression of working people, hence a means to rally popular sentiment against evil. Convinced that he was working on behalf of true American patriotism, Lomax treated folk song as an ideological equivalent of the broadside ballads and abolition songs of earlier days. In a collection compiled by the Lomaxes, father and son, Alan Lomax set down his belief in folk song as a living force. For Lomax, a collector of folk songs was not merely an observer but also an agent with a political goal. In midcentury America, he was not alone in his conviction that folk song was a potent force for political change.

WOODY GUTHRIE

In March 1940 a landmark concert was held at New York's Forrest Theater for the benefit of migrant farm workers. Billed as a "Grapes of Wrath" evening, after John Steinbeck's 1939 novel, the concert was historic because the featured artists were folk musicians. Festivals during the 1930s had placed folk singers and players in front of paying audiences, and some had sung on the radio, at union events and political rallies, and even in nightclubs. Nevertheless, to present them in an evening concert setting, on a New York theater stage and in support of a political cause, was a novel idea. Among the singers who appeared that night, Woody Guthrie, newly arrived in the city, seems to have left the strongest impression.

the Dust Bowl

Born in 1912 in Oklahoma, Guthrie was a talented, prolific writer who also sang and played guitar and managed to avoid formal schooling in any of these pursuits. From his teenage years he lived a wandering life, including stints as a laborer, street singer, and hobo. In the course of his lifetime Guthrie wrote or adapted more than a thousand songs, reflecting his travels and emphasizing the Great Depression, the Dust Bowl drought of the 1930s, New Deal politics, and union organizing. Scornful of music with no message, Guthrie sang his politically inspired songs on picket lines, in marches, and at protest meetings. Alan Lomax, who heard Guthrie for the first time at the "Grapes of Wrath" concert, found him "miraculously" untouched by popular singing styles, a genuine political radical, and a gifted entertainer.

Lomax's respect increased even more as he experienced Guthrie's talent as a songwriter. During a cross-country trip to New York City in early 1940, Guthrie

⤙ Oklahoma-born Woody Guthrie (1912–1967) parlayed genuine folk roots and political radicalism into a prominent place in the folk revival movement that began in the late 1930s.

had come to hate a popular hit that seemed to be everywhere that winter, Irving Berlin's "God Bless America." As Guthrie saw it, Berlin's song—whose text invoked the timeless phrase "home, sweet home," a reference to a song from the early 1800s (see chapter 2)—glossed over social inequality as if it were God's will. In February, shortly after reaching New York, Guthrie wrote a song in six stanzas that answered the falsely inspirational quality of Berlin's hit. The fourth stanza reveals a hard edge of disenchantment:

"This Land Is Your Land"

> Was a big high wall there that tried to stop me
> A sign was painted said: Private Property.
> But on the back side, it didn't say nothing—
> God Blessed America for me.

And the sixth challenges Berlin's song directly:

> One bright sunny morning in the shadow of the steeple
> By the relief office I saw my people—
> As they stood there hungry, I stood there wondering if
> God Blessed America for me.

A few years later, and with changes, Guthrie's number became "This Land Is Your Land," a song hardly less affirmative than Berlin's, and an anthem of the 1960s counterculture.

After the "Grapes of Wrath" concert Lomax invited Guthrie to Washington to record for the Archive of American Folk Song. He soon discovered that the singer had a huge repertory (including "Gypsy Davy," Child ballad no. 200, which Guthrie sang to his own guitar accompaniment). And he learned too that Guthrie used the phonograph to expand his repertory and refine his style. Alan's sister Bess Lomax, who shared a house with Guthrie in 1941, recalled that countless repetitions of blues recordings by Blind Lemon Jefferson and T-Bone Slim helped him work on vocal delivery.

Guthrie recorded his own song "So Long, It's Been Good to Know You" (LG 14.5) at the Library of Congress in March 1940, accompanying himself on guitar. In waltz time and verse-and-chorus form, this ballad takes an unsentimental look at the impact of Depression-era droughts and dust storms on the people of the west Texas plains. Partway through a series of choruses and interludes, Guthrie breaks into storytelling mode over a guitar background. Using the chorus as an ironic punch line, he tells of a preacher who, facing the same hardship his worshipers were going through, decided to "cut price on salvation and sin." Calling his flock together for a message of consolation, he prepared to read his sermon. But finding the meetinghouse too dusty, "he folded his specs and took up collection" before heading out of town, singing, "So long, it's been good to know you."

LG 14.5

Though neither Guthrie's singing nor his Carter-style guitar playing sounds remarkable, both were major influences on the following generation of folk musicians. The unforced vocal delivery, with no attempt to mask his regional accent, allows Guthrie to move easily between speaking and singing. The artless quality of his voice and delivery, and the rolling rhythm that carries him over the rough edges in his singing and playing, set a standard that many folk-revival musicians took as a model of authenticity.

| CD 3.1 | Listening Guide 14.5 | "So Long, It's Been Good to Know You" WOODY GUTHRIE |

SONGWRITER: Woody Guthrie

DATE: 1940

PERFORMER: Woody Guthrie, vocal and guitar

GENRE: folk song

METER: triple

FORM: verse and chorus

WHAT TO LISTEN FOR

- Relaxed, folksy vocal delivery with regional accent
- Carter-style guitar playing
- spoken interlude for storytelling

TIMING	SECTION	COMMENTS
0:00	introduction	4 bars of Carter-style guitar, with a melody similar to the song's chorus.
0:07	chorus	The melody's sing-song, nursery-rhyme quality acts as a foil for the verses to come, signaling that a serious topic will be treated with humor.
0:25	interlude	Immediately after the last word of the chorus Guthrie plays a hammer-on, characteristic of the Carter style.
0:42	verse 1	Guthrie situates his song in Pampa, Texas, where he witnessed the Dust Bowl drought. The implication is that the song is factual and autobiographical.
1:02	chorus	
1:20	interlude	
1:40	spoken episode	Guthrie seems to be picking up the threads of a story already begun, a factual story from his own life.
2:11	verse 2	The mildly anticlerical punch line suggests that the autobiographical nature of the song should not be taken too seriously.
2:32	chorus	
2:49	interlude	A couple of hammer-ons enliven the bass-string melody.
3:01	verse 3	Guthrie moves smoothly from singing to speaking.
3:21	chorus	Return to singing for the final chorus.

NOTE Recorded by Alan Lomax.

Listen & Reflect

1. At least two features of Guthrie's performance could be considered mistakes: (1) when accompanying his singing, he often muffs guitar notes instead of playing them cleanly and clearly, and (2) although his tune implies regular four-bar phrases throughout, he sometimes pauses for an extra bar or two before moving on to the next phrase, as if he weren't sure of the next words. Yet the second "mistake," at least, was widely imitated by Guthrie's admirers. What positive musical effects might be attributed to his less-than-perfect performance technique?

PETE SEEGER AND THE BIRTH OF THE URBAN FOLK REVIVAL

It was during his stay in Washington that Woody Guthrie became the musical mentor of Pete Seeger, a young musician who, like Alan Lomax, came to folk music through inclination rather than birthright, and who was also working at the Archive of American Folk Song. Born to the musicologist Charles Seeger and his first wife, a concert violinist, Pete Seeger was introduced to folk music in the mid-1930s by his father and stepmother Ruth, who were then living in Washington.

Ruth Crawford Seeger had by this time virtually stopped composing the ultramodernist music that had led her to Charles Seeger (see chapter 13). Instead, she was balancing household duties with transcribing melodies that the Lomaxes had recorded for the archive. From this time until her death in 1953, she would produce several volumes of folk song transcriptions, either independently or with the Lomaxes or other collectors. She also promoted the use of folk songs in elementary music education. Meanwhile, Pete, who had imbibed radical politics in his own family circle, dropped out of college after two years, learned the five-string banjo, and moved to Washington. He arrived there at a time when a young man with his background, talent, work habits, and politics could make an impact as a folk musician, a career that until then had not existed.

The New York "Grapes of Wrath" evening in 1940 gave Pete Seeger his first chance to see Woody Guthrie in action and to experience the power of political folk music in a concert setting. Alan Lomax later said that from that night forward, "Pete knew it was his kind of music, and he began working to make it everybody's kind of music." To Seeger, folk styles were perfectly suited to the political messages

🖙 Ruth Crawford Seeger (playing a lap dulcimer), with her husband, Charles Seeger, and their children Michael and Peggy, pictured in Washington around 1937. Both Michael and Peggy would grow up to become influential folk musicians, as would Pete Seeger, one of Charles's sons from his first marriage.

In their own words

Woody Guthrie Tells a Radio Audience the Difference between His Songs and Popular Songs (1944)

I hate a song that makes you think that you are not any good. I hate a song makes you think that you are just born to lose. Bound to lose. No good to nobody. No good for nothing.... Songs that run you down or poke fun at you on account of your bad luck or hard traveling.

I am out to fight those kind of songs to my very last breath of air and my last drop of blood.

I am out to sing songs that'll prove to you that this is your world and that if it's hit you pretty hard and knocked you for a dozen loops, no matter how hard it's run you down or rolled you over, no matter what color, what size you are, how you are built, I am out to sing the songs that make you take pride in yourself and in your work.

that he, Guthrie, and Lomax wanted to convey: unvarnished truths about life, in contrast to the falsehoods of Tin Pan Alley and Broadway.

American folk music had reached a pivotal moment in its historical development. The preparatory stage had been set by the recognition that folk songs did not have to be anonymous works of great antiquity, that recent songs by known songwriters could enter the oral tradition and become part of the folk repertory. Now the concept of who could or could not be a folk musician was undergoing a similar transformation. For the early song catchers, folk musicians were plain people embedded in their traditional communities and cultures. Thanks to the efforts of the Lomaxes and others, some of these folk musicians—such as Woody Guthrie, Leadbelly, and Jean Ritchie—had traveled outside their home communities to perform, sometimes in comparatively formal concert situations, for larger audiences unfamiliar with their music's original contexts and meanings. Along the way, these musicians had learned how to present their songs in a more accessible package, by including spoken introductions and explanations.

The final step in this pivotal transformation was the rise of the "urban folk" singer: a musician who performs folk songs from a traditional culture that is not his or her own. In many cases, these new folk singers of the 1940s learned the songs they performed secondhand, through the work of collectors such as the Lomaxes, though most of them followed up that introduction with fieldwork of their own. In this way, Manhattan-born, Harvard-educated Pete Seeger became a singer of songs only remotely connected with either New York City or Cambridge, Massachusetts.

urban folk singers   Another important factor separated this new breed of folk singers from their traditional forebears: whereas the singers whose songs were collected by Cecil Sharp and Olive Dame Campbell were amateur musicians, the urban folk singers were determined to make their livings as performers. Yet how were these musicians to make a living selling their noncommercial songs?

Early in 1941 Seeger joined with Lee Hays, Millard Lampell, and Guthrie to form the Almanac Singers. Singing about peace, war, and politics, the group set up Almanac House, a cooperative in New York City's Greenwich Village, where they lived and held weekly musical gatherings. They sang at union and political rallies and occasionally on the radio. They also made recordings. The Almanacs have been called the first urban folk-singing group, pursuing a goal stated by Lampell: "We are trying to give back to the people the songs of the workers." Guthrie summarized the group's activist philosophy: "The biggest parts of our song collection are aimed at restoring the right amount of people to the right amount of land and the right amount of houses and the right amount of groceries to the right amount of working folks."

The Almanac Singers possessed the talent and charisma of successful entertainers, though they rejected that label. And as they sang for a widening range of audiences, their music struck a responsive chord, even with listeners who did not share their political outlook. After the United States entered the war in December 1941, the Almanacs added anti-Nazi songs to their repertory. They even auditioned successfully at the Rainbow Room, a swanky nightclub atop a Rockefeller Center skyscraper in midtown Manhattan, singing these words to the Appalachian tune "Old Joe Clark":

> Round and round Hitler's grave
> Round and round we go,
> We're going to lay that poor boy down
> he won't get up no more.
>
> I wish I had a bushel
> I wish I had a peck
> I wish I had old Hitler
> With a rope around his neck.

Cecil Sharp and Robert Winslow Gordon had thought of folk music as coming from the past. In contrast, Pete Seeger, the Lomaxes, and the Almanac Singers approached it as a living force in the present. To Woody Guthrie, performing in something close to his native vernacular, such categories as folklore and folk music hardly existed. To urban folk musicians, on the other hand, the labels marked an identity and a community that they had imagined into being. Folk music by the middle of the century had become a means not only of expressing traditions but also of creating them.

In the interwar years, the labels blues, gospel, country, and folk came to embrace overlapping musical styles, displaying the hybridity characteristic of American music as a whole. The borders between these styles can be hard to pin down. What unites them is their position at the collision of contradictory attitudes toward the creation and ownership of music. On the one hand is a traditionalist stance that sees music as common property to be freely drawn upon by all musicians; from this point of view, new songs are created by taking bits and pieces of old songs and reworking them to fit the expressive needs of the present day. On the other hand is a stance that sees pieces of music as the intellectual property of those who create them; from this point of view, it is fitting that these artistic statements earn a profit as they satisfy the public's expressive needs.

The contrasting goals of these two attitudes have created a tension in America's musical culture that has endured for nearly a century. If anything, the legal stakes surrounding it are higher than ever in the twenty-first century.

QUESTIONS FOR DISCUSSION AND REVIEW

1. What are the differences between classic blues and country blues?

2. What are the similarities and differences between black gospel music, spirituals (see chapter 9), and blues? How did those musical relationships affect the reception of gospel music in Chicago's black churches?

3. Of blues, jazz, gospel music, and country music, which styles allowed women to rise to prominence and which did not? What might be possible reasons for the differences?

4. Summarize the role of communications technology in the development of country music.

5. Although western swing has jazz influences, not everyone agrees that it should be considered a type of jazz. At the same time, Bob Wills insisted that his music should not be confused with "hillbilly music." What evidence supports the argument that western swing is jazz? What evidence supports the argument that it is country music?

6. Compare the attitudes and practices of folk song collectors like John and Alan Lomax with those of A&R men like Ralph Peer.

7. Compare the relationship between singer, song, and audience in three cases: (1) an Appalachian ballad singer before the arrival of Olive Dame Campbell and Cecil Sharp; (2) Leadbelly singing for college students in the Northeast; and (3) Pete Seeger performing at a leftist political rally.

8. Review the opening section of chapter 9 in light of the present chapter. Do you agree or disagree with the following statement, and why? "The urban folk singers and collectors discarded the distorted ideology of Herder and his followers, but they replaced it with the new distortions of communist ideology."

FURTHER READING

Cray, Ed. *Ramblin' Man: The Life and Times of Woody Guthrie.* New York: W.W. Norton, 2004.

George-Warren, Holly. *Public Cowboy No. 1: The Life and Times of Gene Autry.* New York: Oxford University Press, 2007.

Gioia, Ted. *Delta Blues: The Life and Times of the Mississippi Masters Who Revolutionized American Music.* New York: W.W. Norton, 2008.

Harris, Michael W. *The Rise of Gospel Blues: The Music of Thomas Andrew Dorsey in the Urban Church.* New York: Oxford University Press, 1992.

Lieberman, Robbie. *My Song Is My Weapon: People's Songs, American Communism, and the Politics of Culture, 1930–1950.* Urbana: University of Illinois Press, 1989.

Malone, Bill C. *Country Music, U.S.A.* 2d rev. [i.e., 3d] ed. Austin: University of Texas Press, 2002.

Nelson, Scott Reynolds. *Steel Drivin' Man: John Henry, the Untold Story of an American Legend.* New York: Oxford University Press, 2008.

Wolfe, Charles, and Kip Lornell. *The Life and Legend of Leadbelly.* New York: HarperCollins, 1992.

FURTHER VIEWING

Times Ain't Like They Used to Be: Early Rural and Popular American Music, 1928–1935. Sherwin Dunner and Richard Nevins, producers. DVD. Yazoo, 1992. An anthology of short films featuring Jimmie Rodgers, Bob Wills, and other early country, blues, and old-time musicians.

FILM MUSIC, MUSICAL COMEDY, AND SWING BEFORE AND DURING WORLD WAR II

The impact of two new technologies on American music early in the twentieth century—the phonograph and radio—has been noted in the foregoing chapters. This one completes the trilogy with a survey of music for motion pictures, including movie musicals. We then move from Hollywood to Broadway to consider developments in the stage musical circa 1940, before heading to Kansas City for an overview of big band swing and the elevation of jazz singing to one of the United States' characteristic art forms.

FILM MUSIC

One of the most important cultural developments in the years between the world wars was the rise of motion pictures as a popular medium of art and entertainment. The financial success of the movies lured actors, dancers, writers, graphic artists, and musicians from all over the United States, as well as from Europe and the rest of the Americas, to Hollywood, the center of the film industry. The movies offered musicians of many stripes work that paid well, and the special demands of the medium created new kinds of cinematic music.

THE FILM SCORE

From the beginning, silent movies were never truly silent. At first, player pianos and other mechanical instruments were used to cover the noise of the film projector; no attempt was made to coordinate the music to the film. But live musicians, whether a single pianist or organist or a complete theater orchestra, proved far more effective for providing a continuous musical accompaniment. A popular nineteenth-century stage genre, the melodrama, had featured live actors, sparse dialogue, and copious music to accompany the stage action; theater musicians simply transferred the repertory and techniques of matching music to action from melodrama to "photoplays," as the movies were sometimes called. In this way, movie palaces created work for musicians much as live theater had done since colonial times.

Film accompanists generally played whatever they wished, choosing or improvising music that suited the shifting action on-screen. Any type of pre-existing music could be commandeered for the purpose: popular songs, traditional tunes, classical instrumental pieces, or selections from grand opera. Many musicians worked from anthologies of movie music identified by generic mood; the first such collection, published in 1909, consisted of fifty-one short piano pieces, each labeled with a tempo, mood, character, or situation. As an aid to fitting music to a film, studios distributed cue sheets breaking a film down into scenes, with a suggestion for a musical genre or mood appropriate to each scene, such as "Irish jig" or "Plaintive." This practice indicated a growing appreciation of music's role in the cinematic experience and consequently in a movie's commercial success or failure.

Filmmakers and studio executives thus began to exercise increasing control over musical accompaniments. Even before World War I the film studios hired musicians to create or compile musical scores tailored to specific films. These scores were prepared as a set of parts for a theater orchestra, including a conductor's score with cues for coordinating the music to the film, to be distributed to presenters along with the film reels and promotional materials. If a theater orchestra was not available, the score could be used by the pianist or organist.

One of the landmark film scores of the silent era was Joseph Carl Breil's music for *The Birth of a Nation*, director D. W. Griffith's 1915 Civil War epic. Designed to run nonstop through the entire three-hour film, Breil's music mixes original composition with a potpourri of borrowed material: Civil War songs and other patriotic tunes, but also snippets of Beethoven, Grieg, Tchaikovsky, and Wagner. Breil's *leitmotif* score uses the technique of **leitmotif**, in which a musical theme associated with a specific character, object, or situation in the drama recurs whenever its referent is on-screen. Breil's inspiration may have been Wagner's operas, which use leitmotifs extensively, but another likely source of the practice was the melodrama.

With the advent of sound film technology in the late 1920s, it became possible *soundtrack* to record the musical score, now often called the **soundtrack**, in perfect synchronization with the moving picture. (A technological boon for the movies, sound recording was a death knell for theater musicians.) The first feature-length "talkie," *The Jazz Singer* (1927), included a few scenes in which Al Jolson sang and engaged in spoken dialogue with the other actors; his most famous line was the prophetic "You ain't heard nothin' yet." Most of the film, however, is distinguishable from the old-style silent film only in that the orchestral accompaniment is recorded rather than performed live.

The Jazz Singer makes a distinction between the two kinds of music heard in a sound film: **diegetic music**, or **source music**, which is part of the action on-*source music* screen and thus audible to the characters in the story, and **nondiegetic music**, *underscoring* or **underscoring**, which heightens the mood or clarifies plot or character and is inaudible to the characters.

In their first few years, sound movies placed the emphasis on diegetic music, since audiences enjoyed the novelty of hearing the people in the pictures singing and playing instruments. Soon, however, Hollywood composers began to explore the nondiegetic possibilities of the soundtrack's close coordination of music and *Max Steiner* action. One of the first musicians to do so was Max Steiner (1888–1971), a Viennese émigré with a background in operetta and musical comedy who came to Hollywood by way of Broadway (he was one of the orchestrators for the Gershwins'

Lady Be Good! in 1924). Steiner's score for *King Kong* (1933) is an early landmark in sound film: its **title music**, played under the opening credits, functions like an operatic overture, setting the tone for the ensuing drama and introducing important leitmotifs. At its best, as in the sweeping "Tara" theme from *Gone with the Wind* (1939), Steiner's music adds grandeur and emotional intensity to the cinematic experience. At its worst, his music can be busy and intrusive, a holdover from the silent era, when the music had to be continuous from start to finish.

Max Steiner (1888–1971) rehearses the New York Philharmonic for an outdoor concert in 1943.

Steiner's film scores set the tone for what has been called Hollywood's "golden age," from the advent of sound through the 1950s. A number of the golden age's leading film composers were, like Steiner, European émigrés with classical training; some had careers as concert performers and composers in addition to their film work. Among them were the German Franz Waxman (*The Bride of Frankenstein,* 1935), the Hungarian Miklós Rósza (*The Thief of Baghdad,* 1940), and the Ukrainian Dimitri Tiomkin (*High Noon,* 1952). One of the few native-born American contemporaries to match their level of achievement was Alfred Newman (*Wuthering Heights,* 1939)—unlike the Europeans, essentially self-taught as a composer.

Perhaps the most remarkable film composer of this generation was Erich Wolfgang Korngold (1897–1957), who as a child prodigy in his native Vienna won the praise of Gustav Mahler, Richard Strauss, and other eminent musicians. Before the age of twenty Korngold had composed two operas, a ballet, and several orchestral, chamber, and solo piano pieces. When the Austrian director Max Reinhardt came to Hollywood in 1934, he encouraged Korngold to accompany him there. For the next several years, Korngold produced some of the best film scores of the period, including *The Adventures of Robin Hood* (1938), *The Sea Hawk* (1940), and *King's Row* (1941). Korngold's lush, romantic film scores have been called "operas without singing," and their complex, intricate scoring and elaborate systems of leitmotifs make them true successors to the operas of Wagner and Richard Strauss.

Erich Wolfgang Korngold

Korngold's concert music and film scores are essentially identical in style—so much so, in fact, that one of his most attractive concert works, the Violin Concerto in D major, op. 35, composed in 1945, reworks themes from four of his film scores. By the time Jascha Heifetz played the concerto's premiere in 1947, however, Korngold's opulent late-romantic style was considered out of date in the concert hall. Only in recent years has a new generation of violinists taken up Korngold's cause, and the concerto is now a standard part of the virtuoso violin repertory.

THE FILM MUSICAL

Not all film music of the era was classical in flavor. Three film genres used popular music prominently and in pathbreaking ways: the animated cartoon (which also made copious use of classical music), the story musical based on fantasy, and the dance musical.

In 1928 Walt Disney produced a short film picturing a cartoon character called Mickey Mouse as pilot—with Minnie Mouse as passenger—of a boat transporting a collection of animals down a river. At a time when the industry was changing from silent film to sound, the animation of *Steamboat Willie* was made to a metronome's beat, and rhythmic energy pulses through the assortment of whistles, cowbells, and tin pans featured in the soundtrack. The characters find musical instruments in unlikely places: Minnie Mouse cranks a billy goat's tail as if it were a street organ to make the animal sing, while Mickey plays on a cow's teeth as though on a xylophone. Within a decade, Disney began to make feature-length animated films, still relying on music to carry the action, as in *Snow White and the Seven Dwarfs* (1937).

Among movie musicals based on fantasy, perhaps the era's greatest achievement was MGM's *The Wizard of Oz* (1939), which dramatized the children's tale by L. Frank Baum and featured a score by Harold Arlen and E. Y. "Yip" Harburg. The film, made for more than $2.5 million at a time when a loaf of bread and a gallon of gasoline cost six cents each, relied heavily on special effects. In the familiar story, twelve-year-old Dorothy is lifted up by a cyclone from the plains of Kansas and whirled into the magical land of Oz. There she meets several strange companions who join her in a visit to the Wizard, who helps her return home. The Kansas sequences are filmed in sepia-toned black and white, but Dorothy's adventures in Oz, where she encounters a yellow brick road and the Emerald City, appear in color.

"Over the Rainbow," the film's most famous song, has a clear function in the story: it shows the strength of Dorothy's imagination as she pictures a place more interesting to live than the Kansas flatland. Convinced that the film needed a melody here with breadth and sweep, Arlen filled the bill with a ballad based on bold upward leaps. Sung by the sixteen-year-old Judy Garland playing a preadolescent, the song could not revel in the kind of romantic love that dominated the day's popular music. But with Harburg's words sketching a vivid fantasy supported by Arlen's expansive music, the number takes on a grandeur of its own.

🎵 Sixteen-year-old Judy Garland's sophisticated vocal delivery helped make Harold Arlen and Yip Harburg's "Over the Rainbow" a highlight of *The Wizard of Oz* (1939).

By the late 1930s the Hollywood musical had settled on a more or less standard framework: a modern-day romantic comedy that featured four or five songs. The high demand for film musicals drew to southern California, at one time or another, virtually all of Broadway's songwriting talent, lured by the generous salaries, pleasant weather, and relatively light workload (a film score required about one-quarter the songs needed for a Broadway musical). In a typical movie musical at least one song involved some dancing, and in one genre, the **dance musical**, nearly all the songs included dance. The key figure in the dance musical was Fred Astaire, a veteran of vaudeville and Broadway whose assets included accomplished musicianship, a talent for light comedy, and perfection as a dancer, though not the handsomeness of a romantic screen idol.

In 1933 Astaire signed a contract with RKO Radio Pictures, and before long he was paired with actress-dancer Ginger Rogers in a collaboration now recognized as a miracle of Hollywood's studio era. By 1939 Astaire and Rogers had appeared in nine films together and established the dance musical as a genre. Their films stand out not for the quantity of dancing (other dance musicals had just as much or more) but for its high quality and the use of dance to further narration and establish character. Astaire, who as a star won the right to choreograph these dances and even to help edit them on film, was a perfectionist who might spend weeks on a three-minute dance routine. He also brought to the dancing an unparalleled dramatic flair and musical sensibility—his tap dancing was as rhythmically sophisticated as good jazz drumming. The drama is contained within the dancing, the only really serious element in the Astaire-Rogers films. Only rarely do the characters they play show much distinctiveness; the interest and the fun lie in how the couple overcome misunderstandings and other obstacles to a romantic happy ending through singing and dancing.

The excellence of Astaire and Rogers' dancing attracted some of the best collaborators Hollywood could muster, including songwriters Irving Berlin, George and Ira Gershwin, and the team of Jerome Kern and Dorothy Fields. Berlin supplied five songs for *Top Hat* (1935), one of three Astaire-Rogers films on which he worked; all five were popular hits in the year the movie was released, and one, "Cheek to Cheek" (LG 15.1), became a standard.

  In this scene from the 1935 film *Top Hat*, Ginger Rogers and Fred Astaire are dancing to Irving Berlin's "Isn't This a Lovely Day?"

LG 15.1

Like many songs written for film, "Cheek to Cheek" has no verse: more or less continuous underscoring smoothes the transition from speech to song and makes the verse, so important in stage songs, unnecessary. Perhaps in compensation, Berlin creates an unusually expansive chorus, seventy-two bars in length. He doubles the proportions of each section of an *aaba* song from eight bars to sixteen; moreover, he adds an extra eight-bar section before the final *a* (*aabca*). In effect the song has two bridges (*b* and *c*), suggesting two alternative ways that a bridge can provide contrast. Departing from the rhapsodic, expansive mood of the *a* sections, the first bridge strikes a more conversational tone, turning to such unromantic subjects as fishing and hiking. But instead of returning to the *a* section to match the earlier emotional scale, Berlin ratchets up the emotion even further in the second bridge, with its declamatory melody and tension-filled harmonies. The final *a* section is then felt as a relaxation of the intense *c* section.

With those seventy-two bars, Berlin's work on "Cheek to Cheek" was done. Ensuring its integration into the film was the work of other, less celebrated craftsmen: the five arrangers who, under the direction of music supervisor Max Steiner, developed Berlin's song into a six-and-a-half-minute routine including (1) a complete statement of the song as instrumental underscoring for dialogue, (2) Astaire's vocal performance of the complete song, and (3) instrumental accompaniment for a three-minute dance, in which the song's five sections are repeated, reordered, and sometimes truncated to suit the choreography. Both on Broadway and in Hollywood, arrangers played a key role in making the musical numbers the highlight of shows.

CD 3.2	Listening Guide 15.1	"Cheek to Cheek" IRVING BERLIN

DATE: composed 1935; this recording from 1937

PERFORMERS: Fred Astaire with studio orchestra

GENRE: film musical song

METER: duple

FORM: *aabca* chorus, 72 bars (16 + 16 + 16 + 8 + 16)

WHAT TO LISTEN FOR

- romantic ballad in dance rhythm
- Astaire's relaxed, informal vocal delivery
- extension of chorus with second bridge

TIMING	SECTION	TEXT	COMMENTS
0:00	intro		Based on end of chorus's *a* section.
0:06	*a*	Heaven, I'm in heaven . . .	Two-note motive ("Heaven . . .") is manipulated by inverting it and by stringing together in melodic ascent; relaxes downward. Ending breaks from motive.
0:29	*a*	Heaven, I'm in heaven . . .	Literal repeat of melody and accompaniment. Note alternation of strings and saxes over danceable rhythm section, with muted brass "sting" at end.
0:52	*b*	Oh I love to climb a mountain . . .	Jaunty syncopation sets a more relaxed mood. Walking bass and muted trumpet add a jazzy touch, while strings hint at the *a* section's two-note motive.
1:17	*c*	Dance with me . . .	Impassioned melody over a bed of sustained saxes, with dramatic trumpet fanfares.
1:29	*a*	Heaven, I'm in heaven . . .	Literal return to the opening *a*.

NOTE This excerpt from a studio recording fades out after the first full chorus.

Listen & Reflect

1. Compared with his dancing, Fred Astaire's voice seems unremarkable, even ordinary. Yet he was a favorite singer of Irving Berlin and other songwriters. Why might that be?
2. Using a DVD or other resource, view the scene in *Top Hat* that includes "Cheek to Cheek," noting how the song is used both preceding Astaire's singing (as underscoring) and following it (as dance accompaniment). What features of the music make it appropriate for both purposes?

THE MODERNIST FILM SCORE: COPLAND IN HOLLYWOOD

In addition to musicals, other film genres included the occasional on-screen performance of a popular song. Low-budget westerns, for example, mass produced by the minor film studios, featured singing cowboys like Gene Autry crooning country and western songs. It was in a western, in fact, that the next major development in film music took place, shortly before World War II: a shift toward more American-sounding music, often with a modernist slant.

When *Stagecoach* (1939) won two Academy Awards and was nominated for five others, director John Ford established the western as more than B-movie fodder for Saturday matinees; films set in the American West could now be prestige films for the major studios. One of *Stagecoach*'s two Oscars was for best music scoring, indicating that the film's soundtrack would prove influential. The score—the work of a team of studio composers headed by Richard Hageman, a Dutch musician who had conducted at the Metropolitan Opera— was, according to the credits, "based on American folk songs," an accurate enough description if the designation "folk" is taken in its broadest meaning. A tapestry of cowboy songs, minstrel tunes, parlor songs, and gospel hymns, the *Stagecoach* soundtrack counted on "Jeanie with the Light Brown Hair," "The Battle Cry of Freedom," "Shall We Gather at the River," and a fistful of other familiar melodies to trigger emotional associations for the film's viewers.

Stagecoach

By combining the symphonic techniques of the golden-age film score with American folk songs, *Stagecoach* shared in the populist tendencies found in the 1930s music of modernist composers like Roy Harris and Virgil Thomson. Only a year earlier, in 1938, Aaron Copland had used cowboy songs in his ballet *Billy the Kid,* and he would do so again in his ballet *Rodeo* (1942). The key difference lay in the kind of symphonic scoring used: lush and romantic in the film scores, lean and astringent in Copland's ballets. By the 1950s and later, however, western film scores would come to resemble Copland's style almost to the point of parody. The influence of Copland on film music stemmed mostly from his success in working within the Hollywood studio system as a film composer himself.

Copland's cowboy ballets

Copland's first opportunity to try his hand as a movie composer came not from Hollywood but from the Carnegie Corporation, which sponsored the creation of a documentary film to be shown at the 1939 New York World's Fair. *The City* is a half-hour film about urban planning with a strong ideological slant, contrasting an idealized New England village of the past with present-day industrialized slums and closing with a utopian vision of the city of the future. The scenario is perfectly suited to Copland's musical style: pastoral Americana in the outer sections contrast with jarring dissonance for the central depiction of urban blight, the whole framed by modernist fanfares that sound like a call to action.

The City

Critical acclaim for *The City* attracted the attention of Hollywood studios, and soon Copland had a contract to write music for the 1939 film version of John Steinbeck's *Of Mice and Men,* the first of Copland's five scores for feature motion pictures. The 1940 film version of Thornton Wilder's *Our Town* quickly followed. Copland also wrote scores for *The Red Pony,* another Steinbeck adaptation, and *The Heiress,* based on Henry James's novella *Washington Square* (both 1949). More than a decade separates those literary adaptations from Copland's final movie score, for the independent film *Something Wild* (1961).

CHARLES K. FELDMAN presents

MYRNA   ROBERT
LOY · MITCHUM

in *John Steinbeck's*

The RED PONY

A *LEWIS MILESTONE* PRODUCTION

with **LOUIS CALHERN**

and **SHEPPERD STRUDWICK**
and
introducing **PETER MILES** *as* TOM

and **MARGARET HAMILTON** Screen Play by JOHN STEINBECK Music by AARON COPLAND

Produced and Directed by **LEWIS MILESTONE**

A REPUBLIC PRODUCTION

☙ Regarded today as the film's best feature, Aaron Copland's music is barely mentioned in this poster for *The Red Pony* (1949).

In various writings about movie music in the 1940s, Copland distinguished his own efforts from those of his Hollywood predecessors on several counts. Unlike Korngold and company, Copland rejected the notion that a late romantic style was appropriate for all film subjects. He also dismissed the leitmotif as an overworked cliché, too often hammered home in an obvious way. Moreover, he criticized composers like Steiner for matching the music too closely to the screen action, an effect more appropriate for cartoons than for live action pictures—an attitude implied by the industry term **mickey-mousing** to describe such scoring. Finally, another attribute that separates Copland from earlier film composers is his greater reliance on silence; instead of filling a scene with neutral background music that might swell up for the climax of a scene, he withholds the music until the dramatic climax, where its entry can increase the scene's emotional impact.

Recognizing that his movie music was more than background filler, Copland reworked music from all his film scores into orchestral concert works. One of the finest is *The Red Pony Suite,* a series of six movements that had its premiere in Houston in 1948, before the film had been released. The music is perhaps the best thing about the film, an unsuccessful attempt at a "prestige picture" by Republic, a studio that had established itself in the 1930s as a manufacturer of low-budget science fiction serials and B westerns (Republic's biggest star was Gene Autry; see chapter 14). In an attempt to raise its artistic status, Republic's executives took on two highbrow projects in 1948: Orson Welles's version of Shakespeare's *Macbeth,* and *The Red Pony,* using the same artistic team that had filmed Steinbeck's *Of Mice and Men* in 1939. Despite being Republic's most expensive picture to date, *The Red Pony* did poorly at the box office when it was released in 1949, and it failed to earn a single Academy Award nomination. (The Best Music award that year went to Copland's score for *The Heiress.*) Consequently, Copland's music for *The Red Pony* is more familiar today in its concert form than in its original cinematic context.

The score of the concert suite contains the following note by the composer:

Steinbeck's well-known tale is a series of vignettes concerning a ten-year-old boy called Jody, and his life in a California ranch setting. There is a minimum of action of a dramatic or startling kind. The story gets its warmth and sensitive quality from the character studies of the boy Jody, Jody's grandfather, the cow-hand Billy Buck, and Jody's parents, the Tiflins. The kind of emotions that Steinbeck evokes in his story are basically musical ones, since they deal so much with the unexpressed feelings of daily living.

LG 15.2   The suite's opening movement, "Morning on the Ranch" (LG 15.2), carries the following description: "Sounds of daybreak. The daily chores begin. A folk-like

CD 3.3	Listening Guide 15.2	"Morning on the Ranch," from *The Red Pony Suite*
		AARON COPLAND

DATE: 1948

PERFORMERS: New Philharmonia Orchestra; Aaron Copland, conductor

GENRE: film music

METER: changing

FORM: binary (AB) with coda

WHAT TO LISTEN FOR

- broad, grandiose fanfares in slower A
- gentler, folklike music in faster B
- colorful orchestration
- pandiatonic harmony and gradual crescendo near end of B section

TIMING	SECTION	SCREEN ACTION	COMMENTS
0:00	A	Opening credits	Compound duple meter and slow tempo. After a short buildup, strings, trumpets, and woodwinds play fanfare with lowered seventh scale degree.
0:23		Nature at dawn	Soft, sustained tones.
0:51			Overlapping statements of falling pentatonic scale that began the title theme, in clarinet, then violins; gradual crescendo.
1:09			The rising scale of the opening buildup returns.
1:17		Opening credits	The fanfare returns, louder than before.
1:38	B	Morning chores	Low-register flutes play, then repeat, the opening phrase of folklike tune (*a*).
1:51			Contrasting phrase (*b*) in oboe.
2:01			Return of *a* in flutes and strings, with a new concluding phrase (*c*).
2:20			A second folk theme (*d*) makes a fragmentary appearance in the oboe.
2:30			Transition back to *a* with clarinets in thirds.
2:46			Return of *a*, suddenly quiet and now in violins over active accompaniment. Oboe answers with *b*.
3:07		The foal's birth	Theme *a* in high, muted violins, harp, glockenspiel, and celesta, creating a soft, shimmering, pandiatonic sonority.
3:13			Gradual buildup with added instruments: woodwinds and lower strings, then French horns and muted trumpets.
3:25			Brittle piano joins in for *b* over a pulsating accompaniment.

(continued)

| | | CD 3.3 | Listening Guide 15.2 | "Morning on the Ranch," from *The Red Pony Suite*
AARON COPLAND |

TIMING	SECTION	SCREEN ACTION	COMMENTS
3:38			Final, and loudest, statement of *a*, in trombones and open trumpets.
3:50	coda	Galloping pony	Closing theme in the style of a fiddle tune, with boisterous "oom-pah" accompaniment.
4:06		Closing credits	Return of opening fanfare.

Listen & Reflect

1. If you knew nothing about the Steinbeck story or film and heard this music with no explanation of its original purpose, would it make sense on purely musical terms? Why or why not?

2. If possible, view the opening and closing scenes of *The Red Pony* online or on DVD or videocassette. How did Copland restructure the film music for the concert suite, and why? Why would the music as written for the film not work as well in the concert hall? Although Copland avoids "mickey-mousing," how does he shape the music to suit the visual image onscreen?

melody suggests the atmosphere of simple country living." The music draws from the beginning of the movie's soundtrack, which extends through the opening credits to scenes of wildlife stirring at dawn and the morning activities on a California ranch around the turn of the twentieth century. Copland cast this opening music for *The Red Pony* in the antique form of a French overture (ca. 1650–1750): a slow, stately opening, followed by a much livelier section. Copland's slow section comprises the fanfare-like title music and a softer continuation evoking the natural world at dawn. The fast section, depicting morning chores on the farm, repeats folklike melodic phrases with ever-changing orchestration. In the movie this music thins out and fades under dialogue at the breakfast table; for the concert piece Copland jumps to a variation of the folklike melody originally used in the film's closing moments, showing the birth of a foal. A brief coda uses music that in the film represents the galloping foal, now grown, and concludes with a return of the title music.

Rather than borrow actual folk songs, Copland creates original melodies in the style of folk song, using simple rhythms, short phrases, and diatonic scales—not only major and minor but also the modal scales of Anglo-American ballads. The melodies' narrow ranges and highly repetitive structure, however, relate less to traditional American songs and more to the Russian folk tunes used by Igor Stravinsky—a modernist admired highly by Copland and his teacher Nadia

Boulanger—in his 1911 ballet *Petrushka*. The musical depiction of the foal's birth also resembles *Petrushka*'s evocation of a Russian peasant fair: shimmering harp, celesta, glockenspiel, and high strings are gradually joined by the woodwinds and brass in a pulsating wash of **pandiatonic** sound, in which all the notes of the diatonic scale are sounded together.

pandiatonicism

Ironically, it is this musical style—indebted to Stravinsky, a denizen of Paris when Copland was studying there in the 1920s—that came to be emblematic of the American West. Copland never scored a cowboy picture; nevertheless, his manner of applying Russian modernist technique and vocabulary to musical materials from the Anglo-American tradition in his two cowboy ballets, *Billy the Kid* and *Rodeo*, and his music for the two Steinbeck films, both set in California, came to be heard as an evocation of the West. After *The Red Pony*, most Hollywood westerns sported soundtracks with Coplandesque music. Among the best is Elmer Bernstein's music for *The Magnificent Seven* (1960); the memorable title music echoes both Copland and, through him, Stravinsky.

But Copland's influence on Hollywood extended even further, setting the example of an accessible modernist idiom flexible enough to be applied to all sorts of motion pictures. Copland's film scores proved that musically unsophisticated audiences would accept modernist music when it was used intelligently and appropriately for cinematic purposes. Movies, Copland hoped, could be a means of disseminating modernist music to people who might never hear it in a concert hall but who, through this exposure, could come to have a greater appreciation for new musical trends.

In the decades since Copland's Hollywood period, that is exactly what has happened, as movies, and later television programs, have made mass audiences familiar with avant-garde musical techniques that otherwise only a small number of listeners would hear. In that sense, the movie industry has played an important role in dismantling the cultural hierarchy in force earlier in the twentieth century. The music of the United States after World War II would inhabit a much more fluid cultural space, not easily polarized into highbrow and lowbrow.

THE BROADWAY MUSICAL THROUGH WORLD WAR II

Between the onset of the Great Depression and the end of World War II, a significant shift in the aesthetic of the musical comedy placed new demands on show songs. That shift in taste is nowhere more apparent than in the career of Richard Rodgers, which is marked by two long-term collaborations with major lyricists. Between 1919 and 1942 Rodgers worked with Lorenz Hart in the creation of twenty-six Broadway shows and nine Hollywood films, among them some of the most successful musicals of that time: *Jumbo* (1935), *On Your Toes* (1936), *Babes in Arms* (1937), *The Boys from Syracuse* (1938), and *Pal Joey* (1940). Typically for shows of the time, none of these has seen more than the occasional revival since its initial run. Yet the many memorable songs of Rodgers and Hart—"Manhattan," "Blue Moon," "With a Song in My Heart," "Where or When," "My Funny Valentine," "The Lady Is a Tramp," "Bewitched, Bothered, and Bewildered," to name only a few—are evergreen standards.

Rodgers and Hart

Rodgers and Hammerstein

Rodgers had had a troubled partnership with Hart, whose alcoholism and chaotic personal life led to his death in 1943. In the second phase of his career Rodgers teamed up with Oscar Hammerstein II, a veteran creator of books and lyrics both operettas, by Sigmund Romberg and Rudolf Friml, and musical comedies, most notably *Show Boat*, with Jerome Kern. Most of the musicals created by the team of Rodgers and Hammerstein in the 1940s and 1950s enjoyed long runs on Broadway, successful film adaptations, and frequent revivals, both amateur and professional.

The shows of this second partnership, including *Carousel* (1945), *South Pacific* (1949), *The King and I* (1951), and *The Sound of Music* (1959), like all successful musicals before them, contain memorable songs that stand on their own as popular standards, such as "If I Loved You," "Some Enchanted Evening," "Hello Young Lovers," and "My Favorite Things." But for many listeners, the songs of Rodgers and Hammerstein remain strongly tied to the characters and dramatic situations that gave them life. The reason lies in the new aesthetic that these musicals embodied, an aesthetic sometimes summed up in the term **integrated musical**. In an integrated musical, songs are not mere distractions from the advancement of the plot but rather grow out of and further the dramatic situation, at the same time shedding light on the characters' inner lives. Ideally, all of a show's elements—song, dance, acting, costumes, set design, lighting—work together to create a unified artistic whole. Kern and Hammerstein had already taken a giant step in that direction with *Show Boat* (1927; see chapter 11).

the integrated musical

↪ Original theater poster for *Oklahoma!* (1943).

All of the features of the integrated musical are evident in Rodgers and Hammerstein's very first collaboration: *Oklahoma!* (1943). Based on a play from the 1930s and set on a farm in the wide-open spaces of Oklahoma Territory just after 1900 (the territory would not become a state until 1907), *Oklahoma!* explored the old-fashioned virtues of country folk, with melodramatic touches added. Curly, a cowboy, is in love with Laurey, a virtuous young woman. Wanting to make Curly jealous, Laurey attends a box-lunch social with Jud, a brooding ranch hand. But Curly bids everything he owns in an auction for Laurey's picnic basket, and she marries him. Picking a fight with Curly, Jud is killed by accident, and the bride and groom ride off to begin their life together.

Oklahoma! ran on Broadway for 2,248 performances, surpassing all box-office records. Why it had such extraordinary success has been the subject of much speculation. But for Rodgers, the key was that "everything in the production was made to conform to the simple open-air spirit of the story." By working forward from the setting and story rather than backward from standard musical comedy ingredients, Rodgers, Hammerstein, and the other *Oklahoma!* collaborators, including choreographer Agnes de Mille, played with convention in a way that gave the show an atmosphere all its own.

Oklahoma! was also a response to the United States' involvement in World War II, which dominated the national consciousness in 1943. While it may be exaggerating to call it a patriotic musical, Rodgers later commented that the show, featuring country folk from the past with an uncomplicated view of life, aimed to give wartime audiences both pleasure and optimism. These Oklahomans, the show implied, embodied the spirit that would carry the nation through bad times. At a historical moment when the world seemed mad with aggression and brutality, *Oklahoma!* struck a responsive chord by offering audiences a vision of Americans as good-hearted people in a land filled with promise for the future.

The aesthetic of the integrated musical such as *Oklahoma!* is at first sight no different from that of opera and operetta, where music's dramatic function has always been paramount. The similarity is not surprising, considering Hammerstein's background in operetta and as the lyricist-librettist for *Show Boat*, that most operetta-like of musicals. Even in setting and subject matter, some of the Rodgers and Hammerstein musicals indulge in operetta's preference for the long ago and faraway—the South Pacific, Siam, Austria, and (remote at least for 1940s urbanites) Oklahoma Territory circa 1900. Perhaps the most important distinction, then, between operetta and integrated musical is the latter's more insistent demand for songs with the potential to live on as independent popular hits, both as vocal numbers and as instrumentals for social dancing. Rodgers and Hammerstein brought great ingenuity to the challenge of meeting that demand and at the same time fulfilling the dramatic requirements of the integrated musical.

operetta and musical

Their ingenuity is evident in "People Will Say We're in Love" (LG 15.3), which appeared on *Billboard* magazine's popular hit charts three times in 1943, in versions by Bing Crosby and Trudy Erwin (peaking at number 2), Frank Sinatra (at number 3), and Hal Goodman's dance band (number 11; for more on *Billboard* and music charts, see chapter 17). "People Will Say We're in Love" has subsequently been recorded dozens of times by jazz singers and instrumentalists. As it appears in *Oklahoma!* the song displays Hammerstein's deftness in handling what can be an awkward moment in musical theater: the transition from speaking to singing. The scene begins with flirtatious banter between Laurey and Curly, whose budding romance has been the subject of gossiping neighbors. Their spoken lines are filled with folksy locutions intended to evoke the American West. Laurey declares that "most of the talk is that you're stuck on me." Curly responds, "Cain't imagine how these ugly rumors start," and, as Laurey replies "Me neither," four soft chords in the strings signal the beginning of the song.

LG 15.3

Those chords lead directly into the first verse, whose long poetic lines, though metered and rhymed, sustain the conversational tone, but not the rustic dialect, of the preceding dialogue. Rodgers sets these pattering lines in a quick, speechlike rhythm. At the chorus, the lyrics shift to shorter lines (from thirteen syllables to six or seven) and a more elevated tone (e.g., "Your eyes mustn't glow like mine"), inspiring Rodgers to craft a melody with long notes that trace soaring melodic arcs. Although the chorus follows the standard *aaba* format, the first two *a* sections are double the usual length—sixteen bars in place of the usual eight—adding to the chorus's expansive mood.

In sum, the verse has functioned as a way station between the dialogue's homespun local color and the chorus's rhapsodic expression of romantic love.

| CD 3.4 | Listening Guide 15.3 | "People Will Say We're in Love," from *Oklahoma!* RICHARD RODGERS AND OSCAR HAMMERSTEIN II |

GENRE: Broadway show tune

DATE: composed 1943; recorded 1979

PERFORMERS: Christine Andreas and Laurence Guittard, vocals, with studio orchestra

METER: duple

FORM: verse and *aa'ba"* chorus

WHAT TO LISTEN FOR

- informal, folksy tone of verse, in contrast to soaring lyricism of chorus
- expanded proportions of chorus: 16 + 16 + 8 + 8, instead of usual 32 bars
- Broadway-style vocal production, non-operatic yet able to project without electric amplification

TIMING	SECTION		TEXT	COMMENTS
0:00	introduction			Four soft string chords help the first singer find her opening pitch. In a stage production, these chords would underscore the last line of spoken dialogue.
0:05	verse 1		Why do they think up . . .	16 bars: The two characters exchange taunting phrases. The sprightly tempo broadens at end, signaling that the important part of the song is approaching.
0:36	chorus 1	*a*	Don't throw bouquets at me . . .	4 phrases of 4 bars each: 3 varied statements of a six-note motive, each beginning with an ascending leap; phrase 4 is a sinking chromatic line.
1:02		*a'*	Don't sigh and gaze at me . . .	The melody differs from the first *a* only in the last phrase, which now rises to the tonic.
1:27		*b*	Don't start collecting things . . .	8 bars, beginning with an inversion of the opening leap.
1:42		*a"*	Sweetheart, they're suspecting things . . .	8 bars: Shortened a, a variant of phrases 3–4, with one statement of the opening motive, followed by the most emphatic statement of the title phrase.
2:03	verse 2		Some people claim . . .	A return to the lighter mood of verse 1, with the alternation of singers reversed.
2:34	chorus 2		Don't praise my charm too much . . .	Curly sings new lyrics. The singer's breath control is particularly evident at 3:31.

NOTE This recording from the 1979 Broadway revival uses the original 1943 orchestrations by Robert Russell Bennett.

Listen & Reflect

1. When Rodgers collaborated with Hart, he wrote the music first and Hart fitted lyrics to music. With Hammerstein, lyrics generally preceded music. Write out the lyrics of "People Will Say We're in Love." Do they behave on the page like poetry? Why or why not? What features make these words particularly appropriate for singing?

| 🎧 | CD 3.4 | Listening Guide 15.3 | "People Will Say We're in Love," from *Oklahoma!*
RICHARD RODGERS AND OSCAR HAMMERSTEIN II |

2. View a stage performance of the scene in which this song appears, either live, online, or on DVD. What techniques smooth the transition from the end of the song back to dialogue? How do the actors maintain their characters through the song's chorus, where the language is least like the spoken dialogue?

3. Locate a recording of this song by a popular or jazz singer (it has been recorded by Bing Crosby, Frank Sinatra, Ella Fitzgerald, Ray Charles, Nat King Cole, and Nancy Wilson, to name only a handful). How does the vocal technique resemble or differ from that of the Broadway voices heard in this recording?

Sung in its entirety, "People Will Say We're in Love" makes musically explicit the main characters' growing interest in each other. When the verse is omitted, however, as in virtually all the popular and jazz recordings, the song drops everything specific to *Oklahoma!* and behaves like any other standard love song.

Long after its record-setting first run, *Oklahoma!* continues to be revived by professional and amateur theater groups—except for *Show Boat* and perhaps Cole Porter's *Anything Goes* (1934), the oldest musical to enjoy such longevity. What makes the shows of Rodgers and Hammerstein unique is their combination of the theatrical integrity that audiences since that day have come to expect (largely as a result of their influence) with a remarkable propensity for launching hit songs that, after a profitable run on the pop charts, have lived on as standards. The ephemeral musical comedies of the 1920s and 1930s succeeded at the latter, and more recent Broadway shows at the former, but few shows by other songwriters have done both—and, since 1943, all of them have been indebted to the model set by Richard Rodgers and Oscar Hammerstein II.

JAZZ IN THE SWING ERA

By the end of the 1920s the jazz style that had developed in New Orleans had spread from that city throughout the United States and as far abroad as England and France. The presence of New Orleans musicians in New York City—starting as early as the Original Dixieland Jazz Band in 1917 and continuing with shorter-term residencies by Louis Armstrong, Sidney Bechet, and others through the late 1920s—profoundly affected that city's dance bands. With the pre-1920 ragtime styles of James Reese Europe as a starting point, sophisticated dance bands like those of Fletcher Henderson and Duke Ellington embraced the looser, bluesier manner of New Orleans jazz. Meanwhile, dance bands in Chicago, Kansas City, and other urban centers were making similar experiments. By the mid-1930s a new sort of jazz had emerged, and it took its name from a new emphasis on rhythm: **swing**.

Several markers distinguish jazz of the Swing Era (roughly 1935–45) from 1920s jazz: First, there is a more equal emphasis on all four beats in a bar; the

style features

big bands

string bass (ubiquitous, now that the tuba has been phased out) tends to "walk" the bass line, playing on all four beats instead of beats 1 and 3 only. Second, ensembles tend to be larger: the **big band** of thirteen or more players divided into reed, brass, and rhythm sections becomes the norm. Small-ensemble jazz is more often a sideline for musicians working primarily in big bands. Third, solo improvisation is increasingly highlighted, even as it is often confined by elaborate arrangements that discourage "stretching out." Finally, popular songs from Tin Pan Alley and Broadway fill a growing place in the swing repertory, although blues-based compositions are still important. The multi-strain forms of ragtime become a rarity.

The last feature—a repertory increasingly based on popular songs and specialty numbers—changed the nature of the music significantly. For starters, the sophisticated harmonies of songwriters like George Gershwin, Cole Porter, and Richard Rodgers required instrumental soloists to improvise over more demanding chord progressions, in which wide-ranging harmonies moved at a faster pace than in earlier song styles. At the same time, the need to turn thirty-two-bar song structures into three- or four-minute ensemble numbers

arrangers and singers

for recording and dancing inspired arrangers to develop their craft. Many big bands had imaginative staff arrangers who helped shape the band's distinctive sound. And a new kind of singer emerged to present those songs in the context of a swing performance, whether by a small group or a big band. Here we will consider first the expanded role of the instrumentalist, focusing on the Kansas City bandleader Count Basie and his remarkable sideman Lester Young. We will then look at the new role of the singer as song interpreter, focusing on the artistry of Billie Holiday.

COUNT BASIE, LESTER YOUNG, AND KANSAS CITY

In a region that might seem an unlikely place for jazz to have flourished, Kansas City, Missouri, boasted a wide-open nightlife. For a large part of the Midwest and Southwest, Kansas City was a center of commerce and gateway to the markets of the East. Many westerners went there in search of entertainment, which was plentiful because local officials wanted it to be, and the city was controlled by a political faction that protected gambling, prostitution, and, during Prohibition, the selling of liquor. With its variety of good-time venues, Kansas City was a place where jobs for jazz musicians were plentiful, if low-paying.

Bennie Moten

By 1930 a distinctive style of orchestral jazz was developing in Kansas City, especially in a black dance band led by local musician Bennie Moten. Based on a rhythm section that played a driving four beats to the bar, Moten's music relied heavily on the twelve-bar blues and on arrangements based on **riffs**: short musical figures that could be repeated to build up larger sections. The arrangements, written chiefly by Eddie Durham of the trombone section and William "Count" Basie, the pianist, led to performances that blended solo and ensemble passages effectively. Moten's band recorded for Victor in 1932, but they never found much work outside Kansas City, and in the spring of 1935 Bennie Moten died unexpectedly. Then in August of that year big-band jazz entered the public consciousness with a bang when a jazz-oriented white dance band led by clarinetist Benny Goodman opened at the Palomar Ballroom in Los Angeles.

Shortly after Moten's death and Goodman's success on the West Coast, Count Basie formed a nine-piece group and began playing at the Reno Club in Kansas City. Before long, broadcasters on the club's radio hookup brought outside attention to the band. And by 1936 Basie's Midwest group, now managed by a prominent white booking firm, was coming into its own as a swing band with a national following.

Basie was born in 1904 in Red Bank, New Jersey. Indifferent to school, he was drawn to music from an early age. Although piano lessons taught him little about reading music, he learned quickly by ear. Basie quit school before finishing junior high to pursue a career in show business—not to get rich but because "I liked playing music, and I liked the life." He showed an instinct for getting ahead, first in New Jersey and then in Harlem, where he landed a job as pianist with a traveling theater company. When that tour ended, he returned to Harlem and worked in clubs, meeting such local pianists as Thomas "Fats" Waller and Willie "The Lion" Smith, two key figures in the development of ragtime piano into its jazzier descendant, stride.

In 1926 Basie starting touring with a vaudeville act. When engagements ran out in Kansas City in 1927, he remained there, accompanying silent movies at a theater, and in 1929 joining Moten's band. He gained enough experience to form his own band after Moten's death, recruiting local players with a regular engagement. Almost everybody in that band was a good soloist, he remembered, and the group worked mostly off **head arrangements**: arrangements assembled from the ideas (the heads) of band members and learned aurally rather than being written down.

Basie's big break came in 1936 when John Hammond, a producer for Columbia Records working in Chicago, heard the band on the radio. Support from Hammond and Willard Alexander of MCA, a booking agency, helped to transform Basie's local group into a polished, nationally known ensemble. Musicians were added. Singer Billie Holiday was hired to join Jimmy Rushing, a Moten band alumnus who had joined up with Basie the previous year. New arrangements were commissioned. And the band refined its image to please audiences outside the rough-and-ready confines of the Reno Club.

Yet the musical approach that Basie had worked out in Kansas City, and that had caught John Hammond's ear in the first place, remained intact. Basie kept the blues prominent in the band's repertory. Soloists played a key role. Like Ellington (see chapter 12), Basie knew how he wanted each section, and each player, to sound. "I have my own little ideas about how to get certain guys into certain numbers and how to get them out," he said late in life. "I had my own way of opening the door for them to let them come in and sit around awhile. Then I would exit them. And that has really been the formula of the band all down through the years."

At the same time, collaboration was an essential part of the band, in the characteristic sound of its rhythm section, especially after guitarist Freddie Green

The Basie band in 1939. Members pictured here include Lester Young, tenor sax (far right); Walter Page, bass; Jo Jones, drums; and Freddie Green, guitar. Young's unconventional playing posture is evident even at a distance.

head arrangements

John Hammond

the Basie sound

Basie's rhythm section

Big Bands in the Swing Era

One of the most prominent big bands of the 1930s and 1940s was led by Chicago-born Benny Goodman, a virtuoso jazz improviser who worked in New York from 1928 until 1934, when he formed his own dance orchestra. The new Goodman band played in a New York theater, recorded, and began appearing regularly on *Let's Dance,* a late-night NBC radio series. The clarinetist's exacting standards as a leader made his band a model of ensemble discipline and polish, playing a mixture of jazz tunes and popular songs of the day.

In May 1935 Goodman's orchestra began a cross-country tour with only mixed success. But a Los Angeles performance on August 21 attracted large numbers of teenagers who had been listening to the band's late-night broadcasts from New York, which aired earlier in the evening in California and thus drew larger audiences. The young people's electrified response touched off a wave of enthusiasm and nationwide publicity so strong that it has been credited with launching the Swing Era, a new age of popular music and a significant youth-driven musical fashion change. The jazz-oriented dance band was now the preferred popular-music medium and would remain so for the next decade. In 1938 Goodman and his orchestra would acquire some of the classical sphere's prestige when they played a concert of jazz music at Carnegie Hall.

Another clarinetist who led a popular white dance band was Artie Shaw, born in New York's Lower East Side in 1910 and, like Goodman, the son of Eastern European Jewish immigrants. An aficionado of Stravinsky and other modernist classical composers, Shaw developed his jazz bona fides in Harlem nightspots, combining his two interests into well-made instrumental hits like his band's recording of Cole Porter's "Begin the Beguine." The brothers Tommy Dorsey (trombone) and Jimmy Dorsey (clarinet) also led successful big bands in the Swing Era, both jointly and separately. But the most popular of all the white bands was led by trombonist Glenn Miller, whose "In the Mood," "String of Pearls," "Chattanooga Choo Choo," and other hits became for many Americans the favorite popular music of the World War II era.

In addition to the Ellington, Moten, and Basie big bands, other black jazz orchestras of the Swing Era include those of alto saxophonist Jimmie Lunceford and singer Cab Calloway. Both bands featured a strong element of showmanship—novelty songs, dancing, and comedy routines—in addition to first-rate arrangements and top performers. Calloway's band in particular was an incubator for up-and-coming young instrumentalists of the next generation such as Dizzy Gillespie.

joined Basie in 1937. Walter Page's resonant walking bass kept the beat, and Green provided even, on-the-beat guitar chords. The precision and firmness of Page and Green left drummer Jo Jones free to use the bass drum for accents instead of **keeping time** (marking the pulse), as earlier drummers had. Instead, he moved his timekeeping to the **hi-hat**, a pair of pole-mounted cymbals that can be opened and closed with a foot pedal and also be played with sticks or wire **brushes**. Timekeeping on the hi-hat (or alternatively on the suspended **ride cymbal**) lightened the rhythm section's sound without sacrificing intensity. Basie himself had arrived in Kansas City as an experienced stride player who used his left hand as a rhythmic engine. But by the time he and the band headed east in 1936 he had worked out a new, stripped-down piano style that would remain his signature for the rest of his career.

Basie's rhythm section was a four-man accompanying unit, and within it he played his part as a group member to perfection. In opening the door for his soloists, inviting them in to hang around for a while, and then showing them the way out, Basie was acting as an accompanist-in-charge, a role that suited his temperament and personal style. Described as one of the great "comp artists" of all time—to comp, in jazz lingo, is to play a background, usually chordal, as a *comp*lementary ac*comp*anist to a soloist—Basie deftly blended artistic control with restraint as he led from behind.

The chief soloist during the band's early years was tenor saxophonist Lester Young, a Mississippi native who played with Basie from 1936 until 1940. Young was a highly original jazz improviser, a musician of striking individuality. Playing with little vibrato, Young managed a sound both light and intense. He proved that swing did not require high volume and that understatement could be commanding. Young might improvise *against* a tune's phrase structure as well as with it, stay silent on beats where accents were expected, and signify (comment ironically) on musical clichés. The joy of a Lester Young performance, whether with Basie's big band or with a small group drawn from that band (as in *Lester Leaps In,* LG 15.4), lies in the contrasts between the hard-driving rhythm section and Young's cool relaxation, and between the foursquare symmetry of the tune and Young's idiosyncratic, asymmetrical phrases.

By the 1930s it had become standard practice for jazz musicians to improvise new melodies over the chord patterns, or **changes**, of popular songs, which typically fit a thirty-two-bar structure of four equal sections: statement, restatement, contrast, and return (*aaba*). A favorite example was the chord progression of George Gershwin's "I Got Rhythm" (1930), on which many new melodies were composed and given fresh names. The harmonic progression was used so often as a framework that it earned its own name: **rhythm changes**. For *Lester Leaps In* Young composed a new tune based on a repeating riff, which functions as the **head**, a composed thirty-two-bar melody that opens and closes the performance, bracketing a series of improvised solo choruses.

Varying the length of the solos is one way to maintain formal interest within this simple format. Besides taking one or more consecutive choruses, a soloist may take a half chorus, for instance playing *aa,* leaving the second half chorus (*ba*) to another soloist or the full ensemble. Occasionally a soloist takes only the *b* section, or **bridge**. A common device used effectively in this recording is **trading fours**, in which two soloists, or a soloist and the full band, alternate four-bar phrases.

In an interview long after Young's death, Basie mentioned him as a player who could be counted on to swing. The rhythmic energy of the Basie band freed Young to explore asymmetry as a solo improviser. Or perhaps one could say that the rhythmic security provided by Basie and company allowed Young to signify on a more sophisticated, even structural level than would otherwise have been possible. Young was a gifted improviser because he possessed a sovereign command of both vocabulary (melodic inventiveness) and syntax (the adroit placement of notes and phrases in the musical structure). With another supreme master of syntax behind him at the piano, he ventured as a soloist into terrain that no jazz soloist before him had visited.

Lester Young

LG 15.4

rhythm changes

trading fours

| | CD 3.5 | Listening Guide 15.4 | *Lester Leaps In* COUNT BASIE, LESTER YOUNG |

COMPOSER: Lester Young

DATE: 1939

PERFORMERS: Count Basie, piano; Lester Young, tenor sax; Buck Clayton, trumpet; Dicky Wells, trombone; Freddie Green, guitar; Walter Page, bass; Jo Jones, drums

GENRE: Kansas City swing

METER: duple

FORM: series of 32-bar *aaba* choruses

WHAT TO LISTEN FOR

- fast, energetic tempo with walking bass
- the head: a new melody, built from riffs and based on rhythm changes
- Young's relaxed yet intense saxophone sound and melodic ingenuity
- various ways of distributing solos, including trading fours

TIMING	SECTION		COMMENTS
0:00	introduction		4 bars; rhythm section sets the quick tempo. Underneath Basie's melodic line, Page marks four beats per bar with walking bass.
0:03	chorus 1	*a*	Composed melody played in sax with harmony lines in trumpet and trombone. Two nearly identical riff statements.
0:11		*a*	
0:19		*b*	Melody instruments drop out. Guitar and hi-hat contribute to the rhythmic drive.
0:27		*a*	
0:35	chorus 2		Young's solo heats up in the second *a* (0:42), which begins on the blues seventh. Phrase lengths are uneven and unpredictable: phrases often end with a long note played with thick vibrato, in contrast to Young's generally vibrato-less sound.
1:05	chorus 3		Rhythm section plays the first 6 bars of each *a* section in stop-time; for the first *a*, Basie plays melodic counterpoint against Young's ragtime-inspired melody.
1:37	chorus 4		Basie and Young trade fours.
2:09	chorus 5		A different way of trading fours: the band plays a syncopated repeated-note figure (4 bars), Young solos (4 bars), band repeats the syncopated figure (4 bars), Basie solos, carrying his solo through the bridge (4 + 8 bars). The final *a* (2:32) alternates band and Young.
2:40	chorus 6		Similar to chorus 5, now with Basie taking all the solos in spare signature style. An improvised full-ensemble tag fills the last 4 bars (3:07).

Listen & Reflect

1. Listen to a vocal performance of "I Got Rhythm" on CD or online. Then try singing the words and melody of "I Got Rhythm" over *Lester Leaps In*. How easy is it to fit the original song over the Basie group's instrumental?

SONG INTERPRETATION AND THE ART OF JAZZ SINGING

One can hardly imagine a stronger influence on singing styles than the development of electrical recording in 1925. Before the advent of electrical amplification, the most important requirement for a singer was that he or she sing loud enough to be heard over an instrumental accompaniment. Popular vocalists in the pre-microphone era either displayed the semi-operatic style of "trained" singers or projected their voices in an uncultivated "shouting" manner. Al Jolson, whose career skyrocketed before 1920, combined the two to create his personal and widely imitated style. A present-day listener to Jolson's records may find his diction, emoting, and use of stage Negro dialect to be exaggerated and artificial sounding. But from the back of the second balcony, Jolson's fans found his voice clearly audible, his words easy to understand, and his emotional message unmistakable.

Singers who came of age in the early 1920s still tended to emphasize projection along with other vocal qualities. Though remembered today primarily as a trumpet player (see chapter 12), Louis Armstrong sang in public and on records well before 1930, and his singing style deeply influenced many vocalists who came after him. Armstrong's gravelly voice is anything but "cultivated" in the classical sense, yet he uses it to powerful expressive effect. Singing with great rhythmic flexibility, departing from the written melody to improvise his own, adding extra words or syllables or even scat-singing entire phrases, Armstrong used his voice as an extension of his trumpet playing. The result was genuine jazz singing.

Louis Armstrong

Electrical amplification permitted a new singing style: crooning. **Crooners** such as Rudy Vallee sang softly into the microphone with an effect of intimacy, as if a lover were whispering into his sweetheart's ear. When Bing Crosby brought some of Armstrong's jazz sensibility to his own crooning, he became one of the most popular radio and recording artists of the 1930s and after. In the Swing Era, the line between popular singers and jazz singers grew harder to draw, although some singers made greater use of the rhythmic and melodic freedom opened up by Armstrong than others.

crooners

One of the greatest interpreters of the classic American popular song was Billie Holiday. Although she lacked the wide vocal range or dazzling technique of some other singers, Holiday possessed a gift for melodic improvisation and an impeccable rhythmic sense that won her the respect of the jazz instrumentalists who enliven her recordings. Particularly notable is her nuanced **back phrasing**, in which she lags behind the accompaniment for expressive effect.

Billie Holiday

Holiday's expressive song interpretation is evident in her 1945 record of Cole Porter's "What Is This Thing Called Love?" (LG 15.5). Introduced in a 1929 revue, Porter's song went on to establish itself as a jazz standard, a favorite of both singers and instrumentalists. Although Porter wrote a verse for the song, Holiday observes the common practice of omitting it in performance. Instead, after a short introduction she sings the thirty-two-bar *aaba* chorus, which the band then repeats instrumentally, followed by a sixteen-bar half chorus (*ba*).

LG 15.5

Like many classic American popular songs, "What Is This Thing Called Love?" contains oblique references to blues music: each of the four sections of the *aaba* chorus begins on a blue note, but the remainder of the section is not

Billie Holiday (1915–1959) was one of the first musicians to perform publicly with integrated ensembles, including the Artie Shaw Orchestra as well as the unidentified group shown here.

| CD 3.6 | Listening Guide 15.5 | "What Is This Thing Called Love?" BILLIE HOLIDAY |

SONGWRITER: Cole Porter

DATE: composed 1929, recorded 1945

PERFORMERS: Billie Holiday, vocal; 15-piece studio orchestra directed by Specs Powell, drums

GENRE: Swing-era jazz vocal

METER: duple

FORM: *aaba* chorus

WHAT TO LISTEN FOR

- Porter's tune: mix of major and minor, use of blue notes
- Holiday's singing: back phrasing, timbre, subtle variations in the half chorus
- the accompaniment: mix of strings and jazz instrumentation, relaxed dance rhythm

TIMING	SECTION		TEXT	COMMENTS
0:00	introduction			8 bars: muted trumpet, then tenor sax, set an urbane mood over sophisticated harmonies and a soft but insistent rhythm section.
0:16	chorus	*a*	What is this thing called love . . .	32-bar chorus. Holiday stretches the first notes of the melody, immediately beginning to back-phrase, over an active countermelody in the saxes.
		a		
0:50		*b*	I saw you there one wonderful day . . .	Strings add a sweet background at the bridge.
1:06		*a*	That's why I ask the Lawd . . .	The sax countermelody returns.
1:22	chorus	*a*		Muted trumpet solo by Joe Guy.
		a		
1:55		*b*		Electric guitar solo by Tiny Grimes.
2:13		*a*		Sax section.
2:28	half chorus	*b*	I saw you there one wonderful day . . .	Holiday sings the *b* and final *a* sections only, with scoring similar to the first chorus. The final 8 bars are extended to 10 (phrased 6 + 4) to create a sense of closure.
		a'		

Listen & Reflect

1. How does Holiday vary her performance of the second half of the chorus (beginning at 0:49) when it recurs at 2:26? Consider rhythmic, pitch, dynamic, and timbral choices.

(continued)

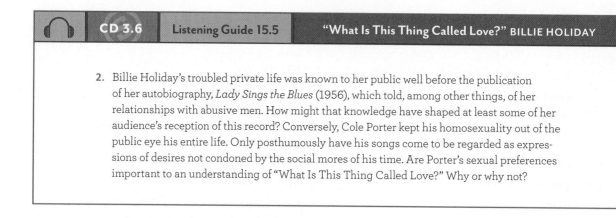

CD 3.6   Listening Guide 15.5   "What Is This Thing Called Love?" BILLIE HOLIDAY

2. Billie Holiday's troubled private life was known to her public well before the publication of her autobiography, *Lady Sings the Blues* (1956), which told, among other things, of her relationships with abusive men. How might that knowledge have shaped at least some of her audience's reception of this record? Conversely, Cole Porter kept his homosexuality out of the public eye his entire life. Only posthumously have his songs come to be regarded as expressions of desires not condoned by the social mores of his time. Are Porter's sexual preferences important to an understanding of "What Is This Thing Called Love?" Why or why not?

particularly bluesy. Instead, Porter creates an ambiguous melodic line that hovers between major and minor modes, as do the harmonies that underpin it. Also like most other songs of its time, it follows the four-beats-to-the-bar rhythm of the era's most popular dance, the foxtrot, making it suitable for dancing as well as listening. When we hear these songs brought to life by a skilled interpreter such as Billie Holiday, we can understand why they became standards for generations of jazz musicians.

QUESTIONS FOR DISCUSSION AND REVIEW

1. Listen to a recording or view a concert performance of Korngold's Violin Concerto. What, if anything, in this piece "sounds like movie music"? Is that an asset or a liability, and why?

2. What are some differences between stage musicals and film musicals?

3. How does the integrated musical resemble earlier stage musicals, and how does it resemble operetta?

4. How does swing differ from earlier jazz styles?

5. What distinguishes Swing Era jazz singing from earlier vocal styles or from later vocal styles with which you are familiar?

FURTHER READING

Banfield, Stephen. "Popular Song and Popular Music on Stage and Film." *In The Cambridge History of American Music,* edited by David Nicholls, 309–44. Cambridge: Cambridge University Press, 1998.

Carter, Tim. *Oklahoma! The Making of an American Musical.* New Haven, CT: Yale University Press, 2007.

Decker, Todd. *Music Makes Me: Fred Astaire and Jazz.* Berkeley and Los Angeles: University of California Press, 2011.

Driggs, Frank, and Chuck Haddix. *Kansas City Jazz from Ragtime to Bebop: A History.* New York: Oxford University Press, 2006.

Goldmark, Daniel. *Tunes for 'Toons: Music and the Hollywood Cartoon.* Berkeley and Los Angeles: University of California Press, 2005.

Kalinak, Kathryn. *How the West Was Sung: Music in the Westerns of John Ford.* Berkeley and Los Angeles: University of California Press, 2007.

McCracken, Allison. "'God's Gift to Us Girls': Crooning, Gender, and the Re-Creation of American Popular Song, 1928–1933." *American Music* 17, no. 4 (1999): 365–95.

Pollack, Howard. *Aaron Copland: The Life and Work of an Uncommon Man.* New York: Holt, 1999.

Schuller, Gunther. *The Swing Era: The Development of Jazz,* 1930–1945. New York: Oxford University Press, 1989.

FURTHER VIEWING

The Red Pony. 1949. 45th anniversary ed. VHS. Republic Pictures, 1994.

TIMELINE: 1939–2009

1939 Igor Stravinsky immigrates to the United States

1940 John Cage invents the prepared piano

1949 The 45-rpm single enters mass production

1950 The Weavers have a no. 1 hit with Leadbelly's "Goodnight Irene"

1951 Alan Freed begins broadcasting *The Moondog Show*

1952 John Cage creates the first American electronic compositions and composes *4'33"*

1954 The first annual Newport Jazz Festival

1955 "Rock around the Clock" becomes the first rock and roll crossover hit

1959 Berry Gordy Jr. founds Motown Records

1959 RCA produces the Mark II, an early electronic music synthesizer

1964 Terry Riley, *In C*

1965 Bob Dylan performs with an electrically amplified rock band at the Newport Folk Festival

1969 Woodstock music festival

1971 Formation of the Philip Glass Ensemble and Steve Reich and Musicians

AMERICA'S MUSIC

SINCE WORLD WAR II

The years immediately after World War II marked a period of separation between classical and popular spheres. A widening gulf stood between the cerebral music of postwar academic composers and the earthy joys of rock and roll. By the beginning of the twenty-first century, however, popular DJs were creating remixes of music by contemporary composers such as Steve Reich. Somewhere during the intervening decades, the popular and classical spheres had moved closer together and found common ground. The site for that merging was the recording studio, an increasing important workplace for musical creativity.

In the meantime, musicians in the traditional sphere found new ways to assert their core value of continuity with the past in an accelerated, fragmented postwar world. Folk musicians in the late twentieth century were as likely as not to have first encountered the music either on records or at multi-ethnic folk festivals. Around the end of the second millennium, "roots music" for most fans was an emblem of a cultural past that existed mostly in the collective imagination, a symbol of an elusive authenticity hard to find in the mediated world of television, instant communication, and Internet.

But if the new communications media made the continuation of traditional music more difficult, it made other forms of music making easier. After the year 2000, a laptop computer could offer more sophisticated music recording and editing capabilities than the most expensive recording studios of earlier days. For both professional and amateur musicians, digital technology opened up new outlets not only for the creation of new music but also for reworkings of existing music. By the second decade of the twenty-first century, those possibilities were being manifested in remixes, mash-ups, and a host of other musical forms that turned listeners from passive consumers to active participants in the process of creating today's dynamic music culture.

◀ DJ Spooky is a hip-hop artist who has collaborated with Baroque music specialists, performance artist Meredith Monk, and heavy metal band Metallica.

1976 An updating of the 1909 Copyright Act extends copyright protection and codifies fair use

1979 The Sugar Hill Gang, "Rapper's Delight"

1981 Music Television (MTV) goes on the air

1983 Wynton Marsalis wins his first two Grammy awards, one in jazz and one in classical music

1987 Founding of the Jazz at Lincoln Center Orchestra

1997 Pulitzer Prize in music goes to Wynton Marsalis's *Blood on the Fields*

1998 The Digital Millenium Copyright Act (DMCA) restricts the concept of fair use

1998 The Sonny Bono Act extends copyright protection to nearly a century after a work's creation

1999 Shootings at Columbine High School lead to public outcry against Marilyn Manson and other violent rock bands

2001 A court decision in favor of the Recording Industry Association of America (RIAA) shuts down Napster, founded two years ealier

2001 Apple introduces iTunes

2006 The Metropolitan Opera introduces "Live in HD" video broadcasts

2009 "We Are One" concert at the Lincoln Memorial

CLASSICAL MUSIC, JAZZ, AND MUSICAL THEATER AFTER WORLD WAR II

In 1946 the United States was the world's chief military power. And as manufacturers turned from weapons to new cars and new houses, the domestic economy boomed, bringing to the postwar era a new level of prosperity. Thousands of military veterans returned to school, supported by the GI "Bill of Rights." Marriage and birth rates rose dramatically, creating the Baby Boom.

But even as peace and prosperity promised a bright future, dangers clouded the postwar mood. African American servicemen returning to the South encountered a segregated society that showed little gratitude for the service they had performed for their country. As veterans returned to the workplace, they displaced the women who had taken factory jobs during the war. The atom bomb, a key factor in ending the war, loomed as a symbol not only of American superiority in science and but also of the perils of progress. The sweetness of victory had turned sour as the United States found itself in a global Cold War. The Soviet Union, a wartime ally, now occupied much of Eastern Europe and was developing into a second global superpower. From 1950 until 1953 U.S. soldiers fought in Korea in a conflict that started as a civil war but soon involved troops from China. Moreover, the Holocaust—the Nazi attempt to rid Europe of Jews and other "undesirables"—left faith in human nature itself badly shaken.

The conflicting realities of prosperity and insecurity, idealism and moral failure, led many postwar artists and intellectuals to a pessimistic outlook. On the international front, new enemies replaced old; at home, Americans grew increasingly conscious that there was no adversary more to be feared than the evil within themselves.

CLASSICAL MUSIC IN THE POSTWAR YEARS

After World War I, a gap had opened between concert audiences and the composers who were exploring the contemporary world through music. By the 1940s a Euro-American modernist tradition had existed for decades, and the end of World War II opened the door to an infusion of new music and ideas. The concert hall's prevailing formula combined edification (through the classics) with virtuoso performance and the notion that art could be glamorous as well as dignified. To change that formula would risk alienating the audience. Was it still reasonable to expect the concert hall to do justice to the classical sphere as it now existed in the United States? And if not, what alternatives might be found? These were some of the questions classical musicians in the United States grappled with after the war.

ÉMIGRÉ COMPOSERS, THE ACADEMY, AND THE CONCERT HALL

The rise of fascism had compelled a number of European musicians to emigrate to the United States. Some composers, such as Erich Wolfgang Korngold in Hollywood and Kurt Weill on Broadway, embraced their new home's musical culture and found their own place within it. Others, such as Arnold Schoenberg and Béla Bartók, did their best to continue their work with no sign that their new surroundings had any influence on their musical style. Schoenberg, at UCLA, and Paul Hindemith, at Yale, joined the ranks of German and Austrian academics who transformed the music departments of American universities in the postwar years. Whether or not they consciously attempted to do so, these émigré musicians had a profound effect on classical music in the United States.

Perhaps the most influential musical émigré was the Russian composer Igor Stravinsky, well established as a leading modernist long before arriving in the United States in 1939. As early as the 1920s American composers had been emulating Stravinsky, many of them—most notably Aaron Copland—through the influence of Nadia Boulanger's tutelage at the Conservatoire Américain at Fontainebleau, in France. Stravinsky was not particularly enthusiastic about American culture in general. One aspect did capture his imagination, though, and had done so long before he came to the United States: African American music, especially ragtime and jazz. That music's influence is apparent in his *Ebony Concerto* (1946), written for the clarinetist Woody Herman and his big band. Mixing blue notes with dissonant harmonies, and Harmon mutes and growls with spiky modernist rhythms, the *Ebony Concerto,* especially as recorded by Herman's band, sounds like a cubist portrait of American jazz.

Igor Stravinsky (1882–1971) in his studio in Los Angeles.

With Stravinsky and other leading European composers now living on American soil, the United States no longer seemed a provincial outpost of European music making. Homegrown classical performers such as conductor-composer Leonard Bernstein also contributed to the country's new musical stature. And a growing number of professional schools were now serving the classical sphere, from conservatories to college and university music departments that expanded their programs as military veterans returned to civilian life.

Performances are the main things musicians have to sell, and the classical sphere's primary marketplace has long been the concert hall: the infrastructure of orchestra and recital halls, opera houses, and the local, regional, and national agencies that recruit their customers. But in the postwar years the academy, while still tied to the work of the concert hall, diversified into subdisciplines

✎ Five of America's leading classical composers of the postwar era were photographed studiously avoiding each other's gaze: (from left, standing) Samuel Barber, Aaron Copland, (from left, seated) Virgil Thomson, Gian Carlo Menotti, and William Schuman.

that together formed an independent force. Grounded in a changing view of music history, some branches of the academy welcomed pre-Bach and modern repertories, which the concert hall had tended to exclude. And in a nation where homegrown classical composers had never played more than a small role in the concert hall, the academy included them in its framework.

Thus the music of new composers, supported by the academy and by commissions, prizes, and fellowships, gained listeners more readily outside than inside the concert hall. The academic environment shared certain features with scientific laboratories. In 1958 Milton Babbitt, a composer on the faculty at Princeton University, likened himself and other "specialist" composers—working outside the confines of general audience esteem, critics' approval, or the skills of most performers—to mathematicians and physicists. Freed from the need to engage with any but a specialist audience, they could explore music in the manner of scientific researchers. At that point, the gap between concert hall and composer widened into a true rift.

The concert hall—the one institution where the priorities of composer, performers, critics, impresarios, and audiences all had to be considered and reconciled—remained the public embodiment of the classical sphere. But the academy's emergence after World War II challenged that position. University teacher-composers could create specialized new music while ignoring impresarios and the general audience—both essential to the concert hall, which relied on the public for support. To a large extent, composition in postwar America reflects the splitting of the classical sphere into two complementary aspects—concert hall and academy—each with its own distinct preferences and goals.

POSTWAR COMPOSITION

The postwar academic environment encouraged compositional approaches that could be rationally explained. Foremost among these was the serial method invented by Arnold Schoenberg in Vienna in the early 1920s. The first and most basic form of serialism is **twelve-tone music**, in which the composer arranges all twelve pitches of the chromatic scale into a particular sequence, or series, also called a **tone row**. Twelve-tone technique substitutes for tonality, which Schoenberg abandoned around 1910, believing that music had long been evolving toward total chromaticism and atonality. Twelve-tone music offers a way to order pitches systematically without the gravitational pull of key centers.

Composers in America approached the twelve-tone technique in a variety of ways. Roger Sessions, who taught composition at the University of California and Princeton, believed with Schoenberg that certain historical laws were inherent in the nature of music; in the postwar years he embraced the twelve-tone method, as did Aaron Copland. The most dramatic proof of serialism's postwar reach, however, came from Igor Stravinsky, long considered the polar opposite of Schoenberg. In the early 1950s Stravinsky discovered the music of Schoenberg's pupil Anton Webern and began writing twelve-tone music himself, as in his ballet *Agon*, which mixes serial and non-serial approaches.

No musician seized more eagerly on the constructive possibilities of twelve-tone technique than Milton Babbitt. Trained as a mathematician as well as a musician, Babbitt found beauty in the idea of a system of rationally ordered sounds. Starting with the work of Schoenberg, Webern, and Alban Berg, he extended their innovations by serializing nonpitch elements as well: rhythm, dynamics, timbre, and register. Babbitt's extensions of the serial principle—sometimes called **integral serialism** or **total serialism**—produced music whose network of internal connections and relationships was formidably complex, despite such plain titles as Three Compositions for Piano (1947) and Composition for Four Instruments (1948). Babbitt was a jazz enthusiast with a deep knowledge and love of classic American popular songs, but with the exception of *All Set* (1957), scored for jazz ensemble, none of this is reflected in his compositions; such interests lay outside the work of the composer as "specialist," conducting research into advanced musical structures much as a chemist or physicist conducts scientific experiments. Babbitt's passion for intellectual control would lead him during the late 1950s into the realm of electronic music.

Milton Babbitt

If a musical Rip Van Winkle had fallen asleep in 1940 and awakened twenty years later, the variety of new music would surely have surprised him. What pre-war commentators had sometimes dubbed an "atonal school" had developed by 1960 into a range of idioms—freely chromatic, twelve-tone, integrally serialized, electronic, chance-based—with only atonality in common. Schoenberg's "emancipation of the dissonance" was now fully on display in the United States, as composers made music out of previously excluded sounds. This emancipation brought fresh energy and excitement to the contemporary music scene.

New works featuring tonal centers, triads, and tuneful melodies had certainly not disappeared, although their vocabulary was expanded with angular melodies, dissonant harmonies, irregular rhythms, and new timbres. Their prominent place in the classical sphere is reflected in the list of Pulitzer Prize winners in music. The first was awarded in 1943 to William Schuman for a cantata, followed in 1944 by Howard Hanson for a symphony, and in 1945 by Aaron Copland for *Appalachian Spring*—all tonal works. During the two postwar decades, only one atonal work—Elliott Carter's String Quartet no. 2 (1960)—won the prize. Awards in other years were for Charles Ives's Symphony no. 3 (composed four decades earlier but only recently premiered); symphonies by Walter Piston; operas by Gian Carlo Menotti, Samuel Barber, Robert Ward, and Douglas Moore; and a film score by Virgil Thomson. Except for Ives, all were stylistically conservative composers.

Pulitzer Prize winners

Against this background of opposing outlooks and fragmented institutions, Elliott Carter emerged during the 1950s as a unique figure: a respected composer who worked his way toward a more and more complex atonal musical style while steering clear of musical systems. Carter, born in New York in 1908, attended Harvard College. In 1932 he went to Paris to continue his schooling in the liberal arts while also studying music with Nadia Boulanger. After the war he began writing music of marked individuality: a piano sonata (1946), a sonata for cello and piano (1948), and his first string quartet (1951). From the piano sonata on, admirers saw each new work as a daring advance. And in 1962 Stravinsky, whose age, eminence, and barbed comments on the musical scene had made him an imposing presence, pronounced Carter's Double Concerto for piano, harpsichord, and small orchestra a masterpiece.

Milton Babbitt (1917–2011) at the RCA Mark II synthesizer.

ELECTRONIC MUSIC

As early as 1917 the Franco-American composer Edgard Varèse had proclaimed: "I dream of instruments obedient to my thought." In 1936 he envisioned creating music directly "on a machine that will faithfully transmit the musical content to the listener." Despite the invention of early electronic instruments such as the theremin (1928), progress toward the realization of Varèse's dream was slow until the magnetic tape recorder was perfected in the late 1940s, after which **electronic music** came into its own.

In 1952 the first American tape music concert took place. The music had been constructed with equipment entirely different from the standard "hardware" of music composition: tape recorders, magnetic tape, splicing materials, generators of sound signals, and devices for filtering sound. While Western music making had always involved some acoustical know-how, electronic music posed different challenges. A new sound palette was available, but to control it required knowledge and experience that few musicians possessed. Most importantly, by creating their works directly on tape, composers were bypassing the performer-interpreter, a key ingredient in earlier music.

Poème électronique

Varèse, nearing seventy when the technology he had imagined came into general use, employed it in *Poème électronique* (1957–58). Collaborating with the Swiss architect Le Corbusier, Varèse composed this work for the Philips Pavilion at the Brussels World's Fair of 1958. Here he realized his longtime dream of creating music to exist in space as well as time. The work was tape-recorded and then played through 425 loudspeakers, arranged so that the sound could sweep across and around the curves of Le Corbusier's building.

the synthesizer

In the early 1950s a studio was established at Columbia University by Columbia professors Vladimir Ussachevsky and Otto Luening and Princeton professors Babbitt and Sessions. Originally, the work in the studio involved recording sounds on tape, rerecording them, and then manually splicing the bits of tape together to create the music itself. In 1959, however, the Radio Corporation of America (RCA) installed the Mark II, an advance model of an electronic sound **synthesizer** that became the heart of the Columbia-Princeton Electronic Music Center. The synthesizer, which constituted and shaped the sounds, reduced the need to rerecord and to splice tape. Further, an instrument able to control precisely such elements as rhythm, dynamics, and timbre as well as pitch proved well suited to Milton Babbitt's ideal of totally organized music. He used the Mark II to create his Composition for Synthesizer (1961) and Ensembles for Synthesizer (1964). He also combined live performance with synthesized sound in such works as *Vision and Prayer* (1961) and *Philomel* (1964). In the meantime, as synthesizer technology became more widespread and affordable, electronic music studios sprang up throughout the United States, one of the most important being the San Francisco Tape Music Center, founded in 1963.

JOHN CAGE

Although Varèse, Babbitt, and others explored the new medium vigorously, John Cage was the first American to complete a tape composition: *Imaginary Landscape no. 5* (1952), followed later that year by the remarkable *Williams Mix*. As early as 1937 the young California-born Cage had predicted that the use of noise to make music would "continue and increase until we reach a music produced through the aid of electrical instruments." Cage's *Imaginary Landscape no. 1*, premiered in 1939, was scored for muted piano, suspended cymbal, and two phonograph turntables—a hint that his imagination was taking a path blazed by ultramodernists like Henry Cowell and others whose experimentalist bent would come to be seen as another kind of American tradition.

Cage's musical interests, like Cowell's, extended westward to Asia as well as eastward to Europe. A student of Arnold Schoenberg's at UCLA, Cage found more inspiration in resisting than in following his teacher's precepts. In the 1930s Cage, along with his fellow Californian Lou Harrison, had begun writing music for ensembles of percussion instruments as a way of exploring new timbres and rhythms while sidestepping the vexed issue of tonality. Unpitched percussion instruments allowed Cage and Harrison to avoid the Western tempered scale, which for more Eurocentric composers had come to represent a stylistic impasse.

While teaching at the progressive Cornish School in Seattle, Cage routinely provided musical accompaniment for the school's modern dance programs. For one occasion in 1940, instead of writing for a group of conventional percussion instruments, Cage devised a sort of one-player percussion orchestra, the **prepared piano**: a grand piano into whose strings are wedged objects made of metal, wood, rubber, and other materials. The added objects not only mute the piano but also radically alter the pitch and timbre of the affected strings. Cage went on to compose several works for prepared piano, most notably the large-scale Sonatas and Interludes (1946–48).

Most of the sixteen sonatas in this hour-long work are in binary form, recalling the keyboard sonatas of the eighteenth-century composer Domenico Scarlatti, and all of them use a structural strategy that Cage explored extensively in his earlier music, **square root form**, using a durational proportion that shapes both small-scale and large-scale divisions. In Sonata no. 2 (LG 16.1), for example, the two parts of the binary form approximate the proportion 1½:2⅜ (or, taking the half-beat as a time unit, 93:147). The A section subdivides into two sections consisting of 62 + 31 half-beats (creating the proportion 1:½), each dividing further into two phrases, the first pair filling 24 + 38 half-beats (1½:2⅜) and the second pair 12 + 19 (1½:2⅜). The B section operates similarly, but with its two main subdivisions creating the proportion 2:⅜. The silences that end most sections and many subsections make the structure easy to follow.

Cage's square root form provides a durational scheme to be filled with musical sounds and silences. The somewhat cold rationality of the scheme contrasts with the playful, colorful sounds of the prepared piano. Inspired by Ananda Coomaraswamy's writings on Indian art and philosophy, Cage stated that his goal in the Sonatas and Interludes was "to express in music the 'permanent emotions' of Indian tradition: the heroic, the erotic, the wondrous, the mirthful, sorrow, fear, anger, the odious and their common tendency toward tranquility." Although it is difficult to state exactly which emotion is expressed by any given sonata, their varied emotional qualities all resolve into the tranquility of the durational scheme.

Cage's interest in music built entirely on durations of sounds was at first based on the polarity of sound and silence. Then, in 1951, Cage realized that he could embrace unintended sounds that were always present, even during silence.

John Cage (1912–1992), composer and explorer of unintended sounds.

LG 16.1

CD 3.7   **Listening Guide 16.1**

Sonata no. 2
JOHN CAGE

DATE: 1946–48
PERFORMER: Philipp Vandré, prepared piano
GENRE: modernist piano piece
METER: primarily duple
FORM: AABB

WHAT TO LISTEN FOR

- varied tone colors of prepared piano
- use of rhythm and timbre, instead of melody and harmony, to create musical structure
- simple binary form combined with more complex square root form
- use of silence to articulate formal divisions

TIMING	SECTION		DURATION
0:00	A	*a*	12 beats.
0:05		*b*	19 beats.
0:15		*c*	6 beats.
0:18		*d*	9½ beats.
0:23	A		Literal repeat; 46½ beats.
0:46	B	*e*	12 beats.
0:51		*f*	19 beats.
1:01		*g*	12 beats.
1:06		*h*	19 beats.
1:16		*i*	4½ beats.
1:19		*j*	7 beats.
1:23	B		Literal repeat; 73½ beats.

NOTE The opening notes of the sonata establish the half-beat unit of measurement.

Listen & Reflect

1. Play this recording for friends who are not familiar with Cage's prepared pianos and ask them to identify the instrument(s) they hear. What are their responses, and what do those responses suggest about Cage's aesthetic goals in writing for prepared piano?

Once he dissolved the split between intention and nonintention, he began avidly exploring the latter. Much of his creative energy went toward setting up mechanical procedures that would bring sounds into compositions independent of his own will, hence with no deliberate link to other sounds.

Cage created *Williams Mix* by collecting a library of both studio-produced and environmentally recorded sounds, then arranging them by a process of random ordering involving charts, chance, and the coin-tossing procedures of the *I Ching* (The Chinese *Book of Changes*, which he had encountered when he began to study Zen Buddhism in the late 1940s). The result sounds random and unintentional, which is just what Cage intended. *Williams Mix* united Cage's interest in technology with a new philosophical outlook he adopted in the early 1950s. The philosophy, religion, and art of the West assumed that humans, created in the image of God, were destined to rule over nature. From a non-Western perspective, however, human beings were simply one of many species of life, and nature itself tended more toward randomness than order. Cage's music from the 1950s on—**chance music** or **aleatoric music** (from the Latin word for dice)—reflects the randomness of natural processes, inspired by a principle found in Indian philosophy: "Art is the imitation of Nature in her manner of operation."

Cage's most famous work, *4'33"* ("four minutes thirty-three seconds"), was composed in 1952, the same year as *Williams Mix,* but copied nature's manner of operation in an entirely different way. Conceived as three movements for piano whose durations—30", 2'23", and 1'40"—were determined by chance methods, *4'33"* prescribed no intentional sounds at all; the pianist sits silently at the keyboard. Cage's "silent" piece invited listeners to pay attention to random sounds in the environment, in effect emptying themselves of expectations. Among other things, *4'33"* could be viewed as a spiritual exercise, a means of quieting the will so that an infinite realm of possibilities may be experienced.

Concert-hall audiences rejected these ideas. Still, Cage had never counted on the concert hall for much support. Nor did he enter academia. From early in his composing career he managed to scrape together a living by collaborating with other artists, chiefly dancers. In the 1940s he served as accompanist for a dance company headed by Merce Cunningham, later becoming its music director and Cunningham's life partner. The early 1950s found him collaborating with other composers, including Morton Feldman, Christian Wolff, Earl Brown, and David Tudor, all of whom assisted him in preparing materials for *Williams Mix.* Meanwhile, Cage had also become a friend and champion of the painters Robert Rauschenberg and Jasper Johns, whose rise to fame as abstract expressionist artists of the New York School helped indirectly to further Cage's own work.

Cage's ideas won him a reputation during the 1950s, if not as a composer, then as either a satirist or a musical anarchist. These opinions persisted well into the 1960s and in some quarters even up to his death in 1992. Yet though often scorned and attacked, Cage also found himself in increasing demand as a lecturer and performer. In Europe, under Cage's influence, the German composer Karlheinz Stockhausen began in the mid-1950s to experiment with chance operations.

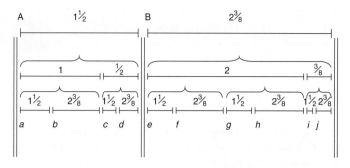

The "square root form" of John Cage's Sonata no. 2 for prepared piano expresses the durational proportion of 1½:2⅜ on both the large scale and the small scale. (The letters *a* through *j* correspond to the sections in Listening Guide 16.1.)

4'33"

Cage's influence

In their own words "

John Cage Explains Why He Writes Music (1957)

And what is the purpose of writing music? One is, of course, not dealing with purposes but dealing with sounds. Or the answer must take the form of paradox: a purposeful purposelessness or a purposeless play. This play, however, is an affirmation of life—not an attempt to bring order out of chaos nor to suggest improvements in creation, but simply a way of waking up to the very life we're living, which is so excellent once one gets one's mind and one's desires out of its way and lets it act of its own accord.

Many younger Americans took Cage's example as a jumping-off point for work of their own. Cage's charisma as a lecturer and raconteur, as well as the visual beauty of his scores, which are masterworks of calligraphy, also enhanced his reputation. *Silence* (1961), the first of several compilations of Cage's lectures and writings, established him as a significant writer on music; winning a wide readership, it has remained in print to this day.

Cage's composing philosophy, which replaces intellectual analysis and the pursuit of one's desires with "purposeless play," offers a radical prescription for emptying the mind, in contrast to academic instruction and the Western musical tradition itself, which both strive to fill it. On the strength of that doctrine of liberation, Cage is often proclaimed a key figure in twentieth-century music. By the time of his death in 1992, Cage's influence was apparent not only in classical music but also in performance art and the more intellectual currents of popular music.

JAZZ IN THE POSTWAR YEARS

If classical composition after World War II continued to win critical respect while its popular appeal shrank, a similar though less drastic process was also at work in postwar jazz. Although rooted in blues and gospel, jazz attracted musicians who pushed the boundaries of technique and expression, earning the attention of critics while challenging the lay listener. Modern pioneers such as Charlie Parker and Dizzy Gillespie were received from the start as virtuosos who were saying something new, in an idiom called **bebop**, which extended the music's vocabulary without losing its swinging rhythm and blues inflections. Historically minded critics placed the new music in a lineage starting in New Orleans and continuing in Chicago, New York, and Kansas City, leading into the big-band music of the Swing Era, which in turn begat bebop. Bebop marked the first phase of the jazz of the postwar period: **modern jazz**.

modern jazz

CHARLIE PARKER AND BEBOP

Charlie Parker, born in Kansas City, Kansas, in 1920, was a musician whose rhythmic originality, harmonic complexity, virtuoso technique, and inventiveness as an improviser helped to bring about changes in style that roused the disapproval of much of the popular music audience. Parker's alto saxophone playing was geared not to the tastes of swing-band fans but to a musical logic of his own, a logic with intense appeal for a small coterie of listeners. Parker seized an artistic freedom that few earlier jazz musicians had enjoyed, but that freedom imposed a burden: how to survive as a popular artist who played music that only a fraction of the jazz audience was ready to accept.

When the war ended and the big bands began to break up, a corps of players remained who were eager to emphasize the listening side of jazz. In the early postwar years, the musicians' originality sparked excitement. Though not nearly on the Swing Era's scale, New York's modern-jazz scene blossomed: uptown in Harlem, downtown in Greenwich Village, but most of all in midtown, on 52nd Street between Fifth and Sixth Avenues. Tenor saxophonist Dexter Gordon later described "The Street," where the top jazz clubs were located, as "the most exciting half a block in the world. Everything was going on—music, chicks, [drug] connections . . . so many musicians working down there side by side." Fans of the music made up in passion what they lacked in numbers. Those who "dug" modern jazz gloried in being "hip" to the music's freedom and intensity and to the young performers, chiefly black, who radiated independence of spirit.

Some commentators suggested parallels between bebop and modernist music. The writer Albert Murray, however, has seen the music differently. Rather than trying to turn dance music into concert music, Murray writes, "Parker was out to swing not less but more. Sometimes he tangled up your feet but that was when he sometimes made your insides dance as never before." That quality of "inner dancing" is apparent in *Yardbird Suite*, a tune Parker wrote and recorded with a small combo in 1946 during an extended stay in California. The tune's title refers humorously both to Parker's nickname—"Yardbird," frequently shortened to "Bird," presumably because of his fondness for chicken—and to the *Firebird* Suite by Stravinsky, one of Parker's favorite modernist composers. Stravinsky's suite is ballet music; in a very different way, *Yardbird Suite* evokes dance as well.

Like many bebop tunes, *Yardbird Suite* is a new melody fitted to an earlier song's chord progression, or changes. Bebop musicians were motivated to write such tunes, which academics later dubbed **contrafacts**, not only by the creative challenge of doing so but also by the financial pressure to avoid paying copyright holders for permission to record the original tunes. The standard format for a bebop record begins (after a short introduction) with a statement of the tune's composed melody, or **head**, followed by a series of improvised solos on the tune's changes, usually with a return to the head as a closing section. Because melodies and titles, not chord progressions, were protected by copyright, and because bebop musicians were sometimes more interested in the harmonic structure of a popular song than in its melody, creating a contrafact offered an alternative to paying permission fees that was both legal and artistically satisfying.

Among the tunes that served as the basis for Parker's contrafacts are Gershwin's "I Got Rhythm," Ray Noble's "Cherokee," and Fats Waller's "Honeysuckle Rose." The model for *Yardbird Suite* (LG 16.2) is "Rosetta," a tune written in 1933 by Earl Hines (the pianist on *West End Blues*, LG 12.4) that was a regional hit in 1937 for Bob Wills and His Texas Playboys. Besides discarding Hines's melody, Parker slightly alters the changes. Where Hines's harmonies begin with a series of chords that slide down the chromatic scale, Parker replaces the second chord with one that lies a **tritone** (three whole steps) away. This **tritone substitution**, a signature feature of bebop harmony, enriches the already expressive vocabulary of the classic

Alto saxophonist Charlie "Bird" Parker and Dizzy Gillespie with bassist Tommy Potter (1950).

bebop contrafacts

LG 16.2

| CD 3.8 | Listening Guide 16.2 | *Yardbird Suite* CHARLIE PARKER |

COMPOSER: Charlie Parker

DATE: 1946

PERFORMERS: The Charlie Parker Septet: Miles Davis, trumpet; Charlie Parker, alto sax; Lucky Thompson, tenor sax; Dodo Marmarosa, piano; Arvin Garrison, guitar; Vic McMillan, bass; Roy Porter, drums

GENRE: bebop

METER: duple

FORM: 32-bar *aaba* choruses

WHAT TO LISTEN FOR

- *aaba* structure of the composed head
- fluid improvised solos with phrases of unpredictable lengths
- conversational quality of musicians' interactions
- role of drummer as both timekeeper and interactive member of ensemble

TIMING	SECTION		COMMENTS
0:00	introduction		Piano alternates two chords a half-step apart over a thrumming pedal point in the bass. Hi-hat provides light beat until the last bar, then snare and kick drums energize the arrival of the head.
0:09	chorus 1 (head)	*a*	The three melody instruments (trumpet, alto sax, tenor sax) in unison.
0:18		*a*	
0:27		*b*	Alto sax solo.
0:36		*a*	Trumpet and tenor return.
0:45	chorus 2		Alto sax solo. At bars 7–8 (0:52) Parker quotes his own tune *Cool Blues*.
1:22	chorus 3	*aa*	Davis's muted trumpet solo contrasts with Parker's more energetic solo by staying in a smaller range and making greater use of silence, or **space**.
1:40		*b*	Tenor sax, with a relaxed solo more characteristic of the Swing Era.
1:49		*a*	Davis returns, turning up the heat with more emphasis on upper register.
1:58	chorus 4	*aa*	Tenor solo features more-convoluted melodic ideas, less symmetrical phrases, and more-intense tone, almost growling.
2:15		*ba*	Electric guitar launches into a fleet single-note solo. In the last bar (2:32), Porter switches from timekeeping on the hi-hat to throw in a pair of triplets on snare and kick drums, propelling the group into the final half chorus.
2:34	half chorus	*b*	Piano begins the bridge with a right-hand melody doubled two octaves lower in the left hand, then switches to quiet chords in the left hand as the right-hand melody continues.
2:42		*a*	Drums usher in the three melody instruments for one last statement of the composed melody's *a* section, with a new rising conclusion to mark the ending.

NOTE Recorded March 28, 1946.

Listen & Reflect

1. The division of this small jazz ensemble into melody instruments and rhythm section is essentially the same as in 1920s New Orleans jazz and 1930s swing. How have the roles of the various instruments changed, and how have they stayed the same?

2. In other words, what, if anything, is new in how the instruments interact?

3. Keeping in mind that this is a mid-tempo bebop record, compare *Yardbird Suite* with *Lester Leaps In* (see LG 15.4), definitely an up-tempo swing record. What are the similarities and differences, not only in the solos but in the role of each instrument in the ensemble?

popular song, creating harmonies that are complex, mysterious, and intriguing for listeners and players alike.

Charlie Parker, at twenty-six, was the senior member of the septet that recorded *Yardbird Suite* in 1946; the youngest, Miles Davis, was nineteen. All seven musicians, to varying degrees, play in styles rooted in swing idioms but with new features associated with bebop. The improvised solos are melodic lines consisting primarily of fast notes (two per beat, at a rapid tempo), in asymmetrical groups that start and stop in unpredictable places within the tune's regular eight-bar phrases. Underpinning the ensemble is a steady walking bass, as in swing, but Vic McMillan's pitch choices reach far beyond the basic notes of the chords, unlike the previous generation of bass players. Like swing drummers, Roy Porter moves the timekeeping function away from the kick (bass) drum up to the ride cymbal; unlike those predecessors, though, he uses the snare and kick drums to "drop bombs," that is, to play accented notes in unexpected places, often with the effect of energizing the following solo. Similarly, the guitar's steady one chord per beat contrasts with the piano's irregular and unpredictable comping. The sum total is a sound that resembles swing but with startling moments of unpredictability.

Parker's contemporaries recognized his superior talent and musicianship, and by 1950 jazz already bore clear signs of his influence. Some of his compositions were by then standards, his recordings were widely known, and saxophonists were not the only players who wore them out with repeated listening, trying to learn from his dense improvising style. Although Parker's heroin addiction and heavy drinking led to erratic performances in the years before his death in 1955 at age thirty-four, his artistic stature was never in doubt. His bold spirit, ready to follow musical logic wherever it might lead, inspired other musicians to push the boundaries further, distancing modern jazz even more from the center of the popular sphere, on which it relied for economic support.

MILES DAVIS AND MODERN TRENDS AFTER BEBOP

Thelonious Monk

Another part of Parker's legacy was the recognition that high technical skill was needed to perform modern jazz. Yet some of those who dominated the music's second decade (1955–65), such as Thelonious Monk, John Lewis, Charles Mingus, and Miles Davis, did not emphasize virtuoso technique. Monk, whose roots as a pianist lay in the Harlem stride school, developed a performing style that made the piano sound more percussive than flowing. And the rhythm of his lean-textured compositions is even more asymmetrical than Lester Young's or Charlie Parker's.

Modern Jazz Quartet

John Lewis, like Monk a pianist-composer, made his mark as leader of the Modern Jazz Quartet (MJQ, with piano, vibraphone, bass, and drums), formed in the early 1950s. Instead of relying chiefly on improvising, Lewis combined composition and improvisation in ways that repaid close listening, as in a concert hall. In doing so, he brought order and form to the materials that brilliant first-generation bebop improvisers like Parker had discovered. The Modern Jazz Quartet, with its relatively soft, introspective sound, opened the concert hall to a new kind of jazz—**cool jazz**—akin to classical chamber music. And Lewis explored that link further by composing Baroque-style "suites" and jazz fugues for the MJQ.

Charles Mingus

Charles Mingus rose to prominence as a bandleader, composer, and virtuoso soloist on the most ungainly of solo instruments, the double bass. After paying his dues as a sideman for musicians as diverse as Louis Armstrong, Duke Ellington, and Charlie Parker, Mingus made his mark as a bandleader with the LP (long-playing record album) *Pithecanthropus Erectus* (1956), whose title track, lasting more than ten minutes, combines blues licks, static harmonies, sudden changes of meter and tempo, and atonal group improvisations in a complex whole that would prove influential on the free-jazz artists of the 1960s (see chapter 18). The 1959 LP *Mingus Ah Um* showcases thick-textured compositions for an eight-piece band including *Goodbye Pork Pie Hat*, an homage to Lester Young, and "Fables of Faubus," a scathing putdown of Arkansas governor Orval Faubus, who in 1957 had forcibly opposed the desegregation of Little Rock's Central High School. Of the second-generation modern-jazz artists, Mingus stands out for carrying forward the orchestral compositional techniques of Duke Ellington while foregrounding a heightened political sensibility that would soon be heard in the music of other jazz musicians, such as Max Roach's 1960 *Freedom Now Suite*.

Miles Davis

Miles Davis, another second-generation master, emerged in the latter 1940s with a lyrical approach that contradicted the image of modern jazz as virtuoso music. By 1954 he had discovered an intensely personal trumpet sound that was often heard in tightly muted playing, close to the microphone. During the 1950s silence and space became basic to Davis's musical vocabulary. The 1950s also saw Davis's collaborations with arranger Gil Evans, who supplemented the traditional jazz combo with more solo instruments, including some not usually associated with jazz, such as flute, French horn, and tuba. On their 1958 album of songs from Gershwin's opera *Porgy and Bess*, Evans's colorful orchestrations create an atmospheric setting for Davis's moody, introspective solos, as on the

LG 16.3

track *Summertime* (LG 16.3). Whereas Davis's work with small combos captures the sometimes competitive spirit of multiple soloists improvising in sequence, his work with Evans puts the Harmon-muted sound of Davis's trumpet front and center, sharing the spotlight with no one.

| CD 3.9 | Listening Guide 16.3 | *Summertime* MILES DAVIS |

SONGWRITER: George Gershwin, arr. Gil Evans

DATE: 1958

PERFORMERS: Miles Davis, trumpet; orchestra conducted by Gil Evans. Instrumentation: solo trumpet; two flutes; two saxophones; three French horns; four trumpets; four trombones; tuba; bass; drums.

GENRE: cool jazz

METER: duple

FORM: 16-bar *abac* choruses

WHAT TO LISTEN FOR

- distinctive timbre of Davis's trumpet with Harmon mute
- introspective, soulful soloing
- colorful use of flutes, French horns, tuba
- mild dissonance of harmonies with added notes

TIMING	SECTION		COMMENTS
0:00	chorus 1 (head)	*aba*	Without introduction, muted trumpet statement of Gershwin's melody. Walking bass and discreet drums; French horns play accompanimental repeating riff, with the tuba joining in at end of *b*, bar 8 (0:15).
0:26		*c*	Momentary shift to the major mode at bar 13 (0:26), with descending chromatic line in the accompaniment. Accompanying riff resumes, now in French horns and low flutes (0:31).
0:35	chorus 2	*aba*	Beginning of chorus 2 blurred by continuation of instrumentation, harmony, riff, and solo trumpet, which begins improvising in last bar of chorus 1. Solo makes use of space, generally falling silent for each statement of the riff in the orchestra.
		c	Sharply rising solo line at the major-mode beginning of the *c* section (1:02).
1:10	chorus 3	*aba*	Flutes join riff. Davis back phrases in the style of Louis Armstrong or Billie Holiday.
		c	Once again, the rising line at *c* (1:37).
1:46	chorus 4	*aba*	Riff in low flutes and French horns. Trumpet solo increasingly impassioned.
		c	At *c* section (2:13), solo begins on a high note and descends.
2:22	chorus 5 (head)		Riff on low flutes alone. Gershwin's melody in trumpet is altered by adding high notes, for a musical and emotional climax.
2:57	coda		Trumpet solo ends with a held note on the fourth degree of the scale, rather than the tonic, leaving the orchestra to resolve the tune at the last moment with a tonic chord—but with a dissonance (the second scale degree) in the flutes.

Listen & Reflect

1. What are some words you would use to describe Davis's sound? In addition to the striking timbre of his playing, what can be said about his melodic ideas (pitch choices), rhythms, dynamics, and so forth?

2. Compare this music for soloist and orchestra with the small ensemble sound of *Yardbird Suite* (LG 16.2). How do the interaction between players and the role of soloing differ in the larger setting? Consider the role of Gil Evans as arranger.

☙ Trumpeter Miles Davis (1926–1991) was a magnetic presence on the jazz scene from the mid-1940s through the 1980s.

hard bop

If cool jazz brought a classical refinement to the language of bebop, a countervailing trend was **hard bop**, which emphasized grittier timbres, heavier rhythms, and a closer connection with jazz's roots in the blues. Groups such as Art Blakey's Jazz Messengers and the quintet led cooperatively by drummer Max Roach and trumpet player Clifford Brown spearheaded the hard bop movement, which flourished on the East Coast and was thought to reflect the harsher, faster pace of urban life, in contrast to the laid-back, West Coast ethos of cool jazz. Gospel-tinged tunes like Horace Silver's "The Preacher" (1955) alluded to the traditions of the black church, inspiring a subset of hard bop called **soul jazz**. By the early 1960s hard bop embraced a diverse array of music, ranging from the intellectual solos of tenor saxophonist Sonny Rollins to the accessible presentation of pop standards by guitarist Wes Montgomery.

soul jazz

POSTWAR LATIN JAZZ AND THE "MAMBO CRAZE"

If hard bop and soul jazz emphasized jazz's roots in the blues and gospel, another type of postwar jazz emphasized what Jelly Roll Morton had called the "Spanish tinge": the Caribbean element that has been present since jazz's earliest manifestations.

Latin American dance music had enjoyed a North American following since the time of Irene and Vernon Castle, before World War I (see chapter 10). The Castle-led fashions for the Argentine tango and the Brazilian maxixe paved the way for a series of dance fads originating in South America and the Caribbean. The Swing Era witnessed the popularity of the rumba, a fast dance of Cuban origin, and the slower beguine, from Guadeloupe and Martinique. Cuban musicians such as Xavier Cugat and Machito (Frank Grillo) found success in New York and Los Angeles leading their own big bands in music that combined Latin music with the swing styles already popular in the United States. Machito in particular influenced bebop pioneer Dizzy Gillespie, and in the late 1940s the two musicians developed a style of fiery Afro-Cuban jazz. Throughout the postwar years, the blend of modern jazz and Caribbean rhythms resulted in new jazz hybrids that kept a firm foothold in the popular sphere.

A Cuban dance that swept the United States in the postwar years was the **mambo**. When "Mambo no. 5," a record by the Mexico City–based Cuban bandleader Pérez Prado, became an unexpected U.S. hit in 1949, its success ushered in a "mambo craze" that lasted well into the 1950s. In addition to records by Cuban musicians, the mambo craze spawned mainstream pop songs like Perry Como's 1954 hit "Papa Loves Mambo." American dancers who found the mambo too difficult were quick to embrace its easier variant, the cha-cha. In fact, a variety of Caribbean dance rhythms became known in the United States as "mambo," which thus functioned as a sort of umbrella term.

One of the most influential musicians to emerge from the mambo craze was Tito Puente, a "Nuyorican"—a native New Yorker of Puerto Rican extraction. Born in 1923, he grew up admiring the Latin dance bands as well as swing musicians like drummer Gene Krupa. The beginning of Puente's career coincided with a large-scale postwar migration of Puerto Ricans to New York that, among other things, provided the background for Leonard Bernstein's *West Side Story*, described later in this chapter. As a young man Puente played **timbales**—the high-pitched tom-toms characteristic of Cuban music—in Machito's jazz band, the Afro-Cubans. After serving in the navy during World War II, he attended Juilliard on the G.I. Bill, where he studied conducting and arranging. He formed his own band in the late 1940s and in 1949 began his long recording career, which lasted until shortly before his death in 2000.

Puente's LP *Dance Mania*, recorded in December 1957 and released in 1958, remains one of the best-selling Latin dance albums. The opening track, "El cayuco" (LG 16.4), displays his signature combination of infectious dance rhythms and complex arrangements. The brief vocal chorus, featuring lead singer Santito Colón, compares the dancer to a *cayuco*, a small canoe, presumably because of the back-and-forth paddling motion. As in much Latin dance music, the lyrics seem secondary to the instrumental music, which layers melody instruments and percussion in a rich polyrhythmic texture. The instrumental sections are

⤷ Mambo king Tito Puente (1923–2000) leads his band from the timbales in the mid-1950s.

Tito Puente

LG 16.4

| CD 3.10 | Listening Guide 16.4 | "El cayuco" TITO PUENTE AND HIS ORCHESTRA |

SONGWRITER: Tito Puente

GENRE: Latin jazz

DATE: 1957

PERFORMERS: Santito Colón, vocalist. Instrumentation: voices, trumpets, saxophones, piano, bass, percussion (multiple players: timbales, congas, bongos, guïro)

METER: duple

FORM: vamps and chorus

WHAT TO LISTEN FOR

- Latin rhythms layered in polyrhythmic ostinatos
- Colorful sound of multiple Latin percussion instruments

TIMING	SECTION	TEXT	COMMENTS
0:00	introduction		2 bars: 3 pickup notes lead to the first downbeat.
0:04	vamp		6 bars: piano *montuno* and Latin percussion for 2 bars, then joined by saxes in repeating 2-bar riff.
0:15			4 bars: trumpets add descant.
0:23	introduction		Return of introduction to signal the chorus.
0:27	chorus	Oye cayuco Oye mi chachacha Pero mira baila baila cayuquin Como tu baila Como tu goza mi chachacha	8 bars: vocal ensemble and solo voice.
0:42	tag		2-bar tag for full band.
0:46	vamp		8 bars: piano and saxes alternate two chords a half-step apart, over an active bass and Latin percussion.
1:01	transition		2-bar transition for full band.
1:04	vamp		8 bars: saxes play a repeating 2-bar riff.
1:20			8 bars: trumpets add a descant.
1:35	transition		2-bar transition for full band.
1:38	introduction		Return of intro to signal another chorus.
1:43	chorus	Oye cayuco . . .	As before.
1:58	tag		As before.
2:02	vamp		4 bars, with new sax riff.
2:09			8 bars, with new trumpet descant over sax riff.
2:25	coda		4 bars based on the introduction, with extended last note.

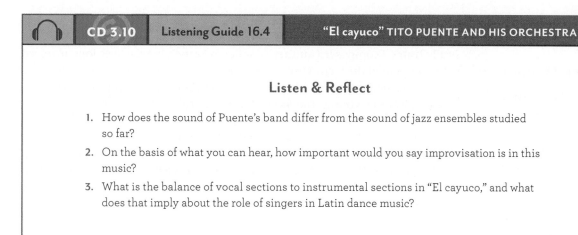

| CD 3.10 | Listening Guide 16.4 | "El cayuco" TITO PUENTE AND HIS ORCHESTRA |

Listen & Reflect

1. How does the sound of Puente's band differ from the sound of jazz ensembles studied so far?
2. On the basis of what you can hear, how important would you say improvisation is in this music?
3. What is the balance of vocal sections to instrumental sections in "El cayuco," and what does that imply about the role of singers in Latin dance music?

essentially vamps, built of repeating two-bar riffs or ostinatos such as the piano *montuno* heard near the beginning of "El cayuco." At a time when other forms of modern jazz were moving away from the dancers that had fueled the Swing Era, Latin jazz bands such as Puente's were maintaining strong ties to their audience's desire to move to the music.

JAZZ LPs AND ARTISTIC PRESTIGE

In the early 1950s jazz recordings began appearing in the 33⅓-rpm long-playing (**LP**) format developed for classical music. The flexibility that LP recording offered jazz musicians influenced the content of their music as well as boosting its prestige. An LP offered the possibility of longer pieces. The relatively high price encouraged repeated listening, which helped fans absorb unfamiliar styles. LPs also came with liner notes by writers—often jazz critics—who might suggest a context for listening. Thanks in part to LP recordings, modern jazz began to develop a fan base that included concertgoers and readers of the magazines, from the *New Yorker* to the trade journal *Down Beat*, that carried jazz criticism and news. Growing numbers of white college-age listeners embraced jazz as their own; a particular favorite of collegiate listeners was the Dave Brubeck Quartet's 1959 LP *Time Out*, which featured tunes with unusual meters, such as *Take Five*, in quintuple meter. And in the summer of 1954 the Newport Jazz Festival, modeled on classical festivals, was founded in Newport, Rhode Island. Jazz was finding a new place on the American scene.

Dave Brubeck

Writers on jazz such as Nat Hentoff and Martin Williams treated the new LPs as an artistic legacy. Indeed, they shaped that legacy into a body of work that, with its great figures, canonic recordings, and style periods, paralleled the tradition of the Western classical sphere. And they did so long before most classical musicians and music lovers showed interest in jazz as an art form. In a day when such labels as "new music" and "contemporary music" pointed to the Eurocentric classical sphere, jazz musicians lacked the institutional support and cultural prestige to convey their own artistic ideas beyond the circle of jazz fans.

the Third Stream

The changing status of jazz encouraged some musicians to focus their energies on the common ground held with the Western classical tradition. The classically trained composer Gunther Schuller, a French horn player long involved with jazz, coined the term **Third Stream** for music that brought jazz techniques into the classical sphere or vice versa, through improvisation or written composition. John Lewis and the Modern Jazz Quartet were already working that territory, as was Charles Mingus. And Schuller himself explored Third Stream possibilities in such works as *Transformation* (1957), for jazz ensemble, which married the sounds of modern jazz with the atonal procedures of serialist music, and *Variants on a Theme of Thelonious Monk* (1960), recorded with an ensemble that included Ornette Coleman and Bill Evans, both of whom would be major figures in later developments in jazz.

BROADWAY MUSICALS IN THE POSTWAR YEARS

On October 7, 1956, the thirty-nine-year-old composer and conductor Leonard Bernstein surveyed American musical theater in a national television broadcast. "For the last fifteen years," he told viewers, "we have been enjoying the greatest period our musical theater has ever known." Bernstein supported his statement with a list of classic Broadway shows: *Pal Joey, Annie Get Your Gun, Oklahoma!, South Pacific, Guys and Dolls*, and *Kiss Me, Kate.* And he illustrated the talent of these shows' creators with examples from Rodgers and Hammerstein's *South Pacific.*

The shows Bernstein called "young classics" all belonged "to an art that arises out of American roots." As he saw it, the best recent shows were neither opera nor light entertainment but a new form somewhere between the two. "We are in a historical position now similar to that of the popular musical theater in Germany just before Mozart came along," he announced. American musical theater needed only for its own Mozart to arrive, which might happen "any second." Bernstein might have had himself in mind: less than a year later, in September 1957, *West Side Story*, with music by Bernstein and lyrics by Stephen Sondheim, opened in New York to the acclaim of critics and audiences.

The high value Bernstein's broadcast placed on American musicals seemed calculated to surprise 1956 viewers. Musicals before that time were largely ignored by music critics, who saw the classical and popular spheres as separated by a firm barrier. Broadway creators submitted their work directly to the judgment of audiences, whose verdict, registered at the box office, was equally direct. Aesthetic decisions were made to trigger positive public responses. If the audience seemed pleased, the decision was right; if not, changes were made. A tryout run preceded a show's Broadway opening so that out-of-town audience response could be used to identify problems, but the makers of musicals took the public pulse even earlier. Alan Jay Lerner, the librettist and lyricist of *My Fair Lady*, wrote that when he and composer Frederick ("Fritz") Loewe finished a song, "we would dash around the neighborhood, looking for 'customers,' as Fritz would say, meaning neighbors for whom to play it. Naturally, our captive audience was complimentary, but somehow we could always tell if the compliments were because of the song or because of the friendship. Very often it influenced us and made us more aware of a weakness."

✎ Composer and conductor Leonard Bernstein (1918–1990) had a strong influence on the public with television appearances that took up serious musical matters in an engaging way.

In his 1967 book *The American Musical Theater: A Consideration*, Lehman Engel, a composer and conductor of Broadway shows, made up his own list of classic musicals from the years 1940–57. The list included the six Bernstein praised in 1956, plus *Brigadoon, My Fair Lady, West Side Story, Carousel,* and *The King and I.* To Engel, what set these musicals apart was not the music, choreography, scenery, or acting but the more realistic stories and better-rounded characters. All the shows on Engel's list succeeded as dramatic wholes. At the same time, like earlier Broadway shows, they contained hit songs that circulated independently. The list leaves no doubt that Rodgers and Hammerstein were supreme masters of the form. It also testifies to the creative powers of two leading composer-lyricists of an earlier day who flourished in the postwar era, when they found the right book. One was Irving Berlin, whose *Annie Get Your Gun* was the leading hit of 1946. The other was Cole Porter, whose *Kiss Me, Kate* (1948) took Shakespeare's *The Taming of the Shrew* as its starting point.

Musical comedy had traditionally revolved around the blossoming of romance: once the heroine and hero declared mutual love, the adventure was over, and so was the show. Although stories and characters grew more realistic, reliance on an old-fashioned view of romantic love persisted in the mid-century years. Convinced that audiences came to the theater to watch two lovers find their way into each other's arms, the makers of musicals held to that time-tested formula, showing little inclination to explore beyond it.

Even the near-operatic *West Side Story*—the only tragic example in Engel's canon, it ends with the hero being shot dead—seems the exception that proves the rule. Modeled after Shakespeare's *Romeo and Juliet,* the story turns on love at first sight. The lovers, Maria and Tony, are affiliated not with Montagues and Capulets but with two rival New York street gangs, the Puerto Rican Sharks and the self-styled "American" (i.e., white) Jets. While most musicals end with the hero and heroine poised to begin a life together, Maria and Tony are denied that chance by a hate-filled society. Yet before he dies they enjoy their moment of bliss, musical theater style, in an updated Balcony Scene. That scene's musical centerpiece is a thirty-two-bar *aaba* song that, as "Tonight," became one of the show's biggest hits.

In the show's score, however, the title "Tonight" is not used until the song is reprised in a later ensemble (LG 16.5). In fact, Bernstein composed the ensemble number first, then saw the wisdom of pulling out Tony and Maria's parts to form a love duet for the earlier Balcony Scene. Originally conceived as a quintet, the "Tonight" ensemble is usually sung by more than five people, with the parts for the two gang leaders reinforced by gang members. The number begins as a pair of minor-key verses sung in alternation by Riff (and his Jets) and Bernardo (and his Sharks), the two joining in unison for the major-key, blues-tinged chorus. A third verse is sung by Bernardo's girlfriend, Anita, but instead of a return to the chorus, Tony breaks in over her last notes with the lyrical song from the Balcony Scene. The Jets, repeating the opening verse, shake Tony out of his reverie, and Riff and Tony converse to fragments of the bluesy chorus. At the same time, Maria sings her reprise of the Balcony Scene song, increasing the number of voices to three. Soon Anita and Bernardo (and his Sharks) join in as well, creating a web of five-voice counterpoint over the pulsating orchestra.

Music makes possible a richness of texture that would be unintelligible in the spoken theater. At the same time, lighting and staging make clear to the audience that the principals are inhabiting different scenes and are not interacting with one another (except for the Jets and Tony). Complex ensembles are high points

West Side Story

LG 16.5

operatic ensembles

CD 3.11	**Listening Guide 16.5**	**"Tonight" Quintet,** from *West Side Story* **LEONARD BERNSTEIN AND STEPHEN SONDHEIM**

DATE: 1957

PERFORMERS: Original Broadway cast recording; Carol Laurence (Maria), Larry Kert (Tony), Chita Rivera (Anita), and ensemble

GENRE: Broadway musical ensemble

METER: mostly duple

FORM: verse and chorus, with interpolated reprises of *aaba* song

WHAT TO LISTEN FOR

- contrast of minor and major modes for dramatic tension
- restless rhythms and blues references in the gangs' music
- lyrical, long-arching melody in the lovers' music ("Tonight")
- polyphonic texture of the second "Tonight" reprise

TIMING	SECTION		TEXT	COMMENTS
0:00	introduction			Angular minor chords, over a three-note repeating figure or **ostinato** in the bass, set anxious mood.
0:06	verse 1		The Jets are gonna have their day Tonight...	Minor mode. Riff and his Jets sing the opening phrase, Bernardo and his Sharks answer, and the Jets continue. Bars lasting only one and a half beats (e.g., "Fair fight") disrupt the duple meter.
0:24	verse 2		We're gonna hand 'em a surprise Tonight...	Sharks and Jets reverse roles.
0:42	chorus		We're gonna rock it tonight...	The two gangs in unison sing the major-mode chorus melody, which emphasizes blues-tinged lowered seventh and third scale degrees. Brass "stings" punctuate phrase endings. After eight bars on the tonic, shift to the subdominant ("Well, they began it"), an allusion to standard blues changes. Stop-time accompaniment with sharp orchestral chords ("stabs").
1:07	verse 3		Anita's gonna get her kicks Tonight...	Return to the minor mode for Anita's solo verse. Marked "sexily," the score indicates that she should swing her rhythms, in contrast to the straight rhythms that have preceded.
1:25	"Tonight" reprise	*a*	Tonight, tonight Won't be just any night...	Shift to major for reprise of "Tonight," song from the earlier Balcony Scene, sung by Tony. The wide intervals and long note durations create lyricism in contrast to the tense verse and chorus. Accompaniment uses a subdued beguine (Latin dance) rhythm.

🎧 CD 3.11	Listening Guide 16.5		**"Tonight" Quintet, from** *West Side Story* **LEONARD BERNSTEIN AND STEPHEN SONDHEIM**

TIMING	SECTION		TEXT	COMMENTS
1:38		a'	Tonight, tonight I'll see my love tonight . . .	Variant a' modulates to the key a minor third higher.
1:51		b	Today The minutes seem like hours . . .	Melody continues ascent to apex ("To-<u>day</u>"), then begins long, slow descent, with violins echoing.
2:04		a''	Oh moon, grow bright . . .	Return to the opening key; music breaks off before the final word as the orchestra returns to agitated introduction music, louder than before.
2:21	verse 4		I'm counting on you to be there Tonight . . .	Return to minor mode, in key a third higher than before; Riff addresses Tony.
2:40	"Tonight" reprise	a	Tonight, tonight Won't be just any night . . .	Shift to major for Maria's reprise. In counterpoint, Riff sings fragments of the chorus melody and Tony responds with fragments of the verse melody.
2:52		a'	Tonight, tonight I'll see my love tonight . . .	Sharks sing fragments of the chorus melody and Anita sings fragments of the verse melody.
3:05		b	Today The minutes seem like hours . . .	Tony joins Maria, with counterpoint from all other participants.
3:18		a''	Oh moon, grow bright . . .	The final moments begin very softly (*pianissimo*), with a dramatic crescendo to the loudest dynamic (*fortissimo*). Reaches conclusion with final word, "Tonight," which Maria sings on a high C.

Listen & Reflect

1. What aspects of the "Tonight" ensemble add to its operatic effect, and what aspects seem definitely non-operatic? How does each set of attributes help or hinder the dramatic situation?

2. Choreographer Jerome Robbins originated the idea for the show and directed the 1961 film version. Robbins's choreography mixes elements of ballet with vernacular theatrical dance, much as Bernstein's music mixes opera and musical comedy styles. After viewing the film's opening sequence on DVD or online, compare its mixture of ballet and street gangs to this ensemble's mixture of opera and street gangs.

in the operas of Mozart and Verdi, but such writing was virtually unknown in the American musical before *West Side Story*. In Leonard Bernstein, at least by implication, Broadway had found its parallel to a Mozart.

Before World War II, some classical musicians had responded to the populist mood of the Great Depression by striving to make their music accessible to a wider audience. After the war, although Samuel Barber, Gian Carlo Menotti, and other composers continued to write in a melodious, inviting style, avant-garde modernists became the dominant voice in the academy, winning an institutional status they had been denied earlier in the century. As musical composition came more and more to resemble scientific experimentation, at least in some quarters, a widening gap separated the audience for classical music from contemporary composers. With the notable exception of Leonard Bernstein, the classical sphere lacked the popularizing efforts of such earlier proponents as Theodore Thomas, Leopold Stokowski, or Aaron Copland.

Perhaps it was no coincidence, then, that other areas of musical expression, such as jazz and the musical theater, developed higher artistic aspirations in the postwar years. Like so many musicians throughout America's history, jazz instrumentalists and Broadway songwriters sought ways to bring their art to its highest level while communicating to a broad general audience. By one means or another, America's musical landscape has always had room for music that embraced both artistic integrity and commercial viability.

QUESTIONS FOR DISCUSSION AND REVIEW

1. What effect did émigré composers have on music in the postwar United States?

2. What factors led to a widening gap between postwar composers and the audience for classical music?

3. Compare the aesthetic stance of John Cage with that of academic composers such as Milton Babbitt.

4. How does bebop differ from swing, and how do those differences account for the shrinking audience for jazz in the postwar years?

5. Compare modern jazz with music in the postwar classical sphere.

6. Is Bernstein's argument for the musical as an American classical art form convincing? Why or why not?

FURTHER READING

Block, Geoffrey. "The Broadway Canon from *Show Boat* to *West Side Story* and the European Operatic Ideal." *Journal of Musicology* 11, no. 4 (autumn 1993): 525–44.

Cage, John. *Silence: Lectures and Writings.* Middletown, CT: Wesleyan University Press, 1961.

DeVeaux, Scott. *The Birth of Bebop.* Berkeley and Los Angeles: University of California Press, 1997.

Gann, Kyle. *No Such Thing as Silence: John Cage's 4'11".* New Haven, CT: Yale University Press, 2010.

Gioia, Ted. *The History of Jazz.* 2d edition. New York: Oxford University Press, 2011.

Horowitz, Joseph. *Artists in Exile: How Refugees from Twentieth-Century Revolution Transformed the American Performing Arts.* New York: HarperCollins, 2008.

Nicholls, David. *John Cage.* Urbana: University of Illinois Press, 2007.

Olsen, Dale, and Daniel E. Sheehy, eds. *The Garland Handbook of Latin American Music.* 2d ed. New York: Routledge, 2008.

Simeone, Nigel. *Leonard Bernstein: "West Side Story."* Surrey, UK: Ashgate, 2009.

Woideck, Carl. *Charlie Parker: His Music and Life.* Ann Arbor: University of Michigan Press, 1996.

"GOOD ROCKING TONIGHT"

Popular and Folk Music after World War II

In 1959 a prestigious university press published a book of essays called *The Art of Jazz*, a title meant to be provocative. Over the past two decades, the editor told his readers, a body of criticism had accumulated around jazz—the kind of writing "that only an art can inspire and that only an art deserves." Gathered in *The Art of Jazz*, these writings focused on the music itself, especially as preserved on record. While far from the most lucrative popular music in the postwar years, jazz was the only one then being taken seriously by critics. Popular music stars received plenty of publicity, but it was a kind that treated them more as celebrities than as artists.

That situation would change in later decades. Today, many writers are critiquing popular music and exploring its history. This new inclination owes much to the example of jazz critics, who, by discussing jazz in a way that only an art deserves, vouched for the music's excellence. But only by treating performances as the equivalent of compositions were they able to claim authority for their judgments. Phonograph records made that possible by turning fleeting performances into permanent works. Fashioned by singers and players in collaboration with composers, arrangers, producers, and technicians, recordings were defined not by musical notation but by their sound; they became the means through which historical trends could be traced, first in jazz, then in other kinds of popular music. Because of the importance of phonograph records as primary documents for popular and folk music in the years after World War II, this chapter also looks at postwar developments in the record industry and in radio and television.

MAINSTREAM POPULAR MUSIC AND THE MASS MEDIA IN THE POSTWAR YEARS

The primary unit of sale in the popular music industry both before and after the war was the **single**—actually a double-sided phonograph record, usually with a marketable song on the A side and a less commercially promising "filler" on the B side.

The old 78-rpm format, ten inches in diameter, remained available through the 1950s, supplemented and eventually superseded by a new format: the **45**, seven inches in diameter, made of sturdier vinyl and spinning at forty-five revolutions per minute. Each side of the 45, like the 78, had a playing time of about three minutes, well suited to popular songs. Manufactured with a larger hole in the center, 45s accommodated the automatic mechanism of the jukebox, an important source of revenue for record companies. The same feature also permitted the stacking of several discs on a home phonograph to play in quick succession, allowing listeners in effect to create their own albums or playlists of favorite records.

the 45

Introduced in 1949, the 45-rpm single, at the lower end of the market, complemented the 33⅓-rpm long-playing record (LP) at the upper end. LPs at first were issued in two formats, either ten or twelve inches in diameter; the former was used largely for jazz, the latter for classical music. By the late 1950s the larger format was used for all types of music, edging out the ten-inch LP in popularity. Each side of the twelve-inch LP could hold about twenty minutes of music: an entire Mozart symphony, several jazz numbers, or about six popular songs. Riding the rising tide of the postwar economic boom, these new formats found tremendous commercial success. Revenues from record sales topped $214 million in 1947, finally surpassing the previous peak, set before the Great Depression, and sales increased to $514 million in 1959.

the LP

New technologies also affected how music was recorded. Chief among these was magnetic tape, developed in Germany during the 1930s and available for commercial use in the United States shortly after the war ended. Tape recording allowed new possibilities in **editing**, as musicians could rerecord unsatisfactory passages and splice the corrected versions into the master tape—the same procedure used in the electronic music studio. Also shared with electronic music was the process of **overdubbing**, in which instrumental and vocal parts could be recorded separately and then superimposed, and the addition of artificial reverberation, or **reverb**, which could make the musicians sound as if they were performing in a massive stone cathedral—or in a tiled bathroom.

studio techniques

A pioneer in the use of these new studio techniques to make popular recordings was the guitarist and inventor Les Paul, whose records sound as if he is playing up to eight separate guitar parts simultaneously. Paul would record some of those tracks with the tape running at half speed, so that when played back at normal speed the part sounds twice as fast and an octave higher—again, a type of tape manipulation borrowed from the electronic music studio.

Les Paul

Another pioneer was Mitch Miller, a classically trained oboist and English horn player. As an A&R man for Mercury Records and then Columbia Records, Miller greatly increased the artistic role of the **record producer**, who oversees the recording process. Whereas previous A&R men had exercised control over the choice of performers and material, Miller extended that control to supervision of the musical arrangement and especially the recording process, exploiting the potentials of the new technologies.

Mitch Miller

In the late 1940s and 1950s Miller produced a series of hits for Mercury and Columbia, many of them novelty songs filled with recording gimmicks, such as "How Much Is That Doggie in the Window?" (1952), which featured Patti Page singing overdubbed harmony to her own lead vocal, punctuated by a yipping dog. Though artistically negligible, Miller's novelty records, like Les Paul's, introduced the idea that a record could deliver a listening experience that could only be constructed bit by bit in the studio. Records were no longer merely literal records of musical performances enacted before a microphone, and a "song" was no longer the notated material that performers bring to life; increasingly, songs were creations of the recording studio. With this redefinition came a shift in artistic control from songwriter to record producer that would have far-reaching consequences for rock music and, later, hip-hop.

In the early 1960s Miller extended his activities into television, a new medium that gained prominence in the postwar era. In *Sing Along with Mitch* he conducted a male chorus—and the audience—in singing old popular songs, reaching as far back as Stephen Foster. The popularity of the show, which had a wide appeal for older audiences, is one indication of the continued relevance of earlier popular styles far into the postwar era.

standards

Standards—songs written as early as the 1920s by Broadway and Tin Pan Alley tunesmiths—were still being performed and remained fundamental to the popular song business. At the end of the 1950s Irving Berlin and Cole Porter, among others, were still making a handsome income from songs they had written in the past, and the Gershwin, Kern, and Hart estates remained lucrative. One reason the older tradition endured was that many of its leading songwriters were still on the scene. Another was the presence of experienced singers who had learned their trade with Swing Era big bands. A third reason was the large adult audience, people who had grown up with the music and still considered it their own. A fourth was that jazz musicians had drawn much of their own repertory from popular song, and listeners were used to hearing their favorite songs in multiple versions. Finally, there was the high quality of so many of the songs. As early as 1925 *Variety* had recognized the uncanny match between words and music that American songwriters were achieving. As the lyricist Yip Harburg put it: "Words make you think thoughts; music makes you feel a feeling; and a song makes you feel a thought."

In the Swing Era, bandleaders hired singers to add variety to the big bands' predominantly instrumental offerings. But after the wartime decline of the big bands, singers emerged as the dominant celebrities in popular music—a process already underway in the 1930s with the success of crooners such as Bing Crosby. Now singers were heard on records produced to highlight their voices over the discreet accompaniment of anonymous studio orchestras. The most influential popular singer of the postwar era was Frank Sinatra, who had first found fame as a singer for Tommy Dorsey's big band.

In the 1940s Sinatra won the adulation of the "bobby-socks brigade"—females aged twelve to sixteen—who screamed in adoration when he appeared onstage. Throngs of bobby-soxers reinforced the idea, first made apparent by Benny Goodman's rise to fame in 1935, that teenage listeners could constitute a profitable market for music tailored to their tastes. By the mid-1950s Sinatra's audience had matured, and so had his artistry. Between 1953 and 1961 Sinatra recorded no fewer than sixteen **concept albums**, LPs in which the individual songs were selected, arranged, and ordered to create a larger artistic

A&R man, record producer, and television sing-along host Mitch Miller (right) in the mid-1960s, smiling for the camera with singer Leslie Uggams and songwriter Irving Berlin, nearly eighty years old and still in the business.

whole. *Frank Sinatra Sings for Only the Lonely* (1958) is one such album. While its *the concept album* twelve songs, all in arrangements by Nelson Riddle, span almost three decades, as a group they maintain a generally melancholy mood, with Riddle's orchestrations providing a contemporary sound. Aimed at adults, a concept album like this one connected songs that had been written separately and testified to the excellence Sinatra found in the work of such songwriting teams as Rodgers and Hart, Harold Arlen and Johnny Mercer, and Sammy Cahn and Jimmy Van Heusen.

Mainstream popular music, rooted in the songwriting and performance styles of the classic American popular song, reached even wider audiences thanks to the new technologies in the record and television industries. (**Mainstream** itself is a relative term, a label for that segment of the nation's culture considered to be predominant or a norm at a particular time.) But the mainstream alone does not account for the huge revenues garnered by the music business in the postwar era. Much of that commercial success was due to innovative developments in music genres originating in the Caribbean and in the southern United States: Latin music (as described in chapter 16), country music, rhythm and blues, and rock and roll.

POSTWAR COUNTRY MUSIC

With prosperity growing in the South, the demand for amusement grew with it. The *Grand Ole Opry* and other radio barn dances (see chapter 11) attracted wide audiences, and jukeboxes reverberated with songs by country entertainers. Country songs also appeared in the popular mainstream. In 1950 "Tennessee Waltz," by the country songwriter and performer Pee Wee King, was turned into a hit record by Mitch Miller, whose production featured Patti Page's signature overdubbed harmony. Sung in a style free of regional traits, the record's mainstream success seemed to indicate that country songwriters' emotional directness could jump barriers of social class and geography.

BILL MONROE AND BLUEGRASS

While postwar country music was proof of the staying power of old styles, themes, and sounds, innovators like Bill Monroe infused the old forms with a new energy. A mandolin virtuoso born in 1911 in the bluegrass state of Kentucky, Monroe established himself on the *Grand Ole Opry*, whose Saturday-night radio broadcasts on Nashville's WSM included a half-hour segment distributed nationally on NBC. The acoustic instruments of Monroe's band—mandolin, five-string banjo, fiddle, guitar, and double bass—preserved the old-fashioned flavor of prewar hillbilly music. Unlike the string bands of the 1930s, however, Monroe's Blue Grass Boys took their numbers extremely fast—much as bebop musicians at the same time often improvised at accelerated speeds—and like jazz performers, they structured their tunes as a series of virtuoso solos. In vocal numbers Monroe pitched his music high, with the tenor's harmony line (which he sang himself) set above the lead and sometimes reaching as far up as the C above

ꙮ Bill Monroe (1911–1996), a key figure in the founding of bluegrass music, performs in the 1970s with the Blue Grass Boys, consisting of his own mandolin, plus fiddle, banjo, guitar, and double bass.

middle C—an intensification of the blended sound of the 1930s brother duos described in chapter 14.

Monroe and his musicians brought an uncommon blend of old and new to country music. Audiences found the music fresh and exciting, even if the songs looked backward in time. Asked in 1977 to define his style, dubbed **bluegrass** in the latter 1950s, Monroe called it "the old southern sound that was heard years ago, many, many years ago in the backwoods, at country dances." Elsewhere he recalled that in writing a fiddle tune called "Land of Lincoln" he made the piece "go the way I thought Abraham Lincoln might have heard it—a tune like he might have heard when he was a boy from some old-time fiddler." Rather than emphasize his own innovations, Monroe's comments invoke the mysterious, mythic simplicity that folk traditions can preserve.

Like the records of the Carter Family a generation earlier, bluegrass was a modern representation of Appalachian folk music, reconstituted for a new audience. Its vocal style was impersonal and stylized in the manner of Anglo-American folk singing, and the high range favored by many singers can be traced back to folk practices from black field hollers to shape-note hymnody. The piercing vocal timbre is a direct legacy from Bill Monroe: the "high lonesome sound" that for many listeners has given the music's deadpan delivery an impassioned edge.

LG 17.1

In a standard bluegrass approach that may seem paradoxical, Monroe's "It's Mighty Dark to Travel" (LG 17.1) is about loneliness but is up-tempo and in major mode. The vocal chorus, sung five times, embodies the Blue Grass Boys' signature sound: Lester Flatt's lead vocal and Monroe's high tenor harmony, sung without vibrato, with a rather nasal timbre, and with perfect intonation. Behind them, the band pours out a steady stream of picked or bowed sixteenth notes. That stream never runs dry, whether during the verses, which Flatt sings alone, or the mandolin's opening statement of the eight-bar chorus melody, or the solos played by the banjo, mandolin, and fiddle. There are contrasts: between verses and choruses, vocal and instrumental statements, and sections that feature different solo instruments. But the ensemble sound and the driving rhythm provide a compelling continuity.

🎧 **CD 3.12**	**Listening Guide 17.1**	**"It's Mighty Dark to Travel"** BILL MONROE AND HIS BLUE GRASS BOYS

SONGWRITER: Bill Monroe

DATE: 1947

PERFORMERS: Bill Monroe, vocal, mandolin; Lester Flatt, vocal, guitar; Earl Scruggs, banjo; Chubby Wise, fiddle; Howard Watts, bass

GENRE: bluegrass

METER: duple

FORM: verse and chorus

WHAT TO LISTEN FOR

- "high lonesome sound" of high-pitched tenor vocal harmonies
- fast tempo and driving rhythm
- same music for verse and chorus
- alternation of virtuosic instrumental solos
- distinctive sound of Earl Scruggs's banjo technique

TIMING	SECTION	TEXT	COMMENTS
0:00	instrumental chorus		Mandolin leads in an instrumental statement of the 8-bar tune. For every sustained note in the melody (as later sung), Monroe plays repeated notes, using a rapid back-and-forth stroke with a flat pick.
0:12	chorus	It's mighty dark for me to travel For my sweetheart she is gone . . .	Vocal duet in close blended harmony.
0:26	instrumental chorus		Fiddle solo, with prominent use of double stops. As in other instrumental choruses, two extra beats at end accommodate the singer's pickup notes into the next verse.
0:39	verse 1	To me she was a little angel Sent down to me from God above . . .	Flatt sings the verse solo, with mandolin filigree as background.
0:51	chorus	It's mighty dark for me to travel . . .	Return to vocal duet; Monroe's mandolin is silent.
1:05	instrumental chorus		Banjo solo featuring Scruggs's influential three-finger style (using metal finger picks), producing a stream of sixteenth notes with syncopated accents.
1:17	verse 2	Many a night we strolled together Talking of our love so fair . . .	Flatt's vocal solo, with mandolin and fiddle in background.
1:30	chorus	It's mighty dark for me to travel . . .	Vocal duet.

(continued)

	CD 3.12	Listening Guide 17.1	"It's Mighty Dark to Travel" BILL MONROE AND HIS BLUE GRASS BOYS

TIMING	SECTION	TEXT	COMMENTS
1:43	instrumental chorus		Mandolin solo, much as at the beginning.
1:56	verse 3	Traveling down this lonesome highway Thinking of my love who's gone...	Flatt's vocal solo, with mandolin, fiddle, and banjo providing furious collective improvisation.
2:08	chorus	It's mighty dark for me to travel...	Vocal duet.
2:22	instrumental chorus		Fiddle solo, in "breakdown" style (see chapter 14).
2:34	chorus	It's mighty dark for me to travel...	Final vocal duet.

Listen & Reflect

1. Like bebop in relation to swing, bluegrass continues earlier string-band styles, but with a generally faster tempo, greater emphasis on virtuosity, and heightened intensity (despite the impassive vocal delivery). What aspects of American life in the 1940s might have contributed to the appeal of these new, supercharged styles?

HANK WILLIAMS AND HONKY-TONK

Western swing, the jazz-inflected dance music of the Southwest, was not the only musical style to arise from the beer halls that offered diversion to people who worked hard and played hard. Another style, emerging just before the war and increasing in popularity through the 1940s and 1950s, took its name from those rough-and-tumble institutions of entertainment: **honky-tonk** music. Like Western swing, honky-tonk used electric guitar and amplified **pedal steel guitar** (an electrified version of the Hawaiian lap guitar, with multiple necks and pedals that change the pitch of certain strings), along with acoustic instruments such as fiddle, to deliver a loud, danceable beat. But in place of jazz influences, honky-tonk hewed closer to traditional ballad styles and kept the emphasis on the singer.

honky-tonk lyrics   The lyrics of honky-tonk songs reflect the concerns of their listeners. Some songs comment on the laboring man's industrialized working conditions, whether coal mining ("Dark as a Dungeon"), truck driving ("Six Days on the Road"), or factory work ("Detroit City"). Other songs touch on themes of alcoholism, adultery, and divorce. Though a few songs celebrate the party atmosphere of the honky-tonk as an escape from reality, most treat their subjects with a moral seriousness that attests to Protestant fundamentalism's strong grip on musicians and listeners alike. Paradoxically, bright tempos, simple major-mode harmonies, and danceable rhythms seem to encourage listeners to dance (and drink) their cares away even as the lyrics offer a pessimistic, guilt-ridden view of the sins of drinking and dancing: "Driving Nails in My Coffin" ("every time I drink a bottle of booze"), "Walking the Floor over You," "Born to Lose." Even humorous songs address topics like domestic violence, infidelity, and divorce: "Pistol Packin' Mama," "Divorce Me C.O.D."

Although dominated by men, honky-tonk music made room for a "Queen of Country Music," Kitty Wells. Her 1952 hit "It Wasn't God Who Made Honky Tonk Angels" was an **answer song**, a response to an earlier hit—in this case, Hank Thompson's "The Wild Side of Life," which accuses women of faithlessness in a chorus beginning: "I didn't know God made honky-tonk angels." Wells's song merely added to the stereotype of the loose-living honky-tonk angel a countervailing stereotype: the long-suffering wife as victim. Still, her answer song unlocked the door for a conversation about women's roles that later country singers like Loretta Lynn and Dolly Parton would swing wide open.

Of the honky-tonk singers and songwriters who emerged in the postwar years, none equaled Hank Williams in popularity and lasting influence. With his western-style outfits and a band called the Drifting Cowboys, Williams, a native of Alabama, molded his Deep South background to the Texan stage persona that was de rigueur for honky-tonk. Williams came to prominence in the late 1940s on radio barn dances, first the *Louisiana Hayride* and then the *Grand Ole Opry*. He briefly had his own radio "song and patter" program, the *Health and Happiness Show*, and appeared on WSM's television broadcasts. Within a few years he had created a body of songs that remain country standards: "Your Cheating Heart," Hey, Good-Lookin'," "I'm So Lonesome I Could Cry," "Cold, Cold Heart," "Jambalaya," and many others. His light, nasal baritone invested his lyrics with emotion, so that listeners felt he had lived the stories his songs related. That sense of authenticity, along with his alcohol-related death at age twenty-nine on New Year's Day 1953, made Hank Williams the country equivalent of the meteoric rock stars who would later, directly or indirectly, follow his example.

Although best known for singing his own songs, Williams sings "Lost Highway" (LG 17.2), a song by Leon Payne, with such conviction that it feels autobiographical. Williams accompanies himself on guitar, playing a characteristic **sock rhythm**: gentle chords on beats 1 and 3 of each bar, alternating with short, accented chords on beats 2 and 4, thus emphasizing the backbeat and encouraging dancing. The stand-up bass lays down a steady foundation on beats 1 and 3, and the texture is filled out by electric guitar (a hollow-bodied instrument enhanced by the mellow sound of a vacuum-tube amplifier), pedal steel guitar (also electrically amplified), and two acoustic instruments, fiddle and mandolin—the latter an unusual member of a honky-tonk band.

Hank Williams (1923–1953), singer, guitarist, and songwriter whose music continued to be a presence in country music long after his early death.

LG 17.2

| CD 3.13 | Listening Guide 17.2 | "Lost Highway" HANK WILLIAMS |

SONGWRITER: Leon Payne

DATE: 1949

PERFORMERS: Hank Williams with the Drifting Cowboys. Instrumentation: electric and acoustic guitars, mandolin, fiddle, pedal steel guitar, bass

GENRE: honky-tonk

METER: duple

FORM: strophic

WHAT TO LISTEN FOR

- relaxed dance rhythm, with sock rhythm emphasizing the backbeat
- prominence of electric guitar, amplified steel guitar, and fiddle
- pentatonic melody
- three-chord (I, IV, V) harmony

TIMING	SECTION	TEXT	COMMENTS
0:00	introduction		4-bar electric guitar solo suggests opening of the vocal melody, then slides down a series of chromatic chords. A sudden silence sets up vocal entrance.
0:06	stanza 1	I'm a rolling stone all alone and lost . . .	In first 16-bar stanza, fills on pedal steel guitar create halo effect around voice.
0:35	stanza 2	Just a deck of cards and a jug of wine . . .	Fiddle fills behind the vocal.
1:03	instrumental stanza		Bluesy guitar solo for bars 1–8, fiddle double stops with pedal steel fills for bars 9–12, guitar for bars 13–16, echoing introduction.
1:32	stanza 3	I was just a lad, nearly twenty-two . . .	Mandolin tremolo fills behind the vocal.
2:01	stanza 4	Now boys don't start your rambling around . . .	Guitar fills behind the vocal.
2:30	tag		4 bars, similar to introduction.

Listen & Reflect

1. What aspects of the performance reinforce the mood of the lyrics, and what aspects seem to work against that mood? What would be the song's effect if the latter aspects were either eliminated or changed to agree with the former?

RHYTHM AND BLUES

At mid-century the music-industry trade magazine *Billboard* tabulated retail and jukebox revenues and radio airplay for popular records by dividing the market into three categories, each with its own chart appearing weekly. The "pop" chart listed mainstream popular records—those thought to appeal primarily to middle-class white listeners, the largest segment of the market. "Country and western" was the new name for what had formerly been called "hillbilly": records that targeted lower-class white audiences in the South and Southwest. The third chart, listing records that aimed to capture the attention of African American music lovers, also underwent a name change, from "race" to **rhythm and blues**. That term, often shortened to **R&B**, is still used to refer to music rooted in the new blues styles that sprang up in the postwar years.

R & B

Like *Billboard*'s other two categories, rhythm and blues encompassed a variety of styles. At one extreme was **Chicago blues**, an electrified version of Mississippi Delta blues performed by musicians who had migrated from the Delta to Chicago. The iconic Chicago bluesman was Muddy Waters (born McKinley Morganfield in Mississippi), whose "Hoochie Coochie Man," "Mannish Boy," and "Got My Mojo Working" exude a swaggering machismo emulated by later generations of rockers and rappers; in the 1960s a British band would take its name from his song "Rollin' Stone." Waters's label, Chess Records, was also the home of such notable blues figures as Little Walter, Bo Diddley, Howlin' Wolf, Etta James, Otis Spann, and Willie Dixon.

Chicago blues

jump bands

At the other extreme of the rhythm and blues spectrum were **jump bands**, scaled-back versions of the big bands of the Swing Era. Under the leadership of musicians like Lionel Hampton, Louis Jordan, and Eddie "Cleanhead" Vinson, jump bands typically consisted of a rhythm section and a front line of two or three melody instruments, such as sax, trumpet, and electric guitar, with vocals supplied by any or all of the instrumentalists. Jump bands specialized in up-tempo blues numbers with elements of piano boogie-woogie and a heavy backbeat mixed in.

Between the rawness of Chicago blues and the tight ensemble precision of the jump bands were a variety of R&B styles, with acts ranging from electrified versions of Texas blues, represented by guitarist T-Bone Walker, to vocal harmony groups like the Orioles and the Dominoes, whose ensemble scat singing inspired the genre label **doo wop**. Also popular were solo vocalists such as Dinah Washington, Ruth Brown, and LaVern Baker, as well as **blues shouters**—men and women who could project over an amplified blues band—like Big Joe Turner, Big Mama Thornton, and Wynonie Harris.

Songwriter Roy Brown recorded "Good Rocking Tonight" in 1947. Though successful, Brown's version was eclipsed the next year when a version by Wynonie Harris (LG 17.3) reached the top of the rhythm and blues charts. Harris's blues shouting, backed by the band's heavy backbeat and a honking tenor sax, is the epitome of postwar R&B.

An increase in the number of companies that produced R&B records points to the music's growing strength in the postwar marketplace. Famous bandleaders like Hampton and Jordan recorded on major labels. But much of the music came from new, independent firms—**indie labels**—including Savoy (founded in 1942 in Newark, New Jersey), King (1944, Cincinnati), Modern (1945, Los Angeles), Atlantic (1947, New York), Chess (1947, Chicago), Peacock (1949, Houston), and Sun (1952, Memphis). Capturing the sound of regional R&B scenes, each of these

Alabama-born Dinah Washington (1924–1963) was one of the most successful R&B singers of the 1950s.

| CD 3.14 | Listening Guide 17.3 | "Good Rocking Tonight" WYNONIE HARRIS |

SONGWRITER: Roy Brown

DATE: 1948

PERFORMERS: Wynonie Harris, vocal, with alto sax, tenor sax, trumpet, piano, bass, drums, hand claps

GENRE: rhythm and blues

METER: duple

FORM: strophic 12-bar blues

WHAT TO LISTEN FOR

- "shouting" vocal style
- "honking" tenor sax style
- dance rhythm with heavy emphasis on backbeat
- fadeout ending

TIMING	SECTION	TEXT	COMMENTS
0:00	introduction		Drum "bomb" begins 8-bar introduction. Rising riff in alto and tenor saxes is answered call-and-response style by growling trumpet. In bars 1, 3, and 5, bass notes on beats 1 and 3 and light cymbal strokes on beat 2 and 4 (the backbeat) set a relaxed groove, alternating with a habanera beat in bars 2, 4, and 6. Bars 7–8 are a solo tenor sax break.
0:14	chorus 1	I heard the news . . .	Harris's raspy voice is backed by walking bass, doubled boogie-style in the piano's left hand, with hand claps on the backbeat.
0:33	chorus 2	Have you heard the news . . .	The lyrics vary only slightly from chorus 1. Harris begins with a bit of back phrasing.
0:52	chorus 3	So meet me in the alley . . .	Lyrics suggest that the pleasures of "good rocking" might be illicit. The band drops out in bars 7–8 for a vocal break that adds to the innuendo.
1:12	chorus 4		Tenor sax solo begins over the end of the preceding chorus. Repeated-note "honking" is characteristic of R&B sax improvisations.
1:32	chorus 5	I got the news . . .	Slight variation of the opening chorus, with vocal break at bars 7–8 as in chorus 3.
1:50	chorus 6	Well, Elder Brown . . .	References to Elder Brown and Deacon Jones suggest that "good rocking" can lead the pious to stray from the straight and narrow.
2:10	chorus 7	Sweet Lorraine . . .	The women mentioned are characters from other songs, ranging from 1928 ("Sweet Lorraine") to 1945 ("Caldonia," an R&B hit for Louis Jordan).
2:29	chorus 8	Hoy, hoy, hoy, hoy . . .	"Hoy hoy" is hipster slang dating back to a 1937 Cab Calloway record. Chorus ends prematurely with a postwar studio effect, the **fadeout**.

| CD 3.14 | Listening Guide 17.3 | "Good Rocking Tonight" WYNONIE HARRIS |

Listen & Reflect

1. Although each chorus follows the traditional 12-bar blues chord progression, the lyrics do not conform to the archetypal AAB format (as in "St. Louis Blues"; see LG 11.1). Instead, certain points in each chorus allow for new lyrics, and others are always the same and thus constitute a refrain. Examine the lyrics and consider their pattern; how might each chorus be described as a verse-and-chorus structure?

indie labels had its own distinctive style, whether the gospel-tinged sound of Atlantic, the electric blues sound of Chess, or the countrified sound of Sun and King. Celebrating bodily joys, rooted in black traditions, yet stylized for distribution in the modern marketplace, postwar rhythm and blues was targeted for black listeners, though most company owners and producers were white.

Rhythm and blues owed much to broadcasting. During the 1930s there had been no such thing as a radio station aimed at black listeners. As black radio began to take shape, however, the new record labels began to serve them. And after the war, across the southern United States black radio matured, with the founding of stations centered on rhythm and blues and also, depending on their location, offering gospel, traditional blues, or jazz. The R&B artists active in recording and broadcasting were also experienced live performers who learned their trade in the theaters, dance halls, clubs, tent shows, and other black venues that made up the "chitlin circuit." Broadcasting increased the diversity of their audience: whites could listen to black radio, and they could buy records by black artists. As one industry figure put it, "you could segregate schoolrooms and buses, but not the airwaves."

black radio

ROCK AND ROLL

No social fact about music in the years after World War II is more noteworthy than the growing influence of teenagers in the marketplace. While the rise of the youthful popular music fan has often been linked to the advent of rock and roll in the 1950s, the careers of Benny Goodman in the 1930s and Frank Sinatra in the 1940s indicate that teenagers had been a growing economic force for two decades before rock and roll. What was new in the postwar era was a growing "generation gap" that did much to transform the popular sphere, especially as a business enterprise. Unlike their parents, who had experienced both the hardships of the Great Depression and the heightened idealism of the World War II years, postwar teenagers came of age in a consumerist society that offered little in the way of unambiguous moral guideposts. Perhaps more openly than ever before, young Americans in those years were searching for social identity.

J. D. Salinger's novel *The Catcher in the Rye* (1951), written from an adolescent's perspective, seemed to speak for the whole postwar generation. Its hero, sixteen-year-old Holden Caulfield, experiences growing up as a process of disillusionment. The adult society described in the book is so corrupt—"phony" is a key word—that only through a teenager's eyes can innocence be glimpsed. Movies also took up the theme, with a young Marlon Brando and an even younger James Dean playing characters who sullenly resisted adult notions of virtue and respectability. Many youngsters, like these characters, felt alienated, and they found reasons to blame older generations for creating a society that evoked such feelings.

Postwar teenagers—at least those in the rapidly swelling middle class—also grew up with money to spend and exposure to an array of media that now included television as well as books, records, movies, newspapers and magazines, and radio. By the 1950s the **mass media**—radio, television, newspapers, magazines, and other modes of communication directed to a broad audience—were introducing Americans to experiences far beyond their own. Within popular music, many middle-class youngsters chose the cultural alternative of downward mobility to claim turf that was supposedly more authentic than that of their elders. "If rock 'n' roll had had no other value," declared a writer who was a teenager in those years, "it would have been enough merely to dent the smug middle-class consciousness of that time."

TEENAGERS AND RADIO

In 1951 white Cleveland disc jockey Alan Freed learned from a local record store owner that white youngsters were buying records previously thought to be exclusively "Negro music." Freed, then working as a classical record host, responded by starting *The Moondog Show*, a youth-oriented program centered on rhythm and blues records and broadcast across the Midwest. As Moondog, Freed won immediate success, speaking the language of his mostly teenage audience. Before long, he was organizing live rhythm and blues shows in Cleveland that attracted racially mixed crowds.

naming the genre

Freed would soon win national fame for introducing white teenagers to rhythm and blues. Perhaps his most lasting contribution was the label he gave the music: **rock and roll**. Freed borrowed the term from African American slang, where it was sometimes used to mean sexual intercourse (as in "good rocking tonight"). Presumably, only insiders knew what the term meant, but decoding the double entendres of R&B records was part of their appeal for white teenagers, who delighted in records like the Dominoes' "Sixty Minute Man" (1951; "I rock 'em, roll 'em all night long") and Bull Moose Jackson's "Big Ten Inch" (1952).

↜ Alan Freed, working in Cleveland in the early 1950s, became one of the first white disc jockeys to play rhythm and blues records for white youth.

That their parents were usually oblivious to such music and its innuendos contributed to the sense of a generation gap.

The general public accepted "rock and roll" as a name that was free of racial overtones and fit the style. In fact, the label has been claimed as a key to the racial crossover. The new name encouraged white acceptance of the music by suppressing its black roots.

A white author later explained that in 1955, when he was twelve years old, he and his friends found rock and roll appealing because it "provided us with a release and a justification that we had never dreamt of." The music made it easy to offend grownups, to mock "the sanctimoniousness of public figures," and to draw a "clear line of demarcation between *us* and *them*."

Although he recorded for Chess, St. Louis native Chuck Berry did not sound like a Chicago bluesman. Instead, his vocal style was racially ambiguous, and some of his songs, such as his first hit, "Maybellene" (1955), were more country than blues. When "Maybellene" caught on with white teenagers, Berry began tailoring his material for younger tastes, writing such songs as "Sweet Little Sixteen" even though he was past his thirtieth birthday. Berry's "School Day" (LG 17.4) is a litany of high school woes contrasted with the liberating power of music. For the song's teenage persona, rock and roll offers a taste of the freedoms of adulthood otherwise just beyond a high school student's reach. Filled with Berry's signature guitar riffs, it is a good example of the primitive, reverb-drenched sound of 1950s indie labels like Chess.

Together with excitement, the new music offered a chance to redefine "us" and "them." By casting their lot with performers like Chuck Berry, Little Richard, Buddy Holly, and Jerry Lee Lewis, white middle-class teenagers could feel as if they were taking a stand for freedom, high spirits, emotional truth, and fun, and against the confining proprieties of middle-class life. The music testified that youth now constituted a social group with its own modes of expression. Moreover, the freedom to draw lines was granted not by parents, teachers, or

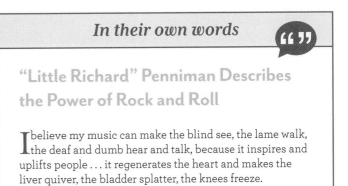

In their own words

"Little Richard" Penniman Describes the Power of Rock and Roll

I believe my music can make the blind see, the lame walk, the deaf and dumb hear and talk, because it inspires and uplifts people . . . it regenerates the heart and makes the liver quiver, the bladder splatter, the knees freeze.

LG 17.4

❧ The flamboyance and unorthodox stage behavior of rock and roll performers such as Little Richard (Richard Penniman, b. 1932) thrilled young fans and outraged their parents.

| CD 3.15 | Listening Guide 17.4 | "School Day" CHUCK BERRY |

SONGWRITER: Chuck Berry

DATE: 1956

PERFORMERS: Chuck Berry, vocal and electric guitar; Johnnie Johnson, piano; Willie Dixon, bass; Fred Below, drums

GENRE: rock and roll

METER: duple

FORM: strophic 12-bar blues

WHAT TO LISTEN FOR

- 12-bar blues structure
- emphatic rhythm to encourage dancing
- teen-oriented lyrics
- prominent blues-based electric guitar playing

TIMING	SECTION	TEXT	COMMENTS
0:00	introduction		One bar of repeated triplet chords sets the tone, followed by 1-bar break that is filled with the pickup notes that begin chorus 1.
0:02	chorus 1	Up in the morning and out to school …	Each short vocal phrase is answered by a response in the guitar, over a chugging beat in the rhythm section.
0:24	chorus 2	Ring, ring goes the bell …	Each vocal chorus begins with pickup notes sung during a break in bar 12 of the previous chorus.
0:46	chorus 3	Soon as three o'clock rolls around …	
1:08	chorus 4	Drop the coin right into the slot …	
1:30	chorus 5		Guitar solo: a series of blues licks emphasizing repeated notes.
1:52	chorus 6	Drop the coin right into the slot …	Repeat of chorus 4.
2:14	chorus 7	Hail, hail rock and roll …	

Listen & Reflect

1. How do Berry's vocal and guitar styles compare with those of Robert Johnson (see LG 14.1)? Likewise, how does his singing with a band compare with Wynonie Harris's (see LG 17.3)?

2. What arguments could be made for and against the following statement? "When the thirty-year-old Chuck Berry wrote a song about high school, he was selling out by merely pandering to the teen market instead of expressing his own artistic ideas."

clergy but by the consumer marketplace. Youngsters in comfortable circumstances could now get a taste of rebellion without actually having to rebel. And in the mid-1950s, no entertainer was better known for redrawing the boundary lines than Elvis Presley.

ELVIS PRESLEY IN MEMPHIS

Elvis Presley, born in 1935 in Mississippi, moved to Memphis with his parents in the late 1940s. Presley's mother and father had little money to spare for their son's musical education. But as a youth with an avid appetite for music, he sampled a wide variety. Elvis was a fan of local black radio, especially WDIA, where B. B. King, a singer and guitar player from the Mississippi Delta, was just starting out as a disc jockey. Memphis was also a place where white gospel quartet singing flourished (see chapter 14). By the mid-twentieth century some quartets were making records and singing on the radio. Though their repertory was all sacred, they were polished performers who bantered with their crowds and sang spiritual songs that listeners could tap their feet to. Gospel quartet music was the center of Presley's musical universe for a time.

Indeed, there seems to have been no kind of music that the young Elvis Presley did not love. He listened to Eddy Arnold, Hank Williams, and other country stars, and to such mainstream pop singers as Teresa Brewer, Bing Crosby, Eddie Fisher, and Perry Como. He attended classical orchestra concerts at an outdoor Memphis park. Dramatic tenor Mario Lanza and the Metropolitan Opera radio broadcasts were also on his menu of listening favorites. Accounts of Presley's early years leave the impression of a painfully shy loner with a rich fantasy life revolving around music. "I just loved music. Music period," he later told an interviewer. Though without formal training or experience as a performer, he nursed an obsessive wish to become a singer. And that desire led him, shortly after he graduated from high school, to the office of Sun Records, founded and run by Sam Phillips.

Sun Records

Phillips, a white native of Florence, Alabama (also the birthplace of W. C. Handy), had moved to Memphis and in 1950 opened a recording studio to provide a place where black entertainers would feel free to play and record their music. Two years later the studio became Sun Records, and by 1953 the Sun label had scored rhythm and blues hits by black artists such as Rufus Thomas and Junior Parker. In that year the eighteen-year-old Elvis Presley showed up at the studio and paid $3.98 plus tax for the chance to be recorded, singing to his own guitar accompaniment. Presley chose a pair of sentimental ballads for the occasion, and Phillips's assistant made a note next to the boy's name: "Good ballad singer. Hold." And that was where Presley's singing career rested for about a year.

In the summer of 1954 Scotty Moore, a guitarist who led a country music band, was looking for a singer to record with, and Sam Phillips suggested Presley. An audition

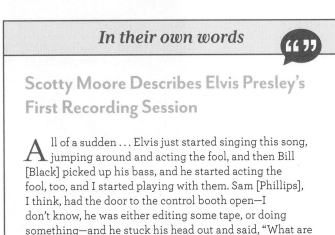

In their own words

Scotty Moore Describes Elvis Presley's First Recording Session

All of a sudden . . . Elvis just started singing this song, jumping around and acting the fool, and then Bill [Black] picked up his bass, and he started acting the fool, too, and I started playing with them. Sam [Phillips], I think, had the door to the control booth open—I don't know, he was either editing some tape, or doing something—and he stuck his head out and said, "What are you doing?" And we said, "We don't know." "Well, back up," he said, "try to find a place to start, and do it again."

was set up at the Sun studio. Toward the end of the session, "this song popped into my mind that I had heard years ago," Elvis later recalled, "and I started kidding around with it." The song was "That's All Right," a rhythm and blues number by Arthur "Big Boy" Crudup, a Mississippi-born bluesman. Surprised that Presley even knew a song by Big Boy Crudup, Sam Phillips was struck even more with the originality, freshness, and exuberance of the performance.

Artistic breakthroughs of such consequence are rare, and eyewitness accounts of them even rarer. This story pinpoints the moment when an artist who would soon number his fans in the millions first glimpsed his realm of personal expression. But it was through musical collaboration that started out with innocent clowning that Presley was able to enter that realm—a process captured on tape by Sam Phillips.

The musical process behind "That's All Right" involved the work of people in many roles: Big Boy Crudup's song, Elvis Presley's singing, Scotty Moore and Bill Black's accompaniment, and, not least, Sam Phillips's recording of the result. In fact, rock and roll itself was grounded in recording. It became popular not so much through live performances as through records played on the radio. That the makers of rock and roll embraced technology from the start is dramatized by Presley's Memphis audition; Sam Phillips was interested not only in how Presley sang but also in how he sounded on tape.

Elvis Presley (1935–1977), singing in Memphis in 1956 to a crowd of ecstatic young listeners.

Phillips knew immediately that something important had happened in Elvis's first recording session. In 1959 he told a Memphis reporter that in the early 1950s "you could sell a half million copies of a rhythm and blues record" but no more, because the appeal to white youngsters was limited. "They liked the music, but they weren't sure whether they ought to like it or not. So I got to thinking how many records you could sell if you could find white performers who could play and sing in this same exciting, alive way." In Elvis Presley, Phillips found what he had been looking for: a white singer who discovered in a black performing style a catalyst for an exciting, charismatic style all his own. Presley's "That's All Right" was the first in a string of 1950s **covers**: rerecordings by white artists of songs originally recorded by black artists. Whether aping the original or altering it more creatively, cover records generally had greater appeal to white audiences, and therefore sold more copies, than the originals.

cover records

Considering the obscurity in which his career began, Presley rose to fame with amazing speed. The arena open to a singer of his background was that of country music, so after his first Sun recording was released, he began touring the South with a troupe headlined by country star Hank Snow. Radio appearances on the *Grand Ole Opry* and the *Louisiana Hayride* were also sandwiched in. The role of professional performer encouraged the shy young man to shed some of his natural inhibitions, unleashing a magnetic, sexually charged onstage presence that worked young audiences into a state of frenzy. But if Presley's showmanship seemed to spring from raw talent and an innate grasp of audience psychology, he also showed an interest in self-improvement. His first manager recalled a day in 1955 when he dropped by the Presley house and found the singer "with a stack of records—Ray Charles and Big Joe Turner and Big Mama Thornton and Arthur 'Big Boy' Crudup—that he studied with all the avidity that other kids focused on their college exams." Presley soon left Sam Phillips's Sun Records for a major label, RCA Victor, and found a new manager. *Billboard*'s comment on the move recognizes Elvis's challenge to the industry's marketing structure: "[Although] Sun has sold Presley primarily as a c.&w. [country and western] artist, Victor plans to push his platters [records] in all three fields—pop, r.&b., and c.&w."

Elvis on stage

Another factor in Presley's rise to fame was his presence on national television. In January 1956 he made the first of several appearances on *Stage Show*, a CBS variety program featuring the swing musicians Tommy and Jimmy Dorsey and their big band. Elvis raced onto the stage and swung into a performance of Joe Turner's "Shake, Rattle, and Roll," complete with acrobatic gyrations and bursting with the sheer joy of performing. By the time he made his last appearance on *Stage Show* in March, he was riding a wave that carried him to Hollywood for a screen test. Records, radio, television, and press coverage had made a national star of a young man who, less than two years earlier, had discovered his musical persona in a recording studio in Memphis. At twenty-one, Presley was the hottest act in show business, though what kind of an act was still open to debate.

Elvis on television

RACE, GENRE, AND ROCK AND ROLL

Elvis Presley rose to stardom on the tide of a cultural phenomenon so strong that the music would probably have happened without him. His main achievement was the huge audience of teenagers that he captured for rock and roll almost overnight.

Rock and roll owed much of its popularity to its differences from the music of Tin Pan Alley. Musical traits included a driving rhythm with a strong backbeat; a fondness for twelve-bar blues form; the use of amplified instruments, especially electric guitar; blues-influenced singing; and vocal sections alternating with instrumental solos for tenor sax, electric guitar, or keyboard. Many early rock and roll hits were white performers' versions of rhythm and blues songs, with lyrics about love and sex. The rather grating singing style of many performers, wholly unsuited to either Western art music or Tin Pan Alley, derived from rural music, white and black.

reactions to rock and roll

Thus rock and roll performers drew a hard line between themselves and Tin Pan Alley or Broadway-style pop, with its kinship to the classical sphere. They also distanced themselves from folk and blues singers by embracing new technology and avidly pursuing commercial success, from jazz musicians by emphasizing fixed versions of pieces that were easily accessible to audiences, and from gospel performers through their secular subject matter. And unlike rhythm and blues and country music, rock and roll was intended for teenage listeners. Ray Charles, whose records ranked high on rhythm and blues popularity charts, insisted that "I never considered myself part of rock 'n' roll." Charles found "a towering difference" between the rockers' music and his own. "My stuff was more adult," he explained. "It was more difficult for teenagers to relate to . . . more serious, filled with more despair than anything you'd associate with rock 'n' roll."

Likewise, rock and roll found little sympathy among established figures in mainstream popular music. Mitch Miller called rock and roll "musical baby food"—harsh words from the man who gave America "How Much Is That Doggie in the Window?" Nonetheless, he had a point: compared to the more sophisticated music and lyrics sung by Ray Charles, Frank Sinatra, or Hank Williams, rock and roll was kid stuff. But music-industry executives found it highly profitable kid stuff.

crossover records

Rock and roll's impact on the music business was revealed by its domination of *Billboard*'s sales charts. But that was only the start. Before the mid-1950s, each *Billboard* chart reflected a discrete market with its own performers, radio stations, and retail outlets. The phenomenon of a **crossover**—a disc's moving from one chart to another—was considered a fluke. Record industry professionals were caught off guard in the summer of 1955 when "Rock around the Clock," by Bill Haley and the Comets, the top single on the pop (i.e., white) chart, also appeared on the rhythm and blues chart. Then Chuck Berry's "Maybellene," which topped the rhythm and blues chart, appeared in the fall on the pop chart and stayed there for fourteen weeks. And then "Heartbreak Hotel," Elvis Presley's first single for RCA Victor, topped both the pop and country charts while also rising to number 5 on the rhythm and blues chart. Rock and roll was proving to be a truly interracial expression. Barriers that had long separated country music, rhythm and blues, and pop seemed in danger of collapsing.

The spectacle of eroding barriers in the music business mirrored a historic change that was under way in American society. As young white listeners reveled in a new, black-inspired popular music, black Americans were entering a new phase in their fight to secure the rights of citizenship. *Brown v. Board of Education* (1954), the Supreme Court decision that declared school segregation illegal, provoked white Southern opposition in an environment that condoned violence, and politicians found ways to encourage the defiance of court orders without actually advocating it.

In the civil rights movement, black Southerners used the weapons of civil disobedience and nonviolent confrontation to fight for civil liberties. They also educated whites about the evils of segregation. In 1955 a boycott led by the twenty-six-year-old Reverend Martin Luther King Jr. succeeded in desegregating public transportation in Montgomery, Alabama. And in the early 1960s "sit-ins" and "freedom marches" came to be standard nonviolent tactics. Black citizens joined forces to secure the equality guaranteed in principle by federal court decisions, and eventually by the landmark Civil Rights Act that Congress passed in 1964, followed by the Voting Rights Act of 1965.

desegregation

It seems no coincidence that in 1954–55, when the laws supporting segregation in the South were being challenged, young white audiences in the South and around the country were embracing black-derived musical styles as their own. Teenagers who bought rock and roll records surely did so more as fans of the music than as champions of racial equality. Yet by accepting rock and roll with enthusiasm, white teenagers endorsed a sensibility shaped by black Americans.

THE URBAN FOLK REVIVAL

Though rock and roll was not explicitly tied to political causes, the same could not be said for folk music in the postwar era. Taking their cue from Woody Guthrie, Alan Lomax, and other politically engaged figures of the prewar years, folk revivalists saw their musical activities as extensions of their political beliefs, whether or not that meant singing songs with overt social messages. The **urban folk revival**—the postwar embrace of traditional music by people outside the communities in which it originated—met the goals of all three spheres of musical activity. While upholding the continuity of the traditional, the revivalists also made an argument for the music's universality; like classical music, but without classical music's agents of notation, formal training, or aesthetic criticism, folk music transcended its circumstances of origin to hold meaning for people of widely varying backgrounds and conditions. And beginning in the postwar years, the revivalists proved that folk music could meet the popular sphere's demands for accessibility.

Nowhere was that accessibility more evident than in the music of the Weavers, a vocal quartet formed in the late 1940s as a successor to the Almanac Singers (see chapter 14). Led by the strong voices and magnetic stage personalities of Pete Seeger and Ronnie Gilbert, the Weavers were singing American and international folk songs at union rallies and on college campuses when they were "discovered" by Gordon Jenkins, a mainstream popular record producer and arranger. Working with Jenkins, the Weavers had a number 1 pop hit in 1950 with "Goodnight Irene," a song by Leadbelly. In the next three years the Weavers had ten other Top 40 hits, but their label, Decca, dropped them summarily when Seeger and quartet member Lee Hays were accused of being communists, a career-busting charge at a time when Cold War tensions were at their height and Senator Joseph McCarthy was fanning the flames of anticommunist sentiment.

the Weavers

Despite the taint of association with communism, folk music continued to be commercially successful in the hands of performers and producers who packaged it with pop trimmings. In 1958 "Tom Dooley," a traditional Appalachian murder ballad, reached number 1 on the pop charts in a version by the Kingston Trio, a group of three clean-cut young men who avoided all but the mildest political commentary. Similarly, Harry Belafonte scored several calypso hits in the 1950s but kept his music separate from his outspoken advocacy of the civil rights movement.

Despite the blacklisting that broke up the Weavers, however, Pete Seeger continued to be a leader among political activists who used music to further progressive causes. Seeger and others wrote **topical songs**—songs, often using preexisting melodies, with new words pertaining to the current scene, whether commenting on specific events or making generalized pleas for peace and justice—for publication in leftist magazines such as *Sing Out!* and *Broadside*. In 1950 *Sing Out!* published "If I Had Hammer," a song written the previous year by Seeger and Lee Hays. The Weavers had recorded the song for Decca, but the record company had backed away from the song's overt politicking and chose not to release it. Not until 1956 did Seeger record a solo version (LG 17.5) for Folkways, a small independent label run by Moses Asch, a devotee of both traditional music and leftist political causes. By that time the song had been adopted by peace activists and was on its way to becoming an anthem of the civil rights movement.

topical songs

LG 17.5

The first three stanzas of "Hammer" differ from one another only in the appearance of two or three new words in each stanza. The fourth stanza merges the imagery of the first three stanzas and gives the key to what otherwise would be enigmatic lyrics. Each stanza is eighteen bars long: the expected sixteen-bar length is extended with a long melisma in the last line that begins with an exuberant upward leap of an octave. The melody is entirely pentatonic with the exception of a single bluesy lowered seventh in bar 6 ("All o-ver this land"), making the tune easy to pick up and sing along with.

FOLK REVIVAL AND FOLK AUTHENTICITY

"If I Had a Hammer" reached a mass audience only in 1962, via a hit record by the popular folk trio of Peter, Paul, and Mary. By that time, following the election of John F. Kennedy to the presidency, the political climate seemed to be moving toward the optimism of JFK's "New Frontier." Amid the social changes of the early 1960s, the flourishing of urban folk music led to the rise of three different approaches: that of *popularizers* (commercialized acts like the Kingston Trio), *politicizers* (social activists like Pete Seeger), and *preservationists* (musicians dedicated to upholding traditional repertories and performance styles). The first group freely altered traditional material to make it more commercially palatable, and the second composed entirely new songs or fit new topical lyrics to old songs. The preservationists, however, sought to perpetuate all they could of the folk traditions they embraced: original lyrics, singing styles, instruments, and earlier ways of playing them. This branch of the urban folk revival drew on the scholarly work of folk song collectors, and one of its most effective proponents was Mike Seeger, the half brother of Pete and son of Charles and Ruth Crawford Seeger.

Mike Seeger

Fascinated with Earl Scruggs's bluegrass banjo style, in the 1950s Mike Seeger and Ralph Rinzler compiled LP anthologies of banjo music with scholarly commentary for Folkways. Then in 1958 Seeger formed a trio, the New Lost City Ramblers, dedicated to performing old tunes in the traditional styles he had been collecting. Each member of the NLCR played multiple string instruments, enabling the group to recreate the sounds of various old-time string bands. They had studied those traditional bands first by listening to old hillbilly and race records, then by traveling south to work directly with old-time musicians who

| CD 3.16 | Listening Guide 17.5 | "If I Had a Hammer" PETE SEEGER |

SONGWRITER: Lee Hays, Pete Seeger

DATE: 1949; recorded in 1956

PERFORMER: Pete Seeger, vocal and banjo

GENRE: urban folk song

METER: duple

FORM: strophic

WHAT TO LISTEN FOR

- pentatonic melody with an added blue note
- melismatic phrase extension at end of each stanza
- cumulative imagery in lyrics, with explanatory final stanza

TIMING	SECTION	TEXT	COMMENTS
0:00	stanza 1	If I had a hammer...	Seeger accompanies his clear, forthright voice with a relaxed but energetic shuffle rhythm on the banjo.
0:26	stanza 2	If I had a bell...	Seeger intensifies the melody with a short melisma on "morning" and a higher apex on "I'd ring out danger."
0:52	stanza 3	If I had a song...	Seeger precedes this stanza by shouting out the first words, as if for a sing-a-long.
1:19	stanza 4	Well, I got a hammer...	The fourth stanza explains the metaphors of the earlier stanzas as a plea for freedom, justice, and love.

NOTE Lyrics are mostly as originally published in *Sing Out!* but with slight alterations introduced by others in the process of oral transmission.

Listen & Reflect

1. How do the lyrics of "If I Had a Hammer" resemble those of camp-meeting hymns from the Second Awakening, as described in chapter 3? How do those shared features encourage participation in group singing?

2. In the space of two words near the end of each stanza—"sisters / All"—the melody quickly moves from its lowest note to its highest. What is the interval between the two? Does that wide interval, unusual in a song designed for group singing by amateur musicians, make the song hard to sing? Why or why not?

the Harry Smith
anthology

were still living, such as Clarence Ashley, whose "Cuckoo Bird" (1929) became a favorite record among postwar folk revivalists.

One influential LP anthology from this period testifies to the revivalists' willingness to accept early race and hillbilly records not as commercial products but as documents of disappearing folk traditions. In 1952 Folkways released the six-LP *Anthology of American Folk Music*, compiled by the eccentric avant-garde filmmaker Harry Smith from his personal collection of race and hillbilly 78s. Augmented by Smith's liner notes, a bizarre mixture of the scholarly, the mystical, and the humorous, the anthology came to have an almost talismanic power among young folk enthusiasts, for whom these obscure records, nearly forgotten though recorded only two or three decades earlier, seemed to speak from an American past both remote and exotic—what the rock critic Griel Marcus would later call "the old, weird America."

the folk counterculture

Ironically, the music in the Harry Smith anthology, though drawn from old commercial recordings, came to represent for many young people an alternative to what they viewed as the crass commercialism of postwar America. They fancied it a link to a more honest, direct, and authentic past. In that respect, the folk revivalists resembled another postwar countercultural movement, that of the Beat poets such as Jack Kerouac and Allen Ginsburg. Although the Beats were taken more with modern jazz than folk music, their denunciation of conformity and materialism resonated with the leftist sympathies of many folk musicians.

That nonconformist spirit linked the folk politicizers with the folk preservationists; and even the popularizers often shared similar antiestablishment values. In fact, although it can be helpful to see the postwar urban folk revival as a blend of three countervailing tendencies, in practice many musicians participated in two or more of these trends, especially after 1960. Joan Baez, for example, one of the most successful folk artists of the early 1960s, combined a traditionalist song repertory and considerable guitar skills with a strikingly beautiful soprano voice that had little to do with traditional vocal styles but had wide popular appeal. When she began to augment her repertory with topical songs such as Richard Fariña's "Birmingham Sunday," about the 1963 bombing of an Alabama church where civil rights activists had met to organize, Baez became a leading proponent of all three trends in the folk revival. In the 1960s, at least partially owing to her influence, a new generation of folk musicians rose to prominence by mixing traditional folk songs and performance styles with newly composed topical songs—soon to be called **protest songs**—presented with a carefully packaged stage deportment that reflected popular sensibilities.

protest songs

BOB DYLAN AND THE GREENWICH VILLAGE FOLK SCENE

One musician who combined old and new forms to comment on current issues was Bob Dylan. Born Robert Zimmerman in Duluth, Minnesota, in 1941, Dylan played rock and roll piano and guitar in high school and got to know folk music mainly from records while briefly attending the University of Minnesota. In 1960 he made a New York pilgrimage to the bedside of an ailing Woody Guthrie, whose records and autobiography, *Bound for Glory*, had made a profound impression on him. Donning the mantle of Guthrie, who a generation earlier had written topical songs with political messages, Dylan began performing in Greenwich Village folk clubs, modeling his singing and guitar playing on Guthrie's style and augmenting his repertory of Guthrie songs with material from the Harry Smith anthology and other LPs. Like his model, Dylan soon discovered that he also had a knack for putting words together, at first fitting them to borrowed tunes. A highlight of his first solo LP, *Bob Dylan* (1961), which consisted mostly of traditional folk songs, was an original "Song to Woody," whose words of tribute to the older musician were sung to the tune of Guthrie's labor song "1913 Massacre."

Greenwich Village, a neighborhood on New York City's Lower West Side, had long been a haven for bohemian artists, poets, and intellectuals. By the late 1950s and early 1960s it had become a focal point for both the Beats and urban folk revivalists. The two countercultural groups had little to do with each other; though both despised what they saw as the artificiality and materialism of mainstream society, in most other respects they cultivated different tastes. Where the Beats were interested in jazz and Eastern religion, experimented with drugs, and condoned a wide range of sexual proclivities, the folkies were more interested in political activism and traditional music as a way to reconnect with an older, more authentic way of life. Bound by the common thread of nonconformity, the two groups seemed to inhabit parallel universes in the Village, intersecting but not interacting. The folk singer Dave Van Ronk recalled that nightclubs would book folk acts to perform after public poetry readings because they were guaranteed to drive out the Beat audience, making room for new customers.

Beats and folkies

A bridge between the two countercultures was Bob Dylan, who shared the musical tastes of the folk revivalists and the literary tastes of the Beats. The years of travel that eventually led Dylan to Woody Guthrie's bedside and Greenwich Village had been inspired in part by Jack Kerouac's novel *On the Road*, which glorified spontaneous road trips fueled by jazz, drugs, and alcohol. Even more influential was the work of Allen Ginsburg, whose long poem *Howl* begins with a lamentation for "the best minds of my generation destroyed by madness." Part 2 of the poem denounces the destroyer of those "angelheaded hipsters": a militaristic consumer society that Ginsburg represents as the pagan god Moloch. A modern-day Jeremiah, the poet unleashes a torrent of vivid imagery:

Bob Dylan

> Moloch whose mind is pure machinery! Moloch whose blood
> is running money! Moloch whose fingers are ten armies!
> Moloch whose breast is a cannibal dynamo! Moloch whose
> ear is a smoking tomb!
> Moloch whose eyes are a thousand blind windows! Moloch whose
> skyscrapers stand in the long streets like endless Jehovahs!
> Moloch whose factories dream and croak in the fog!
> Moloch whose smoke-stacks and antennae crown the cities!

The effect is at once poundingly repetitious and abundantly varied.

Ginsburg's influence is evident in "A Hard Rain's a-Gonna Fall," a song on Dylan's second album, *The Freewheelin' Bob Dylan* (1963), which, unlike the first, consists almost entirely of original compositions. But the song's more obvious model is the old Scottish ballad "Lord Randal" (Child 12), a dialogue between a mother and her son, who returns from a visit to his sweetheart only to realize that he has been poisoned:

*"A Hard Rain's
a-Gonna Fall"*

> "O where ha you been, Lord Randal, my son?
> And where ha you been, my handsome young man?"
> "I ha been at the greenwood; mother, mak my bed soon,
> For I'm wearied wi hunting, and fain wad lie down."

In each stanza of Dylan's song, the mother's questions prompt a flood of apocalyptic visions whose meaning is sometimes obscure but whose sense of impending doom is unmistakable:

> Oh, what did you see, my blue-eyed son?
> And what did you see, my darling young one?
> I saw a newborn baby with wild wolves all around it
> I saw a highway of diamonds with nobody on it
> I saw a black branch with blood that kept drippin'
> I saw a room full of men with their hammers a-bleedin'
> I saw a white ladder all covered with water . . .
> And it's a hard rain's a-gonna fall.

Dylan sings each visionary line to the same short musical phrase. The number of lines varies from stanza to stanza, and the resulting unpredictability creates a tension that finds resolution in the closing refrain, which foretells the fall of a "hard rain." Many listeners understood that rain to be the radioactive fallout that, should the Cold War erupt into a nuclear confrontation, might mark the end of humanity. Dylan, in a radio interview, resisted that interpretation, however, suggesting that the song pointed to a range of injustices that might be washed away in a metaphorical hard rain.

"Blowin' in the Wind"

The opening song on *Freewheelin'*, "Blowin' in the Wind," asks a series of questions, some of them pointedly referring to the civil rights movement: "How many years can some people exist / Before they're allowed to be free?" Dylan underlines his meaning by borrowing from the tune of a Negro spiritual that had become a civil rights anthem, "No More Auction Block." The song, though it poses many questions, offers no solutions. If any answer is to be found, it is blowing in the wind: all around us, yet elusive and hard to grasp. Unlike Pete Seeger, for whom a topical song should be a call to action and therefore must have a clear meaning, Dylan uses the topical song to explore moral ambiguities.

⤷ Twenty-two-year-old Bob Dylan sings "Only a Pawn in Their Game" at a Mississippi voter registration rally in 1963.

✎ The final concert in the 1963 Newport Folk Festival ended with the singing of the spiritual "We Shall Overcome" by many of the participants, including (left to right) Peter, Paul, and Mary (Paul Stookey, Mary Travers, Peter Yarrow), Joan Baez, Bob Dylan, Rutha Mae Harris, Charles Neblett, Cordell Reagon, Bernice Johnson, and Pete Seeger. Standing at Seeger's left but not visible in this picture was actor and folk singer Theodore Bikel.

Dylan's years as a protest singer reached their peak with his third album, *The Times They Are a-Changing* (recorded in 1963 and released early in 1964). The title song is an anthem to the generation gap that throws down the gauntlet to older Americans, declaring that parents cannot really know daughters and sons who have already joined other young comrades in rejecting older values. Dylan's voice—nasal, a bit thin, uncultivated in sound but with clear declamation of the words—evokes Guthrie's spirit, as do his acoustic guitar playing and the song's loping triple meter. Another "us and them" song, "With God on Our Side," sneers at those who would use religion to justify militaristic violence. Like the previous album's "Masters of War," it paints a picture of military leaders as thoroughly evil.

By comparison, "Only a Pawn in Their Game" (LG 17.6) is quite subtle. Its subject is the 1963 murder of Mississippi civil rights activist Medgar Evers. Although the song's opening lines slam home the murder's brutality, it does not go on to denounce the Klansman who pulled the trigger. Rather, it portrays the murderer as himself a victim of manipulation by corrupt politicians and racist ideologues who exploit the poor and ignorant whites who do their dirty work. Dylan first sang the song publicly at a voter registration rally in Greenwood, Mississippi, where he appeared with Pete Seeger. The mostly black audience joined in heartily with Seeger's "If I Had a Hammer," but what they made of Dylan and his song, which replaces the topical song's anticipated call to action with a mood of angry fatalism, remains unknown.

Although Dylan uses the strophic form of the folk ballad in "Only a Pawn in Their Game," he treats it as a flexible container for his lyrics. That is, the music can contract or expand to encompass varying numbers of poetic lines in each stanza. As in "A Hard Rain's a-Gonna Fall," the device used here is a short musical phrase that can be repeated an indefinite number of times to accommodate the varying stanza lengths. Musically, those varying repetitions build tension that is then released in the next phrase, which ends each stanza with the same words, forming a short refrain.

Even as Bob Dylan emerged as the urban folk revival's most successful musician, his songs reveal an artistic personality at odds with that movement. His transition away from the folk revival's ethos may be seen in his appearances at the Newport Folk Festivals of 1963, 1964, and 1965. In the 1963 festival's first

LG 17.6

Dylan at Newport

| CD 3.17 | Listening Guide 17.6 | "Only a Pawn in Their Game" BOB DYLAN |

SONGWRITER: Bob Dylan

DATE: 1963

PERFORMER: Bob Dylan, vocal, guitar

GENRE: protest song

METER: triple

FORM: strophic

WHAT TO LISTEN FOR

- overtly political lyrics, without call to action
- vocal style that favors delivery of lyrics over tonal beauty
- discreet accompaniment with rubato and emphasis on lyrics
- flexible verse lengths accommodating varying numbers of poetic lines per verse

TIMING	SECTION	TEXT	COMMENTS
0:00	stanza 1	A bullet from the back of a bush . . .	A single guitar chord precedes an abrupt vocal entry.
0:19		Two eyes took the aim . . .	A 3-bar musical phrase repeats for three different lines of the lyrics.
0:29	refrain	He's only a pawn in their game.	Each stanza closes with refrain.
0:36	stanza 2	A South politician preaches . . .	
0:54		And the Negro's name . . .	The 3-bar phrase repeats seven times.
1:22	stanza 3	The deputy sheriffs, the soldiers, the governors . . .	
1:42		He's taught in his school . . .	The phrase repeats eight times.
2:09	stanza 4	From the poverty shacks, he looks from the cracks . . .	
2:29		To hang and to lynch . . .	The phrase repeats six times.
2:51	stanza 5	Today, Medgar Evers was buried . . .	
3:10		He'll see by his grave . . .	The phrase repeats four times.

Listen & Reflect

1. Compare Dylan's performance with Woody Guthrie's rendition of "So Long, It's Been Good to Know You" (LG 14.5). Consider vocal style, guitar technique, rhythm and phrasing, and any other aspects that catch your attention.

2. Compare the music, lyrics, and social function of "If I Had a Hammer," the other topical song in this chapter (see LG 17.5), with those of this song.

evening concert, he sang a set of his own topical songs to an appreciative audience. The concert ended with Dylan, Joan Baez, Pete Seeger, and others joining together in the civil rights anthem "We Shall Overcome." In August of that year the same performers gathered to sing during a march on Washington, which culminated in the Reverend Martin Luther King Jr.'s historic "I have a dream" speech on the steps of the Lincoln Memorial.

Dylan's contribution to the Newport Festival of 1964 consisted of two new songs that could have been topical only to him: "It Ain't Me, Babe," and "Mr. Tambourine Man," the latter a swirl of phantasmagoric imagery thought to be inspired by Dylan's experiences with hallucinogenic drugs. The festival that year also included musicians outside the usual folk circle, including the country singer Johnny Cash and Chicago bluesman Muddy Waters. These two musicians, plus Dylan's own determination to move beyond topical songs, pointed the way to elements that the young singer would soon integrate into a fresh personal idiom.

A year later, Dylan's performance with a loudly amplified rock band at the 1965 festival set off howls of protest among the folk community. That concert has long been recognized as a landmark event. Among other things, it signaled Dylan's passage from the folk sphere to the popular sphere. From this time forward, Dylan would be thought of as a rock artist, not a folk singer. With that new persona, he would revolutionize rock music much as he had expanded the conceptions of folk song and folk singer. In popular music after 1960, perhaps no other single figure would be as profoundly influential as Bob Dylan.

QUESTIONS FOR DISCUSSION AND REVIEW

1. What features distinguish the new popular styles of the postwar era—bluegrass, honky-tonk, rhythm and blues, and rock and roll—from mainstream popular music? What similarities tie them to that mainstream?

2. Contrast and compare country music before and after World War II. Do the same for prewar blues and postwar rhythm and blues.

3. In what ways was rock and roll a distinctly new genre in the 1950s? In what ways was it a continuation of earlier styles?

4. What were the principal trends in folk music after World War II? What social and political developments are reflected in the subject matter of the new topical folk songs?

FURTHER READING

Allen, Ray. *Gone to the Country: The New Lost City Ramblers and the Folk Music Revival.* Urbana: University of Illinois Press, 2010.

Cantwell, Robert. *When We Were Good: The Folk Revival.* Cambridge, MA: Harvard University Press, 1996.

Malone, Bill C. *Country Music USA.* 2d rev. ed. Austin: University of Texas Press, 2002.

Palmer, Robert. *Rock & Roll: An Unruly History.* New York: Harmony Books, 1995.

Rosenberg, Neil V. *Bluegrass: A History.* Urbana: University of Illinois Press, 1985.

Shelton, Robert. *No Direction Home: The Life and Music of Bob Dylan.* New York: Morrow, 1986.

Zak, Albin. *I Don't Sound Like Nobody: Remaking Music in 1950s America.* Ann Arbor: University of Michigan Press, 2010.

QUESTIONING AUTHORITY

America's Music in the 1960s

If a single factor may be said to dominate the ethos of the 1960s in the United States, that would be the challenge—from African Americans and from a younger generation, among others—to figures of authority: political figures, business leaders, the military, the clergy, teachers, parents, and the institutions they represented. The civil rights struggle of the 1950s continued into the new decade, winning a major victory with the Civil Rights Act of 1964, which ended segregation in the public schools and outlawed discrimination on the basis of race or gender. But the growing conflict in Southeast Asia and the U.S. government's decision to fight a war in Vietnam meant an increased military draft that changed the lives of a whole generation of younger people, prompting an upheaval within society. Familiar values of the Western world also came under attack, triggering the exploration of non-Western ideas and musical styles. The assassinations of John F. Kennedy, Malcolm X, Martin Luther King Jr., and Robert Kennedy also contributed to the sense that the world was being turned upside down. These developments intensified the "generation gap" that fueled not only the growing youth culture but also many of the musical currents of the 1960s and beyond.

Music in the 1960s reflected the era's social upheavals. Common to all three musical spheres—classical, popular, and traditional—was a sense that the authority of established boundaries was eroding. Since around 1960, in fact, the commonalities among the musical spheres have sometimes seemed to outweigh their differences. For that reason, we have chosen from this point in our narrative to proceed on a more or less decade-by-decade basis, tracing trends that are often shared by classical, popular, and folk music. As this chapter shows, jazz, classical, rock, country, and soul music in the 1960s, as different as they may sound, all reflect in one way or another the tumultuous society in which they flourished.

JAZZ IN THE 1960s

As artistic recognition of jazz blossomed during the 1960s, a wide range of new styles came to the fore, existing alongside older styles like New Orleans jazz and bebop. Some of these were oriented more toward the popular sphere, others toward the classical. But even the more accessible jazz styles were eclipsed in the marketplace by the overwhelming popularity of rock. With more young listeners turning to rock, jazz's economic base continued to decline, even as a new generation of musicians discovered untapped creative possibilities in jazz.

JAZZ SINGERS

Jazz singers have always enjoyed a broader commercial appeal than have instrumentalists. Even jazz's first great soloist, Louis Armstrong, by 1930 was popular at least as much for his singing as for his trumpet playing. Long after Armstrong's groundbreaking Hot Five and Hot Seven recordings in the 1920s (discussed in chapter 12), he continued to win the public's favor through the 1950s by playing concerts with his small ensemble, the All-Stars, and recording a series of vocal duets with Ella Fitzgerald, a singer whose virtuoso technique was matched by her expressive authority. Then in 1964 Armstrong scored the biggest hit of his career with a Broadway show tune, "Hello, Dolly," which rose to number 1 on the pop charts, temporarily displacing the Beatles.

Other jazz singers who enjoyed commercial success in the 1960s included Nat King Cole, Nina Simone, Mel Tormé, and Nancy Wilson. Sarah Vaughan, who had been on the scene since the 1940s, was recognized for her voice's exceptional range, sound, and variety, as well as her excellent control and sense of pitch. Vaughan's achievements may be summed up in a pair of challenges she met: adapting her vocal technique to the demands of rhythmic swing, and capturing the mood of a song and sustaining it without giving up vocal and musical freedom.

SOUL JAZZ

Among the instrumentalists who continued to attract a larger audience were soul jazz artists such as Horace Silver, Cannonball Adderley, Jimmy Smith, and Ramsey Lewis, whose record "The In Crowd" reached number 5 on the pop charts in 1965. Rooted in gospel and blues on the one hand and the hard bop sounds of such artists as Art Blakey on the other, the funky sounds of soul jazz emphasized rhythmic groove and radiated a pride in black ethnicity in tune with the racial politics of the era.

NEW JAZZ HORIZONS

Other jazz artists explored more adventurous directions—sometimes, but not always, alienating audiences not willing to make the effort to understand new musical languages. Bass player Charles Mingus continued to compose freewheeling works for large ensembles that took the collective improvisation of New Orleans jazz into uncharted territory while never losing the hard-driving,

☙ Sarah Vaughan (1924–1990), a remarkable singer by any standard, could use her capacious voice both as a jazz instrument and as a vehicle for words.

gospel-tinged rhythms of hard bop. Saxophonist Ornette Coleman and pianist Cecil Taylor pioneered **free jazz**, which abandoned traditional tunes, repeating chord progressions, and a regular pulse in favor of avant-garde experiments in total freedom that enthralled a small group of devotees but left more-traditional jazz fans scratching their heads. Avant-gardists such as Archie Shepp and Albert Ayler connected free jazz to progressive political and spiritual movements, linked musical authenticity to ethnic pride, and found audiences who shared their ideologies and came to appreciate their musical radicalism.

One innovative jazz style did, however, win favor with a larger audience. In the late 1950s Miles Davis had begun to develop a new style that rejected the complex, rapidly changing harmonies of bebop and replaced them with long, harmonically static stretches based on a single scale or mode. This **modal jazz** filled the entirety of his 1959 album *Kind of Blue*, which eventually became one of the best-selling jazz albums of all time. The opening track, *So What*, is a lengthy improvisation on an original Davis tune that, cast in thirty-two-bar *aaa'a* form, discards traditional chord progressions in favor of a single scale, the **Dorian mode**, which fills the three *a* sections, the only contrast being a modulation up a half step in the *a'* section or bridge. The result is an expansive music with solos that emphasize melodic play rather than tracing harmonic progressions.

modal jazz

One of the musicians on *Kind of Blue* was tenor saxophonist John Coltrane, who already was emerging as a significant artist in his own right. His 1960 album *Giant Steps* featured a title track that, in contrast to modal jazz, pushed the harmonic complexity of bebop to an unprecedented extreme. The quick tempo and complex chord changes of *Giant Steps* remain a standard benchmark for improvising jazz musicians today.

John Coltrane

Coltrane's most popular recording was a modal jazz interpretation of "My Favorite Things" (LG 18.1), a show tune from *The Sound of Music*. Released in 1961, this record revived interest in the soprano sax, hitherto associated chiefly with the traditional New Orleans jazzman Sidney Bechet. Coltrane's "My Favorite Things" was also the first well-known jazz waltz, with three beats, instead of the pop song's usual four, to the bar. Richard Rodgers's minor-key song is in the unusual pattern *aaa'b* (the third *a* is in the major and ends differently from the previous two), with each section comprising sixteen bars, double the usual number because of the tempo and brevity of the waltz bars. Coltrane's quartet simplifies this to *aaa'a* and flattens out the harmony, so that the entire performance is built on an E drone.

LG 18.1

The combination of modal jazz (with its long stretches of harmonic stasis), the minor key (still fairly unusual in jazz), and the nasal wailing of the soprano sax (suggestive of the Indian oboe-like *shenai*) has caused some critics to consider this record to be an early step in an East-West musical hybridization that began in the 1960s. The first of several times Coltrane recorded the tune, this version stretches out for thirteen minutes on LP. The album

---

In their own words

> 66 99

John Coltrane on His Musical Goals

My music is the spiritual expression of what I am—my faith, my knowledge, my being.... When you begin to see the possibilities of music, you desire to do something really good for people, to help humanity free itself from its hangups.... I want to speak to their souls.

| CD 3.18 | Listening Guide 18.1 | "My Favorite Things" JOHN COLTRANE |

SONGWRITERS: Richard Rodgers and Oscar Hammerstein II

DATE: 1961

GENRE: modal jazz

PERFORMERS: John Coltrane, soprano sax; McCoy Tyner, piano; Steve Davis, bass; Elvin Jones, drums

METER: triple

FORM: *aaa'a* chorus with interpolated vamps

WHAT TO LISTEN FOR

- distinctive sound of soprano saxophone
- characteristic sounds of modal jazz: drones, slow-moving harmonies
- expansion of chorus through interpolated vamps

TIMING	SECTION		COMMENT
0:00	introduction		The rhythm section, grounded by the droning bass, sets a minor-key modal groove in waltz time
0:18	head	*a*	16 bars: Although the song as written has moving harmonies in the second half of the *a* section, Davis continues to drone on the tonic note, E, sustaining the modal style.
0:35		vamp	8 bars: Instead of repeating the *a* section directly, the rhythm section vamps on the tonic E, again sustaining the modal style.
0:43		*a*	Repeat of *a*.
1:01		vamp	24 bars: Shift to the tonic major for a brighter quality, giving some of the contrast that a conventional B section would supply; Coltrane solos over the rhythm section.
1:18			References to the melody imply a return of *a*, but this is still vamp.
1:27		*a'*	The ending of this *a* section is slightly different, as in the original song.
1:44		*a*	Instead of Rodgers's *b* section, *a* repeats with no intervening vamp.
2:02		vamp	16 bars.
2:19	chorus 2 (piano solo)		Piano solo for one *a* section and the beginning of a vamp before the fade out marks the end of the single's A side.

NOTE Recorded October 21, 1960, and released the following year on LP and, in truncated form, on 45.

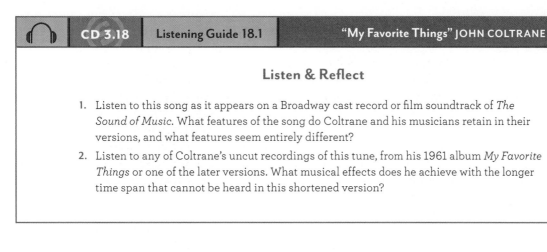

🎧 **CD 3.18**   **Listening Guide 18.1**   **"My Favorite Things"** JOHN COLTRANE

Listen & Reflect

1. Listen to this song as it appears on a Broadway cast record or film soundtrack of *The Sound of Music*. What features of the song do Coltrane and his musicians retain in their versions, and what features seem entirely different?

2. Listen to any of Coltrane's uncut recordings of this tune, from his 1961 album *My Favorite Things* or one of the later versions. What musical effects does he achieve with the longer time span that cannot be heard in this shortened version?

track was trimmed down and cut in two for release on side A (LG 18.1) and B of a 45-rpm single.

Many of Coltrane's later compositions bear titles that reflect his interest in non-Western religions, from African traditions to Islam and Zen Buddhism. Two 1965 albums, *A Love Supreme* and *Ascension*, mark the apex of his efforts to carry jazz into new expressive territory. The first is a four-movement suite that includes Coltrane's overdubbed voice chanting the title phrase as though it were a mantra. The second is a sprawling forty-minute free-jazz improvisation for eleven musicians that captures some of the intensity of his group's live performances in those years.

non-Western influences

Whether improvising the frenetic streams of fast notes that one critic dubbed "sheets of sound" or revealing his gentler, more lyrical side, Coltrane projected a seriousness of purpose that won the respect of musicians both within the jazz world and beyond. Among the many musicians inspired by Coltrane's spiritual approach was his wife, harpist Alice Coltrane, who combined Hindu spiritual practices with her musical activities. And as a later section in this chapter shows, his influence extended beyond the jazz world into the classical sphere.

🎵 John Coltrane (1926–1967) revived interest in the soprano sax around 1960.

CLASSICAL MUSIC IN THE 1960s

On April 6, 1964, a composition for voice and three clarinets was premiered whose symbolic importance far outweighs its length (barely ninety seconds). *Elegy for J.F.K.*, composed by the eighty-one-year-old Igor Stravinsky, mourns the assassination on November 22, 1963, of President John F. Kennedy. Stravinsky, who died in 1971, filled a unique place in American musical life: an embodiment of a musical age governed by axioms thought to be historically necessary. Stravinsky's embrace of serialism in the 1950s had raised it in some circles to near-axiomatic status. And now the Russian-born master, long an American citizen, was using his rarefied art to commemorate the nation's fallen leader.

Samuel Barber

But this moment of quiet homage was also marked by offstage rumblings: the start of a stylistic earthquake that would soon overwhelm the notion of historical necessity in classical composition. To be sure, atonality and serialism were well established. But so were diatonic approaches, as used by Samuel Barber, whose *Antony and Cleopatra* opened New York's new Metropolitan Opera House in 1966, and William Schuman, who continued composing after assuming the presidency of the Lincoln Center for the Performing Arts in 1962. In April 1965 Charles Ives's Symphony no. 4, composed between 1910 and 1916, was heard in full for the first time. That event, suggesting links between Ives and other "experimental" American composers, including Henry Cowell, Harry Partch, Lou Harrison, Conlon Nancarrow, and John Cage, raised new questions about this nation's dependence on the European past. And in 1964 Terry Riley composed *In C*, whose obsessive repetition of simple diatonic fragments outlined another new style that was soon labeled minimalist.

With only Igor Stravinsky left from a past when great composers were thought to define their era's musical values, other kinds of music were also challenging the classical sphere's place atop the nation's musical hierarchy. No longer certain of classical music's place in a larger musical culture, composers in the 1960s searched for new means of expression that reflected the music's new cultural contexts.

serialist orthodoxy

The New York classical scene in the mid-1960s can be seen as having been dominated by three distinct kinds of composers: the composer as intellectual, the composer as experimentalist, and the composer as creator of works for the concert hall. Intellectual composers dominated academia, and in those years being an intellectual meant being a serialist. Composer Jacob Druckman later claimed that "not being a serialist on the East Coast of the United States in the sixties was like not being a Catholic in Rome in the thirteenth century." Though their audience was small, serialists dealt with artistic issues in a way that encouraged support for teaching and composing. Cage and his fellow experimenters, though no less intellectual in their way than the serialists, were less concerned with winning the respect of the academic establishment. Their music, which challenged the very idea of an artwork, attracted patrons who also supported modern dance and avant-garde painting. Finally, a number of composers, including George Rochberg, George Crumb, Jacob Druckman, William Bolcom, Lukas Foss, and David del Tredici, took an approach—sometimes called the **New Romanticism**—that harked back to the European past. They, and more recently Christopher Rouse, Ellen Taaffe Zwilich, John Harbison, Joseph Schwantner, and Joan Tower, among others, have benefited from the resources that orchestras and opera houses can place at a composer's disposal.

THE NEW ROMANTICISM

For composer George Rochberg, the turn away from serialism toward a greater lyricism was motivated by a personal crisis, the death of his twenty-year-old son, Paul Rochberg, in 1964. Beginning with *Music for the Magic Theater* (1965), Rochberg went on to create music that quoted widely from music of the past, from J. S. Bach to Anton Webern and jazz standards, around which the composer wove original music that incorporated those styles while reflecting Rochberg's own personality. Although many serialist composers denounced his newer music for abandoning avant-garde intellectual rigor, other musicians were inspired by his fluid use of quotation. Indeed, the liberal use of quotations became a hallmark of 1960s composition, from German-American conductor and composer Lukas Foss's *Baroque Variations* (1967) to the virtuoso *Sinfonia* (1968) composed for the New York Philharmonic by Luciano Berio, an Italian composer then teaching at the Juilliard School. In its often playful reuses of the past, this quotation-based music was an early harbinger of a new aesthetic attitude that would come to be known as **postmodernism**.

> ### In their own words
>
> **George Rochberg on His Embrace of New Romanticism**
>
> With the loss of my son I was overwhelmed by the realization that death . . . could only be overcome by life itself; and to me this meant through art, by practicing my art as a living thing (in my marrow bone), free of the posturing cant and foolishness abroad these days which want to seal art off from life.

George Crumb

West Virginia–born composer George Crumb created some of the 1960s' most distinctive New Romantic music. With a melodic and harmonic language rooted in Debussy and Bartók, Crumb's music displays a dazzling range of timbral possibilities, from the delicate to the overpowering. He created this palette by using unusual playing techniques—for example, taking to new lengths Cowell's pioneering idea of playing directly on the strings of a piano—and by including instruments unusual in classical music, such as harmonica, musical saw, and tuned water glasses. Another feature of Crumb's music is its element of theater or ritual: various works ask that performers wear masks, move about the stage, and chant or whisper words, numbers, or vocables as if they were magic incantations. These and other effects are evident in several works from the late 1960s, such as *Echoes of Time and the River* (1967), *Songs, Drones, and Refrains of Death* (1968), and *Night of the Four Moons* (1969). They reach their peak in two works from 1970: *Black Angels*, for electrically amplified string quartet, and *Ancient Voices of Children*, a cycle of five songs on texts by the Spanish poet Federico García Lorca.

LG 18.2

The scoring of *Ancient Voices of Children* is unusual and colorful: mezzo-soprano and boy soprano, oboe, harp, piano, and a large assortment of percussion instruments, as well as mandolin, musical saw, harmonica, and toy piano. The text of the fourth song (LG 18.2) is a fragment of a poem by Lorca:

Todas las tardes in Granada, todas
  las tardes se muere un niño.

Each afternoon in Granada, a child
  dies each afternoon.

Crumb's setting includes a quotation of "Bist du bei mir," a song found in a notebook copied out by Anna Magdalena Bach, the wife of German composer J. S. Bach (1685–1750). That song begins with these words:

| | CD 3.19 | Listening Guide 18.2 | "Todas las tardes en Granada," from *Ancient Voices of Children* GEORGE CRUMB |

DATE: 1970

PERFORMERS: Tony Arnold, soprano; Kathryn Dupuy Cooper, harmonica; Hershey Bress, harp; Susan Grace, toy piano; John Kinzie, Mark Foster, William Hill, percussion; David Colson, conductor

GENRE: New Romanticism

METER: changing

FORM: through-composed

WHAT TO LISTEN FOR

- extremely soft dynamic
- unusual and subtle timbres: marimba, humming, harmonica
- traditional chords used in nontraditional juxtapositions
- Bach quotation in toy piano

TIMING	TEXT	TRANSLATION	COMMENTS
0:00			The song begins with an extremely soft C-sharp-major triad sustained on the marimba. After a few seconds, the three percussionists hum, then sing, the three notes of the triad, also entering extremely softly, increasing slightly in volume, then diminishing into silence. At the peak of their crescendo, a barely audible harmonica adds its timbre to the same triad, then also fades to silence.
0:28	Todas las tardes in Granada, todas las tardes se…	Each afternoon in Granada, each afternoon…	The soprano sings the text to a melody that begins simply, with an emphasis on the first three notes of the C-sharp-major scale.
1:01	…muere…	…dies…	On the word "muere" (dies), the melody leaps to a pitch outside the scale—the lowered seventh, B natural—then descends in a series of whole tones that form a dissonant relationship to the sustained marimba chord.
1:14	…un niño.	…a child.	The soprano whispers the last two words. Then the voices and harmonica repeat the opening moments.
1:41			The harp, joined by a stroke on a suspended cymbal, strikes a distantly related triad, G minor (a tritone away from C sharp), and the marimba chord changes to G minor as well.
1:52			The toy piano, in the key of D-flat major (enharmonically identical to C sharp), plays a fragment of "Bist du bei mir," while the marimba continues to sustain the G-minor chord.
2:26			The toy piano breaks off one note from the end; the three voices take up the G-minor chord, then fade into silence.

NOTE Recorded in 2005.

Listen & Reflect

1. The quotation of "Bist du bei mir" could easily be played on a conventional piano. What effect does Crumb obtain by specifying the use of a toy piano?

2. Many commentators have noted the ritualistic character of Crumb's music. Is that evident here? If so, how?

Bist du bei mir, geh ich mit Freuden	If thou art near, I go with joy
zum Sterben und zu meiner Ruh.	To death and to my rest.

Exploring the softest part of the dynamic range, Crumb's music creates a ghostly ambiance in which Lorca's words and an old devotional song hover mysteriously.

MINIMALISM

By 1965, La Monte Young and Terry Riley, both from the western United States, were writing lengthy works based on small amounts of musical material that would point the way for Philip Glass, Steve Reich, and other young composers who fit none of the three niches of New York composers—although the influence of Cage's experimentalist ethos bears strongly on the music of Young, at least. When asked whether any one piece of new music had inspired them to become composers, many musicians born after 1940 point to Terry Riley's *In C* and Steve Reich's *Come Out*. Written in 1964, *In C* became in some ways the anthem of a movement that in the 1970s would borrow its name, **minimalism**, from the visual arts. As applied to music, minimalism denotes music based on a radically reduced amount of musical material and relying on static harmony, patterned rhythms, and repetition.

Terry Riley, In C

Questioned about his work's origins, Riley has described improvisation as one of its main influences. The fifty-three short motives that make up *In C*— each repeated many times over a fast pulse high in the piano—must be played in order by any number of musicians, but each performer decides independently when to move from one motive to the next and therefore how they overlap and fit together. Having grown up playing jazz, Riley was comfortable with the idea of on-the-spot creation. Technology was another influence. *In C* is written for live performers playing an unfixed number of unspecified instruments, but its repetitions sound much like tape loops: lengths of magnetic tape spliced end to end in a circle, so that the recorded sounds repeat indefinitely, an effect Riley and other electronic music composers had been using since the 1950s. A third influence was Riley's outlook on life. "I was a beatnik, and then I turned into a hippie," he told an interviewer. "For my generation," the mid-1960s provided "a first look towards the East, that is, peyote, mescaline, and the psychedelic drugs which were opening up people's attention towards higher consciousness. So I think what I was experiencing in music at that time was another world. Besides just the ordinary music that was going on, music was also able to transport us suddenly out of one reality into another." *In C* was premiered in November 1964 at the San Francisco Tape Music Center by an ensemble of thirteen, including Riley and Steve Reich playing keyboards and the experimentalist composer Pauline Oliveros on accordion.

Steve Reich

Reich's role in the premiere also belongs to the story of minimalism's beginnings. Though not a jazz musician himself, Reich has paid tribute to the impact on his music of trumpeter Miles Davis, drummer Kenny Clarke, and saxophonist John Coltrane. "The jazz influence that's all over my work is not so specific," he said in 1987, "but without the rhythmic and melodic gestures of jazz, its flexibility and nuance, my work is *unthinkable*." His study of West African drumming and Balinese gamelan proved influential as well. He also remembered learning "a tremendous amount from putting [*In C*] together, and I think it had a very strong influence on me."

Reich has described how he stumbled onto the process behind his own musical breakthrough. In 1965 he made tape loops from a short passage of a street preacher's sermon he had recorded in San Francisco. The loops were intended as a way of superimposing one phrase upon another for musical effect, with the help of two tape machines. The unintended result of his experiment was a new type of music he called **phase music**, in which two or more identical parts are played in slightly different tempos.

phase music

Come Out (1966) is based on Reich's new concept of phase music. From an interview with a victim of a police beating in Harlem, who had been told he could receive hospital care only if he were bleeding, Reich chose a single sentence: "I had to, like, let some of the bruise blood come out to show them." Then he tape-looped the last five words. Repeated for more than twelve minutes, and *very* slowly pulled out of phase on several channels, the words are gradually transformed into a new kind of sound material: short, blurred melodic gestures impossible to recognize as human speech. Reich has likened "performing and listening to a gradual musical process" such as this one to "pulling back a swing, releasing it, and observing it gradually come to rest." And he adds: "While performing and listening to gradual musical processes, one can participate in a particularly liberating and impersonal kind of ritual. Focusing in on the musical process makes possible that shift of attention away from *he* and *she* and *you* and *me* outwards towards *it*."

☙ Composer Steve Reich (b. 1936) at the piano around 1970.

Reich has also explained that while fond of the possibilities of taped speech, he prefers live instrumental performance. Early in 1967 he organized a pair of concerts at the Park Place Gallery in New York, a cooperative associated with the geometric, nondecorative "minimal" art of such painters and sculptors as Ellsworth Kelly, Sol LeWitt, and Richard Serra. The concerts were part of an effort by the gallery to promote interchange among experimental artists in different media. The featured new work was a version of *Piano Phase* for four electric pianos, played by Reich and three colleagues, an outcome of the composer's experiment with playing live against a tape loop. From that time forward, several of Reich's pieces have involved either multiple performers on the same instrument or a soloist performing with a multitracked recording of his or her own playing, as in *Violin Phase*, written to be played by four violinists or one violinist with tape.

After one of these concerts, Reich crossed paths with Philip Glass, who in the 1970s would emerge as the most widely recognized minimalist composer, famous for his 1976 opera *Einstein on the Beach* and a series of film scores such as *Koyaanisqatsi* (1982). Along with Riley and Reich, Glass would demonstrate

> ### In their own words
>
> #### Steve Reich on the Discovery of Phase Music
>
> I put headphones on and noticed that the two tape recorders were almost exactly in sync. The effect of this aurally was that I heard the sound jockeying back and forth in my head between my left and right ear, as one machine or the other drifted ahead. Instead of immediately correcting that, I let it go.... what happened was that one of the machines was going slightly faster ... because the left channel was moving ahead of the right channel. I let it go further, and it finally got precisely the relationship I wanted to get to.... It was an accidental discovery.

Philip Glass

minimalism's appeal to a nonspecialist audience, reversing a trend in much twentieth-century classical composition. By reducing the amount of musical material a listener had to digest, minimalist composers moved the focus of listening toward the experience of sound in the moment and change on an expanded time scale. That scale invited a contemplative response that could connect with spirituality, ritual, and an expanding consciousness. These features of the music, along with the use of electrically amplified instruments and voices, made common ground with the youthful counterculture of the 1960s and helped mold the tastes of younger listeners. By incorporating into their work what they had learned from non-Western and vernacular music, especially jazz, the minimalists helped thaw barriers that seemed frozen into place, instilling a new spirit of excitement into the classical music scene.

ROCK IN THE 1960s

Whereas popular music in the 1950s had consisted of a conservative mainstream, represented by singers such as Frank Sinatra, and newer styles emerging on the periphery of the music industry, such as R&B and rock and roll, developments in popular music in the 1960s may be thought of as the intermingling of center and periphery. In other words, mainstream songwriting and studio procedures were adopted by rock and roll, country, and R&B musicians, and at the same time the musical characteristics of those peripheral styles were increasingly heard in mainstream popular songs. By the middle of the decade, in fact, rock and roll, now generally referred to by the shorter label **rock**, *was* the mainstream. In short, the history of rock, country, and R&B—which began to be referred to as **soul music**—in the 1960s is the story of the adoption of mainstream means of production.

SONGWRITING TEAMS, PHIL SPECTOR, AND THE BRILL BUILDING

That process of merging mainstream production methods with newer musical styles had begun in the 1950s with the work of Jerry Leiber and Mike Stoller, a songwriting team in the Tin Pan Alley mold. Leiber and Stoller's new twist was that they wrote for R&B artists such as Big Mama Thornton, whose 1952 record

✑ Three Brill Building songwriters in the early 1960s: Carole King and then-husband Gerry Goffin flank Paul Simon, who, like King, would later have a memorable career as a singer-songwriter.

Phil Spector

the Brill Building

"Will You Love Me Tomorrow"

of their song "Hound Dog" would inspire Elvis Presley's cover version. In addition to their songwriting skills, Leiber and Stoller understood the impact of the studio production techniques of Mitch Miller and other mainstream record producers, and by the late 1950s they were as involved with the recording of their songs as with the writing of them. A series of hit records, especially those for the Coasters and the Drifters, two R&B vocal groups, featured the team's catchy tunes, clever lyrics, and masterful use of the resources of the recording studio, whether the Latin percussion in "Spanish Harlem" (Ben E. King, 1963) or the nuanced balance and tasteful reverb of "On Broadway" (Drifters, 1960).

"On Broadway" included a studio guitar player, Phil Spector, who made the most of his time with Leiber and Stoller, treating it as a sort of apprenticeship for his own writing and producing career. A year later, at age twenty-one, Spector founded his own record company, Philles Records. Whether producing his own songs or those of other writers, Spector invested great care in building up complex instrumental textures in the studio, creating an orchestral wash of timbres known as the **Wall of Sound**. The result was a series of hit records that Spector dubbed his "teenage symphonies."

"Be My Baby," a pop hit in 1963, features the songwriting of Spector, Ellie Greenwich, and Jeff Barry; the naïve but impassioned singing of the Ronettes, one of the many **girl groups** of the time; and the highly skilled playing of a group of L.A. studio musicians nicknamed the Wrecking Crew, most notably the tight, energetic drumming of Hal Blaine. But it is the distinctive Wall of Sound production that makes "Be My Baby" remembered today as a Phil Spector record. Building on the legacy of Les Paul, Mitch Miller, and Leiber and Stoller, Spector raised the role of the record producer to new creative heights.

Greenwich and Barry, like other songwriters associated with Phil Spector, worked in the **Brill Building**, a New York office building that resembled a latter-day Tin Pan Alley, transported uptown from West 28th Street to 1619 Broadway, near 50th Street. There, in tiny cubicles furnished with a piano and not much else, songwriting teams like Carole King and Gerry Goffin, Neil Sedaka and Howard Greenfield, and Doc Pomus and Mort Shuman churned out songs for the teenage market. The tight quarters and poor soundproofing fostered a spirit of competition, and the Brill Building songwriters vied for the attentions of record producers and singing stars. Although much of their work was disposable teen fodder, the best of it displays a high level of craftsmanship and talent.

"Will You Love Me Tomorrow," a 1960 song by King and Goffin, follows the *aaba* format of classic popular songs going back to the 1920s, and the hit record includes an interlude for string orchestra, a nod to the sophisticated accompaniments heard on mainstream pop records. But added to the mix are an insistent drum track, giving the record more of a rock and roll feeling, and the youthful voices of the Shirelles, a girl group. Like many teen-oriented songs, it addresses the concerns of high-schoolers, but here with a new seriousness: the song's persona is a teenage girl questioning her boyfriend's sincerity in asking her for greater sexual intimacy. "Tonight the look of love is in your eyes," she tells him, "but will you love me tomorrow?" A record pitched to teenagers yet tackling a romantic issue with seriousness, "Will You Love Me Tomorrow" straddles the carefree ethos of 1950s rock and roll and the more mature sensibility of 1960s rock.

FUN, FUN, FUN TILL WE GROW UP: ROCK COMES OF AGE

By the late 1950s rock and roll enjoyed a prominent place in the youth culture of the United Kingdom as well as the United States. Some British youngsters encountered African American styles through recordings by southern and Chicago blues artists. Many more took in the sounds of Chuck Berry, Fats Domino, and Elvis Presley. By around 1960 the area of the rough-edged port city of Liverpool alone boasted almost three hundred rock and roll clubs and as many local bands, including one that had begun in 1956 as the Quarrymen and was now called the Beatles.

    Scoring an immediate hit with their first single in 1962, "Love Me Do," the Beatles won such ardent popularity in Britain that their reception earned its own label: "Beatlemania." American Beatlemania began in 1964 with the group's appearance on CBS Television's *Ed Sullivan Show*. The screaming teenagers brought to mind Benny Goodman's performances in the 1930s, Frank Sinatra's in the 1940s, and Elvis Presley's in the 1950s. And their enthusiasm helped to enrich the record industry's coffers through a remarkable sales development: the Beatles' first LP, *Meet the Beatles*, outsold the group's first single by a margin of 3.6 million to 3.4 million, the first time an album had ever sold more copies than its single counterpart. *the Beatles*

    Beatlemania and the ensuing **British Invasion**—the American fascination with British bands in the 1960s, most notably the Beatles and the Rolling Stones—had a lasting effect on American popular music in at least three ways. First, the British musicians' admiration for blues and early rock and roll artists led to a resurgence of interest in those artists in their native land. Second, the Beatles, working closely with record producer George Martin, built on the songwriting and production achievements of people like Carole King and Phil Spector. In the space of only a few years their records trace a skyrocketing development in sophistication and artistry, raising the standards of what a popular song could aspire to be. And third, the success of *Meet the Beatles* signaled a shift away from the single toward the album as the focus of rock musicians' artistic efforts. *the British Invasion*

    All of these factors reflected an artistic exchange between British and American rock musicians. Among other influences, the Beatles found inspiration in one of the most innovative of all rock artists: Bob Dylan. Abandoning folk music for rock, Dylan brought to popular music his nuanced approach to the protest song, replacing a naïve "us and them" sensibility with an understanding that good and evil are intertwined in ways that implicate everyone. And to his earlier literary and musical influences—Woody Guthrie, the Beats, British Romantic poets, and the French symbolist Arthur Rimbaud—Dylan added a deeper engagement with the grotesque and the absurd, with existentialism, and with dreams and hallucinations. In an earlier day, such mental terrain would never have inspired popular songs. But never before had the popular music audience included so many educated young people who were searching avidly for messages. *Bob Dylan*

    Dylan's "Like a Rolling Stone" (1965), in which he sings caustic words to a joyous, gospel-tinged accompaniment, shows the power of this fresh approach to songwriting and performance. Electric guitars, piano, and organ play over a foundation of bass guitar, drums, and tambourine. Dylan's voice slices in over the rolling tide of electrified sound. Too free in form, repetitive in material, and scarce in vocal melody to pass as a standard pop, country, or folk song, this number is an early example of a rock song, differing from 1950s rock and roll *"Like a Rolling Stone"*

A CLOSER LOOK

Surf Music

Surf music was a regional style that emerged in southern California around 1960 and enjoyed widespread popularity in the first half of the 1960s. A pioneer performer was Dick Dale, a guitarist of mixed Lebanese heritage who adapted playing techniques from the *oud*, a Middle Eastern instrument played by his uncle. Along with Middle Eastern scales and borrowings from Mexican mariachi, key elements in the surf sound include solid-body electric guitars, such as the Fender Stratocaster, played with extreme amplification and drenched in reverb, rapid tremolo picking, and use of the **whammy bar**, a device that alters string tension to produce bent pitches and exaggerated vibrato. Dale's 1962 recording of "Miserlou," a Greek song known throughout the Middle East (the title means "Egyptian Girl"), is a classic example of instrumental surf music, along with the Ventures' "Walk, Don't Run" (1960) and the Chantays' "Pipeline" (1963).

in its heavier beat, more adventurous form and content, and tone of worldly experience. (In 2004 *Rolling Stone* magazine placed it at the top of its list of the five hundred greatest rock songs.) "Like a Rolling Stone" lasts six minutes, unusually long for a pop single. The subject is also unusual: an over-protected person being forced out into a cruel world. But even as his lyrics lay out a scenario of existential loneliness, Dylan's music offers a counter-narrative in sound, which can be heard either as gleeful, almost cruel gloating, or simply as the undisguised camaraderie of musicians who are having a wonderful time playing together.

Another model for the Beatles was the Beach Boys, a group led by the singer and songwriter Brian Wilson. The Beach Boys, like the Beatles, began with lighthearted teen fare and developed into a group with more serious artistic aspirations. Wilson and his band members hailed from southern California, and their early songs celebrate the interests of many teenage boys in that sunny climate: girls, cars, and surfboards, best summed up in the title of their 1964 hit "Fun, Fun, Fun." And like the Beatles, Wilson took his songwriting inspiration from 1950s rock-and-rollers, sometimes too much so: the Beach Boys' first Top Ten hit, "Surfin' USA" (1963), leans heavily on Chuck Berry's 1958 "Sweet Little Sixteen," as Berry's lawyers were quick to point out.

Emulating Phil Spector, and using members of the Wrecking Crew for the Beach Boys' recording sessions, Brian Wilson combined his skills as a songwriter with a keen attention to the possibilities of the recording studio. Like those of the Beatles, the Beach Boys' records of the mid- to late 1960s trace the group's rapid development. Spurred on by the Beatles' innovative 1965 album *Rubber Soul*, Wilson threw his talents into the creation of a concept album in which each song would build on its predecessors to achieve an integrated artistic whole, a song cycle of symphonic breadth. *Pet Sounds*, released in 1966, greatly influenced the Beatles' similar effort of 1967, *Sgt. Pepper's Lonely Hearts Club Band*.

LG 18.3   The opening track on *Pet Sounds*, "Wouldn't It Be Nice" (LG 18.3), features thick instrumental textures that resemble Phil Spector's Wall of Sound. The conventional *aaba* song form is expanded by giving each *a* section two distinct subsections, the first eight bars long and the second varying in length at each recurrence. At the bridge, a sudden contrast of timbre underlines the jump to a distant key, an example of Wilson's harmonic sophistication and studio savvy. The lyrics, oriented toward teenagers, take seriously a young person's yearning for maturity. With the artistic achievements of Bob Dylan, the Beatles, and the Beach Boys, rock by the mid-1960s had reached its own maturity.

PSYCHEDELIC MUSIC

Although *Sgt. Pepper's Lonely Hearts Club Band* emulated many aspects of *Pet Sounds*, it differed by placing much greater emphasis on studio sound effects as a simulation of drug experiences. In that way, the Beatles' concept album highlighted the psychedelic movement of late-1960s rock. Beginning as early as 1965

CD 3.20	Listening Guide 18.3	"Wouldn't It Be Nice" THE BEACH BOYS

SONGWRITERS: Brian Wilson, Tony Asher, and Mike Love

DATE: 1966

GENRE: rock

PERFORMERS: The Beach Boys (seven members) and studio musicians; produced by Brian Wilson

METER: duple

FORM: AA'BA"

WHAT TO LISTEN FOR

- rich textures resembling Phil Spector's Wall of Sound
- unusual expansion of *aaba* chorus structure
- distant modulation in bridge, anticipated tonally by the introduction
- tempo changes encourage listening rather than dancing

TIMING	SECTION	TEXT	COMMENTS
0:00	introduction		Prominent harp figure establishes "wrong" key (A major), so that the arrival of the vocal in the tonic (F) is jolting.
0:06	A	Wouldn't it be nice if we were older . . .	Along with the usual rock instruments are accordions, buried deep in the mix.
0:23		You know it's gonna make it that much better . . .	The first A section ends inconclusively, leading smoothly into the second A.
0:33	A'	Wouldn't it be nice if we could wake up . . .	Backing voices add a secondary melodic line.
0:50		The happy times together we'd be spending . . .	
1:00	refrain	Oh, wouldn't it be nice?	Refrain line gives strong closure.
1:05	B	Maybe if we think and wish and hope and pray . . .	Bridge in contrasting key (A major); the harp intro recurs as accompaniment.
1:28	refrain	Oh, wouldn't it be nice?	Return to tonic (F).
1:37	A"	You know it seems the more we talk about it . . .	Instead of a return to the opening, a slowing down, with mandolin tremolos, then a return to the second portion of the A section.
1:57	refrain	Wouldn't it be nice?	
1:59	coda	Good night my baby . . .	A repeating phrase on the tonic harmony leads to a fadeout.

Listen & Reflect

1. How does the subject matter of "Wouldn't It Be Nice" resemble the teen-oriented lyrics of 1950s rock and roll songs, and how does it differ? How does the musical treatment relate to the lyrics?

🔊 Janis Joplin (1943–1970) at New York's Fillmore East in 1968, with visual accompaniment by Joshua Light Show: the epitome of the late-1960s psychedelic rock concert.

with Bob Dylan's "Mr. Tambourine Man," widely received as a song about a drug trip, psychedelic music connected the use of mind-altering drugs with music in two ways. Some songs, such as the Byrds' "Eight Miles High" (1966) and Jefferson Airplane's "White Rabbit" (1967), addressed the topic in their lyrics, usually veiled in metaphor. Other songs, such as "A Day in the Life," the closing track on *Sgt. Pepper*, used the music itself as an analogue for the drug trip, by stressing distorted guitar sounds, "spacey" reverb, sped-up or reversed tape manipulations, and other intentionally unnatural-sounding studio effects.

But psychedelic music was not confined to the recording studio. Rock concerts in the late 1960s acted for some audience members as simulations of drug trips and for others as accompaniments to the same. Such concerts, pioneered in San Francisco, a capital of the youthful counterculture, often included light shows to add a visual element to the high-decibel aural disorientation. Although they made successful albums, San Francisco–based bands such as the Grateful Dead and Big Brother and the Holding Company, whose lead singer was the passionate, gravel-voiced Janis Joplin, made their greatest impact in live performances. For rock audiences, participation in these events could be an expression of a group solidarity, excluding nonfans and creating the sensation of a community favoring "rebellious" personal identities and ready to scorn those outside the tribe.

COUNTRY MUSIC FROM NASHVILLE TO BAKERSFIELD

Country music underwent transformations in the 1960s that paralleled those of rock and roll. And like rock musicians, country artists borrowed the advanced production techniques of mainstream popular music to create records that appealed to a broader, more diverse audience. But many country music lovers saw the trappings of mainstream pop as posing a threat to the music's integrity.

How could a music founded on notions of rural, traditional authenticity survive when dressed up in the slick production techniques of the up-to-date recording studio? Different musicians addressed that question in different ways. Two basic approaches can be seen by comparing the two geographic centers of country music making in the 1960s: Nashville, Tennessee, and Bakersfield, California.

THE NASHVILLE SOUND

Nashville's importance in country music dates as far back as the beginnings of the *Grand Ole Opry* in the 1920s. By the 1950s Nashville was the undisputed capital of the country music industry, the home of numerous songwriters, performers, publishing houses, and record companies. The city thus played a dominant role in country music analogous to New York's position in the Tin Pan Alley years of mainstream popular music.

The basic elements of the 1960s Nashville music scene were already in place in 1956, when Elvis Presley arrived there to record "Heartbreak Hotel" for RCA Victor. Two of the studio musicians who backed him up on that record, guitarist Chet Atkins and pianist Floyd Cramer, would become principal architects of the **Nashville sound** of the 1960s: country-style vocals accompanied by highly polished studio musicians, downplaying traditional instruments such as fiddle and banjo in favor of electric guitar and piano, background singers, and even string sections in the manner of Frank Sinatra records. The songs, many of them products of songwriting teams that worked regularly on publishers' payrolls, treated the time-honored country themes—infidelity, lost love, and wanderlust—with a flair for wordplay reminiscent of the classic popular song. And while some featured artists retained the hard-core country vocal sound of their honky-tonk backgrounds—singers such as Ray Price, George Jones, and Loretta Lynn—others modified their styles to match those of mainstream pop singers like Nat King Cole and Patti Page.

Jim Reeves's "Welcome to My World" (1962) is a classic example of the Nashville sound: a gentle *aaba* love song sung by a mellifluous baritone, accompanied by a small combo featuring vibraphone, Cramer's signature "slip-note" piano in imitation of a guitarist's hammer-ons, and the soft cooing of the Anita Kerr Singers. Another record, Patsy Cline's "Crazy," is filled with features that made it a crossover hit on both country and pop charts in 1961. The trace of rural twang in Cline's vocal gives it an individuality distinct from the singing of her models, pop singers such as Kay Starr and Doris Day. The *aaba* song, with words and music by Willie Nelson—at that time a part of the Nashville establishment, years before developing his Austin outlaw persona—is an homage to Tin Pan Alley songwriters such as Hoagy Carmichael, whose wide-arcing melodies it emulates. Record producer Owen Bradley blends piano and organ with brushed drums, electric bass, and a lightly rhythmic electric guitar backbeat to craft a sound that is urbane, sophisticated, yet somehow not utterly devoid of country-style sincerity and authenticity: a pinnacle of the Nashville sound.

Patsy Cline, "Crazy"

THE BAKERSFIELD SOUND

Meanwhile, a new center for country music was developing far to the west of Nashville: Bakersfield, a midsize city in the San Joaquin Valley of southern California. During the Great Depression, the Dust Bowl ecological crisis had propelled hundreds of thousands of people from the Plains states, particularly Oklahoma, Texas, and Arkansas, to the fertile farms and productive oil fields of the San Joaquin. As described in John Steinbeck's novel *The Grapes of Wrath*, these "Okies," as they were called, retained many aspects of their rural southern folkways, despite their contact with the California-born Chicanos and immigrant populations from Mexico and Europe that already made up a large part of the valley's denizens. A generation later, the children of those Dust Bowl migrants were still replicating the cultural milieu of their parents' home states. Part of that milieu was honky-tonk, the Texas-based music of the beer hall.

Buck Owens

The burgeoning music scene that arose in Bakersfield after World War II thus took honky-tonk as its starting point. As early as 1951 the Bakersfield scene was lively enough to attract studio players from outside the San Joaquin Valley. One of them, Buck Owens, moved to Bakersfield from Arizona in that year; in the decades to come Owens and his band, the Buckaroos, came to define the **Bakersfield sound**. Without turning his back on the traditional honky-tonk sounds of fiddle, pedal steel guitar, and high-pitched vocal harmonies, Owens updated the sound with drums, electric bass, and a twangy Fender Telecaster electric guitar, a solid-body instrument then associated more with rock than with country music, which favored mellower hollow-body guitars. The result was a sound that appealed to country traditionalists who found the Nashville sound too slick, while attracting a younger audience accustomed to the stronger beat of rock and roll. One sign of the crossover appeal of Owens's first big hit, "Act Naturally" (1963), was the appearance two years later of a cover version on the B side of the Beatles' "Yesterday" single.

LG 18.4

The most influential proponent of the Bakersfield sound has been a musician born in 1937 in nearby Oildale, California, to Okie parents. Merle Haggard's early years were inauspicious, and a series of petty crimes showed him what life could be like in a juvenile detention home. An attempted robbery in Bakersfield at age twenty earned him three years in the state prison at San Quentin, where a close look at death row inspired Haggard to go straight and earn his high school equivalency diploma. While in his teens his singing had already attracted the attention of established honky-tonk performers such as Lefty Frizzell, and after his release from prison Haggard began to build a career in the Bakersfield music scene. In 1966 he scored the first of a twenty-year string of number 1 country hits with "I'm a Lonesome Fugitive," by the California-based husband-and-wife songwriting team of Liz and Casey Anderson.

The unpretentious manner of country singer Merle Haggard (b. 1937) was welcomed by working-class listeners.

"Mama Tried" (1968; LG 18.4), Haggard's own composition, is a semi-autobiographical song describing his turn to a life of crime after the death of his father, when Haggard was nine years old. Building on the updated honky-tonk sound of Buck Owens and the Buckaroos, Haggard and his band, the Strangers, add two seemingly contradictory sounds: background singers in the chorus, redolent of the polished Nashville sound, and a fingerpicked acoustic guitar throughout, perhaps an indication of the influence of the urban folk revival and its association of acoustic instruments with authenticity. (**Fingerpicking** is a technique of playing with the individual fingers of the right hand, rather than with a flat pick or by strumming.) "Mama Tried" demonstrates how 1960s country music could embrace stylistic and technological change, expanding the music's expressive range without losing its rural roots.

SOUL MUSIC IN THE 1960s

Beneath the surface unruliness and rebelliousness of 1960s youth culture, the new popular music had opened up an expressive territory in which singers, players, and songwriters found almost limitless possibilities in styles and moods. It was an era when a young musician could aspire to be both artistically serious and commercially successful. Jazz had developed heightened artistic aspirations with the bebop musicians of the 1940s; other popular styles followed suit in the 1960s.

The expansion of expressive possibilities is nowhere more to be found than in soul music, the black popular music of the 1960s. Like soul jazz in relation to hard bop, soul music differed from R&B primarily in the greater infusion of black gospel elements, a stylistic mixture pioneered in the 1950s by Ray Charles, though the term *soul music* did not become widespread until the mid-1960s.

Until the 1960s, white control of the music business had been taken for granted. But with the decade's new patterns of black-white exchange, star performers won more independence, and the balance of power began to shift. Racial interaction changed too. More white singers and players tried to match the emotional intensity of black gospel and blues performers, and more white listeners became their fans.

⤳ James Brown (1933–2006), seen here performing in 1969, earned his reputation as "the hardest-working man in show business."

THE GODFATHER OF SOUL: JAMES BROWN

The career of singer-songwriter-dancer-bandleader James Brown flourished in this climate of black-white exchange. Brown played drums and guitar as a teenager in northeastern Georgia. Deciding to learn piano, he "got all the Hit Parade books and learned all the pop tunes," he later recalled, admiring especially numbers by Bing Crosby and Frank Sinatra. Another inspiration came from the black church, whose atmosphere impressed Brown deeply. He remembered one revival service featuring a preacher who screamed, stamped his feet, and dropped to his knees. "The people got into it with him, answering him and shouting and clapping time." The experience stuck with Brown, who from then on studied preachers closely and imitated them.

Brown's first big break came in the mid-1950s, when he began recording for King Records in Cincinnati. Having scored a national hit with "Please, Please, Please" (1956), he started touring with his vocal group, the Famous Flames, and a large band, and by the early 1960s the James Brown Show was an evening-length revue built around the star's energy. Maintaining a strenuous performing schedule and billed as "the hardest-working man in show business," Brown took a blue-collar approach to his profession. "When you're on stage," he wrote, "the people who paid money to get in are the boss, even if it cost them only a quarter. You're working for them." At the same time, Brown made sure his musicians knew they were working for him; tales of his strict control of every aspect of their performance are legendary. Brown developed a charismatic presence, not only as a singer but also as

| CD 3.21 | Listening Guide 18.4 | "Mama Tried" MERLE HAGGARD |

SONGWRITER: Merle Haggard
DATE: 1968
PERFORMERS: Merle Haggard and the Strangers
GENRE: country
METER: duple
FORM: verse and chorus

WHAT TO LISTEN FOR

- confessional, semi-autobiographical lyrics
- direct, uncomplicated vocal delivery
- Bakersfield sound: twangy electric guitar, light drums
- non-Bakersfield elements: acoustic guitar, background vocals

TIMING	SECTION	TEXT	COMMENTS
0:00	introduction		Solo fingerpicked acoustic guitar sets an intimate mood; electric lead guitar joins in bar 3 to heighten the excitement; in bars 4–5 the drums establish the rhythmic style for the remainder of the song.
0:11	verse 1	The first thing I remember . . .	Bent pitches at the ends of phrases (on "knowing," "blowing"), emphasize the rising melodic line. The lyrics focus on the young child's imagination and wanderlust.
0:31	verse 2	One and only rebel child . . .	The second verse introduces the conflict in values between mother and son.
0:50	chorus	And I turned twenty-one in prison . . .	The melody's highest note falls near the beginning of the chorus ("twenty-one"), closely followed by its lowest note ("no <u>one</u>"). Background singers and more-emphatic drumming, with kick drum and ride cymbal, strengthen melodic climax.
1:11	interlude		Electric guitar solo in the characteristic "twangy" Bakersfield style.
1:20	verse 3	Dear old daddy, rest his soul . . .	Verse focuses on the mother's struggles as a single parent. The accompaniment returns to the more subdued sound of the earlier verses.

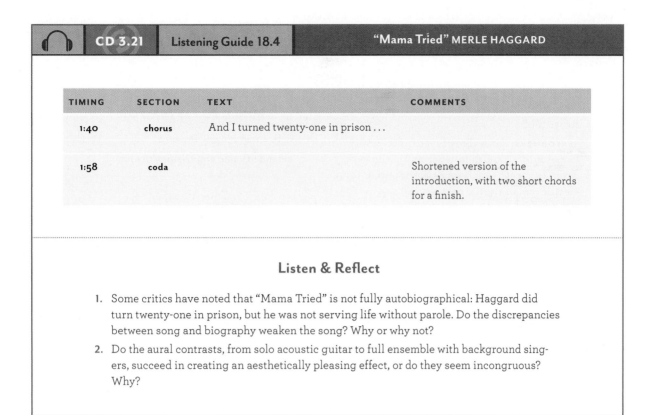

TIMING	SECTION	TEXT	COMMENTS
1:40	chorus	And I turned twenty-one in prison...	
1:58	coda		Shortened version of the introduction, with two short chords for a finish.

Listen & Reflect

1. Some critics have noted that "Mama Tried" is not fully autobiographical: Haggard did turn twenty-one in prison, but he was not serving life without parole. Do the discrepancies between song and biography weaken the song? Why or why not?

2. Do the aural contrasts, from solo acoustic guitar to full ensemble with background singers, succeed in creating an aesthetically pleasing effect, or do they seem incongruous? Why?

an accomplished, athletic dancer who mesmerized audiences with splits, leaps, and other exuberant steps—a style of performance that became a model for Michael Jackson.

By 1964 James Brown was moving away from conventional song structures and toward a new emphasis on movement and dance. "Papa's Got a Brand New Bag" (1965; LG 18.5), more than four minutes long, devotes less than half its length to the lyrics, which celebrate dancing. Originally split into two halves and released on the A and B sides of a 45-rpm single, "Papa" begins with the briefest of intros: a sustained blast from a band that plays with fierce precision from start to finish. Brown sings a pair of vocal choruses in twelve-bar blues form, followed by eight bars of vamp—here a repeated four-beat unit built on a rhythmic bass. After two more choruses, the blues structure disappears, to be replaced by the vamp. The melody instruments interlock polyrhythmically with the bass by attacking the second beat with an explosive accent of three short notes, while the drummer and guitarist regularly accent the backbeat. The vamp churns ahead for the next two and a half minutes to the final fadeout, overlaid by a long tenor sax solo and Brown's shouts of encouragement. (In live performance the singer danced this part of the number.) Brown's commitment to rhythm is unmistakable: the song is used to introduce the vamp instead of the other way around. By this time in his career, Brown later said, "I was hearing everything, even the guitars, like they were drums."

In "Papa's Got a Brand New Bag" and other recordings that followed, Brown virtually invented the style that in the 1970s would be called **funk**, and in the process became the best-selling soul artist of the day. Echoes of Brown's techniques

LG 18.5

CD 3.22   **Listening Guide 18.5**   **"Papa's Got a Brand New Bag"** JAMES BROWN

SONGWRITER: James Brown

DATE: 1965

PERFORMERS: James Brown, vocal; the James Brown Band (alto, tenor, and baritone saxes; trumpets; trombones; electric organ; electric guitar; electric bass; drums)

GENRE: soul music

METER: duple

FORM: strophic 12-bar blues, modified by extended vamps

WHAT TO LISTEN FOR

- tight ensemble polyrhythms
- extended vamp emphasizing rhythm

TIMING	SECTION	TEXT	COMMENTS
0:00	chorus 1	Come here, sisters …	A stabbing chord from the horns, Brown enters on the upbeat, and on the downbeat the full band locks into a tight, bluesy groove. At bar 10 of the 12-bar chorus, Brown sings the title phrase (refrain) as a break (while the band is silent), followed by furious guitar chords in bar 11 and a turnaround in bar 12.
0:24	chorus 2	Come down, brother …	Note the polyrhythmic texture: an active bass line; the horns' two polyrhythmic layers (a low note in the baritone sax on beat 2, then a four-note motive in the other horns); guitar and snare drum in a crisp backbeat.
0:46	vamp	He did the jerk …	New polyrhythmic texture for the 8-bar vamp, built on a single tonic chord: now the horns play a short three-note motive on beat 2. Over that texture, Brown lists some of the latest dance steps.
1:01	chorus 3	Come down, sister …	Return to the texture and 12-bar structure of the earlier choruses.
1:23	chorus 4	Oh and father …	Brown names more dance moves.
1:45	vamp	Hey, come on, hey hey …	Return to the texture of the earlier vamp. (Side A of single fades out at 2:04.)
2:04		I just want you to blow, Maceo …	Brown calls on tenor sax player Maceo Parker to take a solo.
2:08			Tenor sax solo, emphasizing blue notes. Note Brown's calls of encouragement.
3:52		He's doing the jerk …	Return to the words of the first vamp.
4:07		Come here, sister …	The lyrics suggest a possible return to a chorus, but instead the record fades out over the vamp.

🎧	CD 3.22	Listening Guide 18.5	"Papa's Got a Brand New Bag" JAMES BROWN

Listen & Reflect

1. The fadeout ending suggests not that the song has reached a conclusion but that the music continues on, beyond our ability to hear it. In live performance, Brown and his band might stretch this song out for several more minutes. What features of the song encourage that kind of expansive, variable performance? What are some strategies that Brown and his musicians might use to create a longer performance?

were inescapable on black radio of the 1980s. His records were widely sampled in hip-hop of the 1980s and 1990s; one fan's website lists nearly two hundred rap songs that sample a single Brown record, "Funky Drummer" (1970). And his influence has proved international, extending to European synthpop, West African Afro-beat, and Jamaican reggae.

SOUL MUSIC IN MEMPHIS AND DETROIT

Two record companies in particular reflect another kind of black-white interchange: Stax and Motown. Owned by the white brother-and-sister team of Jim Stewart and Estelle Axton, Stax Records in Memphis created soul hits with black singers backed by Booker T. and the MG's, a racially mixed house band led by organist Booker T. Jones. In 1962 Stax released its first record by Otis Redding, a singer from Macon, Georgia, who soon became Stax's best-selling artist. (Redding's records appeared on Stax's sister label, Volt.) In 1965 Jerry Wexler—of New York's Atlantic Records, an indie label fast growing to major status—traveled to Memphis with Wilson Pickett and other Atlantic artists and recorded them with Stax's Booker T. and the MG's. The link with Wexler and Atlantic allowed Stax to improve its distribution. Thus a Memphis firm's combination of black singers, Southern white ownership, national marketing network, and mix of black and white studio musicians gave rise to some of the 1960s' greatest soul music, a genre marketed as quintessentially black.

Stax and Motown

Meanwhile, Motown, a record company founded in Detroit in 1959 by black songwriter Berry Gordy Jr., was becoming one of the most influential in the history of popular music. Motown's records, with performers drawn chiefly from Detroit's black community, combined elements from rhythm and blues, gospel, and rock and roll with the aim of attracting white listeners as well as black. The **Motown sound** relied heavily on mainstream pop trappings, including string sections. At the same time, the records boasted a vital rhythmic core, supplied by a group of jazz-oriented, mostly black studio musicians nicknamed "the Funk Brothers," who, in varying combinations, played uncredited on nearly every Motown record. Of the many members of the Funk Brothers, bassist James Jamerson stands out as an inventive player whose complex, rhythmically active bass lines enlivened virtually all of Motown's hit records.

The company's blend of pop lushness with rhythmic bite and imaginative harmonies proved appealing to white and black listeners alike. In the racial climate of the 1960s and after, white teenage audiences were ready to respond to black performers. Such Motown stars as Diana Ross and the Supremes, Smokey Robinson and the Miracles, the Temptations, Marvin Gaye, Stevie Wonder, and the Jackson Five enjoyed great success in the marketplace.

LG 18.6

Even more than Phil Spector or Stewart and Axton, Berry Gordy exercised control over every aspect of creating a hit record. He not only supervised the work of his staff songwriters, arrangers, producers, vocalists, and instrumentalists, but also took an active role in distribution, marketing, and even the dress and deportment of his singing stars. "I Heard It through the Grapevine" (LG 18.6), the work of two of the company's staff songwriters, the prolific Norman Whitfield and Barrett Strong, is an example of Motown's methods of creating memorable soul records. In a practice not unusual at Motown, it was recorded by more than one artist—in this case, by Smokey Robinson and the Miracles, then by Marvin Gaye, and then by Gladys Knight and the Pips. The third version was the first to be released, in September 1967. Emphasizing Knight's gospel-style vocal, backed with a funky beat and plenty of percussion, it reached number 1 on the R&B charts and number 2 on the pop charts. Just over a year later, Marvin Gaye's more brooding version was released and became one of the most successful Motown singles of all time.

compound AABA form

Like many popular songs from the 1960s to the present, "I Heard It through the Grapevine" is cast in **compound AABA form**. That is, a series of verse-chorus pairs (the A sections) is broken up by a contrasting passage (the B section, or bridge), which typically commences somewhere between halfway and two-thirds through the record. The result combines features of a verse-chorus song, such as "Mama Tried," with the *aaba* structure of the classic popular song, such as "What Is This Thing Called Love?" But whereas the classic *aaba* chorus is a thirty-two-bar unit that typically is stated more than once to fill out a record, the compound AABA structure describes the entire record. Thus, the term *bridge* becomes redefined, no longer as a segment within the chorus, but as a larger contrasting section within the song as a whole.

Significantly, the rise of compound AABA form in the 1960s closely follows the emergence of the songwriter-producer team. One of the first top hits in compound AABA form was "You've Lost That Lovin' Feeling," which reached number 2 on *Billboard*'s Hot 100 chart early in 1965. Sung by the Righteous Brothers, a white duo that specialized in "blue-eyed soul," the song was written by a Brill Building team, Barry Mann and Cynthia Weil, in collaboration with Phil Spector, who produced the record with his characteristic Wall of Sound. The earlier Tin Pan Alley tunesmiths had written songs that were flexible in structure, adaptable to the needs and tastes of performers. In contrast, popular songwriters since 1960 have realized the need to craft a song in the newer sense: a specific recorded performance, typically built up track by track in the recording studio, using all the artifice of modern technology yet exuding an atmosphere of spontaneous music making: a recorded performance that listeners will come to think of as the definitive version.

Compound AABA form is thus one of many aspects of music making profoundly influenced by recording technology in the 1960s. From minimalism to the Nashville sound, and from the records of Phil Spector to those of Berry Gordy, style changes in the 1960s were closely related to activities in the sound studio. Of

Gladys Knight and the Pips (from left: Edward Patten, Bubba Knight, Gladys Knight, William Guest). The poses, costumes, and hairstyles reflect Motown founder Berry Gordy Jr.'s concern that his label's acts should appeal to a broad swath of the popular mainstream.

CD 3.23	Listening Guide 18.6	"I Heard It through the Grapevine" GLADYS KNIGHT AND THE PIPS

SONGWRITERS: Norman Whitfield and Barrett Strong

DATE: 1967

PERFORMERS: Gladys Knight and the Pips; the Funk Brothers (uncredited Motown studio band: tenor sax, piano, electric guitars, electric bass; drums; tambourine)

GENRE: soul music

METER: duple

FORM: compound AABA

WHAT TO LISTEN FOR

- gospel-tinged vocal style
- percussion-heavy, rhythmic instrumental backing
- interaction of female vocal solo and male vocal backup trio
- presence of bridge after second verse-chorus pair: compound AABA

TIMING	SECTION		TEXT	COMMENTS
0:00	introduction			Drums, lightly accompanied by bass, set an energetic tone.
0:09	A	verse 1	I bet you're wond'rin' how I knew . . .	Knight enters with a soulful hum, then delivers the first verse with gospel sincerity; Pips (three male backup singers) respond with countermelody on neutral vowels, all over the band's polyrhythmic groove with an emphatic backbeat.
0:34		chorus	Don't ya know that I heard it through the grapevine . . .	Call and response.
0:52		vamp	Oh yes I am . . .	Short vamp prepares return to the verse.
1:00	A	verse 2	Take a good look at these tears of mine . . .	Electric guitar adds a new layer to the polyrhythmic texture.
1:25		chorus	Instead I heard it through the grapevine . . .	Here and throughout, the simple but extremely accurate tambourine playing adds to the song's gospel intensity.
1:43		vamp		Midway through the vamp, tenor sax **trill** prepares the bridge.
1:52	B	bridge	Go, I gotta go . . .	8 bars of IV chord, with the Pips singing short, energetic phrases while the sax solos.
2:04	A	verse 3	Say believe half of what you see . . .	Knight alters the verse melody to emphasize high notes, while the Pips sing a new, more energetic countermelody.
2:29		chorus	Don't you know that I heard through the grapevine . . .	Knight raises the temperature with impassioned gospel shouting. As a closing gesture, the chorus turns into a vamp, with fadeout.

(continued)

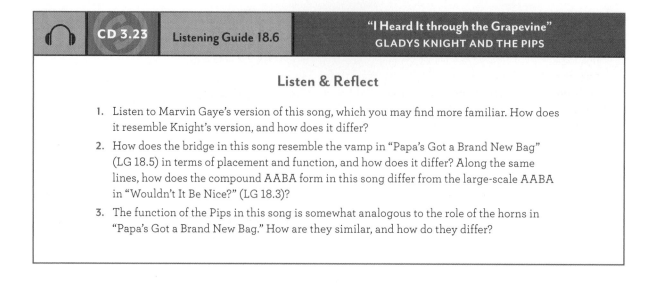

CD 3.23   Listening Guide 18.6   "I Heard It through the Grapevine"
GLADYS KNIGHT AND THE PIPS

Listen & Reflect

1. Listen to Marvin Gaye's version of this song, which you may find more familiar. How does it resemble Knight's version, and how does it differ?

2. How does the bridge in this song resemble the vamp in "Papa's Got a Brand New Bag" (LG 18.5) in terms of placement and function, and how does it differ? Along the same lines, how does the compound AABA form in this song differ from the large-scale AABA in "Wouldn't It Be Nice?" (LG 18.3)?

3. The function of the Pips in this song is somewhat analogous to the role of the horns in "Papa's Got a Brand New Bag." How are they similar, and how do they differ?

the many types of music surveyed in this chapter, 1960s jazz seems to have been the least affected by studio practices (although records have had an important role in the development of jazz at least since the time of Bix Beiderbecke in the 1920s). The half century since the 1960s has seen continued growth in this direction; perhaps as no coincidence, it has also been a time when musicians and their audiences have come to place ever higher value on the elusive concept of authenticity. Ever since the 1960s, musicians have paradoxically turned to technological wizardry to convey messages of direct, unmediated musical expression.

QUESTIONS FOR DISCUSSION AND REVIEW

1. If jazz originated in the realm of popular entertainment, what elements of entertainment, if any, survive in jazz of the 1960s?

2. What were the three trends in East Coast classical music in the 1960s, and how did they relate to or differ from West Coast minimalism?

3. How did 1960s rock differ from 1950s rock and roll?

4. What common factors connect rock, country, and soul music in the 1960s?

5. Compare and contrast the two leading soul music labels, Stax and Motown.

6. What connections might you make between the aesthetic goals of John Coltrane, the minimalists, and psychedelic rock?

FURTHER READING

Gracyk, Theodore. *Rhythm and Noise: An Aesthetics of Rock*. Durham, NC: Duke University Press, 1996.

Frith, Simon. *Sound Effects: Youth, Leisure, and the Politics of Rock 'n' Roll*. New York: Pantheon, 1981.

Reich, Steve. *Writings about Music, 1965–2000*. New York: Oxford University Press, 2002.

Strickland, Edward. *Minimalism: Origins.* Bloomington: Indiana University Press, 1993.

Kirchner, Bill, ed. *The Oxford Companion to Jazz.* New York: Oxford University Press, 2000.

Monson, Ingrid. *Freedom Sounds: Civil Rights Call Out to Jazz and Africa.* New York: Oxford University Press, 2007.

George, Nelson. *Where Did Our Love Go? The Rise and Fall of the Motown Sound.* Urbana: University of Illinois Press, 2007.

Malone, Bill C. *Country Music, U.S.A.* 2d ed. Austin: University of Texas Press, 2002.

CHAPTER 19

"STAYIN' ALIVE"

America's Music in the 1970s

By the 1970s rock was no longer the young upstart it had been two decades earlier. Many rock musicians aspired to the critical status of classical and jazz musicians, with some exploring a fusion of rock and jazz that touched off a firestorm of controversy in jazz circles. Other musicians, sensing that rock was losing touch with its roots, argued for a return to simplicity, a search for authenticity that united musicians as disparate as singer-songwriters and punk rockers. Along similar lines, black popular music saw funk complemented by more accessible disco. Meanwhile, Broadway composers developed musical theater in directions only tangentially related to current pop trends, and classical composers continued to probe the gap between avant-garde music and the broader classical audience they had left behind in the mid-twentieth century. In fact, the problem of exploring new regions of creativity without alienating audiences was common to many areas of music in the 1970s.

While musicians wanted to reach a broad audience, marketing forces continued to devise new categorical schemes to target specific groups. The old categories of "race" and "hillbilly" records attest to the division of audiences on the basis of ethnicity, region, and class; the 1950s category of "rock and roll" introduced the notion of dividing the audience on the basis of age, reifying what in the 1960s would be called the generation gap.

By the 1970s, then, a practice was in place that continues to the present day: the splintering of popular music into ever smaller categories, or **subgenres**, that sometimes tell the historian more about the social affiliations of the music's fans than they do about the music itself. Some observers argue that this fragmentation stems from the music industry's efforts to fine-tune its marketing. Others argue that it is driven by consumers, who use their status as fans to define and express their individual identity and group affiliations. Still others argue that both supply and demand act as twin engines in the creation of subgenres. Whatever the motivating factors, the use of genres and subgenres to define social groups is a key trait of American music in the late twentieth and early twenty-first centuries.

ROCK ENTERS THE 1970s

As the decade began, the wave of psychedelia that had fascinated the youth counterculture of the late 1960s reached its crest. By the mid-1970s, though, following the end of the Vietnam War and President Richard Nixon's resignation in the wake of the Watergate scandal, much of the countercultural movement's energy had dissipated. Rock in those years lost some of its rebellious attitude, resulting in what some critics have called "corporate rock." But an unruly undercurrent persisted, and by the end of the decade the anarchic spirit of early rock and roll reemerged in a new guise: punk rock.

THE RISE OF THE ROCK VIRTUOSO

When rock and roll emerged in the 1950s, teenage listeners had reveled in the crude, sometimes amateurish sounds of musicians who were often self-taught or informally trained. Compared to mainstream pop's polished professionalism and jazz's intellectual complexity, rock and roll's simplicity came as something different. As rock's audiences reached adulthood in the 1960s, however, the music took on much of the sophistication of the genres to which it had formerly stood in opposition. One aspect of that maturation, the use of elaborate studio recording techniques, was discussed in chapter 18. Another aspect was the arrival of a new generation of rock musicians who displayed the sort of ferocious instrumental virtuosity previously associated with classical music and jazz.

In the 1960s perhaps no musician embodied the idea of the electric guitarist as rock hero more dramatically than Jimi Hendrix. By the time of Hendrix's drug-related death in 1970 at age twenty-seven, his example had inspired other musicians to create rock music of dazzling brilliance. In England, Eric Clapton of the band Cream and Jimmy Page of Led Zeppelin, musicians inspired by the Chicago blues of Muddy Waters and other Chess artists, brought Hendrix-style showmanship to their renditions of blues standards and original compositions. In the American South, Duane Allman of the Allman Brothers Band, Allen Collins of Lynyrd Skynyrd, and Billy Gibbons of ZZ Top did likewise. One of the most original, influential, and long-lasting of the guitar heroes is the Mexican-born Carlos Santana, who rose to prominence as the leader of the band Santana, a mix of Latino, black, and white musicians. Emerging in the San Francisco psychedelic scene in the late 1960s, Santana gained national fame at the Woodstock music festival in 1969, and in the next three years would release three landmark albums.

Jimi Hendrix

Carlos Santana

LG 19.1

"Oye como va" (LG 19.1), from Santana's second album, *Abraxas* (a number 1 pop album in 1970), displays the band's blend of blues-based rock improvisation with Latin percussion and rhythms. A cover of a tune introduced in 1962 by Tito Puente, this number is an easygoing celebration of the joys of making and listening to music. The words, "Oye como va, mi ritmo, / Bueno pa' gozar, mulata," may be roughly translated as "Listen to how my groove goes; / It's good for savoring, *mulata*" (a woman or girl of mixed race).

Puente's music for "Oye como va" is built on a striking two-bar chord progression: a minor tonic chord alternates with a major subdominant. In a conventional minor mode, both chords would be minor. The alteration creates the feeling of the Dorian mode, a medieval scale that survives in various types of folk music. Percussion instruments provide layers of dance-inducing polyrhythms,

| CD 3.24 | Listening Guide 19.1 | "Oye como va" CARLOS SANTANA |

SONGWRITER: Tito Puente

GENRE: rock

DATE: 1970

PERFORMERS: Santana; instrumentation: guitar, organ, bass, drums, Latin percussion (two players)

METER: duple

FORM: strophic with vamps

WHAT TO LISTEN FOR

- use of Latin rhythms and percussion instruments with standard rock instruments
- lyrical, expressive electric guitar solos
- dominance of long instrumental solos (guitar, organ) over vocal sections

TIMING	SECTION	TEXT	COMMENTS
0:00	intro/vamp		8 bars, starting with organ and bass to establish a **clave** (an organizing rhythm in Latin music). Bar 4, timbales (high-pitched tom-toms) enter; bar 5, guïro (scraper), conga (a tall Afro-Cuban drum played with the hands) and agogo (cowbell) join to establish a cha-cha rhythm (long-short-short).
0:15			Electric guitar enters with 2-bar phrase, repeated 4 times.
0:30			4 bars of rhythmic unison, followed by silence and a final chord.
0:38	chorus	Oye como va, mi ritmo, Bueno pa' gozar, mulata	The band sings 8-bar chorus in unison over the same 2-bar chord progression heard throughout the song, followed by a 2-bar version of the rhythmic chords that ended the vamp.
0:57	guitar solo		Begins with 8 bars of plangent, slightly distorted playing in the middle register.
1:12			For the next 8 bars the melodic line becomes more intense, moving to a higher register.
1:26			Staying in the high register, guitar suggests a quick triple meter against the basic medium duple meter of the band (4 bars).
1:34			6 bars of rapid repeated chords alternating with a unison melodic phrase in guitar and bass.
1:45	vamp		4-bar return to the introduction.
1:52	interlude		New 8-bar vamp, with sudden drop in volume and changes of texture, featuring the Latin percussion. In bars 7–8 the full band plays repeated chords with a crescendo.

CD 3.24	Listening Guide 19.1		"Oye como va" CARLOS SANTANA

TIMING	SECTION	TEXT	COMMENTS
2:07	organ solo		8 bars begin with held organ tremolo, followed by melodic improvisations highlighting blue notes and generally descending in contour.
2:22			The second 8-bar segment begins with polyrhythms, then continues with more blue notes.
2:37			Organ anticipates the third segment (6 bars) with a return to polyrhythms, expanding the texture to full chords.
2:48	vamp		4-bar return to the introduction, then 2-bar version of the rhythmic chords.
2:59	chorus	Oye como va, mi ritmo, Bueno pa' gozar, mulata	8-bar chorus as before, followed by a 4-bar version of the repeated-chord crescendo that preceded the organ solo.
3:21	guitar solo		Guitar begins with 8 bars of an expressive melody pitched fairly high.
3:36			8 bars: guitar improvises freely in a still higher register, gradually descending to the lower strings.
3:51			8 bars: 2 bars of distorted double stops in the mid-register, then 6 bars of high, clear single notes in the quick triple polyrhythm.
4:06	coda		4 bars: rhythmic chords from the vamp return one last time to end the record emphatically.

Listen & Reflect

1. If you listen to "Oye como va" with good speakers or earbuds, you should be able to appreciate how each instrument is clearly positioned to the right, left, or center. What is the spatial distribution of instruments, and how does the stereo placement affect your experience of this rhythmically complex music?

2. Compare the total duration of the obviously composed sections of the song (the sung choruses, the instrumental unisons, etc.) to the time spent in guitar and organ solos. How does this proportion compare to other popular songs studied so far, and what conclusion might one draw from the difference?

3. Contrast and compare this record with either "El cayuco" (see LG 16.4) or Tito Puente's original recording of "Oye como va." What are the similarities and differences between Puente's style of Latin jazz and Santana's Latin rock? Which do you prefer, and why?

℘ Carlos Santana
(guitar, right, with David
Brown, bass) performs at
Woodstock in 1969.

with solos by Carlos Santana's guitar and the bluesy Hammond B3 organ of Gregg Rolie (who went on to found the band Journey).

ARENA ROCK AND THE PUNK BACKLASH

The 1960s had seen the "British Invasion" of the United States by groups like the Beatles and the Rolling Stones, English bands influenced by American blues and rock and roll and in turn influencing the next generation of American rockers with their innovations. The 1970s, in contrast, was a time of growing separation between British and American rock. The emergent trend in England in the early 1970s was **progressive rock**, typified by concept albums featuring large-scale compositions often based on New Age versions of Eastern spirituality, expressed musically by some of the same Indian-inspired devices used by John Coltrane, such as drones and static harmonies. Although British prog-rock bands such as Yes, Genesis, and Emerson, Lake, and Palmer were popular with U.S. listeners, no American bands made a significant contribution to the movement.

the rock mainstream   Instead, the United States in the 1970s saw the development of a mainstream popular music that, inspired by the psychedelic rock concerts of the 1960s, kept the focus on spectacle while gradually retiring the countercultural ideologies of the hippies. Central to this music was the corporate strategy of tying a band's touring schedule to the release of what their record company hoped to be a mammoth best-selling album. When planned and timed correctly, album sales and ticket sales could reinforce each other synergistically. For groups like Fleetwood Mac and the Eagles—or, at the more cartoonish end of the spectrum, Alice Cooper and Kiss—this strategy led to high-grossing album sales and performances before thousands of enthusiastic fans in high-capacity venues—hence the name **arena rock** to describe this segment of the market. Another name, **album-oriented rock (AOR)**, more accurately describes a late-1970s radio format that favored the longer songs—up to a complete LP side—characteristic of both progressive and arena rock bands.

Despite its commercial success, arena rock failed to win the hearts of young listeners for whom the laid-back soft rock of the Doobie Brothers could not be the soundtrack for any revolution. Those disaffected youth found a music more in tune to their oppositional stance in the discordant sounds of bands that offered a darker view of life. Back in the late 1960s the New York avant-garde art scene (centered on Andy Warhol) had produced the Velvet Underground, whose version of rock was far more pessimistic and rough-edged than that of the arena rockers. At around the same time, Detroit was the home of both the Stooges, with provocative lead singer Iggy Pop, and the MC5, whose "Kick Out the Jams" (1969) was an early harbinger of 1970s **punk**.

Punk in the United States found its first home at CBGB, a rather seedy bar in New York City's Bowery district. CBGB featured performers such as Patti Smith, Television, the Voidoids, and the Ramones. Led by Joey Ramone, the Ramones performed in 1950s-style leather jackets and blue jeans, replicating the sneering poses of early Elvis and Marlon Brando's motorcycle tough in *The Wild Ones*. The Ramones reinvented early 1960s surf rock to create music that was loud, fast, frenetic, and aggressively simpleminded. Each of the songs on their first album, *Ramones* (1976), is less than three minutes long—at a time when guitar heroes and prog-rockers were stretching songs out to fill entire sides of an LP. The group's nihilistic worldview, quirky sense of humor, and infectious blend of teenage fun and rebellion are captured in their lyrics and even titles of songs such as "Now I Wanna Sniff Some Glue" and "I Wanna Be Sedated"—the latter featuring a guitar solo consisting of steady eighth notes on a single pitch.

punk

American punk got a shot in the arm with the arrival of such British punks as the Sex Pistols, the Clash, and Siouxsie and the Banshees, who were reacting against progressive rock in much the same way their American peers were reacting against arena rock. Momentarily reuniting British and American trends, the punks placed high value on simplicity, volume, speed, and a **do-it-yourself (DIY)** attitude that prized raw, amateurish energy over technical command. Their music was assaultive and abrasive, an expression of punk's social values, which placed rebellion and anarchy above any political philosophy.

Perhaps it was inevitable that punk's ferocity would be diluted to reach a wider audience. In the late 1970s some punk acts, such as Blondie and Elvis Costello, modified their sounds and found commercial success as **New Wave** artists, joined by bands such as Devo, the B-52s, and Talking Heads. New Wave bands replaced the angry rebellion of punk with a cool irony more in tune with trends in the visual arts—indeed, Talking Heads consisted of former students from the Rhode Island School of Design. At its best, the New Wave produced songs that were arty and intellectual, like Talking Heads' "Psycho Killer" (1977), where a catchy groove contrasts strangely with lyrics that seem to represent the

Four key figures of 1970s punk and New Wave (left to right): Joan Jett; Debbie Harry of the group Blondie; David Johansen of the New York Dolls; and Joey Ramone of the Ramones.

thoughts of a serial killer, switching at the bridge from English to French, all projected in the nerdy, gulping voice of lead singer David Byrne, who updated Buddy Holly's 1950s geek-rocker persona for a new generation.

Punk launched a reformation movement in rock, seeking to return to the music's roots. Already by the late 1970s that reaffirmation of basics had borne fruit in the New Wave, and after 1980 it would give rise to hardcore punk, grunge, and alternative rock.

SINGER-SONGWRITERS: IN SEARCH OF AUTHENTICITY

If punks sought to purge rock of its venality and regain a more authentic state of anarchic rage, another group of musicians sought authenticity on a different path. In the wake of Bob Dylan's innovations in the 1960s, a generation of **singer-songwriters** carried his work forward in the 1970s by performing their own compositions, often with minimal instrumental accompaniment (a piano or guitar, for example), with lyrics that are often personal, even confessional, in subject matter and tone. Foremost among the singer-songwriters of the 1970s was Dylan himself, whose albums *Blood on the Tracks* (1973) and *Desire* (1976), in particular, contained songs that were widely received as autobiographical accounts of his divorce from his wife Sara; the closing track on *Desire*, "Sara," is hard to read any other way.

Bob Dylan

Dylan had begun in folk music and switched to rock, then found a way to combine the two in *John Wesley Harding* (1968). Singer-songwriters such as James Taylor and Carly Simon began with a folk-rock blend; Carole King and Paul Simon came to the style from a pop background, both making the transition from Brill Building tunesmiths to successful performers of their own confessional songs. And the phenomenon was not confined to the United States: Canada produced Joni Mitchell and Neil Young, and Cat Stevens and Elton John hailed from Great Britain.

Of course, the phenomenon of singers performing their own songs was not new to popular music. Especially in country music, the singer-songwriter had been a dominant figure since the days of Jimmie Rodgers. What was new in the 1970s was the emphasis on intimate self-revelation—self-revelation as an emblem of the music's authenticity, to the extent that listeners were encouraged to blur the separation between singer and song persona. For some singer-songwriters, that tone of authenticity was enhanced through musical references to country idioms, as in the pedal steel guitar that quietly sneaks into Joni Mitchell's song "California," on her 1971 album *Blue*. A more thorough country-rock blend was pioneered by the Byrds in the late 1960s and continued into the 1970s most notably by the trio of David Crosby, Stephen Stills, and Graham Nash, later expanded into a quartet with the addition of Neil Young.

Joni Mitchell

While country singers like Merle Haggard and Johnny Cash had never shied away from confession in their songs, the country musicians closest in spirit to the Dylanesque singer-songwriters were the **outlaw country** artists, based mainly in Austin, Texas. Willie Nelson's transformation from Nashville industry songwriter to confessional singer-songwriter parallels Carole King's similar trajectory from the Brill Building; Nelson's *Red-Headed Stranger* (1975) is a landmark country concept album. Waylon Jennings came to outlaw country from a rock and roll

outlaw country

Dolly Parton's traditionalist image caused many to underestimate her formidable musical skills, a reaction she countered caustically in her song "Dumb Blonde."

background; he had been the drummer in the Crickets, Buddy Holly's band, back in the 1950s. Fellow Texans Kris Kristofferson and Townes Van Zandt brought a refined literary subtlety to their outlaw country songs of alienation and loneliness.

Common to the Austin outlaws was a disdain for what they heard as the slick commercialism of mainstream country, a feeling they shared with the earlier Bakersfield musicians and that resembled in its own way the punks' contempt for progressive and arena rock. Yet successful examples of the singer-songwriter sensibility can be found right in the heart of Nashville's mainstream. Although she sang mostly songs by professional country songwriters, Loretta Lynn had risen to prominence in the 1960s with songs that linked her with a spunky country feminism, a persona she expanded upon in the 1970s with her own songs "Coal Miner's Daughter" (1970) and "The Pill" (1975), the latter a then-shocking song about birth control. Lynn shared her place as a leading female country artist of the 1970s with Tammy Wynette and Dolly Parton.

A native of eastern Tennessee, Dolly Parton moved to Nashville in her late teens and by the latter 1960s was firmly established in two niches in the Music City industry: as a songwriter who produced material for other performers, and as a performer herself, singing her own songs and those of other professional songwriters. First gaining public notice as a featured singer on Porter Wagoner's traditionalist country music television show, Parton recorded her first solo hit in 1970, a lively cover of Jimmie Rodgers's venerable classic "Muleskinner Blues." She followed that hit closely with several others, including original songs such as "Joshua," "Jolene," and "I Will Always Love You," the last also a huge hit in a 1992 cover version by R&B singer Whitney Houston.

Parton's "Coat of Many Colors" (1971; LG 19.2) blends folklike simplicity with up-to-date recording techniques to set a nostalgic tone for an autobiographical story song. The Carter-style guitar picking points to country music's past, while discreet

LG 19.2

| CD 4.1 | Listening Guide 19.2 | "Coat of Many Colors" DOLLY PARTON |

SONGWRITER: Dolly Parton
DATE: 1971
PERFORMERS: Dolly Parton, vocal; studio instrumentalists and background singers
GENRE: country
METER: duple
FORM: verse and modified chorus

WHAT TO LISTEN FOR

- use of Carter-style guitar, organ, background singers to support lyrics' narrative
- modified lyrics in each chorus to support storytelling
- pump-up in second half of song to increase energy

TIMING	SECTION	TEXT	COMMENTS
0:00	introduction		4 bars: Two fingerpicked guitars recall the sound of old Carter Family records. In bar 3, a soft electric bass and a shaker emphasizing the backbeat update the sound.
0:05	verse 1	Back through the years I go wandering once again ...	33 bars: Double the proportions of later verses; the first half will not return. The melody stays in a small range and the harmony uses only three basic chords (I, IV, and V), characteristic of many folk songs; V chord is reserved for second half of verse. Extra bar at the end breaks the symmetry (8 + 8 + 8 + 9).
0:51	verse 2	As she sewed, she told a story ...	17 bars (8 + 9): Sustained organ chords enter with references to the biblical story of Joseph and his coat. As the verse progresses, the bass becomes more active, energizing the motion toward the chorus.
1:15	chorus	My coat of many colors ...	18 bars (9 + 9): Backup singers enter on IV chord, combining with the organ to evoke the sound of a small church choir. Second half of chorus matches music of second half of verse.
1:41	transition		2 bars: Sudden jump to a new key, a whole-step higher: a pop song cliché sometimes called a **pump-up** or **truck driver modulation**.
1:43	verse 3	So with patches on my britches ...	17 bars (8 + 9): Voices and organ drop out, returning to the texture of verse 1.
2:06	verse 4	And oh I couldn't understand it ...	17 bars (8 + 9): Parton's vocal is particularly expressive, dropping at moments nearly into speech and sometimes discreetly back phrasing.

TIMING	SECTION	TEXT	COMMENTS
2:31	chorus	But they didn't understand it . . .	20 bars (9 + 11): Parton alters the first lines of the chorus lyric to deliver the moral of the story, with help from the backup singers and organ. On the last word ("me," 2:54) the tonic chord is delayed by inserting a subdominant chord. The resulting **plagal cadence** (IV–I), especially when played by organ, evokes the "Amen" cadence that ends a Protestant hymn.

Listen & Reflect

1. What musical features connect this song to earlier country songs such as "Can the Circle Be Unbroken" (LG 11.2), and which ones distinguish it as a product of the 1970s?

2. Some listeners may argue that the song is marred aesthetically by its nonstandard English, weak rhymes, and other literary imperfections; others might argue that they contribute positively to the song's air of rural simplicity and authenticity. What do you think? What are some others genres in which nonstandard English might be an asset, not a fault?

3. Compare the subject matter and musical treatment of this song and "Mama Tried" (LG 18.4). Do you find one song more convincing than the other? Why? How is your response affected by knowledge that Merle Haggard did not serve life without parole, but that Dolly Parton's story is, as far as we can determine, factually accurate (the coat she sings about is on display at Dollywood, her theme park in eastern Tennessee)?

percussion and background vocals signal the song's modernity. The deft combination of musical and lyrical elements evokes a simpler time while presenting a traditional moral lesson in the expressive language of 1970s mainstream country.

SOUL, FUNK, AND DISCO IN THE 1970s

African American popular music in the early 1970s underwent transformations similar to those in rock and country music. In all popular genres, to varying degrees, artistic and critical weight shifted from the single to the album; individual songs tended to be longer than the once-standard three minutes and to combine greater formal complexity with more stylistic variety; lyrics tended to stress political engagement, spiritual questioning, or personal confession; and concert spectacle and blockbuster album promotion formed a synergistic bond. Several black artists active in the 1960s continued to flourish as they adjusted to the new commercial and artistic climate, while new artists appeared on the scene, advancing established genres of soul and funk and creating a new genre: disco.

George Clinton onstage in the 1970s.

SOUL AND FUNK IN THE 1970S

James Brown sailed through the early 1970s with a string of hits, including irresistible dance tracks like "Super Bad" and "Get Up (I Feel Like Being a) Sex Machine" (both 1970) that consolidated his title as the Godfather of Soul. Brown also continued to release politically engaged records dealing with issues such as black pride and drug abuse, with "King Heroin" (1972) and "Funky President (People It's Bad)" (1974) adding to the legacy of 1968's "Say It Loud, I'm Black and Proud," in which Brown's vocal is half-sung, half-spoken in a way that recalls Pentecostal preaching and anticipates rap.

Brown's electrifying stage act was a model for rising soul and funk performers such as the Jackson Five and George Clinton. Clinton, a savvy showman and entrepreneur, divided his musical activities between two groups, Parliament and Funkadelic; the former was thought to be the more commercial band and the latter the more experimental, but in fact their stylistic overlap outweighs their differences. Building rich polyrhythmic textures over the supple bass playing of Bootsy Collins, a former member of James Brown's outfit, Clinton's bands, like Sly and the Family Stone before them, brought psychedelic elements from Jimi Hendrix and other rock performers into funk. Clinton's elaborate stage presentations, featuring outlandish costumes, lighting effects, and a glittering spaceship, created a cartoonish science fiction atmosphere that borrowed from the theatrical stage shows of white rock bands like Pink Floyd and Alice Cooper.

George Clinton

Stevie Wonder

Another idea that black artists borrowed from rock was the concept album. Perhaps the first significant soul concept album was Marvin Gaye's *What's Going On* (1971). Following up on its success was the work of Stevie Wonder, who had begun his career at Motown as a thirteen-year-old wunderkind in 1963. As a mature artist in the 1970s, Wonder released such concept albums as *Talking Book* (1972), *Innervisions* (1973), and *Songs in the Key of Life* (1976). George Clinton's Parliament contributed science fiction–themed concept albums such as *The Clones of Dr. Funkenstein* (1976) and *Funkentelechy vs. the Placebo Syndrome* (1977).

Philadelphia soul

Finally, a significant strain of 1970s popular music was **Philadelphia soul**, linked to the Philadelphia International record label and its stable of songwriters, producers, studio musicians, and singers. Much like Motown in the 1960s, Philadelphia soul emphasized smooth, polished performances and danceable rhythms. A song such as the O'Jays' "Love Train" (1973) exemplifies the Philly sound: soaring strings, churning horns, bright guitars, and voices that sometimes are merely one element in a complex texture, all carefully mixed as layers over a tight, energetic rhythm section. With its emphasis on hit records as a producer's art, Philadelphia soul is a significant predecessor of late-1970s disco.

BLAXPLOITATION

A film genre of the 1970s inspired the creation of notable funk-based cinematic scores. That genre, dubbed "**blaxploitation**," retailed images of urban ghetto life as a backdrop for stories focused on crime and punishment with predominantly black casts. One of the films that began the trend, *Sweet Sweetback's Baadasssss Song* (1971), featured a soundtrack by the Chicago-based funk band Earth, Wind, and Fire. Later the same year, *Shaft* became the first high-grossing blaxploitation movie, its success due in part to an Academy Award–winning funk soundtrack by Isaac Hayes, a jazz-influenced former songwriter and session player for the Stax studios in Memphis.

Like *Shaft*, the blaxploitation film *Super Fly* (1972) is remembered today primarily for its funk score, this one by the veteran soul musician Curtis Mayfield. Both of the two hit singles from the movie's soundtrack album combine the political and the personal. "Freddie's Dead" adds antidrug lyrics to the instrumental music for the opening credits, tying them to a minor character in the film. "Superfly" (LG 19.3) describes the title character, a cocaine dealer who follows his own ambiguous morality in an urban setting where the police are more corrupt than the criminals. Like all 1970s funk, "Superfly" emphasizes the **groove**, the use of dance-rhythm ostinatos to establish a sustained mood. (In the context of funk, *groove* is an elusive quality analogous to the term *swing* in jazz: whatever it is, to paraphrase the famous Duke Ellington maxim, the music don't mean a thing if it ain't got it.) In "Superfly," compound AABA form is extended with repeating vamps, which could be expanded even further in live performance so that the song filled many more than the four minutes of this hit single.

LG 19.3

DISCO

The second half of the decade was the era of **disco**, a funk-derived dance music associated with **discotheques**, night spots featuring recorded dance music presided over by disc jockeys, or **DJs**. Originating in New York City's gay scene in the early 1970s, disco emerged nationally with such hits as "Love's Theme" (1974), by Barry White's Love Unlimited Orchestra, and "That's the Way I Like It" (1975), by KC and the Sunshine Band, songs popular with many fans who were unaware of the music's original milieu. Disco was rebranded as heterosexual with the success of 1977's *Saturday Night Fever*, a film starring John Travolta and featuring songs by the Bee Gees, including the hit "Stayin' Alive." But the homosexual subtext never disappeared, as evidenced by the Village People, whose outrageous exaggerations of gay stereotypes fueled such unsubtle songs as "Macho Man" and "YMCA" (both 1978).

Disco was a meticulously crafted studio product, using the resources of recording technology to build up complex polyrhythmic textures, much like funk. Often it was overlaid with sweet strings, as was contemporary soul music, and emphasized Latin dance rhythms and percussion, which it shared with salsa, as Latin dance music generally came to be called in the 1970s. Disco tends to be much more straightforward rhythmically than either funk or salsa, however, with a heavy emphasis on all four beats per bar. A pounding bass drum on every beat—sometimes called **four on the floor**—is a characteristic disco sound. Although tempos in disco vary widely, the biggest hit songs tend to fall within a narrow range of medium tempos. The success of novelty songs like "Disco Duck" (1976) contributed to an impression of vapidity in disco lyrics; in fact, although political topics are rare, a number of songs

In a white polyester suit, John Travolta, the star of *Saturday Night Fever* (seen here with costar Karen Lynn Gorney), epitomized a new model of masculinity in the 1970s.

| CD 4.2 | Listening Guide 19.3 | "Superfly" CURTIS MAYFIELD |

SONGWRITER: Curtis Mayfield

GENRE: funk

DATE: 1972

PERFORMERS: Curtis Mayfield, vocal; studio instrumentalists (guitars, bass, drums, Latin percussions, strings, horns)

METER: duple

FORM: compound AABA

WHAT TO LISTEN FOR

- polyrhythmic texture
- use of extended vamps to emphasize groove
- social commentary in lyrics

TIMING	SECTION		TEXT	COMMENTS
0:00	vamp 1			4 bars: Bass and Latin percussion establish the song's groove.
0:08				4 bars: Hi-hat cymbal, then snare drum, add to the polyrhythmic texture.
0:16				4 bars: Horns, answered by processed guitar, introduce a figure that resembles the riff that will accompany the chorus.
0:24	A	verse 1	Darkest of night With the moon shining bright . . .	8 bars: Horns drop out behind the vocal.
0:40		chorus	Oooh, Superfly . . .	8 bars: Horns reenter.
0:56	A	verse 2	Hard to understand What a hell of a man . . .	8 bars: As before.
1:12		chorus	Oooh, Superfly . . .	8 bars: As before.
1:28	B	bridge	The game he plays he plays for keeps . . .	12 bars: A large-scale polymeter: over 2 bars of steady duple meter in the bass (8 beats, 4 + 4), melody and harmony suggest 2 bars of triple meter and a bar of duple (3 + 3 + 2 beats).
1:52	vamp 2		Tryin' to get over . . .	8 bars: At the last line of lyrics, the bridge switches to a new vamp, which will return at the end of the song.
2:08	vamp 1		Oooh, Superfly . . .	8 bars: What at first sounds like a return of the chorus turns out instead to be a return to the opening vamp.
2:24	A	verse 3	The aim of his role Was to move a lot of blow . . .	8 bars: As before.

🎧 **CD 4.2**	**Listening Guide 19.3**		**"Superfly"** CURTIS MAYFIELD

TIMING	SECTION	TEXT	COMMENTS
2:40	chorus	Oooh, Superfly...	8 bars: As before.
2:56	vamp 1	Superfly...	8 bars: Mayfield chants the title word on the downbeat of every other bar.
3:12	vamp 2	Tryin' to get over...	17 bars: A return of the vamp that closed the bridge.

Listen & Reflect

1. "Superfly" juxtaposes sections with a high level of verbal content (verses), a lower level of verbal content (choruses), and little or no verbal content (vamps). Does that musical device draw your attention toward the words or away from them? Why?

engage social issues either directly, as in Donna Summer's "Bad Girls" (1979), about prostitution, or obliquely, as in Chic's "Good Times" (1979), which places hedonism against an implicit backdrop of late-1970s economic recession.

Hit disco songs were released as standard 45-rpm singles, running about three to four minutes in length. In addition, a new format was created, at first as promotional copies for DJs and later as a commercial product for the general public: the **12-inch single**. The size of an LP, the 12-inch single could hold a longer version of the song, a **dance mix** (or "**club mix**"), which extended the number's length up to eight minutes or more, most notably through long instrumental introductions and interludes. Dance mixes gave the record producer a larger canvas on which to create formal structures based on texture and timbre. With their wide grooves, 12-inch singles allowed DJs to locate segments of a song visually, encouraging the creative juxtaposition of portions of songs, a crucial aspect of hip-hop (see chapter 20).

the dance mix

A parallel could be drawn between disco's popularity with white audiences in the mid-1970s and the rise of rock and roll in the mid-1950s. In both cases, the previously mainstream popular music grew into a listener's music, while the new style offered a more rhythmic music that appealed to people who wanted to dance. Swing, preeminently music for dancing, had by the 1950s morphed into the mainstream pop of Frank Sinatra and Patti Page—fine for listening but, as dance music, rather pallid in comparison to rock and roll. The irony of disco in the 1970s, then, is that the less danceable music it supplanted was rock itself, which, as progressive rock and arena rock, had grown more interesting for listeners but harder to dance to. In that light, disco can be viewed as a part of the reformation movement that also gave rise to punk.

At the time, though, any such comparison would have been hotly contested. Many rock fans—both mainstream and punk—detested disco, as evidenced by the Disco Demolition Night, a promotional event at a Chicago White Sox baseball game in 1979 in which a local radio DJ blew up a crate of disco records in the outfield while near-rioting fans threw LPs as if they were Frisbees. The controversy around disco shows, once again, that genre distinctions often had more to do with the listeners' group affiliations than with the music itself.

JAZZ-ROCK FUSION

With the development of rock virtuosity in the late 1960s, rock albums by groups such as Cream and the Jimi Hendrix Experience came to share features with jazz albums: namely, an emphasis on tracks longer than the typical three to four minutes, with much of that space devoted to lengthy solos. Some rock musicians looked to jazz instrumentalists such as John Coltrane as models who brought a high level of artistry to improvised performance. As early as 1967 the rock band Blood, Sweat, and Tears recorded a cover version of Billie Holiday's classic "God Bless the Child" in an eclectic arrangement that blended rock, jazz, and Latin rhythms.

Miles Davis

At the same time, some jazz artists recognized in rock a kindred aesthetic. In a little more than a decade, rock had evolved from a brash, simplistic alternative to jazz into a style of musical expression that had the potential to match jazz's serious artistic intent. A pioneer in combining elements of both styles into a **jazz-rock fusion**, or simply **fusion**, was trumpeter Miles Davis, who had remained in the forefront of jazz developments since he arrived on the modern jazz scene in the 1940s. His 1968 album *Filles de Kilimanjaro* included an original tune based in part on a Jimi Hendrix composition, and the next year's *In a Silent Way* went even further in the direction of fusion by including the sounds of electric keyboards and distorted, rock-style electric guitar. But Davis's big breakthrough came with 1970's *Bitches Brew*, one of the era's best-selling jazz albums, perhaps because it was often the only jazz record in a rock fan's collection.

Davis's foray into fusion brought a degree of commercial success rare among jazz artists circa 1970, the year Davis's band performed before 600,000 people at the Isle of Wight rock festival—a crowd unthinkable for most jazz acts, which typically played in nightclubs or small concert venues. Some musicians and critics in the jazz community accused Davis of selling out, but the music itself argues otherwise. Apart from the use of electric instruments, Davis's fusion resembles conventional rock less than it does the free jazz of such avant-garde musicians as Ornette Coleman and Cecil Taylor, among the least commercial jazz musicians of the previous decade. Free jazz was one movement within jazz in which

In their own words "

Guitarist Larry Coryell on Rock's Appeal to Late-1960s Jazz Musicians

Everybody was dropping acid and the prevailing attitude was "Let's do something different." We were saying, "We love [jazz guitarist] Wes [Montgomery], but we also love Bob Dylan. We love Coltrane but we also love the Beatles. We love Miles but we also love the Rolling Stones. "

Davis did not participate; his idiosyncratic approach to jazz-rock fusion was his way of entering avant-garde territory on his own terms.

Part of Davis's genius as a fusion artist was his ability to enlist sympathetic musicians who could bridge jazz and rock styles with dexterity and imagination. Several musicians associated with Davis in the late 1960s and 1970s went on to become successful solo acts or formed their own fusion groups. Keyboardist Herbie Hancock formed the Headhunters, keyboardist Chick Corea formed Return to Forever, saxophonist Wayne Shorter and Austrian keyboardist Joe Zawinul formed Weather Report, and pianist Keith Jarrett became one of the most important soloists of the decade.

Another alumnus of Davis's fusion projects was John McLaughlin, a guitarist from Yorkshire who, like many other English musicians of his generation, grew fascinated at a formative age with the records of Muddy Waters and other American bluesmen. After gaining a reputation as a rock guitarist on the British scene, he moved to New York in 1969, where he caught the attention of Miles Davis, who hired him to play on *In a Silent Way* and *Bitches Brew*. Drawn to the classical music and religious traditions of India, McLaughlin formed his own group in 1970 to explore the fusion of jazz, rock, and Indian music. The Mahavishnu Orchestra's first two albums were commercial successes, with the second, *Birds of Fire* (1973), climbing to number 15 on the pop album charts.

The music of the Mahavishnu Orchestra embodies several style features of 1970s jazz-rock fusion. While the harmony tends toward simplicity, other elements gain in importance, especially timbre, rhythm, and melody. The sound emphasizes loud volume, amplified instruments, and rock-influenced drumming. The beat is subdivided into even notes, as in rock, instead of the swinging beat of earlier jazz styles. Meters are often irregular, with bars of five or seven beats supplementing traditional duple and triple meters. Reflecting McLaughlin's interest in Indian classical music, the composed melodies and improvised solos often use unusual scales derived from Indian *ragas*, while also including the pentatonic scales and blue notes common to jazz and rock. Mastering those asymmetrical meters and odd scales requires a high level of musicianship, which also can be heard in virtuoso solo and ensemble playing.

fusion style traits

Birds of Fire (LG 19.4), the opening track from Mahavishnu's second album, displays all these traits. The amplified instruments and conspicuous drumming immerse the listener in a rock-style ambiance. McLaughlin builds his composition on an exotic-sounding scale, sometimes called the "super locrian mode," that resembles certain Indian *ragas*. Throughout the piece that scale is heard at two pitch levels a whole step apart, alternating in one-bar units. The meter, which resembles the *talas* that govern rhythm in Indian music, seems better suited for listening than for dancing: each bar has nine beats, grouped as four plus five. The players demonstrate their virtuosity in both dazzling improvisations and disciplined ensemble performance, especially in McLaughlin's and violinist Jerry Goodman's unison statements of the complicated head. With *Birds of Fire*, the Mahavishnu Orchestra combines the complexity of modern jazz and classical Indian music with the electronically fueled overdrive and mystical overtones of 1970s rock.

☙ Guitarist John McLaughlin and violinist Jerry Goodman of the Mahavishnu Orchestra.

CD 4.3   Listening Guide 19.4

Birds of Fire
MAHAVISHNU ORCHESTRA

COMPOSER: John McLaughlin

DATE: 1973

PERFORMERS: John McLaughlin, guitar; Jerry Goodman, violin; Jan Hammer, keyboards; Rick Laird, bass; Billy Cobham, drums

GENRE: jazz-rock fusion

METER: nine beats per bar, divided 4 + 5

FORM: head (*aaa'b*) alternating with solos

WHAT TO LISTEN FOR

- emphasis on electronic and electrically amplified sounds
- complex rhythm and structure that encourage close listening
- rock-style guitar distortion
- simple alternation of two scales a whole step apart, each lasting one bar

TIMING	SECTION		COMMENTS
0:00	introduction		Widely spaced cymbal crashes are electronically altered to sound like gongs.
0:17			2-bar riff is stated twice in electric guitar, then twice again by guitar and synthesizer in unison.
0:41			A new 2-bar riff, in violin and bass, is added over guitar and synthesizer riff; drums join in to complete the texture.
1:04	head (partial statement)	*a*	Guitar and violin state 4-bar melody in unison; bars 1 and 3 employ pentatonic scales and blues notes, while bars 2 and 4 are sustained notes.
1:15		*a*	4-bar melody repeats.
1:26	guitar solo		Solo begins in middle register then climbs slowly, with increasing reverb, for 8 bars.
1:48			Violin and bass riff enters quietly, then grows in volume over 12 bars as guitar solo becomes more frenetic.
2:18	head	*a*	Violin joins guitar for unison statement of 4-bar melody.
2:28		*a*	Melody repeats.
2:39		*a'*	Third statement of melody varies: the last bar is an upward flurry of rapid notes.
2:48		*b*	New melody rises slowly, in durations that create a triple polymeter over the accompaniment.
3:00	synthesizer solo		Solo begins softly and is quickly submerged under violin and bass riff.
3:11			Synthesizer re-enters loudly, now with distorted timbre and pitch bending that resemble electric guitar more than traditional keyboards. Like the guitar solo, this one also begins in middle register and slowly climbs upward, as riff fades into background.
3:51			As solo increases in intensity, riff returns to foreground as preparation for last statement of head.

	CD 4.3	Listening Guide 19.4	*Birds of Fire* MAHAVISHNU ORCHESTRA

TIMING	SECTION	COMMENTS
4:10	head	Full statement of head, *aaa'b*, as at 2:18, with small melodic variants.
4:52	coda	Riff returns with rising synthesizer arpeggios; fadeout.

Listen & Reflect

1. The same year John McLaughlin recorded this piece, he also collaborated with Carlos Santana on a tribute album to John Coltrane. Compare *Birds of Fire* with Coltrane's "My Favorite Things" (see LG 18.1) and with Santana's "Oye como va" (see LG 19.1). What are the similarities and differences?

MUSICAL THEATER IN THE 1970s

Despite the success of *West Side Story* in the 1950s, the Broadway musical failed to follow up on Leonard Bernstein's assertion that therein lay the road to a truly American operatic form. The most successful shows of the 1960s and 1970s either carried on the tradition of the Rodgers and Hammerstein–style integrated musical, as in Jerry Bock's *Fiddler on the Roof* (1964), or combined the old-fashioned song-and-dance manner of the pre-*Oklahoma!* musical with a Brechtian self-consciousness and ironic self-parody, as in John Kander and Fred Ebb's *Cabaret* (1966) and *Chicago* (1975).

Operatic aspirations, meanwhile, arose not on Broadway but in British rock in the form of the **rock opera**. Despite the name, rock operas like the Who's *Tommy* (1969) and David Bowie's *The Rise and Fall of Ziggy Stardust and the Spiders from Mars* (1972) originated not as theatrical productions but as concept albums, "operatic" only in the sense that a narrative unfolds over several musical numbers with all the words sung, not spoken. The idea of the rock opera was quickly transferred to Broadway, however, in the form of the British composer Andrew Lloyd Webber's *Jesus Christ Superstar* (1971). The same year saw the Broadway opening of American composer Stephen Schwartz's *Godspell*, like *Superstar* based on the New Testament (an unlikely source for a Broadway show), but more akin to the traditional musical, with spoken dialogue and discrete musical numbers, some of which are in a rock style.

rock opera

But the rock idiom proved uncongenial to the Broadway manner of storytelling, and few successful 1970s musicals used the language of rock. African American popular styles fared slightly better thanks to Charlie Smalls's *The Wiz* (1975), an all-black musical version of *The Wizard of Oz* that incorporated soul and gospel styles. Although the Broadway stage production was a success, the 1977 film version, featuring Motown stars Diana Ross and Michael Jackson, was a critical and commercial flop. Instead of embracing new popular styles, then, some of the most significant musical theater of the 1970s developed along a path independent of rock and soul.

Stephen Sondheim

Of the composers of Broadway shows in this last category, the most important and influential is Stephen Sondheim. A New Yorker by birth, Sondheim as a youth found a surrogate father in Oscar Hammerstein II, who mentored him in lyric writing through his teen years. Sondheim's graduate studies in composition with Milton Babbitt focused not on his teacher's recondite serialism but on the techniques of the classic Broadway songwriters they both loved. Between Hammerstein and Babbitt, Sondheim had as thorough and expert a training for the creation of musical theater as one could hope for.

Sondheim's first big break came as lyricist for Bernstein's *West Side Story*; shortly afterward he wrote the lyrics for Jule Styne's successful *Gypsy*. In 1962 he achieved his first Broadway hit as both composer and lyricist with *A Funny Thing Happened on the Way to the Forum*, a bawdy farce set in ancient Rome to give a new twist to an old-fashioned form. But his artistic breakthrough occurred in the early 1970s, with a series of musicals created with the producer and director Hal Prince. *Company* (1970) abandoned traditional linear storytelling, relying instead on a series of vignettes that developed the main character, a no-longer-young bachelor whose married friends advise him to marry and settle down, though their actions suggest he had better do the opposite. *Follies* (1971) used a similar nonlinear format to illuminate the lives of two showbiz couples whose days in the spotlight are long past. In these shows Sondheim perfected his technique of writing songs for theater: while in the traditional integrated musical, songs support the dialogue's exposition, here the songs themselves are the principal means of revealing plot and character.

A Little Night Music

With *A Little Night Music* (1973), based on Ingmar Bergman's 1955 Swedish film comedy *Smiles of a Summer Night*, Sondheim and Prince, with librettist Hugh Wheeler, reverted to more traditional storytelling, though not to the traditional

In this scene from Opera Australia's 2009 production of Stephen Sondheim's 1973 musical *A Little Night Music*, Frederik (Robert Grubb) describes his wife for a less-than-enthralled Désirée (Sigrid Thornton).

format of the integrated musical. Instead, Sondheim's ability to develop character and plot through music and lyrics gives the show a near-operatic quality, despite the use of spoken dialogue. In addition to solo numbers, the show includes ensembles ranging from duets to quintets, including an intricate trio in which three characters sing three quite different songs, titled respectively "Now," "Soon," and "Later," in sequence and then simultaneously. Though Sondheim's music is altogether different in style from Bernstein's *West Side Story, A Little Night Music* comes close to being what Bernstein hoped for: a Broadway equivalent to European opera.

LG 19.5

The act 1 duet "You Must Meet My Wife" (LG 19.5) shows Sondheim's ability to imbue Broadway conventions—here, the standard *aaba* song form—with new dramatic capabilities. Dispensing with a verse, the song launches directly into the chorus, in which the middle-aged Frederik describes his new, much younger bride to his old flame, Désirée. The *aaba* musical structure is then repeated with new lyrics, now in the form of a duet, in which Frederik's praises are undercut by Désirée's acid retorts. A final half chorus (*ba*) brings the conflict to a head when Frederik reveals that his marriage to Anne has not been consummated, provoking Désirée's outraged response. Although the music of the chorus is stated two and a half times with only minor variations, the wide-ranging modulations built into the chorus guarantee a sense of constant motion that supports the continually changing lyrics, which illuminate the characters and represent the change in their relationship during the course of the song. At the same time, Sondheim sustains a comedic mood through his use of far-reaching rhymes, involving such unlikely words and phrases as "mustache" and "cigar butt."

Rather than responding to current popular trends in rock, soul, or funk, Stephen Sondheim found new ways to reinvigorate Broadway conventions, creating an intensely personal style based on the classic show tune but with a new level of artistic craft. Perhaps the apex of Sondheim's work is *Sweeney Todd: The Demon Barber of Fleet Street* (1979), a darkly tragic work that has entered the repertory of several opera companies. But even in the relatively sunny *Into the Woods* (1987), a potpourri of traditional fairy tales, the deft combination of music and lyrics can at moments plumb depths of emotion that make Sondheim's shows, presented as popular theater, a rich portrayal of contemporary experience.

CLASSICAL MUSIC IN THE 1970s

Minimalism, which had arisen in the 1960s in the work of Terry Riley, Steve Reich, and other musicians, had always reflected its creators' experience or interest in jazz, rock, and non-Western musical styles. Now, in the 1970s, minimalism developed into the one genre of new classical music composition that attracted a sizable audience (along with performance art, discussed in chapter 20). With its emphasis on steady pulse, simple tonality, and repetition, minimalism was a type of art music that was intelligible not only to fans of older classical styles but also to listeners more accustomed to the repetitive music of James Brown and other funk artists. Of the minimalists active in the 1970s, none was more accessible to both classical and popular audiences than Philip Glass. Meanwhile, the experimentalist strain in American music remained alive in the work of microtonalist composers.

	CD 4.4	Listening Guide 19.5	"You Must Meet My Wife," from *A Little Night Music* STEPHEN SONDHEIM

DATE: 1973

PERFORMERS: Len Cariou (Fredrik) and Glynis Johns (Désirée)

GENRE: Broadway musical duet

METER: triple

FORM: *aaba* chorus, with one full repeat and one half chorus

WHAT TO LISTEN FOR

- waltz rhythm
- use of lyrics and music to delineate characters
- humorous use of rhyme

TIMING	SECTION		TEXT	COMMENTS
0:00	introduction			Strings and woodwinds establish gentle waltz.
0:06	chorus 1 (64 bars)	*a*	(*Frederik*) She lightens my sadness ...	The melody alternates the raised fourth scale degree (She <u>light</u>ens) with its lowered, typical form (my <u>sad</u>ness). The first *a* section melody ends inconclusively, on the fifth scale degree.
0:30		*a*	She bubbles with pleasure ...	The *a* section repeats a half-step higher, this time concluding firmly on the new tonic.
0:54		*b*	One thousand whims ...	The bridge is harmonically unstable, modulating rapidly in a downward chromatic progression.
1:17		*a*	So sunlike so winning ...	The final *a* section is now stated a whole-step higher than its first appearance.
1:43	interlude (4 bars)		(*Désirée speaks*)	Interlude in the opening key, as underscoring.
1:48	chorus 2 (64 bars)	*a*	(*Frederik and Désirée in alternation*) She sparkles ...	The two characters divide the melody in shifting patterns.
2:07		*a*	She flutters ...	Although Sondheim's score indicates that a few of Désirée's words should be spoken, not sung, Glynis Johns takes liberties and speaks many of her passages.
2:27		*b*	(*Frederik*) She loves my voice ...	Bridge is melodically expansive; Désirée breaks in near the end.
2:46		*a*	(*Frederik and Désirée in alternation*) She dotes on ...	Again the two characters divide the melody.
3:06	half chorus (41 bars)	*b*	(*Frederik*) A sea of whims ...	Désirée breaks in strongly after the startling revelation of Anne's virginity.
3:25		*a*	(*Frederik and Désirée in alternation*) She's monstrous ...	Now Désirée leads the exchange of voices. Her rising anger motivates a change in the music, and in the 16th bar the *a* section ends on a dissonant diminished chord.

🎧 CD 4.4	Listening Guide 19.5	"You Must Meet My Wife," from *A Little Night Music* STEPHEN SONDHEIM

TIMING	SECTION	TEXT	COMMENTS
3:45		(*Désirée*) I must meet your wife . .	In a 9-bar extension, the tempo slows and the dynamic drops to *piano* as Désirée's anger gives way to resignation.

NOTE Original Broadway cast recording.

Listen & Reflect

1. What features of this recording would support a description of the performers as "singing actors" rather than "acting singers"? What is gained in this style of performance, and what is lost?

PHILIP GLASS AND *EINSTEIN ON THE BEACH*

The new techniques and musical languages that proliferated in the twentieth century presented difficult challenges for performance, and composers have long complained that standard ensembles such as symphony orchestras are ill-equipped to do justice to new music. At the end of the 1960s Steve Reich and Philip Glass, along with several other musicians, took the unusual step of forming an ensemble to perform their own works in a way that ensures both adequate rehearsal and sympathetic interpreters ready to pour heart and soul into the music and its performance.

🖎 A scene from a 2012 performance of Philip Glass's 1976 opera *Einstein on the Beach*.

In 1971 Reich and Glass split up to form separate ensembles. Containing between five and eight players, each of these groups sounded more like an orchestra than like chamber music, for players doubled each other's lines, and, especially in Glass's works, the music was amplified by the use of synthesizers and microphones. The music's tonal simplicity, rhythmic interest, and, in Glass's case, rock-like timbres proved keys to the public appeal of minimalism.

the Philip Glass Ensemble

Glass has described the Philip Glass Ensemble as the cornerstone of his career. He supported the ensemble by working as a cab driver, plumber, and furniture mover rather than teaching, as a more conventionally minded classical composer might have done. From the first concert on, he paid his players, which kept the ensemble together, while guaranteeing concerts of high quality. Glass also bet on his music's appeal by refusing to let anyone else perform it. "I felt that if I had a monopoly on the music, that as the music became known there would be more work for the ensemble"—again, an attitude more characteristic of a jazz or rock bandleader than a classical composer. He committed the group to twenty concerts a year after discovering that this would qualify his players for unemployment insurance. Glass worked day jobs until 1978, when grants and commissions finally allowed him to concentrate more fully on composition.

Comfortable with the idea of making art that makes money, Glass has also argued that he and his colleagues restored something valuable to American musical life by returning to "the idea that the composer *is* the performer." He has also expressed a long-standing desire to transcend the gulf separating classical and popular spheres. "I personally know that I didn't want to spend my life writing music for a handful of people. . . . I wanted to play for thousands of people; I was always interested in a larger audience."

Einstein on the Beach

In November 1976 *Einstein on the Beach*, a "portrait opera" and collaboration between Glass and theater director Robert Wilson, was staged in New York. Wilson's concept was to wean theater away from narrative, reorienting it more toward visual imagery and spectacle. As a result, the opera offers neither a plot nor any singing characters. Singing is prominent in the work, but the soprano soloist and the chorus sing only numbers and solfège syllables. According to Glass, people who attended performances could be counted on to bring their own story with them.

Glass's opera has turned out to be historically significant. For one thing, while opera has long enjoyed a prominent place in American musical life, few American-composed operas have caused much excitement. *Einstein* was different. The Wilson-Glass collaboration introduced a brand of theatricality that, while reflecting a contemporary spirit, was also musically accessible. At the same time, the idea of a new American opera drew audiences, sparked debate, and made the opera house a center for artistic ferment.

MICROTONALITY

In addition to minimalism, a quite different kind of musical experimentalism reached fruition in the 1970s. At least as far back as Charles Ives, maverick musicians have questioned Western music's standard division of the octave

equal temperament

into twelve equidistant half steps, the **equal temperament** that emerged in eighteenth-century Europe as the approved system of tuning pianos and organs. An experimentalist minority has long explored the possibilities of **microtonality**, narrowly defined as the use of intervals smaller than a half step, and more broadly, as using any pitches not found on an equal-tempered piano. There are several broad categories of microtonal writing. Some composers simply subdivide the equal tempered system to create a system with quarter steps, sixth steps, and so on. Others return to the simple numeric ratios that create basic musical intervals like the fifth and the third, in some form of **just intonation**, the tuning of frequencies as they appear in the overtone series, rather than in the approximations required by equal temperament. Some composers have used still other means to compute pitches numerically. Some adopt or modify musical systems of non-Western cultures. And many composers simply "bend" pitches, as is done in the blues.

just intonation

Ives, along with other early twentieth-century modernists, experimented with doubling the number of pitches per octave by splitting each half step into two **quartertones**. Ives did this by writing music for two pianos tuned in equal temperament but with one instrument pitched a quartertone higher than the other. The resulting music at first sounds simply out of tune but can begin to reveal a beauty of its own.

The Californian Lou Harrison (1914–2003) took his inspiration from Indonesian and other non-Western musics with tuning systems based on ideas distinct from those of equal temperament, sometimes writing for non-Western instruments such as the pitched percussion instruments of the **gamelan**, an Indonesian ensemble, as well as for conventional Western instruments either retuned or requiring the performers to learn how to produce the slightly different intervals his music required. His *Concerto in Slendro* (1961) calls for piano, harp, and percussion tuned in a pentatonic scale in just intonation, while the violin soloist must learn to locate those pitches on the instrument's fingerboard. (*Slendro* is an Indonesian term for such a scale, though American listeners are likely to associate Harrison's concerto with the sound of Chinese classical music, which uses a similar scale.)

Lou Harrison

The American composer who explored microtonality most thoroughly was Harry Partch (1901–1974), the son of former missionaries in China who raised him in various parts of the American Southwest. Partch listed Chinese, Mexican, and Yaqui Indian music among his early influences. A pianist trained in the Western classical traditions, he was dissatisfied with the piano's inability to reproduce the intervals he heard in the music he loved. Extensive reading in acoustics and music history acquainted him with the long history of Western tuning systems, and he became convinced that equal temperament constituted a wrong turn in the development of music in the West. During the Great Depression of the 1930s he began to build his own musical instruments and refine a system of just intonation that divided the octave into forty-three discrete pitches. For part of that time he lived as a hobo, riding freight trains and working as a transient laborer.

Harry Partch

In the 1940s Partch created a variety of string and percussion instruments, trained other musicians in how to play them, and began to compose ambitious works for large ensembles. His 1949 book *Genesis of a Music* sets forth his tuning system and the philosophy behind it, as well as describing his musical instruments and some of his compositions. His last major composition, *Delusion of the Fury* (1966), is a grand theatrical work combining drama, dance, singing, and the spectacular sound and visual appearance of his orchestra.

Of the younger musicians who worked with Harry Partch, the one who has gone furthest to create his own microtonal music is Ben Johnston. Born in Georgia in 1926, Johnston became intrigued by acoustics as a youth. In 1949 he encountered Partch's just-published *Genesis of a Music*, and a year later he was in

Ben Johnston

California assisting Partch as a carpenter and musician. On the faculty of the University of Illinois from 1951 to 1986, Johnston began to compose microtonal music only in 1960, beginning with works for specially tuned piano, including a *Sonata for Microtonal Piano* (1964) that derives some of its pitch material from classic popular songs such as "What Is This Thing Called Love?" A *Suite for Microtonal Piano* (1978) includes a movement titled "Blues." Other works require wind and string players to play with highly refined intonation; to indicate subtleties of pitch, Johnston expands the traditional sharp and flat signs (raising and lowering a pitch by a half step respectively) to a total of ten signs, indicating relative degrees of raising and lowering a written pitch.

LG 19.6   Johnston's String Quartet no. 4 (LG 19.6) is a set of **variations** on the folk hymn tune NEW BRITAIN, better known as "Amazing Grace" (see chapter 3). The four string players begin with two simple statements of the melody in **Pythagorean tuning**, a system favoring perfectly tuned fourths and fifths (according to the overtone series) over thirds and sixths; the sonority, open and rather stark, is distinctly different from equal temperament, where no intervals are favored, so that all intervals are slightly out of tune relative to the natural overtones. Attributed to the ancient Greek mathematician Pythagoras, Pythagorean tuning was widely used through the Middle Ages in Europe, and is also the basis for classical Chinese scales.

The following variations add more pitches, organized in scales of various tunings. Moreover, the rhythmic relationships mirror the pitch relationships. For instance, the frequency ratio of the Pythagorean fifth is 3:2, and in the first variation the cello, using double and triple stops, plays two simultaneous lines, one moving at the rate of three notes to every two notes in the other. The score's highly precise notation allows Johnston to control minute fluctuations in tempo and even construct passages in which the four instrumentalists play in different but coordinated tempos, a technique of **metric modulation** pioneered by Elliott Carter.

The piece's melodic ideas also reflect changes in the tuning system from variation to variation. The sixth variation uses "undertones," the reciprocals of the overtone series; in other words, instead of beginning with a low note and building pitches above it in the ratios of the overtone series, Johnston begins with a high note and builds pitches below it in a mirror inversion of the overtone series. In a melodic analogy, "Amazing Grace" is heard in melodic inversion; that is, the rise and fall of the tune is inverted, or played "upside down."

Microtonal music continues to attract musicians eager to look beyond the twelve pitches of the piano keyboard. Among other benefits, it has opened up Western classical music to the tuning systems of other cultures, ranging from the blues (since blue notes can be thought of as microtonal adjustments to the equal-tempered scale) to the traditional musics of Asia and Africa.

QUESTIONS FOR DISCUSSION AND REVIEW

1. · How do developments in rock in the early 1970s resemble developments in modern jazz in the 1940s and 1950s, and how do they differ?

2. What are the stylistic features of punk rock, and how do they distinguish punk from other 1970s trends? What makes punk a "reformation" movement in rock history?

3. What are some similarities and differences between funk and disco?

DATE: 1973

PERFORMERS: Kepler Quartet

GENRE: microtonal music

METER: changing

FORM: theme and variations

WHAT TO LISTEN FOR

- "Amazing Grace" melody in all variations, more recognizable in some than in others
- different resonance of different tuning systems used
- complex cross-rhythms, multiple simultaneous tempos, and metric modulation

TIMING	SECTION	COMMENTS
0:00	theme first statement	Two statements of the "Amazing Grace" melody in Pythagorean tuning, using only the notes of the pentatonic scale (fourths and fifths are pure, major thirds are quite wide—listen to the interval between the second and third notes of the tune). The first statement is played by the upper three instruments without vibrato, sounding medieval.
0:42	second statement	First violin plays an octave higher; cello adds depth; the setting is slightly florid, more like folk fiddling, and light vibrato adds warmth.
1:22	variation 1	Still using only the pentatonic scale, rhythmic complications are introduced: 2-against-3 cross-rhythms at various rates of speed (3:2 is the **frequency** ratio of the pure fifth, the basis of Pythagorean tuning).
2:03	variation 2	The first violin plays the tune using the complete major scale, and the whole ensemble switches to just intonation, with the sweet sound of pure thirds and sixths. Added to the 3-against-2 rhythms are 5-against-4 rhythms (5:4 is the frequency ratio of the pure major third).
2:45	variation 3	The rhythm is simplified as the pitch material expands to include the seventh **partial**, which sounds a bit like a blue note (as in the second bar).
3:14	variation 4	Rhythm becomes extremely complex, with all four instruments playing in different tempos. For example, the viola and cello are playing in two tempos with the strict ratio 35:36.
4:16	variation 5	The rhythm settles down as the instruments explore the very small intervals (microtones) created through the overlay of multiple tuning schemes. A minor-key version of the melody is audible in the second violin.
5:16	variation 6	Again the rhythm is simplified as the pitch material expands, now to introduce "undertones." First violin's melody is based on an inversion of "Amazing Grace."
5:52	variation 7	An eerie blur of soft, rapid notes in rhythmic ratios such as 7:8:9:10. At 6:29 the cello plays "Amazing Grace" in high-pitched **harmonics**.
7:42	variation 8	All twenty-two pitches of the previous scales are combined in a rapturous final variation, with trills and tremolos. At 9:02 the pitch material is simplified to a diatonic scale, while the cross-rhythms reflect the frequency ratios of a dominant seventh chord (2:3:5:7). The final statement of "Amazing Grace" (9:34) is in sweet-sounding just intonation flavored with seventh-partial blue notes on the IV chords ("Amazing Grace, how <u>sweet</u> the sound").

(continued)

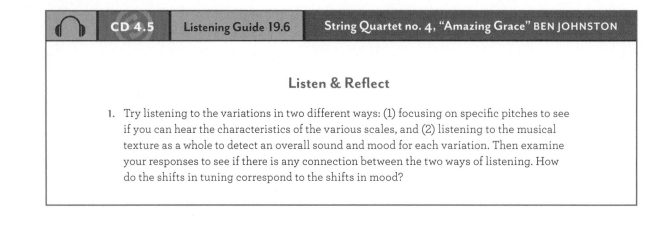

Listen & Reflect

1. Try listening to the variations in two different ways: (1) focusing on specific pitches to see if you can hear the characteristics of the various scales, and (2) listening to the musical texture as a whole to detect an overall sound and mood for each variation. Then examine your responses to see if there is any connection between the two ways of listening. How do the shifts in tuning correspond to the shifts in mood?

4. What is jazz-rock fusion? How does it resemble jazz? How does it resemble rock?

5. How does musical theater fit into the larger picture of American music in the 1970s?

6. Who are some of the principal figures in microtonal music, and what seem to be their aesthetic goals and means of achieving those goals?

FURTHER READING

Banfield, Stephen. *Sondheim's Broadway Musicals.* Ann Arbor: University of Michigan Press, 2003.

Echols, Alice. *Hot Stuff: Disco and the Remaking of American Culture.* New York: W.W. Norton, 2010.

Gann, Kyle. *American Music in the Twentieth Century.* New York: Schirmer Books, 1997.

Holt, Fabian. *Genre in Popular Music.* Chicago: University of Chicago Press, 2007.

Kronengold, Charles. "Exchange Theories in Disco, New Wave, and Album Oriented Rock." *Criticism* 50, no. 1 (winter 2008): 43–82.

Lawrence, Tim. *Love Saves the Day: A History of American Dance Culture, 1970–1979.* Durham, NC: Duke University Press, 2004.

Stimeling, Travis D. *Cosmic Cowboys and New Hicks: The Countercultural Sounds of Austin's Progressive Country Music Scene.* New York: Oxford University Press, 2011.

AMERICA'S MUSIC IN THE 1980s

The 1970s was a time when musical audiences seemed to splinter into ever-smaller factions, as evidenced in the growing number of popular music subgenres. Throughout the decade, that process was increasingly reflected in the larger culture. The election of Ronald Reagan to the presidency in 1980 coincided with an intense period of "culture wars," characterized by a polarizing of conservative and liberal political affiliations. Already in the late 1970s, advances won by ethnic minorities, women, and gays led to backlash movements: the discrediting of affirmative action as a "quota" system, a growing distrust that immigrants were "stealing" jobs from native-born Americans, and the rise of the religious right and the Moral Majority, a political lobbying group that espoused evangelical Christian values. An anti-intellectual ethos throughout the 1980s cast suspicion on professors, artists, and others who favored the social changes that were afoot.

Yet trends within music during the 1980s suggest a relaxing of the tensions of the so-called culture wars. The aesthetic issues of the 1970s were framed as dichotomies: music could be simple or complex, elaborate or primal, ambitious or accessible. In the music of the 1980s those dichotomies seemed to fade, or at least grew less emotionally fraught for both musicians and audiences. In their place was a new emphasis on eclecticism and hybridity, as well as a celebration of differences for the variety they could bring to our collective musical culture. Across the many styles of American music, the 1980s can be considered a postmodern moment, when musicians took a more relaxed posture to both their own musical traditions and the traditions of others.

POSTMODERNISM

As discussed in chapter 16, the years after World War II witnessed a widening gap between popular musical styles and the new music being composed for the concert hall and especially for the setting of the academic music department. Within the classical sphere, moreover, a smaller yet significant divide separated academic composers from experimentalists working outside educational institutions. Of the former group, the epitome was Milton Babbitt, who in the 1950s had made the case for university-based composers to dedicate themselves to research that might expand the language of music, in the manner of research scientists and mathematicians. From Babbitt's point of view, appealing to a general audience ought to be no more necessary for a composer than for a physicist.

Of those outside academia, the minimalists in particular sought to explore new musical ideas while communicating with a broader slice of the musical audience. Minimalism, especially the music of Philip Glass, marks the start of a larger historical trend toward the reuniting of popular and classical spheres that continues to the present day. That movement within music can be seen as part of the larger cultural phenomenon of **postmodernism**.

POSTMODERNISM IN THE ACADEMY

Within the academy before 1980, writing music with popular appeal was often regarded as retrogressive. Although the hegemony of Babbitt-style serialism was less pervasive than the stories of some veterans of those years may suggest, academic composers in the 1960s and 1970s generally avoided traditional tonality, writing music that either was atonal or used tonality in unconventional ways, as in the music of George Crumb or Ben Johnston. University composers who embraced the New Romanticism most fully, such as George Rochberg, often found themselves ostracized by their professional colleagues.

Many of those colleagues subscribed to the idea that music was historically "progressing" toward ever more complex means of expression. That modernist notion fostered a difficult relationship with music of the past: composers could admire and love the music of past masters but shied away from emulating it for fear of being imitators. Moreover, some modernists tended toward a high-mindedness that discouraged reference to popular styles for fear of eclecticism, a bugbear of late modernist aesthetics. These attitudes could result in new music whose complexity exceeded the listening capacities of all but the most specialized audience.

In fact, however, many academic composers in the century's latter years grew more tolerant and pluralistic in outlook. As already noted, since the 1960s a handful of composers, notably Crumb and Rochberg, had developed highly personal musical languages that combined tonality and atonality, mixing earlier classical styles with non-Western elements and cutting-edge contemporary idioms. Following their example, composers during the last third of the twentieth century grew more open to stylistic admixtures.

William Bolcom

One composer who has successfully bridged the gap between academia and popular styles is William Bolcom, long on the faculty at the University of Michigan. Trained in serialism, Bolcom began his career writing avant-garde concert works. On the side, however, he participated in the revival of interest in Scott Joplin, wrote a few Joplin-inspired rags of his own, most notably *Graceful Ghost* (1970), and launched a separate career as accompanist for his wife, singer Joan Morris, devoted especially to English-language popular songs of all eras. Beginning in the 1980s, he combined the various strains of his compositional life in a series of eclectic compositions drawing on a wide range of cultivated and vernacular idioms. His Violin Concerto in D Major (1984) requires a soloist with a command of both classical virtuosity and the style and panache of a jazz violinist such as Joe Venuti. The concerto moves fluidly from Stravinskyan modernism to ragtime and Gershwinesque lyricism. In the same year, Bolcom's massive setting of William Blake's *Songs of Innocence and Experience* for solo singers, chorus, and orchestra, a mixture of modernist music with elements of rock, soul, country, and reggae, won the Pulitzer Prize for music.

Three years later, the 1987 Pulitzer Prize went to another academic composer, John Harbison, for his sober, uncompromisingly modernist sacred motet *The Flight into Egypt.* Even while composing that work, however, Harbison, a professor at MIT, was embracing a more expansive tonal language in his Symphony no. 2 (1987). By the time of his 1999 opera *The Great Gatsby*, Harbison could conceive a musical setting for F. Scott Fitzgerald's novel that moves freely from 1920s dance styles to spiky modernist idioms in a language that is expressive and intensely personal.

John Harbison

This shift in composers' attitudes required letting go of any notion that music history outlines a story of progress. The increased interest in early music (from the Middle Ages to Bach), a trend encouraged by university music departments, had demonstrated that great music has been created in all historical epochs. The expansion of the usable past opened the door to the appropriation of older musical styles in new compositions, such as the telling quotation of Bach in George Crumb's *Ancient Voices of Children*. Another long-held attitude that lost credence was the notion that popular styles are, by definition, aesthetically inferior to "serious" music. This shift owed much to the phonograph, which preserved the work of such performers as Louis Armstrong and Billie Holiday. Together, these attitudes broadened the range of styles on which composers could draw for inspiration or material.

postmodern attitudes

Although traces of these new artistic attitudes were present throughout the modernist period, their emergence as a predominant trait in new music composition led in the 1980s to the application of a new term to describe the phenomenon. Rather than a repudiation of modernism, postmodernism may be thought of as both a continuation and a questioning of modernist values. Perhaps the chief characteristic of musical postmodernism is its questioning of dividing lines: between past and present, classical and popular, and creators and consumers. Composers working from a postmodern stance may use quotations and other allusions to various musical styles, often to ironic or "distanced" effect. Rather than trying to resolve the incongruities among the various idioms brought together in the same composition, a postmodern composer is likely to play on their differences, embracing multiple meanings that may be contingent on the time, place, and social context of the act of performance.

musical postmodernism

POSTMODERNISM OUTSIDE THE ACADEMY

Harbison, after studying at Harvard in the 1950s, had gone on to graduate work at Princeton and taught at MIT for many years before taking a step toward postmodernism. Born a decade later, the composer John Adams had a different experience as an undergraduate at Harvard in the 1960s. The young Adams was disturbed by the gulf that separated the serialist music he was studying in the classroom from the records of the Beatles and Jimi Hendrix he was listening to in his dorm room. As a teacher at the San Francisco Conservatory of Music in the 1970s, he worked

John Adams

✎ Richard Nixon (James Maddalena) and Pat Nixon (Janis Kelly) descend from Air Force One in the English National Opera's 2006 production of John Adams's 1987 opera *Nixon in China*.

in the tape studio and created music, both electronic and for live instruments, in a minimalist style influenced by Terry Riley, Steve Reich, and Philip Glass. By the 1980s he had moved on to a style that combined minimalism's rhythmic energy, diatonic tonality, and love of repetition with a more varied sound palette drawn from romantic orchestral music, big-band jazz, rock, and modernist music—what may be called a **postminimalist** style.

Nixon in China

Adams's most significant work of the 1980s is his opera *Nixon in China*, premiered by the Houston Grand Opera in 1987. With a libretto by Alice Goodman inspired by President Richard Nixon's historic visit to Beijing in 1972, *Nixon in China* brought minimalism into the musical mainstream, reaching a far wider audience than even Glass's successful *Einstein on the Beach* of the preceding decade. The opera's music ranges in style from the overt minimalism of its opening to the foxtrot-inspired moment when First Lady Pat Nixon recalls her youth, and to the highly eclectic pastiche that accompanies a parody of a communist Chinese revolutionary ballet. Derided by some critics as a sensational attention-getter that would have no lasting value, *Nixon in China* has been revived by several opera companies worldwide and seems to be taking its place in the standard operatic repertoire.

performance art

Some of the most compelling postmodernist music of the 1980s was created in the context of **performance art**, which grew out of the "happenings" staged in the 1960s by artists inspired by John Cage, in which groups of performers would engage in seemingly irrational behavior that broke down the barrier between performers and audience. Pioneering performance artists include Pauline Oliveros, the dancer-filmmaker-composer Meredith Monk, and the multimedia artist Laurie Anderson.

Laurie Anderson

A composer entirely outside the academic music world, Laurie Anderson came from a background in the visual arts to become an important performance artist, combining visual images, music, movement, and words to create an all-encompassing aesthetic experience. Anderson's first major composition involved a Cage-inspired reversal of roles. In the small town of Rochester, Vermont, where local tradition demanded that listeners at outdoor concerts in the village park applaud by honking the horns of the cars and trucks in which they sat, Anderson presented a piece in 1972 in which the horns were the musical instruments, which she conducted from the park's gazebo. In the 1970s she invented the "tape-bow violin," a stringless violin with a tape recorder's playback head where the bridge would be and a bow that replaced the horsehair with magnetic tape on which she had previously recorded sounds such as her own voice. A downbow plays the tape forward, an upbow backward; changing the speed of the bow changes the speed and pitch of the recorded sounds. In performance she could thus create electronically altered music while simultaneously singing, speaking, and dancing.

In 1981 a record of Anderson's song "O Superman" became an unexpected crossover hit, rising to number 2 on British pop charts. A minimalist composition in which tape loops and electronic instruments accompanied Anderson's voice, processed to sound both masculine and robotlike, "O Superman" featured enigmatic poetry that didn't faze listeners raised on Bob Dylan and his followers. On the contrary, the rhythmic electronic sound and impassive, ironic text brought "O Superman" closer to New Wave pop than to academic postmodernism. The success of "O Superman," which was written as a small part of an ambitious live performance work called *United States*, brought Anderson a record deal with Warner Brothers and the chance to make a concert film, *Home of the Brave* (1986). Despite that period of notoriety and her long-term partnership with singer Lou Reed, whose band the Velvet Underground inspired the punk rock movement, Anderson has never really fit into the popular music scene. Rather, she is best viewed as a performance artist whose work has affinities with both popular and classical spheres.

Laurie Anderson in concert in 1987.

FILM MUSIC GOES POSTMODERN

In the decades after World War II, Hollywood film scores came increasingly to reflect the aesthetic stance established by Aaron Copland. The lush romanticism of the "golden age" gave way to a leaner, more astringent modernism, sometimes using small instrumental ensembles instead of full orchestras. Long stretches of more or less continuous underscoring, along with the use of leitmotifs associated with the main characters, became less common as films made greater use of silence and diegetic music.

One of the leading postwar film composers, Bernard Herrmann, developed a personal style that combined qualities of the golden age with the new Coplandesque aesthetic. Herrmann's colorful scores for action, fantasy, and science fiction films such as *Journey to the Center of the Earth* (1959) and *Jason and the Argonauts* (1963) call for large orchestras used in highly imaginative ways, emphasizing percussion, unusual instrumental groupings (such as ten harps), and unconventional instruments, such as the theremin, an electronic instrument featured in *The Day the Earth Stood Still* (1951). But Herrmann is best remembered for his decade-long collaboration with director Alfred Hitchcock; his tense, modernist music for *Psycho* (1960), using only string instruments, altered

Bernard Herrmann

jazz film scores

filmgoers' notions of what a horror film score should sound like and has been one of the most influential soundtracks of all time.

The 1960s and early 1970s saw the demise of the golden-age film score, as Hollywood composers turned to jazz and other popular styles in addition to a more dissonant, modernist idiom. Notable jazz scores included Duke Ellington's for *Anatomy of a Murder* (1959) and Quincy Jones's for *In Cold Blood* (1967). Characteristic of this more economical aesthetic is Argentinean American composer Lalo Schifrin's music for *Cool Hand Luke* (1967), much of which is played by a small bluegrass-style ensemble featuring acoustic guitar and banjo. The most familiar example of Shifrin's jazz-influenced music is his theme for the television series *Mission: Impossible*, which ran from 1966 to 1973.

all-diegetic scores

Some films went so far as to limit themselves to diegetic music. *The Last Picture Show* (1971), set in small-town Texas in the early 1950s, uses only country and popular songs by Hank Williams, Bob Wills, and others, which the characters listen to on jukeboxes, car radios, and the like. The music in *Five Easy Pieces* (1970), in which Jack Nicholson portrays a concert pianist alienated from his musical family, consists only of piano pieces by Bach, Mozart, and Chopin played by characters onscreen and the Tammy Wynette records that fascinate Nicholson's unrefined waitress girlfriend.

JOHN WILLIAMS: A RETURN TO THE GOLDEN AGE

A major pendulum swing occurred in the mid-1970s with the film scores of John Williams. An established film composer and Oscar-winner for his music for Stephen Spielberg's horror thriller *Jaws*, Williams drew on his enormous stylistic range to create an entirely different kind of soundtrack for the first of George Lucas's *Star Wars* movies in 1977. For that film, which evoked the nonstop adventure of 1930s movie serials featuring science fiction heroes Buck Rogers and Flash Gordon, Williams paid homage to the golden-age scores of Erich Korngold and Max Steiner. In the context of mid-1970s Hollywood scoring practices, audiences could detect a tone of affectionate parody in *Star Wars*' lush orchestration, romantic harmony, nearly continuous underscoring, occasional mickey-mousing, and memorable leitmotifs.

⤷ C-3PO, the protocol droid from *Star Wars*, rehearses the Boston Pops under the watchful eye of composer and conductor John Williams.

The popularity of Williams's music for *Star Wars* and other action-adventure films of the next decade, including the *Superman* and *Indiana Jones* movies, soon made the grandiose golden-age orchestral score the default sound of cinematic fantasy, science fiction, and adventure—often without the irony of using such music for stories set in the present or future.

In the meantime, a countervailing trend in film scoring placed ever greater emphasis on using movies to launch hit songs. Although movie musicals and the popular music industry had worked in tandem since the beginning of sound film, a postwar phenomenon was the hit single that gained popularity through its use in a nonmusical film. By the 1980s it had become a common practice to have at least one scene in a movie, often a wordless montage, that used a song in a rock or dance-oriented style, typically unrelated to the rest of the movie's soundtrack. Hit songs launched in this way included Bananarama's "Cruel Summer" (*The Karate Kid*, 1983), Patti LaBelle's "New Attitude" (*Beverly Hills Cop*, 1984), and Orchestral Manoeuvers in the Dark's "If You Leave" (*Pretty in Pink*, 1986).

Linking a movie with a hit song was just one aspect of the commercial practice of film tie-ins. A blockbuster movie could also generate sales of T-shirts, action figures, fast-food promos, and a variety of other ancillary products, which in turn acted as advertising to promote the film; the corporate term for this kind of marketing was "synergy." Central to the strategy was the idea of the "high concept" film, easily marketed on the strength of its stars and a premise that is either already familiar to moviegoers or reducible to a few words or a single image. A classic high-concept movie poster of the 1980s showed the diminutive Danny DeVito and muscleman Arnold Schwarzenegger, in matching suits and sunglasses, under a one-word title: *Twins*. That was all audiences needed to understand the comedy's premise. Filmmakers, critics, and moviegoers interested in the medium's artistic potential deplored high-concept films and their synergistic marketing. Veteran film composers in particular denounced studio pressure to incorporate a hit song as a commercially driven ploy that made a musically coherent sound world for the picture unlikely.

marketing synergy

DANNY ELFMAN: REINTERPRETING THE GOLDEN AGE

In at least one high-concept film of the 1980s, however, a composer took the studios' demands for synergy as an artistic challenge and found a postmodernist solution that involved both golden era–style underscoring and songs by a current pop star. For his 1989 movie *Batman*, the first in a long-running film series, director Tim Burton turned to two musicians to create the soundtrack. The Minneapolis-born pop star Prince, one of the decade's most successful musicians, wrote a series of danceable songs, one of which, "Batdance," rose to the top of the pop charts before the film had been released. At the same time, Burton's longtime collaborator Danny Elfman composed an orchestral score in a style closely linked to 1980s superhero adventure movies.

From one point of view, Elfman's background made him ideally suited for the job. As a youth growing up in Los Angeles, he was inspired by golden-age film composers (he cites Herrmann's music for *The Day the Earth Stood Still* as a particularly strong childhood influence), and alongside his early film work he played in a quirky, eclectic New Wave band called Oingo Boingo.

But Elfman, much like Irving Berlin, lacked many of the tools that come with academic training. His music reading and notation skills are limited; for example, he reads and writes only in the treble clef (not unusual for a guitarist), and his command of standard music notation is faulty. Some industry insiders accuse him of being a "hummer": the kind of musician who relies on ghostwriters to fill out his meager musical ideas. But his track record over a long career suggests otherwise. Even when he works with different orchestrators, Elfman's music has distinctive stylistic traits.

Elfman's first feature film scores for Tim Burton—two Pee Wee Herman movies and *Beetlejuice*—recall classic cartoon music: manaically, energetic, colorfully

Elfman and Tim Burton

Danny Elfman's soundtrack for Tim Burton's *Batman* (1989) contrasts golden age–style leitmotif for Batman (Michael Keaton) and self-consciously postmodern pastiche for the Joker (Jack Nicholson).

orchestrated, and shifting restlessly between a wide range of styles. One of Elfman's most familiar pieces in that idiom, a sort of comic-book counterpart to John Adams's postminimalism, is his theme music for the animated television series *The Simpsons*, which premiered in 1989. The dark, brooding score for *Batman* thus represents a departure for Elfman. Like film composers of the golden age such as Steiner and Korngold, Elfman wrote the *Batman* score in a largely romantic harmonic and melodic language, using the resources of a symphony orchestra, and like those composers he relied on leitmotif technique. But whereas a golden-age film score would contain several leitmotifs, the *Batman* score has only one, associated with the title character. The only other distinctive melody is a love theme for Bruce Wayne and his love interest, and it is simply a variation on the "Bat-theme."

In contrast, the music accompanying the film's villain, the Joker, is a postmodernist stew of Prince's pop songs, a grotesque waltz, and a syrupy arrangement of Stephen Foster's "Beautiful Dreamer." Moreover, the Joker is aware of his music, both when it is diegetic (as when he enters a room carrying a boom box) and when it is not (as when he dances to and seems to conduct the waltz). As an anarchic trickster figure, the Joker refuses to abide by a basic rule of nondiegetic music: the convention that the audience hears it but the characters do not. The Joker allows Elfman to turn the commercial necessity of incorporating Prince's songs into a virtue. The clash of musical styles that results is used to intensify the conflict between hero and villain.

Elfman's treatment of Batman/Bruce Wayne's music, though more in the golden-age tradition, runs counter to 1980s expectations. An audience familiar with John Williams's film scores would expect the opening title music for an adventure movie to be loud, brassy, marchlike, in a major key, and emphasizing "heroic" upward melodic leaps—an apt description of Williams's title music for *Star Wars*, *Superman*, and *Raiders of the Lost Ark*. Instead, *Batman*'s title music (LG 20.1) begins softly, in the lowest registers of the orchestra, in a minor key, with an uncertain meter, and with a melody that rises mostly by step and emphasizes a falling "sigh" figure—music one might expect at the start of a horror movie. Even when a more energetic march rhythm takes over, the music repeatedly modulates downward through a series of minor keys. Rather than set the optimistic tone of a typical adventure movie, Elfman's title music prepares the audience for a hero who is socially alienated, troubled, and unstable. Unexpected things about this character are suggested before he even appears onscreen.

CDS, MTV, AND POP SPECTACLE

The late 1970s saw a sharp decline in record sales, with the LP market shrinking by 10 percent or more throughout the industrialized nations. Some observers blamed the downturn on the worldwide recession following the mid-1970s oil crisis, and others on the public's widespread use of blank audiocassettes to copy music in violation of copyright laws. Still others argued that the market

| CD 4.6 | Listening Guide 20.1 | Title music from *Batman* DANNY ELFMAN |

DATE: 1989
PERFORMERS: Sinfonia of London; Shirley Walker, conductor
GENRE: film music
METER: changing
FORM: through-composed

WHAT TO LISTEN FOR

- scored for traditional symphony orchestra
- unified by five-note "Bat-theme"
- emphasis on minor keys, frequent downward modulations

TIMING	SECTION	COMMENTS
0:00	slow	Low-register French horns softly intone the five-note minor-mode "Bat-theme" twice over an almost inaudible tonic pedal point in the basses; irregular rhythm obscures any sense of meter.
0:12		English horn enters with a more rhythmically stable version of the Bat-theme in canon with the French horns. Glockenspiel (bells) plays a repeating four-note descending figure derived from the Bat-theme, establishing a duple meter.
0:19		A distant bass-drum stroke and growing volume from the lower instruments, playing the Bat-theme in canon, set an ominous tone.
0:40		The crescendo reaches its peak as the Bat-theme is extended by one note, a "tail" that resolves chromatically to a new, unexpected chord, the first departure from the sustained tonic triad; the entrance of a pipe organ heightens the gothic mood.
0:47	march	Return to the tonic as brass establish an urgent march tempo, much faster than the preceding.
0:50		French horns, then woodwinds, transform the Bat-theme into a march; a sudden drop down a whole step is signaled by a trumpet fanfare.
1:01		Another drop of a whole step, as strings and low brass introduce a new, more sustained version of the Bat-theme; falling arpeggios drop the key down a further half step.
1:13		The key lurches downward a major third.
1:20	lyrical development	At the gong stroke, the tempo increases, but the volume decreases and the martial rhythm falls away; modulation down a perfect fifth. A series of canonic statements of the Bat-theme from low to high, ending with the chromatic tail first heard at 0:40.
1:39		At the second statement of the chromatic tail, shift to remote key a tritone away.
1:45		A pair of statements of the Bat-theme include the chromatic tail, harmonized with a dissonance reminiscent of Tchaikovsky.
1:58		The second dissonance resolves unconventionally, with a modulation up a whole step. A new idea alternates two chords, with an upper-register accompaniment figure derived from the Bat-theme.

(continued)

TIMING	SECTION	COMMENTS
2:11	triple meter	Clear statements of the Bat-theme, now in triple meter, with gradual crescendo.
2:25		Percussion and sharp, staccato chords for full orchestra lead to a final, unstable diminished chord and a gong stroke.

Listen & Reflect

1. How does the *Batman* title music resemble the romantic orchestral techniques heard in Amy Beach's *Gaelic* Symphony (see LG 8.1), and how does it differ?
2. Compare this music with Aaron Copland's title music for *The Red Pony*, which makes up most of the first movement from *The Red Pony Suite* (LG 15.2).

for long-playing records had reached a saturation point and that the industry strategy of segmenting the market, as described in chapter 19, was starting to backfire, reducing profits instead of increasing them.

the CD

Breathing new life into the record industry in the early 1980s was a new format: the **compact disc (CD)**. Record companies promised music lovers that the new digital format offered longer playing times than LPs (true), greater audio fidelity (debatable), and virtual indestructibility (too good to be true). Introduced in 1983, the CD gradually replaced the LP over the next decade, spurred in part by the practice of reissuing older albums in the new format, with digital mastering and bonus tracks thrown in to lure buyers into purchasing music they already owned on vinyl.

the music video

In addition to the CD, the most significant new medium to emerge from the 1980s was the **music video**, a miniature movie designed to accompany a popular record. The idea goes back to the 1940s and the short-lived phenomenon of "soundies," three-minute musical films designed to be played on a coin-operated jukebox containing a small projector; the soundies, some of which featured such big-name performers as Cab Calloway and Louis Jordan, usually consisted of performers lip-synching to their records before the camera in an imitation of live performance, often with dancers.

Early attempts to create short films that involved more than lip-synching include a couple of sequences in the Beatles movie *Help!* (1965) and Bob Dylan's innovative prologue to *Don't Look Back* (1967), a documentary about his 1965 tour of Great Britain. In the latter, "Subterranean Homesick Blues" accompanies images of a blasé-looking Dylan displaying a series of hand-lettered cue cards containing key words from the song. Far more modest in budget than later music videos, Dylan's visual complement to his own song hints at the artistic possibilities of combining music and image. For the next decade and a half, record companies occasionally made promotional videos to boost the popularity of their acts, but with no obvious venue for their distribution, these early music videos, which usually consisted of unimaginative lip-synching, played only a small part in the marketing of popular music.

MUSIC TELEVISION (MTV)

Spurring further artistic development was the launch in 1981 of Music Television (MTV), a cable channel designed to broadcast nothing but music videos. Cable television had emerged in the 1970s as a way to bring network broadcasts to regions where conventional antenna reception was poor; consequently, MTV was at first seen primarily by viewers in the Midwest and South, parts of the country distant from cutting-edge popular trends. Only gradually, with the growing success of premium cable channels such as Home Box Office (HBO), did MTV and other cable channels come to be a fixture in most American homes with television sets.

At the time, the idea of a channel devoted to music videos seemed strange to most people both inside and outside the music industry. Record companies thought of videos as promotional tools for bands—as advertisements for records, where the real money was to be made. A cable channel that aired nothing but commercials struck most people as a folly. But the audience for MTV rapidly grew, and by the mid-1980s MTV took its place alongside radio as an effective way to launch a hit record.

At first, MTV was at the mercy of the record companies and would air just about anything the major labels sent its way. As the number of videos grew and they began to compete for airtime, however, the artistic quality of the visual images began to matter. In short time, some musicians and filmmakers realized that music videos could aspire to the artistic level of the songs themselves. The video for Michael Jackson's "Billie Jean" (1983), a five-minute homage to classic Hollywood film noir, simultaneously raised the artistic status of the music video, brought widespread attention to MTV, and made Jackson a solo pop star of the first magnitude. For a follow-up, Jackson collaborated with the feature film director John Landis to create a fourteen-minute narrative video for the title song from his blockbuster album *Thriller*. That landmark ushered in the so-called golden age of music video—an era, extending into the early 1990s, when record companies put their full financial and technological resources into supporting the making of videos as meticulously crafted as the studio-created music they helped promote.

Close on the heels of Jackson's successes came the second major music video star of the 1980s, Madonna Louise Ciccone. Her debut album, *Madonna* (1984), was followed a year later by her breakthrough *Like a Virgin*, by which time she was a

Madonna (b. 1958) and Michael Jackson (1958–2009), the first music video superstars.

constant presence on television as well as radio. Both Jackson and Madonna were talented dancers as well as singers; they both also made full use of the medium of television through their use of costumes and hairstyles.

THE POP MAINSTREAM AND ITS ALTERNATIVES

As the early careers of Michael Jackson and Madonna indicate, heavy rotation on MTV was one marker of inclusion in the mainstream of popular music in the 1980s. One genre that figured prominently in the early years of MTV was New Wave. The success of videos by bands like the imaginatively geeky Devo indicated how easily New Wave, an outgrowth of the punk rebellion, had accommodated itself to the mainstream. But popular music in the 1980s encompassed more than the coolly ironic New Wave bands and dance-oriented musicians featured on MTV; also part of the mainstream (or at least perceived to be so) was **heavy metal**, which preserved rock's anarchic energy. Meanwhile, on the fringes of the pop scene were a variety of bands that also kept alive rock's antiauthoritarian flame, playing a variety of styles such as **hardcore punk** and other genres loosely collected under the general terms "college rock," "indie rock," and—the name that eventually stuck—**alternative rock**.

heavy metal   Heavy metal, perceived by its fans as the "true" mainstream of rock, is rooted in the aggressive styles of such late 1960s–early 1970s rock bands as Iron Butterfly and Steppenwolf (whose 1968 song "Born to Be Wild" contains the phrase "heavy metal thunder," possibly the origin of the name). Heavy metal is characterized by extremely loud volume levels, a thundering beat, and long, virtuosic guitar solos that show the influence of guitar heroes like Jimi Hendrix and Carlos Santana. The lyrics tend to focus on dark imagery—death, the occult, and the gothic—linking heavy metal with 1970s progressive rock. Although some heavy metal bands self-consciously dressed down to resemble the white working-class males who made up the large majority of their fans, others affected the outrageous costumes and stage effects of 1970s British glam rockers like David Bowie and arena rockers like Alice Cooper and Kiss. By the late 1980s such over-the-top fashions had earned some groups the nickname **hair bands**.

The earliest phases of heavy metal can be traced to a number of British and American bands. By 1980, however, the geographic center of heavy metal innovation was definitely Los Angeles, where the concentration of recording studios had attracted a large number of rock instrumentalists. Chief among the early L.A. metal bands were Van Halen and Mötley Crüe. Their commercial success paved the way for the enormously popular Guns N' Roses. Among the more inventive heavy metal bands to emerge in 1980s Los Angeles are Metallica and Megadeth, bands whose early focus on very fast tempos earned their music the nickname "speed metal," but whose more varied later music is more often called "thrash metal." Both bands have produced songs longer than the usual three minutes, with changing tempos and textures, which, along with lyrics exploring political and ethical issues, represent an updating of progressive rock. At the same time, though, thrash metal's fast tempos, aggressive volume, and snarling vocal delivery tie the music to punk. In fact, the coining by fans and critics of ever narrower categories—black metal, death metal, doom metal,

↳ Dave Mustaine of Megadeth, seen here performing in 2007, personifies the continued importance of the guitar hero in heavy metal.

power metal—disguises the fact that the similarities between these styles are more significant than the differences.

Los Angeles was also an important center for hardcore punk. Like their fore-bears the Ramones and the Sex Pistols, hardcore punk bands played songs that were short, fast, and loud, with lead singers shouting angry, anarchistic, nihilist lyrics. Unlike the 1970s punk bands, however, they were more inclined to indulge in instrumental solos—always within very short song formats—featuring more complex drumming and exploration of guitar effects such as extreme distortion. Their stage dress tended to be the same slovenly jeans and T-shirts they wore on the street, a sort of antifashion fashion statement. Virtually none of the hardcore bands signed contracts with the major labels; instead, they created their own independent labels to issue self-produced vinyl LPs and **EPs** (ten- or twelve-inch 45-rpm "extended play" records, typically containing four to six songs and thus longer than a single but shorter than an LP).

Ignored by the major labels, hardcore punk bands tended to have regional followings, and the hardcore phenomenon was not so much a national movement as it was the sum of several local scenes. Probably the first and most influential scene was in Los Angeles, where Black Flag was formed in the late 1970s; by

hardcore punk

the early 1980s the band had been joined by Bad Religion, the Circle Jerks, and Suicidal Tendencies. To the north, the Dead Kennedys were central to the San Francisco hardcore punk scene, while in Washington, D.C., Bad Brains held a similar position in East Coast hardcore.

college/indie/
alternative rock

Local music scenes throughout the United States gave rise to an assortment of bands whose music lay somewhere between MTV-style mainstream accessibility and the confrontational stance of hardcore punk and heavy metal. The success of R.E.M., originally a group of students at the University of Georgia, made Athens, Georgia, a mecca for bands who made attractive pop music that managed to project an "underground" sensibility. Because records by groups like R.E.M., Hüsker Dü, and 10,000 Maniacs received heavy rotation on the playlists of college radio stations, their sound became labeled *college rock*. Because those records generally appeared on small, independent labels, another term widely used was *indie rock*. By the end of the decade this music was more often referred to as *alternative rock*, an umbrella term for a range of musical tendencies that would become a major force in the 1990s. One indication of how diverse the non-mainstream pop scene could be was Sonic Youth, which began as a hardcore punk band but began to expand its range toward both mainstream pop and the "downtown" avant-gardism of the minimalists and performance artists.

HIP-HOP

Perhaps the most important musical innovation of the late twentieth century, **hip-hop**, also emerged from a local music scene: in this case, black and Latino neighborhoods of New York City.

Beginning in the 1970s, DJs at dance parties in the Bronx developed a range of techniques for manipulating records by using two turntables and an audio mixer, which controlled how much each turntable would be amplified by the sound system. Those techniques, later dubbed **turntablism**, include:

- **scratching**: manually moving a record back and forth under the playback stylus to produce percussive rhythmic effects
- **cutting** or **looping**: alternating between two copies of the same record to repeat one section of a song over and over
- **beatmatching**: adjusting the speed of one turntable so that the record played on it matches exactly the tempo of a record on the other turntable, allowing dancers to continue uninterruptedly from song to song and allowing the DJ to move seamlessly back and forth between songs
- **beat juggling**: combining the above techniques to create new music from snippets of prerecorded music

In addition to deft turntable skills, expert DJs possessed extensive record collections and an encyclopedic knowledge of their contents, enabling them to choose songs to match the mood of the dancers and even to manipulate the dancers' reactions, shaping a dance party into a coherent musical experience. A key element was the use of looping to extend through repetition a favorite part of a song, usually an instrumental passage or **break**, into an occasion for ecstatic dancing. The dancers, **b-boys** and **b-girls**, developed a vocabulary of gymnastic moves that came to be called **b-boying** or breaking by its practitioners and, by the general public, **break dancing**.

At first the DJ, with the help of a microphone, would offer spoken patter and shouts of encouragement to heighten the celebratory mood of a dance party. As turntablism grew more complex, this role was often handed over to an **MC**, who, as the name indicates, acted as a master of ceremonies. In short time the MC's patter developed into **rap**, the vocal component of hip-hop music and, along with DJing, b-boying, and graffiti, one of the four pillars of hip-hop culture.

MCs used rhyme and meter to raise rap into a half-spoken, half-sung form of oral poetry. Rap draws on African American traditions of rhythmically intoned speech, including the oratory of black Pentecostal preachers; **toasting**, the telling of humorous stories often boasting about the narrator's exploits; and **the dozens**, or **dirty dozens**, a game of exchanging humorous insults, a source as well of the innumerable jokes beginning "Yo momma . . ." Rap also benefited

DJs and MCs

DJ Grandmaster Flash at the turntables in the 1980s.

from early explorations into poetry recitations with jazz accompaniment dating back to the Beats and continued in the 1970s by the Last Poets and by Gil Scott-Heron, both of whom stressed social commentary reflecting the black nationalist movement of the 1960s. The 1973 album *Hustlers Convention* features jazz and funk musicians, notably Kool and the Gang, backing recitations by Lightnin' Rod, one of the Last Poets, that use the methods of toasting to recount the rise and fall of a young ghetto criminal. In its funky rhythms, unvarnished portrayals of ghetto life, and earnest social message, *Hustlers Convention* is a forerunner of much of the rap music that was yet to come.

The MC's rapping went hand in hand with the DJ's ability to extract, alter, and extend instrumental breaks from records—in short, to spontaneously create a rhythmic instrumental accompaniment, or **beat**, for the MC. Caribbean immigrants figured prominently in the ranks of early hip-hop DJs, and their beats drew on the similar practices found in dub, a Jamaican genre dating back to the late 1960s. By the end of the 1970s DJs in the South Bronx such as Kool Herc (a Jamaican immigrant), Grandmaster Flash (born in Barbados), and Disco Wiz (born in the South Bronx to a Puerto Rican father and a Cuban mother), either doing their own rapping or working with early MCs such as Cowboy and Melle Mel, had attracted enthusiastic audiences to their live performances. In fact, their art was intrinsically about live performance. The combination of DJing and MCing was something one did *with* records, not something to be done *on* records.

"Rapper's Delight"

That changed in 1979 with the release of "Rapper's Delight," the first commercially successful hip-hop record. "Rapper's Delight" was the result of efforts by Sylvia Robinson, a producer, singer, and guitarist who in the 1950s had scored an R&B hit, "Love Is Strange," as half of the duo Mickey and Sylvia. As a co-owner of Sugar Hill Records, Robinson assembled a group of MCs and named them the Sugar Hill Gang. She recorded their rapping over a backing of studio musicians recreating the instrumental break from Chic's current disco hit "Good Times." The breakaway success of "Rapper's Delight" proved that rap could be captured on vinyl and that doing so could turn a profit. At the same time, it marked a shift in the music's center of gravity from the DJ to the MC. Because live interaction with dancers, a significant part of the DJ's craft, had no place in recorded hip-hop, the DJ came to be seen as merely providing a backdrop for the rapping. Likewise, as MCing came to be less about acting as master of ceremonies than about crafting rap performances, attention increasingly turned to the work of **rappers**, as MCs were now more likely to be called.

As record labels scrambled to sign rap artists in the 1980s, the rappers in turn began to craft songs with meatier content than the feel-good party rhymes of "Rapper's Delight." As early as 1982 rap had produced its first hit single with

LG 20.2

social commentary: "The Message" (LG 20.2), credited to Grandmaster Flash and the Furious Five, who performed it in concert even though only one of the furious Five, Melle Mel, appears on the record. Sylvia Robinson and producer Duke Bootee (Ed Fletcher) wrote the first half of the rap, and Melle Mel (Melvin Glover) wrote the second half, an extended toast much in the style of *Hustlers Convention*. Duke Bootee also created the instrumental track with a synthesizer and a **drum machine**, a device that imitates percussive sounds and sound effects, such as the shattering glass that introduces the rapping in "The Message." On top of the ominous-sounding minor-mode beat, the gritty depiction of ghetto life set the tone for much rap to come.

CD 4.7	Listening Guide 20.2	"The Message" GRANDMASTER FLASH AND THE FURIOUS FIVE

SONGWRITERS: Sylvia Robinson, Ed Fletcher, and Melvin Glover

DATE: 1982

PERFORMERS: Duke Bootee (Ed Fletcher) and Melle Mel (Melvin Glover)

GENRE: rap

METER: duple

FORM: verse and chorus, with vamps and interlude

WHAT TO LISTEN FOR

- use of synthesizer and drum machine
- rhythmic, intoned speech (rapping) instead of singing
- socially conscious lyrics about ills of ghetto life

TIMING	SECTION	TEXT	COMMENTS
0:00	introduction		After 2 bars of drum machine, 16 bars of synthesized texture establish a groove that is sustained throughout the song. In lieu of harmonic motion, a rising and falling pentatonic melody creates a sense of question-and-answer.
0:43	chorus (partial)	It's like a jungle sometimes...	
0:52	vamp		Staccato repeated chords create an expectant mood for the beginning of the rap, ushered in by the sound of breaking glass.
1:02	verse 1	Broken glass everywhere...	Melle Mel describes intolerable ghetto conditions.
1:21	chorus	Don't push me...	The emphatic delivery creates a triple-meter polyrhythm against the beat.
1:30		It's like a jungle...	Only one statement.
1:35	verse 2	Standing on the front stoop...	The story of a woman who descends from dancer to prostitute to street person.
1:59	chorus	Don't push me...	
2:09		It's like a jungle...	Two statements.
2:18	verse 3	My brother's doing bad on my mother's TV...	A lighter story about too much television progressively darkens with references to debt, drug addiction, and insanity.
2:47	chorus	Don't push me...	
2:57		It's like a jungle...	Two statements.
3:06	vamp		8 bars of the repeated chords, marking the halfway point.

(continued)

		"The Message" GRANDMASTER FLASH AND THE FURIOUS FIVE
CD 4.7	Listening Guide 20.2	

TIMING	SECTION	TEXT	COMMENTS
3:25	interlude		8 bars of the introduction.
3:44	verse 4	My son said, "Daddy..."	Bad schools foster bad attitudes and gang violence.
4:23	chorus	Don't push me...	"Say what?" replaces the dry laugh.
4:32		It's like a jungle...	Four statements.
4:51	verse 5	A child is born...	Melle Mel's high-energy rapping tells the short life story of a would-be gangsta.
5:58	chorus	Don't push me...	
6:08		It's like a jungle...	The final two statements are the most emphatic, punctuated by rhythmic laughs.
6:18	coda	Yo, Mel...	A miniature play in which the Furious Five are questioned by the police and apparently arrested for the crime of hanging out on the street.

Listen & Reflect

1. What similarities and differences can you note between "The Message" and Curtis Mayfield's "Superfly" (LG 19.3)?

the sampler

"The Message," with its combination of studio-generated beats and socially conscious rapping, set the pattern for later 1980s rap groups. Public Enemy explored the use of **samplers**—digital devices that manipulate recorded sounds in synthesizer-like ways—to create rhythmic loops of prerecorded sound, replicating a DJ's beat juggling to build up dense beats for the politically charged rapping of leader Chuck D. At the same time, the eclectic tastes of DJ Afrika Bambaataa, who combined Afrocentric imagery with European and Japanese electronic dance music, inspired other rap artists to extend the range of musical influences in hip-hop. In 1986 Run-DMC's cover of Aerosmith's "Walk This Way" blended boastful rapping with hard-rock guitars, creating a crossover hit that spurred white interest in rap and revitalized the popularity of Aerosmith (who participated in the record and the amusing video that promoted it). "Walk This Way" is also an early example of what would eventually become a hip-hop staple, the song with rapped verses and a sung chorus.

By the end of the 1980s hip-hop had come to be a national phenomenon, with emergent local scenes in Philadelphia, Los Angeles, Atlanta, and other cities. As new styles arose from those scenes, and as the audience for hip-hop became increasingly suburban and white, hip-hop would continue to develop and expand its range of musical styles and lyrical subject matter.

As diverse as American music of the 1980s may be, a common thread can be traced through all of the music described in this chapter: the thread of postmodernism. Musicians as different as Laurie Anderson, John Adams, Danny Elfman, and Grandmaster Flash share a creative approach to music of the past and a willingness to explore new territories without discarding useful traditions. Likewise, all of these musicians are unafraid to stretch beyond boundaries of genre and to bring into their music influences from other musical styles.

At the same time that postmodern attitudes were shaping many aspects of American arts late in the twentieth century, traditional music—folk music—came to occupy a new space in the general culture of the United States. The next chapter considers the role of traditional music in contemporary society, where traditions whirl together in the postmodern blender.

QUESTIONS FOR DISCUSSION AND REVIEW

1. What are the aesthetic premises of postmodernism, and how do they differ from the tenets of modernism?

2. What are the major phases of film music in the second half of the twentieth century, and who are the film composers associated with each phase?

3. How did MTV's emphasis on visual spectacle influence popular music in the 1980s?

4. What are the specific techniques that distinguish hip-hop from earlier musical styles? How are those techniques indicative of the live performance contexts in which they emerged?

FURTHER READING

Cateforis, Theodore. *Are We Not New Wave? Modern Pop at the Turn of the 1980s.* Ann Arbor: University of Michigan Press, 2011.

Chang, Jeff. *Can't Stop, Won't Stop: A History of the Hip Hop Generation.* New York: St. Martin's Press, 2005.

Charnas, Dan. *The Big Payback: The History of the Business of Hip-Hop.* New York: New American Library, 2010.

Halfyard, Jante K. *Danny Elfman's "Batman": A Film Score Guide.* Lanham, MD: Scarecrow Press, 2004.

Katz, Mark. *Groove Music: The Art and Culture of the Hip-Hop DJ.* New York: Oxford University Press, 2012.

Kramer, Jonathan. "The Nature and Origins of Musical Postmodernism." In *Postmodern Music/Postmodern Thought*, edited by Judy Lochhead and Joseph Auner, 13–26. New York: Routledge, 2002.

Ross, Alex. "Oscar Scores." *New Yorker,* March 9, 1998. Online at http://www.therestisnoise .com/2004/05/oscar_scores.html.

Strickland, Edward. *American Composers: Dialogues on Contemporary Music.* Bloomington: Indiana University Press, 1991.

Tschmuck, Peter. "The Recession in the Music Industry: A Cause Analysis." *Music Business Research,* March 29, 2010. Online at http://musicbusinessresearch.wordpress.com/.

CHAPTER 21

AMERICAN ROOTS MUSIC

Many genres of American music have flourished for decades, even centuries, before spreading beyond the confines of the community of their origin. In particular, music sung in languages other than English has been slow to break out of its native social setting. The latter part of the twentieth century, however, has seen widespread interest in music previously thought to have limited appeal for broader audiences.

An agent in the dissemination of this traditional music has been the folk festival. As far back as the 1930s the National Folk Festival began its annual series of multiethnic events. At first held in Washington, D.C., the festival eventually rotated to a new city every few years, often spawning a local festival in its wake. The 1976 American bicentennial boosted further interest in folk music, which since that time has often been referred to as **roots music**, distinguishing it from the music of the urban folk revival (discussed in chapter 17).

This chapter samples only a few traditions of roots music. We have chosen examples with some traits in common: all have been around for many decades, all originated in the contact between two or more ethnic groups, all are sung in languages other than English, and all have seen their audience grow considerably in recent years, often due to their inclusion in multiethnic folk festivals.

THE MUSIC OF PANTRIBALISM

Alliances among American Indian nations have a long history, intensifying in the late nineteenth century and early twentieth century as Indians worked together to fend off cultural collapse in the face of white conquest. This movement toward pantribalism, also called pan-Indianism or intertribalism, led to a greater exchange of cultural traditions and beliefs among Native peoples. With new pantribal institutions came new music, blending characteristics of different Native traditions. Three notable instances of pantribal music are the songs associated with the Ghost Dance, the peyote religion, and the powwow.

The Ghost Dance religious movement emerged in 1889 under the leadership of Wovoka, a Paiute shaman who taught that the dance would revive Indians who had died in battle and restore the dwindling buffalo herds, thus allowing the religion's followers to repulse the whites who had been systematically exterminating the buffalo as a tactic in the Plains Indian Wars. The religion swept through Great Basin and Plains tribes, who resisted confinement to reservations even though the destruction of their main food sources was leading to starvation. Although the U.S. government outlawed the Ghost Dance in 1890, proponents preserved its practices, and many recordings of Ghost Dance songs were made in the twentieth century, some as late as 1980. The songs display features of Great Basin music: they are sung unaccompanied with a relaxed, open vocal quality; they frequently have paired phrases (*aa bb cc*, etc.); and they stress words over vocables.

the Ghost Dance

The peyote religion, later named the Native American Church, is based on a northern Mexican religious practice dating back to pre-Columbian times. Peyotism was adopted by Apaches in the eighteenth century, and in the late nineteenth and twentieth centuries it spread throughout Native North America in the wake of the collapse of the Ghost Dance. Blending Christian elements and indigenous shamanic practices, church members hold prayer meetings, beginning early in the evening and continuing through the next morning, with prayer, songs, ritual smoking, and the ingestion of peyote, a cactus traditionally used for its psychoactive properties. Peyote songs, sung solo with accompaniment of water drum and rattles, resemble traditional Apache songs in some respects but are unique in the vocable refrain that closes every stanza, "he ye no we," found in no other Indian song type.

the Native American Church

The most visible aspect of pantribalism today is the intertribal powwow, a major expression of Indian cultural identity. The powwow originated in the rituals of men's societies in Prairie tribes such as the Kansa, Pawnee, and Omaha, in which feasting, dancing, and music celebrated military exploits. By the 1860s the ceremonies had spread to the Northern Plains tribes, where they became known as the Grass Dance or Omaha Dance, and gradually added practices borrowed from other tribes and newly created ones too. In the early twentieth century white observers began to call such a ceremony a "powwow," using a name derived from the Algonkian word *pauau*, meaning a healer or a healing ritual. By the mid-twentieth century the name was widely used by Indians as well.

the intertribal powwow

Intertribal powwows date back at least to the Ponca Powwow, which began in the late 1870s in Indian Territory (part of present-day Oklahoma). These early intertribal festivals encouraged the sharing of traditional songs and dances among Ponca, Omaha, Osage, Pawnee, and other tribes. Some of the tribes were originally from the Southern Plains, while others had been relocated there. Relocation itself was a strong encouragement toward pantribalism in the first place. Although the Bureau of Indian Affairs strongly discouraged traditional Indian dancing during the 1890s, there is some evidence that powwows occurred on the Flathead Indian Reservation in Montana and elsewhere in that decade. In the early 1900s the powwow began to resemble its modern form, partially as a result of Indian participation in World War I; homecoming ceremonies honored returning war veterans as modern-day warriors who had fought alongside members of other tribes. Flag ceremonies and the honoring of veterans remain essential elements of many powwows today.

An ensemble of singers, or *drum*, at a modern powwow.

Although the format varies from place to place, music and dance form the core of any powwow, along with arts and crafts, food, raffles, and the honoring of respected guests. War Dances involve many dancers, each with his or her own choreography and costume. Other dances, such as the Men's Traditional and the Women's Jingle Dress, have more prescribed steps and dress. Social, exhibition, and contest dances, in which participants compete for prizes, round out the program.

An ensemble of singers, called a drum, provides the music while seated around a large double-headed bass drum, which all members play with padded drumsticks. Traditionally, only men play the drum; women may stand in an outer ring and join in the singing. All-women and mixed-gender drums are more recent phenomena. The music is derived from Plains Indian styles and features tense, nasal singing in the upper register (more so in the Northern Plains than the Southern Plains style), heavy pulsations on sustained tones, portamento, terraced melodic descents, and texts that rely on vocables.

LG 21.1

The War Dance song on the accompanying track (LG 21.1) was recorded in August 1975 by Cherokee ethnomusicologist Charlotte Heth at the sixth annual Kihekah Steh Powwow in Skiatook, Oklahoma, a suburb of Tulsa. The thirteen male singers who formed the drum for this intertribal performance represent a variety of Indian nations now living in Oklahoma, including the Pawnee, Ponca, Sac and Fox, Quapaw, Osage, and Kiowa. Only the last three are native to the Southern Plains; the others were relocated from the Northern Plains in the late 1800s. This song was part of the Flag Parade that brought the 1975 powwow to a close.

War Dance song structure

War Dance songs are typically sung a few times in succession before the drum moves on to a new song. Each time through a song, called a **push**, has a set form. The leader begins with a *lead*, and the ensemble (often a second singer, then the full group) repeats and extends the leader's phrase: this is the *second*. The lead and second form the first part of the push: *aa'*. The full ensemble then continues with the *chorus*, which comprises two contrasting phrases, *bc*. The lead begins on the melodic apex, the music describes a terraced descent, and the chorus ends on the melodic nadir.

🎧 CD 4.8	Listening Guide 21.1		War Dance song TRADITIONAL

DATE: recorded August 1975

PERFORMERS: Adam Pratt, leader; twelve other singers.

GENRE: Southern Plains powwow song

METER: duple

FORM: a series of *aa' bc bc* pushes

WHAT TO LISTEN FOR

- melody using gapped scale and terraced descent
- Southern Plains vocal style: somewhat tense, mid-register, unison
- honor beats at specific point in each push
- role of women's voices

TIMING	STATEMENT	SECTION	COMMENTS
0:00	push 1	*a* lead	The leader begins on the apex.
0:05		*a'* second	A second voice, then the full ensemble, repeats and extends the lead phrase.
0:16		*bc* chorus	Two new phrases, continuing downward and ending on the nadir.
0:28		honor beats	Three accented drumbeats, separated by weak beats.
0:29		*bc* second chorus	
0:41	push 2		The leader begins before the end of the preceding push, and the rest of the drum overlaps with his lead. At the second chorus, women's ululations (1:09).
1:18	push 3		The pitch is higher and the drumming more emphatic.
1:53	push 4		The pitch remains high while the drumming rises and falls in intensity.
2:29	tail	*bc*	The chorus is sung one last time, softly, with gentle drumbeats. Five loud beats mark the end of the song.

NOTE Field recording by Charlotte Heth, Skiatook, Oklahoma.

Listen & Reflect

1. Hearing the structure of Plains Indian songs is not easy at first for non-Indians. If you are new to powwows and their music, try listening for the leader's voice signaling the beginning of each push. Then listen for the honor beats around the midpoint of each push. If you are familiar with this style, how does this song compare with other powwow songs you've heard?

2. After you have familiarized yourself with this War Dance song, see if you can hear a similar structure in other powwow songs. Some recordings are listed at the end of this chapter, and others can be found online—or better yet, attend a powwow.

At the conclusion of the chorus, the singers play three emphatic drumbeats, separated by weaker beats: these **honor beats** show respect for the dancers or sometimes memorialize a person mentioned in the song. Then the ensemble repeats the chorus, *bc*, completing one full push.

The leader may begin a push just before the previous push has ended. (Likewise, in subsequent pushes the lead and second may overlap.) Or the leader may signal a series of consecutive loud beats (three, five, or seven) at the end of a push. After the final push, a *tail* consisting of one last repetition of the chorus marks the end of the song.

The music is sung in unison at full volume, in the moderately tense, mid-register vocal style of the Southern Plains. On the second push, a group of women joins in briefly with a wailing **ululation,** adding a new layer to the vocal texture and raising the pitch for the third and fourth pushes. Heth writes: "The solemn tone befits the ending of this important annual event."

In the twentieth century the "vanishing Americans" reestablished their presence on the national scene as a minority within a large population of other cultures. And as Indians managed to reconstruct a sense of peoplehood, music helped to provide continuity, especially in the intertribal powwow, an amalgam of diverse elements that feels to participants like a cultural whole. The competing obligations to remain loyal to older ways that society has dismissed, to keep outraged memory alive, to adjust to modern life, and to come together in a celebratory way with other Indians, have marked the consciousness of modern American Indians with a profound tension that fuels their cultural renewal.

◈ Flaco Jiménez sings and plays *norteño* on the button accordion.

NORTEÑO (TEX-MEX)

One type of music cultivated by Tejanos, or Texans of Mexican descent, is known to Spanish-speakers as *norteño* (music from northern Mexico and north of the Mexican border) and to English-speakers as **Tex-Mex.** Drawing on traditional Mexican genres such as *mariachi, rancheras*, and *corridos*, Tejano musicians developed *norteño* by incorporating the music of the German, Czech, and Polish immigrants who settled in south Texas and northern Mexico in the nineteenth century. Along with **banda** (played by wind bands with military-style instrumentation), **tejano** (a style closer to mainstream pop, made popular in the early 1990s especially by the Latina singer Selena), and more recently **nortec** (electronic dance music that samples *norteño* and *banda*), *norteño* is a type of roots music that has in recent decades increased its audience to include non-Hispanic listeners.

The most common form of *norteño* is performed by a standard ensemble called a *conjunto norteño*; thus the music itself is often called **conjunto** ("group"). The lead instrument, a button accordion, reveals the music's German influences, while the *bajo sexto*, a type of twelve-string guitar, points to its Mexican roots. Rounding out the ensemble is an electric bass and drums, indicating the influence of mid-twentieth-century popular styles such as rhythm and blues. The four instrumentalists share vocals, often in the close harmonies of traditional Mexican songs. *Conjuntos* play polka-style dance music with lyrics reflecting the realities of life on both sides of the Texas-Mexican border.

"Soy de San Luis" (LG 21.2) was written by Santiago Jiménez, part of a multi-generational family of *norteño* musicians. Its lively polka rhythms encourage the listener not to take too seriously the song persona's plight: a native of San Luis Potosí, Mexico, he has crossed the border to Texas, where there is plenty of work, but in San Antonio he meets a young Texan woman (*tejanita*) who bosses him around, takes his money, accepts gifts from other men, and winds up south of the border and asking him for more money. In disgust, he leaves her to the devil and goes back home, where men wear the pants.

LG 21.2

The recording here is by Santiago's elder son, Leonard "Flaco" Jiménez, perhaps the best-known *norteño* musician, famous for his collaborations with rock stars such as the Rolling Stones and Bob Dylan. In the 1990s he was a member of the Texas Tornados, a bilingual Tex-Mex "supergroup" that also included Tejano country singer Freddy Fender and white rockers Augie Meyers and Doug Sahm. His recording of "Soy de San Luis" stays close to traditional *norteño* style, evident in the flashy *adornos* or instrumental interludes between stanzas; nevertheless, his use of blues licks suggest that he does not restrict himself to traditional Mexican and German influences.

CAJUN AND ZYDECO MUSIC

As discussed in chapters 4, 5, and 12, music in New Orleans developed in a unique way thanks to the city's blend of French, Spanish, Anglo-American, African, and Caribbean influences. But that rich interaction was not limited to New Orleans; rural Louisiana was the site of similar interchanges. Whereas the urban music culture of New Orleans was oriented toward the classical and popular spheres, rural music making in Louisiana has retained closer ties to the traditional sphere. That is especially evident in the music of the state's Cajun population and in the zydeco music of rural black Louisianans.

Cajuns are the descendants of Acadians, the residents of the portion of France's North American empire once called Acadia—present-day Nova Scotia and nearby territories. When the British took possession of Acadia in 1710, French-speaking refugees began to flee, and many more left in the Great Expulsion during the French and Indian War in the 1760s. The many thousands of Acadian refugees who settled in Louisiana (still a French possession at that time) became known as Cajuns. Many became farmers, while others specialized in fishing the swamps and bayous prevalent in the state's southern parishes, where most Cajuns live today. While they retained many traditional folkways—including their language, a dialect known as Cajun French—over time they absorbed influences from their neighbors of Spanish, English, and African descent.

Cajun music, like the French Canadian music from which it is descended, is centered on fiddle-based dance music that resembles Celtic reels and jigs.

Cajun music

	CD 4.9	Listening Guide 21.2	"Soy de San Luis" FLACO JIMÉNEZ

SONGWRITER: Santiago Jiménez

DATE: 1990

INSTRUMENTATION: vocals, accordion, bajo sexto, electric bass, drums

GENRE: conjunto

METER: duple

FORM: strophic

WHAT TO LISTEN FOR

- Mexican-style vocals harmonized in parallel thirds
- German-style polka rhythm and prominent accordion
- blue notes in *adornos*

TIMING	SECTION	TEXT	TRANSLATION	COMMENTS
0:00	introduction			Accordion, then full band, set a slow, expectant mood.
0:04	stanza 1	Voy a cantar estos versos porque yo no soy de aquí...	I'm going to sing these verses because I'm not from here...	The polka rhythm is established as the stanza begins.
0:38	adorno			A short accordion solo shows a German influence.
0:47	stanza 2	Me encontré a una tejanita y de ella me enamoré...	I met a little Texan girl and fell in love with her...	Vocal harmony in thirds.
1:21	adorno			A longer accordion solo begins in polka style, then introduces a long blue note (1:28) and finishes in a bluesier style.
1:41	stanza 3	Todo el dinero me quita a bailar se va al salon...	She takes all my money and goes dancing at the bar...	
2:13	adorno			Mixture of polka and blues.
2:26	stanza 4	Ya me voy para mi tierra aunque pobre es mi nación...	I'm going back to my land even though it's a poor nation...	
3:00	coda			The brief coda goes out with a descending chromatic scale.

| CD 4.9 | Listening Guide 21.2 | "Soy de San Luis" FLACO JIMÉNEZ |

Listen & Reflect

1. How might this song be heard differently by Spanish speakers and non-Spanish speakers? If you have access to the bilingual version recorded in the 1990s by the Texas Tornados, listen for the similarities and differences. How do they change the song's impact?

(Scottish colonists were an important part of the population of Acadia.) In the nineteenth century Cajuns adopted the ten-button diatonic accordion as a lead melody instrument alongside the fiddle, and new dances like the waltz and two-step supplemented reels and jigs. Guitar was added for chordal backup and triangle and spoons for percussion.

Although 78-rpm records of Cajun music date back to the 1920s, the music was little known outside Louisiana until the Balfa Brothers, led by fiddler Dewey Balfa, played the Newport Folk Festival in the 1960s. The group Beausoleil, formed by fiddler Michael Doucet in 1975 and still active today, brought Cajun music, sung in both French and English, to a much wider audience in the 1980s.

Meanwhile, rural French-speaking black Louisianans, or Creoles, adapted Cajun music to their own culture by bringing in African and Caribbean influences, a process that probably began well before 1900. The result is **zydeco**, a name probably derived from the Creole dialect's pronunciation of "les haricots"; "Les haricots sont pas salés" (The green beans aren't salty) is the title of a song about hard times, when one can't afford salt pork to flavor vegetables. In place of the ten-button diatonic accordion, zydeco musicians prefer either a larger version with thirty-one buttons, resembling the instrument used in *conjunto*, or the piano accordion. Either one gives the player access to blue notes not obtainable on the smaller Cajun instrument. Instead of triangle and spoons, zydeco percussion features a washboard, whose player rubs a spoon or bottle opener against the corrugated metal, or a ***frottoir***, a washboard-like instrument that the player wears like a vest. Since the mid-twentieth century, zydeco bands show the influence of rhythm and blues in their use of electric guitar, electric bass, and drum set.

Zydeco combines Cajun-style dance music with Afro-Caribbean syncopation and blues-derived intonation and blue notes. Its history on records begins in the 1950s with Clifton Chenier, the first great zydeco master, a singer and performer on the piano accordion, to which he brought an intense R&B energy. Boozoo Chavis was another early recording artist. But zydeco did not reach a wide audience until the 1980s, when Buckwheat Zydeco and Rockin' Dopsie became well known both with their own bands and through collaboration with rock stars Eric Clapton and Paul Simon. In 1982 the first Grammy awarded to a zydeco musician went to Queen Ida (Ida Lewis Guillory), born in Louisiana in 1929 but raised in San Francisco's small black Creole community. Her performance of "Ful il sa" (LG 21.3), a song by her brother, Al Rapone, demonstrates the foot-stomping

zydeco

LG 21.3

☙ Queen Ida (b. 1929) performing at the 1985 San Francisco Blues Festival.

SONGWRITER: Al Rapone

DATE: 1990

PERFORMERS: Queen Ida and the Bon Temps Zydeco Band; instrumentation: vocals, accordion, electric guitar, electric bass, drums, *frottoir*

GENRE: zydeco

METER: duple

FORM: combination of binary dance tune and verse-and-chorus song

WHAT TO LISTEN FOR

- heavy dance rhythm, reinforced by electric instruments and drums
- instruments typical of zydeco: accordion, *frottoir*
- alternation of instrumental dance tune and verse-and-chorus song in Creole

TIMING	SECTION		COMMENTS
0:00	binary tune	aa	After five pickup notes in the accordion, the full band enters with a strong duple beat.
0:16		b	The second half of the dance tune is played only once here.
0:24	verse 1		Queen Ida's gravelly vocal is heard clearly over the band. The high guitar chords and *frottoir* add upper-register brightness to the ensemble sound.
0:40	chorus		Other band members add their voices.
0:48	binary tune	aa	As before.
1:04		b′b′b	The second half of the tune is played three times, the first two times in a variant form.
1:28	verse 2		The added reverb on Queen Ida's vocal helps it stand out in the texture.
1:44	chorus		As before.
1:53	binary tune	aa	As before.
2:09		bb	The original version of the second half is now played twice: the only time the tune is played in "standard" *aabb* form.
2:25	chorus		As before.
2:34	binary tune	b″b″	Two new variants on the tune's second half. Emphatic close on two loud chords.

Listen & Reflect

1. What elements of this music—song structure, instrumental techniques and textures, vocal style, and so on—resemble their counterparts in any of the traditional or popular songs studied up to now? For example, compare the variants of the binary dance tune with the performance of "Money Musk" (LG 2.2), or the use of solo and combined voices with the nineteenth-century songs in chapter 6.

ᕪ Slack key guitar
master Ledward Kaapana
(b. 1948).

energy of her Bon Temps Zydeco Band. It combines two simple traditional song forms: the instrumental portions are a binary dance, and the vocal portions follow the familiar verse-and-chorus format.

SLACK KEY GUITAR

The music of Hawai'i reveals a range of native adaptations of music brought to the islands by immigrant groups in the nineteenth century. Hawaiian musicians acquired the guitar and similar stringed instruments from the *paniolo*—the Hawaiian term (from *español*) for the Spanish and Portuguese workers on sugar plantations and Mexican *vaqueros* who worked on cattle ranches. From the Portuguese *cavaquinho*, a small, four-stringed guitar, native Hawaiians developed the 'ukulele. Another nineteenth-century Hawaiian innovation is the lap steel guitar, an instrument later adopted by country musicians, as described in chapter 11, and further developed into the pedal steel guitar. One important genre of Hawaiian music uses a standard guitar, however, though in a variety of nonstandard tunings: **slack key** takes its name from the practice of turning the tuning pegs to lower the pitch of selected strings.

By the time slack key guitar was first recorded in the 1940s, it had blended traditional Hawaiian music with harmonies influenced by Christian hymns and the mainland American popular music that had poured into the islands following Hawai'i's annexation by the United States in 1898. At the start of the twentieth century Hawaiian musicians had appropriated the popular songs of Tin Pan Alley to create a style they called *hapa haoli* (half white), which in turn sparked a mainland fad for things Hawaiian in the 1910s and 1920s. It is *hapa haoli*, the mixture of Hawaiian and mainland pop, that most non-Hawaiians think of as Hawaiian music. Slack key draws on all of these influences, including *hapa haoli*, but is its own distinct genre.

Almost all slack key pieces require retuning the guitar, usually by lowering some strings from their standard tuning so that the six strings form a major chord, sometimes with an added note (a sixth or seventh).

E A D G B E (conventional tuning) $\longrightarrow$ D G D G B D (taro patch tuning)

$\longrightarrow$ C G E G A E (Mauna Loa tuning)

$\longrightarrow$ C F C E A C (double slack F)

The retunings allow the guitarist to play combinations of notes that do not easily lie under the left hand in standard tuning. The other main element in the characteristic sound of slack key is the fingerpicking technique, in which the thumb plays an independent bass line on the lower strings, alternating low notes on the beat with middle-register notes between the beats, while the other fingers play melodies and chords on the upper strings.

LG 21.4   For "Wai okeaniani" (LG 21.4), Ledward Kaapana, one of the great slack key masters to emerge in the 1980s, uses "taro patch," in which the open strings

| | CD 4.11 | Listening Guide 21.4 | | "Wai okeaniani" LEDWARD KAAPANA |

SONGWRITER: traditional

DATE: 1992

PERFORMER: Ledward Kaapana

GENRE: slack key guitar

METER: duple

FORM: strophic

WHAT TO LISTEN FOR

- resonant sound of acoustic guitar in slack key tuning
- characteristic Hawaiian vocal technique: wide vibrato, somewhat tense, mid- to lower register
- relaxed but insistent rhythm
- highly polished fingerpicking technique

TIMING	SECTION	COMMENTS
0:00	introduction	4 bars: two statements of the turnaround that closes each stanza.
0:06	stanza 1	10 bars: two 4-bar phrases, followed by an unvarying 2-bar instrumental turnaround. The simple three-chord progression (I, IV, and V) resembles that found in blues and Anglo-American folk songs.
0:23	stanza 2	
0:42	guitar solo 1	10 bars: same phrase and harmonic structure as in the sung stanzas, including the turnaround. In contrast to the simple diatonic melody of the sung portions, solo begins with chromatically decorated notes. At the halfway point, a short bass run displays **palm muting**, an important technique in both acoustic and electric guitar playing.
0:58	stanza 3	
1:15	stanza 4	
1:33	guitar solo 2	20 bars: Equivalent of 2 stanzas. Begins delicately in the upper register and works its way downward. Second stanza like solo 1 but more elaborately ornamented.
2:07	stanza 5	
2:24	stanza 6	
2:42	guitar solo 3	20 bars: Another pair of solo stanzas display Kaapana's quiet virtuosity, using a variety of right-hand and left-hand techniques.
3:15	stanza 7	Kaapana repeats the second phrase, for a total of 12 bars.
3:40	tag	4 bars: Turnaround is extended by playing it twice, with a short extension the second time.

(continued)

| CD 4.11 | Listening Guide 21.4 | "Wai okeaniani" LEDWARD KAAPANA |

Listen & Reflect

1. As described in chapter 11, significant exchanges took place between early country musicians and Hawaiian musicians in touring tent-rep shows in the South. One can only speculate as to whether Maybelle Carter's techniques influenced Hawaiian musicians or vice versa. Compare slack key guitar with Carter-style guitar, as in "Can the Circle Be Unbroken" (LG 11.2). What relationship can you hear between the two?

2. How would you characterize Kaapana's singing? Consider range, register, and vocal tension. Also, how does the voice complement or clash with the instrumental sonority?

form a G major chord (actually an F-sharp major chord in the performance heard here, since the entire instrument is tuned a half-step flat). The words to this traditional song, sung in Hawaiian, comment on the beauty of the islanders' natural surroundings. This performance, recorded for Smithsonian/Folkways Records, took place as part of a multiethnic folk festival in Virginia in 1992.

KLEZMER

The influx of 20 million immigrants to the United States between 1880 and 1920 ushered in a new era in American ethnic history. Though significant numbers came from China and Japan, and smaller numbers from nations throughout the world, by far the most immigrants came from Europe. Of these, the two largest groups were Italians and Eastern European Jews. Although Jewish communities had been part of the American fabric since colonial times, the arrival of large groups of Yiddish-speaking Jews, fleeing the pogroms in Russia and Poland, forever altered the face of American Jewish ethnicity. Most European immigrants arrived in the United States via Ellis Island, and many of these settled in New York City's Lower East Side. Tenements became ethnic enclaves, where languages, religious customs, foods, and other traditional practices could be preserved and the process of assimilation to a new culture thereby eased.

American klezmer   Among the cultural practices retained by Yiddish-speaking American Jews was a type of secular music developed in the Russian and Austro-Hungarian empires and in Romania and associated particularly with wedding celebrations. A musician who played this type of music was called a *klezmer* (plural *klezmorim*, from the Hebrew phrase for "vessels of song"), and in the United States that term was extended to the music itself. **Klezmer** is a living repertory of traditional Jewish songs and dances, such as *freylekhs* and *zhoks*, to which new pieces are continually added ("klezmer" is also used to refer to the musical style). In Eastern Europe the instrumentation typically emphasized violin and folk instruments such as the *tsimbl*, a hammered dulcimer. In its American incarnation, the typical klezmer band resembles a theater orchestra of the vaudeville era, which was also the era of peak Jewish immigration: the melody is carried by violin, trumpet, and clarinet, with lower brass and piano filling out the texture and with a foundation supplied by string bass and sometimes drums. More distinctively American instruments like banjo and saxophone are occasionally heard on old klezmer records as well, and accordion and other instruments are also not unusual.

As the change in instrumentation suggests, American *klezmorim* were open to influences from American popular music. In this respect they were not far removed from such Jewish immigrants and children of immigrants as Irving Berlin and George Gershwin, who immersed themselves in popular music and found success on Tin Pan Alley. Even the more traditional *klezmorim* found ways to bring jazz and popular song into their repertory. By the 1920s and 1930s, stars of Yiddish theater and film, which flourished especially in New York City, were singing songs that sounded like a sort of Jewish jazz, and in the 1930s and 1940s klezmer-derived songs like "And the Angels Sing" and "Bay mir bistu sheyn" were crossover big-band swing hits.

↪ The Klezmer Conservatory Band recreates the sound and spirit of early twentieth-century klezmer.

Following the Holocaust, however, klezmer's association with that historical tragedy, combined with the dwindling number of Yiddish speakers, led to a quick decline in the music's popularity among Jewish listeners. Then, in the wake of the urban folk revival, a younger generation of musicians exploring their musical roots rediscovered the music and sought out surviving past masters such as clarinetist Dave Tarras. Revivalist klezmer bands began to form in the 1970s, and by the 1980s klezmer was once again alive and well. Today a second wave of klezmer revival is taking the music in new directions, with groups like the Klezmatics incorporating contemporary jazz, punk, and Middle Eastern music into their original repertory.

the revival of klezmer

The Klezmer Conservatory Band, founded in 1979, revives the jazzier, more theatrical side of American klezmer. Their rendition of "Oy, s'iz gut" (LG 21.5) is a tribute to Molly Picon, the Yiddish theater and film star who introduced the song in the 1937 musical *Mayn Malkele*. The music uses a minor mode with a raised fourth scale degree, a major mode with a lowered seventh scale degree, and melodic phrases that emphasize the interval of an augmented second (e.g., E flat to F sharp), all of which resemble various modes used in synagogue cantillation. Otherwise, the song follows the conventions of a typical classic American popular song: an introductory verse (here sung in the middle as an interlude) and a thirty-two-bar *aaba* chorus. The performance swings like 1930s jazz, and the second chorus has jazzlike two-bar breaks, though the solos that fill them are in a traditional klezmer style, with elaborate melodic embellishments and a driving, nonswinging rhythm. At the bridge in the second chorus, the band drops the swing style and plays the eight bars as a traditional *freylekh*, a fast dance of Bulgarian origin.

LG 21.5

A few common traits link many types of roots music. Most function as an emblem of ethnic pride for a designated social group. At the same time, most show traces of contact with other social groups, and any notion of ethnic "purity" is contrary to the reality of the music's history. Moreover, many types of roots music have

| CD 4.12 | Listening Guide 21.5 | "Oy, s'iz gut" KLEZMER CONSERVATORY BAND |

SONGWRITERS: Jacob Jacobs and Abraham Ellstein

DATE: 1937; recorded 1997

PERFORMERS: Instrumentation: vocal, clarinet, trumpet, trombone, violin, bass, piano, drums

GENRE: klezmer

METER: duple

FORM: *aaba* chorus with verse

WHAT TO LISTEN FOR

- alternation of swing rhythm with *parlando* verse and *freylekh* bridge in second chorus
- solos in two-bar breaks, as in early jazz, but played in klezmer style
- vocal sung in Yiddish
- minor mode and occasional augmented second as musical signifiers of Jewish ethnicity

TIMING	SECTION		TEXT	TRANSLATION	COMMENTS
0:00	introduction				4 bars establish "Jewish-sounding" minor key with swing rhythm.
0:05	chorus	*a*	Oy, s'iz gut! ...	Oh, it's good to sit with your beloved, Oh, it's good when your head is a-spinning, Oh, it's good to tell your girl you love her.	The melody outlines the minor tonic triad, then quick notes touch on the raised fourth scale degree. The first *a* section ends with a 2-bar clarinet break in klezmer style.
0:17		*a*	Oy, si'z gut! ...	Oh, it's good, as my mother used to say, Oh, it's good to carry a secret in your heart, Oh, it's good to be the master of your own home.	
0:28		*b*	Oy, kh'hob shoyn dem bestn simen ...	Oh, I just knew you were really fine. Oh, since he came along he's become a part of me.	In the relative major, but with a flatted seventh that resembles a Jewish liturgical mode.
0:41		*a*	Oy, si'z gut! ...	Oh, it's good to hear words of love, Oh, it's good that no one is here to interfere, My heart is beating at this moment. Oh, it's good!	A return of the opening melody rounds out the 32-bar *aaba* chorus.

| CD 4.12 | Listening Guide 21.5 | "Oy, s'iz gut" KLEZMER CONSERVATORY BAND |

TIMING	SECTION		TEXT	TRANSLATION	COMMENTS
0:54	verse		Kinder libe fargest nit keyner...	Young love is never forgotten, It seeps into your bones, That's what my mother used to say. She would become so happy When she'd talk about her own wedding. How the wedding jester recited so beautifully, As he exhorted the bride to cry. The musicians serenaded the bride and groom. If only I could have such a wedding.	The verse is taken slowly, in *parlando* (speechlike) rhythm. The stepwise melody includes "Jewish-sounding" augmented seconds.
1:47	chorus	*a*	Oy, s'iz gut!...	Oh, it's good when the clarinet plays, Oh, it's good when the fiddle answers,	The altered chorus now trades 2 bars of singing with 2-bar breaks for solo instruments in klezmer style.
1:59		*a*	Oy, s'iz gut!...	Oh, it's good when the trumpet blasts, Oh, it's good when the roaring bass sounds.	Trumpet and an ensemble bass line fill the last two breaks.
2:10		*b*			The bridge is played instrumentally in the style of a *freylekh*.
2:23		*a*	Oy, s'iz gut!...	Oh, it's good to hear words of love, Oh, it's good that no one will ever break us apart, This very minute my heart is pounding with excitement. Oh, it's good!	A return to the swing style for the final *a* section, which is extended into a short coda.

NOTE Translation from liner notes for the Klezmer Conservatory Band, *Dancing in the Aisles* (Rounder CD 3155, 1997).

Listen & Reflect

1. Of the examples of roots music heard in this chapter, this song comes the closest to mainstream popular music, though of a self-consciously old-fashioned variety. What does placing "Oy, s'iz gut" under the umbrella of "roots music" say about that label, what it means, and how it is used?

benefited from the folk festival as an institution that both conserves and disseminates the music, bringing it to new audiences in a way that ideally is for the good of the musicians who create it.

The roots revival indicates the heightened value placed on traditional music in recent decades. Like popular music, folk music has proved to have lasting value for listeners of a sort that used to be ascribed only to classical music. One result of that higher valuation is a further blurring of the distinctions that once were held between the classical, popular, and folk spheres. As the next chapter will disclose, that breakdown of hierarchies has led in our own time to a vibrant musical culture that is filled with possibilities for new musical innovations.

QUESTIONS FOR DISCUSSION AND REVIEW

1. How does the category "roots music" differ from earlier definitions of "folk music" as discussed in chapters 9, 14, and 17? How do these changing definitions reflect larger societal changes in the nineteenth and twentieth centuries?

2. The introduction to this chapter states that each type of music discussed here "originated in the contact between two or more ethnic groups." What evidence supports that statement for powwow music, *norteño*, zydeco, slack key guitar, and klezmer?

3. Does the roots revival represent a countervailing trend to the 1980s' emphasis on eclecticism and hybridity, or does the transformation of roots music from subculture to the larger musical culture reinforce that emphasis?

FURTHER READING

Browner, Tara C. "Making and Singing Pow-wow Songs: Text, Form, and the Significance of Culture-based Analysis." *Ethnomusicology* 44 (2000): 214–33.

Chew Sánchez, Martha I. *Corridos in Migrant Memory*. Albuquerque: University of New Mexico Press, 2006.

Koskoff, Ellen, ed. *The Garland Encyclopedia of World Music*. Vol. 3. *The United States and Canada*. New York: Garland, 1998.

Sandmel, Ben. *Zydeco!* Jackson: University Press of Mississippi, 1999.

Slobin, Mark, ed. *American Klezmer: Its Roots and Offshoots*. Berkeley and Los Angeles: University of California Press, 2002.

Zotigh, Dennis W. "Moving History: The Evolution of the Powwow." Oklahoma City: Oklahoma Historical Society Folklife Center, 1991. Online at http://www.okhistory.org/research/folkarticles/MovingHistory.pdf.

FURTHER LISTENING AND VIEWING

Friedman, Susan. *Ki ho'alu: That's Slack Key Guitar*. Cambridge, MA: Rounder Records, 1995. Videocassette.

Into the Circle: An Introduction to Native American Powwows. Produced by Scott Swearingen and Sandy Rhoades. State Arts Council of Oklahoma. Tulsa, OK: Full Circle Communications, 1992. Videocasette.

Powwow Songs: Music of the Plains Indians. New World Records, 1986.

REMIX

America's Music since 1990

From the start of this exploration of America's music, we have used the conceptual model of three spheres of musical activity: the classical, the popular, and the folk or traditional. At some points in history the model fits quite well and at others not so well. Some kinds of music making belong firmly in one sphere, while others seem to straddle two or even all three. The most recent developments in the history of America's music suggest that the three spheres can now overlap to such an extent that the similarities among music styles, as varied as those styles may be, are no less significant than the differences. The convergence of classical, popular, and traditional elements indicates that the United States has a dynamic music culture that continues to develop in fresh ways. Distinctive traits defining each sphere persist nonetheless, and the sense of negotiating boundaries is part of what makes certain kinds of new music eventful.

JAZZ: AMERICA'S CLASSICAL MUSIC?

Since the 1960s jazz has seen both a proliferation of styles and a shift in the music's cultural position. Alongside the development of free jazz and fusion, described in earlier chapters, a family of musical approaches coalescing in the wake of bebop and post-bop styles came to be known as mainstream jazz, or **straight-ahead jazz**. Keepers of the straight-ahead flame included such musicians as Dizzy Gillespie, Thelonious Monk, Sarah Vaughan, Sonny Rollins, and Art Blakey. Older artists such as Earl Hines, Coleman Hawkins, and Roy Eldridge continued to work in the idioms they had helped to establish decades earlier. During the 1960s, too, Duke Ellington continued to find the big band an arena open to fresh musical creativity.

As straight-ahead jazz proved its artistic worth as a music to be composed and studied as well as performed and listened to, the notion of formal instruction took hold in the United States. Programs of jazz study were established in schools and colleges beginning in the 1960s, and by the end of the 1970s a quarter million

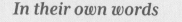

In their own words

Dr. Billy Taylor on Jazz as a Classical Music

Jazz is America's classical music. It is both a way of spontaneously composing music and a repertoire, which has resulted from the musical language developed by improvising artists. Though it is often fun to play, jazz is *very serious* music. As an important musical language, it has developed steadily from a single expression of the consciousness of *black* people into a *national* music that expresses American ideals and attitudes to Americans and to people from other cultures all around the world.

people were studying jazz formally. Today many—perhaps even most—professional jazz musicians have some amount of formal jazz training. Moreover, in a move unprecedented for any music in the popular sphere, musicians and institutions devoted to jazz now are eligible for grants from government agencies and private foundations. The idea of grants for jazz musicians is a symptom of the music's position in the twenty-first century: recognized as artistically important but largely overlooked by the audience for popular music.

Schools have not been the only institutions to embrace jazz. The Smithsonian Institution set up a jazz program in 1970. Important record reissues followed, and so did Smithsonian-sponsored concerts by ensembles reconstructing jazz performances of the past. Those concerts gave birth to the **jazz repertory movement**: a trend since the 1980s to view jazz as a music with a history that has produced, chiefly in the form of phonograph recordings, a body of masterpieces worth preserving. In the latter particular, if not in its unwritten sources, it resembles the European classical repertory. An influential 1986 article by pianist and educator Billy Taylor titled "Jazz: America's Classical Music" marked a defining moment in jazz's passage through folk, popular, and classical spheres. By the standards used to measure value in classical music, jazz now fitted that description.

the jazz repertory movement

One of the premier jazz repertory ensembles is the Jazz at Lincoln Center Orchestra. Organized in 1987, the group presents historically minded concerts that are the centerpiece of a jazz program at New York's Lincoln Center for the Performing Arts, the home of the New York Philharmonic, the Metropolitan Opera, the Juilliard School, and other organizations associated with the classical sphere. In the 1990s the jazz program was formally instituted as Jazz at Lincoln Center, and in 2004 it moved into a newly designed performing arts complex containing three performance spaces, an education center, and a museum-like hall of fame.

Wynton Marsalis

Jazz at Lincoln Center's director since its inception has been Wynton Marsalis, perhaps the best-known figure in jazz today. A native of New Orleans, Marsalis, born in 1961, shares Taylor's view that jazz is not only an African American inheritance but also a broader reflection of American character. Backed by a pedigree that includes professional training at the Juilliard School and performances of many classical works, Marsalis has presented himself as an artist working within the jazz tradition's strict standards—that is, the evolutionary stream beginning with ragtime and blues and followed by such styles as New Orleans, Chicago, New York (the dance orchestras of Duke Ellington and Fletcher Henderson), Kansas City swing, bebop, and more recent spin-offs from the straight-ahead mainstream grounded in the rhythmic innovations of the 1940s and 1950s and in the ethos and tonal framework of the blues.

Marsalis won two Grammy awards in 1983, one for best classical solo performance and one for best jazz solo performance, and repeated that achievement the next year. In 1997 the Pulitzer Prize in music composition was awarded for

Trumpeter-composer Wynton Marsalis, director of New York's Jazz at Lincoln Center Orchestra.

the first time to a jazz work: Marsalis's oratorio *Blood on the Fields*, an epic work for vocal soloists and jazz ensemble. By then he had written a series of ambitious multimovement compositions, beginning with *In This House, on This Morning*, which was commissioned by Jazz at Lincoln Center, premiered in 1992, and released as a two-CD set in 1994. Scored for seven players, the piece is an instrumental depiction of a Sunday worship service in a Southern black church, from sunrise prayers to the home-cooked meal that follows the service. Its twenty-one separate sections, grouped into three large parts, span nearly two hours in performance.

Although many of those sections draw on the expressive power of the jazz tradition's rhythmic groove, the opening, "Devotional" (LG 22.1), is in free tempo. "Devotional" also introduces musical material that will be heard in later sections: especially the wide-ranging six-note figure played first by the soprano saxophone, then the double bass, then the trumpet, and finally again by the soprano sax as the section nears its end. This figure is used in "Devotional" as a blues-like call, representing a deacon who leads the prayers, with the other instruments suggesting the responses from the congregation: a bluesy eighth-note piano figure, two or three bell-like piano chords, and hushed chords from the rest of the players. Only twice does the drummer join in the ensemble, as if an in-tempo section is about to start. Both times, after a brief polyrhythmic moment, a unifying call returns and the beat again becomes flexible. While "Devotional" is not intended as a free-standing piece, it provides an example of how non-swinging jazz elements can be used to introduce a large-scale musical structure.

LG 22.1

In a milieu of strong-minded individuals, it is no surprise that Marsalis's stance has drawn criticism, especially since he became a dispenser of patronage through Jazz at Lincoln Center. Many musicians have disagreed with his historicist approach to a tradition that since the 1950s has evolved into a broad range of musical styles,

the Wynton controversy

CD 4.13	Listening Guide 22.1	"Devotional," from *In This House, on This Morning*
		WYNTON MARSALIS

PERFORMERS: Wynton Marsalis Septet: Wynton Marsalis, trumpet; Wycliffe Gordon, trombone; Wessell Anderson and Todd Williams, saxophones; Eric Reed, piano; Reginald Veal, bass; Herlin Riley, drums

DATE: 1992

GENRE: jazz concert piece

METER: indefinite, changing

FORM: through-composed

WHAT TO LISTEN FOR

- references to blues and gospel music
- use of dissonant harmonies and indefinite, changing meters and tempos
- expanded role of rhythm section

TIMING	COMMENTS
0:00	Solo soprano sax sounds the six-note "call to worship" motive.
0:10	Piano responds with a bluesy gospel lick, with tambourine in the background.
0:16	The "congregation" responds, with the tenor sax "testifying."
0:32	Piano chords resemble the sound of church bells.
0:44	Solo bowed bass sounds the "call"; the ensemble adds its "amen."
1:13	Piano "bells."
1:18	Music becomes more rhythmically active, as the drums start to keep time.
1:25	New repeated-note motive in soprano sax over gospel piano.
1:37	Solo bass and ensemble call and response.
1:48	Piano "bells."
1:55	Instruments enter one by one, stacking up loud, dissonant chords, concluding with a gospel-flavored cadence.
2:15	Six-note "call" in trumpet, harmonized in block chords, with gospel piano response.
2:37	Repeated-note motive in soprano sax returns.
2:45	Faster version of the "call," with gospel piano response.
2:55	Slower version of the "call," in dissonant harmony.
3:16	Piano "bells" slowly fade.

🎧 CD 4.13	Listening Guide 22.1	*"Devotional," from In This House, on This Morning* WYNTON MARSALIS

Listen & Reflect

1. What aspects of "Devotional" remind you of any of the blues, gospel, and jazz music studied in earlier chapters? What aspects remind you of modernist classical music? Do those different aspects seem to merge smoothly or stand in opposition to one another, and why?

2. What arguments can you make that "Devotional" supports the idea that jazz is now a classical music, not a popular music? How might you argue the opposite: that "Devotional" shows how jazz remains in the popular sphere?

linked chiefly by improvisation. Some have also challenged his image of jazz musicians. As clarinetist Don Byron has put it: "One of the fallacies of the Wynton era is that jazz cats don't listen to rap." For trumpeter Lester Bowie, the tradition is far broader than Marsalis has granted. Jazz, Bowie said shortly before his death in 1999, is "not simple music anymore. So it does belong in the concert hall. But it also belongs in the street, on the farm, it needs equal access everywhere, the same as country western, rap, anything. Because jazz is all of these."

Marsalis told an interviewer in 1984 that a society's ultimate achievement "is the establishment of an art form . . . indigenous to that society." He explained that during the 1940s, jazz musicians, including Armstrong, Parker, Ellington, and Monk, "introduced an entire range of mood and emotion into the vocabulary of Western music, an entirely new way of phrasing, an entirely new way of thinking in the language of music" that "perfectly captures the spirit and tone of America." Their contribution, however, went unrecognized. For one thing, racism and economic inequality had marginalized jazz. For another, improvisation was thought to rely more on intuition than on intellect. And for yet another, cultural standards had slipped to the point that "anything can pass for art." Marsalis blamed the mass media for promoting a popular culture with everything reduced to the lowest common denominator. And he challenged his colleagues to fight for standards: "We musicians should never forget that it is our job to educate people, to stand up for excellence and quality." In his view, the excellence and quality of jazz are democratic and characteristically American because the music combines a vernacular base with a hunger for artistic exploration. "To me," Marsalis declared, "the test of true greatness in an artist is the ability to write or perform music that is on the very highest level but can also appeal to common people. That's the problem Beethoven, Stravinsky, Charlie Parker, and Louis Armstrong all faced."

Marsalis's comments reveal a belief in hierarchy: jazz *deserves* to be part of an educational agenda; Ellington's artistry places him on an *equal* footing with such European composers as Beethoven and Stravinsky. But perhaps the most striking notion of all is that *no music is more thoroughly American than jazz*—that is, the blues-based strain of jazz championed by Marsalis—whose civilizing force has provided a much-needed boost to the nation's sense of humanity.

jazz and cultural hierarchy

The artistic recognition that jazz has received in recent years testifies not only to its new position in American music but also to the way the elements of jazz cut across the three spheres of music. Rooted in black folk music, jazz has also relied on the popular sphere for repertory and forms; the careers of jazz musicians are still mostly carried on in the popular sphere's marketplace, but some have identified with the traditional sphere (chiefly African) and others more with the classical concert hall and the academy. Finally, once jazz is recorded, it can be analyzed historically, culturally, and technically with the help of approaches developed in the classical sphere. Works that pass muster may then be treated as part of a transcendent musical legacy. Thus a music that was once socially controversial, linked in the minds of some with a lack of schooled musicianship and sometimes with unreliable conduct, enjoys today the respected status due a full-fledged art form.

ROCK, ROOTS, AND REBELLION

By the 1990s the cyclic pattern of rock history—rebellion, commodification, and reformation—showed signs of accelerating into a nonstop spin. Rock and roll had originated in the 1950s as a rebellious "outsider" music—chiefly because it was aimed at a teenage market, for which no previous musical style had been created. But by the 1970s, as the story goes, it had accommodated itself to the mainstream popular music industry so fully that its listeners began to find it a toothless lion, still capable of an occasional roar but with no bite. Punk rock, the 1970s reformation movement that restored rock's outsider status, had by the end of the decade already smoothed its rough edges to become MTV-friendly New Wave. The hardcore punk reformation of the 1980s likewise combed its hair and became radio-friendly college rock. By the end of the 1980s heavy metal and rap had found a home on MTV. Today, rebellion, commodification, and reformation describe not successive developmental stages but rather different aspects of a segmented musical marketplace.

Since the 1990s a highly polished mainstream music, aimed at teens and even preteens, has shared the media with an array of outsider music, such as alternative rock, jam bands, singer-songwriters, and roots musicians of various stripes. Although anticommercialism is a common posture in outsider music, some musicians have found it to be highly profitable, raising the uncomfortable possibility that the anti-mainstream stance is now part of the mainstream, and that nonconformity is the new orthodoxy—in which case, the very notion of a "mainstream" is called into question.

ALTERNATIVE ROCK AND ITS ALTERNATIVES

From the 1990s to the present day, alternative rock has been in a state of seemingly permanent rebellion against what its adherents consider to be a crassly commercial, inauthentic mainstream. In contrast to such popular 1990s mainstream acts as the Backstreet Boys, *NSYNC, and Britney Spears, alternative rock is distinguished by a set of values derived from punk: the musical texture is dominated by loud, distorted guitars; song lyrics tend to be angry and nihilistic; displays of virtuosity are rejected in favor of a deliberately amateurish, do-it-yourself aesthetic; and clothing and hairstyles tend to be ostentatiously unostentatious.

All of these characteristics are on display in **grunge**, the alternative rock that emerged in Seattle in the late 1980s and found widespread popularity in the early 1990s. The band that brought grunge to the national scene was Nirvana, whose leader, Kurt Cobain, born in 1967, was hailed by the media as a spokesperson for his generation, much as Bob Dylan had been labeled in the 1960s. Nirvana's "Smells Like Teen Spirit," a number 1 pop hit in 1992, sets a mood of cynicism and despair with its opening words, "Load up on guns and bring your friends / It's fun to lose and to pretend." The chorus articulates disaffection and passivity: "I feel stupid and contagious / Here we are now, entertain us." The music, an insistent two-bar phrase that repeats with no variation other than instrumentation and dynamics, adds to the mood of futility. This, grunge argued, was the dominant ethos of Generation X. Only two years later Cobain was dead from a self-inflicted gunshot wound.

grunge

If Nirvana took hopelessness to a fatal extreme, other alternative rock acts were able to tone down the nihilism and achieve remarkable longevity. Pearl Jam and Green Day are two veteran bands that originated in grunge and have continued to the present day, modifying their sound and aesthetic stance along the way. Each band has also sold over 60 million records, making them two of the most popular and commercially successful acts at the turn of the century. Therein lies the paradox of alternative rock: as the most prominent and profitable genre in rock today, just what is it an alternative to?

Other rock musicians pursued different alternatives to the glitzy artifice of mainstream pop. One descendant of heavy metal is **industrial rock**, best represented by the "group" Nine Inch Nails, actually the overdubbed, studio-created music of an individual musician, Trent Reznor; after creating an album in the studio, Reznor assembles a band to perform the music live on tours. He augments heavily distorted guitars and pounding drums with electronic sounds and eerily processed vocals to express a dark, pessimistic worldview. Even his quieter moments maintain an unsettled atmosphere, as in "Hurt," a 1994 song that reached a wider audience in a cover version recorded by country singer Johnny Cash in 2002, only a year before his death.

Another industrial act is Marilyn Manson, a band that updated the 1970s stage persona of Alice Cooper: both bands used the same name for the group and for the (male) lead singer, both made provocative fashion statements, both shared heavy metal's fascination with the grotesque and occult, and both were the targets of outraged moral watchdogs who argued that their music was detrimental to young audiences. In a 1996 press conference William Bennett, formerly George H. W. Bush's "drug czar," denounced Marilyn Manson, along with Nine Inch Nails and other groups, as an assault on decency. When it became rumored that the Colorado teenagers responsible for the shootings at Columbine High School in 1999 had been avid fans of violent bands and video games, Marilyn Manson was so heavily attacked in the press that the band canceled their performances in mid-tour. But after a short hiatus the furor died down and the group resumed recording and touring, though in the post–September 11, 2001, cultural climate Marilyn Manson's acts of provocation have lost the power to shock that they had in the 1990s.

Marilyn Manson in concert: for many parents in the 1990s a symptom of civilization's decline and fall.

rap metal

Whereas Marilyn Manson updated the more theatrical branch of heavy metal that had spawned the 1980s hair bands, other groups emulated Metallica and Megadeth in saving the flamboyance for the music itself. An important new development was **rap metal**, which combined the assaultive instrumental textures of heavy metal with rapped vocals. Rage Against the Machine pioneered rap metal in the early 1990s, adding funk rhythms and scratching to the mix. By the end of the decade one of the most innovative bands was System of a Down, whose four members are of Armenian descent and bring the rhythmic complexity of Middle Eastern music to rap metal, especially in the work of Beirut-born drummer John Dolmayan.

jam bands

roots rock

Many musicians reached further back than heavy metal for inspiration. **Jam bands** such as Phish and the Dave Matthews Band continued the legacy of the 1960s-era Grateful Dead by focusing on live performance more than recording, touring incessantly, and developing instrumental virtuosity in long solos. Other artists pursued **roots rock**, which, as the name implies, combined a return to earlier rock sounds with the roots revival's interest in folk music. Roots rockers include the Wallflowers (led by Bob Dylan's son Jakob Dylan) and Counting Crows. Sheryl Crow has probably had the longest-lasting influence; she is also among the significant number of female singer-songwriters to emerge since 1990.

WOMEN SINGER-SONGWRITERS

As male-female relations changed in late twentieth-century America, women began to explore a widening range of identities. Music has been involved in that exploration. In the early 1960s, for example, girl groups spoke powerfully to young women, who were bombarded with contradictory messages from parents, teachers, and the mass media. The songs of girl groups allowed teens to play at being the defiant rebel as well as the docile girlfriend. "Sweet Talkin' Guy," a Chiffons record from 1960 about a deceitful, irresistible charmer, sent the message that it's normal to want to yield to such boys as well as to try to resist them.

Movies, literature, and fashion in the 1960s proclaimed a new openness about sexuality. That openness followed a breakthrough in contraception: the 1960 appearance on the market of the birth control pill. Women could now engage more freely in sexual activity without worrying about unwanted pregnancies. With fertility under their control through contraception and early-term abortion, legalized in 1973, growing numbers of married women pursued careers outside the home, and family roles changed accordingly. The women's movement of the 1960s and 1970s challenged the idea that women are truly fulfilled only through child care and housework.

As discussed in chapter 13, songwriters in the 1920s began celebrating romantic love between unattached individuals. But rock introduced other views of love. Where the characters in earlier love songs longed for connection, those in rock songs also perceived that male-female relations involve power. Though women may have been freed from earlier stereotypes, they were assigned new ones, still subordinate to men, including the flower child, earth mother, and idealized prostitute. The tension between sexual freedom and restraint persisted.

Whatever the balance of power between males and females today, since the 1990s the popular media have tended to portray young modern women as independent, even untamable, rejecting the view that their identity revolves around duty. *Trouble Girls: The Rolling Stone Book of Women in Rock* (1997), written and edited entirely by women, touts the need for women to speak their mind and to confront misogyny. In the preface, a prominent female rock critic of the 1960s endorses truth telling, wherever it leads: "Music that boldly and aggressively laid out what the singer wanted, loved, hated—as good rock & roll did—challenged me to do the same, and so, even when the content was antiwoman . . . the form encouraged my struggle for liberation." Around the same time that *Trouble Girls* appeared, the punk-inspired **riot grrrl** movement was at its height, with groups like Bikini Kill and Sleater-Kinney proving that women could rock just as hard as men.

Following in the footsteps of rock, folk, and country songwriters like Carole King, Joni Mitchell, Laura Nyro, Loretta Lynn, and Dolly Parton, women singer-songwriters since 1990 have continued to explore new aspects of feminine identity, one facet of the late-century phenomenon of third-wave feminism (the first wave being the pre-1920 suffrage movement and the second wave being the 1970s women's movement). The third wave's more fluid concepts of gender roles and sexuality are evident in the songs of Tori Amos, Liz Phair, and the Canadians Alanis Morrisette and Sarah McLachlan. Two artists whose careers began in the 1980s, Suzanne Vega and Michelle Shocked, are representative of the **anti-folk** movement, a category that embraces singer-songwriters whose sound is too edgy or punk to be considered part of the folk tradition.

Another anti-folk musician is Ani DiFranco, who projects a vibrant feminism on albums such as *Not a Pretty Girl* (1995). Resisting corporate inauthenticity, DiFranco turned down major label contracts, instead forming her own record company, Righteous Babe. DiFranco's label distributes not only her own records but also those of other hard-to-classify singer-songwriters, such as Anaïs Mitchell, whose *Hadestown* (2010) is a concept album (Mitchell calls it a "folk opera," the same term Gershwin applied to *Porgy and Bess*) that retells the Greek myth of Orpheus and Eurydice in a postapocalyptic setting that resembles the 1930s Great Depression.

Just as rock spawned alternative rock and folk gave rise to anti-folk, country music encountered its own oppositional movement in the 1990s: alternative country, or **alt.country**. Inspired by an older generation of country rockers like Gram Parsons and Texas "outlaw" musicians Joe Ely and Jimmie Dale Gilmore, alt.country blends traditional country elements with roots rock and punk, whose oppositional stance and do-it-yourself aesthetic it emulates. Sometimes alt.country is referred to as *No Depression*, the name of a magazine devoted to the music since its inception in 1995, and which in turn takes its name from the Carter Family song "No Depression in Heaven." Because of its wide range of stylistic resources, from honky-tonk to bluegrass and rockabilly, alt.country is also known by the label **Americana**.

The one element studiously avoided by alt.country musicians is the sound of contemporary mainstream country, as produced by the country music establishment in Nashville. The Nashville scene, from an alt.country perspective, represents all that is false, slick, and deracinated in our present-day music culture. Alt.country musicians seek to restore authenticity by reconnecting with traditionalist roots, filtered through an ironic, postmodernist sensibility.

The riot grrrl movement took its name from a *zine*: a small-circulation publication, usually reproduced on photocopiers. Like the music, zines were important in creating and supporting a subcultural identity for their readership.

alt.country

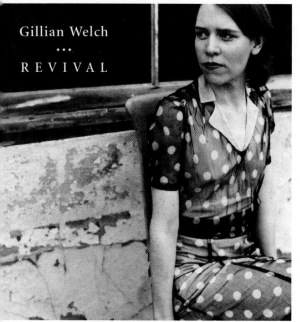

Gillian Welch
• • •
R E V I V A L

The cover of *Revival* (1996) represents Gillian Welch (b. 1967) as a figure from the Great Depression.

Along with singer-songwriters Steve Earle and Lucinda Williams, one of the most influential alt.country artists is Gillian Welch, who brings an unusual pedigree to country music. The daughter of two television screenwriters, Welch grew up in Los Angeles and attended the University of California at Santa Cruz, where she played bass and drums in goth and psychedelic bands. After studying songwriting at the Berklee College of Music in Boston, she moved to Nashville in 1992 with her musical collaborator David Rawlings. There they gained the attention of T-Bone Burnett, a veteran of Bob Dylan's 1970s Rolling Thunder Revue and the producer of several successful roots rock and country albums. Burnett produced Welch's first two albums, *Revival* (1996) and *Hell among the Yearlings* (1998), and included Welch in his soundtrack for the Coen brothers film *O Brother Where Art Thou?* (2000). When a larger corporation bought out Welch's label, Almo, which also recorded British electronica artist Imogen Heap and the alternative rock band Garbage, Welch formed her own independent label, Acony, on which she has released her subsequent work.

"Orphan Girl" (LG 22.2) the first track on Welch's debut album, exemplifies her characteristic songwriting, performance, and production style. The song's structure is bone simple, with rudimentary harmonies and a folklike melody sung in an untrained voice with a rural southern accent. Combined with a Carter-style acoustic guitar and a harmonizing backup vocal, the effect is of an old-time hillbilly record. Enhancing that effect is the intentionally low-fidelity audio quality, which Burnett obtained by tracking down vintage recording equipment purported to have been used by Hank Williams. "We wanted the record to sound real and tough," Welch explained, "real and small, with everything mashed together and one thing fighting through another. It gives the songs character."

But the song's production is deceptively simple-sounding and includes instruments that would have been unfamiliar to the country icons Welch invokes. The discreet backup one might expect from a second acoustic guitar is played instead on a six-string bass guitar (essentially an electric guitar tuned one octave lower). Near the end of the track, a distorted electric guitar seems to beam down from an alternative rock universe. And throughout, watery organ chords emanate from an Optigan, an early-1970s electronic keyboard designed for amateurs that used prerecorded optical soundtracks, like those used in motion pictures, to generate sound. Like its professional counterpart, the Mellotron, the Optigan provides some of the "vintage synthesizer" sounds prized by present-day electronics antiquarians.

LG 22.2   "Orphan Girl" thus evokes the past, but which past is intended: 1930s Carter Family, 1950s Hank Williams, or 1970s analog synthesizers? The combination of sonic elements suggests that Welch uses them as costumes for a musical masquerade, much like the Depression-era polka-dot dress she wears on the album's cover. Even the song's sacred overtones are part of the act; in one of her gospel songs, "Rock of Ages," Welch mistakenly refers to the four Gospel writers—Matthew, Mark, Luke, and John—as "prophets," revealing herself as an outsider in relation to the religious traditions from which Southern white gospel music springs. Piety, like the rural poverty and deprivation that haunt the characters in her songs, appears to be just another mask she wears. But to dismiss Welch as a mere poseur is to miss the point of her postmodernist pastiche. Coming from

| CD 4.14 | Listening Guide 22.2 | "Orphan Girl" GILLIAN WELCH |

SONGWRITER: Gillian Welch

DATE: 1996

PERFORMERS: Gillian Welch, vocal, acoustic guitar; David Rawlings, vocal, electric guitar, six-string bass, Optigan; T-Bone Burnett, Optigan

GENRE: alt.country

METER: duple

FORM: verse and chorus

WHAT TO LISTEN FOR

- "old-timey" sound of Carter-style guitar
- vocal style and lyrics suggestive of 1930s country
- understated yet sophisticated production indicative of song's 1990s origin

TIMING	SECTION	LYRICS	COMMENT
0:00	introduction		4 bars: Carter-style guitar suggests a Depression-era setting. Very quiet organ (Optigan) chords add a subliminal religious aura.
0:07	verse 1	I am an orphan …	8 bars: Welch's unvarnished voice sings a folklike melody whose rises and falls resemble Hank Williams's "Lost Highway." Six-string electric bass adds a very soft bass line played on the upper strings.
0:23	chorus	I have no mother …	The 11-bar chorus is less a separate section than an extension of the verse. Note the extra beat in bar 9, reminiscent of the extra beats in the Carter Family's "Can the Circle Be Unbroken."
0:46	verse 2	I have had friendships …	
1:03	chorus	I know no mother …	Rawlings adds country-style vocal harmonies in the choruses and for occasional lines in verses.
1:27	interlude (instrumental chorus)		Guitar plays a slightly modified version of the chorus melody on the lower strings. As in earlier sections, organ chords swell near the end, only to recede as the next section begins.
1:50	verse 3	But when he calls me …	Welch modifies the first two phrases to end on a clipped high note.
2:06	chorus	I'll meet my mother …	
2:30	interlude		Like the first interlude, with the addition of a countermelody on the upper strings of the electric bass.
2:53	verse 4	Blessed savior …	

(continued)

		CD 4.14	Listening Guide 22.2		"Orphan Girl" GILLIAN WELCH

TIMING	SECTION	LYRICS	COMMENT
3:09	chorus	Be my mother...	At the last phrase, crescendo of distorted electric guitar and organ to reach the song's peak volume.
3:34	coda	I am an orphan girl	The last line of the chorus is repeated on a plagal ("Amen") cadence, IV–I; voices and guitars drop out, leaving an organ chord that fades to silence.

Listen & Reflect

1. Contrast and compare "Orphan Girl" with "Can the Circle Be Unbroken" (LG 11.2), "Mama Tried" (LG 18.4), and "Coat of Many Colors" (LG 19.2). How does each song convey, or fail to convey, a feeling of authenticity? How does knowledge of the singers' actual life experiences affect your reception of the songs?

2. Each chorus begins with slightly altered lyrics. Why, and what is the effect?

outside the tradition on which she comments, Welch adopts a traditionalist stance to disguise what in fact is innovative music making. It is left to the listener to try to figure out what that traditionalist rhetoric has to do with the actual music.

HIP-HOP, THE DIGITAL REVOLUTION, AND REMIX CULTURE

As hip-hop entered its second decade as a national and international phenomenon, it acquired new shades of cultural significance. Whereas earlier hip-hop DJs and MCs had been communicating within tight-knit social groups, big-name rap stars were now portraying lifestyles unfamiliar to many of their listeners. In this new, larger context, misunderstandings were certain to arise. Yet hip-hop also became a musical language embraced by a multitude of people worldwide who saw in the African American experience parallels with their own conditions.

With the rise of digital information technology, the technical processes used in the creation of hip-hop raised legal questions about copyright and ownership, questions made even more vexing by the rise of peer-to-peer downloading technology. In the first decade of the twenty-first century, the sampling practices of hip-hop gave rise to a broader artistic movement incorporating remixes and mash-ups (see below), calling into question basic notions of originality and artistic creation.

HIP-HOP SINCE 1990

At the end of the 1980s, as New York–based groups like Public Enemy and Boogie Down Productions were advancing rap with socially conscious, often militant lyrics, a superficially similar school of rap was emerging in Los Angeles. West Coast rap broke on the national scene with "I'm Your Pusher," a 1987 single by rapper Ice-T that sampled "Pusherman" from Curtis Mayfield's soundtrack for *Super Fly*. As graphic as Grandmaster Flash's "The Message" and even angrier, the new genre, dubbed **gangsta rap**, earned greater notoriety with *Straight Outta Compton*, a 1989 album by N.W.A. (Niggaz with Attitude). The album's first two tracks in particular, the title song and "Fuck Tha Police," alarmed the parents of the white suburban youth who made up much of the audience for gangsta rap.

The racial and economic disparity between creators and consumers of gangsta rap probably had much to do with its bad reputation. Although the songs sought to raise political awareness of ghetto inequities, at least in the movement's early phases, their effect on listeners far removed from those realities was to glorify the criminal activities described in the lyrics. But as gangsta rap grew in popularity in the 1990s, its lyrics became difficult to read in any other way. West Coast rap set low standards for subject matter, not only romanticizing criminality but also endorsing misogyny, homophobia, and a materialistic outlook unparalleled for crassness and cynicism. An assessment of its musical value is thus hampered by its frequently objectionable lyrics and by a sense, too, that those lyrics trade on the most lamentable black stereotypes in order to pander to an affluent white audience. For the historically minded, the white reception of gangsta rap, regardless of its creators' intentions, raises the specter of minstrelsy and its racist legacy.

That said, much of musical interest can be found in the work of the artists associated with Death Row Records, an L.A. label launched in the 1990s. A member of N.W.A. who signed onto Death Row as a solo artist was Dr. Dre, an innovative DJ, producer, and rapper. Dre's 1993 album *The Chronic* expands the musical range of hip-hop beats by exploring more-relaxed tempos and greater textural variety, a style called **G-funk**. A track like "Let Me Ride" (a reference to "Swing Down Chariot," a gospel song based on the spiritual "Swing Low, Sweet Chariot") displays Dr. Dre's G-funk beat, built on samples from George Clinton and James Brown: a repetitious, hypnotic groove; complex, funky bass line; straightforward drum machine; sparse, synthesized chords; female background vocals; and a high, burbling synthesizer line that twines sinuously around Dre's rhythmically varied rapping.

The Chronic also introduced Dr. Dre's protégé Snoop Doggy Dogg (later Snoop Lion), a virtuoso rapper. Snoop's relaxed vocal style swerves around the beat with a playful unpredictability reminiscent of the jazz phrasing of Louis Armstrong and Billie Holiday. His humor and musicality brought him success as a headliner, beginning with *Doggystyle*, a 1996 album produced by Dr. Dre. The other major rapper on Death Row, Tupac Shakur, in contrast, delivered socially conscious lyrics in an intense style that harked back to Public Enemy's Chuck D, enlivened with the rhythmic flexibility of West Coast rap.

꧂ Snoop Dogg and Tupac Shakur, two foundational members of West Coast rap, at the MTV awards in 1996.

G-funk

Tupac and Biggie

The East Coast counterpart to Death Row Records was Big Boy, founded in 1993 by rapper Puff Daddy (later Diddy). Big Boy's most profitable act was a son of Jamaican immigrants, the Notorious B.I.G., also known as Biggie Smalls, whose *Ready to Die* (1995) played the familiar gangsta tropes, which were by no means confined to West Coast rap. A rivalry between the East and West Coast factions came to a climax when Tupac Shakur was the victim of a drive-by shooting in 1996. Although his feud with Biggie was well known, the latter's connection to the shooting was never substantiated, and six months later Biggie himself was fatally wounded by a drive-by assassin.

Eminem

But gangsta rap was far from dead as a genre. From Detroit came Dr. Dre's second important protégé, Eminem, the first white artist to sustain a career in hip-hop. Eminem's first big success, 1999's *The Slim Shady LP*, introduced his alter ego, Slim Shady, a figure who could verbalize hostility and aggression too extreme for the unmasked Eminem (who already is the stage persona of Marshall Mathers). Like minstrelsy's Jim Crow and Zip Coon, Slim Shady allowed a white performer to use the vocabulary of black music to express thoughts that transgress social mores. And transgress them he did, to the consternation of many listeners. On *The Marshall Mathers LP* (2000), which dropped the Slim Shady persona, Eminem turned to more-personal subject matter, especially his mother and his former wife, whom he excoriated with the same misogynist venom on display in his earlier work. Characteristic of the inverted logic of turn-of-the-century mass media, the public uproar against Eminem only furthered his career, which continued to move forward until 2005, when he entered a drug rehabilitation program. When he began to release new material in 2009, the albums sold reasonably well but critical reception was lukewarm.

mainstream hip-hop

While gangsta rap garnered media attention, other artists were pursuing a more family-friendly sound. MC Hammer built on his late-1980s success with a string of early 1990s hits that, apart from dissing other rappers in a wholesome version of the dozens, had nothing that moral watchdogs would find objectionable; indeed, by the late 1990s Hammer had become a Pentecostal television minister. Also popular with young listeners and their parents was Fresh Prince, a cheerful rapper who showed acting talent in his television series *Fresh Prince of Bel Air* and went on to a major film career under his real name, Will Smith. Hammer and Smith demonstrated that there was cultural space for styles of rap that could

regional scenes

have more mainstream appeal. Later rappers like Jay-Z and 50 Cent emerged from the East Coast gangsta scene but were able to modify their messages to reach that mainstream audience. The New York–based collective Wu Tang Clan proved influential for later artists like Kanye West. The midwestern and southern hip-hop scenes produced Nelly and the duo Outkast, as well as such regional styles as crunk and snap.

alternative hip-hop

Like rock and country, hip-hop also has a contrarian branch: **alternative hip-hop**. The term arose as a way to distinguish artists that fit neither the gangsta nor mainstream categories. As an umbrella term, it embraces such diverse acts as De La Soul, Arrested Development, A Tribe Called Quest, and the Roots. As with their rock and country counterparts, however, the crossover success of such one-time alternative acts as Outkast, the Gorillaz, and Gnarls Barkley indicates just how porous a boundary separates the alternative from the mainstream. Likewise, the commercial success of female rappers such as Salt-n-Pepa, Queen Latifah, Lauryn Hill, and Missy Elliott has not yet dispelled the common perception that strong women in hip-hop remain somehow "alternative."

The early 2000s witnessed the spread of hip-hop outside the United States. In Europe, Africa, and Asia, socially conscious rappers have used the music to plead the cause of groups facing discrimination, from Turkish immigrants in Germany to Palestinians. Within the United States, only one imported genre related to hip-hop has reached a wider audience: **reggaeton**, a blend of hip-hop with Latin American and Caribbean influences, including the Jamaican dance-hall music that inspired hip-hop in the first place. Popular throughout Latin America, reggaeton in the United States is associated particularly with Colombian singer Shakira and Puerto Rican acts such as Daddy Yankee and Calle 13. All of these artists are more versatile than the reggaeton label implies, ranging widely through hip-hop, electronica, and various Latin styles such as cumbia and salsa. In the second decade of the twenty-first century, hip-hop has become a world-wide phenomenon that in turn is giving rise to new genres.

reggaeton

THE DIGITAL REVOLUTION I: THE SAMPLING WARS

Ever since hip-hop's inception in the 1970s, prerecorded music has been an important element in its sound. Indeed, the DJ techniques that are the foundation of hip-hop are entirely dependent on prerecorded music. That posed no legal problems as long as hip-hop was purely a live-performance art, but the advent of rap records in 1979 changed the situation.

Since the 1909 Copyright Act, mentioned in chapter 7 in connection with John Philip Sousa, music publishers have sought to retain control over the "mechanical rights" to their music—a term that at first applied to player pianos and other music machines as well as phonographs. A 1976 updating of copyright law addressed the technological changes that had taken place since 1909, extended the length of copyright protection, and codified a doctrine of **fair use**: the concept that no formal permission is needed when a work of art or literature is copied or quoted for purposes of criticism, parody, scholarship, and similar limited use. For example, when videocassette recorders became popular in the 1980s, the Supreme Court decided that taping television broadcasts for later viewing fell within the definition of fair use. What falls outside that definition is the copying of a work for commercial gain, as in the making of bootleg CDs and DVDs, actions that are clearly unethical.

fair use

Taking fragments of prerecorded music and assembling them into hip-hop beats falls into a gray area regarding fair use and plagiarism (the latter involves not crediting a source, while "fair use" concerns the economic value of intellectual property). As long as the practice was confined to DJs spinning records at a dance, it drew little attention from the music industry. But after "Rapper's Delight" turned hip-hop into a highly remunerative recorded art, the music entered new legal territory. Because hip-hop records in the early years used first studio musicians, and later drum machines and synthesizers, to recreate DJ-style beats without actually using earlier recordings, music publishers generally ignored their use of elements from earlier songs. That changed in the latter 1980s with the first affordable samplers (see chapter 20), which could lift snippets—"samples"—from other artists' records and manipulate them digitally with much greater ease, control, and complexity. For the next few years, hip-hop beats consisted of dense tapestries of sounds sampled from earlier records: this is the sound of groups as diverse as Public Enemy, De La Soul, and the Beastie Boys.

plagiarism

This "golden age" of sampling ended with a December 1991 court decision in favor of a music publisher that sued a rapper for unauthorized use of a 1970s soft rock song. Some legal historians now view this case as a lost opportunity to establish sampling as within the bounds of fair use. Instead, the rapper's record label, Warner Brothers, pursued a weak defense strategy and lost resoundingly, setting a legal precedent that made unauthorized sampling too risky. And because publishers tended to set exorbitant licensing fees, authorized sampling became prohibitively expensive in many instances. Creators of the sampled songs reacted in various ways, from outrage at what they saw as theft to delight at what they saw as an act of homage; many older artists were happy to receive partial songwriting credit and a share of royalties, whatever they thought of the new song's quality.

sampling practices 	Since 1992, then, hip-hop artists have taken any of a number of paths in the creation of hip-hop beats. First, the wealthiest hip-hop artists simply pay the high fees for authorized samples. Second, some choose samples from obscure artists whose songs are less expensive to clear. Third, some producers, such as Dr. Dre, prefer to use studio musicians to recreate the sound of earlier songs, much as in the first rap records; Dre argues that he does this as much for aesthetic reasons as for legal ones. Fourth, a handful of producers build their beats "from the ground up," using no sampling or borrowing of any kind. Finally, many artists choose to flout the law, digitally altering unauthorized samples to make them unrecognizable to the copyright holders. In short, current standards of copyright protection have encouraged a subversive, "outlaw" approach to the creation of hip-hop.

THE DIGITAL REVOLUTION II: THE DOWNLOADING WARS

the Sonny Bono Act 	Two pieces of legislation in 1998 made copyright protection even more stringent. The Sonny Bono Act—named after a recently deceased congressman who had been a folk-rock singing star in the 1960s—extended copyright protection beyond the limits of the 1976 law. Under the new act, anything created after 1923 that was still copyright protected in 1998 will remain so until at least 2019; that includes almost everything by George Gershwin, Cole Porter, and other long-dead song-
the DCMA 	writers. The second law, the Digital Millennium Copyright Act (DMCA), gives copyright holders veto power over all uses of their work, even those that constitute fair use. It authorizes the use of digital rights management (DRM) tools to restrict how consumers use electronic media such as sound recordings—for example, the content scramble system that makes it difficult to rip a DVD to a computer hard drive.

the MP3 	The DCMA was in part a response to new digital technology that in the 1990s was making electronic media easier to disseminate. One of these, the **MP3**, compressed audio files to much more manageable sizes that took less computer memory to store and, more importantly, could more easily travel across the Internet. Music fans began to share recorded music online, and by the end of the decade, 17 million MP3s were being downloaded onto personal computers every day. Because searching for MP3s was slow and laborious, Shawn Fanning, an eighteen-year-old student at Northeastern University in Boston, developed a utility that made it easier for users to locate MP3s and download them directly
p2p networks 	from other users' computers—a **peer-to-peer (p2p)** file-sharing network. When his utility, Napster, went online in 1999, it quickly developed a devoted following, and in a short time it had some 25 million users and indexed 80 million songs.

Napster users did not pay for the music they downloaded, but for that matter neither did they receive payment for the music they owned and allowed others to copy. The utility was arguably a sort of collective digital lending library in which each user was both lender and borrower. Fair use has always embraced the lending of books, CDs, and so on—indeed, public libraries institutionalize that concept. Just as libraries did not put bookstores out of business, Napster's supporters argued, p2p networks do not stop people from buying CDs. Likewise, they argued, since the advent of the cassette recorder in the 1970s music lovers have compiled "mix tapes" of favorite songs for friends and family, and p2p networks are merely an extension of that practice. But their argument stretches that aspect of fair use to the breaking point, unless a user has 25 million friends and family members. Some observers, such as Chuck D of Public Enemy, likened Napster to radio, for decades a medium where listeners could hear music "for free" without putting record companies out of business. An important difference, however, is that musicians earn royalties from radio play but not from file sharing.

Unsurprisingly, the record companies did not see Napster in such a benevolent light, and neither did some musicians with major label contracts. In 2000 Metallica sued Napster for copyright infringement, and shortly afterward Dr. Dre did the same. Though both cases were settled out of court, a successful lawsuit filed by the Recording Industry Association of America (RIAA), the music industry's lobbying organization, shut Napster down in 2001. But the death of Napster was not the death of p2p networks, and since that time music fans have migrated from one relatively short-lived p2p to another.

In retrospect, this was clearly a moment when the music industry needed to reimagine its business model. Since its inception in the 1800s, the popular music industry has been predicated on the commodification of music into material objects that can be marketed and sold: first sheet music, then piano rolls, then phonograph records from the Edison cylinder to the CD. But since the 1990s recorded music in the form of digital audio files can be downloaded to personal computers, MP3 players, and other devices, without the purchase of any physical object. Although legal pay-per-download sites such as iTunes emerged immediately after the closure of Napster, the use of digital rights management locks (the legacy of the Digital Millennium Copyright Act) makes legally downloaded files cumbersome to use. Moreover, a generation of music lovers has grown up in a post-Napster world and, rightly or not, considers recorded music something that should be freely downloadable. The result is an economic climate in which the music industry, slow to respond to technological and cultural change, is in a state of crisis.

Napster

Napster's shutdown

iTunes

DIY REBORN: REMIXES AND MASH-UPS

Napster marked a new development in America's music culture, a shift from a "broadcast" or one-to-many model, in which corporations create music and distribute it to the public, to a many-to-many model, in which individuals can take an active role in the making and dissemination of music. The ease and affordability of file sharing has allowed the Internet to become a medium for exchanging not only music produced by the major labels but also music created by users themselves. A host of websites, from MySpace and SoundCloud to last.fm and YouTube, have allowed musicians without record company contracts to upload their own music with the hope of attracting a following. These musicians make little or no money through downloading; instead, the goal is to create a market for concerts and merchandise such as collectible deluxe CDs. In some cases, it works: the band Dispatch gained a following on Napster and went on to tour nationally to capacity audiences. In 2007 they played three sold-out shows in Madison Square Garden, the first band without backing from a major label to do so.

The quality of do-it-yourself recorded music has benefited from affordable sound recording and editing software, which allows a laptop to take the place of the racks of expensive audio equipment that once was within the means only of professional recording studios. The same technology also makes it possible to *the remix*   manipulate the recorded music of other artists. One result is the **remix**, in which a recorded song is altered by adding, subtracting, or changing the dynamic balance between textural layers; revising the song's structure, generally by lengthening it through repetition or interpolation; shifting the pitch or tempo of the original; or combining any or all of these techniques. The practice dates back to the disco era, when record companies would release "extended mixes"—six- or seven-minute versions of songs whose radio versions were closer to the three-minute mark—for the use of club DJs. Hip-hop DJs, of course, were creating their own extended mixes by looping breaks, and their manipulation of vinyl on turntable set the pattern for later remixes, which use digital technology to expand the ways in which a song may be altered. Club DJs may, for example, alter the tempo of a slow ballad to make it more suitable for dancing.

But remixes can be more than simple reworkings of dance music. The Cana*John Oswald*   dian John Oswald, who began creating sound collages in the 1970s, alters popular songs to create avant-garde electronic music that defamiliarizes the familiar, a process he calls "plunderphonics." "A plunderphone," he wrote in 1985, "is a recognizable sonic quote, using the actual sound of something familiar which has already been recorded. Whistling a bar of [Edgard Varèse's] 'Density 21.5' is a traditional musical quote. Taking Madonna singing 'Like a Virgin' and rerecording it backwards or slower is plunderphonics, as long as you can reasonably recognize the source. The plundering has to be blatant though."

Oswald's 1988 *Plunderphonics* EP displays his remixing aesthetic. One track features Dolly Parton covering a 1950s doo-wop song, "The Great Pretender," her voice altered to sound first like a chipmunk, then like herself, and then like a masculine baritone, accompanied by an eerie electronic soundscape. Other tracks similarly defamiliarize Elvis Presley, Count Basie, and Igor Stravinsky. In every case, the source material is recognizable, but in no way would anyone mistake Oswald's work for a mere copy of the original. Rather, his collages create new meaning by commenting on the originals.

Oswald's aesthetic of creating new music from recognizable sources informs *the mash-up*   another type of musical recycling, the **mash-up**, in which tracks from two or more songs are combined to create a new song. Although the idea of the mash-up goes back to 1950s novelty songs, the use of the technique for more than comic purposes probably begins with DJ Shadow's *Endtroducing.....*, a 1996 album consisting entirely of samples from a wide array of popular music and jazz. Mash-ups became more widely known in 2004, with the rapid proliferation on the Internet of DJ Danger Mouse's *The Grey Album*, a mash-up of the vocal tracks from Jay-Z's *Black Album* with heavily processed instrumental tracks from the 1968 album officially called *The Beatles* but generally known as *The White Album*.

Danger Mouse   Because Danger Mouse had not cleared the instrumental tracks, the holder of the Beatles' copyrights, EMI, cited the Digital Millenium Copyright Act to halt distribution of *The Grey Album*, though no listener would consider it a commercial replacement for the Beatles songs, the unfair use that the DMCA was designed to prevent. In response, a number of websites coordinated an offer of free downloads of *The Grey Album* on February 24, 2004, a date they called "Grey Tuesday," one of the first acts of electronic civil disobedience to protest stringent copyright protection laws. The album, EMI's reaction, and the Grey Tuesday protest brought Danger Mouse notoriety and sparked interest in his next venture, the alternative hip-hop duo Gnarls Barkley, whose other half is singer and rapper Cee Lo Green.

The most prominent mash-up artist in the second decade of the century is Girl Talk. He began releasing mash-ups in 2002 while still a college student and continued while working as a biomedical technician, not becoming a full-time professional musician until 2007. As a live DJ and as a recording artist, Girl Talk creates complex collages of a dozen or more songs, highly danceable and depending for their full effect on the listener's recognition of the sources. Instead of copyrighting his works, he licenses them through Creative Commons, an organization that promotes alternatives to traditional copyrights; the licenses allow users to make their own derivative works based on Girl Talk's, such as the music videos that proliferate on YouTube and other Internet video sites. His albums are available only as downloads, and rather than set a fixed price he asks users to pay what they choose.

If Girl Talk confined his mash-ups to live performance, he could probably fly under the radar of the record companies whose recordings he samples. His albums, in contrast, seem deliberately to invite litigation. Yet as of this writing, no lawsuit has been brought against him. Some commentators believe that his opponents hesitate to do so for fear that he might win in court, establishing a precedent that construes the artistic reuse of prerecorded music as fair use. Many of his fans see him as a copyright-law provocateur, a folk hero for remix culture.

Paradoxically, in one sense remixes and mash-ups are a reversion to the earliest phase of the popular music industry: the sheet music era. Sheet music invites users to take liberties with the music, altering it to conform to their own tastes and abilities. The technological breakthroughs at the turn of the present century have allowed users to treat sound recordings in the same way. Although it has happened in a way that John Philip Sousa might never have imagined, remix culture has ended the passivity that the March King feared the phonograph would induce. Amateur music making, though far removed from the community choruses and town bands of Sousa's day, is alive and well.

Mash-up artist Girl Talk in performance, 2008.

CLOSING THE GAP: CLASSICAL MUSIC IN THE TWENTY-FIRST CENTURY

Perhaps no twentieth-century condition did more to fragment the world of classical music than the gap between composer and audience. Beginning with the rise of modernism in the 1910s, exploring new musical territory was often considered a higher artistic goal for a composer than communicating with general audiences. Commenting wryly on "The Gap," composer and journalist Kyle Gann wrote in 1997: "We pretend to lament its existence, but actually, we have become so proud of it that, when music doesn't put up barriers to the audience's comprehension or patience, we accuse it of not being authentically twentieth-century." As Gann saw it, the rise of academia after World War II widened "The Gap" even further. Favoring the intellectual side of composition, it put a damper on expression and ignored audience response. Late in the century, though, the situation began to change as more accessible approaches such as minimalism attracted new audiences. More performers and composers today seem interested in engaging listeners' emotions, inspiring hope for a classical sphere in the new millennium that is not so sharply divided against itself.

CLASSICAL PERFORMANCE SINCE 1990

A number of performers in recent years have broken away from the formality of the traditional classical recital in search of more-immediate ways to form connections with their listeners. Classical musicians are more likely now than in the past to speak to audiences from the stage, dress with more imagination and personal style, and engage in educational outreach and other programs that break down the barrier between performer and audience. A leading

Yo-Yo Ma

example is Chinese American cellist Yo-Yo Ma, perhaps the best-known classical instrumentalist in the world today. Ma is not only a master of the standard cello repertory but also a musical omnivore, collaborating in a huge variety of musical traditions with other musicians, from Appalachian fiddle tunes with bluegrass performer Mark O'Connor to the tangos of Astor Piazzola with Argentinean musicians. In 2000 his playing was featured in the score for the film *Crouching Tiger, Hidden Dragon*, written by the Chinese classical composer Tan Dun. In 1998 Ma founded his ongoing Silk Road Project, which promotes collaborations among musicians from the regions historically joined by the trade routes known as the Silk Road: Europe, North Africa, the Middle East, South Asia, China, and Southeast Asia.

Institutions as well as individuals have begun to close the gap as well. In 2006 New York's Metropolitan Opera launched a series of high-definition video broadcasts of live performances from the stage of the Met to specially equipped movie theaters around the country. Although more expensive than a regular movie ticket, admission is considerably more affordable than a seat at the Met; more important,

"Live in HD"

the "Live in HD" programs bring world-class opera to audiences far removed from New York or other cultural centers. With high-quality audio and video, imaginative camera work, English-language subtitles, and intermission features such as backstage interviews, the HD broadcasts have proven to be more than mere substitutes for live performance, and their phenomenal success has helped to expand the audience for opera in the twenty-first century.

Alan Gilbert

In 2007 the New York Philharmonic Orchestra appointed as its next music director Alan Gilbert. At his debut in September 2009 he was forty-two—the second youngest (after Leonard Bernstein) to hold that post in the history of the orchestra. Both of his parents were NYPO violinists, and his mother, Yoko Takebe, continued playing in the orchestra after her son's appointment. An advocate for American music and new composition, Gilbert has experimented with the format of the orchestra's concerts, for example presenting modern operas in full stagings. He has also brought on to the orchestra's staff as artist-in-residence the baritone Thomas Hampson, whose Hampsong Foundation promotes art song in America.

Also in 2007, the Los Angeles Philharmonic Orchestra took the remarkable step of appointing as its music director the twenty-six-year-old conductor of a Venezuelan youth orchestra, Gustavo Dudamel. The Simon Bolivar Youth Orchestra is the flagship ensemble of El Sistema, the government-financed program that has brought music education to some 250,000 impoverished Venezuelan children, in the process adding a surprisingly high number of gifted musicians to the world of classical music. Dudamel, a product of El Sistema, is a champion of music as an agent for social change, and his presence in Los Angeles bodes well for the success of efforts to establish in the United States a music education program inspired by El Sistema.

🎵 Venezuelan conductor Gustavo Dudamel brings his high-energy style to the podium of the Los Angeles Philharmonic Orchestra.

CLASSICAL COMPOSITION SINCE 1990

Seven conditions divide the musical world of contemporary American composers from that of older composers:

1. European music of the 1700s and 1800s (Bach to Debussy) has lost much of its privileged position.

2. If Americans have a common musical culture, it comes from radio and television, mass media that play a smaller role in the lives of younger generations than of older generations.

3. Because so much music is now created digitally, musical notation is fading in importance.

4. Few scores are published today, but recorded music is easy to distribute; therefore, new music is more likely than ever before to be judged by how it sounds.

5. Thanks to digital samples, the most elemental musical unit, which used to be the individual note, may now be a complex of sounds or a quotation.

6. Because exposure to popular music is almost universal, composers who hope to reach a live audience rarely write without referring to pop's musical conventions.

7. Today's audience for classical music, as for all kinds of music, has splintered into many different groups, each increasingly cut off from the others.

In general, younger classical composers are inclined to accept the world as they find it and to ground their work in conditions they encounter in everyday life. Influence seems to be passing away from composers who see themselves as champions of quality in an age of quantity. Traditional barriers of nationality, culture, and economics are disappearing, and the supply of music grows increasingly out of proportion to the demand. An almost limitless capacity exists to gather, record, reshape, and circulate musical sound. In a culture of such abundance, the idea of composing as a private activity, walled off within

🎵 Hilary Hahn (b. 1979) has championed several American violin concertos, including that of Jennifer Higdon.

the classical sphere's contemporary wing, seems more parochial than praiseworthy.

One of the most widely performed composers active today is Jennifer Higdon. Growing up in Georgia and Tennessee, Higdon heard little classical music until she was in college; from the first, she was more interested in modernist music than the traditional classical repertory. Her music is unabashedly romantic: tonal, melodic, and with a rhythmic verve and colorful sense of timbre. In 2010 she was awarded the Pulitzer Prize for her Violin Concerto, composed for Hilary Hahn, her former student at the Curtis Institute in Philadelphia. (Hahn, an exemplar of the new generation of classical performers, has also recorded American violin concertos by Samuel Barber and two Los Angeles émigrés, Arnold Schoenberg and Erich Wolfgang Korngold.)

Also representative of new trends in classical music is the Argentinean American composer Osvaldo Golijov. Born in Buenos Aires to a family of Eastern European Jewish descent, Golijov lived in Israel for a few years before emigrating in 1986 to the United States, where he studied composition at the University of Pennsylvania with George Crumb. For the past two decades he has been based in Massachusetts, where he teaches composition at the College of the Holy Cross in Worcester. A number of Golijov's works incorporate the sounds of klezmer, most notably *The Dreams and Prayers of Isaac the Blind* (1994), a chamber work for clarinet and string quartet. One of his most ambitious works to date is *La Pasión según San Marcos* (2000), an epic work for vocal soloists, choir, orchestra, and dancers. In it he combines Latin American popular and folk music, from tango to salsa, with Afro-Cuban rhythms and Brazilian *capoeira*; much of the orchestral writing could be described as postminimalist, while the harmonies are sometimes on the verge of atonality.

Another Spanish-language work based on the New Testament is John Adams's opera-oratorio *El Niño* (2000), which uses music, dance, and film to recast the Nativity story as a tale of undocumented immigrants. *El Niño* is a worthy addition to the string of politically engaged works that Adams began in the 1980s with *Nixon in China* and continued with the 1991 opera *The Death of Klinghoffer*, about the 1985 hijacking of the passenger liner *Achille Lauro* by members of the Palestine Liberation Organization. Since 2000 he has also composed *On the Transmigration of Souls* (2002), a commemorative symphony commissioned by the New York Philharmonic shortly after the September 11, 2001, terrorist attacks, and the

Doctor Atomic

opera *Doctor Atomic* (2005), about the scientists at work on the World War II–era Manhattan Project at Los Alamos, New Mexico, which led to the creation of the atomic bomb. In all of these works, Adams writes in a postminimalist style that combines propulsive rhythms and clear if unconventional tonality with colorful orchestration and glittering textures. Adams has impressively demonstrated that serious music on serious topics can appeal to wide audiences, and his music has enjoyed frequent revivals and successful recordings.

Steve Reich

Like Adams, Steve Reich has occasionally touched on political themes in his music since his earliest works, as in *Come Out* (1966), discussed in chapter 18.

But *Different Trains* (1988), for string quartet and tape, combines the political and the personal. Its subject is the transcontinental train rides the composer took as a child in the 1940s between New York and California to visit his separated parents. The adult Reich reflects that had he been living in Europe at that time, he might have been riding different trains, the ones that took Jews to the Nazi death camps. Combining rich string textures with recorded voices, including those of Holocaust survivors, in a compositional style that resembles minimalism but is more expansive and emotionally resonant, *Different Trains* is a powerful example of late twentieth-century composition.

In the twenty-first century, Reich has continued to compose works that consolidate his position as a leading American composer. Among the celebrations of Reich's seventieth birthday in October 2006 was the premiere of his *Daniel Variations*, for voices, clarinets, pianos, string quartet, and percussion. The piece commemorates the life of Daniel Pearl, an American journalist who was kidnapped and murdered in Pakistan by Al-Qaeda terrorists in 2002. After Pearl's parents approached Reich in 2004 about writing music in their son's memory, Reich began work on a piece that, like *Different Trains*, would have political overtones but would focus on individual experiences and emotions. He agreed with Pearl's parents that the piece should be a celebration of Pearl's efforts to bring understanding and reconciliation to the world's cultures.

Reich decided on a four-movement structure in which the first and third movements set texts from the biblical book of Daniel and the second and fourth set words spoken by Pearl himself. The text of the last movement (LG 22.3) is "I sure hope Gabriel likes my music, when the day is done"—a reference to a recording by jazz violinist Stuff Smith that Pearl owned. Reich does not quote the Stuff Smith song but commemorates Pearl's love of jazz and bluegrass fiddling (he was an amateur violinist) by giving a prominent role to the string instruments.

As in *Different Trains*, Reich expands the language of minimalism to create a rhythmically pulsating, glowing texture. Pianos and vibraphones play chords that combine notes of the diatonic scale into pleasingly crunchy pandiatonic dissonances over a slow-moving bass line that outlines a gradual progression through four distinct tonal centers. Against this backdrop, voices, clarinets, and strings weave long melodic lines that repeat with continual small changes, generally by lengthening or shortening individual notes. As the music steadily unfolds over its ten-minute duration, the repeated text becomes a mantra, the prayer not only of Daniel Pearl but also of the composer as he nears his seventieth birthday and looks back over a long career of music making.

> ## *In their own words*   💬
>
> ### Steve Reich, Interviewed Shortly before the Premiere of His *Daniel Variations*
>
> *Daniel Variations* is a homage to someone who stands beautifully and grotesquely at the same time as a symbol of thousands of innocent victims who were murdered while trying to really give a fair shake to all concerned. . . . So win, lose, or draw in terms of the reaction to the piece, I'm glad I did it. And I hope that the family likes it. And I hope Danny likes it. And I sure hope Gabriel likes my music.

Daniel Variations

LG 22.3

CD 4.15   **Listening Guide 22.3**   *Daniel Variations,* **fourth movement**
STEVE REICH

DATE: 2006

PERFORMERS: Los Angeles Master Chorale;
Grant Gershon, conductor. Instrumentation:
2 sopranos; 2 tenors; 2 clarinets; 4
vibraphones; bass and kick drum, tam-tam
(not heard in this movement); 4 pianos;
string quartet

GENRE: classical concert work for large
ensemble

METER: triple, with occasional duple bars

FORM: four sections, each a variant of a
single additive process

WHAT TO LISTEN FOR

- minimalist earmarks: steady pulse, slowly unfolding processes, repetition
- diatonic pitch material but nontraditional harmonies
- melodies in closely spaced rhythmic canons
- lyrics in nonpoetic, "everyday" tone

TIMING	SECTION	COMMENTS
0:00	**part 1**	12 bars in triple meter: pianos and vibraphones play rhythmically pulsating pandiatonic chords in G major.
0:23		Pianos and vibes repeat the 12 bars, with addition of a melody in two-part harmony in clarinets and strings.
0:46		12 bars repeat, with the melody echoed by added instruments in close rhythmic canon.
1:09		12 bars repeat, with addition of soprano and tenor voices: "I sure hope . . ."
1:32		Final repetition of 12 bars, with addition of second soprano and tenor in close rhythmic canon.
1:56	**part 2**	Same process, now in B-flat major and 14-bar sections.
2:23		Melody instruments enter.
2:50		Melody instruments in canon.
3:17		Voices enter.
3:45		Voices in canon.
4:13	**part 3**	The process begins again, now in D-flat major; 14-bar sections, with an extra beat in bar 4.
4:40		Melody instruments enter.
5:09		Melody instruments in canon.
5:36		Voices enter.
6:04		Voices in canon.

🎧 **CD 4.15**	**Listening Guide 22.3**	***Daniel Variations*, fourth movement** **STEVE REICH**

TIMING	SECTION	COMMENTS
6:32	part 4	The process begins for a final time, in 20-bar sections; the first 3 bars are in E major, with the remaining in G major.
7:10		Melody instruments enter.
7:50		Melody instruments in canon.
8:30		Voices enter.
9:10		Voices in canon.
9:50		As voices arrive at the last word, the closing sonority is sustained through a slow diminuendo, ending very softly.

Listen & Reflect

1. Compare the sound of Reich's pandiatonicism with that of Aaron Copland's, at the foal's birth in *The Red Pony Suite* (LG 15.2, especially at 3:08). Do the two share anything in common?

2. What evidence is there, if any, of Reich's early work in electronic music, as described in chapter 18? Does *Daniel Variations* fit the description of minimalism in that chapter? Why or why not?

3. How does Reich's choice and setting of text compare with any of the other politically or socially conscious music discussed in this book?

CONCLUSION: *E PLURIBUS UNUM*

The United States has been blessed with a wealth of musical traditions. The problem in the twenty-first century lies in the amount of attention any given musician may hope to claim. The choices of so-called leisure activities are legion: music, drama, literature, dance, and the visual arts; television, radio, movies, and video games; sports as participation and spectatorship; travel; cooking and restaurant-going; even shopping; and of course, the ever-present Internet. New music in an unfamiliar idiom, whether classical, popular, or some hybrid, has only a tiny chance of winning attention beyond a small circle of connoisseurs. Nevertheless, musicians continue to create new music.

As earlier chapters have chronicled, one effect of the dominance of recorded sound in our culture has been the elevation of popular music to the status once reserved for classical music. The best recordings of the past have retained their artistic value and relevance for later generations. That means that, like classical

↪ The gap narrows: hip-hop's DJ Spooky and composer Steve Reich, photographed by a blogger who describes them as "my-fav-musicians."

composers, musicians in the popular sphere can take the long view of history, knowing that posterity has often judged artists more truly than their own contemporaries and that present-day indifference may not be fatal to the life of one's work. At the same time, as the present chapter has argued, musicians in the classical sphere, raised in America's consumer culture and unashamed to call it their own, have explored new ways to create music that seeks to close the gap separating them from the general public not in some indeterminate future but *now*.

Although it is still too early to say, we might hazard a guess that the history of America's music in the twenty-first century will be one of the narrowing and ultimate closing of "The Gap"—not just the gap between classical composers and their audiences but also the gap between the classical, popular, and traditional spheres. Maybe that January 2009 concert at the Lincoln Memorial described in this book's introduction had it right after all: despite the fragmenting of audiences in a time when broadcasting seems more like "narrowcasting," and despite the huge variety of music available to anyone with an Internet connection, Americans really do share one enormous, interconnected musical culture. We *are* one.

QUESTIONS FOR DISCUSSION AND REVIEW

1. What arguments could be made to support the concept of a "women's music" that connects musicians as diverse as Tori Amos, Ani DiFranco, and Gillian Welch, and what arguments could be made against it?

2. What is the "authenticity" that seems so important to so many popular music movements of the past half century or more, from the urban folk revival to punk, alternative rock, and alt.country?

3. What are some arguments in favor of strict enforcement of current copyright laws, and what are some arguments in favor of changing those laws? How does your own downloading behavior and that of your friends affect your perception of those arguments? If you are a musician, how does that affect your perception?

4. What are the technical differences between sampling, remixing, and mash-up?

5. What is "The Gap," and what are some indications in our current music culture that it is closing?

FURTHER READING

Adams, John. *Hallelujah Junction: Composing an American Life*. New York: Farrar, Straus and Giroux, 2008.

Caponi, Gena Dagel, ed. *Signifyin(g), Sanctifyin', and Slam Dunking: A Reader in African American Expressive Culture*. Amherst: University of Massachusetts Press, 1999.

Chang, Jeff. *Can't Stop, Won't Stop: A History of the Hip-hop Generation*. New York: St. Martin's Press, 2005.

Covach, John, and Andrew Flory. *What's That Sound? An Introduction to Rock and Its History*. 3d ed. New York: W.W. Norton, 2012.

DeVeaux, Scott, and Gary Giddins. *Jazz*. New York: W.W. Norton, 2009.

Fox, Pamela. "Time as 'Revelator': Alt.Country Women's Performance of the Past." In *Old Roots New Routes: The Cultural Politics of Alt.Country Music*, ed. Pamela Fox and Barbara Ching, 134–53. Ann Arbor: University of Michigan Press, 2009.

Horowitz, Joseph. *Classical Music in America: A History*. New York: W.W. Norton, 2007.

Katz, Mark. *Capturing Sound: How Technology Has Changed Music*. Rev. ed. Berkeley and Los Angeles: University of California Press, 2010.

Rose, Tricia. *Black Noise: Rap Music and Black Culture in Contemporary America*. Hanover, NH: Wesleyan University Press and University Press of New England, 1994.

Sinnreich, Aram. *Mashed Up: Music, Technology, and the Rise of Configurable Culture*. Amherst: University of Massachusetts Press, 2010.

Taylor, William "Billy." "Jazz: America's Classical Music." *The Black Perspective in Music* 14, no. 1 (winter 1986): 21–25.

GLOSSARY

12-inch single. A 45-rpm single the size of an LP and typically holding a longer version of a popular song, such as a dance mix.

45. See *single.*

A&R. "Artists and repertoire"; the segment of the record industry focused on locating new artists and songs.

aaba **form.** A common song structure, consisting of statement, restatement, contrast, and return.

accelerando. A gradual increase in tempo.

accent. Emphasis on a beat or note.

album-oriented rock (AOR). A 1970s radio format that emphasized mainstream and progressive rock.

aleatoric music. See *chance music.*

alt.country. A style that blends traditional country music elements with roots rock and punk; sometimes called "Americana."

alternative hip-hop. A broad category embracing artists that fit neither the gangsta nor mainstream categories.

alternative rock. Since the 1980s, any rock style whose proponents hold an oppositional stance to the "mainstream."

Americana. See *alt.country.*

amplitude. The distance a vibrating object moves with each oscillation, audible as its dynamic level.

ancient music. Nineteenth-century term for simple psalm and hymn tunes composed much earlier.

answer song. A popular song written in response to an earlier song.

anthem. An elaborate choral work, often with biblical text.

anti-folk. A category that embraces singer-songwriters whose sound is too edgy or punk to be considered part of the folk tradition.

arco. Performance direction to sound the strings with the bow; cf. *pizzicato.*

arena rock. A mainstream popular music genre of the 1970s.

arpeggio. Musical figure in which the notes of a chord are played one after another instead of simultaneously.

atonality. The avoidance of any clear key center.

augmentation. Playing a melody with each note "stretched out" in slower rhythm.

B side. The back side of a 78-rpm or 45-rpm single; also called the flip side.

b-boying. A style of dancing to hip-hop often called "break dancing" by the general public.

b-boys and **b-girls.** Break dancers.

back phrasing. In jazz, intentionally lagging behind the accompaniment for expressive effect.

backbeat. An emphasis on beats 2 and 4 in four-beat duple meter.

Bakersfield sound. A 1960s popular style that updates traditional honky-tonk music with drums, electric bass, and rock-style electric guitar.

ballad. 1. A narrative song in strophic form. 2. A popular song in medium or slow tempo with lyrics expressing a romantic sentiment.

ballad opera. A theater work whose songs consist of new words set to familiar tunes.

banda. Mexican American music played by wind bands with military-style instrumentation.

bar. A grouping of beats (usually two, three, or four); also called *measure.*

barbershop quartet. A style of four-part singing for men in which a lead voice carries the melody, higher and lower voices (tenor and baritone) add harmony lines, and a bass voice provides harmonic underpinning and occasional countermelodies.

barrelhouse piano. See *boogie woogie.*

baser. Any of the singers in a ring shout who respond to the songster's lead.

beat. 1. A steady pulse, dividing musical time into equal units. 2. In hip-hop, the instrumental accompaniment for an MC or rapper.

beat juggling. In hip-hop, combining the various techniques of turntablism essentially to create new music from snippets of prerecorded music.

beatmatching. In hip-hop, adjusting the speed of one turntable so that the record played on it matches exactly the tempo of a record on another turntable.

bebop. A jazz style, developed in the 1940s, that extended the music's melodic and harmonic vocabulary without losing its swinging rhythm and blues inflections.

benefit concert. In the 1700s and early 1800s, a concert intended to reap a profit for an individual performer.

big band. A large jazz ensemble, typically of thirteen or more players, divided into reed, brass, and rhythm sections.

binary form. A musical structure of two sections, or strains, usually repeated: *aabb.*

blaxploitation. A 1970s film genre featuring funk soundtracks, urban ghetto settings, stories focused on crime and punishment, and predominantly black casts.

block chords. A texture in which all voices or instruments move in identical rhythm.

blue note. A lowered or "bent" version of the third, seventh, and sometimes fifth scale degrees in the major scale.

blue yodel. Song genre associated with Jimmie Rodgers that combines elements of blues with yodeling.

bluegrass. Mid-twentieth-century country style derived from earlier string band music.

blues. African American traditional music featuring blue notes, blues progressions, and often the 12-bar blues chorus structure.

blues chorus. In blues, music corresponding to one stanza of lyrics, often twelve bars in length.

blues progression. A standard chord progression for the 12-bar blues; in its simplest form, tonic (I) for four bars, subdominant (IV) for two bars, tonic for two bars, dominant (V) for two bars, and tonic for the final two bars.

blues shouter. A big-voiced singer who can project over an amplified rhythm and blues band.

bones. A rhythm instrument made of segments of bone that are clicked together in one hand like castanets; traditional in Irish music, American minstrel bands, and other styles.

boogie woogie. A style of blues piano emphasizing a heavily rhythmic left hand.

book. The script for a musical comedy, equivalent to an opera's *libretto.*

bop. See *bebop.*

border blaster. A radio station with a powerful signal, owned by a U.S. citizen but located just across the Rio Grande from Texas and thus exempt from U.S. broadcasting regulations.

bottleneck guitar. A technique of playing the guitar with a glass or metal slide on the fretboard.

brass band. The typical nineteenth-century American wind ensemble, consisting of brass and Janissary instruments, with optional woodwinds.

break. 1. In popular music, a brief solo moment during which the accompaniment is silent. 2. In hip-hop, a brief instrumental passage, typically extended by a DJ by cutting.

break dancing. See *b-boying.*

break strain. A section in a march or related form characterized by alternations of high and low instruments and unsettled harmony.

breakdown. In country music, a fast instrumental performance of a traditional fiddle tune or a new composition in the style of a fiddle tune.

bridge. 1. The *b* section of an *aaba* song chorus. 2. After 1960, a contrasting section occurring in the second half of a popular song.

Brill Building. An office building at 1619 Broadway in New York City, in the 1960s a center for popular songwriting and publishing; by extension, the style of music favored by Brill Building writers and publishers.

British Invasion. The American fascination with the Beatles and other British bands in the 1960s.

broadside ballads. Dating from colonial times, verses commenting on current events matched with a familiar tune, printed on sheets called broadsides, and sold in the marketplace.

brushes. Wire brushes used in place of drumsticks to produce a softer sound.

burlesque. 1. In the 1800s, an onstage parody of a familiar stage work such as an opera. 2. In the twentieth century, a stage entertainment emphasizing low comedy and female display.

cadence. The closing gesture that ends a phrase.

cadenza. An unaccompanied solo in free rhythm.

Cajun music. Music of Cajuns (descendants of French Canadians living in Louisiana), emphasizing dance rhythms and often using button accordion, fiddle, guitar, triangle, and spoons.

cakewalk. An African American dance, popular in the late 1800s and early 1900s, resembling a fancy march step.

call and response. A musical practice in which a leader's musical phrase is answered by the group.

camp meeting. A gathering at which worshipers camp out for several days of prayer and singing.

canon. A composition or section of a composition in which a melody is stated in multiple voices or instruments entering one after the other, as in a round.

cantabile. In a singing manner.

Carter style. Guitar performance style associated with Maybelle Carter, featuring "thumb-and-brush" picking and the use of hammer-ons.

CD. See *compact disc.*

chance music. Music in which random processes are used to determine, wholly or in part, the composition, performance, or both.

changes. Jazz term for *chord progression.*

Chicago blues. An electrified version of Mississippi Delta blues.

Child ballad. Any of the 305 traditional English and Scottish ballads collected by Francis James Child.

chord. A group of pitches sounded simultaneously.

chord progression. A series of chords.

chorus. 1. In a song, a section that repeats with unvaried, or only slightly varied, words; cf. *verse.* 2. See *blues chorus.*

chromatic scale. The collection of all twelve pitches within the octave.

classic American popular song. A popular song written between ca. 1920 and 1955, especially one that has become a standard.

classic blues. See *vaudeville blues.*

classical sphere. The realm of musical activity built around composers' music: music embodied in written scores, which performing musicians strive to play and sing as the notation directs so that the artistic substance fashioned by the composer is translated into sound; cf. *popular sphere, traditional sphere.*

clave. An organizing rhythmic pattern in Latin music.

club mix. See *dance mix.*

coda. A musical composition's closing section. See also *tag.*

collective improvisation. Simultaneous improvisation, especially by the front-line players in a New Orleans jazz ensemble.

collegium musicum. A group of people gathered to make music.

comic opera. 1. In the 1700s, a spoken play with a rather large amount of specially composed music. 2. In the 1800s and 1900s, a synonym for *operetta.*

comp. In jazz, to play chords as accompaniment to a soloist.

compact disc. A digital recording format on optical disc, in use since the 1980s.

compass. The distance between the highest and lowest pitches in a melody. Also called *range.*

compound AABA form. A post-1960 popular song structure in which a series of verse-chorus pairs (the A sections) is broken up by a contrasting passage (the B section, or bridge).

compound meter. A meter in which each beat is divided into three equal parts.

concept album. An LP (or later format) in which the songs are composed or selected, arranged, and ordered to create a larger artistic whole.

conga. A tall Afro-Cuban drum played with the hands.

conjunct. Moving mostly by step (said of a melody).

conjunto. (Lit. "group.") 1. A *norteño* ensemble consisting of button accordion, *bajo sexto* (a type of twelve-string guitar), electric bass, and drums. 2. The German-influenced music played by a *conjunto.*

consonance. A chord or interval that sounds pleasing and harmonious.

contra dance. A style of New England folk dance in which couples dance in two facing lines.

contrafact. A jazz composition created by fitting a new melody to an existing song's chord progression.

cool jazz. A modern jazz style emphasizing soft dynamics and introspective moods.

coon song. A type of popular song in the late 1800s and early 1900s that depicts African Americans in racially stereotyped caricatures.

cornet. A brass instrument, similar to the trumpet but with a mellower, softer tone.

counterpoint. 1. See *polyphony.* 2. Specifically, the technique of composing polyphonic music.

country blues. A style of blues associated with rural southern musicians.

country dance. A forerunner of square dancing and later New England *contra dancing.*

country music. Popular music rooted in traditional music styles of the rural white South, including the blues.

couple dance. A courtly dance of French origin such as the gavotte, the bourrée, or the minuet.

cover. Since the 1950s, a new recording of a previously recorded popular song.

crescendo. A gradual increase in volume.

crooner. A performer who sings softly into the microphone with an effect of intimacy.

crossover. A record that performs well on more than one *Billboard* chart.

cutting. In hip-hop, alternating between two copies of the same record to repeat one section of a song over and over; also called "looping."

cutting contest. A semi-private occasion on which two or more performing musicians pit their skills as improvisers against each other.

dance mix. A version of a popular song that extends its length, for instance by adding long instrumental introductions and interludes.

dance musical. A film musical in which nearly all the musical numbers also involve dance.

deacon. In psalmody, a leader who reads the psalm, line by line, to the congregation, which then sings each line back in alternation.

deceptive cadence. A phrase ending that sounds as if it will be final but at the last moment substitutes a "wrong" chord for the expected one.

decrescendo. A gradual decrease in volume.

Delta blues. A type of country blues associated with musicians from the Mississippi River Delta.

descant. A countermelody above the main melody.

diatonic scale. Any scale that consists of seven pitches separated by a mixture of whole steps and half steps, e.g., major and minor scales.

diegetic music. In film, music that is part of the action onscreen and thus audible to the characters; also called "source music."

diminished triad. A chord consisting of a root and the pitches a minor third and diminished fifth above the root, such as occurs in a minor key using the second, fourth, and sixth scale tones.

diminuendo. See *decrescendo*.

dirty dozens. A traditional African American game of exchanging humorous insults.

disco. A 1970s funk-derived dance music associated with discotheques.

discotheque. A night spot featuring recorded dance music.

disjunct. Moving mostly by leap (said of a melody).

dissonance. A chord or interval that sounds harsh and unsettled.

dissonant counterpoint. A modernist musical texture comprising two or more independent lines of melody that clash consistently with each other.

DIY. See *do-it-yourself*.

DJ. A "disc jockey," someone who plays records for a listening public, such as on the radio or at dances.

do-it-yourself (DIY) A punk and post-punk aesthetic that encourages active, not passive, consumption of cultural products and often prizes raw, amateurish energy over technical command.

dominant. The fifth degree of a diatonic scale or the chord built on that degree.

doo-wop. In rhythm and blues, a style of vocal harmony featuring ensemble scat singing.

Dorian mode. A mode resembling the minor scale but with a raised sixth degree, with steps in the pattern whole-half-whole-whole-whole-half-whole.

dotted rhythm. The regular alternation of long and short notes.

double stop. The technique of bowing two strings of a violin or other bowed instrument simultaneously.

downbeat. The first beat in a bar, usually carrying the most emphasis.

dozens. See *dirty dozens*.

drum machine. A digital device, introduced in the 1980s, that imitates percussive sounds and sound effects.

duple meter. A meter of two or four beats per bar.

dynamics. Volume, meaning degrees of loudness or softness as a musical element.

editing. A recording studio practice of rerecording unsatisfactory passages and splicing the corrected versions into the master tape.

electronic music. Music created by manipulating recorded acoustic or electronically generated sounds, for example, altering their pitch or timbre.

EP. A seven-inch "extended play" 33⅓-rpm record, typically containing four songs.

equal temperament. The division of the octave into twelve equidistant half steps, standard for keyboard instruments since the late 1700s.

ethnomusicology. A scholarly discipline that uses fieldwork as its basis and emphasizes ethnography, recording, transcription, and cultural and musical analysis.

event song. A narrative ballad of the 1800s or 1900s based on a recent event.

fadeout. A terminal diminuendo effected in the recording studio.

fair use. The legal concept that no formal permission is needed when a work of art or literature is copied or quoted for limited purposes including criticism, parody, and scholarship.

fasola. A system of four-syllable solmization associated with shape-note singing.

fermata. In music notation, an indication of a held note or chord.

field holler. An agricultural work song for a solitary singer.

field music. Military music involving fifes and drums.

fill. In jazz, rock, and other popular styles, a brief instrumental passage played while a singer rests.

film musical. A musical comedy either written expressly for the movies or adapted for the screen from a stage musical.

fingerpicking. The playing of a guitar or other plucked string instrument directly with the individual fingers of the right hand, rather than with a pick.

folk hymn. A hymn in which religious words are set to a secular tune.

folk sphere. See *traditional sphere.*

forte. A loud dynamic.

four on the floor. A loud bass drum stroke on every beat of a bar in four-beat duple meter, a characteristic sound in disco.

fourth. The interval between two scale degrees separated by two intervening degrees.

free jazz. Modern jazz style reliant on improvisation and avoiding traditional tunes, repeating chord progressions, and regular pulse.

frequency. The speed at which a sounding object is vibrating, heard as pitch.

front line. In a New Orleans jazz ensemble, the melody instruments, such as cornet, clarinet, and trombone.

frottoir. In zydeco, a washboard-like instrument of corrugated metal that the player wears like a vest.

fuging tune. A psalm or hymn tune containing at least one "fuging" section, where individual voice parts enter at different times with a similar melody.

full cadence. A phrase ending that sounds final, as at the end of a piece.

fundamental. The lowest partial in the overtone series.

funk. Black popular style of the 1970s featuring complex polyrhythmic textures.

fusion. See *jazz-rock fusion.*

G-funk. A style of beat pioneered by Dr. Dre for gangsta rap, featuring relaxed tempos, varied textures, hypnotic grooves, complex bass lines, and high-pitched synthesizer countermelodies.

gallery orchestra. In the worship of early Calvinist Protestants, a group of instrumentalists in the rear balcony, or gallery, of a meeting house.

gamelan. An Indonesian percussion orchestra.

gangsta rap. West Coast hip-hop genre of the 1980s whose lyrics focus on criminal behavior.

gapped scale. A scale in which some adjacent pitches are separated by at least a minor third; the pentatonic scale is one type of gapped scale.

girl group. Any of the female vocal harmony groups popular in the early 1960s.

glee. An unaccompanied song for three or more solo singers.

gospel hymn. A sacred song in a popular style and format.

gospel music. A form of sacred music that draws on popular styles, such as blues (in black gospel) or gospel hymns and barbershop quartet singing (in white gospel).

groove. The use of dance-rhythm ostinatos to establish a sustained mood.

grunge. An alternative rock style of the early 1990s, originating in Seattle, that often expresses sentiments of cynicism, despair, and futility.

habanera. A long-long-short rhythm characteristic of Caribbean-derived music.

hair band. Any 1980s heavy metal band that affected the outlandish hair and costumes of British glam rock.

half cadence. A phrase ending that sounds inconclusive.

half chorus. A musical unit consisting of half of a popular song's thirty-two-bar *aaba* chorus, either *aa* or *ba.*

half step. The smallest interval in the chromatic scale; also called a semitone.

hammer-on. Guitar technique of plucking a string just before forcefully placing a left-hand finger behind a fret.

hard bop. A modern jazz style emphasizing gritty timbres, heavily accented rhythms, and a close connection with jazz's roots in the blues.

hardcore punk. A 1980s version of punk featuring longer solos, more complex drumming, and guitar effects such as extreme distortion.

Harmon mute. A type of trumpet or trombone mute producing a pinched, nasal timbre.

harmonic. The resulting sound when a string instrument is plucked or bowed while the performer lightly touches the string at any of several points that mute the fundamental and emphasize an upper partial.

Harmoniemusik. A German term sometimes translated as "band of music"; military music performed by pairs of wind instruments (oboes, horns, bassoons, occasionally flutes or clarinets).

harmony. A collection of tones sounded simultaneously; the art of connecting chords into chord progressions.

Hawaiian guitar. See *steel guitar.*

head. In jazz performance, a statement of the tune's composed melody.

head arrangement. An unwritten arrangement assembled from the ideas of band members.

heavy metal. A popular genre characterized by extremely loud volume levels, guitar virtuosity, a heavy beat, and lyrics that focus on dark imagery.

heterophony. A musical texture in which multiple voices simultaneously vary the same melody.

hi-hat. A pair of pole-mounted cymbals that can be opened and closed with a foot pedal.

hillbilly record. A phonograph record marketed primarily to rural southern white buyers.

hip-hop. Black and Latino popular music rooted in the performance practices of 1970s Bronx DJs and MCs.

homophony. Either of two musical textures: block chords or melody and accompaniment.

honky-tonk. 1. A nightclub featuring beer and dancing. 2. A postwar country music style associated with honky-tonks.

honor beats, In powwow music, a series of emphatic drumbeats separated by weaker beats, showing respect for the dancers or sometimes memorializing a person mentioned in the song.

hornpipe. A country dance tune, like the reel, in simple duple meter.

hymn. Sacred verse written in the style of a metrical psalm, or the musical setting for such text.

hymn texture. See *block chords.*

hymnal. A tunebook with multi-stanza hymn texts printed in full with the music.

hymnody. The practice of writing and singing hymns.

impresario. A manager who organizes concerts and operatic performances, books tours, and handles an artist's business affairs.

indie label. Any small, independent record company.

industrial rock. A 1990s style emphasizing heavily distorted guitars, pounding drums, electronic sounds, and processed vocals to express a morbid worldview.

integral serialism. The technique of serializing both pitch and nonpitch elements such as rhythm, dynamics, timbre, and register.

integrated musical. A musical comedy in which the songs grow out of and further the dramatic situation, working with other elements such as dance, acting, costumes, set design, and lighting to create a unified artistic effect.

interlocutor. Master of ceremonies for a minstrel show.

interpolation. In musical comedy and operetta, a song added to a show's original score, not necessarily by the original show's principal composer and lyricist.

interval. The distance between two pitches.

intonation. The quality of being in tune.

inversion. Reversing the direction of intervals in a melody, thus playing or singing it "upside down."

iterative form. A musical form in which stanzas repeat with same words and music.

jam band. Any rock group that focuses on live performance featuring long instrumental solos more than on recording.

Janissary instruments. Triangle, cymbals, and bass drum.

jazz. An American music originating in the early twentieth century, with roots in the traditional sphere (folk music), chiefly African; developed further in the popular sphere as a blend of improvisation and composition (performers' music); and over time also recognized, with the help of recordings, as a classical art form (composers' music).

jazz repertory movement. A trend since the 1980s to recreate outstanding jazz performances of the past, using phonograph recordings as primary sources.

jazz-rock fusion. A style, arising in the late 1960s, that combines elements of jazz and rock.

jig. A country dance tune in compound duple meter.

jug band. An instrumental ensemble that mixes string instruments with homemade or toy instruments like kazoo, washtub bass, spoons, washboard, and ceramic jug, the last played as a wind instrument.

jukebox. A coin-operated phonograph, typically found in a public place.

jump band. A scaled-back version of a Swing Era big band that plays rhythm and blues.

just intonation. The tuning of intervals in simple numerical ratios, as they appear in the overtone series.

keeping time. Marking the pulse, part of the drummer's job in jazz and popular styles.

key. A way to characterize a passage of music according to the diatonic scale it uses and that scale's tonic pitch; e.g., F-sharp major, G minor.

Klangfarbenmelodie. Literally, "tone color melody"; a melody that is a succession of not only pitches but also timbres.

klezmer. A living repertory of traditional Eastern European Jewish songs and dances, and the style of playing that repertory.

leap. An interval larger than a step.

legato. Smooth, connected (notes of a melody, etc.).

leitmotif. In opera or film music, a recurring theme associated with a specific character, object, or situation.

libretto. (Lit. "little book.") The words for an opera.

lick. A jazz term for a melodic gesture longer than a motive and shorter than a phrase.

light opera. See *operetta.*

lining out. The practice of singing with a deacon or precentor.

looping. See *cutting.*

LP. The 33⅓-rpm long-playing phonograph record, developed in the late 1940s initially for classical music and accommodating roughly twenty-five minutes of music per side.

mainstream. That segment of the nation's culture considered to be predominant or a norm at a particular time.

major scale. A diatonic scale with steps in the pattern whole-whole-half-whole-whole-whole-half, corresponding to the white keys of the piano from C to C.

major triad. A chord consisting of a root and the pitches a major third and perfect fifth above it, corresponding to the fourth, fifth, and sixth partials of the overtone series, or to the first, third, and fifth degrees in the major scale.

mambo. A Caribbean dance, popular in the United States in the mid-twentieth century.

mash-up. An artistic product in which tracks from two or more prerecorded songs are combined to create a new song.

mass media. All forms of communication directed to a broad audience, such as radio, television, newspapers, and magazines.

MC. In hip-hop, a master of ceremonies, someone who takes over a DJ's job of providing patter.

measure. See *bar.*

medicine show. Free entertainment designed to attract customers for a traveling patent medicine peddler's sales pitch.

melisma. Multiple notes sung on a single syllable.

melodic contour. A melody's rise and fall.

melodrama. A nineteenth-century stage genre featuring sparse dialogue and music to accompany the stage action.

melody. The succession of tones in a piece of music that, by virtue of its coherence, intelligibility, and attractiveness, most readily catches a listener's ear.

melody and accompaniment. A texture in which one melodic line is supported by other musical activity that is subordinate to it.

meter. The number of beats per bar, e.g., *duple* (for two or multiples of two) or *triple* (for three or multiples of three).

metric modulation. A twentieth-century compositional device for coordinating different tempos by means of a common note duration.

metrical psalm. A psalm translated into metrical, rhymed English.

mickey-mousing. In film, matching the music extremely closely to the screen action, an effect more appropriate for cartoons than for live action pictures.

microtonality. Any system of intonation that uses pitches other than the twelve pitches of equal temperament.

minimalism. A style of music composition based on a radically reduced amount of musical material, thus relying on static harmony, patterned rhythms, and repetition.

minor scale. A diatonic scale with steps in the pattern whole-half-whole-whole-half-whole-whole, corresponding to the white keys of the piano from A to A.

minor triad. A chord consisting of a root and the pitches a minor third and perfect fifth above it, corresponding to the first, third, and fifth degrees in the minor scale.

minstrelsy. Blackface entertainment, originating in the nineteenth century, that purports to represent the lives of southern slaves.

modal jazz. Modern jazz style featuring harmonically static stretches based on a single scale or mode.

mode. Any of the diatonic scales used in older European music and in folk music; in addition to the minor and major scales, these include two other somewhat major-sounding modes and two somewhat minor-sounding modes.

modern jazz. An umbrella term for all of the jazz styles developed after World War II.

modernism. Twentieth-century aesthetic movement that, in music, emphasizes fragmented melodies, dissonant harmonies, and irregular rhythms.

modulation. The movement from one key to another.

monophony. A musical texture consisting of a single, unaccompanied melodic line.

motive. A brief thematic element.

Motown sound. A style of 1960s soul music, associated with Motown Records, that resembles mainstream pop in its use of smooth vocals and string sections.

MP3. A compressed digital audio file format that takes relatively little computer memory to store and travels easily across the Internet.

music video. A short video designed to accompany a popular record.

musical. See *musical comedy*.

musical comedy. A spoken play with songs and dances in a popular style.

mute. Any object that reduces the volume and alters the timbre of an instrument.

Nashville sound. A 1960s popular style featuring country-style vocals, polished instrumental and vocal backings, and the downplaying of traditional instruments such as fiddle and banjo in favor of electric guitar, piano, and string sections.

New Romanticism. A postmodern style of composition that incorporates modernist and premodernist elements, often making use of quotation.

New Wave. A late-1970s offshoot of punk music emphasizing ironic distance.

nondiegetic music. In film, music that heightens the mood or clarifies plot or character and is inaudible to the characters; also called underscoring.

nortec. Mexican American electronic dance music that samples *norteño* and *banda*.

norteño. Musical style of northern Mexico and Texas combining Mexican and German elements.

note. The musical notation for a tone; informally, synonymous with *tone*.

novelty song. A comic popular song, often topical in subject matter.

octave. The interval between a pitch and one with exactly twice (or half) its frequency.

old-time music. String band style typical of pre–World War II country music.

Old Way. The style of lining-out favored by New England congregations before the rise of Regular Singing.

open. Unmuted (for a trumpet or other brass instrument).

opera. A theatrical genre in which all, or nearly all, of the words are sung instead of spoken; cf. *comic opera* and *operetta*.

operetta. A form of musical theater similar to opera but lighter in theme and musical style, with spoken dialogue.

ophicleide. Any member of a now-obsolete family of keyed brass instruments.

oratorio. A large-scale religious work for chorus, solo singers, and orchestra.

ostinato. A repeating melody, rhythm, or chord progression used as a structural element.

out chorus. The final chorus in a jazz performance.

outlaw country. Austin-based 1970s country music that appropriated the countercultural stance, if not the sounds, of rock.

overdubbing. A recording studio practice in which instrumental and vocal parts are recorded separately and then superimposed.

overtone. A note of the overtone series higher than the fundamental.

overtone series. The complement of partials that make up the sound of any single tone, heard as timbre.

p2p. See *peer-to-peer*.

palm muting, A technique in both acoustic and electric guitar playing in which the side or palm of the right hand mutes the strings, creating a staccato effect.

pandiatonicism. Musical effect or style in which all the notes of the diatonic scale are sounded together.

parlor song. Nineteenth-century song intended for home music making.

partial. Any constituent element of the overtone series.

pasticcio. A theater work whose songs consist of borrowings from other stage works.

patting juba. A transformation of African drumming practice, using the human body as a substitute for percussion instruments.

pedal point. A long-held note with changing harmonies over or around it.

pedal steel guitar. An amplified steel guitar equipped with pedals that allow rapid changes of tuning.

peer-to-peer (p2p). Any communications system that allows users equal access, facilitating the creation of a file-sharing network.

pentatonic scale. A scale of five pitches; most frequently, a five-pitch scale that corresponds to five of seven notes of a diatonic scale and avoids half steps (and thus can be produced by the black notes of the piano).

performance art. An artwork consisting of a performance that typically combines multiple means of expression, such as theater, dance, music, and visual art.

persona. The character who seems to be singing or narrating a song to the audience; the song's "I."

phase music. A minimalist style in which two or more identical parts are played in slightly different tempos.

Philadelphia soul. A 1970s style linked to the Philadelphia International record label, reminiscent of the Motown sound and a predecessor of disco.

phrase. A grouping of two or more bars into a larger musical unit.

piano. A soft dynamic.

pickup note. A note preceding the first downbeat of a phrase.

pitch. The highness or lowness of a tone, the result of a tone's frequency.

pizzicato. Performance direction to pluck the strings of a bowed instrument such as the violin; cf. *arco*.

plagal cadence. A cadence in which the subdominant triad precedes the tonic (IV–I); sometimes called an "Amen" cadence.

plunger-and-growl. Brass technique using plunger and pixie mutes and humming or gargling while playing.

plunger mute. The rubber end of a plumber's helper, used to partially open and close the bell of a trumpet or trombone.

polyphony. A musical texture with two or more independent melodic lines.

polyrhythm. A texture in which each instrument maintains a distinctive rhythmic pattern, which interlocks with the other instruments' rhythms to create a complex texture.

popular sphere. The realm of musical activity associated with performers' music: music that, sketched in outline form by the composer, invites performers to use the original composition as a starting point, singing and playing it as they choose, with accessibility to particular audiences as their primary goal; cf. *classical sphere, traditional sphere*.

postminimalism. A style that combines minimalism's rhythmic energy, diatonic tonality, and use of repetition with a sound palette drawn from romantic orchestral music, big band jazz, rock, and modernist music.

postmodernism. In music, the mixing of modernist and premodernist styles in a way that emphasizes their contrasts.

precentor. See *deacon*.

prepared piano. A grand piano into whose strings are wedged objects made of metal, wood, rubber, and other materials.

program. Extramusical content (a story, picture, or person) described in music.

progressive rock. A British music of the 1970s typified by concept albums featuring large-scale compositions often based on New Age versions of Eastern spirituality.

protest song. See *topical song*.

psalm. A sacred song in the Hebrew Scripture (Old Testament).

psalmody. 1. The practice of singing psalms in worship. 2. In colonial and early Federal America, the general practice of sacred singing in singing schools, as well as worship.

psalter. A book of metrical psalms.

pump-up. A sudden upward key change in the second half of a popular song, intended to produce the effect of heightened energy.

punk. An aesthetic movement of the 1970s that emulated the nihilistic, anarchistic energy of early rock and roll.

push. In powwow music, one iteration of a song.

Pythagorean tuning. A musical system based on fourths and fifths that are tuned perfectly (according to the overtone series); the resulting thirds and sixths are impure.

quartertone. A microtonal interval one-half the size of a semitone.

R&B. See *rhythm and blues*.

race record. A phonograph record marketed primarily to African American buyers.

radio barn dance. A regularly scheduled live performance of country music for radio broadcast.

ragtime. African American popular style emerging in the 1890s that emphasizes irregular syncopations played over a steady, marchlike accompaniment.

ragtime song. In the ragtime era, any song with the words "rag" or "ragtime" in its title.

range. See *compass*.

rap. The vocal component of hip-hop music.

rap metal. A popular style of the 1990s that combined the assaultive instrumental textures of heavy metal with rapped vocals.

rapper. A performer and writer of rap; cf. *MC*.

recapitulation. The return of opening material after intervening material in a musical form.

record producer. An executive who oversees the recording process, often with a measure of artistic control.

reel. A country dance tune in simple duple meter.

refrain. Words that repeat verbatim at the end of each stanza or verse in a song or hymn.

reggaeton. A Spanish-language blend of hip-hop with Latin American and Caribbean influences.

register. Any one part of the total compass of an instrument, voice, or melody.

Regular Singing. Singing by rule, as encouraged by the musical literacy movement of eighteenth-century New England.

remix. An alteration of a recorded song by changing the balance between layers of the texture; revising the structure by repetition, interpolation, or other means; shifting the pitch or tempo; or combining any of these techniques.

responsorial texture. See *call and response*.

reverb. The addition of artificial reverberation to a recording.

revue. A variety stage entertainment, often with an overarching theme.

rhapsody. A classical composition with a loose form, meant to sound somewhat improvisatory.

rhythm. Duration; the temporal aspect of music.

rhythm and blues. Postwar electrified blues and related styles.

rhythm changes. The harmonies of George Gershwin's "I Got Rhythm," used as a standard chord progression for improvisation.

rhythm section. In jazz and popular music, a group of instruments, such as piano, drums, guitar, and bass, that provides the harmonic and rhythmic underpinning for melody instruments or voices.

ride cymbal. A suspended cymbal used for keeping time.

riff. A short musical figure that is repeated to build up a larger section, whether as foregrounded melodic material or as a background for solo improvisation.

ring shout. An African American practice of religious singing and dancing.

riot grrrl. Any member of a punk-inspired feminist movement of the 1990s.

ritornello. A recurring section in a classical composition.

rock. Post-1960 rock and roll.

rock and roll. A musical category that packaged postwar country and R&B styles for a teenage audience.

rock opera. An extended narrative composition in a rock idiom, whether a stage work or concept album.

root. The note on which a triad or other chord is built.

roots music. Since the 1970s, an umbrella term for a variety of American folk, blues, and country styles.

roots rock. A 1990s style that combines a return to earlier rock sounds with the roots revival's interest in folk music.

rubato. Rhythmic elasticity in performance.

sampler. A digital device, introduced in the 1980s, used to create rhythmic loops of prerecorded sound.

saxhorn. Any member of a family of mellow-toned brass instruments invented by Adolph Sax.

scale. A collection of pitches arranged in order from lowest to highest within an octave, used as the basic material for a composition or improvisation.

scale degree. Any single pitch in a scale.

scat singing. Jazz singing on vocables instead of words.

scherzo. A fast-tempo instrumental movement of light character, commonly an inner movement in a four-movement symphony.

scientific music. Nineteenth-century term for music based on theoretical knowledge.

scratching. In hip-hop, manually moving a record back and forth under the playback stylus to produce percussive rhythmic effects.

semitone. See *half step*.

serialism. Compositional technique in which all twelve notes available within the octave are arranged into a fixed pattern or row, which is then manipulated to generate a stream of constantly changing pitches unified by their derivation from the original row.

shape notes. A system of notation in which shaped note heads indicate scale degrees.

shout. See *ring shout*.

shouter. A dancer in a ring shout.

show song. A song specifically written for a musical comedy or revue.

simple meter. A meter in which each beat is divided into two equal parts.

singer-songwriter. A musician who writes and performs songs, typically in a folk or popular style and with personal content, often delivered in a confessional tone.

singing school. A course of instruction devoted to teaching the rudiments of singing and note reading, focused on sacred music.

single. A double-sided phonograph record, rotating at either 78 or 45 revolutions per minute, usually with a marketable song on the A side and less commercially promising "filler" on the B side.

skip. See *leap*.

slack key. Style of Hawaiian music that uses a standard acoustic guitar in nonstandard tunings.

slide guitar. See *bottleneck guitar.*

sock rhythm. In country music, gentle chords on beats 1 and 3 of each bar, alternating with short, accented chords on beats 2 and 4.

solfège. See *solmization.*

solmization. The practice in singing of assigning a particular syllable to each scale degree.

sonata. A classical instrumental genre in three or four movements, typically with no descriptive program.

song catcher. A folk song collector of the early twentieth century.

song plugger. A pianist, employed by a Tin Pan Alley publisher, who demonstrates new songs for potential performers.

songster. 1. A printed collection of song texts, usually without music. 2. The leader in a ring shout.

soul jazz. An offshoot of hard bop emphasizing ties to gospel music.

soul music. Post-1960 rhythm and blues.

soundtrack. The musical score for a sound film.

source music. See *diegetic music.*

space. In jazz improvisation, the expressive use of silence.

spiritual. An African American sacred song rooted in the experience of slavery.

Sprechstimme. A vocal technique halfway between singing and speaking.

square root form. A compositional strategy, developed by John Cage, in which a single durational proportion shapes both small-scale and large-scale divisions of time.

standard. A classic American popular song that remains in the repertories of singers and instrumentalists.

stanza. Any one of several recurring units in a song's lyrics, all with a similar metrical structure so that the same music may be used for each stanza; cf. *verse.*

steel guitar. A guitar modified so the strings are well above the fingerboard, held in the lap and played with a slide; also called a *Hawaiian guitar.*

step. The interval between two adjacent notes in a scale; may be a *whole step* or *half step (semitone).*

sticker. In the ring shout, a musician who keeps time with a broom handle or other stick.

stop-time. A musical device, used in ragtime, jazz, and other popular styles, in which in-tempo silences interrupt the steady marking of the beat in the bass and drums.

straight-ahead jazz. Mainstream jazz rooted in bebop and its related styles.

strain. A section in a multisectional form such as a march, rag, or country dance tune.

stride. A ragtime-based solo jazz piano style, developed in the 1910s and flourishing in the 1920s and 1930s, based on virtuosic inventiveness in the right hand and a rhythmically driving left hand.

string band. An ensemble of two or more players of string instruments, who may sing as well.

strophe. See *verse.*

strophic form. A song form in which multiple stanzas are sung to the same music.

subdominant. The fourth degree of a diatonic scale or the chord built on that degree.

subgenre. Any of the myriad fine stylistic distinctions characteristic of more recent popular music culture.

subscription. In publishing, a commercial practice in which a publisher raises capital by offering copies of a book at a pre-publication discount.

subscription concert. A concert or concert series in which tickets are sold in advance.

surf music. A southern Californian rock style of the 1960s that emphasizes loud electric guitars, heavy reverb, rapid tremolo picking, and the use of Middle Eastern scales and borrowings from Mexican mariachi.

swing. 1. Jazz in the style popularized ca. 1935–45. 2. The rhythmic lilt characteristic of swing music.

syncopation. The accenting of a beat or part of a beat that is usually unaccented.

synthesizer. A musical instrument that generates sound electronically.

tag. In popular music, a brief musical gesture added at the end of a piece whose material already sounds complete; cf. *coda.*

tailgate. A style of trombone playing associated with New Orleans jazz, with frequent smears and a mixture of countermelody in the tenor range and doubling of the bass line.

tejano. Any of a range of Mexican-American styles resembling mainstream pop.

tempo. Musical term for pace, especially of the music's rhythmic pulse.

tent-repertory show (tent-rep). A traveling troupe of vaudeville entertainers performing in a tent for rural audiences.

ternary form. Three-part form, ABA.

Tex-Mex. See *norteño.*

texture. The interactions between multiple melodic, harmonic, and rhythmic layers.

theme and variations. Musical form in which an initial section, or theme, is repeated in a series of varied versions.

third. The interval between two scale degrees separated by one intervening degree.

Third Stream. An aesthetic movement that sought to bring jazz techniques into the classical sphere and vice versa.

through-composed form. A musical structure in which the composer continually spins out new music instead of literally repeating sections of music.

timbre. See *tone color*.

Tin Pan Alley. Nickname for the publishing district around W. 28th St. in New York City, and by extension for the popular music industry ca. 1890–1950s.

title music. Music played under the opening credits of a film and often functioning as an overture.

toasting. Traditional African American practice of telling humorous stories often boasting about the narrator's exploits.

tonal. Having or using tonality.

tonality. The perceived hierarchy among scale degrees and the chords built on them, centered on the tonic.

tone. A single musical sound; a note.

tone cluster. A chord consisting of several closely spaced pitches, such as those created by pressing adjacent piano keys.

tone color. The quality of sound that enables a listener to distinguish between different musical instruments or voices; also called *timbre*.

tone poem. A single-movement symphonic work whose multiple sections, in contrasting tempos and characters, suggest a *program*.

tone row. In serialism, an ordering of the twelve pitches of the chromatic scale into a sequence that is then manipulated to produce the pitch content of a composition.

tonic. The first degree of a diatonic scale or the chord built on that degree; the generating note from which the other notes are built.

topical song. In the urban folk revival, a song, often using a preexisting melody, with new words that comment on current political or social issues.

total serialism. See *integral serialism*.

trading fours. A device in which two jazz soloists, or a soloist and the full band, alternate four-bar phrases.

traditional sphere. The realm of musical activity connected with particular customs and ways of life,

relying on oral transmission and preserved as "folk music" in the name of cultural continuity; cf. *classical sphere, popular sphere*.

transcription. 1. A notated documentation of a performance. 2. An arrangement of a composition for different instrumental forces.

tremolo. 1. A figure of rapidly repeated notes, executed on bowed instruments with a rapid back-and-forth motion of the bow, and on keyboard instruments, with a rapid alternation of two notes, often an octave apart.

triad. A chord consisting of a root and pitches a third and fifth above it.

trill. A rapid, unmeasured oscillation between two tones a scale degree apart.

trio. A middle strain of a multisectional march or rag form, typically marked by a modulation to the subdominant key.

triple meter. A meter of three beats per bar.

tritone. The interval of three whole steps (six half steps), which divides the octave symmetrically.

tritone substitution. The replacement of a chord with a chord whose root lies a tritone away from the original chord's; a signature feature of bebop harmony.

truck driver modulation. See *pump-up*.

tune. See *melody*.

tunebook. A published collection of psalm or hymn tunes.

turnaround. A dominant chord (V), or a series of chords ending on the dominant, played at the end of a blues chorus or other musical section to signal a repetition.

turntablism. The techniques of a hip-hop DJ, such as scratching, cutting, and beat matching.

twelve-bar blues. A common chorus structure in the blues, consisting of three four-bar phrases and following a standard blues progression.

twelve-tone music. See *serialism*.

ultramodernism. A twentieth-century aesthetic movement that called for a radical break with traditional musical styles.

ululation. A high-pitched, wavering howl.

underscoring. See *nondiegetic music*.

unison. Multiple voices or instruments sounding the same pitch; monophony.

upbeat. The beat preceding a downbeat.

urban folk revival. The twentieth-century aesthetic movement in which traditional music was embraced by people outside the communities in which it originated.

vamp. A short section of music meant to be repeated until a fresh musical statement is ready to be introduced.

variations. See *theme and variations.*

vaudeville. Variety stage entertainment of the late 1800s and early 1900s presenting a succession of short acts.

vaudeville blues. A style of 1920s blues performance with female vocal soloists accompanied by either piano or small jazz-style ensemble.

verse and chorus. A song structure in which verses alternate with a repeated chorus.

verse. The section of a verse-and-chorus song that repeats with new words each time.

vibrato. A minute, rapid variation of pitch, used to lend expressivity to singing and playing.

vocable. A nonsemantic syllable used in singing.

walkaround. A section of a minstrel show in which performers cavorted in what was taken to be the manner of Southern plantation hands.

walking bass. In jazz and popular music, a bass line with a note played firmly on each beat of the bar in four-beat duple meter.

Wall of Sound. The thick instrumental texture associated with 1960s popular recordings produced by Phil Spector.

waltz. 1. A couple dance in triple meter. 2. A favorite form of instrumental dance music in the 1800s and 1900s. 3. A favored gait for popular songs in the early days of Tin Pan Alley (from the 1880s through the 1910s).

western swing. A type of music originating in the Southwest combining country, jazz, and other styles.

whammy bar. A device that alters an electric guitar's string tension to create exaggerated vibrato and other pitch effects.

whole step. The interval equal to two half steps.

work song. A song that helps workers fulfill their tasks by pacing their activity, coordinating their movements, and rallying their spirits.

zydeco. Music of rural French-speaking black Louisianans, or Creoles, that combines Cajun music with African and Caribbean influences.

CREDITS

Courtesy New England Conservatory; page 188: Library of Congress; page 189: Corbis; page 192: Corbis; page 196: The Charles Ives Papers, Yale University Music Library; page 197: The Charles Ives Papers, Yale University Music Library; page 202: © Lebrecht Music & Arts; page 209: National Museum of American History, Smithsonian Institution, Washington; page 210: Idaho State Historical Society, #2771; page 212: MPI/Getty Images; page 213: State Historical Society of North Dakota, photo by Frank Bennett Fiske; page 217: © EFDSS; page 222: Courtesy of the Braun Research Library, Autry National Center of the American West, Los Angeles; page 226: Corbis; page 233: New York Public Library, Music Division; page 235: Wikimedia; page 238: New York Public Library, Music Division; page 239: The Granger Collection; page 243: Library of Congress, Music Division; page 245: Baldwin H. Ward/Corbis; page 249: Frank Driggs Collection/Corbis; page 250: © Corbis; page 254: GAB Archive/Redferns/Getty Images; page 258: © Pictorial Press Ltd/Alamy; page 261: Frank Driggs Collection/Getty Images; page 268: Frank Driggs Collection/Getty Images; page 270: Frank Driggs Collection/Getty Images; page 275: New York Public Library, Music Division; page 276: The Granger Collection; page 283: © Bettmann/Corbis; page 287: Courtesy of the New Orleans Jazz Club Collection of the Louisiana State Museum; page 291: William Ransom Hogan Jazz Archives, Tulane University Library; page 295: Corbis; page 297: The Granger Collection; page 299: Frank Driggs Collection/Getty Images; page 300: © Bettmann/Corbis; page 301: Music Division, The New York Public Library for the Performing Arts, Astor, Lennox and Tilden Foundations; page 306: Richard Tucker/Pix Inc./Time Life Pictures/Getty Images; page 307: Alamy; page 308: Corbis; page 313: The Granger Collection; page 318: The Granger Collection; page 329: © Bettmann/Corbis; page 330: Archive Photos/Getty Images; page 336: Robert Johnson Estate/Hulton Archive/Getty Images; page 339: © Ted Williams/Corbis; page 345: GAB Archive/Redferns/Getty Images; page 346: GAB Archive/Redferns/Getty Images; page 347: Collection of Steve Hathaway, westernswing.com; page 349: Smithsonian Institution, Courtesy of the Alan Lomax Archive, New York; page 350: Getty Images; page 354: Frank Driggs Collection/Getty Images; page 357: Library of Congress; page 363: Michael Ochs Archives/Getty Images; page 364: Silver Screen Collection/Hulton Archive/Getty Images; page 365: © Bettmann/Corbis; page 368: Everett Collection Inc; page 372: The Granger Collection; page 377: © JazzSign/Lebrecht Music & Arts; page 382: Charles Hewitt/Getty Images;

page 386: Stephanie Berger, © 2012, All Rights Reserved; page 389: © Boosey & Hawkes Collection/ArenaPal/The Image Works; page 390: © Bettmann/Corbis; page 391: Bruce H. Frisch; page 393: Herve Gloaguen/Gamma-Rapho/Getty Images; page 397: Frank Driggs Collection/Getty Images; page 402: © Bettmann/CORBIS; page 403: Frank Driggs Collection/Getty Images; page 406: GAB Archive/Redferns/Getty Images; page 414: Private collection of Leslie Uggams; page 416: Courtesy of Country Music Hall of Fame; page 419: Alamy; page 421: Album/Newscom; page 424: Hulton Archive/Getty Images; page 425: © Michael Ochs Archives/Corbis; page 428: © Bettmann/CORBIS; page 436: RB/Redferns/Getty Images; page 437: The Estate of David Gahr/Getty Images; page 442: Metronome/Getty Images; page 445: Michael Ochs Archives/Getty Images; page 450: Michael Ochs Archives/Getty Images; page 452: Michael Ochs Archives/Getty Images; page 456: © Elliott Landy/Corbis; page 458: © Henry Diltz/Corbis; page 459: Julian Wasser/Time & Life Pictures/Getty Images; page 464: RB/Redferns/Getty Images; page 472: Tucker Ransom/Getty Images; page 473: Roberta Bayley/Redferns/Getty Images; page 475: Michael Ochs Archives/Getty Images; page 478: Richard E. Aaron/Redferns/Getty Images; page 479: Michael Ochs Archives/Getty Images; page 483: David Redfern/Redferns/Getty Images; page 486: William West/AFP/Getty Images; page 489: © Brooklyn Academy of Music, Stephanie Berger; page 498: © Tristram Kenton/Lebrecht Music/Lebrecht Music & Arts; page 499: © Lynn Goldsmith/Corbis; page 500: Tom Herde/The Boston Globe via Getty Images; page 502 (top): © Murray Close/Sygma/Corbis; page 502 (bottom): © Murray Close/Sygma/Corbis; page 505: DMI/Time Life Pictures/Getty Images; page 507: © Starstock/Photoshot/iPhoto/Newscom; page 509: David Corio/Michael Ochs Archives/Getty Images; page 516: © Luc Novovitch/Alamy; page 518: Ebet Roberts/Redferns/Getty Images; page 522: Jon Sievert/Michael Ochs Archives/Getty Images; page 524: © Colleen Ricci; page 527: Courtesy of the Klezmer Conservatory Bank, photo by Kathy Chapman; page 533: David Redfern/Redferns/Getty Images; page 537: © Rune Hellestad/Corbis; page 539: Courtesy of the Fales Library, NYU and Allison Wolfe + Molly Neuman; page 540: Photo by John Patrick Salisbury, courtesy Acony Records; page 543: Ke.Mazur/WireImage/Getty Images; page 549: Taylor Hill/FilmMagic/Getty Images; page 550: Copyright © 2009 Photo by Lawrence K. Ho/Los Angeles Times. Reprinted with Permission; page 552: picture-alliance/Newscom; page 553: Photo by Ines Philipp.

INDEX

Italic page numbers indicate illustrations. Page numbers followed by c indicate chronology entries.